CURRENT LAW STATUTES ANNOTATED
1987

VOLUME ONE

AUSTRALIA AND NEW ZEALAND
The Law Book Company Ltd.
Sydney : Melbourne : Perth

CANADA AND U.S.A.
The Carswell Company Ltd.
Agincourt, Ontario

INDIA
N. M. Tripathi Private Ltd.
Bombay
and
Eastern Law House Private Ltd.
Calcutta and Delhi

M.P.P. House
Bangalore

ISRAEL
Steimatzky's Agency Ltd.
Jerusalem : Tel Aviv : Haifa

MALAYSIA : SINGAPORE : BRUNEI
Malayan Law Journal (Pte.) Ltd.
Singapore and Kuala Lumpur

PAKISTAN
Pakistan Law House
Karachi

CURRENT LAW
STATUTES
ANNOTATED
1987

VOLUME ONE

EDITOR IN CHIEF

PETER ALLSOP, C.B.E., M.A.
Barrister

GENERAL EDITOR

KEVAN NORRIS, LL.B.
Solicitor

ASSISTANT GENERAL EDITORS

GILLIAN BRONZE, LL.B.

SUSAN SHUAIB, B.A.

LONDON

SWEET & MAXWELL   STEVENS & SONS

EDINBURGH

W. GREEN & SON

1988

Published by
SWEET & MAXWELL LIMITED
and STEVENS & SONS LIMITED
of 11 New Fetter Lane, London,
and W. GREEN & SON LIMITED
of St. Giles Street, Edinburgh,
and Printed in Great Britain
by The Eastern Press Ltd.,
London and Reading

ISBN This Volume only : 0 421 39650 4
As a set : 0 421 39680 6

CONTENTS

CHRONOLOGICAL TABLE

VOLUME ONE

STATUTES

c.1. Teachers' Pay and Conditions Act 1987

2. Licensing (Restaurant Meals) Act 1987

3. Coal Industry Act 1987

4. Ministry of Defence Police Act 1987

5. Rate Support Grants Act 1987

6. Local Government Finance Act 1987

7. Social Fund (Maternity and Funeral Expenses) Act 1987

8. Consolidated Fund Act 1987

9. Animals (Scotland) Act 1987

10. Broadcasting Act 1987

11. Gaming (Amendment) Act 1987

12. Petroleum Act 1987

13. Minors' Contracts Act 1987

14. Recognition of Trusts Act 1987

15. Reverter of Sites Act 1987

16. Finance Act 1987

17. Appropriation Act 1987

18. Debtors (Scotland) Act 1987

19. Billiards (Abolition of Restrictions) Act 1987

20. Chevening Estate Act 1987

21. Pilotage Act 1987

22. Banking Act 1987

23. Register of Sasines (Scotland) Act 1987

24. Immigration (Carriers' Liability) Act 1987

25. Crown Proceedings (Armed Forces) Act 1987

INDEX OF SHORT TITLES

VOLUME ONE

References are to chapter numbers of 1987

VOLUME ONE

TEACHERS' PAY AND CONDITIONS ACT 1987

(1987 c. 1)

An Act to repeal the Remuneration of Teachers Act 1965; to make temporary provision with respect to the remuneration and other conditions of employment of school teachers and as to certain arrangements for settling the remuneration and other conditions of employment of teachers in further education; and for connected purposes.

[2nd March 1987]

PARLIAMENTARY DEBATES
Hansard: H.C. Vol. 106, col. 539; Vol. 107, cols. 38, 358, 445, 447; Vol. 111, col. 433; H.L. Vol. 482, col. 1302, Vol. 483, cols. 369, 1121, 1256; Vol. 484, cols. 427, 861.

Termination of existing arrangements

1.—(1) The Remuneration of Teachers Act 1965 is repealed.

(2) The remuneration of teachers shall continue to be determined, and paid to teachers by local education authorities, in accordance with the scales and allowances in payment, and other provisions in force, immediately before the passing of this Act until those provisions are superseded—

(a) in the case of school teachers, by provisions having effect under this Act;

(b) in the case of teachers in further education, by provisions agreed between, or settled in a manner agreed between, teachers and their employers.

Interim Advisory Committee on School Teachers' Pay and Conditions

2.—(1) The Secretary of State shall appoint an Interim Advisory Committee on School Teachers' Pay and Conditions to examine and report to him on such matters relating to the remuneration and other conditions of employment of school teachers in England and Wales as he may refer to them.

(2) The members of the Committee shall include persons having relevant knowledge of or experience in education.

(3) Schedule 1 has effect with respect to the constitution and proceedings of the Committee.

(4) The Secretary of State may give directions to the Committee with respect to matters referred to them as to considerations to which they are to have regard and financial or other constraints to which their recommendations are to be subject, and as to the time within which they are to report to him.

(5) Where a matter has been referred to the Committee, they shall give notice of the matter and of any relevant direction—

(a) to such associations of local education authorities as appear to them to be concerned and to any local education authority with whom consultation appears to them to be desirable,

(b) to such bodies representing the interests of governors of voluntary schools as appear to them to be concerned, and

(c) to such organisations representing school teachers as appear to them to be concerned,

and shall afford them a reasonable opportunity of submitting evidence and representations with respect to the issues arising.

(6) The report of the Committee to the Secretary of State shall contain their recommendations on the matter referred to them and such other advice relating to that matter as they think fit.

(7) The Secretary of State shall, upon receiving a report from the Committee, arrange for it to be published.

Power of Secretary of State to make provision by order

3.—(1) Where the Advisory Committee has reported to the Secretary of State on any matter, he may, after consulting—

(a) such associations of local education authorities as appear to him to be concerned and any local education authority with whom consultation appears to him to be desirable,

(b) such bodies representing the interests of governors of voluntary schools as appear to him to be concerned, and

(c) such organisations representing school teachers as appear to him to be concerned,

make provision by order made by statutory instrument giving effect to the recommendations of the Committee, with or without modification, or making such other provision with respect to that matter as he thinks fit.

(2) An order which contains a statement that it gives effect without any material modification to recommendations of the Committee shall be subject to annulment in pursuance of a resolution of either House of Parliament; and an order which does not contain such a statement shall not be made unless a draft of the order has been laid before and approved by resolution of each House of Parliament.

(3) An order may, instead of containing the provision to be made, refer to provisions set out in a document published by Her Majesty's Stationery Office and direct that those provisions shall have effect or, as the case may be, be amended in accordance with the order.

(4) An order may make different provision for different cases, including different provision for different areas.

(5) An order may, in particular, as regards remuneration—

(a) confer discretion on the local education authority with respect to any matter;

(b) make provision as to the aggregate amount of allowances payable to teachers in a school;

(c) set lower and upper limits on the number or proportion of teachers in a school to be paid on specified scales or who are at any specified time to be paid any specified allowance;

(d) provide for the designation of schools in relation to which special provisions apply;

(e) provide for the determination of any questions arising as to the interpretation or application of the provisions set out or referred to in the order;

(f) make retrospective provision, but not so as to require the reduction of a teacher's pay in respect of a past period;

(g) provide that to the extent specified in the order matters may be settled by agreement between, or in a manner agreed between, teachers and local education authorities.

(6) The effect of an order is—

(a) so far as it relates to remuneration, that the remuneration of teachers to whom the order applies shall be determined, and paid to teachers by local education authorities, in accordance with the scales and other provisions set out or referred to in the order, and

(b) so far as it relates to conditions of employment other than remuneration, that the provisions set out or referred to in the order shall have effect as terms of the contracts of employment of teachers to whom the order applies;

and the provisions of a teacher's contract of employment shall have, or continue to have, effect only so far as consistent with those provisions.

(7) The Secretary of State may by order made by statutory instrument coming into force on or before 1st October 1987, without any report of the Advisory Committee but after consulting—

(a) such associations of local education authorities as appear to him to be concerned and any local education authority with whom consultation appears to him to be desirable.

(b) such bodies representing the interests of governors of voluntary schools as appear to him to be concerned, and

(c) such organisations representing school teachers as appear to him to be concerned,

make such provision as he thinks fit with respect to the remuneration and other conditions of employment of school teachers in England and Wales.

(8) Any such order shall be subject to annulment in pursuance of a resolution of either House of Parliament; and subsections (3) to (6) apply to such an order as they apply to an order under subsection (1).

(9) The first order under this section may include provision as regards remuneration in respect of the period between 1st April 1986 and the passing of this Act.

Arrangements for settling remuneration and other conditions of employment of teachers in further education

4.—(1) Any arrangements for settling for the whole of England and Wales any matter relating to the remuneration and other conditions of employment of teachers in further education, or any description of such teachers, shall be such that every organisation which—

(a) was represented immediately before the passing of this Act on the Burnham Further Education Committee, and

(b) has members whose conditions of employment may be affected, is afforded a reasonable opportunity of participating in the process.

(2) The "Burnham Further Education Committee" means the committee set up in pursuance of section 1 of the Remuneration of Teachers Act 1965 to consider the remuneration payable to teachers in further education.

(3) It is the duty of the parties to any such arrangements to take any steps necessary to secure that the requirements of this section are complied with.

(4) This section applies to arrangements notwithstanding that they were made before the passing of this Act and any steps required to be taken in relation to such arrangements shall be taken before anything is done in pursuance of the arrangements after the passing of this Act.

Financial provisions

5. There shall be paid out of money provided by Parliament any expenses of the Secretary of State under this Act and any increase attributable to this Act in the sums so payable under any other Act.

Duration of Act

6.—(1) This Act shall expire on 31st March 1990 unless continued in force under this section.

(2) The Secretary of State may by order made—

    (a) in the case of the first order, on or before 31st December 1989, and

    (b) in the case of any subsequent order, before the end of the calendar year before the 31st March on which this Act is due to expire,

provide that this Act shall continue in force for a further year.

(3) On the expiry of this Act any order under section 3 in force immediately before expiry shall continue to have effect in accordance with section 3(6) in relation to any contract of employment entered into before the expiry until superseded by provisions agreed between, or settled in a manner agreed between, teachers and their employers.

(4) An order under this section shall be made by statutory instrument which shall not be made unless a draft of the order has been laid before and approved by resolution of each House of Parliament.

Interpretation

7.—(1) In this Act—

    "Advisory Committee" means the Interim Advisory Committee on School Teachers' Pay and Conditions appointed under section 2;

    "contract of employment", in relation to a teacher, means the contract, whether a contract of service or for services, under which he performs his duties as teacher;

    "school teacher" means—

        (a) a teacher in a primary or secondary school maintained by a local education authority, or

        (b) a person employed by a local education authority as a teacher in the provision of primary or secondary education,

    other than a person employed as a teacher in an establishment maintained by a local authority in the exercise of a social services function;

    "teacher in further education" means a teacher paid by a local education authority who is—

        (a) employed in an establishment of further education, or

        (b) otherwise employed by a local education authority for the purposes of their functions relating to further education,

    other than a teacher seconded to a body which reimburses the employing authority the amount of his salary.

(2) This Act shall be construed as one with the Education Act 1944.

Short title, &c.

8.—(1) This Act may be cited as the Teachers' Pay and Conditions Act 1987.

(2) The enactments mentioned in Schedule 2 are repealed to the extent specified.

(3) This Act extends to England and Wales only, except for paragraph 4 of Schedule 1 (amendment as to House of Commons disqualification) which extends to the whole of the United Kingdom.

SCHEDULES

Section 2(3)   SCHEDULE 1

CONSTITUTION AND PROCEEDINGS OF ADVISORY COMMITTEE

Membership of Committee

1.—(1) The Advisory Committee shall consist of not less than five or more than nine members, who may be appointed as full-time or part-time members.

(2) Members shall hold and vacate office in accordance with their terms of appointment, subject to the following provisions.

(3) A member may resign his membership by notice in writing to the Secretary of State.

(4) The Secretary of State may by notice in writing to the member concerned remove from office a member who—

(a) has become bankrupt or made an arrangement with his creditors,

(b) is incapacitated by physical or mental illness, or

(c) has been absent from two or more consecutive meetings of the Committee otherwise than for a reason approved by the Committee,

or who is in the opinion of the Secretary of State otherwise unable or unfit to perform his duties as member.

Chairman and Deputy Chairman

2.—(1) The Secretary of State shall appoint one of the members of the Advisory Committee to be Chairman and may appoint one of them to be Deputy Chairman.

(2) The persons so appointed shall hold and vacate those offices in accordance with their terms of appointment, subject to the following provisions.

(3) The Chairman or Deputy Chairman may resign his office by notice in writing to the Secretary of State.

(4) If the Chairman or Deputy Chairman ceases to be a member of the Committee, he also ceases to be Chairman or Deputy Chairman.

Financial provisions

3.—(1) The Secretary of State may pay the Chairman, Deputy Chairman and members of the Advisory Committee such remuneration, and such allowances in respect of expenses properly incurred by them in the performance of their duties, as he may determine.

(2) The Secretary of State may determine to pay in respect of a person's office as Chairman, Deputy Chairman or member of the Advisory Committee—

(a) such pension, allowance or gratuity to or in respect of that person on his retirement or death, or

(b) such contributions or other payment towards the provision of such a pension, allowance or gratuity,

as the Secretary of State may determine.

(3) Where a person ceases to be a member of the Advisory Committee otherwise than on the expiry of his term of office and it appears to the Secretary of State that there are special circumstances which make it right for him to receive compensation, the Secretary of State may determine to make a payment to him by way of compensation of such amount as the Secretary of State may determine.

(4) As soon as may be after making a determination under sub-paragraph (2) or (3) the Secretary of State shall lay before each House of Parliament a statement of the amount payable in pursuance of the determination.

(5) The consent of the Treasury is required for any determination of the Secretary of State under this paragraph.

House of Commons disqualification

4. In Part III of Schedule 1 to the House of Commons Disqualification Act 1975 (disqualifying offices), insert at the appropriate place—

"A member of the Interim Advisory Committee on School Teachers' Pay and Conditions appointed under section 2 of the Teachers' Pay and Conditions Act 1987 who is in receipt of remuneration.".

Proceedings of the Committee

5.—(1) The quorum of the Advisory Committee and the arrangements relating to their meetings shall be such as the Committee may determine.

(2) The validity of proceedings of the Committee is not affected by any vacancy among the members or any defect in the appointment of any member.

Section 8(2)

SCHEDULE 2

REPEALS

Chapter	Short title	Extent of Repeal
1965 c.3.	Remuneration of Teachers Act 1965.	The whole Act.
1975 c.71.	Employment Protection Act 1975.	In Part IV of Schedule 16, paragraph 11.
1986 c.1.	Education (Amendment) Act 1986.	Section 2.

LICENSING (RESTAURANT MEALS) ACT 1987*

(1987 c. 2)

An Act to relax the day-time restrictions concerning the hours during which intoxicating liquor may be served with meals in restaurants; and for connected purposes.　　　　　　　　　　　[2nd March 1987]

GENERAL NOTE

This Act has the effect of allowing those who serve table meals in restaurants, hotels, etc., to continue serving intoxicating liquor, throughout the afternoon, to patrons who require it as an "ancillary" to their meal.

Under the previous law, it was necessary for such service to cease at 3 p.m. (although the thirty-minute "drinking up" time applicable in such cases allowed consumption to continue until 3.30 p.m.—see s.63(1)(*b*) of the main Act). This was felt by many to be a serious restriction on trade, particularly for those in the tourist industry, and the amendments introduced by the present Act arose from a Bill introduced in the House of Lords by Viscount Montgomery of Alamein.

The original Bill contained provision for the total deregulation of permitted hours when intoxicating liquor was served along with table meals, but this proposal was withdrawn following opposition during the Second Reading in the Lords. The present Act makes no change in the permitted hours in the evening, nor does it alter the system of control over restaurants, etc., exercised by licensing justices (or by magistrates' courts in the case of registered clubs which provide such a service). In the language of s.68 of the main Act, this Act simply gives, to those serving "table meals" in "a part of the premises usually set apart for the service of" such meals the right to continue serving intoxicating liquor as an "ancillary" to such meals throughout the afternoon. The traditional afternoon break in hours has therefore disappeared in such cases.

The effect of s.95 of the main Act is that where the licensing justices are satisfied that the premises for which a restaurant licence or a residential and restaurant licence is being granted will only be used for the service of either the mid-day meal or the evening meal, then the permitted hours in such premises may be limited to the lunchtime or evening sessions, as appropriate. S.1(2) of the new Act amends the wording of s.95 of the main Act so that the permitted hours may be made to begin or end at the start of the second period of permitted hours for the day (*i.e.* 5.30 p.m. in most areas).

By virtue of s.2(*b*) of the new Act, any restriction of this type already in existence when the Act comes into force will automatically operate by reference to the start of the second period of permitted hours.

S.68 of the main Act allows proprietors and registered clubs to apply extended afternoon hours without application to the licensing justices or magistrates, although s.69 requires 14 days' notice to the police before such hours will be effective and gives the licensing justices or magistrates the right to forfeit this privilege where it is held that the premises no longer qualify. The effect of s.2(*a*) of the new Act is that, subject to this possible forfeiture, those establishments which at the commencement of the Act were serving intoxicating liquor until 3 p.m. may now do so throughout the afternoon. It remains unclear, from the wording of s.2(*a*), whether they must give 14 days' notice to the police before doing so.

Scotland

The Act does not apply to Scotland.

Northern Ireland

The Act does not apply to Northern Ireland.

PARLIAMENTARY DEBATES

Hansard: H.L. Vol. 482, col. 23; Vol. 483, cols. 248, 619, 880, 1404; H.C. Vol. 111, col. 562.

---

* Annotations by David Field, B.A., Solicitor, Head of the Department of Law, Napier College, Edinburgh.

Relaxation of day-time restrictions on hours during which intoxicating liquor may be served with meals in restaurants, etc.

1.—(1) In section 68 of the Licensing Act 1964 (extension of permitted hours in restaurants, etc.) in subsection (1)(*a*) for the words from "(if any)" to the end of the paragraph there shall be substituted the words "between the first and second parts of the general licensing hours;".

(2) In section 95 of that Act (permitted hours in premises for which restaurant or residential and restaurant licence is in force)—

(a) in subsection (1), for the words "afternoon break" there shall be substituted the words "start of the second part of the general licensing hours"; and

(b) in subsection (3), for the words "afternoon break" there shall be substituted the words "second part of the general licensing hours".

Transitional provisions

2. On the commencement of this Act—

(a) section 68(1)(a) of the Licensing Act 1964, as amended by section 1(1) above, shall apply (subject to section 69 of that Act) to any premises to which that paragraph applied immediately before the commencement of this Act; and

(b) any condition in force immediately before the commencement of this Act under section 95 of the said Act of 1964 shall take effect as a condition restricting the permitted hours in the premises so as to exclude any time after the start of the second part of the general licensing hours (within the meaning of that Act), or any time before it, as the case requires.

Short title, commencement and extent

3.—(1) This Act may be cited as the Licensing (Restaurant Meals) Act 1987.

(2) This Act shall come into force at the end of the period of two months beginning with the date on which it is passed.

(3) This Act does not extend to Scotland or Northern Ireland.

COAL INDUSTRY ACT 1987

(1987 c. 3)

ARRANGEMENT OF SECTIONS

British Coal Corporation

An Act to change the name of the National Coal Board to the British Coal Corporation; to make new provision with respect to grants by the Secretary of State to the Corporation; to make provision for securing further participation by organisations representing employees in the coal industry in the management of trusts and other bodies connected with that industry and in the management of superannuation schemes for such employees; and for other purposes connected therewith.

[5th March 1987]

PARLIAMENTARY DEBATES
Hansard: H.C. Vol. 105, col. 220; Vol. 106, col.151; Vol. 108, col. 429; H.L. Vol. 483, col. 714; Vol. 484, col. 402; Vol. 485, cols. 154, 441.
The Bill was considered by Standing Committee on December 2 to 16, 1986.

British Coal Corporation

British Coal Corporation

1.—(1) The body corporate established by sections 1 and 2 of the Coal Industry Nationalisation Act 1946 with the name of the National Coal Board shall be known instead as "the British Coal Corporation"; and in this Act the British Coal Corporation is referred to as "the Corporation".

(2) The enactments mentioned in Schedule 1 to this Act shall have effect with the amendments there specified which are consequential on subsection (1) above.

(3) For any reference to the National Coal Board in any other enactment or in any instrument or other document there shall, as respects any time after the coming into force of this section, be substituted a reference to the Corporation.

Grants to the Corporation

Deficit grants to British Coal Corporation

2.—(1) The Secretary of State may, with the approval of the Treasury, make grants to the Corporation out of money provided by Parliament with a view to reducing or eliminating any group deficit for the financial years of the Corporation ending in March 1988 and 1989.

(2) In this section "group deficit" means, in relation to a financial year of the Corporation, any deficit shown in any consolidated profit and loss account of the Corporation and any of their subsidiaries prepared by the Corporation in accordance with a direction given by the Secretary of State in respect of that year under section 8(1) of the Coal Industry Act 1971.

(3) Grants under subsection (1) above—
  (a) may be made subject to such conditions as the Secretary of State may with the approval of the Treasury determine; and
  (b) may be made in advance of the preparation in respect of any financial year of the Corporation mentioned in that subsection of any such consolidated profit and loss account as is mentioned in subsection (2) above, if it appears to the Secretary of State that there will be a group deficit for that year.

(4) The aggregate of the grants made under subsection (1) above shall not exceed £100 million but the Secretary of State may with the approval of the Treasury by order increase or further increase that amount subject to a maximum of £200 million.

(5) The power to make an order under subsection (4) above shall be exercisable by statutory instrument and no such order shall be made unless a draft of the order has been laid before, and approved by a resolution of, the House of Commons.

Grants for workforce redeployment and reduction, etc.

3.—(1) The Secretary of State may make grants to the Corporation out of money provided by Parliament towards any eligible expenditure of the Corporation or any of their wholly-owned subsidiaries which is expenditure which relates to costs falling to be charged to any consolidated profit and loss account of the Corporation and any of their subsidiaries prepared in accordance with a direction given under section 8(1) of the Coal Industry Act 1971 in respect of a relevant financial year of the Corporation.

(2) Expenditure is eligible for the purposes of this section—
  (a) if it is of a kind specified in relation to the relevant financial year in question in an order made by the Secretary of State with the approval of the Treasury; and
  (b) to the extent that it does not exceed the amount of the costs mentioned in subsection (1) above to which it relates or such larger amount as the Secretary of State and the Corporation may with the approval of the Treasury agree.

(3) An order under subsection (2)(a) above—
  (a) may only specify expenditure of a kind which falls within one or more of the descriptions of expenditure mentioned in Schedule 2 to this Act;
  (b) shall restrict the amount which may be paid under this section by way of grant in respect of the relevant financial year in question in such manner as the Secretary of State considers appropriate; and

(c) may impose different such restrictions in relation to different kinds of expenditure.

(4) In this section "relevant financial year" means a financial year—

(a) which is the financial year ending in March 1988 or March 1989 or any financial year ending not later than March 1992 which is specified for the purposes of this subsection by an order made by the Secretary of State with the approval of the Treasury; and

(b) in which the Corporation are redeploying and reducing the number of their employees with a view to—

(i) adjusting the future supply of coal or a particular kind of coal produced by the Corporation or any of their wholly-owned subsidiaries to meet the likely demand for it; or

(ii) reducing the Corporation's costs in producing coal or a particular kind of coal.

(5) Not more than one financial year may be specified in any order made under subsection (4)(a) above.

(6) The aggregate of the grants made under subsection (1) above shall not exceed £300 million, but the Secretary of State may, with the approval of the Treasury, by order increase or further increase that amount to an amount not exceeding £750 million.

(7) Grants may be made under subsection (1) above towards eligible expenditure of the Corporation in advance of the preparation of such an account as is mentioned in that subsection if it appears to the Secretary of State that the expenditure—

(a) relates to any costs falling to be charged to that account; and

(b) does not exceed the amount which should properly be entered in that account in respect of those costs or such larger amount as he and the Corporation may with the approval of the Treasury agree.

(8) The Secretary of State may, with the approval of the Treasury, give directions to the Corporation as to the manner in which the amount of any expenditure is to be determined for the purposes of this section.

(9) References in this section and in Schedule 2 to this Act to expenditure include references to costs incurred by providing goods or services.

(10) The power to make an order under this section shall be exercisable by statutory instrument and no such order shall be made unless a draft of the order has been laid before, and approved by a resolution of, the House of Commons.

Pit closure grants: cessation and transitional provisions

4.—(1) Section 6 of the Coal Industry Act 1977 (grants in respect of pit closures) shall cease to have effect, but without prejudice to the payment of any grant under that section in respect of relevant expenditure actually incurred during any period specified in subsection (3) of that section.

(2) The Secretary of State may, with the approval of the Treasury, make grants to the Corporation out of money provided by Parliament towards any relevant expenditure of the Corporation in a financial year of the Corporation ending after March 1987 being expenditure which—

(a) relates to costs falling to be charged to a consolidated profit and loss account of the Corporation and any of their subsidiaries prepared in respect of any period specified as mentioned in subsection (1) above in accordance with a direction given under section 8(1) of the Coal Industry Act 1971; or

(b) relates to obligations undertaken by the Corporation in any such

period and has been approved by the Secretary of State and the Treasury for the purpose of this paragraph;
but grants may only be made under this subsection towards expenditure within paragraph (a) above to the extent that the expenditure does not exceed the amount of the costs to which it relates or such larger amount as the Secretary of State and the Corporation may with the approval of the Treasury agree.

(3) Grants under subsection (2) above towards expenditure in any financial year shall not exceed one-half of the expenditure in that year which would apart from this subsection be eligible for such grants.

(4) In this section "relevant expenditure" has the same meaning as in the said section 6.

Participation by representative organisations

Coal industry trusts

5.—(1) If, on application to the Charity Commissioners by an employee organisation, it appears to them—
  (a) that the members of the organisation or the members and their dependants constitute a substantial proportion of those who may benefit under a trust to which this section applies; and
  (b) that neither the organisation nor its members are entitled to appoint any of the trustees of the trust,
the Charity Commissioners may by order make a scheme making such amendments of the provisions regulating the trust as they consider appropriate for the purpose of securing fair representation amongst the trustees of those persons employed in the coal industry who may benefit under the trust.

(2) A scheme under subsection (1) above in respect of a trust may—
  (a) make such provision as to the manner in which the trustees are to be appointed as the Charity Commissioners consider appropriate;
  (b) restrict or remove any person's right to appoint a trustee;
  (c) remove any trustee; and
  (d) make such further amendments of the provisions regulating the trust (whether or not for the purpose mentioned in subsection (1) above) as the Charity Commissioners consider appropriate.

(3) This section applies to any trust for purposes which are exclusively charitable according to the law of England and Wales—
  (a) which is a trust of property wholly or partly representing an application of money from the miners' welfare fund constituted under section 20 of the Mining Industry Act 1920 or the body known as the Coal Industry Social Welfare Organisation;
  (b) which is a trust expressed to be for the benefit of—
    (i) persons currently or formerly employed in the coal industry or any class of such persons or their dependants; or
    (ii) members of the mining community in general or of the mining community of a particular area,
    whether or not any other persons are also beneficiaries; or
  (c) under the terms of which all or a majority of the trustees are appointed by the body mentioned in paragraph (a) above or are appointed by the Corporation and an employee organisation.

(4) In this section "an employee organisation" means an organisation with which such an agreement as is mentioned in section 46 of the Coal Industry Nationalisation Act 1946 (agreements for establishment of machinery for settlement of terms and conditions of employment etc.) has been made or with which the Charity Commissioners are satisfied that consultations are being or have been held for the purposes of that section.

(5) References in this section to the trustees of a trust include references to the members of any body a function of which is to hold property subject to the trust or to perform any administrative functions in relation to the trust and, in relation to the members of such a body, references in this section to the appointment of trustees shall be construed as references to any corresponding procedure under the provisions relating to the constitution of the body.

(6) Where any functions relating to a trust are exercisable by more than one body of trustees, for the purposes of subsection (1)(b) above the Charity Commissioners may disregard or have regard only to the members of one of those bodies.

(7) The Charity Commissioners shall not exercise their powers under this section in any case which they consider, by reason of any special question of law or of fact which it may involve, more fit to be adjudicated on by the court (within the meaning of the Charities Act 1960).

(8) Sections 18(3), (8), (10) to (12), 19(1) to (7) and 21 of the Charities Act 1960 shall apply in relation to the powers of the Charity Commissioners and the making of schemes under this section as they apply to their powers and the making of schemes under that Act (but with the omission from section 19(6) of the reference to a reference from the Secretary of State and the substitution in that section for the reference to section 18 of that Act of a reference to this section) and sections 40(1) to (4) and 42 of that Act shall apply to orders and decisions under this section as they apply to orders and decisions under that Act.

(9) Nothing in this section shall affect any other powers exercisable by the Charity Commissioners or the High Court in relation to any trust to which this section applies.

(10) In the application of this section to Scotland—

    (a) for the reference in subsection (3) to purposes which are exclusively charitable according to the law of England and Wales there shall be substituted a reference to purposes which are charitable, benevolent or philanthropic (whether or not they are charitable within the meaning of any rule of law);

    (b) references to the Charity Commissioners shall be construed as references to the Court of Session; and

    (c) subsections (7) and (8) above shall be omitted.

Other social welfare bodies

6.—(1) If it appears to the Secretary of State after receiving representations from the Corporation that there is any organisation representing a substantial proportion of their employees or of any class of them which does not enjoy full participation in any relevant social welfare body, that is to say—

    (a) membership of the body;

    (b) the right to vote on decisions affecting its affairs; and

    (c) the right to participate in the management of its affairs in such other ways, if any, as appear to the Secretary of State to be appropriate,

he may by order make such amendments of the constitution of the body as he considers appropriate for all or any of the following purposes, namely—

    (i) to entitle the organisation to be a member of the body;

    (ii) to confer on it the right to vote on decisions affecting its affairs; and

    (iii) to confer on it the right to participate in the management of the body in any other way.

(2) In this section "relevant social welfare body" means any body—

(a) which for the time being exercises functions in connection with the promotion of the social welfare of persons currently or formerly engaged in the coal mining industry or the dependants of such persons; and

(b) whose constitution provides for the Corporation and one or more organisations representing a substantial proportion of their employees or of any class of them to participate in the management of the body's affairs.

(3) An order under this section in respect of a relevant social welfare body which is a company may provide that the company shall be taken to have passed in general meeting on such day or days as may be specified in the order such resolutions as may be so specified in connection with the consolidation and reclassification of unissued shares and their allotment to such persons as the Secretary of State thinks appropriate; and any requirements compliance with which is necessary for the passing or implementation of those resolutions shall be taken to have been complied with.

(4) An order under this section in respect of a relevant social welfare body may make such consequential, transitional and supplemental amendments of the constitution of the body as the Secretary of State considers appropriate.

(5) An order under this section shall not amend the provisions regulating any trust to which section 5 above applies but, subject as aforesaid, shall have effect notwithstanding any provision to the contrary in any enactment or in the constitution of the body in question.

(6) Before making an order under this section the Secretary of State shall consult the Corporation and any organisation which appears to him after consultation with the Corporation to represent a substantial proportion of their employees or of any class of them (other than any organisation representing employees who are also represented by another organisation which he has consulted).

(7) The fact that a provision relating to the constitution of a body has been added or amended by an order under this section shall not preclude its subsequent alteration or deletion in accordance with any relevant powers.

(8) Any person who is a party to an agreement to which a relevant social welfare body is a party which regulates the establishment by it of committees for the discharge of its functions in relation to particular areas may terminate the agreement by giving notice in writing to the other parties to the agreement not later than two months before the date specified in the notice as the date on which the termination is to take effect (but without prejudice to any right of any party to such an agreement to terminate it at shorter notice).

(9) References in this section to membership or a right enjoyed by an organisation include membership or a right enjoyed by any person as a nominee or on behalf of the organisation.

(10) The power to make an order under this section shall be exercisable by statutory instrument and an instrument containing such an order shall be subject to annulment in pursuance of a resolution of either House of Parliament.

(11) The power to make an order under this section may only be exercised once as respects any relevant social welfare body unless it is exercised—

(a) before an order previously made under this section has come into force; and

(b) so as to amend or revoke that order;

but for the purposes of this subsection the making of an order which is annulled under subsection (10) above or quashed under section 8 below shall be disregarded.

Superannuation schemes, etc.

7.—(1) If, after receiving representations from the Corporation, the Secretary of State considers that a scheme established under section 37 of the Coal Industry Nationalisation Act 1946 (provisions as to superannuation etc. rights) does not provide for participation in any function conferred under the scheme by any organisation which appears to him to represent a substantial proportion of the members of the scheme, the Secretary of State may by order make such amendments of the scheme as he considers appropriate to secure such participation by that organisation.

(2) Before making an order amending a scheme under this section the Secretary of State shall consult the Corporation and any organisation which appears to him to represent a substantial proportion of the members of the scheme (other than any organisation representing members who are also represented by another organisation which he has consulted).

(3) References in this section to the members of a scheme do not include members who have ceased to be liable to pay contributions under the scheme.

(4) References in this section to participation by an organisation include participation by any person as a nominee or on behalf of the organisation.

(5) An order under this section shall not make any amendment of a scheme of the kind which requires the consent of the Occupational Pensions Board under section 50(1) of the Social Security Pensions Act 1975 (alteration of rules of contracted-out schemes).

(6) An order amending a scheme under this section may make—

(a) such consequential and supplementary amendments of the scheme; and

(b) without prejudice to paragraph (a) above, such amendments of any provisions in the scheme relating to the quorum necessary for the making of decisions relating to the scheme,

as the Secretary of State considers appropriate.

(7) The fact that a provision of a scheme has been added or amended by an order under this section shall not preclude its subsequent alteration or deletion in accordance with the scheme.

(8) The power to make an order under this section shall be exercisable by statutory instrument and an instrument containing such an order shall be subject to annulment in pursuance of a resolution of either House of Parliament.

(9) The power to make an order under this section may only be exercised once as respects any scheme unless it is exercised—

(a) before an order previously made under this section has come into force; and

(b) so as to amend or revoke that order;

but for the purposes of this subsection the making of an order which is annulled under subsection (8) above or quashed under section 8 below shall be disregarded.

Proceedings for questioning validity of orders under sections 6 and 7

8.—(1) If any person is aggrieved by an order made under section 6 or 7 above and desires to question its validity on the ground that the order is not within the powers of the Secretary of State or that any requirements under that section have not been complied with in relation to it he may, within 42 days beginning with the date on which a copy of the statutory instrument containing the order is laid before Parliament (or if such copies are laid on different days, with the later of the two days), make an application to the court under this section.

(2) If on an application under this section the court is satisfied that the order was not within those powers or that the interests of the applicant have been substantially prejudiced by a failure to comply with those requirements in relation to the order the court may quash the order.

(3) Except as provided by this section, the validity of such an order shall not be questioned in any legal proceedings whatever.

(4) In this section "the court" means—

    (a) in relation to England and Wales, the High Court;

    (b) in relation to Scotland, the Court of Session.

Supplementary

Interpretation

9. In this Act—

    "the Corporation" means the British Coal Corporation;

    "subsidiary" and "wholly-owned subsidiary" shall be construed in accordance with section 736 of the Companies Act 1985.

Short title, commencement, repeals and extent

10.—(1) This Act may be cited as the Coal Industry Act 1987.

(2) Sections 6 to 8 of this Act shall come into force at the end of the period of two months beginning with the day on which it is passed.

(3) The enactments specified in Schedule 3 to this Act are hereby repealed to the extent specified in the third column of that Schedule.

(4) The provisions of this Act do not extend to Northern Ireland except for the provisions of Schedules 1 and 3 affecting enactments which extend there.

SCHEDULES

SCHEDULE 1

BRITISH COAL CORPORATION: CONSEQUENTIAL AMENDMENTS

The Coal Industry Nationalisation Act 1946

1.—(1) In section 1(1) and (2) of the Coal Industry Nationalisation Act 1946 for the words "National Coal Board" and "the Board" there shall be substituted respectively the words "British Coal Corporation" and "the Corporation".

(2) In section 2(1) of that Act for the words "The Board" and "National Coal Board" there shall be substituted respectively the words "The Corporation" and "British Coal Corporation".

(3) For the word "Board" wherever it occurs in sections 1(3) and (4), 2(2) to (8), 3, 4, 27, 28, 29(2), 30, 31, 36, 37, 38(2), 46 to 54 and 64(9) of and Schedule 2A to that Act and in section 38(3) in the second place where it occurs there shall be substituted the word "Corporation".

(4) In sections 30, 37 and 46 of that Act for the word "Board's" wherever it occurs there shall be substituted the word "Corporation's".

The Coal Industry Act 1949

2. In section 1 of the Coal Industry Act 1949 for the word "Board" wherever it occurs there shall be substituted the word "Corporation".

The Miners' Welfare Act 1952

3. In the Miners' Welfare Act 1952—

    (a) in sections 13 and 14 for the word "Board" wherever it occurs there shall be substituted the word "Corporation"; and

(b) in section 16 after the definition of "the Commission" there shall be inserted—
" 'the Corporation' means the British Coal Corporation".

The Landlord and Tenant Act 1954

4. In the definition of "statutory undertakers" in section 69(1) of the Landlord and Tenant Act 1954 for the words "National Coal Board" there shall be substituted the words "British Coal Corporation".

The Coal-Mining (Subsidence) Act 1957

5. In the Coal-Mining (Subsidence) Act 1957—
  (a) in section 1(2) for the words "the National Coal Board (in this Act referred to as 'the Board')" there shall be substituted the words "the British Coal Corporation (in this Act referred to as 'the Corporation')";
  (b) in sections 1(3) to (5), 2 to 13, 15 and Schedules 1 and 2 for the word "Board" wherever it occurs there shall be substituted the word "Corporation";
  (c) in section 17(1) for the definition of "the Board" there shall be substituted—
  " 'the Corporation' means the British Coal Corporation".

The Public Records Act 1958

6. In Part II of the Table in paragraph 3 of Schedule 1 to the Public Records Act 1958 there shall be inserted at the appropriate place the words "British Coal Corporation".

The Opencast Coal Act 1958

7. In the Opencast Coal Act 1958—
  (a) in section 3(1) for the word "Board" in the first place where it occurs there shall be substituted the words "British Coal Corporation (in this Act referred to as 'the Corporation')";
  (b) in section 14A(6)(a) for the words "National Coal Board" there shall be substituted the words "British Coal Corporation";
  (c) for the word "Board" wherever else it occurs and the word "Board's" wherever it occurs there shall be substituted respectively the words "Corporation" and "Corporation's"; and
  (d) in section 51(1) after the definition of "compulsory rights order" there shall be inserted—
  " 'the Corporation' means the British Coal Corporation".

The Coal Industry Act 1962

8. In section 2 of the Coal Industry Act 1962 for the words from the begininng to "the Board" there shall be substituted the words "The financial year of the British Coal Corporation".

The Licensing Act 1964

9. In section 56(3)(a) of the Licensing Act 1964 for the words "National Coal Board" there shall be substituted the words "British Coal Corporation".

The Continental Shelf Act 1964

10. In section 1(2) of the Continental Shelf Act 1964 for the words "National Coal Board" there shall be substituted the words "British Coal Corporation".

The Coal Industry Act 1965

11.—(1) In section 1(1) of the Coal Industry Act 1965 for the words "the National Coal Board (hereafter in this Act referred to as 'the Board')" there shall be substituted the words "the British Coal Corporation (hereafter in this Act referred to as 'the Corporation')".

(2) In sections 1(2) to (6), 2(3) and 4 for the word "Board", wherever it occurs, there shall be substituted the word "Corporation" and in sections 1(4)(b) and 2(3) for the word "Board's" there shall be substituted the word "Corporation's".

The Mines (Working Facilities and Support) Act 1966

12. In paragraphs 3(1) and 4(2) of the Table in section 1 and in sections 4(5) and 9 of the Mines (Working Facilities and Support) Act 1966 for the words "National Coal Board" wherever they occur there shall be substituted the words "British Coal Corporation".

The Building Control Act 1966

13. In the Schedule to the Building Control Act 1966 for the words "National Coal Board" there shall be substituted the words "British Coal Corporation".

The Industrial Development Act 1966

14. In Schedule 2 to the Industrial Development Act 1966 for the words "National Coal Board" there shall be substituted the words "British Coal Corporation".

The National Coal Board (Additional Powers) Act 1966

15.—(1) In section 1(1) of the National Coal Board (Additional Powers) Act 1966 for the words "National Coal Board (hereafter in this Act referred to as 'the Board')" there shall be substituted the words "British Coal Corporation (hereafter in this Act referred to as 'the Corporation')".

(2) In section 1(1)(b) to (e) and (2) of that Act for the word "Board", wherever it occurs, there shall be substituted the word "Corporation".

The Coal Industry Act 1967

16. In section 4 of the Coal Industry Act 1967—
   (a) for the word "Board" where it first occurs there shall be substituted the words "British Coal Corporation";
   (b) for the word "Board" in the second and third place where it occurs and the word "Board's" there shall be substituted respectively the words "Corporation" and "Corporation's".

The Gaming Act 1968

17. In section 52(2)(a) of the Gaming Act 1968 for the words "National Coal Board" there shall be substituted the words "British Coal Corporation".

The Coal Industry Act 1971

18.—(1) In sections 4, 6, 7, 8 and 9 of the Coal Industry Act 1971 for the words "Board" and "Board's" wherever they occur there shall be substituted respectively the words "Corporation" and "Corporation's".

(2) In section 10(3) of that Act for the definition of "the Board" there shall be substituted—
   " 'the Corporation' means the British Coal Corporation".

The Town and Country Planning Act 1971

19. In sections 192(1)(a), 216(2), 264(4)(b) and 273(1) and (2) of the Town and Country Planning Act 1971 for the words "National Coal Board" wherever they occur there shall be substituted the words "British Coal Corporation" and in section 273(1) of that Act the words "the Board" and "that Board" there shall be substituted respectively the words "the Corporation" and "that Corporation".

The Town and Country Planning (Scotland) Act 1972

20. In sections 181(1)(a), 205(2), 251(3)(b) and 259(1) and (2) of the Town and Country Planning (Scotland) Act 1972 for the words "National Coal Board" wherever they occur there shall be substituted the words "British Coal Corporation" and in section 259(1) of that Act for the words "the Board" and "that Board" there shall be substituted respectively the words "the Corporation" and "that Corporation".

The Coal Industry Act 1973

21.—(1) In sections 2(2) and 10 of the Coal Industry Act 1973 for the word "Board" there shall be substituted the words "British Coal Corporation".

(2) In section 2(3) to (7) of that Act for the word "Board" there shall be substituted the word "Corporation".

The Local Government Act 1974

22. In paragraph 6 of Schedule 3 to the Local Government Act 1974 for the words "National Coal Board" there shall be substituted the words "British Coal Corporation".

The Control of Pollution Act 1974

23. In section 25 of the Control of Pollution Act 1974 for the words "the National Coal Board" and the words "the Board" wherever they occur there shall be substituted respectively the words "the British Coal Corporation" and "the Corporation".

The House of Commons Disqualification Act 1975

24. In Part II of Schedule 1 to the House of Commons Disqualification Act 1975 there shall be inserted at the appropriate place the words "The British Coal Corporation".

The Northern Ireland Assembly Disqualification Act 1975

25. In Part II of Schedule 1 to the Northern Ireland Assembly Disqualification Act 1975 there shall be inserted at the appropriate place the words "The British Coal Corporation".

The Local Government (Scotland) Act 1975

26. In Paragraph 6 of Schedule 1 to the Local Government (Scotland) Act 1975 for the words "National Coal Board" there shall be substituted the words "British Coal Corporation".

The Statutory Corporations (Financial Provisions) Act 1975

27. In Schedule 2 to the Statutory Corporations (Financial Provisions) Act 1975 for the words "National Coal Board" there shall be substituted the words "British Coal Corporation".

The Coal Industry Act 1975

28.—(1) In section 1(1) of the Coal Industry Act 1975 for the words "National Coal Board (in this Act referred to as 'the Board')" there shall be substituted the words "British Coal Corporation (in this Act referred to as 'the Corporation')".

(2) For the words "Board" and "Board's" wherever they occur in that Act (except in sections 1(4), 2(5), (6), (8), paragraphs 2(a) and 3(c) of Schedule 1 and in the first place they occur in section 3(8)) there shall be substituted the words "Corporation" and "Corporation's".

The Welsh Development Agency Act 1975

29. In paragraph (b) of the definition of "statutory undertakers" in section 27(1) of the Welsh Development Agency Act 1975 for the words "National Coal Board" there shall be substituted the words "British Coal Corporation".

The National Coal Board (Finance) Act 1976

30.—(1) In section 2 of the National Coal Board (Finance) Act 1976 for the words "Board" and "Board's" wherever they occur there shall be substituted respectively the words "Corporation" and "Corporation's.

(2) In section 4(2) of that Act for the definition of "the Board" there shall be substituted—

  " 'the Corporation' means the British Coal Corporation".

The Local Government (Miscellaneous Provisions) Act 1976

31. In sections 15(3) and 26(6)(b) of the Local Government (Miscellaneous Provisions) Act 1976 for the words "National Coal Board" there shall be substituted the words "British Coal Corporation".

The Land Drainage Act 1976

32. In section 112(2)(a) of the Land Drainage Act 1976 for the words "National Coal Board" there shall be substituted the words "British Coal Corporation".

The Development of Rural Wales Act 1976

33. In paragraph (b) of the definition of "statutory undertakers" in section 34(1) of and in paragraph 8 of the Table in paragraph 56(3) of Schedule 3 to the Development of Rural Wales Act 1976 for the words "National Coal Board" there shall be substituted the words "British Coal Corporation".

The Coal Industry Act 1977

34.—(1) In sections 7, 9 and 10 of the Coal Industry Act 1977 for the word "Board", wherever it occurs, there shall be substituted the word "Corporation".

(2) In section 11 of that Act for the word "Board's" in subsection (1) and for the word "Board" wherever it occurs there shall be substituted respectively the words "Corporation's" and "Corporation".

(3) In section 14(1) of that Act after the definition of "the Board" there shall be inserted—

" 'the Corporation' means the British Coal Corporation".

The Ancient Monuments and Archaeological Areas Act 1979

35. In section 61(2)(b) of the Ancient Monuments and Archaeological Areas Act 1979 for the words "National Coal Board" there shall be substituted the words "British Coal Corporation".

The Coal Industry Act 1980

36. In subsection (1) of section 2 of the Coal Industry Act 1980 for the word "Board" there shall be substituted the words "the British Coal Corporation" and in subsections (2) and (3) of that section for that word wherever it occurs there shall be substituted the word "Corporation".

The Overseas Development and Co-operation Act 1980

37. In section 2(4) and (5) of and Part III of Schedule 1 to the Overseas Development and Co-operation Act 1980 for the words "National Coal Board" there shall be substituted the words "British Coal Corporation".

The Local Government, Planning and Land Act 1980

38. In paragraph (b) of the definitions of "statutory undertakers" in sections 108(1), 120(3) and 170(1) of and in paragraph 14 of Schedule 16 to the Local Government, Planning and Land Act 1980 for the words "National Coal Board" there shall be substituted the words "British Coal Corporation".

The Highways Act 1980

39. In section 290 of the Highways Act 1980, in subsections (5) and (7) for the words "National Coal Board" there shall be substituted the words "British Coal Corporation" and in subsection (5) for the words "that Board" there shall be substituted the words "that Corporation".

The Acquisition of Land Act 1981

40. In paragraph (a) of the definition of "statutory undertakers" in section 17(4) and in section 29(2)(b) and (c) of the Acquisition of Land Act 1981 for the words "National Coal Board" there shall be substituted the words "British Coal Corporation".

The Coal Industry Act 1982

41. In section 3 of the Coal Industry Act 1982 for the words "Board" and "Board's" wherever they occur there shall be substituted respectively the words "Corporation" and "Corporation's" and in section 5 of that Act for the definition of "the Board" there shall be substituted—

" 'the Corporation' means the British Coal Corporation".

The Iron and Steel Act 1982

42. In section 30 of the Iron and Steel Act 1982 for the words "National Coal Board" in both places where they occur there shall be substituted the words "British Coal Corporation".

The Civic Government (Scotland) Act 1982

43. In section 123(1) of the Civic Government (Scotland) Act 1982 for the words "National Coal Board" there shall be substituted the words "British Coal Corporation".

The National Audit Act 1983

44. In Part I of Schedule 4 to the National Audit Act 1983 there shall be inserted at the appropriate place the words "The British Coal Corporation".

The Housing Defects Act 1984

45. In paragraph 1 of Schedule 4 to the Housing Defects Act 1984 for the words "National Coal Board" there shall be substituted the words "British Coal Corporation".

The Roads (Scotland) Act 1984

46. In subsections 3(b) and (4) of section 140 of the Roads (Scotland) Act 1984 for the words "National Coal Board" there shall be substituted the words "British Coal Corporation" and in the said subsection (3)(b) for the word "Board's" there shall be substituted the word "Corporation's".

The Housing Act 1985

47. In section 573(1) of the Housing Act 1985 for the words "National Coal Board" there shall be substituted the words "British Coal Corporation".

The Weights and Measures Act 1985

48. In paragraph 28(1) and (3) of Schedule 5 to the Weights and Measures Act 1985 for the words "National Coal Board" there shall be substituted the words "British Coal Corporation".

The Agricultural Holdings Act 1986

49. In paragraph 8(1)(a) of Part II of Schedule 3 to the Agricultural Holdings Act 1986 for the words "National Coal Board" there shall be substituted the words "British Coal Corporation".

Section 3   SCHEDULE 2

SECTION 3 GRANTS: ELIGIBLE EXPENDITURE

1. Expenditure which is related to persons who leave the employment of the Corporation or of a wholly-owned subsidiary of the Corporation by virtue of redundancy or early retirement.

2. Expenditure on payments made to or for the benefit of employees of the Corporation or of a wholly-owned subsidiary of the Corporation, or on the provision for them of housing or transport, by virtue of their work or place of employment being changed.

3. Expenditure on the maintenance of existing social welfare activities (within the meaning of the Miners' Welfare Act 1952).

4. Expenditure on the maintenance of existing arrangements for the provision of concessionary coal (that is to say, coal or other solid fuel supplied free of charge or at reduced prices) or other benefits to former employees of the Corporation or any wholly-owned subsidiary of the Corporation who have reached normal retirement age or their dependants.

5. Expenditure on the provision of retraining for persons who are to leave or have left the employment of the Corporation or any wholly-owned subsidiary of the Corporation by virtue of redundancy or incapacity.

6. Expenditure on the promotion of new employment in coal mining areas and of new employment for such persons as are mentioned in paragraph 5 above (whether in such areas or elsewhere).

                 SCHEDULE 3

REPEALS

PART I

PIT CLOSURE GRANTS

Chapter	Short title	Extent of repeal
1976 c.1.	The National Coal Board (Finance) Act 1976.	Section 2(5).
1977 c.39.	The Coal Industry Act 1977.	Section 6. Schedule 2. In Schedule 4, paragraph 5.
1980 c.50.	The Coal Industry Act 1980.	Section 6.
1982 c.15.	The Coal Industry Act 1982.	Section 3(3).
1983 c.60.	The Coal Industry Act 1983.	Section 3.
1985 c.27.	The Coal Industry Act 1985.	Section 2.

The repeals in the Part of this Schedule do not affect grants under section 6 of the Coal Industry Act 1977 in respect of expenditure actually incurred in any period specified in subsection (3) of that section.

PART II

OTHER REPEALS

Chapter	Short title	Extent of repeal
6 & 7 Eliz.2 c.51.	The Public Records Act 1958.	In Part II of the Table in paragraph 3 of Schedule 1, the words "National Coal Board"
6 & 7 Eliz.2 c.69.	The Opencast Coal Act 1958.	In section 51(1), the definition of "the Board".
1967 c.91.	The Coal Industry Act 1967.	In section 7(1), the definition of "the Board".
1975 c.24.	The House of Commons Disqualification Act 1975.	In Part II of Schedule 1, the words "The National Coal Board".
1975 c.25.	The Northern Ireland Assembly Disqualification Act 1975.	In Part II of Schedule 1, the words "The National Coal Board".
1980 c.50.	The Coal Industry Act 1980.	In section 10, the definition of "the Board".
1983 c.44.	The National Audit Act 1983.	In Part I of Schedule 4, the words "The National Coal Board".

MINISTRY OF DEFENCE POLICE ACT 1987

(1987 c. 4)

An Act to make fresh provision for the Ministry of Defence Police.

[5th March 1987]

PARLIAMENTARY DEBATES
Hansard: H.L. Vol. 482, cols. 233, 946; Vol. 483, cols. 126, 818; Vol. 485, col. 520; H.C. Vol. 109, col. 275; Vol. III, col. 169.
The Bill was considered by Standing Committee B on February 10 and 12, 1987.

The Ministry of Defence Police

1.—(1) There shall be a police force to be known as the Ministry of Defence Police and consisting—

(a) of persons nominated by the Secretary of State; and

(b) of persons who at the coming into force of this Act are special constables by virtue of appointment under section 3 of the Special Constables Act 1923 on the nomination of the Defence Council.

(2) A person nominated under subsection (1) above shall—

(a) in England and Wales be attested as a constable by making the declaration required of a member of a police force maintained under the Police Act 1964 before a justice of the peace;

(b) in Scotland make the declaration required of a person on appointment to the office of constable of a police force maintained under the Police (Scotland) Act 1967 before a person before whom such a declaration may be made by a person appointed to that office; and

(c) in Northern Ireland be attested as a constable by taking and subscribing the oath required of a member of the Royal Ulster Constabulary before a justice of the peace.

(3) The Secretary of State shall appoint a chief constable for the Ministry of Defence Police, and they shall operate under the chief constable's direction and control.

(4) The Secretary of State shall have power—

(a) to suspend a member of the Ministry of Defence Police from duty; and

(b) to terminate a person's membership.

(5) The Secretary of State shall appoint a committee, to be known as the Ministry of Defence Police Committee, to advise him with respect to such matters concerning the Ministry of Defence Police as he may from time to time require and may make regulations concerning membership and the procedure of the Committee.

(6) The power to make regulations conferred by subsection (5) above shall be exercisable by statutory instrument which shall be subject to annulment in pursuance of a resolution of either House of Parliament.

Jurisdiction

2.—(1) In any place in the United Kingdom to which subsection (2) below for the time being applies, members of the Ministry of Defence Police shall have the powers and privileges of constables.

(2) The places to which this subsection applies are—

    (a) land, vehicles, vessels, aircraft and hovercraft in the possession, under the control or used for the purposes of—

        (i) the Secretary of State for Defence;

        (ii) the Defence Council;

        (iii) a headquarters or defence organisation; or

        (iv) the service authorities of a visiting force;

    (b) land, vehicles, vessels, aircraft and hovercraft which are—

        (i) in the possession, under the control or used for the purposes of an ordnance company; and

        (ii) used for the purpose of, or for purposes which include, the making or development of ordnance or otherwise for naval, military or air force purposes;

    (c) land, vehicles, vessels, aircraft and hovercraft which are—

        (i) in the possession, under the control or used for the purposes of a dockyard contractor; and

        (ii) used for the purpose of, or for purposes which include, providing designated services or otherwise for naval, military or air force purposes;

    (d) land which is in the vicinity of land mentioned in any of paragraphs (a) to (c) above and on which a constable of the police force for the police area in which the first-mentioned land is situated, or, in Northern Ireland, of the Royal Ulster Constabulary, has asked the Ministry of Defence Police to assist him in the execution of his duties; and

    (e) land where the Secretary of State has agreed to provide the services of the Ministry of Defence Police under an agreement notice of which has been published in the appropriate Gazette.

(3) Members of the Ministry of Defence Police shall also have the powers and privileges of constables in any place in the United Kingdom to which subsection (2) above does not for the time being apply, but only—

    (a) in relation to Crown property, international defence property, ordnance property and dockyard property;

    (b) in relation to persons—

        (i) subject to the control of the Defence Council;

        (ii) employed under or for the purposes of the Ministry of Defence or the Defence Council; or

        (iii) in respect of whom the service courts and service authorities of any country may exercise powers by virtue of section 2 of the Visiting Forces Act 1952;

    (c) in relation to matters connected with anything done under a contract entered into by the Secretary of State for Defence for the purposes of his Department or the Defence Council; and

    (d) for the purpose of securing the unimpeded passage of any such property as is mentioned in paragraph (a) above.

(4) Subsections (1) to (3) above shall have effect in the territorial waters adjacent to the United Kingdom as they have effect in the United Kingdom, but as if the references in subsections (1) and (3) to the powers and privileges of constables were references to the powers and privileges of constables in the nearest part of the United Kingdom.

(5) In this section—

    "appropriate Gazette" means—

(i) in relation to land in England or Wales, the London Gazette;

(ii) in relation to land in Scotland, the Edinburgh Gazette, and

(iii) in relation to land in Northern Ireland, the Belfast Gazette;

"Crown property" includes property in the possession or under the control of the Crown and property which has been unlawfully removed from its possession or control;

"designated services" means services designated under subsection (1) of section 1 of the Dockyard Services Act 1986;

"dockyard contractor" means a company which is a dockyard contractor as defined by subsection (13) of that section;

"dockyard property" means property which—

(a) belongs to a dockyard contractor, is in its possession or under its control or has been unlawfully removed from its possession or control; and

(b) is (or was immediately before its removal) used to any extent for the purpose of providing designated services or otherwise for naval, military or air force purposes;

"headquarters", "defence organisation" and "visiting force" mean respectively a headquarters, defence organisation or visiting force to which the Visiting Forces and International Headquarters (Application of Law) Order 1965, or any order replacing that Order, applies;

"international defence property" means property which belongs to, is in the possession or under the control of or has been unlawfully removed from the possession or control of a headquarters, a defence organisation or the service authorities of a visiting force;

"ordnance company" means a company in which there is for the time being vested any property, right or liability which has at some time been the subject of a transfer by virtue of a provision made under section 1(1)(a) of the Ordnance Factories and Military Services Act 1984;

"ordnance property" means property which—

(a) belongs to an ordnance company, is in its possession or under its control or has been unlawfully removed from its possession or control; and

(b) is (or was immediately before its removal) used to any extent for the purpose of, or for purposes including, the making or development of ordnance or otherwise for naval, military or air force purposes;

"service authorities" means naval, military or air force authorities; and

"vessel" includes any ship or boat or any other description of vessel used in navigation.

Defence Police Federation

3.—(1) There shall continue to be a Defence Police Federation.

(2) The Federation shall represent members of the Ministry of Defence Police in all matters affecting their welfare and efficiency, other than questions of discipline affecting individuals, except as provided by subsection (3) below, and questions of promotion affecting individuals.

(3) The Federation may represent a member of the Ministry of Defence Police at any disciplinary proceedings or on an appeal from any such proceedings.

(4) Except on an appeal to the Secretary of State or as provided by section 4 below, a member of the Ministry of Defence Police may only be represented under subsection (3) above by another member of that force.

(5) The Federation shall act through branches and regional and national committees; and the Federation and every branch and committee thereof shall be entirely independent of and unassociated with, any body or person outside the police service, but may employ persons outside the police service in an administrative or advisory capacity.

(6) The Secretary of State may, after consultation with the management committee of the Federation, by regulations prescribe the constitution and proceedings of the Federation or authorise the Federation to make rules concerning such matters relating to their constitution and proceedings as may be specified in the regulations and, without prejudice to the generality of that power, regulations under this subsection may make provision—

(a) with respect to the membership of the Federation;

(b) with respect to the raising of funds by the Federation by subscription and the use and management of funds derived from subscription; and

(c) with respect to the manner in which representations may be made by the Federation to the Ministry of Defence Police Committee and the Secretary of State.

(7) The power to make regulations conferred by this section shall be exercisable by statutory instrument which shall be subject to annulment in pursuance of a resolution of either House of Parliament.

Representation at disciplinary proceedings

4.—(1) On the hearing of a disciplinary charge against a member of the Ministry of Defence Police of the rank of chief superintendent or below the punishment of dismissal, requirement to resign or reduction in rank may not be awarded unless he has been given an opportunity to elect to be legally represented at the hearing.

(2) Where a member of the Ministry of Defence Police so elects, he may be represented at the hearing, at his option, either by counsel or by a solicitor.

(3) Except in a case where a member has been given an opportunity to elect to be legally represented and has so elected, he may only be represented at the hearing of a disciplinary charge by another member of the force.

(4) The Secretary of State shall by regulations specify—

(a) a procedure for notifying a member of the Ministry of Defence Police of the effect of subsections (1) to (3) above;

(b) when he is to be so notified and when he is to give notice whether or not he wishes to be legally represented at the hearing.

(5) Regulations under subsection (4) above shall be made by statutory instrument and a statutory instrument containing any such regulations shall be subject to annulment in pursuance of a resolution of either House of Parliament.

(6) If a member of the Ministry of Defence Police—

(a) fails without reasonable cause to give notice in accordance with the regulations that he wishes to be legally represented; or

(b) gives notice in accordance with the regulations that he does not wish to be legally represented,

any such punishment as is mentioned in subsection (1) above may be awarded without his being legally represented.

(7) If a member of the Ministry of Defence Police has given notice in

accordance with the regulations that he wishes to be legally represented, the case against him may be presented by counsel or a solicitor whether or not he is actually so represented.

Impersonation, etc.

5.—(1) Any person who with intent to deceive impersonates a member of the Ministry of Defence Police, or makes any statement or does any act calculated falsely to suggest that he is such a member, shall be guilty of an offence and liable on summary conviction to imprisonment for a term not exceeding six months or to a fine not exceeding level 5 on the standard scale, or to both.

(2) Any person who, not being a member of the Ministry of Defence Police, wears any article of the uniform of the Ministry of Defence Police in circumstances where it gives him an appearance so nearly resembling that of a member as to be calculated to deceive shall be guilty of an offence and liable on summary conviction to a fine not exceeding level 3 on the standard scale.

(3) Any person who, not being a member of the Ministry of Defence Police, has in his possession any article of uniform of the Ministry of Defence Police shall, unless he proves that he obtained possession of that article lawfully and has possession of it for a lawful purpose, be guilty of an offence and liable on summary conviction to a fine not exceeding level 1 on the standard scale.

(4) In this section "article of uniform" means any article of uniform or any distinctive badge or mark or document of identification usually issued to members of the Ministry of Defence Police, or any thing having the appearance of such an article, badge, mark or document.

Causing disaffection

6. Any person who causes, or attempts to cause, or does any act calculated to cause, disaffection amongst the members of the Ministry of Defence Police, or induces or attempts to induce, or does any act calculated to induce, any member of the Ministry of Defence Police to withhold his services or to commit breaches of discipline, shall be guilty of an offence and liable—

   (a) on summary conviction, to imprisonment for a term not exceeding six months or to a fine not exceeding the statutory maximum, or to both;

   (b) on conviction on indictment, to imprisonment for a term not exceeding two years or to a fine or to both.

Consequential amendments and repeals

7.—(1) In section 3 of the Special Constables Act 1923—

   (a) in subsection (1)—

      (i) for the words "the Defence Council", there shall be substituted the words "an authority who by virtue of any enactment are authorised to make nominations under this section"; and

      (ii) the words from "both" to "Force" shall cease to have effect; and

   (b) in subsection (2), for the word "department", in both places where it occurs, there shall be substituted the word "authority".

(2) In paragraph 1 of Schedule 2 to the Emergency Laws (Miscellaneous Provisions) Act 1947—

   (a) in sub-paragraph (1) there shall cease to have effect—

      (i) the words "nominated by the Defence Council";

      (ii) the words "so nominated";

      (iii) the word "other";

      (iv) the words "the Defence Council, the Secretary of State for Defence or"; and

      (v) the words "or are for the time being used for or in connection with naval, military or air force purposes"; and

  (b) in sub-paragraph (2)—

      (i) for the words "the Defence Council" there shall be substituted the words "an authority who by virtue of any enactment are authorised to make nominations under section 3 of the Special Constables Act 1923"; and

      (ii) there shall cease to have effect the words "the Defence Council, the Secretary of State for Defence or" and the words "or are specified by the Defence Council to be, for the time being, used for or in connection with naval, military or air force purposes".

(3) In Schedule 3 to the Atomic Energy Authority Act 1954 in the paragraph dealing with section 3 of the Special Constables Act 1923, for the words "so" to the end there shall be substituted the words "and, in relation to those premises, the Authority may make nominations under that section.".

(4) In paragraph 4 of Schedule 1 to the Nuclear Installations Act 1965—

  (a) the following sub-paragraph shall be substituted for sub-paragraph (1)—

      (1) Section 3 of the Special Constables Act 1923 shall have effect as if all premises in the occupation or under the control of the specified body corporate were under the control of the Authority."; and

  (b) sub-paragraph (2) shall cease to have effect.

(5) Section 11 of the Ordnance Factories and Military Services Act 1984 and Schedule 3 to that Act (both of which relate to special constables) shall cease to have effect.

(6) In subsection 3(1) of the Dockyard Services Act 1986, paragraph (a) (application of section 3 of the Special Constables Act 1923 to land in a designated dockyard) shall cease to have effect.

Short title, commencement and extent

8.—(1) This Act may be cited as the Ministry of Defence Police Act 1987.

(2) This Act shall come into force at the end of the period of two months beginning with the date on which it is passed.

(3) The provisions of this Act, except section 7(1)(2)(a) and (6), extend to Northern Ireland, and section 7(2)(b) only so extends.

RATE SUPPORT GRANTS ACT 1987*

(1987 c. 5)

An Act to make further provision as to the calculation of entitlement to block grant under Part VI of the Local Government, Planning and Land Act 1980.   [12th March 1987]

INTRODUCTORY NOTE
  The purpose of this Act is to abolish the procedure known as grant recycling. Under Part VI of the Local Government, Planning and Land Act 1980, the Secretary of State, in a Rate Support Grant Report, determines principles for the grant-related poundage schedule which distributes the aggregate amount of block grant payable to local authorities on the basis of their estimated expenditure. When information is available about actual expenditure, the Secretary of State, in supplementary reports, redetermines the distribution of block grant. In so doing he has hitherto been required to ensure that the aggregate amount of block grant is the same as the aggregate amount specified in the original report. The effect was that the amount of block grant payable to a local authority might fluctuate during the financial year as a result of the expenditure decisions of other local authorities and create uncertainty for local authorities as a whole.
  The Act is designed to remove this uncertainty by making further provision for calculating block grant for 1987/8 and subsequent years.

PARLIAMENTARY DEBATES
  Hansard: H.C. Vol. 108, col. 1046; Vol. 109, col. 1006; Vol. 111, col. 831; H.L. Vol. 485, cols. 655, 1007.
  The Bill was considered by Standing Committee A on February 17 and 19, 1987.

Exclusion of adjustments of block grant by reference to total expenditure or aggregate amount available

1.—(1) For the year beginning on 1st April 1987 and any subsequent year the Secretary of State, in the exercise of his powers under Part VI of the Local Government, Planning and Land Act 1980—
  (a) may determine principles for calculating grant-related poundages for the Rate Support Grant Report and any supplementary report on the basis of such assumptions as he thinks fit about the total expenditure of local authorities and the Receiver for the Metropolitan Police District; but
  (b) in determining such principles for a supplementary report—
    (i) need not take into account information as to the total expenditure which has been or will be incurred by such authorities and the Receiver; and
    (ii) shall not be concerned to ensure that the aggregate amount of block grant is the same as any amount previously calculated as the aggregate amount available for it.
  (2) The aggregate amount of block grant payable out of money provided by Parliament in pursuance of a supplementary report may accordingly be more or less than any amount previously calculated as the aggregate amount available for it.
  (3) Different assumptions may be made under this section in relation to different authorities or different descriptions of authorities.
  (4) In this section "total expenditure" means—
    (a) in relation to local authorities, total expenditure for the purposes of Part VI of the Local Government, Planning and Land Act 1980; and

---

* Annotations by Reginald Jones, Barrister, former Inspector of Audit, District Audit Service.

(b) in relation to the Receiver for the Metropolitan Police District, the Receiver's total expenditure, as defined in paragraph 1(1) of Schedule 2 to the Local Government Finance Act 1982.

(5) Section 62 of the Local Government, Planning and Land Act 1980 and paragraph 11 of Schedule 1 to the Rate Support Grants Act 1986 shall cease to have effect except in relation to years beginning before 1st April 1987.

DEFINITION
"total expenditure": subs. (4).

GENERAL NOTE
This section enables the Secretary of State to determine principles for calculating grant-related poundages for the Rate Support Grant Report on the basis of such assumptions as he thinks fit about the total expenditure of local authorities and provides also that in determining such principles for a supplementary report the Secretary of State shall not be concerned to ensure that the aggregate amount of block grant is the same as any amount which was previously calculated: subss. (1)–(4).

It also provides that section 62 of the Local Government, Planning and Land Act 1980 (adjustments for matching amount available for block grant) shall cease to have effect for financial years from 1987/8 onwards: subs. (5).

Classes of authorities

2. The references in sections 57(1), 58(1) and 62(2) of the Local Government, Planning and Land Act 1980 to local authorities belonging to the appropriate class shall have effect, and be treated as always having had effect, as references to local authorities of a description which brings them within a class referred to in one or other of the paragraphs of section 53(5), as that subsection falls to be treated for the purposes of section 59.

GENERAL NOTE
This section clarifies the meaning of the words "the appropriate class" in relation to a local authority so that where that expression is referred to in ss.53(5), 57(1), 58(1), 59(9), (10) and (11), and 62(2) of the Local Government, Planning and Land Act 1980, it has the same meaning.

Short title and extent

3.—(1) This Act may be cited as the Rate Support Grants Act 1987.

(2) This Act extends to England and Wales only.

LOCAL GOVERNMENT FINANCE ACT 1987*

(1987 c. 6)

ARRANGEMENT OF SECTIONS

PART I

ENGLAND AND WALES

PART II

SCOTLAND

PART III

GENERAL

An Act to validate things done by the Secretary of State in connection with, and to make further provision as to, rate support grants and the limitation or reduction of rates and precepts of local authorities; and for connected purposes. [12th March 1987]

---

* Annotations by Reginald Jones, Barrister, former Inspector of Audit, District Audit Service.

PARLIAMENTARY DEBATES
  Hansard: H.C. Vol. 107, col. 1365; Vol. 108, cols. 36, 602, 904; Vol. 109, cols. 36, 67;
Vol. 112, col. 419; H.L. Vol. 483, col. 1512; Vol. 484, col. 569; Vol. 485, cols. 11, 102, 725,
940.

GENERAL NOTE
  The purposes of the Act are to validate the practice adopted since 1981–2 in calculating
relevant expenditure and total expenditure for block grant and rate limitation, to allow that
practice to continue on a proper basis, and to set rate and precept limits for 1987–8.
  "Relevant expenditure", under s.54(5) of the Local Government, Planning and Land Act
(the 1980 Act) is the expenditure to be defrayed from the rate fund of a local authority after
excluding certain items and netting off miscellaneous income such as fees and charges.
  "Total expenditure", under s.56(8) of the 1980 Act, is, broadly, relevant expenditure less
specific grants, and is thus essentially the expenditure to be defrayed from the rate fund less
income other than rate support grant and rates or precepts. An authority's "total expenditure" is the basis for the calculation of its entitlement to block grant and for the determination
of any rate limitation under the Rates Act 1984.
  The way in which relevant and total expenditure had been calculated in practice was not
now considered to comply with the statutory definitions. In particular, expenditure shown
in the accounts as having been debited to accounts such as the Housing Revenue Account,
or to special funds established under para. 16 of Sched. 13 to the Local Government Act
1972, had not been treated as relevant and total expenditure, though such accounts and
funds are in law sub-divisions of the rate fund. Similarly, contributions to such accounts and
funds had been treated as relevant and total expenditure, though they are not in law
expenditure falling to be defrayed from the rate fund.
  The Act deals with this situation by validating things already done for rate support grant
and rate limitation purposes, and by providing for the future a new method of calculating
relevant and total expenditure which broadly reflects what has been done in the past.
  The Act also provides formulae in accordance with which the Secretary of State is to
determine maximum rates or precepts for 1987–8 in relation to authorities designated under
s.2 of the Rates Act 1984.

PART I

ENGLAND AND WALES

Rate support grant: future years

GENERAL NOTE
  Ss.1–3 and Sched. 1 provide, for 1987–8 and subsequent years, a new method of calculating
relevant and total expenditure which broadly reflects what has been done in practice for
previous years. Ss.1 and 2 and Sched. 1 provide for the keeping by local authorities of a rate
fund revenue account. S.3 defines relevant and total expenditure by reference to the items
of account debited and credited to the rate fund revenue account.

Rate fund revenue accounts

  1.—(1) Every local authority shall keep for each year an account, to be
known as—
  (a) a general rate fund revenue account, in the case of a district council
       or London borough council,
  (b) a county fund revenue account, in the case of a county council,
  (c) a general fund revenue account, in the case of a joint authority or
       the Inner London Education Authority, or
  (d) a revenue account in respect of the general rate, in the case of the
       Common Council or the Council of the Isles of Scilly.
  (2) In this Part of this Act "rate fund revenue account" means an
account kept by virtue of subsection (1) above.
  (3) The items of account debited to the rate fund revenue account of an
authority shall include all items of defined revenue expenditure, and the

items of account credited to the rate fund revenue account of an authority shall include all items of defined revenue income; and the proper practices to be observed in compiling accounts shall have effect accordingly.

(4) For the purposes of subsection (3) above defined revenue expenditure is all expenditure which is (or is to be) met by the authority concerned and which is of a revenue nature, other than—

(a) expenditure which by virtue of any enactment, or the proper practices to be observed in compiling accounts, must be debited to an account mentioned in subsection (6) below, or

(b) expenditure which in accordance with those practices can be, and is, debited to an account so mentioned.

(5) For the purposes of subsection (3) above defined revenue income is all income which is (or is to be) received by the authority concerned and which is of a revenue nature, other than—

(a) income which by virtue of any enactment, or the proper practices to be observed in compiling accounts, must be credited to an account mentioned in subsection (6) below, or

(b) income which in accordance with those practices can be, and is, credited to an account so mentioned.

(6) The accounts are the following accounts kept by the authority concerned—

(a) any account listed in Schedule 1 to this Act, and

(b) any other account specified in respect of the year concerned by the Secretary of State.

(7) Where the authority concerned is the Common Council expenditure does not fall within subsection (4) above unless (in addition to meeting the provisions of that subsection) it falls to be defrayed out of the general rate or out of income falling to be credited in aid of the general rate.

(8) Where the authority concerned is the Common Council income does not fall within subsection (5) above unless (in addition to meeting the provisions of that subsection) it is income from the general rate or income falling to be credited in aid of the general rate.

(9) This section shall have effect in relation to future years.

DEFINITIONS
"local authority": s.12(2).
"joint authority": s.12(2).
"year": s.12(5)(a).
"rate fund revenue account": s.1(2).
"future years": s.12(5)(d).
"Inner London Education Authority": s.12(3)(b).
"Common Council": s.12(4).

GENERAL NOTE
This section requires local authorities to keep for the financial year 1987–8 and subsequent financial years a rate fund revenue account. The section provides for certain defined items of account which must be included in the rate fund revenue account (subss. (3)–(5)) and provides that expenditure and income properly debited or credited to the accounts listed in Sched. 1, or to any other account specified by the Secretary of State, should not be debited or credited to the rate fund revenue account.

The accounts listed in Sched. 1 are accounts the contents of which according to traditional accounting practices have been excluded from an authority's main revenue account.

The defined items to be included in the rate fund revenue account are those of a revenue nature, other than items which must or can be included, in accordance with proper accounting practices, in the accounts specified in Sched. 1 or by the Secretary of State.

Rate fund revenue accounts: further provisions

2.—(1) The practices to be observed in deciding as regards a particular year the matters mentioned in subsection (2) below shall be the practices mentioned in subsection (3) below.

(2) The matters are—
(a) what expenditure or income is of a revenue nature for the purpose of debiting or crediting items of account to a rate fund revenue account,
(b) which of the following items of account are to be debited or credited to a rate fund revenue account, namely, items which are not items of expenditure or income and items which are items of expenditure or income but are not of a revenue nature,
(c) whether a particular item of account is to be debited or credited to a rate fund revenue account for the year concerned or to such an account for some other year, and
(d) other matters in connection with the compilation of a rate fund revenue account.

(3) The practices are the proper practices applicable to accounts (by whatever name known) kept by local authorities for the year beginning in 1986 for the entry of items of the same kind as those falling to be entered in rate fund revenue accounts, but taking into account variations of practice occurring from time to time.

(4) The Secretary of State may specify in respect of any year kinds of expenditure or income which are to be regarded as of a revenue nature for the purpose of debiting or crediting items of account to a rate fund revenue account.

(5) Before making a specification under subsection (4) above the Secretary of State shall consider the practices mentioned in subsection (3) above, but such a specification may override those practices.

(6) Subsection (1) above shall have effect subject to section 1(3) above and to any specification under subsection (4) above.

DEFINITIONS
"rate fund revenue account": s.1(2).
"local authority": s.12(2).
"year": s.12(5)(a).

GENERAL NOTE
This section provides that in deciding specified and other matters relating to the rate fund revenue account authorities must use the currently applicable proper accounting practices: subss. (1), (3).

The specified matters are: (*a*) what items are of a revenue nature; (*b*) to what extent the accounts may include items not of a revenue nature and items other than expenditure and income (*e.g.* contributions to special funds); (*c*) the year in which items should be included in the account: subs. (2).

The Secretary of State may specify kinds of expenditure and income which are to be regarded as of a revenue nature. In doing so he may override proper accounting practices, though he must consider them: subss. (4), (5).

Meaning of local authorities' expenditure

3.—(1) For the purposes of Part VI of the 1980 Act relevant expenditure of a local authority in relation to any future year is the aggregate of the debit items of account for the year—
(a) reduced by the aggregate of the credit items of account for the year, and
(b) adjusted by making such additions or subtractions (or both) as are specified in respect of the year concerned by the Secretary of State.

(2) For the purposes of subsection (1) above the debit items of account for a year are the items of account (whether of expenditure or otherwise but excluding excepted items) debited to the authority's rate fund revenue account for the year.

(3) For the purposes of subsection (1) above the credit items of account for a year are the items of account (whether of income or otherwise but

excluding excepted items) credited to the authority's rate fund revenue account for the year.

(4) For the purposes of subsection (2) above the following are excepted items—

(a) items of account representing sums falling to be paid to another local authority, or the Receiver, by virtue of a precept or other instrument, and

(b) items of account representing expenditure under section 1(1) of the Education Act 1962 (awards for university and comparable courses).

(5) For the purposes of subsection (3) above the following are excepted items—

(a) items of account representing relevant grants to the authority, and

(b) items of account representing rate support grants to the authority.

(6) Subsection (1) above shall have effect subject to any enactment (whenever passed) having the effect that anything is, or is not, to be treated for the purposes of Part VI of the 1980 Act as relevant expenditure of a local authority in relation to the year concerned.

(7) For the purposes of Part VI of the 1980 Act the total expenditure of a local authority in relation to any future year is the expenditure which is for those purposes the authority's relevant expenditure in relation to the year—

(a) reduced by the amount of any item of account which is credited to the authority's rate fund revenue account for the year and represents a relevant grant to the authority, and

(b) adjusted by making such additions or subtractions (or both) as are specified in respect of the year concerned by the Secretary of State.

(8) The Secretary of State may specify in respect of the year concerned the manner in which, and the factors by reference to which, the amount of any addition or subtraction specified under subsection (1) or (7) above shall be calculated; and an addition or subtraction specified under subsection (1) or (7) above may or may not represent an item of account debited or credited to the authority's rate fund revenue account for the year.

(9) In relation to any future year subsections (7) and (8) above shall have effect instead of the definition of "total expenditure" in section 56(8) of the 1980 Act.

(10) For the purposes of subsections (5) and (7) above relevant grants are grants mentioned in section 54(2)(a), (b) or (c) of the 1980 Act other than those mentioned in sub-paragraph (i), (ii) or (iii) of section 54(2)(a).

DEFINITIONS
"relevant expenditure": subs. (1).
"total expenditure": subs. (7).
"relevant grants": subs. (10).
"rate fund revenue account": s.1(2).
"local authority": s.12(2).
"year": s.12(5)(a).
"the receiver": s.12(4).
"future year": s.12(5)(d).
"the 1980 Act": s.12(1).

GENERAL NOTE
This section defines, for the year 1987–8 and subsequent years, "relevant expenditure" and "total expenditure" for the purposes of Part VI of the 1980 Act (Rate Support Grant). For the reasons for the change see General Note at the beginning of this Act, above.

"Relevant expenditure" is now defined, in effect, as the debits less the credits to the rate fund revenue account, subject to (a) the exclusion of "excepted items", (b) adjustments specified by the Secretary of State, and (c) statutory provisions: subss. (1)–(3), (6).

"Excepted items" are expenditure on precepts and mandatory education awards, and income from rate support grants and other "relevant grants" specified in subs. (10) (which include the bulk of specific and supplementary grants): subs. (4), (5), (10).

"Total expenditure" is defined, in effect, as relevant expenditure reduced by the "relevant grants" specified in subs. (10) and adjusted as specified by the Secretary of State: subss. (7), (8).

The result is that relevant expenditure and total expenditure can be calculated in the same way as they have been, in practice, in the past.

Rate support grant: other years

Validation for past and general provision for future

4.—(1) Anything done by the Secretary of State before the passing of this Act for the purposes of the relevant provisions in relation to any of the initial years or intermediate years shall be deemed to have been done in compliance with those provisions.

(2) In subsection (1) above "the relevant provisions" means Part VI of the 1980 Act, section 8 of and Schedule 2 to the Local Government Finance Act 1982, sections 2 and 3 of the Education Act 1986 and section 2 of the Rate Support Grants Act 1986.

(3) Any basic block grant calculation made after the passing of this Act in relation to any of the initial years shall be made by reference to the contents of, and the information taken into account by the Secretary of State in making, the last supplementary report made for the year concerned before the passing of this Act; and this subsection shall be applied separately in England and Wales.

(4) For the purposes of subsection (3) above a basic block grant calculation is a calculation made for the purposes of section 66(2) of the 1980 Act of an amount of block grant payable, without taking account of section 63 of and Schedule 10 to that Act (education adjustments).

(5) In relation to any intermediate year—

(a) after the passing of this Act relevant and total expenditure of a local authority shall be calculated for the purposes of Part VI of the 1980 Act in accordance with section 5 below, and

(b) anything done (including an adjustment made) after the passing of this Act for those purposes shall, to the extent that it involves relevant or total expenditure of a local authority, be done by reference to expenditure so calculated.

(6) Subsection (1) above shall have effect notwithstanding any decision of a court (whether before or after the passing of this Act) purporting to have a contrary effect.

DEFINITIONS
"relevant provisions": subs. (2).
"basic block grant calculation": subs. (4).
"initial years": s.12(5)(b).
"intermediate years": s.12(5)(c).
"1980 Act": s.12(1).
"supplementary report": s.12(2).

GENERAL NOTE
This section validates anything done by the Secretary of State in relation to 1981–2 to 1986–7 for the purposes of rate support grant: subss. (1), (2). This applies notwithstanding any decision of a court (whether before or after the Act) purporting to have a contrary effect: subs. (6).

For 1981–2 and 1982–3 (and in Wales for 1983–4), for which rate support grant supplementary reports intended to be final have been made, the grant calculations are to be made on the basis of those reports and their supporting information: subss. (3), (4).

Further provision as to future

5.—(1) Section 3 above shall apply in relation to intermediate years as it applies in relation to future years, and in its application by virtue of this section subsections (2) and (3) below shall apply.

(2) In subsections (1), (7) and (9) the references to a future year shall be read as references to an intermediate year.

(3) In subsections (2), (3), (7) and (8) the references to items debited (or credited) to the authority's rate fund revenue account for the year shall be read as references to items which would by virtue of sections 1 and 2 above have been debited (or credited) to the account the authority would have been required to keep under those sections for the year if they had had effect in relation to the year.

(4) In the application (by virtue of subsection (3) above) of sections 1 and 2 above in relation to an intermediate year, section 2 shall have effect as if for subsection (3) there were substituted—

"(3) The practices are the proper practices applicable to the account (by whatever name known) kept by the local authority concerned for the year concerned for the entry of items of the same kind as those falling to be entered in rate fund revenue accounts; and if those practices allow for more than one course of action the course actually taken shall be deemed to have been taken."

(5) In the application (by virtue of subsection (3) above) of sections 1 and 2 above in relation to an intermediate year beginning in 1983, 1984 or 1985, section 1 shall have effect as if for "a joint authority" in subsection (1)(c) there were substituted "the Greater London Council."

(6) This section shall have effect as regards anything falling to be done after (but not as regards anything done before) the passing of this Act.

DEFINITIONS
"intermediate years": s.12(5)(c).
"future years": s.12(5)(d).
"rate fund revenue account": s.1(2).
"year": s.12(5)(a).
"local authority": s.12(2), (3).

GENERAL NOTE
The effect of this section, as applied by s.4(5), is that for 1984–5 to 1986–7 (and for 1983–4 in England), relevant and total expenditure are to be calculated in the same way as for 1987–8 and subsequent years.

Rates

Validation of past acts

6.—(1) For the purposes of any order made before the passing of this Act under section 2(3) of the 1984 Act any total of relevant expenditure there mentioned shall be deemed to have been estimated in compliance with the provisions of Part VI of the 1980 Act.

(2) Anything done by the Secretary of State before the passing of this Act for the purposes of Part I of the 1984 Act in relation to the financial year beginning in 1985 or that beginning in 1986 shall be deemed to have been done in compliance with the provisions of that Part.

(3) For the purposes of section 7 below and Schedule 2 to this Act—

(a) any designation of an authority under section 2 of the 1984 Act in relation to the financial year beginning in 1987, and

(b) any determination and notification under section 3(1) and (3) of that Act of a level for an authority's total expenditure in that year, shall, if made before the passing of this Act, be deemed to have been made in compliance with the provisions of Part I of the 1984 Act.

(4) This section shall have effect notwithstanding any decision of a court (whether before or after the passing of this Act) purporting to have a contrary effect.

DEFINITIONS
"1984 Act": s.12(1).
"financial year": s.12(5)(e).

GENERAL NOTE
This section validates anything already done by the Secretary of State for the purposes of rate limitation under the Rates Act 1984: subss. (1)–(3). It is to have effect notwithstanding any decision of a court (before or after the Act) which purports to have a contrary effect: subs. (4).

Restrictions on rating and precepting

7.—(1) This section applies to authorities designated before the passing of this Act under section 2 of the 1984 Act in relation to the financial year beginning in 1987, whether actually designated by the Secretary of State or deemed by virtue of section 68(6) of the Local Government Act 1985 (new authorities) to have been designated.

(2) In relation to that financial year the powers and duties of such an authority (a designated authority) in respect of the making of a rate or issuing a precept for that year, as the case may be, shall have effect subject to section 8 below but not to the provisions of Part I of the 1984 Act.

(3) Any duty of the Secretary of State under Part I of the 1984 Act shall not apply in relation to that financial year.

(4) For the purposes of section 8 below the maximum limit in relation to a designated authority shall be determined in accordance with Schedule 2 to this Act.

(5) As soon as is reasonably practicable after the Rate Support Grant Report for the financial year beginning in 1987 has been laid before the House of Commons, the Secretary of State shall serve on each designated authority a notice stating—

  (a) the maximum limit determined by him in relation to the authority in accordance with Schedule 2 to this Act,
  (b) the amount which in accordance with that Schedule he estimates as BG in relation to the authority (a component of the maximum limit),
  (c) the version of the valuation lists, and the other information relating to hereditaments and rateable values, by reference to which he calculates RV in relation to the authority (another component of the maximum limit), and
  (d) the amount which in accordance with that Schedule he estimates as DBG in relation to the authority (in a case where DBG is a component of the maximum limit in relation to the authority).

DEFINITIONS
"1984 Act": s.12(1).
"designated authority": subss. (1), (2).
"financial year": s.12(5)(e).
"Rate Support Grant Report": s.12(2).
"maximum limit": Sched. 2, para. 1.
"BG" and "RV": Sched. 2, para. 2(3), (5).
"DBG": Sched. 2, para. 4(1).

GENERAL NOTE

Because of the need to pass this Act, the Department of the Environment were unable to proceed with rate and precept limitation for 1987–8 in accordance with the normal timetable under the Rates Act 1984. This section and Sched. 2 therefore provide for rate and precept limitation for authorities designated under the 1984 Act to be determined for 1987–8 in accordance with a formula for each class of authority. The Secretary of State said at Second Reading (*Hansard*, H.C. Vol. 108, col. 36) that the formulae contained broadly the same factors as are necessary to calculate rate and precept limits under normal procedures and reflect, as far as possible, the decisions which would have been taken under those procedures.

The procedure for imposing maximum rates and precepts for 1987–8 is also necessarily different from the normal procedure under the Rates Act 1984. For that year the provisions of Part I of the 1984 Act are not to apply to the powers and duties of designated authorities as to the making of rates and precepts (except that s.7 of the 1984 Act (certificates of compliance) applies as amended): subs. (2), Sched. 4, para. (8). Nor are the duties of the Secretary of State under Part I of the 1984 Act applicable: subs. (3).

The 1987–8 procedure is set out in subs. (5) and s.8. Subs. (5) requires the Secretary of State to serve notice on each designated authority stating the maximum limit of rate or precept poundage determined for that authority in accordance with Sched. 2 (para. (a); together with supporting information (paras. (b)–(d))).

Sanctions

8.—(1) If a designated authority makes a rate, whether before or after the passing of this Act but before a notice has been served on it, and the amount in the pound of the rate (exclusive of any excluded part) exceeds the maximum limit, the authority shall make a substituted rate before the expiry of the permitted period.

(2) If a designated authority issues a precept, whether before or after the passing of this Act but before a notice has been served on it, and the amount in the pound of the precept exceeds the maximum limit, the authority shall issue a substituted precept before the expiry of the permitted period.

(3) If a designated authority fails to comply with subsection (1) or (2) above the rate made or precept issued before the service of the notice shall be deemed not to have been validly made or issued.

(4) A rate made by a designated authority (under subsection (1) above or otherwise) after a notice has been served on it shall be invalid if the amount in the pound of the rate (exclusive of any excluded part) exceeds the maximum limit.

(5) A precept issued by a designated authority (under subsection (2) above or otherwise) after a notice has been served on it shall be invalid if the amount in the pound of the precept exceeds the maximum limit.

(6) A rate shall be invalid if any part of the rate is made for giving effect to a precept which is invalid under subsection (5) above.

(7) In a case where a rate (or precept) is levied otherwise than at a uniform rate in the pound this section shall have effect as if—

(a) references to the amount in the pound of the rate (or precept) were to the product of the rate (or precept) levied, and

(b) references to the maximum limit were to the product of a rate (or precept) levied at a uniform rate in the pound equal to the maximum limit.

(8) For the purposes of subsection (1) above the permitted period is the period of 6 weeks beginning with the day on which a notice is served on the authority; and for the purposes of subsection (2) above the permitted period is the period of one month beginning with the day on which a notice is served on the authority.

(9) For the purposes of this section an excluded part of a rate is any part made for giving effect to—

(a) a precept issued to the rating authority concerned by another authority referred to in section 1(3) of the 1984 Act or by the Receiver, or

(b) a levy made on the rating authority concerned under section 13 of the London Regional Transport Act 1984.

(10) References in this section to a notice are to a notice served under section 7(5) above.

(11) This section applies only in relation to rates for, and precepts in respect of, the financial year beginning in 1987.

DEFINITIONS
"designated authority": s.7(1)(2).
"notice": subs. (10).
"excluded part": subs. (9).
"maximum limit": Sched. 2, para. 1.
"permitted period": subs. (8).
"the Receiver": s.12(4).

GENERAL NOTE
If a designated authority has made a rate or precept before the issue of a notice under s.7(5) and the poundage for its own requirements exceeds the maximum limit specified in the notice, the authority must make a substituted rate or precept within a specified period of the service of the notice (six weeks for a rate, one month for a precept). If it does not do so the original rate or precept will be invalid: subss. (1)–(3), (8), (9).

A rate or precept issued after service of a notice will be invalid if the poundage for the authority's own requirements exceeds the maximum limit specified in the notice: subss. (4), (5). A rate which includes an invalid precept will itself be invalid: subs. (6).

Subs. (7) makes provision for rates or precepts levied otherwise than at uniform poundage.

Miscellaneous and general

Power of specifying: general

9.—(1) Subsections (2) to (5) below apply to any power to specify under section 1(6), 2(4) or 3(1), (7) or (8) above.

(2) The power includes power to specify in respect of any of the intermediate years (in relation to which sections 1 to 3 above apply by virtue of section 5 above).

(3) The power includes power to revoke or amend a specification made under the power.

(4) Before exercising the power the Secretary of State shall consult such associations of local authorities as appear to him to be concerned and any local authority with whom consultation appears to him to be desirable.

(5) The power may be exercised differently for England and Wales.

(6) Any power to specify under section 2(4) or 3(1), (7) or (8) above shall be exercised in accordance with principles to be applied to all local authorities.

DEFINITIONS
"intermediate years": s.12(5)(c).
"local authorities": s.12(2), (3).

GENERAL NOTE
This section makes detailed provision concerning the Secretary of State's power to specify matters relating to the rate fund revenue account (ss.1(6), 2(4)) and to relevant and total expenditure (s.3(1), (7), (8)).

The power includes powers to specify for intermediate years (subs. (2)) and to revoke or amend specifications (subs. (3)). It may be exercised differently for England and Wales (subs. (5)), but except in relation to s.1(6) it must be exercised in accordance with principles to be applied to all local authorities: subs. (6). The exclusion from this provision of the power under s.1(6) to specify accounts to be excluded from the rate fund revenue account enables this power to be tailored to the individual circumstances of each authority.

Before exercising any power to specify, the Secretary of State must consult local authority associations which appear to him to be concerned and such individual local authorities as he thinks desirable: subs. (4).

Special provisions as to rate support grant

10. Schedule 3 to this Act (which contains special provisions as to rate support grant) shall have effect.

Amendments and repeals

11.—(1) Schedule 4 to this Act (which contains amendments) shall have effect.

(2) The enactments mentioned in Schedule 5 to this Act are repealed to the extent specified in column 3, but subject to the provision at the end of the Schedule.

Interpretation

12.—(1) In this Part of this Act "the 1980 Act" means the Local Government, Planning and Land Act 1980 and "the 1984 Act" means the Rates Act 1984.

(2) In this Part of this Act "joint authority", "Rate Support Grant Report" and "supplementary report" have the same meanings as in Part VI of the 1980 Act, "local authority" means any body which is a local authority for the purposes of that Part, and "trading undertaking" has the same meaning as in section 72(3)(e) of that Act.

(3) For the purposes of this Part of this Act as it applies in relation to an intermediate year beginning in 1983, 1984 or 1985—

(a) "local authority" also includes the Greater London Council and the Inner London Education Authority within the meaning of section 30 of the London Government Act 1963,

(b) references to the Inner London Education Authority in section 1(1)(c) above, paragraph (c) below and paragraph 3(10) of Schedule 3 to this Act shall be construed as references to the Inner London Education Authority within the meaning of section 30 of that Act,

(c) the Greater London Council and the Inner London Education Authority shall be taken to be separate local authorities, and

(d) "local authority" does not include a joint authority or the Inner London Education Authority established by section 18 of the Local Government Act 1985.

(4) In this Part of this Act "the Common Council" means the Common Council of the City of London and "the Receiver" means the Receiver for the Metropolitan Police District.

(5) For the purposes of this Part of this Act—

(a) "year" means a period of 12 months beginning with 1st April,

(b) initial years are (as regards England) years beginning in 1981 and 1982 or (as regards Wales) those beginning in 1981, 1982 and 1983,

(c) intermediate years are (as regards England) years beginning in 1983, 1984, 1985 and 1986 or (as regards Wales) those beginning in 1984, 1985 and 1986,

(d) future years are the year beginning in 1987 and subsequent years, and

(e) "financial year" means a period of 12 months beginning with 1st April.

PART II

SCOTLAND

Ascertainment of expenditure for purposes of redetermination of needs element

13.—(1) The validity of anything done, whether before of after the passing of this Act, by the Secretary of State under or for the purposes of paragraph 1 or 3 of Part I of Schedule 1 to the Local Government (Scotland) Act 1966 in relation to the financial year 1983–84 or any subsequent financial year shall not be called in question in any legal proceedings on the ground that in ascertaining the actual expenditure or the estimated expenditure of a local authority the Secretary of State took into account the transfer of any sum between the authority's general fund and any special fund or account maintained by them under any enactment.

(2) Except where the context otherwise requires, an expression used in this section and in the Local Government (Scotland) Act 1966 has in this section the same meaning as it has in that Act.

GENERAL NOTE
   This section relates only to Scotland. It provides that any apportionment by the Secretary of State of the needs element of rate support grant for 1983–4 or any subsequent financial year shall not be called in question on the ground that he took into account a transfer between an authority's general fund and any special fund or account.

Ascertainment of expenditure etc. for purposes of section 5 of Local Government (Scotland) Act 1966

14.—(1) The validity of anything done after the passing of this Act by the Secretary of State in relation to any rate determined by any local authority shall not be called in question in any legal proceedings on the ground that in ascertaining, for the purposes of section 5 of the Local Government (Scotland) Act 1966, the total estimated expenses mentioned in section 108(2) of the Local Government (Scotland) Act 1973 the Secretary of State took into account the transfer of any sum between the authority's general fund and any special fund or account maintained by them under any enactment.

(2) Except where the context otherwise requires, an expression used in this section and in the Local Government (Scotland) Act 1966 has in this section the same meaning as it has in that Act.

GENERAL NOTE
   This section relates only to Scotland. It provides that, for the future, action of the Secretary of State in respect of a local authority's rate shall not be called in question on the ground that in estimating expenditure for the purpose of s.5 of the Local Government (Scotland) Act 1966, he took into account a transfer between an authority's general fund and any special fund or account. (S.5 of the 1966 Act empowers the Secretary of State to lay before Parliament a report proposing a reduction in an authority's rate.)

PART III

GENERAL

Expenses

15. There shall be paid out of money provided by Parliament any increase attributable to this Act in the sums payable out of money so provided under any other Act.

Citation and extent

16.—(1) This Act may be cited as the Local Government Finance Act 1987.

(2) Part I of this Act extends to England and Wales only.

(3) Part II of this Act extends to Scotland only.

(4) This Act does not extend to Northern Ireland.

SCHEDULES

Section 1   SCHEDULE 1

LIST OF ACCOUNTS

1. The Housing Revenue Account.

2. The Housing Repairs Account.

3. Any account of a trading undertaking (whether the undertaking is owned by the authority concerned individually or as a member of a joint committee).

4. Any account of any fund established under section 15(1) of the Public Libraries and Museums Act 1964.

5. Any account kept by virtue of section 2(2) of the Local Authorities (Goods and Services) Act 1970.

6. Any account of any fund known as a superannuation fund and maintained under regulations made under section 7 of the Superannuation Act 1972.

7. Any account of a loans fund established under paragraph 15 of Schedule 13 to the Local Government Act 1972.

8. Any account of any fund established under paragraph 16 of Schedule 13 to the Local Government Act 1972.

9. Any account of any lottery fund within the meaning of section 8 of the Lotteries and Amusements Act 1976.

10. Any account kept by virtue of section 10(1)(i) of the 1980 Act (direct labour organisations).

11. Any account kept by virtue of section 55(1) of the Road Traffic Regulation Act 1984 (parking places).

12. Any account kept by virtue of section 3(4)(a)(i) of the Further Education Act 1985.

13. Any account of any fund known as a metropolitan debt administration fund and operated under any order made under section 66 of the Local Government Act 1985.

DEFINITION
   "trading undertaking": s.12(2).

GENERAL NOTE
   See general note to s.1.

Section 7   SCHEDULE 2

RATES: MAXIMUM LIMIT

1.—(1) The maximum limit in relation to a designated authority shall be determined by applying the appropriate formula (found in accordance with paragraph 6 below).

(2) The maximum limit in relation to a designated authority shall be expressed in pence; and parts of pence shall be calculated to two decimal places only, after adding one hundredth where (apart from this sub-paragraph) there would be not less than one thousandth.

2.—(1) This paragraph applies for the purposes of paragraph 6 below.

(2) EL is the level for the authority's total expenditure in the relevant financial year which before the passing of this Act was determined and notified to the authority under section 3(1) and (3) of the 1984 Act.

(3) BG is the aggregate of the amount (if any) of block grant which the Secretary of State estimates will be payable to the authority for the relevant financial year, where the estimate—

(a) is made by reference to the contents of, and the information taken into account by him in making, the relevant Report, and

(b) is made without taking into account the effect (if any) of sections 62 and 63 of the 1980 Act (adjustments).

(4) E is the contribution (if any) payable to the authority in respect of the relevant financial year under any scheme under section 66 of the London Government Act 1963 (equalisation of rates).

(5) RV is the aggregate of the rateable values of the hereditaments in the area of the authority; and for this purpose the rateable value of a hereditament is—

(a) in the case of a hereditament for which a method of ascertaining its rateable value for the purposes of Part VI of the 1980 Act is provided in the relevant Report, the value so ascertained, and

(b) in any other case, the rateable value ascribed to the hereditament in the valuation lists on 1st April 1986,

ignoring any changes in the valuation lists, and any other information relating to hereditaments and rateable values, not notified to the Secretary of State before 20th December 1986.

(6) T is the amount (if any) determined by applying the formula—

$$\frac{A}{B} \times M \times 12$$

(7) GRE is the amount shown as grant-related expenditure in relation to the authority in the relevant Report.

(8) R is the amount determined by applying the formula—

$$\left((GRE \times 1{\cdot}09) - (EL \times 1{\cdot}02) + BG - DBG \right) \times \frac{100}{RV}$$

3.—(1) This paragraph applies for the purposes of paragraph 2(6) above.

(2) A is the amount (if any) which before 20th December 1986 the authority submitted under section 65 of the 1980 Act (information) as the amount the authority estimates as its expenditure on education for the financial year beginning in 1986 (taking, if more than one such amount was submitted before that date, the latest to be so submitted).

(3) B is the amount shown as grant-related expenditure in relation to the authority in the Rate Support Grant Report for England for the financial year beginning in 1986.

(4) M is the figure shown as the multiplier in relation to the authority in the relevant Report.

(5) For the purposes of sub-paragraph (2) above any amount submitted by the authority as an amount it estimates as its expenditure by way of debt charges, or by way of provision for pay and price changes, or on school meals and milk, shall be ignored.

4.—(1) For the purposes of paragraph 2(8) above DBG is the aggregate of the amount (if any) of block grant which the Secretary of State estimates will be payable to the authority for the relevant financial year, where the estimate—

(a) is made on the assumptions that the authority's total expenditure in relation to the relevant financial year is equal to GRE × 1·09, and that the gross rateable value of its area is equal to RV,

(b) is made by reference to the contents of the relevant Report, and

(c) is made without taking into account the effect (if any) of sections 62 and 63 of the 1980 Act (adjustments).

(2) For the purposes of paragraph 2(8) above and sub-paragraph (1) above EL, BG, RV and GRE have the same meanings as in paragraph 6 below.

5. In this Schedule "the relevant financial year" means the financial year beginning in 1987 and "the relevant Report" means the Rate Support Grant Report for England for that financial year.

6.—(1) In the case of an authority actually designated by the Secretary of State (as opposed to one deemed to have been designated) the appropriate formula is, if the authority was also designated under section 2 of the 1984 Act in relation to the financial year beginning in 1986—

$$\left((EL - (BG + E)) \times \frac{100}{RV} \right) + T$$

(2) In the case of an authority actually designated by the Secretary of State (as opposed to one deemed to have been designated) the appropriate formula is, if the authority was not also designated under section 2 of the 1984 Act in relation to the financial year beginning in 1986 and if in the case of the authority GRE × 1·09 does not exceed EL × 1·02—

$$\left(\frac{((EL \times 1{\cdot}02) - (BG + E)) \times 100}{RV} \right) + T$$

(3) In the case of an authority actually designated by the Secretary of State (as opposed to one deemed to have been designated) the appropriate formula is, if the authority was not also designated under section 2 of the 1984 Act in relation to the financial year beginning in 1986 and if in the case of the authority GRE × 1·09 exceeds EL × 1·02—

$$\left(\frac{((EL \times 1{\cdot}02) - (BG + E)) \times 100}{RV} \right) + T + R$$

(4) In the case of a metropolitan county police authority or the Northumbria Police Authority the appropriate formula is—

$$\left(\frac{(EL \times 1{\cdot}04) - BG}{} \right) \times \frac{100}{RV}$$

(5) In the case of a metropolitan county fire and civil defence authority or the London Fire and Civil Defence Authority the appropriate formula is—

$$\left(\frac{(EL \times 1{\cdot}025) - BG}{} \right) \times \frac{100}{RV}$$

(6) In the case of a metropolitan county passenger transport authority the appropriate formula is—

$$\left(\frac{(EL \times 1{\cdot}02) - BG}{} \right) \times \frac{100}{RV}$$

(7) In the case of the Inner London Education Authority the appropriate formula is—

$$\left(\frac{(EL \times 1{\cdot}006) - BG}{} \right) \times \frac{100}{RV}$$

DEFINITIONS
  "designated authority": s.7(1), (2).
  "EL", "BG", "E", "RV", "T", "GRE", "R": para. 2.
  "A", "B", "M": para. 3.
  "DBG": para. 4.
  "relevant financial year": para. 5.
  "relevant Report": para. 5.

GENERAL NOTE
  See general note to s.7.

Section 10   SCHEDULE 3

RATE SUPPORT GRANT: SPECIAL PROVISIONS

Consultation

1.—(1) Sub-paragraphs (2) and (3) below apply as regards the Rate Support Grant Report for England for the year beginning in 1987 and the Rate Support Grant Report for Wales for that year.

(2) If the Secretary of State proposes to include in such a Report any specification under section 1(6), 2(4) or 3(1), (7) or (8) of this Act in respect of that year, section 60(5) of the 1980 Act shall not require consultation to be made (as regards that Report) as to any matter relating to such a specification.

(3) The requirements of section 60(5) of the 1980 Act may be satisfied (as regards such a Report) by consultation before the passing of this Act; and the requirement in section 54(4) of that Act to consult may be satisfied (as regards a determination to be specified in such a Report) by consultation before the passing of this Act.

(4) Sub-paragraphs (5) and (6) below apply as regards—
    (a) the first supplementary report proposed to be made after the passing of this Act for England for the year beginning in 1985,
    (b) the first supplementary report proposed to be so made for England for the year beginning in 1986, and

(c) the first supplementary report proposed to be so made for Wales for the year beginning in 1986.

(5) If the Secretary of State proposes to include in such a report any specification under section 1(6), 2(4) or 3(1), (7) or (8) of this Act in respect of the year concerned, section 60(5) of the 1980 Act (as applied by section 61(2)) shall not require consultation to be made (as regards that report) as to any matter relating to such a specification.

(6) The requirements of section 60(5) of the 1980 Act (as applied by section 61(2)) may be satisfied (as regards such a report) by consultation before the passing of this Act; and the requirement in section 54(4) of that Act to consult may be satisfied (as regards a fresh determination to be specified in such a Report) by consultation before the passing of this Act.

(7) Sub-paragraphs (2) and (3) above also apply as regards any Report proposed to be made in substitution (directly or indirectly) for any Report mentioned in sub-paragraph (1) above.

(8) Sub-paragraphs (5) and (6) above also apply as regards any report proposed to be made in substitution (directly or indirectly) for—

(a) the first supplementary report made after the passing of this Act for England for the year beginning in 1985,

(b) the first supplementary report so made for England for the year beginning in 1986, or

(c) the first supplementary report so made for Wales for the year beginning in 1986.

(9) In a case where sub-paragraph (2) or (5) above applies, section 9(4) of this Act shall not apply in relation to the exercise of the power to specify.

Certain matters to be disregarded

2.—(1) In making any determination or doing any other thing (other than making an excepted specification) after the passing of this Act for the purposes of any relevant report, the Secretary of State shall leave out of account information and representations received by him on or after the relevant date.

(2) In this paragraph "relevant report" means any report as regards which paragraph 1(2) and (3) above or 1(5) and (6) above apply.

(3) In this paragraph "the relevant date" means 20th December 1986 in the case of—

(a) the Rate Support Grant Report for England for the year beginning in 1987,

(b) any Report proposed to be made in substitution (directly or indirectly) for the Report mentioned in paragraph (a) above,

(c) the report mentioned in paragraph 1(4)(b) above, or

(d) any report proposed to be made in substitution (directly or indirectly) for the report mentioned in paragraph 1(8)(b) above.

(4) In this paragraph "the relevant date" means 11th December 1986 in the case of—

(a) the report mentioned in paragraph 1(4)(a) above, or

(b) any report proposed to be made in substitution (directly or indirectly) for the report mentioned in paragraph 1(8)(a) above.

(5) In this paragraph "the relevant date" means 4th December 1986 in the case of—

(a) the Rate Support Grant Report for Wales for the year beginning in 1987,

(b) any Report proposed to be made in substitution (directly or indirectly) for the Report mentioned in paragraph (a) above,

(c) the report mentioned in paragraph 1(4)(c) above, or

(d) any report proposed to be made in substitution (directly or indirectly) for the report mentioned in paragraph 1(8)(c) above.

(6) In this paragraph "an excepted specification" means a specification made under section 1(6), 2(4) or 3(1), (7) or (8) of this Act.

Total expenditure 1985–86

3.—(1) In doing any of the acts mentioned in sub-paragraph (2) below the Secretary of State shall treat the relevant amount as the amount of an English local authority's total expenditure in relation to the relevant year.

(2) The acts are—

(a) making any determination or doing any other thing after the passing of this Act for the purposes of any relevant report, and

(b) making under section 66(1) of the 1980 Act the first estimate and notification to be made after the passing of this Act as regards the authority concerned for the relevant year.

(3) Where an amount estimated as an authority's total expenditure in relation to the relevant year was submitted to the Secretary of State by the authority—

(a) before 11th December 1986, and

(b) in response to a requirement made under section 65 of the 1980 Act in April 1986,

for the purposes of this paragraph the relevant amount is (as regards the authority) the amount submitted.

(4) Where in the case of an authority no amount was submitted as mentioned in sub-paragraph (3) above but an amount estimated as the authority's total expenditure in relation to the relevant year was submitted to the Secretary of State by the authority—

(a) before 11th December 1986, and

(b) in response to a requirement made under section 65 of the 1980 Act in February 1985,

for the purposes of this paragraph the relevant amount is (as regards the authority) the amount mentioned in sub-paragraph (5) or (6) below (as the case may be).

(5) Where sub-paragraph (4) above applies in the case of an authority which is not a local education authority, the amount is the amount submitted.

(6) Where sub-paragraph (4) above applies in the case of an authority which is a local education authority, the amount is the amount submitted as adjusted by a method determined by the Secretary of State; and the method shall be determined in accordance with principles to be applied to all authorities affected by the adjustment.

(7) Where in the case of an authority more than one amount was submitted as mentioned in sub-paragraph (3) above, for the purposes of that sub-paragraph the amount submitted shall be taken to be the latest to be so submitted.

(8) In this paragraph "the relevant year" means the year beginning in 1985.

(9) For the purposes of this paragraph relevant reports are—

(a) the report mentioned in paragraph 1(4)(a) above, and

(b) any report proposed to be made in substitution (directly or indirectly) for the report mentioned in paragraph 1(8)(a) above.

(10) In its application in relation to the Greater London Council, the Inner London Education Authority or a metropolitan county council, this paragraph shall have effect as if the second reference to the authority in sub-paragraph (3) included a reference to the London Residuary Body or (as the case may be) the body established for the metropolitan county by section 57(1)(b) of the Local Government Act 1985.

Total expenditure 1986–87

4.—(1) Sub-paragraph (2) below applies where before the relevant date a local authority submitted to the Secretary of State an amount which it estimates as its total expenditure in relation to the relevant year.

(2) In doing any of the acts mentioned in sub-paragraph (3) below the Secretary of State shall treat the amount submitted as the amount of the authority's total expenditure in relation to the relevant year.

(3) The acts are—

(a) making any determination or doing any other thing after the passing of this Act for the purposes of any relevant report, and

(b) making under section 66(1) of the 1980 Act the first estimate and notification to be made after the passing of this Act as regards the authority concerned for the relevant year.

(4) For the purposes of sub-paragraph (2) above—

(a) if the authority and the Secretary of State agreed before the relevant date an amount to replace any amount submitted, the amount submitted shall be taken to be the amount agreed, and

(b) subject to paragraph (a) above, if more than one amount was submitted before the relevant date, the amount submitted shall be taken to be the latest to be so submitted.

(5) In this paragraph "the relevant year" means the year beginning in 1986.

(6) For the purposes of this paragraph relevant reports are—

(a) the report mentioned in paragraph 1(4)(b) above and that mentioned in paragraph 1(4)(c) above, and

(b) any report proposed to be made in substitution (directly or indirectly) for the report mentioned in paragraph 1(8)(b) above or that mentioned in paragraph 1(8)(c) above.

(7) In this paragraph "the relevant date" means 20th December 1986 in the case of an English authority, or 4th December 1986 in the case of a Welsh authority.

Total expenditure 1986–87 (further provisions)

5.—(1) Sub-paragraph (2) below applies where before the relevant date a local authority submitted to the Secretary of State an amount which it estimates as its total expenditure in relation to the year beginning in 1986.

(2) Where, in making any determination or doing any other thing after the passing of this Act for the purposes of any Report as regards which paragraph 1(2) and (3) above apply the Secretary of State wishes to take into account the authority's total expenditure in relation to the year beginning in 1986, he shall treat the amount submitted as the amount of its total expenditure in relation to that year.

(3) For the purposes of sub-paragraph (2) above—

    (a) if the authority and the Secretary of State agreed before the relevant date an amount to replace any amount submitted, the amount submitted shall be taken to be the amount agreed, and

    (b) subject to paragraph (a) above, if more than one amount was submitted before the relevant date, the amount submitted shall be taken to be the latest to be so submitted.

(4) In this paragraph "the relevant date" means 20th December 1986 in the case of an English authority, or 4th December 1986 in the case of a Welsh authority.

Teachers' remuneration

6.—(1) In making any determination or doing any other thing after the passing of this Act for the purposes of any Report as regards which paragraph 1(2) and (3) above apply, the Secretary of State shall leave out of account the matters mentioned in sub-paragraph (2) below.

(2) The matters are scales and allowances which relate to the remuneration of school teachers and provide for remuneration greater than the aggregate of—

    (a) the remuneration in payment in December 1986, and

    (b) 3·75 per cent. of the remuneration mentioned in paragraph (a) above (3·75 per cent. being the approximate increase in the GDP deflator for 1987–88, as predicted in the Autumn Statement 1986 presented to Parliament by the Chancellor of the Exchequer in November 1986).

(3) In making any determination or doing any other thing after the passing of this Act for the purposes of—

    (a) the report mentioned in paragraph 1(4)(b) above or that mentioned in paragraph 1(4)(c) above, or

    (b) any report proposed to be made in substitution (directly or indirectly) for the report mentioned in paragraph 1(8)(b) above or that mentioned in paragraph 1(8)(c) above,

the Secretary of State shall leave out of account the matters mentioned in sub-paragraph (4) below.

(4) The matters are scales and allowances which relate to the remuneration of school teachers and provide for remuneration greater than the remuneration in payment in December 1986.

(5) In this paragraph "school teacher" means—

    (a) a teacher in a primary or secondary school maintained by a local education authority, or

    (b) a person employed by a local education authority as a teacher in the provision of primary or secondary education, other than a person employed as a teacher in an establishment maintained by a local authority in the exercise of a social services function.

Rateable values 1985–86

7.—(1) In doing any of the acts mentioned in sub-paragraph (2) below the Secretary of State shall—

    (a) take into account information relating to hereditaments in the area of an English local authority and their rateable values if the information falls within sub-paragraph (4) below, and

    (b) leave out of account information relating to such hereditaments and their rateable values if the information does not fall within sub-paragraph (4) below.

(2) The acts are—

    (a) making any determination or doing any other thing after the passing of this Act for the purposes of any relevant report, and

(b) making under section 66(1) of the 1980 Act the first estimate and notification to be made after the passing of this Act as regards the authority concerned for the year beginning in 1985.

(3) For the purposes of this paragraph relevant reports are—
    (a) the report mentioned in paragraph 1(4)(a) above, and
    (b) any report proposed to be made in substitution (directly or indirectly) for the report mentioned in paragraph 1(8)(a) above.

(4) The information referred to in sub-paragraph (1) above is that which was taken into account in making the last supplementary report made before the passing of this Act for England for the year beginning in 1985.

Rateable values 1986–87.

8.—(1) In doing any of the acts mentioned in sub-paragraph (2) below the Secretary of State shall—
    (a) take into account information relating to hereditaments in the area of an English local authority and their rateable values if the information falls within sub-paragraph (4) below, and
    (b) leave out of account information relating to such hereditaments and their rateable values if the information does not fall within sub-paragraph (4) below.

(2) The acts are—
    (a) making any determination or doing any other thing after the passing of this Act for the purposes of any relevant report, and
    (b) making under section 66(1) of the 1980 Act the first estimate and notification to be made after the passing of this Act as regards the authority concerned for the year beginning in 1986.

(3) For the purposes of this paragraph relevant reports are—
    (a) the report mentioned in paragraph 1(4)(b) above, and
    (b) any report proposed to be made in substitution (directly or indirectly) for the report mentioned in paragraph 1(8)(b) above.

(4) The information referred to in sub-paragraph (1) above is that which was taken into account in making the Rate Support Grant Report for England for the year beginning in 1986.

General

9. References in this Schedule to making determinations or doing other things for the purposes of a report include references to making or doing them with a view to the inclusion of anything in a report whether or not the inclusion is required by any enactment.

10.—(1) Paragraph 6 above shall have effect subject to paragraphs 4 and 5 above.

(2) Part VI of the 1980 Act shall have effect subject to paragraphs 2 to 8 above.

GENERAL NOTE

This Schedule makes miscellaneous and consequential provision in respect of rate support grant. It enables the Secretary of State to make the Rate Support Grant Report for 1987–8, and certain supplementary reports, with modified requirements as to consultation and after leaving out of account certain information and representations which would otherwise have to be taken into account. The object is to minimise delay which would otherwise have been caused by the necessity for passing this Act.

Section 11   SCHEDULE 4

AMENDMENTS

Local Government, Planning and Land Act 1980

1.—(1) Section 54 of the 1980 Act shall be amended as mentioned in sub-paragraphs (2) and (3) below.

(2) In subsection (1) for "in respect of their" there shall be substituted "and the Receiver in respect of", subsections (5) and (6) shall be omitted, and in subsection (7) the words "for the Metropolitan Police District" and the words from "and to the extent that" to the end shall be omitted.

(3) At the end there shall be inserted—
    "(9) In this section "relevant expenditure" in relation to any year means—

(a) the aggregate of all local authorities' relevant expenditure in relation to the year, plus

(b) the Receiver's total expenditure for the year (within the meaning of Schedule 2 to the Local Government Finance Act 1982).

(10) But to the extent that, in any year, any expenditure of the Receiver or of a combined police authority is met by any grants mentioned in subsection (7)(a) or (b) above, that expenditure shall be treated for the purposes of this section as relevant expenditure in relation to that year.

(11) In this section "the Receiver" means the Receiver for the Metropolitan Police District."

2.—(1) Section 56 of the 1980 Act shall be amended as mentioned in sub-paragraphs (2) and (3) below.

(2) In subsections (6) and (7) for "the total expenditure to be incurred by them during" there shall be substituted "their total expenditure in relation to".

(3) In subsection (8), in the definition of grant-related expenditure, after "notional" there shall be inserted "total".

3. In section 58(5) of the 1980 Act after "in their" there shall be inserted "total".

4. The following shall be substituted for section 65 of the 1980 Act—

"Information

65.—(1) Each local authority shall submit to the Secretary of State in respect of each year, in such form and by such date as he may specify, such of the information mentioned in subsection (2) below as he may from time to time require for the purposes of this Part of this Act, section 8 of the Local Government Finance Act 1982, section 2 of the Rate Support Grants Act 1986 and sections 1 and 2 of the Local Government Finance Act 1987.

(2) The information is information as to the following matters—

(a) the expenditure incurred, or to be incurred, by the authority during the year,

(b) their relevant expenditure in relation to the year,

(c) their total expenditure in relation to the year, and

(d) their accounts for the year.

(3) The information required under subsection (1) above may include any of the following—

(a) what the authority calculate as the amount of expenditure incurred, or likely to be incurred, by them during the year,

(b) what the authority calculate as the amount, or likely amount, of their relevant expenditure in relation to the year,

(c) what the authority calculate as the amount, or likely amount, of their total expenditure in relation to the year,

(d) what the authority calculate as the amount of any addition or subtraction to be made in relation to the year by virtue of any specification under section 3(1) or (7) of the Local Government Finance Act 1987, and

(e) information about the items of account which are likely to be (as well as those which have been) debited or credited to the authority's accounts for the year.

(4) Where no or no sufficient information as to the matters mentioned in subsection (2) above has been submitted to the Secretary of State in respect of a year, whether under subsection (1) above or otherwise, he may for the purpose of making a supplementary report, an adjustment under section 62 above or an estimate under section 66(1) below make such assumptions as to those matters as he thinks appropriate.

(5) Where any information as to any of the matters mentioned in subsection (2) above is submitted to the Secretary of State under subsection (1) above after the date specified by him, or otherwise than under that subsection, he may for any of the purposes mentioned in subsection (4) above disregard it if he considers that it is not reasonably practicable to take it into account for that purpose."

Social Security and Housing Benefits Act 1982

5. In section 34(2) of the Social Security and Housing Benefits Act 1982 for the words from "count" to the end there shall be substituted "be treated for the purposes of Part VI of the Local Government, Planning and Land Act 1980 (rate support grant) as relevant expenditure of the authority in relation to the year concerned."

Local Government Finance Act 1982

6.—(1) Section 3 of the Local Government Finance Act 1982 (substituted rates and precepts) shall be amended as mentioned in sub-paragraphs (2) and (3) below.

(2) In subsection (4) for "any authority" there shall be substituted "or section 8 of the Local Government Finance Act 1987, any authority to which the duty in section 8(1) of that Act does not apply and".

(3) In subsections (5) and (7) after "this section" there shall be inserted "or section 8 of the Local Government Finance Act 1987".

7. In section 8 of the Local Government Finance Act 1982 (adjustments of distribution of block grant) the following shall be inserted after subsection (4)—

"(4A) If guidance issued for the purposes of section 59(6)(cc) of the said Act of 1980 is guidance by reference to total expenditure, and if representations in the following behalf are made to the Secretary of State by any association of local authorities or by any local authority, he may—

(a) in the Rate Support Grant Report made for any year under section 60 of that Act, or

(b) in a supplementary report made for any year under section 61 of that Act,

provide that items of any description or amount shall be disregarded in calculating total expenditure for the purposes of the said section 59(6)(cc) and of determining under subsection (3)(c) above whether or the extent to which local authorities have or have not complied (or have or have not taken steps to comply) with the guidance."

Rates Act 1984

8.—(1) Section 7 of the 1984 Act (certificates of compliance) shall be amended as mentioned in sub-paragraphs (2) and (3) below.

(2) In subsection (1) for "this Part of this Act" there shall be substituted "section 8(4) of the Local Government Finance Act 1987".

(3) In subsections (2) and (3) for "this Part of this Act" there shall be substituted "section 8(5) of the Local Government Finance Act 1987".

(4) In section 7(2) of this Act the words "but not to the provisions of Part I of the 1984 Act" shall have effect subject to this paragraph.

9. In section 19(2) of the 1984 Act for ", "Rate Support Grant Report" and "total expenditure"" there shall be substituted "and "Rate Support Grant Report" ", and after section 19(2) of that Act there shall be inserted—

"(2A) For the purposes of this Act the total expenditure of a local authority in relation to any financial year is the expenditure which is its total expenditure in relation to the year for the purposes of Part VI of the Local Government, Planning and Land Act 1980 by virtue of section 3 of the Local Government Finance Act 1987."

Local Government Act 1985

10. In paragraph 2(1)(b) of Schedule 15 to the Local Government Act 1985 for "section 54(5)" there shall be substituted "Part VI".

Social Security Act 1986

11. In section 30(10) of the Social Security Act 1986 for the words from "count" to the end there shall be substituted "be treated for the purposes of Part VI of the Local Government, Planning and Land Act 1980 (rate support grant) as relevant expenditure of the authority in relation to the year."

General

12.—(1) The amendments in paragraphs 6 and 8 above shall have effect only in relation to rates for, and precepts in respect of, the financial year beginning in 1987.

(2) The amendment in paragraph 9 above shall have effect in relation to the financial year beginning in 1988 and subsequent financial years.

(3) The other amendments in this Schedule—

(a) shall have effect in relation to each of the future years, and

(b) shall have effect in relation to each of the intermediate years as regards anything falling to be done after (but not as regards anything done before) the passing of this Act,

to the extent that the provisions amended have effect (apart from this Act) in relation to the future year or intermediate year concerned.

SCHEDULE 5

REPEALS

Chapter	Short title	Extent of repeal
1976 c.32.	Lotteries and Amusements Act 1976.	Section 8(3).
1980 c.65.	Local Government, Planning and Land Act 1980.	In section 54, subsections (5) and (6), in subsection (7) the words "for the Metropolitan Police District" and the words from "and to the extent that" to the end, and in subsection (8) the definition of rate fund.
		In section 56, in subsection (8) the definition of total expenditure, in subsection (10) the words "giving a direction under subsection (8) above or", and subsection (11).
		Section 68(4).
1982 c.32.	Local Government Finance Act 1982.	In section 9, subsections (2) and (3). In Schedule 2, paragraphs 3 and 9.
1985 c.51.	Local Government Act 1985.	Section 69(3).
1986 c.50.	Social Security Act 1986.	In Schedule 10, paragraph 52(2).
1986 c.54	Rate Support Grants Act 1986.	In Schedule 1, paragraph 13.

The repeals in this Schedule—

    (a) shall have effect in relation to each of the future years, and

    (b) shall have effect in relation to each of the intermediate years as regards anything falling to be done after (but not as regards anything done before) the passing of this Act,

to the extent that the provisions repealed have effect (apart from this Act) in relation to the future year or intermediate year concerned.

SOCIAL FUND (MATERNITY AND FUNERAL EXPENSES) ACT 1987

(1987 c. 7)

An Act to empower the Secretary of State to prescribe, under section 32(2)(a) of the Social Security Act 1986, amounts, whether in respect of prescribed items or otherwise, to meet maternity expenses and funeral expenses.   [17th March 1987]

PARLIAMENTARY DEBATES
  Hansard: H.C. Vol. 108, col. 1127; Vol. 109, col. 1171; Vol. 110, col. 81; H.L. Vol. 484, col. 515; Vol. 485, cols. 367, 1193, 1317.

Amendment of section 32(2) of Social Security Act 1986

1. In section 32(2)(a) of the Social Security Act 1986 the words "of prescribed amounts, whether in respect of prescribed items or otherwise," shall be inserted before "to meet".

Short title etc.

2.—(1) This Act may be cited as the Social Fund (Maternity and Funeral Expenses) Act 1987.

(2) An Order in Council under paragraph 1(1)(b) of Schedule 1 to the Northern Ireland Act 1974 (legislation for Northern Ireland in the interim period) which states that it is made only for purposes corresponding to those of this Act—

   (a) shall not be subject to paragraph 1(4) and (5) of that Schedule (affirmative resolution of both Houses of Parliament); but

   (b) shall be subject to annulment in pursuance of a resolution of either House.

(3) Subsections (1) and (2) above extend to Northern Ireland, but this Act does not otherwise so extend.

CONSOLIDATED FUND ACT 1987

(1987 c. 8)

Apply certain sums out of the Consolidated Fund to the service of the years ending on 31st March 1986 and 1987. [25th March 1987]

PARLIAMENTARY DEBATES
Hansard: H.C. Vol. 113, col. 173; H.L. Vol. 486, cols. 147, 181.

Issue out of the Consolidated Fund for the year ending 31st March 1986

1. The Treasury may issue out of the Consolidated Fund of the United Kingdom and apply towards making good the supply granted to Her Majesty for the service of the year ending on 31st March 1986 the sum of £392,730,629·84.

Issue out of the Consolidated Fund for the year ending 31st March 1987

2. The Treasury may issue out of the Consolidated Fund of the United Kingdom and apply towards making good the supply granted to Her Majesty for the service of the year ending on 31st March 1987 the sum of £1,277,764,000.

Short title

3. This Act may be cited as the Consolidated Fund Act 1987.

ANIMALS (SCOTLAND) ACT 1987*

(1987 c. 9)

ARRANGEMENT OF SECTIONS

An Act to make provision for Scotland with respect to civil liability for injury or damage caused by animals, the detention of straying animals and the protection of persons or livestock from animals; and for connected purposes. [9th April 1987]

PARLIAMENTARY DEBATES
Hansard: H.L. Vol. 482, col. 644; Vol. 483, cols. 530, 1256; Vol. 484, col. 12; Vol. 486, col. 297; H.C. Vol. 110, col. 1232; Vol. 112, col. 664.
The bill was considered by the Second Scottish Standing Committee on March 11, 1987.

INTRODUCTION AND GENERAL NOTE

Reform of the law on civil liability for damage by animals has had a lengthy period of gestation. The Law Reform Committee for Scotland in 1963 (Cmnd. 2185), having noted a "remarkable amount of judicial disagreement," recommended that the ordinary principles of negligence be applied to the exclusion of the common law rule of strict liability based upon foreknowledge of vice. In England a similar recommendation (but incorporating a shift of the burden of proof) by the Goddard Committee (Cmd. 8746 (1953)) came to nothing; however, following the Law Commission Report (*Civil Liability for Animals*, Law Com. No. 13, 1967) the Animals Act 1971 introduced a statutory form of strict liability based upon knowledge of the likelihood of damage attributable to abnormal characteristics known to the keeper. (See North *The Modern Law of Animals* (1972); Carey Miller "A Statutory Substitute for Scienter" 1973 J.R. 61.) The Royal Commission on Civil Liability and Compensation for Personal Injury (Cmnd. 7054 (1978), I, para. 1626) suggested that the English Animals Act be extended to Scotland but, in August 1982, the Scottish Law Commission published a consultative memorandum (No. 55) on the subject. This was followed by a report (Scot. Law Com. No. 97), published in November 1985. A draft bill was annexed to the report and, in all substantive respects, the Act corresponds with the draft.

New provisions as to strict liability for injury or damage caused by animals

1.—(1) Subject to subsection (4) and (5) below and section 2 of this Act, a person shall be liable for any injury or damage caused by an animal if—

(a) at the time of the injury or damage complained of, he was a keeper of the animal;

(b) the animal belongs to a species whose members generally are by virtue of their physical attributes or habits likely (unless controlled or restrained) to injure severely or kill persons or animals, or damage property to a material extent; and

(c) the injury or damage complained of is directly referable to such physical attributes or habits.

---

* Annotations by Dr. D. L. Carey Miller, University of Aberdeen.

(2) In this section "species" includes—
(a) a form or variety of the species or a sub-division of the species, or the form or variety, identifiable by age, sex or such other criteria as are relevant to the behaviour of animals; and
(b) a kind which is the product of hybridisation.
(3) For the purposes of subsection (1)(b) above—
(a) dogs, and dangerous wild animals within the meaning of section 7(4) of the Dangerous Wild Animals Act 1976, shall be deemed to be likely (unless controlled or restrained) to injure severely or kill persons or animals by biting or otherwise savaging, attacking or harrying; and
(b) any of the following animals in the course of foraging, namely—
cattle, horses, asses, mules, hinnies, sheep, pigs, goats and deer,
shall be deemed to be likely (unless controlled or restrained) to damage to a material extent land or the produce of land, whether harvested or not.
(4) Subsection (1) above shall not apply to any injury caused by an animal where the injury consists of disease transmitted by means which are unlikely to cause severe injury other than disease.
(5) Subsection (1) above shall not apply to injury or damage caused by the mere fact that an animal is present on a road or in any other place.
(6) For the purposes of the Law Reform (Contributory Negligence) Act 1945, any injury or damage for which a person is liable under this section shall be treated as due to his fault as defined in that Act.
(7) Subsections (1) and (2) of section 3 of the Law Reform (Miscellaneous Provisions) (Scotland) Act 1940 (contribution among joint wrongdoers) shall, subject to any necessary modifications, apply in relation to an action of damages in respect of injury or damage which is brought in pursuance of this section as they apply in relation to an action of damages in respect of loss or damage arising from any wrongful acts or omissions; but nothing in this subsection shall affect any contractual, or (except as aforesaid) any other, right of relief or indemnity.
(8) The foregoing provisions of this section and section 2 of this Act replace—
(a) any rule of law which imposes liability, without proof of a negligent act or omission, on the owner or possessor of an animal for injury or damage caused by that animal on the ground that the animal is *ferae naturae* or is otherwise known to be dangerous or harmful;
(b) the Winter Herding Act 1686;
(c) section 1(1) and (2) of the Dogs Act 1906 (injury to cattle or poultry).

GENERAL NOTE
This introduces and defines the scope of a new form of strict liability which—as subs. (8)(a) specifically provides—replaces any common law rule imposing liability because an animal is *ferae naturae*, or on the basis of proof that it is known to be dangerous or harmful. But the possibility of an alternative claim based upon the ordinary principles of negligence remains (see subs. (8)(a) and *Henderson* v. *John Stuart (Farms)*, 1963 S.C. 245, 248) and, of course, knowledge of vicious or dangerous propensity may be a factor in the proof of negligence.
Subs. (1) provides for the liability of the keeper (defined in s.5) where the animal belongs to a species which, by reason of physical attributes or habits, means that uncontrolled members are likely to cause severe injury (or death) or material damage to property, and where the injury or damage—not necessarily serious in nature—directly resulted from the attributes or habits concerned. The subsection, it is submitted, envisages strict liability applicable to predictable injury or damage caused by an animal belonging to a group which manifests the particular risk.
The problem of classification in terms of risk is aided by two provisions: first, by subs. (3)(a) providing that dogs and dangerous animals, within the meaning of the Dangerous

Wild Animals Act 1976, are deemed likely to cause harm, to humans or other animals, by direct vicious conduct; and, secondly, by subs. (3)(b) providing that the grazing animals listed are likely, in the course of foraging, to cause damage to land or the produce of land. It should be noted that the words "injury" and "harry" are defined in s.7 and this clarifies the scope of the loss covered in s.1. From the point of view of sheep-worrying by dogs it is significant that "injury" includes any abortion and "harrying" includes chasing in such a way as may be likely to cause injury.

An innovatory aspect of the Act is its cross-referencing to the Dangerous Wild Animals Act 1976 to establish a counterpart category for the purpose of the application of strict liability to wild animals. S.7(4) of the Dangerous Wild Animals Act defines "dangerous wild animals" by reference to a list contained in the Schedule which may be periodically updated by order of the Secretary of State. One may compare this solution with that of the English Animals Act 1971 (s.6(2)) providing an open-ended definition of dangerous species as a species not commonly domesticated in Britain, whose fully grown members have characteristics making them likely, unless restrained, to cause severe damage, or that any damage they may cause is likely to be severe.

Subs. (2) clarifies the intended scope of "species"; a matter of importance in cases in which the pursuer seeks to establish the defender's strict liability but cannot rely upon one of the deeming provisions in subs. (3). The word is given a wide—and even loose—meaning with the apparent intention of aiding a pursuer in a claim under subs. (1). On the basis of s.1(2)(a) "species" includes, as potentially separate species, not only different breeds of the same species, but also sub-groupings which are distinct from the point of view of risk, because of particular circumstances or conditions. Accordingly, it may be possible, within a given class, to justify a distinction between males and females, mature and young, females with young and other adults and so on. (See Scot. Law Com. No. 97, paras. 4.7 and 4.8 on the point that it should be open to a pursuer to argue, in any way, that special rules apply to a particular class.) Subs. (2)(b) is specific in including hybrid animals, the intention being to avoid any scientific criteria in terms of which hybrids are not classified as species.

Subs. (4), read with s.7, limits the extent of liability under the section by excluding injury in the form of disease transmitted by a means unlikely to cause severe injury. Accordingly, if an infection is merely passed on there will be no liability but disease which results from an act likely to cause severe injury, typically a bite, is actionable.

Subs. (5) excludes from the sphere of strict liability the situation of the passive involvement of an animal through its mere presence. The important point here is that road accidents involving livestock remain a matter for the ordinary law of negligence which, of course, has the flexibility to reflect the different emphases which may be justified depending upon the locality, in which the accident occurs. (See *Gardiner* v. *Miller,* 1967 S.L.T. 29.)

Subs. (6)—read with s.2, subss. (1)(a) and (3)(a), in effect providing for the partial defence of contributory negligence—makes possible an apportionment of damages in appropriate circumstances. Where joint-wrongdoers are involved (*e.g.* owner and possessor of an animal) subs. (7) provides for the possibility of an action for contribution or the conjoining of defenders under third party procedure. (The aim being that "a complete settlement of the claims of all parties . . . be expeditiously achieved in the one process." Scot. Law Com. No. 97, para. 4.20.)

Subs. (8) clarifies the scope of s.1 in setting out the prior rules of strict liability which are replaced by the Act. Clearly, the most important aspect is the substitution of the statutory form for the common law principles of strict liability while—as indicated above—leaving intact the ordinary concept of fault in so far as this may be applicable. The rule under s.1 achieves comprehensiveness in also displacing certain legislation providing for strict liability in respect of particular forms of damage by animals; in the case of the Winter Herding Act 1686, damage by straying livestock and, in the case of the Dogs Act 1906, loss occasioned by a dog to cattle or poultry. The formal repeal of this legislation is provided for in s.8(2) and the Schedule.

Although the legislation displaces existing forms of strict liability it is worth noting that the doctrine of *res ipsa loquitur* remains potentially applicable where negligence is alleged. (This follows from the fact that the ordinary principles of fault are untouched by the legislation: see s.1(8)(a) and Scot. Law Com. No. 97, para. 3.13). In so far as a prima facie case of negligence may be established by the invocation of this doctrine to proof of the event which caused harm it seems that, in some circumstances, the claimant may have open to him either action under s.1, or what would amount to an alternative form of strict liability at common law. Moreover, in respect of injury or damage not covered by the deeming provisions in s.1(3), recourse to the common law of delict may be hardly more demanding, in terms of proof, than what would have to be established under s.1(1)(b). One thinks, for example, of the application of *res ipsa loquitur* to the case of a bolting horse—see *Snee* v. *Durkie* (1903) 6 F. 42; *Hendry* v. *M'Dougall,* 1923 S.C. 378.

Exceptions from liability under section 1

2.—(1) A person shall not be liable under section 1(1) of this Act if—

   (a) the injury or damage was due wholly to the fault of—

      (i) the person sustaining it; or

      (ii) in the case of injury sustained by an animal, a keeper of the animal;

   (b) the person sustaining the injury or damage or a keeper of the animal sustaining the injury willingly accepted the risk of it as his; or

   (c) subject to subsection (2) below, the injury or damage was sustained on, or in consequence of the person or animal sustaining the injury or damage coming on to, land which was occupied by a person who was a keeper, or by another person who authorised the presence on the land, of the animal which caused the injury or damage; and, either—

      (i) the person sustaining the injury or damage was not authorised or entitled to be on that land; or (as the case may be)

      (ii) no keeper of the animal sustaining the injury was authorised or entitled to have the animal present on that land.

(2) A person shall not be exempt from liability by virtue of subsection (1)(c) above if the animal causing the injury or damage was kept on the land wholly or partly for the purpose of protecting persons or property, unless the keeping of the animal there, and the use made of the animal, for that purpose was reasonable, and, if the animal was a guard dog within the meaning of the Guard Dogs Act 1975, unless there was compliance with section 1 of that Act.

(3) In subsection (1) above—

   (a) in paragraph (a) "fault" has the same meaning as in the Law Reform (Contributory Negligence) Act 1945;

   (b) in paragraph (c) "authorised" means expressly or impliedly authorised.

GENERAL NOTE

The defences available against a claim under s.1(1) are set out in s.2 and the actual measure of strict liability emerges from reading the two sections together.

Subs. (1)(a) provides for the defence of fault of the pursuer. Given that, in terms of subs. (3)(a), "fault" has the meaning of the Law Reform (Contributory Negligence) Act 1945, this introduces the concept of contributory negligence. It is significant that the legislation does not curtail the application of the defence of fault of the pursuer to match the special risk involved in the keeping of a dangerous animal but, of course, any such limitation would be incompatible with the equitable device of apportionment.

Subs. (1)(b) makes possible the defence of voluntary assumption of risk on the model of s.2(3) of the Occupiers' Liability (Scotland) Act 1960.

Subs. (1)(c), read with subss. (2) and (3)(b), deals with the not unusual situation of a person, or another animal, being injured—by the defender's animal—on land where the presence of the injured person or animal was not authorised. In this subsection the legislation prescribes the obviously justifiable condition that the animal which caused the injury was kept by the occupier of the land, or by another party whose presence was authorised (e.g. a seasonal grazing tenant). Subs. (2) precludes the operation of the defence of unauthorised presence if the animal was kept for purposes of protection unless this was reasonable and, in so far as applicable, there was compliance with the requirements of the Guard Dogs Act 1975 regarding control and warning. This sensible provision, the broad counterpart of s.5(3) of the Animals Act 1971 (see *Cummings* v. *Granger* [1977] 1 All E.R. 104), means that the defence of unauthorised presence of the pursuer is available only where the defender can show that the keeping of the animal concerned, for the purposes of protection, was justifiable in the circumstances.

Detention of straying animals

3.—(1) Without prejudice to section 98 of the Roads (Scotland) Act 1984, where an animal strays on to any land and is not then under the control of any person, the occupier of the land may detain the animal for the purpose of preventing injury or damage by it.

(2) Part VI of the Civic Government (Scotland) Act 1982 (lost and abandoned property) shall apply in relation to an animal, other than a stray dog, detained under subsection (1) above as it applies in relation to any property taken possession of under section 67 of that Act subject to the omission from section 74 of the words from "or livestock" to "129 of this Act" and to any other necessary modifications; and section 4 of the Dogs Act 1906 shall, subject to any necessary modifications, apply to a stray dog detained under subsection (1) above as it applies to a stray dog taken possession of under that section.

GENERAL NOTE

Subs. 1 permits the occupier of land to detain a straying animal, but only to prevent injury or damage by it. S.98 of the Roads (Scotland) Act 1984 providing for the detention of animals on public roads, by the roads authority or by a constable, is not affected by this provision. S.5(2)(a) provides that the detainer under these circumstances will not be liable as keeper of the animal concerned, however, the wording of this exemption leaves the court with a discretion to determine that the holding has in fact become possession for the purpose of liability; clearly, the logic of the exception would not necessarily extend to protracted detention or a change in the *animus* of the detainer and, in this regard, the duty to deal with the animal as provided by subs. (2) may be relevant.

Subs. (2) provides for the disposal of animals detained under subs. (1) by applying the legislation generally applicable to lost or abandoned property and, in respect of dogs, s.4 of the Dogs Act 1906 providing for the delivery of stray dogs to the police.

Killing of, or injury to, animals attacking or harrying persons or livestock

4.—(1) Subject to subsection (2) below, in any civil proceedings against a person for killing or causing injury to an animal, it shall be a defence for him to prove—

(a) that he acted—
   (i) in self-defence;
   (ii) for the protection of any other person; or
   (iii) for the protection of any livestock and was one of the persons mentioned in subsection (3) below; and
(b) that within 48 hours after the killing or injury notice thereof was given by him or on his behalf at a police station or to a constable.

(2) There shall be no defence available under subsection (1) above to a person killing or causing injury to an animal where the killing or injury—

(a) occurred at or near a place where the person was present for the purpose of engaging in a criminal activity; and
(b) was in furtherance of that activity.

(3) The persons referred to in subsection (1)(a)(iii) above are—

(a) a person who, at the time of the injury or killing complained of, was a keeper of the livestock concerned;
(b) the owner or occupier of the land where the livestock was present; and
(c) a person authorised (either expressly or impliedly) to act for the protection of the livestock by such a keeper of the livestock or by the owner or occupier of the land where the livestock was present.

(4) A person killing or causing injury to an animal ("the defender") shall be regarded, for the purposes of this section, as acting in self defence or for the protection of another person or any livestock if, and only if—

(a) the animal is attacking him or that other person or that livestock and (whether or not the animal is under the control of anyone) the defender has reasonable grounds for believing that there are no other practicable means of ending the attack; or

(b) the defender has reasonable grounds for believing—
  (i) that the animal is about to attack him, such person or livestock and that (whether or not the animal is under the control of anyone) there are no other practicable means of preventing the attack; or
  (ii) that the animal has been attacking a person or livestock, is not under the control of anyone and has not left the vicinity where the attack took place, and that there are no other practicable means of preventing a further attack by the animal while it is still in that vicinity.

(5) In subsection (4) above "attack" or "attacking" includes "harry" or "harrying".

(6) In this section—
  "livestock" means any animals of a domestic variety (including in particular sheep, cattle and horses) and, while they are in captivity, any other animals.

GENERAL NOTE

This section replaces s.129 of the Civic Government (Scotland) Act 1982—an interim measure following s.9 of the Animals Act 1971—in regulating the right to destroy or injure an animal which is an actual or potential threat to a person or to "livestock" (widely defined, in subs. (6), to include any domestic animal or any other animal in captivity). Subs. (2) excludes the availability of any defence under the section from one who kills or injures an animal in the context of a criminal escapade. Regarding the destruction of an animal which is a threat to livestock—the most important practical aspect of this section—subs. (3) establishes the category of persons accorded this right. Subs. (4) defines the circumstances in which the defence of preventive action will be available to one who destroys or injures an animal whether in self-defence, in the defence of another, or in the defence of livestock. The significant aspect of this defence is the unambiguous requirement (". . . if, and only if . . .") of proof by the defender that reasonable grounds existed for believing that there were no other practicable means of ending or preventing the attack or a further attack, depending upon the circumstances. The defence is available regardless of whether or not the animal destroyed or injured was under the control of anyone. This clarification of the right to take action against an offending animal, even if a party in charge of the animal is present, is important—especially to those concerned with the protection of livestock from worrying by dogs.

It is submitted that there is no reason in principle why the defence available under this section should not apply where the preventive measures taken by the defender involve the use of his animal.

Meaning of a keeper of an animal

5.—(1) Subject to subsection (2) below, for the purposes of this Act a person is a keeper of an animal if—
  (a) he owns the animal or has possession of it; or
  (b) he has actual care and control of a child under the age of 16 who owns the animal or has possession of it.

(2) For the purposes of this section—
  (a) a person shall not be regarded as having possession of an animal by reason only that he is detaining it under section 3 of this Act or is otherwise temporarily detaining it for the purpose of protecting it or any person or other animal or of restoring it as soon as is reasonably practicable to its owner or a possessor of it;
  (b) if an animal has been abandoned or has escaped, a person who at the time of the abandonment or escape was the owner of it or had it in his possession shall remain its owner or shall be regarded as continuing to have possession of it until another person acquires its ownership or (as the case may be) comes into possession of it; and
  (c) the Crown shall not acquire ownership of an animal on its abandonment.

GENERAL NOTE

This section gives various meanings to the word "keeper" for the purposes of liability under s.1. In so far as more than one party may, in a particular case, qualify as "keeper" liability will be joint and several. (See Scot. Law Com. No. 97, Recommendation 13.) The broad notion of "keeper" reflects the policy that concomitant with the justification for strict liability is the desirability that an innocent victim should have a remedy. (See Scottish Law Commission No. 97, para. 4.20). The same approach appears from the rule that where a child under 16 is owner or possessor strict liability is imposed not only on the child but also on the person who has actual care and control of the child. (See s.6(3)(b) of the Animals Act 1971).

S.5(2)(a), exempting from the class of possessor one who detains an animal to prevent injury or damage, has been mentioned in the annotation to s.3; but it may be noted that the wording of subs. (2)(a), and in particular the words "temporarily" and "as soon as is reasonably practicable", gives an indication of the degree of detention necessary to constitute possession.

Subs. (2)(b) is intended to prevent a hiatus in ownership or possession caused by the abandonment or escape of an animal which, were it not for this provision, might leave a victim without a remedy because, from a proprietary point of view, no party can be identified as keeper at the time the injury or damage was caused.

Application to Crown

6. This Act binds the Crown, but this section shall not authorise proceedings to be brought against Her Majesty in her private capacity.

Interpretation

7. In this Act, unless the context otherwise requires—
"animal" does not include viruses, bacteria, algae, fungi or protozoa;
"harry" includes chase in such a way as may be likely to cause injury or suffering; and "harrying" shall be construed accordingly;
"injury" includes death, any abortion or other impairment of physical or mental condition and any loss of or diminution in the produce of an animal and, subject to section 1(4) of this Act, disease.

Transitional provision and repeals

8.—(1) This Act shall apply only in relation to injury or damage caused after the commencement of the Act.

(2) The enactments mentioned in the Schedule to this Act are hereby repealed to the extent specified in the third column of that Schedule.

Short title, commencement and extent

9.—(1) This Act may be cited as the Animals (Scotland) Act 1987.

(2) This Act shall come into force at the end of a period of 2 months beginning with the date on which it is passed.

(3) This Act extends to Scotland only.

Section 8(2)   SCHEDULE

ENACTMENTS REPEALED

Chapter	Short title	Extent of repeal
1686 c.21.	The Winter Herding Act 1686.	The whole Act.
6 Edw. 7 c.32.	The Dogs Act 1906.	In section 1, subsections (1) to (3).
18 and 19 Geo. 5. c. 21.	The Dogs (Amendment) Act 1928.	In section 1(1) the words "in both places where that word occurs".
1982 c.45.	The Civic Government (Scotland) Act 1982.	Section 129, except as it has effect for the purposes of section 74 of that Act.

BROADCASTING ACT 1987

(1987 c. 10)

An Act to alter the maximum period for which programmes may be provided under contracts with the Independent Broadcasting Authority.

[9th April 1987]

PARLIAMENTARY DEBATES

Hansard: H.L. Vol. 482, cols. 234, 937; Vol. 483, col. 1035; Vol. 484, col. 12; H.C. Vol. 110, col. 662; Vol. 113, col. 637.

The Bill was considered by Standing Committee B from February 24 to March 3, 1987.

Amendment of 1981 Act

1.—(1) Section 19 of the Broadcasting Act 1981 (programme contracts) shall be amended as mentioned in subsections (2) and (3) below.

(2) In subsection (2)(aa) (DBS contracts limited to twelve years) for "twelve" there shall be substituted "fifteen".

(3) The following shall be inserted after subsection (2)—

"(2A) But in the case of a contract to which this subsection applies the relevant maximum period for the purposes of subsection (1) is the period expiring on 31st December 1992.

(2B) Subsection (2A) applies to a contract—

    (a) which is for the provision of television programmes for broadcasting otherwise than in a DBS service or an additional teletext service, and

    (b) under which at least one of the programmes is to be provided before 1st January 1993".

Short title and extent

2.—(1) This Act may be cited as the Broadcasting Act 1986.

(2) This Act extends to Northern Ireland.

GAMING (AMENDMENT) ACT 1987*

(1987 c. 11)

An Act to amend section 18 of the Gaming Act 1968 with respect to the hours for gaming [9th April 1987]

PARLIAMENTARY DEBATES

Hansard: H.L. Vol. 483, cols. 279, 775, 1463; Vol. 484, col. 334; H.C. Vol. 111, col. 1201; Vol. 113, col. 721.

GENERAL NOTE

This modest Act extends and standardises Sunday morning closing hours for premises licensed for gaming under Pt. II of the Gaming Act 1968. Casinos in London will be permitted to remain open until 4 a.m. instead of 3 a.m., and those in the rest of Great Britain will likewise be permitted to remain open until 4 a.m., instead of 2 a.m., thus making permitted closing hours uniform throughout the week, and throughout Great Britain.

The Act gives effect to a recommendation of the Report of the Royal Commission on Gambling (Cmnd. 7200 (1978), para. 1869). The Act was sponsored by Lord Harris of Greenwich, and was supported by the Gaming Board for Great Britain, the British Casino Association, and the government.

COMMENCEMENT

The Act shall come into force on such day as the Secretary of State may by statutory instrument appoint.

EXTENT

The Act does not extend to Northern Ireland.

Amendment of section 18 of Gaming Act 1968

1.—(1) Section 18 of the Gaming Act 1968 (gaming on Sundays) shall be amended as follows.

(2) For subsection (1) there shall be substituted the following—

"(1) In England and Wales no gaming shall take place on any Sunday between the hours of four in the morning and two in the afternoon on any premises in respect of which a licence under this Act is for the time being in force".

(3) In subsection (2), for the words "two in the morning" there shall be substituted the words "four in the morning".

(4) Subsection (3) shall be repealed.

GENERAL NOTE

S.1(3) permits gaming in Scotland to be conducted until 4 a.m. on a Sunday morning, but without any change in the 7.30 p.m. opening time on Sunday evening.

S.1(4) repeals references to the "inner London area" consequent upon the uniformity of closing time.

Short title, commencement and extent

2.—(1) This Act may be cited as the Gaming (Amendment) Act 1987.

(2) This Act shall come into force on such day as the Secretary of State may by order made by statutory instrument appoint.

(3) This Act does not extend to Northern Ireland.

DEFINITION

"Secretary of State": one of Her Majesty's Principal Secretaries of State, Interpretation Act 1978, Sched. I.

---

* Annotations by David R. Miers, LL.M., D.Jur., Senior Lecturer in Law, University College, Cardiff.

PETROLEUM ACT 1987

(1987 c. 12)

ARRANGEMENT OF SECTIONS

PART I

ABANDONMENT OF OFFSHORE INSTALLATIONS

PART II

LICENSING

PART III

MISCELLANEOUS

Safety zones

Pipe-lines

Refineries

PART IV

SUPPLEMENTARY

An Act to make provision in respect of the abandonment of offshore installations and submarine pipe-lines and in respect of safety zones around offshore installations; to amend the Petroleum (Production) Act 1934 and to make provision in respect of licences under that Act; to amend the law relating to pipe-lines; to repeal sections 34 to 39 of the Petroleum and Submarine Pipe-lines Act 1975; and for connected purposes. [9th April 1987]

PARLIAMENTARY DEBATES
Hansard: H.C. Vol. 105, col. 220; Vol. 105, col. 27; Vol. 110, col. 369; H.L. Vol. 484, col. 744; Vol. 485, col. 984; Vol. 486, cols. 19, 745, 902.
The Bill was considered by Standing Committee B on December 2 to January 22, 1987.

PART I

ABANDONMENT OF OFFSHORE INSTALLATIONS

Preparation of programmes

1.—(1) The Secretary of State may by written notice require—
  (a) the person to whom the notice is given, or
  (b) where notices are given to more than one person, those persons jointly,
to submit to the Secretary of State a programme setting out the measures proposed to be taken in connection with the abandonment of an offshore installation or submarine pipe-line (an "abandonment programme").

(2) A notice under subsection (1) shall either specify the date by which the abandonment programme is to be submitted or provide for it to be submitted on or before such date as the Secretary of State may direct.

(3) A notice under subsection (1) may require the person to whom it is given to carry out such consultations as may be specified in the notice before submitting an abandonment programme.

(4) An abandonment programme—
  (a) shall contain an estimate of the cost of the measures proposed in it;
  (b) shall either specify the times at or within which the measures proposed in it are to be taken or make provision as to how those times are to be determined;
  (c) if it proposes that an installation or pipe-line be left in position or not wholly removed, shall include provision as to any continuing maintenance that may be necessary.

(5) A person who submits an abandonment programme to the Secretary of State under this section shall at the same time pay to him such fee in respect of his expenditure under this Part of this Act as may be determined in accordance with regulations under section 11.

(6) The Secretary of State may exercise his powers under this section notwithstanding that an abandonment programme has previously been submitted for the installation or pipe-line in question, but only if he rejected that programme under section 4 or has withdrawn his approval of it under section 7.

Persons who may be required to submit programmes

2.—(1) A notice under section 1(1) shall not be given to a person in relation to the abandonment of an offshore installation unless at the time when the notice is given he is within any of the following paragraphs—
  (a) the person who has registered the installation pursuant to section

2 of the Mineral Workings (Offshore Installations) Act 1971 or, if there is no such person, the person having the management of the installation or of its main structure;

(b) a person who is a concession owner in relation to the installation for the purposes of that Act, or who was a concession owner for those purposes when an activity within section 12(2) of that Act was last carried on from, by means of or on the installation;

(c) a person outside paragraphs (a) and (b) who is a party to a joint operating agreement or similar agreement relating to rights by virtue of which a person is within paragraph (b);

(d) a person outside paragraphs (a) to (c) who owns any interest in the installation otherwise than as security for a loan;

(e) a company which is outside paragraphs (a) to (d) but is associated with a company within any of those paragraphs.

(2) A notice under section 1(1) shall not be given to a person in relation to the abandonment of a submarine pipe-line unless at the time when the notice is given he is within any of the following paragraphs—

(a) a person designated as the owner of the pipe-line by an order made by the Secretary of State in pursuance of section 33(3) of the Petroleum and Submarine Pipe-lines Act 1975;

(b) a person outside paragraph (a) who owns any interest in the whole or substantially the whole of the pipe-line, otherwise than as security for a loan;

(c) a company which is outside paragraphs (a) and (b) but is associated with a company within one of those paragraphs.

(3) The Secretary of State may by written notice require a person appearing to the Secretary of State to be within any of the paragraphs of subsection (1) or (2) to give him, within such time as may be specified in the notice, the name and address of every other person whom the recipient of the notice believes to be within any of those paragraphs in relation to the installation or pipe-line concerned.

(4) A person who without reasonable excuse fails to comply with a notice under subsection (3) shall be guilty of an offence.

(5) For the purposes of this section, one company is associated with another if one of them controls the other or a third company controls both of them; and one company controls another if it possesses or is entitled to acquire—

(a) one half or more of the issued share capital of the company,

(b) such rights as would entitle it to exercise one half or more of the votes exercisable in general meetings of the company,

(c) such part of the issued share capital of the company as would entitle it to one half or more of the amount distributed if the whole of the income of the company were in fact distributed among the shareholders, or

(d) such rights as would, in the event of the winding up of the company or in any other circumstances, entitle it to receive one half or more of the assets of the company which would then be available for distribution among the shareholders,

or if it has the power, directly or indirectly, to secure that the affairs of the company are conducted in accordance with its wishes.

(6) In determining whether, by virtue of subsection (5), one company controls another, the first-mentioned company shall be taken to possess—

(a) any rights and powers possessed by a person as nominee for it, and

(b) any rights and powers possessed by a company which it controls (including rights and powers which such a company would be taken to possess by virtue of this paragraph).

Section 1 notices: supplementary provisions

3.—(1) The Secretary of State shall not before 1st July 1988 give a notice under section 1(1) to a person within paragraph (d) or (e) of section 2(1) or paragraph (b) or (c) of section 2(2).

(2) Subject to subsection (4), the Secretary of State shall not give a notice under section 1(1) in relation to an offshore installation to a person within paragraph (d) or (e) of section 2(1) if the Secretary of State has been and continues to be satisfied that adequate arrangements (including financial arrangements) have been made by a person or persons within paragraph (a), (b) or (c) to ensure that a satisfactory abandonment programme will be carried out.

(3) Subject to subsection (4), the Secretary of State shall not give a notice under section 1(1) in relation to a submarine pipe-line to a person within paragraph (b) or (c) of section 2(2) if the Secretary of State has been and continues to be satisfied that adequate arrangements (including financial arrangements) have been made by a person or persons within paragraph (a) to ensure that a satisfactory abandonment programme will be carried out.

(4) Subsections (2) and (3) shall not apply if there has been a failure to comply with a notice under section 1(1) or if the Secretary of State has rejected a programme submitted in compliance with such a notice.

(5) The Secretary of State shall not give a notice to a person under section 1(1) without first giving him an opportunity to make written representations as to whether the notice should be given.

(6) Where the Secretary of State has given a notice under section 1(1) in relation to an installation or pipe-line, he may at any time before the programme required by it is submitted withdraw the notice or give (subject to the preceding provisions of this section) a further notice under section 1(1) (whether in substitution for or in addition to any notice already given); and if he does so he shall inform the recipients of any other notices which have been given in relation to that installation or pipe-line and not withdrawn.

(7) Neither the withdrawal of a notice given under section 1(1) nor the giving of a further notice shall relieve the recipient of any other notice of his duty to submit a programme (jointly, in a case where more than one notice is given and not withdrawn, with the recipients of the other notices).

Approval of programmes

4.—(1) The Secretary of State may either approve or reject a programme submitted to him under section 1.

(2) If he approves a programme, the Secretary of State may approve it with or without modifications and either subject to conditions or unconditionally.

(3) Before approving a programme with modifications or subject to conditions, the Secretary of State shall give the persons who submitted the programme an opportunity to make written representations about the proposed modifications or conditions.

(4) If he rejects a programme, the Secretary of State shall inform the persons who submitted it of his reasons for doing so.

(5) The Secretary of State shall act without unreasonable delay in reaching a decision as to whether to approve or reject a programme.

Failure to submit programmes

5.—(1) If a notice under section 1(1) is not complied with, or if the Secretary of State rejects a programme submitted in compliance with such a notice, the Secretary of State may himself prepare an abandonment programme for the installation or pipe-line concerned.

(2) With a view to exercising his powers under subsection (1) of this section, the Secretary of State may by written notice require any of the persons to whom notice was given under section 1(1) to provide him, within such time as may be specified in the notice, with such records and drawings and such other information as may be so specified.

(3) A person who without reasonable excuse fails to comply with a notice under subsection (2) shall be guilty of an offence.

(4) The Secretary of State may recover from any of the persons to whom a notice was given under section 1(1) any expenditure incurred by the Secretary of State in preparing an abandonment programme under this section, and any fee that would have been payable on the submission of a programme by those persons.

(5) A person liable to pay any sum to the Secretary of State by virtue of subsection (4) shall also pay interest on that sum for the period beginning with the day on which the Secretary of State notified him of the sum payable and ending with the date of payment.

(6) The rate of interest payable in accordance with subsection (5) shall be a rate determined by the Secretary of State as comparable with commercial rates.

(7) Where the Secretary of State prepares an abandonment programme under this section, he shall inform the persons to whom notice was given under section 1(1) of its terms; and when he has done so, the following provisions of this Part of this Act shall have effect as if the programme had been submitted by those persons and approved by the Secretary of State.

Revision of programmes

6.—(1) Where the Secretary of State has approved a programme submitted to him under section 1—

(a) either he or the persons who submitted it acting together may propose an alteration to the programme or to any condition to which it is subject, and

(b) either he or any of those persons may propose that any person who by virtue of section 8 has a duty to secure that the programme is carried out shall cease to have that duty, or that a person who does not already have that duty shall have it (either in addition to or in substitution for another person).

(2) In the case of a proposal of the kind mentioned in subsection (1)(b), any person who would if the proposed change were made have a duty to secure that the programme is carried out must be a person who—

(a) if the programme relates to an offshore installation, is within paragraph (a), (b), (c), (d) or (e) of section 2(1) when the proposal is made, or has been within one of those paragraphs at some time since the giving of the first notice under section 1(1) in relation to the installation, and

(b) if the programme relates to a submarine pipe-line, is within paragraph (a), (b) or (c) of section 2(2) when the proposal is made, or has been within one of those paragraphs at some time since the giving of the first notice under section 1(1) in relation to the pipe-line.

(3) The Secretary of State shall not propose that a person who is or has been within paragraph (d) or (e) (but no other paragraph) of section 2(1) or paragraph (b) or (c) (but not paragraph (a)) of section 2(2) shall have a duty to secure that a programme is carried out unless it appears to the

Secretary of State that a person already under that duty has failed or may fail to discharge it.

(4) A proposal under subsection (1) shall be made by written notice given—

    (a) if the proposal is the Secretary of State's, to each of the persons by whom the programme was submitted, and

    (b) in any other case, to the Secretary of State;

and a person giving notice to the Secretary of State shall at the same time pay to him such fee in respect of his expenditure under this Part of this Act as may be determined in accordance with regulations under section 11.

(5) Where the Secretary of State has made a proposal under subsection (1)(a), he shall give an opportunity to make written representations about it to each of the persons who submitted the programme.

(6) Where a proposal has been made under subsection (1)(b), the Secretary of State shall give an opportunity to make written representations about it to every person (other than one who made the proposal) who will if the proposed change is made—

    (a) have a duty to secure that the programme is carried out, or

    (b) cease to have that duty.

(7) The Secretary of State shall determine whether a change proposed under subsection (1) is to be made and shall then give notice of his determination, and of his reasons for it, to—

    (a) every person who, before the determination was made, had a duty to secure the carrying out of the programme, and

    (b) any person who has that duty as a result of the determination.

(8) Where the Secretary of State determines that a change proposed in accordance with this section shall be made, this Part of this Act shall thereafter have effect as if the programme had been approved by the Secretary of State after being submitted under section 1 with the alterations, or as the case may be by the persons, specified in the determination.

Withdrawal of approval

7.—(1) The Secretary of State may at the request of one or more of the persons who submitted an abandonment programme withdraw his approval of the programme.

(2) If a request under subsection (1) is made by some but not all of the persons who submitted the programme, the Secretary of State shall give the others an opportunity to make written representations as to whether his approval should be withdrawn.

(3) The Secretary of State shall after determining whether to withdraw his approval of an abandonment programme give notice of his determination to each of the persons who submitted the programme.

Duty to carry out programmes

8. Where an abandonment programme is approved by the Secretary of State, it shall be the duty of each of the persons who submitted it to secure that it is carried out and that any conditions to which the approval is subject are complied with.

Default in carrying out programmes

9.—(1) If an abandonment programme approved by the Secretary of State is not carried out or a condition to which the approval is subject is not complied with, the Secretary of State may by written notice require any of the persons who submitted the programme to take such remedial action as may be specified in the notice within such time as may be so specified.

(2) A person who fails to comply with a notice given to him under subsection (1) shall be guilty of an offence unless he proves that he exercised due diligence to avoid the failure.

(3) If a notice under subsection (1) is not complied with, the Secretary of State may carry out the remedial action required by the notice, and may recover any expenditure incurred by him in doing so from the person to whom the notice was given.

(4) A person liable to pay any sum to the Secretary of State by virtue of subsection (3) shall also pay interest on that sum for the period beginning with the day on which the Secretary of State notified him of the sum payable and ending with the date of payment.

(5) The rate of interest payable in accordance with subsection (4) shall be a rate determined by the Secretary of State as comparable with commercial rates.

Financial resources

10.—(1) At any time after the Secretary of State has given a notice under section 1(1) to any person and before he has approved an abandonment programme for the installation or pipe-line concerned, he may by written notice require that person within such time as may be specified in the notice—

(a) to provide such information relating to the financial affairs of that person, and

(b) to supply copies of such documents relating to those affairs,

as may be so specified.

(2) In order to satisfy himself that a person who has a duty to secure that an abandonment programme is carried out will be capable of discharging that duty, the Secretary of State may at any time by written notice require that person, within such time as may be specified in the notice—

(a) to provide such information, and

(b) to supply copies of such documents,

as may be so specified.

(3) A person who—

(a) without reasonable excuse fails to comply with a notice under subsection (1) or subsection (2), or

(b) in purported compliance with such a notice provides information which he knows to be false in a material particular or recklessly provides information which is false in a material particular,

shall be guilty of an offence.

(4) If the Secretary of State is not satisfied that a person will be capable of discharging the duty imposed on him by section 8, he may by written notice, after consulting the Treasury, require that person to take such action as may be specified in the notice within such time as may be so specified.

(5) The Secretary of State shall not give notice to a person under subsection (4) without first giving him an opportunity to make written representations as to whether the notice should be given.

(6) A person who fails to comply with a notice under subsection (4) shall be guilty of an offence unless he proves that he exercised due diligence to avoid the failure.

Regulations

11.—(1) The Secretary of State may make regulations relating to the abandonment of offshore installations and submarine pipe-lines.

(2) Without prejudice to the generality of subsection (1), regulations under this section may—

(a) prescribe standards and safety requirements in respect of the dismantling, removal and disposal of installations and pipe-lines;

(b) prescribe standards and safety requirements in respect of anything left in the water in cases where an installation or pipe-line is not wholly removed;

(c) make provision for the prevention of pollution;

(d) make provision for inspection, including provision as to the payment of the costs of inspection;

(e) make provision as to the determination of the amount of any fees that are payable to the Secretary of State under this Part of this Act.

(3) Regulations under this section may include provision making it an offence, in such cases as may be prescribed in the regulations, to contravene the regulations.

(4) Where regulations under this section create an offence, they shall make provision as to the mode of trial and punishment of offenders; but—

(a) any provision as to punishment on summary conviction shall not authorise a fine exceeding the statutory maximum or imprisonment, and

(b) any provision as to punishment on conviction on indictment shall not authorise imprisonment for a term exceeding two years.

(5) Before making regulations under this section the Secretary of State shall consult organisations in the United Kingdom appearing to him to be representative of those persons who will be affected by the regulations; and he shall not make regulations relating to the amount of any fees without the consent of the Treasury.

(6) Regulations under this section shall be made by statutory instrument, which shall be subject to annulment in pursuance of a resolution of either House of Parliament.

Offences: penalties

12. A person guilty of an offence under section 2, 5, 9 or 10 shall be liable—

(a) on summary conviction, to a fine not exceeding the statutory maximum;

(b) on conviction on indictment, to imprisonment for a term not exceeding two years, or to a fine, or to both.

Offences: general

13.—(1) Proceedings for an offence under section 2, 5, 9 or 10 or under regulations made under section 11 shall not be instituted in England and Wales except—

(a) by the Secretary of State or by a person authorised in that behalf by the Secretary of State, or

(b) by or with the consent of the Director of Public Prosecutions.

(2) Proceedings for an offence under section 2, 5, 9 or 10 or under regulations made under section 11 shall not be instituted in Northern Ireland except—

(a) by the Secretary of State or by a person authorised in that behalf by the Secretary of State, or

(b) by or with the consent of the Director of Public Prosecutions for Northern Ireland.

(3) Where an offence committed by a body corporate under section 2, 5, 9 or 10 or under regulations made under section 11 is proved to have

been committed with the consent or connivance of, or to be attributable to any neglect on the part of, any director, manager, secretary or other similar officer of the body corporate or any person who was purporting to act in any such capacity, he as well as the body corporate shall be guilty of that offence and shall be liable to be proceeded against and punished accordingly.

(4) Where the affairs of a body corporate are managed by its members, subsection (3) shall apply in relation to acts and defaults of a member in connection with his functions of management as if he were a director of the body corporate.

(5) If an offence under section 9 or under regulations made under section 11 is committed outside the United Kingdom, proceedings for the offence may be taken, and the offence may for all incidental purposes be treated as having been committed, in any place in the United Kingdom.

(6) Section 3 of the Territorial Waters Jurisdiction Act 1878 (restriction on prosecutions) shall not apply to proceedings for an offence to which subsection (1) of this section applies.

(7) In section 27 of the Oil and Gas (Enterprise) Act 1982 (which restricts prosecutions for certain offences), at the end of subsection (2) (which excludes offences under certain enactments from the operation of that section) there shall be added—

"(g) Part I of the Petroleum Act 1987".

Validity of Secretary of State's acts

14.—(1) If any person is aggrieved by any of the acts of the Secretary of State mentioned in subsection (2) and desires to question its validity on the ground that it was not within the powers of the Secretary of State or that the relevant procedural requirements had not been complied with, he may within 42 days of the day on which the act was done make an application to the court under this section.

(2) The acts referred to in subsection (1) are—

(a) the giving of a notice under section 1(1);
(b) the approval of a programme under section 4;
(c) the rejection of a programme under section 4;
(d) a determination under section 6;
(e) a determination under section 7;
(f) the giving of a notice under section 10(4).

(3) If on an application under this section the court is satisfied that the act in question was not within the powers of the Secretary of State or that the applicant has been substantially prejudiced by a failure to comply with the relevant procedural requirements, the court may quash the act.

(4) Except as provided by this section, the validity of any of the acts of the Secretary of State referred to in subsection (1) shall not be questioned in any legal proceedings whatever.

(5) In this section "the relevant procedural requirements"—

(a) in relation to the giving of a notice under section 1(1), means the requirements of section 3(5);
(b) in relation to the approval of a programme under section 4, means the requirements of section 4(3);
(c) in relation to the rejection of a programme under section 4, means the requirements of section 4(4);
(d) in relation to a determination under section 6, means the requirements of section 6(5), (6) and (7);
(e) in relation to a determination under section 7, means the requirements of section 7(2);
(f) in relation to the giving of a notice under section 10(4), means the requirements of section 10(5).

(6) In this section, "the court" means—
    (a) in relation to England and Wales, the High Court;
    (b) in relation to Scotland, the Court of Session;
    (c) in relation to Northern Ireland, the High Court.

Notices

15. Any notice or other communication authorised or required to be given by this Part of this Act may be sent by post (but this is without prejudice to any other method of transmission).

Interpretation of Part I

16.—(1) In this Part of this Act—
    "abandonment programme" has the meaning given by section 1;
    "offshore installation" has the same meaning as in the Mineral Workings (Offshore Installations) Act 1971;
    "submarine pipe-line" means a pipe-line within the meaning of section 33 of the Petroleum and Submarine Pipe-lines Act 1975 which is in, under or over waters in—
    (a) the territorial sea adjacent to the United Kingdom, or
    (b) an area designated under section 1(7) of the Continental Shelf Act 1964.

(2) This Part of this Act—
    (a) so far as it applies to individuals, applies to them whether or not they are British citizens, and
    (b) so far as it applies to bodies corporate, applies to them whether or not they are incorporated under the law of any part of the United Kingdom.

PART II

LICENSING

Existing licences

17.—(1) Where a licence granted under section 2 of the Petroleum (Production) Act 1934 before the coming into force of this section incorporates any of the model clauses mentioned in Schedule 1 to this Act, the model clauses as incorporated in the licence shall have effect with the amendments provided for by that Schedule.

(2) Any provision of a licence which is amended by subsection (1) may be altered or deleted by an instrument under seal executed by the Secretary of State and the licensee.

(3) A reference in any document to a provision of a licence which is amended by subsection (1) shall, except so far as the nature of the document or the context otherwise requires, be construed as a reference to the provision as so amended.

(4) It is hereby declared that where a licence granted under section 2 of the Petroleum (Production) Act 1934 before the coming into force of this section refers to any provision of Part I of the Oil Taxation Act 1975, the reference (unless the contrary intention appears) is to that provision as it has effect for the time being for the purposes of petroleum revenue tax.

Future licences

18.—(1) The model clauses mentioned in Schedule 2 to this Act (clauses prescribed for incorporation in certain licences granted under section 2 of the Petroleum (Production) Act 1934) shall have effect with the amendments provided for by that Schedule.

(2) The model clauses amended by this section may be varied, revoked, modified or excluded as if the amendments had been made by regulations under section 6 of the Petroleum (Production) Act 1934.

Northern Ireland territorial waters

19.—(1) In section 1(2) of the Petroleum (Production) Act 1934 (which defines the area within which Her Majesty has exclusive rights to petroleum so as to include United Kingdom territorial waters adjacent to Great Britain) the words "adjacent to Great Britain" shall be omitted.

(2) In section 3(1) of that Act, after the words "shall apply" there shall be inserted the words "(in England and Wales and Scotland)".

Annual reports

20. The Secretary of State shall not be required to prepare a report under section 1(5) of the Continental Shelf Act 1964 (annual reports relating to licences under the Petroleum (Production) Act 1934) for the financial year ending on 31st March 1987 or for any subsequent financial year.

PART III

MISCELLANEOUS

Safety zones

Automatic establishment of safety zones

21.—(1) Subject to subsections (3) and (4), there shall be a safety zone around every installation which, or part of which, is in waters to which subsection (7) applies if—

  (a) it is stationed there so that any of the activities mentioned in subsection (2) may be carried out on, from or by means of it, or
  (b) it is being assembled at a station where it is to be used for such a purpose, or
  (c) it remains or is being dismantled at a station where it has been used for such a purpose.

(2) The activities referred to in subsection (1) are—

  (a) the exploitation or exploration of mineral resources in or under the shore or bed of waters to which subsection (7) applies;
  (b) the storage of gas in or under the shore or bed of such waters or the recovery of gas so stored;
  (c) the conveyance of things by means of a pipe, or system of pipes, constructed or placed on, in or under the shore or bed of such waters;
  (d) the provision of accommodation for persons who work on or from an installation satisfying the condition in paragraph (a), (b) or (c) of subsection (1).

(3) Subsection (1) shall not apply to an installation in respect of which an order under section 22 has effect, or to one which—

  (a) is connected with dry land by a permanent structure providing access at all times and for all purposes, or
  (b) does not project above the sea at any state of the tide.

(4) The Secretary of State may by order exclude any installation or any description of installation from the operation of subsection (1), and may do so generally or by reference to specified activities or locations or in any other way.

(5) A safety zone established by subsection (1) shall extend to every point within 500 metres of any part of the installation (ignoring any moorings) and to every point in the water which is vertically above or below such a point.

(6) A safety zone established by subsection (1) may extend to waters outside waters to which subsection (7) applies.

(7) The waters to which this subsection applies are—

    (a) tidal waters and parts of the sea in or adjacent to the United Kingdom up to the seaward limits of the territorial sea, and

    (b) waters in an area designated under section 1(7) of the Continental Shelf Act 1964.

Establishment of safety zones by order

22.—(1) The Secretary of State may by order establish a safety zone around any installation which, or part of which, is stationed in waters to which subsection (7) of section 21 applies, or is being assembled or dismantled in such waters.

(2) The area of a safety zone established by an order under this section shall be defined in the order and may extend outside waters to which subsection (7) of section 21 applies, but shall not extend to any point which would be outside a zone defined in accordance with subsection (5) of that section.

(3) An order under this section may be made in anticipation of an installation's arriving at its station, so as to come into force when it does so.

Safety zones: offences

23.—(1) Where by virtue of this Act there is a safety zone around an installation, no vessel shall enter or remain in the zone except—

    (a) in the case of a safety zone established by an order under section 22, in accordance with that order, or

    (b) in that or any other case, in accordance with regulations made or a consent given by the Secretary of State.

(2) If a vessel enters or remains in a safety zone in contravention of subsection (1) then, subject to subsection (3), its owner and its master shall each be guilty of an offence and liable—

    (a) on summary conviction, to a fine not exceeding the statutory maximum;

    (b) on conviction on indictment, to imprisonment for a term not exceeding two years or to a fine or to both.

(3) It shall be a defence for a person charged with an offence under this section to prove that the presence of the installation or the existence of the safety zone was not, and would not on reasonable enquiry have become, known to the master.

(4) Where the commission by any person of an offence under this section is due to the act or default of some other person, that other person shall also be guilty of that offence and shall be liable to be proceeded against and punished accordingly.

(5) Where an offence committed by a body corporate under this section is proved to have been committed with the consent or connivance of, or to be attributable to any neglect on the part of, any director, manager, secretary or other similar officer of the body corporate or any person who was purporting to act in any such capacity, he as well as the body corporate shall be guilty of that offence and shall be liable to be proceeded against and punished accordingly.

(6) Where the affairs of a body corporate are managed by its members,

subsection (5) shall apply in relation to acts and defaults of a member in connection with his functions of management as if he were a director of the body corporate.

(7) Proceedings for an offence under this section may be taken, and the offence may for all incidental purposes be treated as having been committed, in any place in the United Kingdom.

(8) In this section "vessel" includes a hovercraft, submersible apparatus (within the meaning of section 16(2) of the Merchant Shipping Act 1974) and an installation in transit; and "master"—

(a) in relation to a hovercraft, means the captain,

(b) in relation to submersible apparatus, means the person in charge of the apparatus, and

(c) in relation to an installation in transit, means the person in charge of the transit operation.

Safety zones: supplementary

24.—(1) For the purposes of sections 21 to 23—

(a) any floating structure or device maintained on a station by whatever means, and

(b) any apparatus or works treated as associated with a pipe or system of pipes by section 33 of the Petroleum and Submarine Pipe-lines Act 1975 (but not anything else within the definition of pipe-line in that section),

shall be taken to be an installation.

(2) Any power to make orders or regulations under sections 21 to 23 shall be exercisable by statutory instrument, and a statutory instrument containing an order under section 21 or regulations under section 23 shall be subject to annulment in pursuance of a resolution of either House of Parliament.

(3) Sections 21 to 23—

(a) so far as they apply to individuals, apply to them whether or not they are British citizens, and

(b) so far as they apply to bodies corporate, apply to them whether or not they are incorporated in any part of the United Kingdom.

(4) Section 21 of the Oil and Gas (Enterprise) Act 1982, and any orders made under it, shall cease to have effect when this section comes into force (but without prejudice to the anticipatory exercise, by virtue of section 13 of the Interpretation Act 1978, of any power conferred by this Act).

(5) In section 22 of the Oil and Gas (Enterprise) Act 1982 (application offshore of the criminal law etc.), for subsection (3) there shall be substituted—

"(3) Where a body corporate is guilty of an offence by virtue of an Order in Council under this section and that offence is proved to have been committed with the consent or connivance of, or to be attributable to any neglect on the part of, any director, manager, secretary or other similar officer of the body corporate or any person who was purporting to act in any such capacity, he as well as the body corporate shall be guilty of that offence and shall be liable to be proceeded against and punished accordingly.

(3A) Where the affairs of a body corporate are managed by its members, subsection (3) shall apply in relation to acts and defaults of a member in connection with his functions of management as if he were a director of the body corporate.

(3B) Proceedings for anything that is an offence by virtue of an Order in Council under this section may be taken, and the offence may for all incidental purposes be treated as having been committed, in any place in the United Kingdom."

(6) In section 27 of the Oil and Gas (Enterprise) Act 1982 (which restricts prosecutions for certain offences)—

(a) in subsection (1), paragraph (d) shall be omitted, and

(b) in subsections (3) and (4), for the words "section 21 above" there shall be substituted the words "section 23 of the Petroleum Act 1987".

Pipe-lines

Construction authorisations

25.—(1) Schedule 1 to the Pipe-lines Act 1962 (applications for construction authorisations) shall have effect with the following amendments in relation to applications made after the coming into force of this section.

(2) In paragraph 6(1) (which provides for the modification of the proposed route of a pipe-line), for the words from "or along a modified route" onwards there shall be substituted the words "or, subject to paragraph 6A below, along a modified route."

(3) After paragraph 6 there shall be inserted—

"6A.—(1) A pipe-line construction authorisation shall not authorise the execution of works for the placing of the proposed pipe-line along a modified route unless the applicant has given a notice relating to the modified route to—

(a) every local planning authority within whose area any modification of the route occurs, and

(b) any person specified by the Minister.

(2) A notice under sub-paragraph (1) shall state the time within which objections to the modification can be sent to the Minister and shall contain such other particulars as the Minister may direct.

(3) The time stated in accordance with sub-paragraph (2) shall not be less than 28 days from the date on which the notice is served or such shorter time (being not less than 14 days) as the Minister may direct.

(4) Where a local planning authority makes an objection in accordance with a notice under sub-paragraph (1) and does not withdraw it, the Minister shall cause a public inquiry to be held with respect to the objection and shall before granting the application consider the report of the person who held the inquiry.

(5) Where a person other than a local planning authority makes an objection in accordance with a notice under sub-paragraph (1) and does not withdraw it, the Minister shall either—

(a) cause a public inquiry to be held with respect to the objection, or

(b) afford to the person making the objection an opportunity of appearing before and being heard by a person appointed by the Minister for the purpose;

and shall in either case consider the resulting report.

6B. The Minister may if he thinks fit cause a public inquiry to be held with respect to an application for the grant of a pipe-line construction authorisation whether or not any objection to the application, or to any modification of the route proposed in it, is made or maintained."

(4) Paragraph 4(2) (which is superseded by paragraph 6B) shall be omitted.

Availability of funds

26.—(1) After section 26 of the Pipe-lines Act 1962 there shall be inserted—

> "**Availability of funds**
>
> 26A.—(1) The Secretary of State may at any time by notice served on the owner of a pipe-line prohibit the use or testing of the pipe-line, or of any length of the pipe-line, unless there are satisfied such requirements as may be specified in the notice for the purpose mentioned in subsection (2).
>
> (2) The purpose referred to in subsection (1) is that of ensuring that funds are available to discharge any liability that may arise in respect of damage attributable to the release or escape of anything from the pipe-line or length.
>
> (3) If, before the expiration of twelve weeks from the date on which a notice is served on any person under subsection (1), he serves a counter-notice on the Secretary of State objecting to the notice, the Secretary of State shall afford him an opportunity of appearing before and being heard by a person appointed by the Secretary of State for the purpose.
>
> (4) Before the expiration of twelve weeks from the date on which any hearing under subsection (3) is concluded, the Secretary of State shall consider the objection and the report of the person appointed to hear the objector and, by notice served on the objector,—
>
> > (a) quash the notice objected to, or
> > (b) confirm it without modification, or
> > (c) confirm it with such modification as appears to the Secretary of State to meet the objection.
>
> (5) The quashing of a notice served under subsection (1) shall not affect the previous operation of the notice or be taken to prevent the service of a fresh notice.
>
> (6) If a pipe-line is used or tested in contravention of a prohibition imposed by a notice under this section then, unless he shows that he used due diligence to avoid contravention, the owner shall be guilty of an offence.
>
> (7) A person guilty of an offence under this section shall be liable—
>
> > (a) on summary conviction, to a fine not exceeding the statutory maximum;
> > (b) on conviction on indictment, to a fine."

(2) In sections 58(4) and 59(5) of the Pipe-lines Act 1962, at the appropriate places in the lists of provisions of that Act, there shall be inserted the words "section 26A".

Compulsory acquisition of rights

27. In section 2 of the Mines (Working Facilities and Support) Act 1966 (which enables a court to grant certain rights ancillary to mining)—

    (a) in subsection (1)(b) (under which the rights that may be granted for the purpose of the conveyance of minerals are limited to the extent provided by subsection (1A)), for the words from "minerals" to "purpose of the" there shall be substituted the words "or conveyance of minerals or the"; and

    (b) subsection (1A) shall cease to have effect.

Refineries

Construction of refineries

28. Sections 34 to 39 of the Petroleum and Submarine Pipe-lines Act 1975 (control of construction and extension of refineries) shall cease to have effect.

PART IV

SUPPLEMENTARY

Expenses

29. There shall be paid out of money provided by Parliament any expenditure incurred by the Secretary of State under this Act and any increase attributable to this Act in the sums so payable under any other Act.

Repeals

30. The enactments mentioned in Schedule 3 to this Act are hereby repealed to the extent specified in the third column of that Schedule.

Commencement

31.—(1) Subject to subsection (2), this Act shall come into force at the end of the period of two months beginning with the day on which it is passed.

(2) The following provisions of this Act—

    (a) sections 17 and 18, and Schedules 1 and 2, and

    (b) sections 21 to 24, and the repeals of section 21 and in section 27 of the Oil and Gas (Enterprise) Act 1982,

shall come into force on such day as the Secretary of State may appoint by order made by statutory instrument, and different days may be appointed for different purposes.

(3) An order under subsection (2) may make such transitional provision and savings as appear to the Secretary of State to be necessary or expedient.

Short title and extent

32.—(1) This Act may be cited as the Petroleum Act 1987.

(2) Sections 25, 26 and 27 of this Act do not extend to Northern Ireland, but otherwise this Act extends there.

SCHEDULES

Section 17   SCHEDULE 1

AMENDMENT OF EXISTING LICENCES

Part II of Schedule 2 to the 1975 Act

1.—(1) The model clauses set out in Part II of Schedule 2 to the Petroleum and Submarine Pipe-lines Act 1975 as amended by the Oil and Gas (Enterprise) Act 1982 (clauses incorporated in production licences for seaward areas) shall have effect with the following amendments (which relate to royalty payments, royalty in kind, carrying back of costs, arbitration and measurement etc. of petroleum).

(2) In clause 9(1)—

    (a) for "paragraphs (2) to (4)" there shall be substituted "paragraph (1A)"; and

    (b) after "clauses" there shall be inserted "9A,".

(3) In clause 9, for paragraphs (2) to (4) there shall be substituted—

    "(1A) Paragraph (1) of this clause shall not apply to a chargeable period in which the Licensee delivers petroleum to the Minister in pursuance of clause 11 of this licence; but if the petroleum delivered has a value of less than 12½ per cent. of the aggregate of—

    (a) the value of the petroleum delivered (ignoring any such excess as is mentioned in paragraph (11) of this clause), and

    (b) the value of the petroleum relating to that period,

he shall pay to the Minister a royalty of an amount equal to the difference."

(4) In clause 9(5), for "clause 10" there shall be substituted "clauses 9A and 10".

(5) In clause 9, after paragraph (7) there shall be inserted—

    "(7A) A notice under paragraph (7) of this clause may, if the Minister thinks fit, provide for the costs in respect of which a sum is ascertained for the purposes of paragraph (5)(b) to include, to such extent as may be specified in the notice,—

    (a) costs incurred in relation to assets which have ceased to be used in connection with the conveying or treating of petroleum;

    (b) costs incurred after the end of the chargeable period to which the sum relates.

    (7B) If a notice under paragraph (7) of this clause contains a provision relating to costs incurred after the end of a chargeable period, sub-paragraph (b) of paragraph (7) shall have effect in relation to a dispute concerning such costs as if the chargeable period there referred to were that in which the costs were incurred."

(6) In clause 9, for paragraph (8) there shall be substituted—

    "(8) Subject to paragraphs (9) and (10) of this clause, the value of petroleum delivered to the Minister in pursuance of clause 11 of this licence shall be ascertained for the purposes of this clause and clause 9A on such basis (or, where petroleum of more than one kind is delivered, such bases) as the Minister and the Licensee agree.

    (9) If the Minister and Licensee fail to agree on the value of any petroleum delivered to the Minister in pursuance of clause 11 of this licence, it shall be ascertained on such basis as the Minister may specify as fair in a notice in writing given by him to the Licensee.

    (10) The Licensee may, during the period of 28 days beginning with the day on which he receives a notice from the Minister under paragraph (9) of this clause, refer to arbitration in the manner provided by clause 40 of this licence any question as to whether the basis of valuation specified in the notice is fair.

    (11) In this clause and clauses 9A, 10 and 11A, references to petroleum delivered to the Minister in pursuance of clause 11 include references to any excess over the quantity required to be delivered by a notice served in pursuance of paragraph (1) of that clause."

(7) After clause 9, there shall be inserted—

    "9A. If in any chargeable period the Licensee delivers to the Minister in pursuance of clause 11 of this licence petroleum having a value greater than 12½ per cent. of the aggregate of—

    (a) the value of the petroleum delivered (ignoring any such excess as is mentioned in clause 9(11) of this licence), and

    (b) the value of the petroleum relating to that period,

the Minister shall pay to the Licensee a sum equal to the difference."

(8) In clause 10(1), for sub-paragraph (e) there shall be substituted—

    "(e) the amount which the Licensee estimates will be the sum ascertained as respects that period for the purposes of clauses 9(5)(b) of this licence (ignoring, in a case where they might otherwise be taken into account in the estimate, any costs incurred after the end of the period)".

(9) In clause 10(3), for "9(3) or (4)" there shall be substituted "9(1A)".

(10) In clause 10(4)—

    (a) for "paragraphs (2) to (4)" there shall be substituted "paragraph (1A)"; and

    (b) for "paragraph (2)" there shall be substituted "paragraph (1A)".

(11) In clause 10(6)—

    (a) the words from "and a sum" to "petroleum" shall be omitted; and

    (b) for "that clause" there shall be substituted "clause 9 of this licence".

(12) In clause 10, after paragraph (7) there shall be inserted—

    "(7A) If, after the date when the Minister gave notice to the Licensee in pursuance of paragraph (6) of this clause or this paragraph in respect of a chargeable period, it appears to the Minister that as a result of costs incurred after the end of the period there is an increase in the sum to be taken into account by virtue of clause 9(5)(b) of this licence, and accordingly a reduction in the amount payable by the Licensee in respect of that period, he may give notice in writing to the Licensee specifying the reduced amount; and where he does so he shall forthwith pay to the Licensee an amount equal to the difference between the reduced amount and the total amount already paid by the Licensee in pursuance of this clause in respect of the period."

(13) In clause 10(8)—

    (a) for "or (7)" (in both places) there shall be substituted ", (7) or (7A)"; and

    (b) after "may" there shall be inserted ", during the period of 28 days beginning with the day on which the Licensee receives the notice,".

(14) In clause 10, for paragraph (9) there shall be substituted—

"(9) An amount in respect of interest shall be payable when a notice is given under paragraph (5), (6), (7) or (7A) of this clause, and that amount shall be calculated in such manner as the Minister may specify from time to time in a notice in writing given by him to the Licensee; but—

    (a) a notice in pursuance of this paragraph shall provide for amounts by way of interest to be calculated by applying a rate of interest which is for the time being a commercial rate of interest;

    (b) any such amount in respect of interest shall be disregarded in calculating for the purposes of paragraph (5), (6), (7) or (7A) of this clause any amount already paid by the Licensee in pursuance of this clause;

    (c) where costs of the kind mentioned in clause 9(7A)(b) of this licence are taken into account, they shall not affect the amount of interest payable in respect of any period ending earlier than two months after the chargeable period in which they were incurred."

(15) In clause 10, after paragraph (9) there shall be inserted—

"(9A) If a payment is made by the Minister in pursuance of clause 9A of this licence more than two months after the end of the chargeable period to which the payment relates, an amount in respect of interest on the payment from the end of those two months shall also be payable by him to the Licensee.

(9B) Interest under paragraph (9A) of this clause shall be calculated in such manner as the Minister may specify from time to time in a notice in writing given by him to the Licensee (but sub-paragraph (a) of paragraph (9) of this clause shall apply to such a notice as it applies to a notice under paragraph (9))."

(16) In clause 10(11), for "or (7)" there shall be substituted ", (7) or (7A)".

(17) In clause 11A(1)—

    (a) for "a notice served by virtue of clause 11(1)" there shall be substituted "clause 11";

    (b) for "the delivery and treatment of the" there shall be substituted "conveying and treating";

    (c) for "clause 9(7)" there shall be substituted "clause 9(7) to (7B)"; and

    (d) for "for the reference to paragraph (5)(b) of that clause there were substituted a reference" there shall be substituted "references to clause 9(5)(b) were references".

(18) In clause 11A, after paragraph (4) there shall be inserted—

"(4A) If, after the date when the Minister gave notice to the Licensee in pursuance of paragraph (4) of this clause or this paragraph in respect of a chargeable period, it appears to the Minister that as a result of costs incurred after the end of the period there is an increase in the amount payable by him in pursuance of this clause in respect of the period, he may give notice in writing to the Licensee specifying the increased amount; and where he does so he shall forthwith pay to the Licensee an amount equal to the difference between the increased amount and the total amount already paid by the Minister in pursuance of this clause in respect of the period."

(19) In clause 11A(5)—

    (a) for "or (4)" there shall be substituted ", (4) or (4A)";

    (b) after "paragraph (4)" there shall be inserted "or (4A)"; and

    (c) after "may" there shall be inserted ", during the period of 28 days beginning with the day on which the Licensee receives the notice,".

(20) In clause 11A, for paragraph (6) there shall be substituted—

"(6) An amount in respect of interest shall be payable when a notice is given under paragraph (3), (4) or (4A) of this clause, and that amount shall be calculated in such manner as the Minister may specify from time to time in a notice in writing given by him to the Licensee; but—

(a) a notice in pursuance of this paragraph shall provide for amounts by way of interest to be calculated by applying a rate of interest which is for the time being a commercial rate of interest;

(b) any such amount in respect of interest shall be disregarded in calculating for the purposes of paragraph (3), (4) or (4A) of this clause any amount already paid by the Minister in pursuance of this clause;

(c) where costs of the kind mentioned in clause 9(7A)(b) of this licence are taken into account, they shall not affect the amount of interest payable in respect of any period ending earlier than two months after the chargeable period in which they were incurred."

(21) In clause 11A(7), for "or (4)" there shall be substituted ", (4) or (4A)".

(22) In clause 12, after paragraph (1) there shall be inserted—

"(1A) If and to the extent that the Minister so directs, the duty imposed by paragraph (1) of this clause shall be discharged separately in relation to petroleum won and saved—

(a) from each part of the licensed area which is an oil field for the purposes of the Oil Taxation Act 1975,

(b) from each part of the licensed area which forms part of such an oil field extending beyond the licensed area, and

(c) from each well producing petroleum from a part of the licensed area which is not within such an oil field.

(1B) If and to the extent that the Minister so directs, the preceding provisions of this clause shall apply as if the duty to measure or weigh petroleum included a duty to ascertain its quality or composition or both; and where a direction under this paragraph is in force, the following provisions of this clause shall have effect as if references to measuring or weighing included references to ascertaining quality or composition."

Part II of Schedule 3 to the 1975 Act

2.—(1) The model clauses set out in Part II of Schedule 3 to the Petroleum and Submarine Pipe-lines Act 1975 as amended by the Oil and Gas (Enterprise) Act 1982 (clauses incorporated in production licences for landward areas) shall have effect with the following amendments (which relate to royalty payments, royalty in kind, carrying back of costs, arbitration and measurement etc. of petroleum).

(2) In clause 9(1), for "paragraphs (2) to (4)" there shall be substituted "paragraph (1A)".

(3) In clause 9, for paragraphs (2) to (4) there shall be substituted—

"(1A) Paragraph (1) of this clause shall not apply to a chargeable period in which the Licensee delivers petroleum to the Minister in pursuance of clause 11 of this licence; but if the petroleum delivered has a value of less than the relevant percentage of the aggregate of—

(a) the value of the petroleum delivered (ignoring any such excess as is mentioned in paragraph (7F) of this clause), and

(b) the value of the petroleum relating to that period,

he shall pay to the Minister a royalty of an amount equal to the difference."

(4) In clause 9(5), for "clause 10" there shall be substituted "clauses 9A and 10".

(5) In clause 9, after paragraph (7) there shall be inserted—

"(7A) A notice under paragraph (7) of this clause may, if the Minister thinks fit, provide for the costs in respect of which a sum is ascertained for the purposes of paragraph (5)(b) to include, to such extent as may be specified in the notice,—

(a) costs incurred in relation to assets which have ceased to be used in connection with the conveying or treating of petroleum;

(b) costs incurred after the end of the chargeable period to which the sum relates.

(7B) If a notice under paragraph (7) of this clause contains a provision relating to costs incurred after the end of a chargeable period, sub-paragraph (b) of paragraph (7) shall have effect in relation to a dispute concerning such costs as if the chargeable period there referred to were that in which the costs were incurred."

(6) In clause 9, before paragraph (8) there shall be inserted—

"(7C) Subject to paragraphs (7D) and (7E) of this clause, the value of petroleum delivered to the Minister in pursuance of clause 11 of this licence shall be ascertained for the purposes of this clause and clause 9A on such basis (or, where petroleum of more than one kind is delivered, such bases) as the Minister and the Licensee agree.

(7D) If the Minister and the Licensee fail to agree on the value of any petroleum delivered to the Minister in pursuance of clause 11 of this licence, it shall be ascertained on such basis as the Minister may specify as fair in a notice in writing given by him to the Licensee.

(7E) The Licensee may, during the period of 28 days beginning with the day on which he receives a notice from the Minister under paragraph (7D) of this clause, refer to arbitration in the manner provided by clause 38 of this licence any question as to whether the basis of valuation specified in the notice is fair.

(7F) In this clause and clauses 9A, 10 and 11A, references to petroleum delivered to the Minister in pursuance of clause 11 include references to any excess over the quantity required to be delivered by a notice served in pursuance of paragraph (1) of that clause."

(7) In clause 9(8), for the definition of "royalty petroleum" there shall be substituted—
" 'relevant percentage', in relation to a chargeable period, means the effective rate at which, apart from any notice under clause 11 of this licence, royalty would be payable for that period in pursuance of paragraph (1) of this clause;".

(8) After clause 9, there shall be inserted the following—
"9A.—(1) If in any chargeable period the Licensee delivers to the Minister in pursuance of clause 11 of this licence petroleum having a value greater than the relevant percentage of the aggregate of—
    (a) the value of the petroleum delivered (ignoring any such excess as is mentioned in clause 9(7F) of this licence), and
    (b) the value of the petroleum relating to that period,
the Minister shall pay to the Licensee a sum equal to the difference.

(2) In this clause, 'chargeable period' and 'relevant percentage' have the same meanings as in clause 9 of this licence."

(9) In clause 10(1), for sub-paragraph (e) there shall be substituted—
    (e) the amount which the Licensee estimates will be the sum ascertained as respects that period for the purposes of clause 9(5)(b) of this licence (ignoring, in a case where they might otherwise be taken into account in the estimate, any costs incurred after the end of the period)".

(10) In clause 10(2), for "fraction" there shall be substituted "percentage".

(11) In clause 10(3), for "9(3) or (4)" there shall be substituted "9(1A)".

(12) In clause 10(4)—
    (a) for "paragraphs (2) to (4)" there shall be substituted "paragraph (1A)"; and
    (b) for "paragraph (2)" there shall be substituted "paragraph (1A)".

(13) In clause 10(6)—
    (a) the words from "and a sum" to "petroleum" shall be omitted; and
    (b) for "this clause" there shall be substituted "clause 9 of this licence".

(14) In clause 10, after paragraph (7) there shall be inserted—
"(7A) If, after the date when the Minister gave notice to the Licensee in pursuance of paragraph (6) of this clause or this paragraph in respect of a chargeable period, it appears to the Minister that as a result of costs incurred after the end of the period there is an increase in the sum to be taken into account by virtue of clause 9(5)(b) of this licence, and accordingly a reduction in the amount payable by the Licensee in respect of that period, he may give notice in writing to the Licensee specifying the reduced amount; and where he does so he shall forthwith pay to the Licensee an amount equal to the difference between the reduced amount and the total amount already paid by the Licensee in pursuance of this clause in respect of the period."

(15) In clause 10(8)—
    (a) for "or (7)" (in both places) there shall be substituted ", (7) or (7A)"; and
    (b) after "may" there shall be inserted ", during the period of 28 days beginning with the day on which the Licensee receives the notice,".

(16) In clause 10, for paragraph (9) there shall be substituted—
"(9) An amount in respect of interest shall be payable when a notice is given under paragraph (5), (6), (7) or (7A) of this clause, and that amount shall be calculated in such manner as the Minister may specify from time to time in a notice in writing given by him to the Licensee; but—
    (a) a notice in pursuance of this paragraph shall provide for amounts by way of interest to be calculated by applying a rate of interest which is for the time being a commercial rate of interest;
    (b) any such amount in respect of interest shall be disregarded in calculating for the purposes of paragraph (5), (6), (7) or (7A) of this clause any amount already paid by the Licensee in pursuance of this clause;

(c) where costs of the kind mentioned in clause 9(7A)(b) of this licence are taken into account, they shall not affect the amount of interest payable in respect of any period ending earlier than two months after the chargeable period in which they were incurred."

(17) In clause 10, after paragraph (9) there shall be inserted—

"(9A) If a payment is made by the Minister in pursuance of clause 9A of this licence more than two months after the end of the chargeable period to which the payment relates, an amount in respect of interest on the payment from the end of those two months shall also be payable by him to the Licensee.

(9B) Interest under paragraph (9A) of this clause shall be calculated in such manner as the Minister may specify from time to time in a notice in writing given by him to the Licensee (but sub-paragraph (a) of paragraph (9) of this clause shall apply to such a notice as it applies to a notice under paragraph (9))."

(18) In clause 10(10)—

(a) for "'royalty petroleum'" there shall be substituted "'relevant percentage'"; and
(b) the definition of "the relevant fraction" and the word "and" preceding it shall be omitted.

(19) In clause 10(11), for "or (7)" there shall be substituted ", (7) or (7A)".

(20) In clause 11A(1)—

(a) for "a notice served by virtue of clause 11(1)" there shall be substituted "clause 11";
(b) for "the delivery and treatment of the" there shall be substituted "conveying and treating";
(c) for "clause 9(7)" there shall be substituted "clause 9(7) to (7B)"; and
(d) for "for the reference to paragraph (5)(b) of that clause there were substituted a reference" there shall be substituted "references to clause 9(5)(b) were references".

(21) In clause 11A, after paragraph (4) there shall be inserted—

"(4A) If, after the date when the Minister gave notice to the Licensee in pursuance of paragraph (4) of this clause or this paragraph in respect of a chargeable period, it appears to the Minister that as a result of costs incurred after the end of the period there is an increase in the amount payable by him in pursuance of this clause in respect of the period, he may give notice in writing to the Licensee specifying the increased amount; and where he does so he shall forthwith pay to the Licensee an amount equal to the difference between the increased amount and the total amount already paid by the Minister in pursuance of this clause in respect of the period."

(22) In clause 11A(5)—

(a) for "or (4)" there shall be substituted ", (4) or (4A)";
(b) after "paragraph (4)" there shall be inserted "or (4A)"; and
(c) after "may" there shall be inserted ", during the period of 28 days beginning with the day on which the Licensee receives the notice,".

(23) In clause 11A, for paragraph (6) there shall be substituted—

"(6) An amount in respect of interest shall be payable when a notice is given under paragraph (3), (4) or (4A) of this clause, and that amount shall be calculated in such manner as the Minister may specify from time to time in a notice in writing given by him to the Licensee; but—

(a) a notice in pursuance of this paragraph shall provide for amounts by way of interest to be calculated by applying a rate of interest which is for the time being a commercial rate of interest;
(b) any such amount in respect of interest shall be disregarded in calculating for the purposes of paragraph (3), (4) or (4A) of this clause any amount already paid by the Minister in pursuance of this clause;
(c) where costs of the kind mentioned in clause 9(7A)(b) of this licence are taken into account, they shall not affect the amount of interest payable in respect of any period ending earlier than two months after the chargeable period in which they were incurred."

(24) In clause 11A(7), for "or (4)" there shall be substituted ", (4) or (4A)".

(25) In clause 12, after paragraph (1) there shall be inserted—

"(1A) If and to the extent that the Minister so directs, the duty imposed by paragraph (1) of this clause shall be discharged separately in relation to petroleum won and saved—

(a) from each part of the licensed area which is an oil field for the purposes of the Oil Taxation Act 1975,

12–21

(b) from each part of the licensed area which forms part of such an oil field extending beyond the licensed area, and

(c) from each well producing petroleum from a part of the licensed area which is not within such an oil field.

(1B) If and to the extent that the Minister so directs, the preceding provisions of this clause shall apply as if the duty to measure or weigh petroleum included a duty to ascertain its quality or composition or both; and where a direction under this paragraph is in force, the following provisions of this clause shall have effect as if references to measuring or weighing included references to ascertaining quality or composition."

Schedule 4 to the 1976 Regulations

3.—(1) The model clauses set out in Schedule 4 to the Petroleum (Production) Regulations 1976 as amended by the Oil and Gas (Enterprise) Act 1982 (clauses incorporated in production licences for landward areas) shall have effect with the following amendments (which relate to royalty payments, royalty in kind, arbitration and measurement etc. of petroleum).

(2) In clause 9(1), for "paragraphs (2) to (4)" there shall be substituted "paragraph (1A)".

(3) In clause 9, for paragraphs (2) to (4) there shall be substituted—

"(1A) Paragraph (1) of this clause shall not apply to a chargeable period in which the Licensee delivers petroleum to the Minister in pursuance of clause 11 of this licence; but if the petroleum delivered has a value of less than the relevant percentage of the aggregate of—

(a) the value of the petroleum delivered (ignoring any such excess as is mentioned in paragraph (6D) of this clause), and

(b) the value of petroleum relating to that period,

he shall pay to the Minister a royalty of an amount equal to the difference."

(4) In clause 9(5), for "clause 10" there shall be substituted "clauses 9A and 10".

(5) In clause 9, after paragraph (6) there shall be inserted—

"(6A) Subject to paragraphs (6B) and (6C) of this clause, the value of petroleum delivered to the Minister in pursuance of clause 11 of this licence shall be ascertained for the purposes of this clause and clause 9A on such basis (or, where petroleum of more than one kind is delivered, such bases) as the Minister and the Licensee agree.

(6B) If the Minister and the Licensee fail to agree on the value of any petroleum delivered to the Minister in pursuance of clause 11 of this licence, it shall be ascertained on such basis as the Minister may specify as fair in a notice in writing given by him to the Licensee.

(6C) The Licensee may, during the period of 28 days beginning with the day on which he receives a notice from the Minister under paragraph (6B) of this clause, refer to arbitration in the manner provided by clause 39 of this licence any question as to whether the basis of valuation specified in the notice is fair.

(6D) In this clause and clauses 9A and 10, references to petroleum delivered to the Minister in pursuance of clause 11 include references to any excess over the quantity required to be delivered by a notice served in pursuance of paragraph (1) of that clause."

(6) In clause 9(7), for the definition of "royalty petroleum" there shall be substituted—

"'relevant percentage', in relation to a chargeable period, means the effective rate at which, apart from any notice under clause 11 of this licence, royalty would be payable for that period in pursuance of paragraph (1) of this clause;".

(7) After clause 9, there shall be inserted—

"9A.—(1) If in any chargeable period the Licensee delivers to the Minister in pursuance of clause 11 of this licence petroleum having a value greater than the relevant percentage of the aggregate of—

(a) the value of the petroleum delivered (ignoring any such excess as is mentioned in clause 9(6D) of this licence), and

(b) the value of the petroleum relating to that period,

the Minister shall pay to the Licensee a sum equal to the difference.

(2) In this clause, 'chargeable period' and 'relevant percentage' have the same meanings as in clause 9 of this licence."

(8) In clause 10(2), for "fraction" there shall be substituted "percentage".

(9) In clause 10(3), for "9(3) or (4)" there shall be substituted "9(1A)".

(10) In clause 10(7), after "may" there shall be inserted ", during the period of 28 days beginning with the day on which the Licensee receives the notice,".

(11) In clause 10(8)(b), for "or (5)" there shall be substituted ", (5) or (6)".

(12) In clause 10, after paragraph (8) there shall be inserted—

"(8A) If a payment is made by the Minister in pursuance of clause 9A of this licence more than two months after the end of the chargeable period to which the payment relates, an amount in respect of interest on the payment from the end of those two months shall also be payable by him to the Licensee.

(8B) Interest under paragraph (8A) of this clause shall be calculated in such manner as the Minister may specify from time to time in a notice in writing given by him to the Licensee (but sub-paragraph (a) of paragraph (8) of this clause shall apply to such a notice as it applies to a notice under paragraph (8))."

(13) In clause 10(9)—

    (a) for "'royalty petroleum'" there shall be substituted "'relevant percentage'"; and

    (b) the definition of "the relevant fraction" and the word "and" preceding it shall be omitted.

(14) In clause 12, after paragraph (1) there shall be inserted—

"(1A) If and to the extent that the Minister so directs, the duty imposed by paragraph (1) of this clause shall be discharged separately in relation to petroleum won and saved—

    (a) from each part of the licensed area which is an oil field for the purposes of the Oil Taxation Act 1975,

    (b) from each part of the licensed area which forms part of such an oil field extending beyond the licensed area, and

    (c) from each well producing petroleum from a part of the licensed area which is not within such an oil field.

(1B) If and to the extent that the Minister so directs, the preceding provisions of this clause shall apply as if the duty to measure or weigh petroleum included a duty to ascertain its quality or composition or both; and where a direction under this paragraph is in force, the following provisions of this clause shall have effect as if references to measuring or weighing included references to ascertaining quality or composition."

Schedule 5 to the 1976 Regulations

4.—(1) The model clauses set out—

    (a) in Schedule 5 to the Petroleum (Production) Regulations 1976 as amended by the Oil and Gas (Enterprise) Act 1982;

    (b) in that Schedule as amended by the Petroleum (Production) (Amendment) Regulations 1978 and the 1982 Act; and

    (c) in that Schedule as amended by the 1978 Regulations, the Petroleum (Production) (Amendment) Regulations 1980 and the 1982 Act,

(clauses incorporated in production licences for seaward areas) shall have effect with the following amendments (which relate to royalty payments, royalty in kind, arbitration and measurement etc. of petroleum).

(2) In clause 9(1)—

    (a) for "paragraphs (2) to (4)" there shall be substituted "paragraph (1A)"; and

    (b) for "clause 10" there shall be substituted "clauses 9A and 10".

(3) In clause 9, for paragraphs (2) to (4) there shall be substituted—

"(1A) Paragraph (1) of this clause shall not apply to a chargeable period in which the Licensee delivers petroleum to the Minister in pursuance of clause 11 of this licence; but if the petroleum delivered has a value of less than the appropriate percentage of the aggregate of—

    (a) the value of the petroleum delivered (ignoring any such excess as is mentioned in paragraph (10) of this clause), and

    (b) the value of the petroleum relating to that period,

he shall pay to the Minister a royalty of an amount equal to the difference."

(4) In clause 9(5), for "clause 10" there shall be substituted "clauses 9A and 10".

(5) In clause 9, for paragraph (7) there shall be substituted—

"(7) Subject to paragraphs (8) and (9) of this clause, the value of petroleum delivered to the Minister in pursuance of clause 11 of this licence shall be ascertained for the purposes of this clause and clause 9A on such basis (or, where petroleum of more than one kind is delivered, such bases) as the Minister and the Licensee agree.

(8) If the Minister and the Licensee fail to agree on the value of any petroleum delivered to the Minister in pursuance of clause 11 of this licence, it shall be

ascertained on such basis as the Minister may specify as fair in a notice in writing given by him to the Licensee.

(9) The Licensee may, during the period of 28 days beginning with the day on which he receives a notice from the Minister under paragraph (8) of this clause, refer to arbitration in the manner provided by clause 41 of this licence any question as to whether the basis of valuation specified in the notice is fair.

(10) In this clause and clauses 9A and 10, references to petroleum delivered to the Minister in pursuance of clause 11 include references to any excess over the quantity required to be delivered by a notice served in pursuance of paragraph (1) of that clause".

(6) After clause 9, there shall be inserted—

"9A. If in any chargeable period the Licensee delivers to the Minister in pursuance of clause 11 of this licence petroleum having a value greater than the appropriate percentage of the aggregate of—

    (a) the value of the petroleum delivered (ignoring any such excess as is mentioned in clause 9(10) of this licence), and

    (b) the value of the petroleum relating to that period,

the Minister shall pay to the Licensee a sum equal to the difference."

(7) In clause 10(3), for "9(3) or (4)" there shall be substituted "9(1A)".

(8) In clause 10(7), after "may" there shall be inserted ", during the period of 28 days beginning with the day on which the Licensee receives the notice,".

(9) In clause 10(8)(b), for "or (5)" there shall be substituted ", (5) or (6)".

(10) In clause 10, after paragraph (8) there shall be inserted—

"(8A) If a payment is made by the Minister in pursuance of clause 9A of this licence more than two months after the end of the chargeable period to which the payment relates, an amount in respect of interest on the payment from the end of those two months shall also be payable by him to the Licensee.

(8B) Interest under paragraph (8A) of this clause shall be calculated in such manner as the Minister may specify from time to time in a notice in writing given by him to the Licensee (but sub-paragraph (a) of paragraph (8) of this clause shall apply to such a notice as it applies to a notice under paragraph (8))."

(11) In clause 12, after paragraph (1) there shall be inserted—

"(1A) If and to the extent that the Minister so directs, the duty imposed by paragraph (1) of this clause shall be discharged separately in relation to petroleum won and saved—

    (a) from each part of the licensed area which is an oil field for the purposes of the Oil Taxation Act 1975,

    (b) from each part of the licensed area which forms part of such an oil field extending beyond the licensed area, and

    (c) from each well producing petroleum from a part of the licensed area which is not within such an oil field.

(1B) If and to the extent that the Minister so directs, the preceding provisions of this clause shall apply as if the duty to measure or weigh petroleum included a duty to ascertain its quality or composition or both; and where a direction under this paragraph is in force, the following provisions of this clause shall have effect as if references to measuring or weighing included references to ascertaining quality or composition."

Schedule 4 to the 1982 Regulations

5.—(1) The model clauses set out in Schedule 4 to the Petroleum (Production) Regulations 1982 (clauses incorporated in production licences for landward areas) shall have effect with the following amendments (which relate to royalty payments, royalty in kind, arbitration and measurement etc. of petroleum).

(2) In clause 9(1), for "paragraphs (2) to (4)" there shall be substituted "paragraph (1A)".

(3) In clause 9, for paragraphs (2) to (4) there shall be substituted—

"(1A) Paragraph (1) of this clause shall not apply to a chargeable period in which the Licensee delivers petroleum to the Minister in pursuance of clause 11 of this licence; but if the petroleum delivered has a value of less than the relevant percentage of the aggregate of—

    (a) the value of the petroleum delivered (ignoring any such excess as is mentioned in paragraph (6D) of this clause), and

    (b) the value of the petroleum relating to that period,

he shall pay to the Minister a royalty of an amount equal to the difference."

(4) In clause 9(5), for "clause 10" there shall be substituted "clauses 9A and 10".

(5) In clause 9, after paragraph (6) there shall be inserted—

"(6A) Subject to paragraphs (6B) and (6C) of this clause, the value of petroleum delivered to the Minister in pursuance of clause 11 of this licence shall be ascertained for the purposes of this clause and clause 9A on such basis (or, where petroleum of more than one kind is delivered, such bases) as the Minister and the Licensee agree.

(6B) If the Minister and Licensee fail to agree on the value of any petroleum delivered to the Minister in pursuance of clause 11 of this licence, it shall be ascertained on such basis as the Minister may specify as fair in a notice in writing given by him to the Licensee.

(6C) The Licensee may, during the period of 28 days beginning with the day on which he receives a notice from the Minister under paragraph (6B) of this clause, refer to arbitration in the manner provided by clause 39 of this licence any question as tc whether the basis of valuation specified in the notice is fair.

(6D) In this clause and clauses 9A and 10, references to petroleum delivered to the Minister in pursuance of clause 11 include references to any excess over the quantity required to be delivered by a notice served in pursuance of paragraph (1) of that clause."

(6) In clause 9(7), for the definition of "royalty petroleum" there shall be substituted—

"'relevant percentage', in relation to a chargeable period, means the effective rate at which, apart from any notice under clause 11 of this licence, royalty would be payable for that period in pursuance of paragraph (1) of this clause;".

(7) After clause 9, there shall be inserted—

"9A.—(1) If in any chargeable period the Licensee delivers to the Minister in pursuance of clause 11 of this licence petroleum having a value greater than the relevant percentage of the aggregate of—

(a) the value of the petroleum delivered (ignoring any such excess as is mentioned in clause 9(6D) of this licence), and

(b) the value of the petroleum relating to that period,

the Minister shall pay to the Licensee a sum equal to the difference.

(2) In this clause, 'chargeable period' and 'relevant percentage' have the same meanings as in clause 9 of this licence."

(8) In clause 10(2), for "fraction" there shall be substituted "percentage".

(9) In clause 10(3), for "9(3) or (4)" there shall be substituted "9(1A)".

(10) In clause 10(7), after "may" there shall be inserted ", during the period of 28 days beginning with the day on which the Licensee receives the notice,".

(11) In clause 10(8)(b), for "or (5)" there shall be substituted ", (5) or (6)".

(12) In clause 10, after paragraph (8) there shall be inserted—

"(8A) If a payment is made by the Minister in pursuance of clause 9A of this licence more than two months after the end of the chargeable period to which the payment relates, an amount in respect of interest on the payment from the end of those two months shall also be payable by him to the Licensee.

(8B) Interest under paragraph (8A) of this clause shall be calculated in such manner as the Minister may specify from time to time in a notice in writing given by him to the Licensee (but sub-paragraph (a) of paragraph (8) of this clause shall apply to such a notice as it applies to a notice under paragraph (8))."

(13) In clause 10(9)—

(a) for "'royalty petroleum'" there shall be substituted "'relevant percentage'"; and

(b) the definition of "the relevant fraction" and the word "and" preceding it shall be omitted.

(14) In clause 12, after paragraph (1) there shall be inserted—

"(1A) If and to the extent that the Minister so directs, the duty imposed by paragraph (1) of this clause shall be discharged separately in relation to petroleum won and saved—

(a) from each part of the licensed area which is an oil field for the purposes of the Oil Taxation Act 1975;

(b) from each part of the licensed area which forms part of such an oil field extending beyond the licensed area, and

(c) from each well producing petroleum from a part of the licensed area which is not within such an oil field.

(1B) If and to the extent that the Minister so directs, the preceding provisions of this clause shall apply as if the duty to measure or weigh petroleum included a duty to ascertain its quality or composition or both; and where a direction under this paragraph is in force, the following provisions of this clause shall have effect as if references to measuring or weighing included references to ascertaining quality or composition."

Schedule 5 to the 1982 Regulations

6.—(1) The model clauses set out in Schedule 5 to the Petroleum (Production) Regulations 1982 (clauses incorporated in production licences for seaward areas) shall have effect with the following amendments (which relate to royalty payments, royalty in kind, arbitration and measurement etc. of petroleum).

(2) In clause 8(1)—

    (a) for "paragraphs (2) to (4)" there shall be substituted "paragraph (1A)"; and

    (b) for "clause 9" there shall be substituted "clauses 8A and 9".

(3) In clause 8, for paragraphs (2) to (4) there shall be substituted—

"(1A) Paragraph (1) of this clause shall not apply to a chargeable period in which the Licensee delivers petroleum to the Minister in pursuance of clause 10 of this licence; but if the petroleum delivered has a value of less than the appropriate percentage of the aggregate of—

    (a) the value of the petroleum delivered (ignoring any such excess as is mentioned in paragraph (10) of this clause), and

    (b) the value of the petroleum relating to that period,

he shall pay to the Minister a royalty of an amount equal to the difference."

(4) In clause 8(5), for "clause 9" there shall be substituted "clauses 8A and 9".

(5) In clause 8, for paragraph (7) there shall be substituted—

"(7) Subject to paragraphs (8) and (9) of this clause, the value of petroleum delivered to the Minister in pursuance of clause 10 of this licence shall be ascertained for the purposes of this clause and clause 8A on such basis (or, where petroleum of more than one kind is delivered, such bases) as the Minister and the Licensee agree.

(8) If the Minister and the Licensee fail to agree on the value of any petroleum delivered to the Minister in pursuance of clause 10 of this licence, it shall be ascertained on such basis as the Minister may specify as fair in a notice in writing given by him to the Licensee.

(9) The Licensee may, during the period of 28 days beginning with the day on which he receives a notice from the Minister under paragraph (8) of this clause, refer to arbitration in the manner provided by clause 40 of this licence any question as to whether the basis of valuation specified in the notice is fair.

(10) In this clause and clauses 8A and 9, references to petroleum delivered to the Minister in pursuance of clause 10 include references to any excess over the quantity required to be delivered by a notice served in pursuance of paragraph (1) of that clause."

(6) After clause 8, there shall be inserted—

"8A. If in any chargeable period the Licensee delivers to the Minister in pursuance of clause 10 of this licence petroleum having a value greater than the appropriate percentage of the aggregate of—

    (a) the value of the petroleum delivered (ignoring any such excess as is mentioned in clause 8(10) of this licence), and

    (b) the value of the petroleum relating to that period,

the Minister shall pay to the Licensee a sum equal to the difference."

(7) In clause 9(3), for "8(3) or (4)" there shall be substituted "8(1A)".

(8) In clause 9(7), after "may" there shall be inserted ", during the period of 28 days beginning with the day on which the Licensee receives the notice,".

(9) In clause 9(8)(b), for "or (5)" there shall be substituted ", (5) or (6)".

(10) In clause 9, after paragraph (8) there shall be inserted—

"(8A) If a payment is made by the Minister in pursuance of clause 8A of this licence more than two months after the end of the chargeable period to which the payment relates, an amount in respect of interest on the payment from the end of those two months shall also be payable by him to the Licensee.

(8B) Interest under paragraph (8A) of this clause shall be calculated in such manner as the Minister may specify from time to time in a notice in writing given by him to the Licensee (but sub-paragraph (a) of paragraph (8) of this clause shall apply to such a notice as it applies to a notice under paragraph (8))."

(11) In clause 11, after paragraph (1) there shall be inserted—

"(1A) If and to the extent that the Minister so directs, the duty imposed by paragraph (1) of this clause shall be discharged separately in relation to petroleum won and saved—

(a) from each part of the licensed area which is an oil field for the purposes of the Oil Taxation Act 1975,

(b) from each part of the licensed area which forms part of such an oil field extending beyond the licensed area, and

(c) from each well producing petroleum from a part of the licensed area which is not within such an oil field.

(1B) If and to the extent that the Minister so directs, the preceding provisions of this clause shall apply as if the duty to measure or weigh petroleum included a duty to ascertain its quality or composition or both; and where a direction under this paragraph is in force, the following provisions of this clause shall have effect as if references to measuring or weighing included references to ascertaining quality or composition."

Schedule 4 to the 1984 Regulations

7.—(1) The model clauses set out in Schedule 4 to the Petroleum (Production) (Landward Areas) Regulations 1984 (clauses incorporated in appraisal licences for landward areas) shall have effect with the following amendments (which relate to arbitration, royalty payments and measurement etc. of petroleum).

(2) In clause 9(6), after "may" there shall be inserted ", during the period of 28 days beginning with the day on which the Licensee receives the notice,".

(3) In clause 9(7)(b), for "or (4)" there shall be substituted ", (4) or (5)".

(4) In clause 10, after paragraph (1) there shall be inserted—

"(1A) If and to the extent that the Minister so directs, the duty imposed by paragraph (1) of this clause shall be discharged separately in relation to petroleum won and saved—

(a) from each part of the licensed area which is an oil field for the purposes of the Oil Taxation Act 1975,

(b) from each part of the licensed area which forms part of such an oil field extending beyond the licensed area, and

(c) from each well producing petroleum from a part of the licensed area which is not within such an oil field.

(1B) If and to the extent that the Minister so directs, the preceding provisions of this clause shall apply as if the duty to measure or weigh petroleum included a duty to ascertain its quality or composition or both; and where a direction under this paragraph is in force, the following provisions of this clause shall have effect as if references to measuring or weighing included references to ascertaining quality or composition."

Section 18   SCHEDULE 2

AMENDMENT OF MODEL CLAUSES

Schedule 5 to the 1982 Regulations

1.—(1) The model clauses set out in Schedule 5 to the Petroleum (Production) Regulations 1982 (clauses for incorporation in production licences for seaward areas) shall have effect with the following amendments (which relate to calculation and payments of royalty, royalty in kind, arbitration and measurement etc. of petroleum).

(2) In clause 1, after paragraph (2) there shall be inserted—

"(3) Any clause of this licence which refers to any provision of Part I of the Oil Taxation Act 1975 shall, unless the contrary intention appears, be construed as referring to that provision as it has effect for the time being for the purposes of petroleum revenue tax".

(3) In clause 8(1)—

(a) for "paragraphs (2) to (4)" there shall be substituted "paragraph (1A)"; and

(b) for "clause 9" there shall be substituted "clauses 8A and 9".

(4) In clause 8, for paragraphs (2) to (4) there shall be substituted—

"(1A) Paragraph (1) of this clause shall not apply to a chargeable period in which the Licensee delivers petroleum to the Minister in pursuance of clause 10 of this licence; but if the petroleum delivered has a value of less than the appropriate percentage of the aggregate of—

    (a) the value of the petroleum delivered (ignoring any such excess as is mentioned in paragraph (10) of this clause), and

    (b) the value of the petroleum relating to that period,

he shall pay to the Minister a royalty of an amount equal to the difference."

(5) In clause 8(5), for "clause 9" there shall be substituted "clauses 8A and 9".

(6) In clause 8, for paragraph (7) there shall be substituted—

"(7) Subject to paragraphs (8) and (9) of this clause, the value of petroleum delivered to the Minister in pursuance of clause 10 of this licence shall be ascertained for the purposes of this clause and clause 8A on such basis (or, where petroleum of more than one kind is delivered, such bases) as the Minister and Licensee agree.

(8) If the Minister and the Licensee fail to agree on the value of any petroleum delivered to the Minister in pursuance of clause 10 of this licence, it shall be ascertained on such basis as the Minister may specify as fair in a notice in writing given by him to the Licensee.

(9) The Licensee may, during the period of 28 days beginning with the day on which he receives a notice from the Minister under paragraph (8) of this clause, refer to arbitration in the manner provided by clause 40 of this licence any question as to whether the basis of valuation specified in the notice is fair.

(10) In this clause and clauses 8A and 9, references to petroleum delivered to the Minister in pursuance of clause 10 include references to any excess over the quantity required to be deliverd by a notice served in pursuance of paragraph (1) of that clause."

(7) After clause 8, there shall be inserted—

"8A. If in any chargeable period the Licensee delivers to the Minister in pursuance of clause 10 of this licence petroleum having a value greater than the appropriate percentage of the aggregate of—

    (a) the value of the petroleum delivered (ignoring any such excess as is mentioned in clause 8(10) of this licence), and

    (b) the value of the petroleum relating to that period,

the Minister shall pay to the Licensee a sum equal to the difference."

(8) In clause 9(3), for "8(3) or (4)" there shall be substituted "8(1A)".

(9) In clause 9(7), after "may" there shall be inserted ", during the period of 28 days beginning with the day on which the Licensee receives the notice,".

(10) In clause 9(8)(b), for "or (5)" there shall be substituted ", (5) or (6)".

(11) In clause 9, after paragraph (8) there shall be inserted—

"(8A) If a payment is made by the Minister in pursuance of clause 8A of this licence more than two months after the end of the chargeable period to which the payment relates, an amount in respect of interest on the payment from the end of those two months shall also be payable by him to the Licensee.

(8B) Interest under paragraph (8A) of this clause shall be calculated in such manner as the Minister may specify from time to time in a notice in writing given by him to the Licensee (but sub-paragraph (a) of paragraph (8) of this clause shall apply to such a notice as it applies to a notice under paragraph (8))."

(12) In clause 11, after paragraph (1) there shall be inserted—

"(1A) If and to the extent that the Minister so directs, the duty imposed by paragraph (1) of this clause shall be discharged separately in relation to petroleum won and saved—

    (a) from each part of the licensed area which is an oil field for the purposes of the Oil Taxation Act 1975,

    (b) from each part of the licensed area which forms part of such an oil field extending beyond the licensed area, and

    (c) from each well producing petroleum from a part of the licensed area which is not within such an oil field.

(1B) If and to the extent that the Minister so directs, the preceding provisions of this clause shall apply as if the duty to measure or weigh petroleum included a duty to ascertain its quality or composition or both; and where a direction under this paragraph is in force, the following provisions of this clause shall have effect as if references to measuring or weighing included references to ascertaining quality or composition."

Schedule 4 to the 1984 Regulations

2.—(1) The model clauses set out in Schedule 4 to the Petroleum (Production) (Landward Areas) Regulations 1984 (clauses for incorporation in appraisal licences for landward areas) shall have effect with the following amendments (which relate to calculation and payments of royalty, arbitration and measurement etc. of petroleum).

(2) In clause 1, after paragraph (2) there shall be inserted—

"(3) Any clause of this licence which refers to any provision of Part I of the Oil Taxation Act 1975 shall, unless the contrary intention appears, be construed as referring to that provision as it has effect for the time being for the purposes of petroleum revenue tax."

(3) In clause 9(6), after "may" there shall be inserted ", during the period of 28 days beginning with the day on which the Licensee receives the notice,".

(4) In clause 9(7)(b), for "or (4)" there shall be substituted ", (4) or (5)".

(5) In clause 10, after paragraph (1) there shall be inserted—

"(1A) If and to the extent that the Minister so directs, the duty imposed by paragraph (1) of this clause shall be discharged separately in relation to petroleum won and saved—

(a) from each part of the licensed area which is an oil field for the purposes of the Oil Taxation Act 1975,

(b) from each part of the licensed area which forms part of such an oil field extending beyond the licensed area, and

(c) from each well producing petroleum from a part of the licensed area which is not within such an oil field.

(1B) If and to the extent that the Minister so directs, the preceding provisions of this clause shall apply as if the duty to measure or weigh petroleum included a duty to ascertain its quality or composition or both; and where a direction under this paragraph is in force, the following provisions of this clause shall have effect as if references to measuring or weighing included references to ascertaining quality or composition."

Schedule 5 to the 1984 Regulations

3.—(1) The model clauses set out in Schedule 5 to the Petroleum (Production) (Landward Areas) Regulations 1984 (clauses for incorporation in development licences for landward areas) shall have effect with the following amendments (which relate to calculation and payments of royalty, royalty in kind, arbitration and measurement etc. of petroleum).

(2) In clause 1, after paragraph (2) there shall be inserted—

"(3) Any clause of this licence which refers to any provision of Part I of the Oil Taxation Act 1975 shall, unless the contrary intention appears, be construed as referring to that provision as it has effect for the time being for the purposes of petroleum revenue tax."

(3) In clause 8(1), for "paragraphs (2) to (4)" there shall be substituted "paragraph (1A)".

(4) In clause 8, for paragraphs (2) to (4) there shall be substituted—

"(1A) Paragraph (1) of this clause shall not apply to a chargeable period in which the Licensee delivers petroleum to the Minister in pursuance of clause 10 of this licence; but if the petroleum delivered has a value of less than the relevant percentage of the aggregate of—

(a) the value of the petroleum delivered (ignoring any such excess as is mentioned in paragraph (6D) of this clause), and

(b) the value of the petroleum relating to that period,

he shall pay to the Minister a royalty of an amount equal to the difference."

(5) In clause 8(5), for "clause 9" there shall be substituted "clauses 8A and 9".

(6) In clause 8, after paragraph (6) there shall be inserted—

"(6A) Subject to paragraphs (6B) and (6C) of this clause, the value of petroleum delivered to the Minister in pursuance of clause 10 of this licence shall be ascertained for the purposes of this clause and clause 8A on such basis (or, where petroleum of more than one kind is delivered, such bases) as the Minister and the Licensee agree.

(6B) If the Minister and the Licensee fail to agree on the value of any petroleum delivered to the Minister in pursuance of clause 10 of this licence, it shall be ascertained on such basis as the Minister may specify as fair in a notice in writing given by him to the Licensee.

(6C) The Licensee may, during the period of 28 days beginning with the day on which he receives a notice from the Minister under paragraph (6B) of this clause, refer to arbitration in the manner provided by clause 37 of this licence any question as to whether the basis of valuation specified in the notice is fair.

(6D) In this clause and clauses 8A and 9, references to petroleum delivered to the Minister in pursuance of clause 10 include references to any excess over the quantity required to be delivered by a notice served in pursuance of paragraph (1) of that clause."

(7) In clause 8(7), for the definition of "royalty petroleum" there shall be substituted—

'relevant percentage', in relation to a chargeable period, means the effective rate at which, apart from any notice under clause 11 of this licence, royalty would be payable for that period in pursuance of paragraph (1) of this clause;".

(8) After clause 8, there shall be inserted—

"8A—(1) If in any chargeable period the Licensee delivers to the Minister in pursuance of clause 10 of this licence petroleum having a value greater than the relevant percentage of the aggregate of—

(a) the value of the petroleum (ignoring any such excess as is mentioned in clause 8(6D) of this licence), and

(b) the value of the petroleum relating to that period,

the Minister shall pay to the Licensee a sum equal to the difference.

(2) In this clause, 'chargeable period' and 'relevant percentage' have the same meanings as in clause 8 of this licence."

(9) In clause 9(2), for "fraction" there shall be substituted "percentage".

(10) In clause 9(3), for "8(3) or (4)" there shall be substituted "8(1A)".

(11) In clause 9(7), after "may" there shall be inserted ", during the period of 28 days beginning with the day on which the Licensee receives the notice,".

(12) In clause 9(8)(b), for "or (5)" there shall be substituted ", (5) or (6)".

(13) In clause 9, after paragraph (8) there shall be inserted—

"(8A) If a payment is made by the Minister in pursuance of clause 8A of this licence more than two months after the end of the chargeable period to which the payment relates, an amount in respect of interest on the payment from the end of those two months shall also be payable by him to the Licensee.

(8B) Interest under paragraph (8A) of this clause shall be calculated in such manner as the Minister may specify from time to time in a notice in writing given by him to the Licensee (but sub-paragraph (a) of paragraph (8) of this clause shall apply to such a notice as it applies to a notice under paragraph (8))."

(14) In clause 9(9)—

(a) for " 'royalty petroleum' " there shall be substituted " 'relevant percentage' "; and

(b) the definition of "the relevant fraction" and the word "and" preceding it shall be omitted.

(15) In clause 11, after paragraph (1) there shall be inserted—

"(1A) If and to the extent that the Minister so directs, the duty imposed by paragraph (1) of this clause shall be discharged separately in relation to petroleum won and saved—

(a) from each part of the licensed area which is an oil field for the purposes of the Oil Taxation Act 1975,

(b) from each part of the licensed area which forms part of such an oil field extending beyond the licensed area, and

(c) from each well producing petroleum from a part of the licensed area which is not within such an oil field.

(1B) If and to the extent that the Minister so directs, the preceding provisions of this clause shall apply as if the duty to measure or weigh petroleum included a duty to ascertain its quality or composition or both; and where a direction under this paragraph is in force, the following provisions of this clause shall have effect as if references to measuring or weighing included references to ascertaining quality or composition."

SCHEDULE 3

Repeals

Chapter	Short title	Extent of repeal
1934 c.36	The Petroleum (Production) Act 1934.	In section 1(2), the words "adjacent to Great Britain". Section 11(3).
1962 c.58.	The Pipe-lines Act 1962.	In section 47(3), the words "an objection to", in each place where they occur. In Schedule 1, paragraph 4(2).
1964 c.29.	The Continental Shelf Act 1964.	Section 1(5).
1966 c.4.	The Mines (Working Facilities and Support) Act 1966.	Section 2(1A).
1975 c.74.	The Petroleum and Submarine Pipe-lines Act 1975.	Sections 34 to 39.
1981 c.36.	The Town and Country Planning (Minerals) Act 1981.	Section 33.
1982 c.23.	The Oil and Gas (Enterprise) Act 1982	Section 21. In section 27(1), paragraph (d) and the word "and" preceding it. In Schedule 3, paragraph 29.

MINORS' CONTRACTS ACT 1987*

(1987 c. 13)

An Act to amend the law relating to minors' contracts.

[9th April 1987]

PARLIAMENTARY DEBATES
Hansard: H.L. Vol. 482, cols. 345, 709; Vol. 483, cols. 8, 817; H.C. Vol. 110, col. 1030; Vol. 114, col. 275.
The Bill was considered by Standing Committee A on March 17, 1987.

GENERAL NOTE

This Act is based on recommendations of the Law Commission published in their Report on Minors' Contracts (Law Com. No. 134) and seeks to remove certain restrictions on the enforceability of contracts entered into by minors. Before the coming into force of this Act the law concerning minors' contracts was mainly governed by the Infants Relief Act 1874, which was generally considered to be unsatisfactory, and the common law which to a large extent reflected historical considerations which are no longer of practical significance. The Minors' Contracts Act attempts to simplify and improve the law in this area by repealing the Infants Relief Act, by giving the court some discretionary powers to require restitution of property in obvious cases of unjust enrichment and by giving prominence, once more, to common law rules. There are, undoubtedly, still problems with the common law as it exists. The aim of this legislation is to make the law in this area easier to understand while reforming within the ambit of present principles.

The Act is not expected to have any effect on public expenditure or public service manpower nor are there any EEC implications.

Disapplication of Infants Relief Act 1874 etc.

1.—(1) The following enactments shall not apply to any contract made by a minor after the commencement of this Act—

    (a) the Infants Relief Act 1874 (which invalidates certain contracts made by minors and prohibits actions to enforce contracts ratified after majority); and

    (b) section 5 of the Betting and Loans (Infants) Act 1892 (which invalidates contracts to repay loans advanced during minority).

GENERAL NOTE

S. 1 of this Act disapplies the Infants Relief Act 1874 and s.5 of the Betting and Loans Act 1892 in relation to contracts made after June 9, 1987.

Subs. (a)

The Infants Relief Act 1874 had only two substantive sections, which, it has been said, caused problems incommensurate with its length. It affected the common law in two important ways. Firstly, in s.1, it provided that contracts of loan, contracts for goods other than necessaries and contracts for accounts stated entered into by a minor, should be rendered "absolutely void". The section caused difficulties because its wording was ambiguous and its effect uncertain. Critics questioned the extent to which the word "absolutely" added to the meaning of the section and suggested that the contracts that fell within it were not selected on a coherent basis. The result was that, at times, judges were reluctant to give the words of the section their literal meaning. Its disapplication will result in the contracts specified being subject to the rules of the common law and will allow the rules of "qualified enforceability" to prevail once more.

Secondly, in s.2, the Infants Relief Act 1874 imposed a bar on proceedings to enforce ratification of contracts on the minor attaining majority, but allowed that a new contract with fresh consideration could be made, despite the fact that it incorporated exactly the same promises. Not surprisingly, this led at times to very artificial results since the line dividing ratification from a new contract to do the same thing was sometimes very thin. The principle behind the provision was that minors should not be pressurized into making legal on majority what was previously not legal, but the rule as to new contracts did little to uphold it. The position now is that, after attaining majority a minor can ratify contracts

---

* Annotations by Linda Mulcahy, LL.B.

that are unenforceable against him or voidable at his option. According to the common law rules now in force ratification is confirmation of an earlier promise and does not require fresh consideration. It is a unilateral act.

Subs. (b)

This subsection provides a follow up to the last by repealing s.5 of the Betting and Loans (Infants) Act 1892. S.5 provided that a new contract entered into by a minor, after attaining majority, to pay a debt due under a void loan, contracted in infancy, is itself void. The disapplication of this section makes effective any new agreement and negotiable instrument in connection with it, to repay a loan advanced during minority.

Guarantees

2. Where—
   (a) a guarantee is given in respect of an obligation of a party to a contract made after the commencement of this Act, and
   (b) the obligation is unenforceable against him (or he repudiates the contract) because he was a minor when the contract was made,

the guarantee shall not for that reason alone be unenforceable against the guarantor.

DEFINITIONS

"repudiates": use has been made of this word because it is the one customarily used in cases where a minor is entitled to escape liability before or within a reasonable time after his majority.

GENERAL NOTE

This section makes a guarantee of a minor's contractual obligation enforceable against the guarantor even though the main contractual obligation is not enforceable against the minor. It has no authority in relation to contract goods that are "necessaries" since there is an enforceable obligation on the minor to pay a reasonable price for such goods anyway. It ensures that the guarantee of an unenforceable minor's contract is as effective as if the minor had been an adult. Prior to this section coming into force, s.1 of the Infants Relief Act 1874 had the effect of invalidating guarantees on the basis that the main contract itself was rendered "absolutely void". This created inconsistencies since indemnities, often only distinguished from guarantees on the basis of technicalities bearing no relation to the substance of the transaction, were not affected by the Act of 1874. Moreover there were not always good reasons to justify the invalidation of guarantees since they often operated to the advantage of the minor and the other party to the contract.

It has been suggested that a repeal of s.1 of the Infants Relief Act 1874 might, by itself, have achieved the same result as s.2 of this Act, by providing that contracts which came within the section and guarantees of such contracts are no longer rendered void but merely unenforceable against a minor. However, there is no clear authority on the effect at common law of a guarantee of an unenforceable minor's contract and so s.2 of this Act was drafted to ensure that the desired result was achieved.

The effect of the actual guarantee of a contractual obligation voidable by the minor depends very much on the terms of the guarantee. It has, however, been made clear in the section that it will not be unenforceable solely because of the repudiation of the main contract. This provision was thought to be required for two reasons. Firstly it might be relevant to obligations incurred by a minor prior to repudiation. The law is, at present uncertain as to exactly what obligations are enforceable against a minor. Secondly, it is possible that it will be relevant to obligations incurred after repudiation if the guarantee is worded to cover such an obligation.

S.2 does not alter the circumstances in which a guarantor who has honoured the guarantee is entitled to recover against the minor. He is in the same position as any of the minors' creditors. Neither does it effect the guarantee of an obligation incurred by a minor prior to June 9, 1987, even if the guarantee was given after that date.

Restitution

3.—(1) Where—
   (a) a person ("the plaintiff") has after the commencement of this Act entered into a contract with another ("the defendant"), and

· (b) the contract is unenforceable against the defendant (or he repudiates it) because he was a minor when the contract was made,

the court may, if it is just and equitable to do so, require the defendant to transfer to the plaintiff any property acquired by the defendant under the contract, or any property representing it.

(2) Nothing in this section shall be taken to prejudice any other remedy available to the plaintiff.

GENERAL NOTE

S.3 provides that where a minor has acquired property under a contract that is unenforceable against him or which he has repudiated on the grounds of his minority then he may be required by the court, where they think it "just and equitable" to do so, to return the property, or property representing that which he has acquired. This power to make restitution does not affect any other remedy available to the party and may be in addition to it.

The section aims to provide a remedy in cases where an unscrupulous minor obtains goods and refuses to pay for them. Prior to the coming into force of this section a minor could do just that with virtual impunity. The section does not attempt to cover every case of unjust enrichment but rather the most obvious cases of abuse. To do otherwise would be to complicate the law unnecessarily.

The most important effect of the section is that it extends the power of the court to order restoration of property by a minor. This remedy was previously confined to cases where the minor fraudulently induced the other party to enter into the contract. There is no attempt to specify the circumstances in which the court may exercise its discretion except that it must be just and equitable to do so. The advantage of such wording is that these are principles with which the courts are familiar and which they are at liberty to develop. It should however, be noted that the court's power is limited to ordering the minor to return the property acquired or property representing it. Thus, the minor may be required to offer up goods acquired in exchange. But if he has consumed or disposed of the goods or their proceeds he cannot be required to compensate the other party.

Consequential amendment and repeals

4.—(1) In section 113 of the Consumer Credit Act 1974 (that Act not to be evaded by use of security) in subsection (7)—

(a) after the word "indemnity", in both places where it occurs, there shall be inserted "or guarantee";

(b) after the words "minor, or" there shall be inserted "an indemnity is given in a case where he"; and

(c) for the word "they" there shall be substituted "those obligations".

(2) The Infants Relief Act 1874 and the Betting and Loans (Infants) Act 1892 are hereby repealed (in accordance with section 1 of this Act).

GENERAL NOTE

This section provides for the repeals and amendments to other legislation as a result of the Minors' Contracts Act coming into force.

Subs. (1)

This subsection relates to s.113 of the Consumer Credit Act 1974. S.113 contains important provisions designed to prevent evasion of the Act by the use of securities. S.113(1) allows that however the security is expressed the surety cannot be called upon to pay more than the debtor or hirer would be obliged to in the circumstances. S.113(7) creates an exception where the security takes the form of a contract of indemnity with the creditor or owner and the debtor or hirer is not of full legal capacity because he is, for instance, a minor. Subs. 7 was designed to ensure that where the debtor or hirer is not of full legal capacity that s.113(1) does not produce the effect that a contract of indemnity becomes unenforceable merely by reason of his minority, as it would have done if it had been a contract of guarantee. In line with s.2 of this Act the word "guarantee" has been inserted where appropriate so that the use of the words "indemnity" and "guarantee" are now interchangeable for the purposes of the Act as far as they relate to minors' contracts. The position now is that where the debtor or hirer is a minor, a contract of indemnity or guarantee that he enters into is not rendered unenforceable by s.113(1) merely by reason of his minority.

The amendment does not affect the operation of the section insofar as it relates to other forms of contractual incapacity. Thus in other areas the line distinguishing indemnities from guarantees is preserved.

Subs. (2)

This subsection repeals the Infants Relief Act 1874 and the Betting and Loans (Infants) Act 1892. This is done in accordance with s.1 of this Act with the effect that the repealed provisions will still apply to contracts entered into before June 9, 1987. The whole of the Betting and Loans (Infants) Act 1892 is repealed by this subsection because the only sections of it that are still in force in England and Wales are s.5, repealed by s.1 of this Act, and s.8 which relates to the short title of the Act.

Short title, commencement and extent

5.—(1) This Act may be cited as the Minors' Contracts Act 1987.

(2) This Act shall come into force at the end of the period of two months beginning with the date on which it is passed.

(3) This Act extends to England and Wales only.

GENERAL NOTE

Subs. (2)

This subsection provides that the Act shall come into force two months after April 9, 1987, *i.e.* June 9, 1987.

Subs. (3)

This subsection restricts the application of the Act to England and Wales. The effect of this is that the Infants Relief Act 1874 which applied to England, Wales and Northern Ireland prior to the passing of this Act shall henceforth only apply to Northern Ireland, while the Betting and Loans (Infants) Act which applied to England, Wales, Northern Ireland and Scotland prior to the coming into force of this Act shall continue to apply in Scotland and Northern Ireland.

RECOGNITION OF TRUSTS ACT 1987*

(1987 c. 14)

An Act to enable the United Kingdom to ratify the Convention on the law applicable to trusts and on their recognition which was signed on behalf of the United Kingdom on 10th January 1986.

[9th April 1987]

PARLIAMENTARY DEBATES
Hansard: H.L. Vol. 482, cols. 345, 938; Vol. 483, cols. 8, 818; H.C. Vol. 111, col. 1129; Vol. 114, col. 275.
The Bill was considered by Standing Committee A on March 17, 1987.

GENERAL NOTE
This Act enables the United Kingdom to ratify the Convention on the law applicable to trusts and on their recognition which was adopted in draft by the Hague Conference on Private International Law on October 20, 1984, Cmnd. 9494 (1984). Professor Von Overbeck, the rapporteur of the committee of experts which drafted the Convention, has written a report published by the Hague Conference so as to assist in the understanding and interpretation of the Convention. There is also an article in (1987) 36 I.C.L.Q. 260 written by Dr. D. J. Hayton, the annotator.

The Convention does not introduce the concept of the trust into the domestic law of States that do not already have the trust ("non-trust" States). It does establish common conflicts of law principles on the law applicable to trusts, such principles to be applied by trust States and non-trust States alike. These flexible principles in Arts. 6 and 7, subject to safeguards for the *lex situs* and *lex fori* in Arts. 15, 16 and 18, reflect what are considered to be the current U.K. principles.

The Convention further requires States to recognise foreign trusts as such, rather than by analogues in their own domestic law if the trust is an alien concept. Pragmatically, the Convention stresses the major consequences of recognising a trust validly created under the applicable law. This will greatly assist non-trust States to deal fairly, expeditiously and effectively with trust issues arising within their jurisdiction. Adoption of the Convention by non-trust States will reassure trustees worrying whether their beneficiaries' interests may be prejudiced by purchasing foreign assets directly or through nominees.

COMMENCEMENT
The Act comes into force on a day to be appointed, perhaps in October 1987.

EXTENT
The Act extends to Northern Ireland.

Applicable law and recognition of trusts

1.—(1) The provisions of the Convention set out in the Schedule to this Act shall have the force of law in the United Kingdom.

(2) Those provisions shall, so far as applicable, have effect not only in relation to the trusts described in Articles 2 and 3 of the Convention but also in relation to any other trusts of property arising under the law of any part of the United Kingdom or by virtue of a judicial decision whether in the United Kingdom or elsewhere.

(3) In accordance with Articles 15 and 16 such provisions of the law as are there mentioned shall, to the extent there specified, apply to the exclusion of the other provisions of the Convention.

(4) In Article 17 the reference to a State includes a reference to any

---

* Annotations by D. J. Hayton, LL.D., Barrister, who headed the U.K. delegation to the Fifteenth Session of the Hague Conference (1984).

country or territory (whether or not a party to the Convention and whether or not forming part of the United Kingdom) which has its own system of law.

(5) Article 22 shall not be construed as affecting the law to be applied in relation to anything done or omitted before the coming into force of this Act.

GENERAL NOTE

While subs. (1) imports into U.K. law the provisions of the Convention set out in the Schedule to the Act, subs. (2) extends those provisions beyond the trusts described in Arts. 2 and 3 of the Convention. The first extension is to any other trusts of property arising under the law of any part of the U.K. This ensures that U.K. courts have one set of rules for all trusts arising under the law of any part of the U.K. whether in writing or orally or by automatic operation of statute (*e.g.* Law of Property Act 1925, ss.34–36, Administration of Estates Act 1925, s.33) or by specific action under a statute like the Mental Health Act 1983, s.96(1)(*d*). The other extension is to any other trusts of property arising by virtue of a judicial decision, whether in the U.K. or elsewhere. This ensures compliance with the U.K.'s EEC obligations as incorporated in the Civil Jurisdiction and Judgments Act 1982 and prevents any problems arising over the extent to which judicial decisions (*e.g.* as to constructive trusts) may or may not take a trust outside Arts. 2 and 3.

Subs. (3) clears up what U.K. lawyers might regard as an ambiguity created by the use, in Arts. 15 and 16, of the clause "This Convention does not prevent the application of . . .": it emphasises the overriding nature of Arts. 15 and 16.

Subs. (4) deals with the fact that many States contain territorial units with their own separate systems of law. Art. 23 of the Convention which deals with this in more convoluted fashion has not been adopted in the Schedule to the Act.

Subs. (5) ensures, *ex abundante cautela,* that the Act does not affect the law to be applied in relation to anything done or omitted before the coming into force of the Act, though the Act applies to trusts regardless of the date on which they were created (Art. 22).

Extent

2.—(1) This Act extends to Northern Ireland.

(2) Her Majesty may by Order in Council direct that this Act shall also form part of the law of the Isle of Man, any of the Channel Islands or any colony.

(3) An Order in Council under subsection (2) above may modify this Act in its application to any of the territories there mentioned and may contain such supplementary provisions as Her Majesty considers appropriate.

(4) An Order in Council under subsection (2) above shall be subject to annulment in pursuance of a resolution of either House of Parliament.

Short title, commencement and application to the Crown

3.—(1) This Act may be cited as the Recognition of Trusts Act 1987.

(2) This Act shall come into force on such date as the Lord Chancellor and the Lord Advocate may appoint by an order made by statutory instrument.

(3) This Act binds the Crown.

SCHEDULE

CONVENTION ON THE LAW APPLICABLE TO TRUSTS AND ON THEIR RECOGNITION

CHAPTER I—SCOPE

Article 1

This Convention specifies the law applicable to trusts and governs their recognition.

GENERAL NOTE

The Convention is an "open" or "universal" one since tremendous difficulties would arise if it were restricted to relations between contracting States and some aspects of a trust involved a contracting State whilst some did not or if exercise of powers might take a trust in and out of the Convention.

Article 2

For the purposes of this Convention, the term "trust" refers to the legal relationship created—inter vivos or on death—by a person, the settlor, when assets have been placed under the control of a trustee for the benefit of a beneficiary or for a specified purpose.
A trust has the following characteristics—
    (a) the assets constitute a separate fund and are not a part of the trustee's own estate;
    (b) title to the trust assets stands in the name of the trustee or in the name of another person on behalf of the trustee;
    (c) the trustee has the power and the duty, in respect of which he is accountable, to manage, employ or dispose of the assets in accordance with the terms of the trust and the special duties imposed upon him by law.
The reservation by the settlor of certain rights and powers, and the fact that the trustee may himself have rights as a beneficiary, are not necessarily inconsistent with the existence of a trust.

GENERAL NOTE

This Article describes a "trust" by its central characteristics so as to include the classic Anglo-American trust where there is the distinction between legal ownership in the trustees and equitable ownership in the beneficiaries. It also includes the trust in Scotland or India where such distinction does not exist. It is capable of including trust-like concepts that have developed or may yet develop in other countries.

The final paragraph recognises that whilst A cannot hold on trust for A, A can transfer assets to A and B to hold on trust for such of A, B their spouses and issue as the trustees see fit, and A can reserve to himself powers such as a power of revocation or a power to add other relatives to the class of discretionary beneficiaries.

Article 3

The Convention applies only to trusts created voluntarily and evidenced in writing.

GENERAL NOTE

Trusts need not be created in writing so long as they are evidenced in writing. Signed writing of the settlor is not required. A letter from the trustees may suffice, as, presumably, may a court decree specifying the terms of a disputed trust.

Trusts need to be created voluntarily in the sense that they are created, whether gratuitously or for value, by the exercise of free will.

If a voluntary trust evidenced in writing fails after some time so that an "automatic" resulting trust arises such trust is within the Convention. If a "presumed" resulting trust arises in S's favour where she purchases property in the name of T (or of S and T) it would seem that subsequent written evidence would bring the trust within the Convention.

A constructive trust imposed by a court decision without reference to, or against the intention of, a person is excluded from the Convention as not "created voluntarily" by a person (see Art. 2). Art. 20 enables a State (as the U.K. has done in s.1(2) above) to extend the Convention to trusts of property declared by judicial decisions.

Where persons voluntarily intend to create a trust which cannot take effect as an express trust because of failure to comply with statutory formalites (*e.g. Grant* v. *Edwards* [1986] Ch. 638, C.A.) but the court intervenes to vindicate the express trust by imposing a constructive trust to prevent the defendant fraudulently keeping the property for himself alone, then the trust should fall within the Convention.

Trusts automatically arising by operation of law (such as the statutory trust for sale arising on an intestacy or on land being purchased by co-owners) or specifically created under a statutory jurisdiction like ss.95 and 96 of the Mental Health Act 1983, fall outside the Convention, though s.1(2) above extends the Convention to such trusts arising under the law of any part of the U.K.

In the case of divorce settlements if H voluntarily settles property on W and their children, knowing that otherwise the court will be likely to order him to make a similar settlement, the settlement will be within the Convention. It ought to make no difference if H makes the settlement pursuant to a court order (as indicated in the Von Overbeck Report, para. 49): s.1(2) makes it clear that such trusts are included.

Article 4

The Convention does not apply to preliminary issues relating to the validity of wills or of other acts by virtue of which assets are transferred to the trustee.

GENERAL NOTE

An instrument or act is necessary to get a trust off the ground just as a rocket-launcher is needed to launch a rocket. Only when the trust has been effectively "launched" does the Convention apply. It does not apply to antecedent issues of form, capacity or validity which may wholly or partly vitiate the instrument or act which purports to subject assets to a trust.

Article 5

The Convention does not apply to the extent that the law specified by Chapter II does not provide for trusts or the category of trusts involved.

GENERAL NOTE

In the remarkable case of the applicable law under Arts. 6 or 7 being the law of a State that does not have in its domestic law the concept of the trust then the Convention does not apply. If such applicable law only has a concept similar to the charitable trust then the Convention will only apply to charitable trusts (as opposed to private trusts) governed by that law.

CHAPTER II—APPLICABLE LAW

Article 6

A trust shall be governed by the law chosen by the settlor. The choice must be express or be implied in the terms of the instrument creating or the writing evidencing the trust, interpreted, if necessary, in the light of the circumstances of the case.

Where the law chosen under the previous paragraph does not provide for trusts or the category of trust involved, the choice shall not be effective and the law specified in Article 7 shall apply.

GENERAL NOTE

There may be an express or implied choice of applicable law by the person establishing the original trust, but, first, the hurdle in Art. 4 must be surmounted and then safeguards are provided by Arts. 15, 16 and 18. There will for example be an implied choice if the trust instrument excludes, qualifies or extends expressly mentioned provisions of a particular State's trust law.

One law may be chosen to govern one aspect of a trust (*e.g.* matters of validity, assets in Scotland) and another law to govern another aspect (*e.g.* matters of administration, assets in Manitoba) (see Art. 9).

An express choice of U.K. law or U.S.A. law or Canadian law or Australian law will be a nullity: reference must be to a territory with its own system of law, *e.g.* Scotland, California, Ontario, Queensland. To avoid *renvoi* problems a choice of a territory's conflicts of law rules cannot be effective since only a territory's domestic law may be chosen (see Art. 17).

Article 7

Where no applicable law has been chosen, a trust shall be governed by the law with which it is most closely connected.

In ascertaining the law with which a trust is most closely connected reference shall be made in particular to—

(a) the place of administration of the trust designated by the settlor;
(b) the situs of the assets of the trust;
(c) the place of residence or business of the trustee;
(d) the objects of the trust and the places where they are to be fulfilled.

GENERAL NOTE

If the form and contents of the trust instrument are not themselves sufficient to reveal a settlor's express or implied choice of law then they will be taken into account in ascertaining the law with which the trust is most closely connected, as will other relevant factors including those mentioned in (a), (b), (c) and (d). In an *inter vivos* trust the domicile or habitual residence of the settlor when creating the trust will be one relevant factor. In a testamentary trust the testator's domicile at his death has had much significance since the *lex domicilii* governs the validity of the will, though it does not necessarily have to govern the validity of trust provisions contained in the will (see *Re Lord Cable's Will Trusts* [1976] 3 All E.R. 417, at 431 and *Chellaram* v. *Chelleram* [1985] 1 All E.R. 1043 at 1056).

Article 8

The law specified by Article 6 or 7 shall govern the validity of the trust, its construction, its effects and the administration of the trust.

In particular that law shall govern—

(a) the appointment, resignation and removal of trustees, the capacity to act as a trustee, and the devolution of the office of trustee;
(b) the rights and duties of trustees among themselves;
(c) the right of trustees to delegate in whole or in part the discharge of their duties or the exercise of their powers;
(d) the power of trustees to administer or to dispose of trust assets, to create security interests in the trust assets, or to acquire new assets;
(e) the powers of investment of trustees;
(f) restrictions upon the duration of the trust, and upon the power to accumulate the income of the trust;
(g) the relationships between the trustees and the beneficiaries including the personal liability of the trustees to the beneficiaries;
(h) the variation or termination of the trust;
(i) the distribution of the trust assets;
(j) the duty of trustees to account for their administration.

GENERAL NOTE

This illustrates various trust issues that may arise and which are to be governed by the applicable law or laws determined under Arts. 6, 7 and 9. No attempt is made to characterise such issues as matters of validity or of construction or of administration since this is a difficult, underdeveloped and relatively uncharted area where any attempt at consensus would be premature and bound to fail. Such characterisation is left to the relevant applicable law. If the law of England or Scotland should be the "mother" law governing validity then such law should determine whether any particular trust issue is one of validity, construction or administration: on this distinction see Underhill and Hayton, *Law of Trusts and Trustees* (14th ed., 1987) pp.837–838.

The theoretically unlimited jurisdiction of the English court under the Variation of Trusts Act 1958 has been restricted to what was generally the *de facto* practical jurisdiction. The court (see *Re Paget's Settlement* [1965] 1 W.L.R. 1046) used to give careful consideration to the question whether it was in fact proper to exercise the jurisdiction where there were substantial foreign elements in the case, taking into account the effectiveness of any court order and whether there was any possibility of "limping" trust provisions valid by English law under the 1958 Act but void under some other applicable law governing validity. Now, variation of beneficial interests is possible only if authorised by the law governing validity of the trust.

Article 9

In applying this Chapter a severable aspect of the trust, particularly matters of administration, may be governed by a different law.

GENERAL NOTE

This recognises that a settlor may legitimately pick and choose different laws to govern different aspects of his trust, *e.g.* English law to govern English assets, New York law to govern New York assets, or Irish law to govern validity of the trust, Scots law to govern construction of the trust and English law to govern administration of the trust. The interests of other States which might otherwise be prejudiced by such freedom of choice are safeguarded by Arts. 15, 16 and 18.

Article 10

The law applicable to the validity of the trust shall determine whether that law or the law governing a severable aspect of the trust may be replaced by another law.

GENERAL NOTE

To have sufficient flexibility to cope with changing family, economic or social conditions it is common for a settlor expressly to provide for the trustees (perhaps with the consent of some designated "Protector") to have power to replace the law governing the whole trust or part of the trust or governing validity or governing administration by another law from time to time, so long as such law is the law of a State with its own domestic law of trusts. Whether there may be some implied power of replacing the governing law to some extent can be a difficult question. Art. 10 recognises that it is the "mother" law applicable to the validity of the trust which determines whether that law or the law governing a severable aspect of the trust (*e.g.* administration matters) may be replaced by another law.

CHAPTER III—RECOGNITION

Article 11

A trust created in accordance with the law specified by the preceding Chapter shall be recognised as a trust.

Such recognition shall imply, as a minimum, that the trust property constitutes a separate fund, that the trustee may sue and be sued in his capacity as trustee, and that he may appear or act in this capacity before a notary or any person acting in an official capacity.

In so far as the law applicable to the trust requires or provides, such recognition shall imply in particular—

(a) that personal creditors of the trustee shall have no recourse against the trust assets;
(b) that the trust assets shall not form part of the trustee's estate upon his insolvency or bankruptcy;
(c) that the trust assets shall not form part of the matrimonial property of the trustee or his spouse nor part of the trustee's estate upon his death;
(d) that the trust assets may be recovered when the trustee, in breach of trust, has mingled trust assets with his own property or has alienated trust assets. However, the rights and obligations of any third party holder of the assets shall remain subject to the law determined by the choice of law rules of the forum.

GENERAL NOTE

This emphasises the effects of recognising a trust. The qualifying clause prefacing the third paragraph caters for special situations like those covered by the Insolvency Act 1986, ss.339–344, 423–425 which may enable creditors to have recourse to trust assets.

The very last sentence drastically curtails the right to trace assets where such assets are disposed of in a State that does not have the trust in its domestic law. This application of the general principle that the *lex situs* determines transfer of title to property makes the right to trace meaningless, except to the extent that a transferee's actual knowledge of a breach of trust may make it possible to take advantage of rules of the *lex situs* concerning fraud.

Article 12

Where the trustee desires to register assets, movable or immovable, or documents of title to them, he shall be entitled, in so far as this is not prohibited by or inconsistent with the law of the State where registration is sought, to do so in his capacity as trustee or in such other way that the existence of the trust is disclosed.

GENERAL NOTE

This enables a trustee, if he wishes, to register his entitlement to trust assets *qua* trustee so far as this is not prohibited by or inconsistent with the *lex situs*, *e.g.* the Companies Act 1985, s.360. A trustee should so register if such registration is a pre-condition if the beneficiaries' interests are to be preferred to creditors' interests.

Article 14

The Convention shall not prevent the application of rules of law more favourable to the recognition of trusts.

CHAPTER IV—GENERAL CLAUSES

Article 15

The Convention does not prevent the application of provisions of the law designated by the conflicts rules of the forum, in so far as those provisions cannot be derogated from by voluntary act, relating in particular to the following matters—
  (a) the protection of minors and incapable parties;
  (b) the personal and proprietary effects of marriage;
  (c) succession rights, testate and intestate, especially the indefeasible shares of spouses and relatives;
  (d) the transfer of title to property and security interests in property;
  (e) the protection of creditors in matters of insolvency;
  (f) the protection, in other respects, of third parties acting in good faith.
If recognition of a trust is prevented by application of the preceding paragraph, the court shall try to give effect to the objects of the trust by other means.

GENERAL NOTE

Regardless of the applicable law of the trust under the Convention, there must be applied the mandatory rules to entitlement to assets that happen to be held on trust. Thus a trust that has survived Art. 4 may still fall foul of Art. 15 where the conflicts rules of the *lex fori* refer to the *lex fori* or the *lex situs* or the *lex loci solutionis* and such *lex* has mandatory rules in the sense that they cannot be derogated from by voluntary act.

There is much uncertain scope for Art. 15 to be applied so as to negate much of the promotional effect of Art. 11. It is to be hoped that the central crucial role of Art. 11 will place a heavy onus on anyone invoking Art. 15 to establish an exceptional case for application of a rule as mandatory.

Article 16

The Convention does not prevent the application of those provisions of the law of the forum which must be applied even to international situations, irrespective of rules of conflict of laws.

GENERAL NOTE

This states the obvious: the court will apply the extra-special mandatory rules of the *lex fori* designed to protect the interests of the State, *e.g.* in preventing the export of currency, cultural heritage objects, arms, technical equipment.

Article 17

In the Convention the word 'law' means the rules of law in force in a State other than its rules of conflict of laws.

GENERAL NOTE
This excludes the doctrine of *renvoi* in accordance with the general practice for Hague Conventions.

Article 18

The provisions of the Convention may be disregarded when their application would be manifestly incompatible with public policy.

GENERAL NOTE
This affords scope for intervention by the *lex fori* where it has a sufficiently strong interest to invoke public policy in the fundamental ordre public sense (see Chapter 4 by D. C. Jackson in *Contract Conflicts* (P. M. North ed., 1982)) to justify disregarding other provisions in the Convention.

Article 22

The Convention applies to trusts regardless of the date on which they were created.

GENERAL NOTE
All trusts created before or after the Convention comes into force are covered. *Ex abundante cautela* (since it seems the modern formulation of conflicts rules in the Convention reflects the position already reflected in case law or likely to be reflected in future case law but for this 1987 Act), s.1(5) makes it clear that the entry into force of the 1987 Act is not to affect the law to be applied in relation to anything done or omitted before such entry into force.

REVERTER OF SITES ACT 1987*

(1987 c. 15)

An Act to amend the law with respect to the reverter of sites that have ceased to be used for particular purposes; and for connected purposes.

[9th April 1987]

PARLIAMENTARY DEBATES

Hansard: H.L. Vol. 482, cols. 344, 984; Vol. 483, cols. 484, 714; H.C. Vol. 111, col. 243; Vol. 114, col. 276.

The Bill was considered by Standing Committee A on March 17, 1987.

INTRODUCTION AND GENERAL NOTE

In 1978 the Law Commission was asked to consider the provisions for reverter contained in a number of nineteenth-century statutes (notably, the School Sites Act 1841, the Literary and Scientific Institutions Act 1854, and the Places of Worship Sites Act 1873). The Law Commission's Report No. 111 (Property Law—Rights of Reverter) which incorporated the report of a working party, was presented to Parliament in November 1981. While the Reverter of Sites Act 1987 departs in a significant number of respects from some recommendations of the working party (and ignores others), it nevertheless attempts to tackle the central problems which were first brought to the attention of those involved in the law reform process in the 1970's.

The background

Prior to the provision of compulsory education by the state, schools were endowed mainly from private sources. The purpose behind the School Sites Act 1841 was to encourage private landowners to convey to trustees small plots of land for the provision of schools for the poor (and school teachers' houses) by providing a simplified and cheap form of conveyance. In relation to conveyances made under the authority of the Act land which ceased to be used for the purposes for which it had been granted automatically reverted to the grantor. This pattern was followed with regard to sites for museums and libraries (Literary and Scientific Institutions Act 1854) and for churches and chapels (Places of Worship Sites Act 1873). It is thought that there are altogether about 5,000 sites governed by these Acts, over 2,000 of them being school sites.

Under the 1925 legislation, a determinable fee is normally an equitable interest (Law of Property Act 1925, s.1(3)), the creation of which brings about a strict settlement governed by the Settled Land Act 1925 (s.1(1)(ii)(c)). By virtue of s.7(1) of the Law of Property Act 1925, however, a determinable fee simple created under the School Sites Act 1841 and similar enactments is declared to be a fee simple absolute in possession for the purpose of the Law of Property Act 1925. It has been taken for granted that the effect of s.7(1) is to prevent the creation of a strict settlement.

Reported litigation illustrates that genuine problems were posed by the reverter provisions when a site ceased to be used for the specified charitable purposes. A central issue was: what happened to the legal estate? According to the pre-1926 law, when a site was no longer used for the purposes for which it had been granted both the beneficial interest and the legal estate automatically shifted to the person entitled on reverter (*e.g. Att.-Gen.* v. *Shadwell* [1910] 1 Ch. 92); no conveyance from the trustees was required. The position after 1925 was less clear, as a result of an apparent conflict between s.7(1) of the Law of Property Act 1925 which provides that a fee simple which is liable to be divested (such as under the School Sites Act 1841) "remains liable to be divested as if this Act had not been passed," and s.3(3) of the same Act which states that where by reason of a statutory or other right of reverter a person becomes entitled to require a legal estate to be vested in him "the estate owner whose estate is affected shall be bound to convey or create such legal estate as the case may require."

In the case of *Re Clayton's Deed Poll* [1980] Ch. 99 (Allen & Christie (1981) 45 Conv. 186) it was held that the effect of s.3(3) of the Law of Property Act 1925 was that on the cesser of the stipulated use only the beneficial interest passed to the person entitled in reverter, the trustees continuing to hold the legal estate (on bare trust). The alternative (and better) view was that s.7(1) had the effect of preserving the 1926 position, so that on cesser

---

* Annotations by Jonathan Hill, Lecturer in Law, University of Bristol.

of the relevant use the legal estate automatically shifted to the revertee (*Re Ingleton Charity* [1956] Ch. 585; *Re Chavasse's Conveyance* (April 14, 1954, unreported)—in neither of these cases was s.3(3) of the Law of Property Act 1925 referred to; *Re Rowhook Mission Hall, Horsham* [1985] Ch. 62 (discussed by Evans, (1984) 100 LQ.R. 528) in which Nourse J. expressly declined to follow *Re Clayton's Deed Poll*).

Where the identity of the person entitled in reverter was known it made little difference whether or not the legal estate switched to the revertee automatically. (The *Re Clayton's Deed Poll* approach was less convenient since to acquire the legal estate the revertee would have to call for a conveyance from the trustees.) However, where the revertee was unascertained the difference between the two views became much more significant.

As a trustee cannot obtain a title by adverse possession against his beneficiaries (Limitation Act 1980, s.21), the effect of *Re Clayton's Deed Poll* (if correct) was to leave the trustees with a *damnosa hereditas*. After reverter the trustees became trustees of a private trust, and therefore it seems that they could not abandon the land. But they would have no funds with which to meet their responsibilities since they could not properly deal with the legal estate in order to raise the necessary money without a Court Order. Of course *Re Clayton's Deed Poll* also called into question the validity of numerous titles assumed (on the basis of *Re Ingleton Charity* and *Re Chavasse's Conveyance*) to have been acquired by adverse possession.

One of the significant attractions of the traditional view (endorsed in *Re Rowhook Mission Hall, Horsham*) was that if, when the site ceased to be used for the stipulated purposes, the revertee could not be found the trustees might obtain good possessory title after twelve years. In such a case the trustees would hold the legal estate on the original trusts (the purpose of which had necessarily failed) and a *cy-près* scheme could be sought. (In the period immediately following the decision in *Re Clayton's Deed Poll* the Charity Commissioners understandably ceased to make *cy-près* schemes after reverter had occurred.)

In addition to the uncertainties which resulted from the conflicting interpretations of ss.3(3) and 7(1) of the Law of Property Act 1925, neither approach provided an entirely satisfactory answer to the question of how to prevent the reverter provisions leading to the sterilisation of valuable areas of land. According to *Re Clayton's Deed Poll*, although the legal estate remained vested in the trustees, it was doubtful whether they had the power of sale, and in any event the indefinite preservation of the revertee's equitable interest would significantly reduce the attractiveness of the site. The traditional view based on the pre-1926 law posed fewer problems since ultimately the trustees might acquire good possessory title. However, in the short term the land might be difficult to sell as a purchaser would be running the risk of the revertee reclaiming possession of the land before title by adverse possession could be established.

The basic scheme of the 1987 Act

In the recommendations of the working party it was proposed that a system similar to that set up by the Commons Registration Act 1965 should be adopted (Law Com. No. 111, para. 86). For a period of three years revertees would be entitled to protect their interests by registration (para. 89). Failure to register during this period would result in the revertee's claim being barred, thereby leaving the trustees holding the site with an indefeasible title in favour of the charity (para. 90(a)). Even when rights of reverter were registered, it was proposed that such rights should cease to exist altogether if reverter had not taken place within eighty years of the setting up of the system (para. 98). Given that it was assumed that in a large proportion of cases there would be no registration, the effect of the proposed scheme would be tantamount to the expropriation of rights of reverter without compensation. The working party admitted that "[a] solution involving expropriation is never one to be adopted lightly" (para. 73).

The 1987 Act does not follow these recommendations. During the second reading of the Bill in the House of Lords, Lord Hailsham noted that the solution suggested by the working party "was felt by some to be unduly draconian and almost to amount to expropriation, and the report was accordingly not adopted" (*Hansard*, H.L. Vol. 486, col. 986). A central feature of the Act is the preservation, and in certain respects enhanced protection of rights of reverter. The basic structure of the Act (contained in ss.1–3) involves departing from the traditional approach to ss.3(3) and 7(1) of the Law of Property Act 1925 by providing that when a site ceases to be used for the purposes which it was originally granted the charitable trustees shall continue to hold the legal estate, but attempting to overcome the problems posed by the interpretation of ss.3(3) and 7(1) advocated in *Re Clayton's Deed Poll*. First, when the site ceases to be used for the specified purposes, there is no automatic shifting of the legal estate to the revertee; the trustees continue to hold the legal estate—on trust for sale—for the revertee (s.1). Secondly, after having complied with a procedure designed to ascertain the identity of the revertee entitled to the land (s.3), the trustees may apply to the Charity Commissioners to have the interests of the revertee extinguished (s.2). Thirdly, in certain circumstances a revertee whose rights have been extinguished will be entitled to compensation (s.2(4)).

While the Act provides a new regime for rights of reverter, the pre-Act law is important in that the legislative schemes established in the nineteenth-century provide the backdrop against which the Act operates. The working party identified a number of serious flaws in the drafting of the legislation relating to reverter of sites; the various statutes do not give unequivocal answers to questions such as: when does reverter occur? what reverts? and to whom does the site revert? Unfortunately these questions are not addressed by the 1987 Act, and therefore some of the problems which existed before the commencement of this Act will continue.

The Act does not expressly resolve the conflicting interpretations of ss.3(3) and 7(1) of the Law of Property Act 1925. Nevertheless, from the report of the working party, and the terms of the Act itself, it is clear that the correct view of s.7(1) of the Law of Property Act 1925 is that it preserved the pre-1926 position to the extent that when a site ceased to be used for the specified purpose the legal estate shifted to the revertee automatically (as explained in *Re Rowhook Mission Hall, Horsham*). This can be seen from s.1(4), which preserves the application of limitation principles to the period before the entry into force of the Act (which would be meaningless if the approach taken *Re Clayton's Deed Poll* was correct), and s.8(2) which amends s.3(3) of the Law of Property Act 1925 by repealing the words which had been described by Nourse J., on the basis of the traditional view of s.7(1) of the Law of Property Act 1925, as "superfluous" (*Re Rowhook Mission Hall, Horsham* [1985] Ch. 62 at 78).

ABBREVIATION
Law Com.: Law Commission Report.

Right of reverter replaced by trust for sale

1.—(1) Where any relevant enactment provides for land to revert to the ownership of any person at any time, being a time when the land ceases, or has ceased for a specified period, to be used for particular purposes, that enactment shall have effect, and (subject to subsection (4) below) shall be deemed always to have had effect, as if it provided (instead of for the reverter) for the land to be vested after that time, on the trust arising under this section, in the persons in whom it was vested immediately before that time.

(2) Subject to the following provisions of this Act, the trust arising under this section in relation to any land is a trust to sell the land and to stand possessed of the net proceeds of sale (after payment of costs and expenses) and of the net rents and profits until sale (after payment of rates, taxes, costs of insurance, repairs and other outgoings) upon trust for the persons who but for this Act would from time to time be entitled to the ownership of the land by virtue of its reverter.

(3) Where—

    (a) a trust in relation to any land has arisen or is treated as having arisen under this section at such a time as is mentioned in subsection (1) above; and

    (b) immediately before that time the land was vested in any persons in their capacity as the minister and churchwardens of any parish,

those persons shall be treated as having become trustees for sale under this section in that capacity and, accordingly, their interest in the land shall pass and, if the case so requires, be treated as having passed to their successors from time to time.

(4) This section shall not confer any right on any person as a beneficiary—

    (a) in relation to any property in respect of which that person's claim was statute-barred before the commencement of this Act, or in relation to any property derived from any such property; or

(b) in relation to any rents or profits received, or breach of trust committed, before the commencement of this Act;

and anything validly done before the commencement of this Act in relation to any land which by virtue of this section is deemed to have been held at the time on trust for sale shall, if done by the beneficiaries, be deemed, so far as necessary for preserving its validity, to have been done by the trustees.

(5) Where any property is held by any persons as trustees of a trust which has arisen under this section and, in consequence of subsection (4) above, there are no beneficiaries of that trust, the trustees shall have no power to act in relation to that property except—

(a) for the purposes for which they could have acted in relation to that property if this Act had not been passed; or

(b) for the purpose of securing the establishment of a scheme under section 2 below or the making of an order under section 2 of the Education Act 1973 (special powers as to trusts for religious education).

(6) In this section—

"churchwardens" includes chapel wardens;

"minister" includes a rector, vicar or perpetual curate; and

"parish" includes a parish of the Church in Wales;

and the reference to a person's claim being statute-barred is a reference to the Limitation Act 1980 providing that no proceedings shall be brought by that person to recover the property in respect of which the claim subsists.

DEFINITIONS

"churchwardens": s.1(6).

"land": s.7(2).

"minister": s.1(6).

"parish": s.1(6).

"relevant enactment": s.7(1).

GENERAL NOTE

Subss. (1) and (2)

These subsections establish the trust for sale mechanism when land granted by conveyances under the authority of the School Sites Act 1841, the Literary and Scientific Institutions Act 1854 or the Places of Worship Sites Act 1873 is no longer used for the purposes for which it was granted. Instead of the legal estate automatically shifting to the revertee (as would have been the case before the commencement of the Act), those in whom the legal estate was vested prior to reverter (normally the charitable trustees) continue to hold the legal estate (s.1(1)), but on trust for sale for the revertee (s.1(2)).

The imposition of the trust for sale resolves a major conveyancing problem by ensuring that after the circumstance giving rise to reverter has occurred someone will be able to give good title to a purchaser. Before the entry into force of this Act, it was assumed that the effect of s.7(1) of the Law of Property Act 1925 was to shift the legal estate to the revertee automatically on cesser of the stipulated purposes; if the revertee was unascertainable, the land was difficult to sell until the trustees acquired good possessory title (*i.e.* when the rights of the revertee became statute-barred). Under subss. (1) and (2) when the circumstance giving rise to reverter occurs the trustees immediately become trustees for sale, and therefore they can give good title to a purchaser, as long as the equitable interest of the revertee is overreached (which will be the case if the requirements of s.2 of the Law of Property Act 1925 are complied with).

Subss. (1) and (2) have retrospective effect in the sense that where reverter has occurred prior to the entry into force of the Act the legal estate is nevertheless deemed to have been held (since reverter) on trust for sale. (See subs. (4) for important qualifications to subs. (1)).

When the land ceases, or has ceased for a specified period, to be used for particular purposes. According to s.2 of the School Sites Act 1841 and s.4 of the Literary and Scientific Institutions Act 1854 when the land "or any part thereof" ceases to be used for the relevant purposes then the land reverts. S.1 of the Places of Worship Sites Act 1873, however, provides that reverter occurs when the land "or any part thereof" ceases "for a year at one time" to be used as a place of worship.

Unresolved problems

A number of issues raised by the nineteenth-century legislation were identified by the working party and are not unresolved by the Act:

(1) When does reverter occur? (Law Com. No. 111, paras. 22–6.)

Subs. (1) provides for the trust for sale to arise when the site would have reverted according to the terms of the relevant statute. Cesser of use is a question of fact, and there may be situations in which there is room for argument as to what constitutes cesser. It seems clear that intentional or enforced permanent discontinuance of the charitable use constitutes cesser. While it is less clear what the position would be where it is intended that discontinuance of the specified purposes will be temporary, it is possible that there will be cesser if resumption of the authorised use is unlikely, or the intended period of unauthorised use is substantial.

(2) What reverts? (Law Com. No. 111, paras. 27–8.)

As a result of subs. (1) and (2) those persons who but for this Act would have been entitled to the land on reverter become beneficiaries behind a trust for sale. But if, for example, part of a site ceases to be used for the designated purposes does a trust for sale arise in relation only to that part of the site, or to the whole? The Act fails to tackle the issue, notwithstanding that the working party noted that when counsel had been approached by trustees on this point conflicting opinions had been obtained (para. 27). It is suggested that the best solution would be acceptance of the working party's proposal that part-cesser should lead to part-reverter (para. 102(3)).

(3) To whom does the site revert? (Law Com. No. 111, paras. 29–37.)

It is unclear from the wording of the statutory provisions whether the land reverts to the grantor (or his successors) or to the grantor's neighbouring land. (At the time that the relevant legislation was enacted it seems likely that it was not expected that the estates out of which the sites were granted would be broken up.)

In *Re Cawston's Conveyance* [1940] Ch. 27 the Court of Appeal held, in relation to a site which had never formed part of a larger estate, that the land should revert to the successors of the grantor. As the working party pointed out it is not at all clear whether *Re Cawston's Conveyance* is authority for the proposition that the site always reverts to the grantor, or whether it only applies where the site was not part of a larger unit of land (para. 33). In a case relating to St. Andrew's Mission Church, Llanfairmarthafarneithaf (decided by Llangefni, Holyhead and Menai Bridge County Court in 1966), the dispute between the grantor's heirs and the owners of the neighbouring land from which the site had been severed was resolved in favour of the latter (para. 33 (and n. 33)). Reported litigation also lends some support to the view that where a site was granted out of a larger estate the land reverts to the owners of the rest of the estate rather than the representatives of the grantor (*Dennis* v. *Malcolm* [1934] Ch. 244; *Att.-Gen.* v. *Shadwell* [1912] 1 Ch. 92).

The problems with this view are considerable since the nineteenth-century legislation gives no guidance as to how to identify the estate to which the land is to revert. The working party therefore recommended that the law should be clarified by declaring that reverter should operate in all cases in favour of the original grantor (unless the original grant was made by a lord of the manor as such, in which case the land should revert to the lord of the manor at the date of reverter) (para. 103). Given the absence of binding authority to the contrary, it is open to the courts to follow the working party's recommendation.

Subs. (3)

When reverter occurs the trust for sale which arises under subs. (1) will normally be a private trust, and therefore it would follow that the trustees' title would devolve in accordance with the ordinary law (rather than under s.7 of the School Sites Act 1841 (as amended by the 1844 Act) which provides that the grant of a school site to an incumbent and his churchwardens upon trust for the education of poor people vests the site in those persons and their successors). A consequence of this would be that the minister and churchwardens at the time of the reverter might be regarded as continuing indefinitely as trustees in their personal capacity (Law Com. No. 111, para. 47). Subs. (3) prevents this inconvenient result: where the minister and churchwardens were, immediately prior to reverter, trustees in an *ex officio* capacity, after reverter they continue to hold the legal estate in that capacity, so that their successors automatically replace them as trustees for sale (and they are regarded as having done so in those cases where reverter has occurred before the commencement of the Act).

Subs. (4)

Limitation

One of the unsatisfactory aspects of the interpretation of s.7(1) of the Law of Property Act 1925 favoured in *Re Clayton's Deed Poll* was that by denying the automatic shifting of the legal estate to the revertee when the land ceased to be used for the specified purposes, the trustees were prevented from acquiring title by adverse possession. By virtue of subs. (4)(a) rights of reverter may have become statute-barred prior to the commencement of the Act, and therefore trustees may have acquired possessory title by twelve years adverse possession prior to the entry into force of the Act.

However, as a result of the imposition of a trust for sale on behalf of the revertee (s.1(1) and (2)), the effect of s.21 of the Limitation Act 1980 (which prevents a trustee acquiring title by adverse possession against his beneficiaries) is to prevent a revertee's claim being barred by lapse of time where the circumstance giving rise to reverter either occurs after, or has occurred less than twelve years before, the commencement of this Act. (But see the procedure laid down in s.2 for the extinguishment of rights of reverter.)

The period between reverter and the entry into force of the Act

The effect of subs. (1) is to regard the revertee as having been entitled only in equity after the circumstance giving rise to reverter has occurred. Subs. (1) would, if left without qualification, call into question the title of anyone who had taken a conveyance of the legal estate from a revertee after the land had ceased to be used for the specified purposes. The final part of subs. (4) validates transactions entered into by the revertee after cesser of the specified purposes, by deeming transactions which would be invalid if carried out by a beneficiary, but valid if executed by trustees for sale, to have been executed by the trustees.

Subs. (5)

Subject to the express exception contained in subs. (5)(b) (which empowers the trustees to apply to the Charity Commissioners (under s.2) or the Secretary of State (under s.2 of the Education Act 1973) to have a scheme established), if the rights of the revertee have become barred through lapse of time, the trustees' powers are limited by subs. (5)(a) to those which they would have had under the pre-Act law. This has the effect of ensuring that the trustees remain subject to the original charitable trusts. In *Re Ingleton Charity* [1956] Ch. 585 it was held that where trustees continue in possession of land after reverter they remain trustees on the trusts named in the deed of grant.

Charity Commissioners' schemes

2.—(1) Subject to the following provisions of this section and to sections 3 and 4 below, where any persons hold any property as trustees of a trust which has arisen under section 1 above, the Charity Commissioners may, on the application of the trustees, by order establish a scheme which—

(a) extinguishes the rights of beneficiaries under the trust; and

(b) requires the trustees to hold the property on trust for such charitable purposes as may be specified in the order.

(2) Subject to subsections (3) and (4) below, an order made under this section—

(a) may contain any such provision as may be contained in an order made by the High Court for establishing a scheme for the administration of a charity; and

(b) shall have the same effect as an order so made.

(3) The charitable purposes specified in an order made under this section on an application with respect to any trust shall be as similar in character as the Charity Commissioners think is practicable in all the circumstances to the purposes (whether charitable or not) for which the trustees held the relevant land before the cesser of use in consequence of which the trust arose; but in determining the character of the last-mentioned purposes the Commissioners, if they think it appropriate to do so, may give greater weight to the persons or locality benefited by the purposes than to the nature of the benefit.

(4) An order made under this section on an application with respect to any trust shall be so framed as to secure that if a person who—

(a) but for the making of the order would have been a beneficiary under the trust; and

(b) has not consented to the establishment of a scheme under this section,

notifies a claim to the trustees within the period of five years after the date of the making of the order, that person shall be paid an amount equal to the value of his rights at the time of their extinguishment.

(5) The Charity Commissioners shall not make any order under this section establishing a scheme unless—

(a) the requirements of section 3 below with respect to the making of the application for the order are satisfied or, by virtue of subsection (4) of that section, do not apply;

(b) one of the conditions specified in subsection (6) below is fulfilled;

(c) public notice of the Commissioners' proposals has been given inviting representations to be made to them within a period specified in the notice, being a period ending not less than one month after the date of the giving of the notice; and

(d) that period has ended and the Commissioners have taken into consideration any representations which have been made within that period and not withdrawn.

(6) The conditions mentioned in subsection (5)(b) above are—

(a) that there is no claim by any person to be a beneficiary in respect of rights proposed to be extinguished—

(i) which is outstanding; or

(ii) which has at any time been accepted as valid by the trustees or by persons whose acceptance binds the trustees; or

(iii) which has been upheld in proceedings that have been concluded;

(b) that consent to the establishment of a scheme under this section has been given by every person whose claim to be a beneficiary in respect of those rights is outstanding or has been so accepted or upheld.

(7) The Charity Commissioners shall refuse to consider an application under this section unless it is accompanied by a statutory declaration by the applicants—

(a) that the requirements of section 3 below are satisfied with respect to the making of the application or, if the declaration so declares, do not apply; and

(b) that a condition specified in subsection (6) above and identified in the declaration is fulfilled;

and the declaration shall be conclusive for the purposes of this section of the matters declared therein.

(8) A notice given for the purposes of subsection (5)(c) above shall contain such particulars of the Commissioners' proposals, or such directions for obtaining information about them, and shall be given in such manner, as they think sufficient and appropriate; and a further such notice shall not be required where the Commissioners decide, before proceeding with any proposals of which notice has been so given, to modify them.

DEFINITIONS

"outstanding": s.7(3).

"proceedings that have not been concluded": s.7(4).

"relevant land": s.7(1).

GENERAL NOTE

Ss.2–4 are complicated and technical: s.2 regulates the scheme-making powers of the Charity Commissioners; s.3 lays down the procedure which the trustees must follow before applying to the Charity Commissioners under s.2; s.4 sets out a procedure whereby appeals may be brought against schemes made under s.2, and deals with the publicity requirements of schemes ordered under s.2 which must be complied with by the Charity Commissioners.

The effect of s.1 is to transform the persons who were holding the legal estate immediately prior to reverter into trustees for sale either for the revertee, or (if the rights of the revertee were statute-barred before the commencement of the Act) for the original charitable purposes. In either case, the fact that reverter has taken place indicates that the original purposes of the trust have failed, and as under s.13(5) of the Charities Act 1960 charity trustees have a duty to secure the effective use of charity property, when the circumstance giving rise to reverter has occurred the trustees for sale ought to apply to have a *cy-près* scheme established.

The trustees for sale have two possible courses of action: an application under s.2 to the Charity Commissioners, or (in the case of certain trusts for religious education) an application to the Secretary of State under s.2 of the Education Act 1973 (as amended by ss.5(1) and 8(3) of this Act). In relation to cases falling within the scope of s.2 of the Education Act 1973 the jurisdiction of the Charity Commissioners and the Secretary of State overlaps, but s.5(3) prevents problems arising if trustees for sale apply to both the Charity Commissioners and the Secretary of State.

Subs. (1)

When the revertee is unascertained, but his claim was not statute-barred before the commencement of the Act, the most straightforward solution is for the Charity Commissioners to order a scheme which would (*inter alia*) extinguish the rights of the revertee behind the trust for sale. This possibility is provided for by subs. (1)(a). However, expropriation of the revertee's rights cannot be justified merely on grounds of convenience, and substantial protection of the revertee's rights is provided by subss. (4)–(8) and s.3.

Subs. (2)

The scheme-making powers of the High Court are regulated by ss.13–16 and 22 of the Charities Act 1960.

Subs. (3)

The *cy-près* doctrine enables the property of a charity which has failed to be applied for other charitable purposes as near as possible to those intended by the donor. The problem which arises in the context of sites granted under the various nineteenth-century enactments is that it may be difficult to devise a useful scheme which reflects the original purposes, especially if the purposes outlined in the deed of grant were very narrowly circumscribed. For example, when a village school closes, and the local children attend a new school in a nearby town, a scheme for educational purposes within the precise terms of the original trust may be of little value to the local community.

The purpose of this subsection is to give the Charity Commissioners a broad discretion, by allowing them to define the purposes of the original trust in such a way as to enable them to order a scheme under subs. (1), which will be as useful as possible to the community. For example, when a local school closes, by virtue of subs. (3) the Charity Commissioners may, when defining the purposes of the original grant, give weight to the fact that the original trust was for the benefit of the young people of the locality, rather than being required to have regard exclusively to the educational nature of the original trust.

Subss. (4)–(8)

These subsections are designed to ensure that the rights of a revertee are protected. This is done in a variety of ways:

—the Charity Commissioners may not *consider* an application unless the trustees for sale have signed a declaration to the effect that they have complied with the procedure outlined in s.3 (or that they are exempted from having to do so by virtue of s.3(4)), and that one of the two conditions in subs. (6) is fulfilled (subs. (7));

—the Charity Commissioners shall not *establish* a scheme unless (a) s.3 has been complied with; (b) one of the conditions laid down in subs. (6) is satisfied; (c) they have, by public notice, invited representations on their proposals; and (d) they have considered any representations they have received (subs. (5));

—an order under subs. (1) which has the effect of extinguishing the rights of a revertee must be framed in such a way as to enable a revertee who has not consented to the scheme to receive compensation from the trust (to the value of the beneficial interest behind the trust for sale at the time of the making of the order) if he notifies the trustees within five years of the making of the order (subs. (4)).

As a result of this compensation provision trustees ought to take out insurance to cover the possibility of a previously unascertained revertee making a claim within the five year period following the making of the order.

In some ways the position of revertees has been improved by the Act. Before the commencement of the Act if the revertee made no attempt to recover possession of the site after reverter his claim might become statute-barred, the trustees acquiring title by adverse possession (*Re Rowhook Mission Hall, Horsham*). (If a revertee's claim was statute-barred before the commencement of this Act, the Act does not operate to revitalise the revertee's interest (s.1(4)). However, where at the entry into force of the Act either the circumstance giving rise to reverter has not yet occurred or the revertee's claim to the site is not yet barred, as a result of the imposition of a trust for sale the revertee's rights will continue to be enforceable unless and until extinguished by an order of the Charity Commissioners (under s.2(1)) or the Secretary of State (under s.2 of the Education Act 1973). In relation to orders of the Charity Commissioners, compensation is available if the revertee gives notice to the trustees within five years of the order, and this could be more than twelve years after cesser of the specified purposes.

The fact that a scheme cannot be ordered unless one of the conditions laid down in subs. (6) is satisfied effectively means that where the identity of the revertee is known and he asserts his rights, these rights cannot be extinguished without his consent.

Subs. (8) deals with the contents of the public notice required under subs. (5)(c).

Applications for schemes

3.—(1) Where an application is made under section 2 above by the trustees of any trust that has arisen under section 1 above, the requirements of this section are satisfied with respect to the making of that application if, before the application is made—

(a) notices under subsection (2) below have been published in two national newspapers and in a local newspaper circulating in the locality where the relevant land is situated;

(b) each of those notices specified a period for the notification to the trustees of claims by beneficiaries, being a period ending not less than three months after the date of publication of the last of those notices to be published;

(c) that period has ended;

(d) for a period of not less than twenty-one days during the first month of that period, a copy of one of those notices was affixed to some object on the relevant land in such a position and manner as, so far as practicable, to make the notice easy for members of the public to see and read without going on to the land; and

(e) the trustees have considered what other steps could be taken to trace the persons who are or may be beneficiaries and to inform those persons of the application to be made under section 2 above and have taken such of the steps considered by them as it was reasonably practicable for them to take.

(2) A notice under this subsection shall—

(a) set out the circumstances that have resulted in a trust having arisen under section 1 above;

(b) state that an application is to be made for the establishment of a scheme with respect to the property subject to the trust; and

(c) contain a warning to every beneficiary that, if he wishes to oppose the extinguishment of his rights, he should notify his claim to the trustees in the manner, and within the period, specified in the notice.

(3) Where at the time when the trustees publish a notice for the purposes of subsection (2) above—

(a) the relevant land is not under their control; and

(b) it is not reasonably practicable for them to arrange for a copy of the notice to be affixed as required by paragraph (d) of subsection (1) above to some object on the land,

15–9

that paragraph shall be disregarded for the purposes of this section.

(4) The requirements of this section shall not apply in the case of an application made in respect of any trust if—

(a) the time when that trust is treated as having arisen was before the commencement of this Act; and

(b) more than twelve years have elapsed since that time.

DEFINITION
"relevant land": s.7(1).

GENERAL NOTE
This section is designed to ensure that before a scheme is ordered under s.2(1) efforts are made to locate revertees—entitled in equity as a result of s.1(1)—so that they may assert their rights. If a revertee does claim to be a beneficiary under the trust for sale (and falls within s.2(6)(a)) a scheme cannot be ordered unless he consents to it (s.2(5)(b) and (6)(b)).

Subss. (1)–(3)
Subs. (1) lists a number of measures which the trustees must take so that revertees are given a reasonable opportunity of discovering that the trust for sale under s.1 has arisen, and that an application to the Charity Commissioners is being made:

—notices must be put in the national and local press (subs. (1)(a));
—subject to the exception contained in subs. (3), a notice must be affixed to the land (subs. (1)(d));
—trustees must consider what other steps they could take to trace revertees, and they must take such steps as they consider reasonably practicable (subs. (1)(e)).

Subs. (2) sets out the details which must be contained in the notices required by subs. (1). Beneficiaries must be warned that if they wish to oppose the extinguishment of their rights they must inform the trustees, and subs. (1)(b) and (c) provides that they are to be given at least three months from the publication of the final notice in the press (required by subs. (1)(a)) to make a claim.

Subs. (4)
Where the revertee's claim has been statute-barred before the commencment of the Act there would be no point in requiring the trustees for sale to comply with the procedure provided for in subs. (1)–(3). Subs. (4) exempts the trustees for sale from the s.3 procedure when the circumstance giving rise to reverter has occurred before the commencement of the Act, and more than twelve years have elapsed since that time.

It should be noted that this subsection includes within its scope situations in which the claim of the revertee will not be statute-barred. Where reverter has occurred less than twelve years before the commencement of the Act, the imposition of a trust for sale by s.1 prevents the revertee's claim becoming statute-barred (Limitation Act 1980, s.21), but when more than twelve years since reverter have elapsed subs. (4) will excuse the trustees from having to comply with the procedure laid down in subs. (1)–(3).

In all cases involving reverter after the commencement of the Act the trustees for sale will have to follow the procedure outlined in subs. (1)–(3).

Provisions supplemental to ss.2 and 3

4.—(1) Where an order is made under section 2 above—

(a) public notice of the order shall be given in such manner as the Charity Commissioners think sufficient and appropriate; and

(b) a copy of the order shall, for not less than one month after the date of the giving of the notice, be available for public inspection at all reasonable times at the Commissioners' office and at some convenient place in the locality where the relevant land is situated;

and a notice given for the purposes of paragraph (a) above shall contain such particulars of the order, or such directions for obtaining information about it, as the Commissioners think sufficient and appropriate.

(2) Subject to subsection (3) below, an appeal against an order made under section 2 above may be brought in the High Court by any of the following, that is to say—

   (a) the Attorney General;
   (b) the trustees of the trust established under the order;
   (c) a beneficiary of, or the trustees of, the trust in respect of which the application for the order had been made;
   (d) any person interested in the purposes for which the last-mentioned trustees or any of their predecessors held the relevant land before the cesser of use in consequence of which the trust arose under section 1 above;
   (e) any two or more inhabitants of the locality where that land is situated.

(3) An appeal shall not be brought under subsection (2) above against any order—
   (a) after the end of the period of three months beginning with the day following the date on which public notice of the order is given; or
   (b) without either a certificate by the Charity Commissioners that it is a proper case for an appeal or the leave of the High Court,
unless it is brought by the Attorney General.

(4) Sections 40 and 42 of the Charities Act 1960 (supplemental provisions with respect to orders and appeals) shall apply in relation to, and to appeals against, orders under section 2 above as they apply in relation to, and to appeals against, orders under that Act.

(5) Trustees of a trust which has arisen under section 1 above may pay or apply capital money for any of the purposes of section 2 or 3 above or of this section.

DEFINITION
  "relevant land": s.7(1).

GENERAL NOTE

Subss. (1)–(3)
  The purpose of these subsections is to allow a range of people to appeal to the High Court against an order made by the Charity Commissioners under s.2(1). Subs. (1) requires the Charity Commissioners to give public notice of the order, so that interested parties (listed in subs. (2)) can discover whether there is something about the scheme to which they take exception. The list in subs. (2) does not include beneficiaries entitled under the trust for sale arising under s.1; once a scheme is ordered under s.2(1) a revertee may notify the trustees of his claim (and may be entitled to compensation under s.2(4)), but he may not challenge the order.
  Subss. (2) and (3) in substance reproduce s.18(10)–(12) of the Charities Act 1960 (as explained in *Childs* v. *Att.-Gen.* [1973] 1 W.L.R. 497). While these provisions do not expressly limit the right of appeal to questions of law, the court will not interfere with the Charity Commissioners' discretion unless the scheme contains something wrong in principle or wrong in law (*Re Campden Charities* (1881) 18 Ch.D. 310).
  Except in relation to appeals brought by the Attorney General, an appeal must be brought within a three month time limit (subs. (3)(a)), and it must have the consent of the Charity Commissioners or leave of the court (subs. (3)(b)). R.S.C., Ord. 108, r.3(1) provides that an application to the court shall not be made for leave to appeal against an order of the Charity Commissioners unless the applicant has requested the Commissioners to grant a certificate that it is a proper case for an appeal and they have refused to do so.
  In addition to there being a right of appeal under s.4 the court may, on an application for judicial review, make an order of certiorari, quashing a scheme ordered under s.2(1), if, for example, the Charity Commissioners have exceeded their jurisdiction. However, where a statutory appeals procedure provides an appropriate alternative remedy to judicial review an applicant ought to avail himself of that remedy of appeal before seeking judicial review (*R.* v. *Secretary of State for the Home Department, ex p. Swati* [1986] 1 All E.R. 717). Therefore, the court would be unlikely to entertain an application in relation to an order of the Charity Commissioners unless the applicant had already exhausted his rights of appeal under s.4(2). (In *R.* v. *Charity Commissioners for England and Wales* [1897] 1 Q.B. 407 mandamus was refused where an applicant had failed to use the alternative statutory remedy under the Charitable Trusts Act 1853.)

Subs. (4)

Supplementary provisions

The Charity Commissioners may include in any order under the Act such incidental or supplementary provisions as they think expedient for carrying into effect the objects of the order (Charities Act 1960, s.40(1)). The Commissioners may give public notice of the making or contents of any order (Charities Act 1960, s.40(2)). At any time within twelve months after the making of an order, the Charity Commissioners may discharge it if they are satisfied that it was made by mistake or on misrepresentation or otherwise contrary to the Act (Charities Act 1960, s.40(3)).

Procedure

S.42(1) of the Charities Act 1960 provides for the making of rules of court to deal with appeals under the Act. The relevant rules (originally established by Rules of the Supreme Court (No. 5), 1960 (S.I. 1960 No. 2328)) are now to be found in R.S.C., Ord. 108 (Rules of the Supreme Court (Revision) 1965 (S.I. 1965 No. 1776) as amended by Rules of the Supreme Court (Amendment) 1972 (S.I. 1972 No. 813), Rules of the Supreme Court (Amendment No. 2) 1982 (S.I. 1982 No. 1111) and Rules of the Supreme Court (Amendment No. 3) 1982 (S.I. 1982 No. 1786)).

S.42(2) of the 1960 Act provides that the Attorney General is entitled to appear and be heard in any appeal against an order of the Charity Commissioners.

The effect of s.42(3) of the 1960 Act was that an appeal against an order of the Charity Commissioners was heard and determined by a single judge. This is now provided for by R.S.C., Ord. 108, r.5(1); s.42(3) of the 1960 Act was repealed by the Administration of Justice Act 1977 (s.32(4) and Sched. 5, Pt. IV).

Orders under the Education Act 1973

5.—(1) An order made under section 2 of the Education Act 1973 (special powers as to certain trusts for religious education) with respect to so much of any endowment as consists of—

    (a) land in relation to which a trust under section 1 above has arisen or will arise after the land ceased or ceases to be used for particular purposes; or

    (b) any other property subject to a trust under that section,

may extinguish any rights to which a person is or may become entitled as a beneficiary under the trust.

(2) The Secretary of State shall not by an order under section 2 of the said Act of 1973 extinguish any such rights unless he is satisfied that all reasonably practicable steps to trace the persons who are or may become entitled to any of those rights have been taken and either—

    (a) that there is no claim by any person to be a person who is or may become so entitled—

        (i) which is outstanding; or

        (ii) which has at any time been accepted as valid by the trustees or by persons whose acceptance binds or will bind the trustees; or

        (iii) which has been upheld in proceedings that have been concluded; or

    (b) that consent to the making of an order under section 2 of the said Act of 1973 has been given by every person whose claim to be such a person is outstanding or has been so accepted or upheld.

(3) Where applications for the extinguishment of the rights of any beneficiaries are made with respect to the same trust property both to the Secretary of State under section 2 of the said Act of 1973 and to the Charity Commissioners under section 2 above, the Commissioners shall not consider, or further consider, the application made to them, unless the Secretary of State either—

    (a) consents to the application made to the Charity Commissioners being considered before the application made to him; or

    (b) disposes of the application made to him without extinguishing the rights of one or more of the beneficiaries.

(4) Trustees of a trust which has arisen under section 1 above may pay or apply capital money for the purposes of any provision of this section or section 2 of the said Act of 1973.

DEFINITIONS
"land": s.7(2).
"outstanding": s.7(3).
"proceedings that have been concluded": s.7(4).
"Secretary of State": Education Act 1944, s.1(1) as amended by State Education and Science Order, 1964 (S.I. 1964 No. 490) and Transfer of Functions (Wales) Order, 1970 (S.I. 1970 No. 1536).

GENERAL NOTE
S.2 of the Education Act 1973 empowers the Secretary of State (either the Secretary of State for Education and Science, or the Secretary of State for Wales, who is responsible for primary and secondary education in matters only affecting Wales) to make new provisions with regard to the use of certain endowments where the premises of a voluntary school (defined by s.9(2) of the Education Act 1944) have ceased or are likely to cease to be used for a voluntary school. Endowments fall within the scope of s.2 of the 1973 Act if they have been held wholly or partly for the provision at the school of religious education of a *particular* denomination. A significant number of cases arise in which orders under s.2 of the 1973 Act cannot be made because attachment to a particular denomination is lacking. The working party gave the example of trusts for schools established by the British and Foreign Schools Society which often required only "Christian" education (Law Com. No. 111, para. 59, n. 63). In these cases the trustees will have to apply to the Charity Commissioners under s.2(1) of this Act.
Where on cesser of the specified purposes a trust for sale arises under s.1 of this Act the Secretary of State's powers are regulated by this section. Under subs. (1) the Secretary of State may extinguish the rights of the revertee; subs. (2) seeks to protect the interests of the revertee.

Subs. (1)
Under s.2 of the 1973 Act (as originally enacted) the Secretary of State could only exclude the operation of a right of reverter before the school closed (while it could be said that the land was "liable to revert"). The working party noted that this posed particular difficulties in practice (Law Com. No. 111, para. 60), and this subsection (along with s.8(3)—and the Schedule—which repeals part of s.2(3) of the 1973 Act) rectifies the problem. Now the Secretary of State may extinguish rights of reverter either before or after the trust for sale arises under s.1.

Subs. (2)
Although this subsection is similar in purpose to s.2(4)–(8), there are differences between the two schemes for protecting the revertee's rights. In particular, there is no express provision for the compensation of revertees whose rights are extinguished by an order of the Secretary of State (*cf.* s.2(4)).
Rather than replicate the detailed provisions contained in s.2(5)–(8) which must be followed before a scheme under s.2(1) can be ordered by the Charity Commissioners, this subsection provides that the Secretary of State may make an order under s.2(1) of the 1973 Act if he is satisfied that all reasonable practicable steps have been taken to trace the revertee and either no one has claimed the land as revertee (subs. (2)(a)) or the revertee has consented to the making of the order (subs. (2)(b)). (Subs. (2)(a) and (b) reproduce the conditions in s.2(6).)

Subs. (3)
This subsection is designed to prevent conflicts arising in cases where trustees for sale under s.1 have made applications for a scheme extinguishing the revertee's rights both to the Charity Commissioners (under s.2 of this Act) and to the Secretary of State (under s.2 of the Education Act 1973).
The Charity Commissioners may not consider the application unless the Secretary of State consents to their doing so (subs. (3)(a)), or the Secretary of State has already considered the application and has declined to extinguish all the rights of reverter (subs. (3)(b)).

Clarification of status etc. of land before reverter

6.—(1) Nothing in this Act shall require any land which is or has been the subject of any grant, conveyance or other assurance under any relevant enactment to be treated as or as having been settled land.

(2) It is hereby declared—

(a) that the power conferred by section 14 of the School Sites Act 1841 (power of sale etc.) is exercisable at any time in relation to land in relation to which (but for the exercise of the power) a trust might subsequently arise under section 1 above; and

(b) that the exercise of that power in respect of any land prevents any trust from arising under section 1 above in relation to that land or any land representing the proceeds of sale of that land.

DEFINITIONS
"land": s.7(2).
"relevant enactment": s.7(1).

GENERAL NOTE

Subs. (1)

Despite the broad definition of a strict settlement in s.1 of the Settled Land Act 1925, it has been assumed that, as a consequence of s.7(1) of the Law of Property Act 1925 the grant of a determinable fee under the School Sites Act 1841 or other similar enactments does not create a settlement governed by the Settled Land Act. Subs. (1) expressly confirms this generally held belief.

Subs. (2)

S.14 of the School Sites Act 1841 provides that, in relation to a site under the Act, when "it shall be deemed advisable to sell or exchange the same for any other more convenient or eligible site, it shall be lawful for the trustees . . . by direction or with the consent of the managers and directors of the said school . . . to sell or exchange the said land or building . . . and to apply the money arising from such sale or given on such exchange in the purchase of another site . . ."

Once a site ceases to be used for the specified purposes a trust for sale arises under s.1, and if the land is sold the rights of the revertee can be overreached and transferred into the proceeds of sale. But, what is the legal position if the trustees sell a school site under the powers conferred by s.14 of the 1841 Act while the school is still operating? Does the reverter proviso apply (thereby making the sale wholly self-defeating) or can the trustees override the right of reverter?

It had been assumed that if a site was sold under s.14 any right of reverter was destroyed (Law Com. No. 111, para. 42). This assumption is confirmed by subs. (2) which declares that when a school site is sold under the powers conferred by s.14 of the School Sites Act 1841 the rights of the revertee are overridden, and no trust for sale will arise in relation either to the original site, or a new site acquired with the proceeds of the sale of the original site.

Construction

7.—(1) In this Act—

"relevant enactment" means any enactment contained in—

(a) the School Sites Acts;

(b) the Literary and Scientific Institutions Act 1854; or

(c) the Places of Worship Sites Act 1873;

"relevant land", in relation to a trust which has arisen under section 1 above, means the land which but for this Act would have reverted to the persons who are the first beneficiaries under the trust.

(2) In this Act references to land include references to—

(a) any part of any land which has been the subject of a grant, conveyance or other assurance under any relevant enactment; and

(b) any land an interest in which (including any future or contingent interest arising under any such enactment) belongs to the Crown, the Duchy of Lancaster or the Duchy of Cornwall.

(3) For the purposes of this Act a claim by any person to be a beneficiary under a trust is outstanding if—

(a) it has been notified to the trustees;

(b) it has not been withdrawn; and

(c) proceedings for determining whether it should be upheld have not been commenced or (if commenced) have not been concluded.

(4) For the purposes of this Act proceedings shall not, in relation to any person's claim, be treated as concluded where the time for appealing is unexpired or an appeal is pending unless that person has indicated his intention not to appeal or, as the case may be, not to continue with the appeal.

Consequential amendments, repeals and saving

8.—(1) The Secretary of State shall not make a determination under paragraph 7 of Schedule 1 to the Education Act 1946 (payment to local education authority of proceeds of sale of voluntary school) in respect of any property subject to a trust which has arisen under section 1 above unless he is satisfied that adequate steps have been taken to protect the interests of the beneficiaries under the trust.

(2) In section 3(3) of the Law of Property Act 1925 (right of certain persons to creation of legal estate), the words "of a statutory or other right of reverter, or" (which are unnecessary) shall be omitted.

(3) The enactments mentioned in the Schedule to this Act are hereby repealed to the extent specified in the third column of that Schedule.

(4) The repeals contained in the Schedule to this Act shall not affect the operation at any time after the commencement of this Act of so much of any order made before the commencement of this Act under section 2 of the Education Act 1973 as has excluded the operation of the third proviso to section 2 of the School Sites Act 1841.

DEFINITION

"voluntary school": Education Act 1944, s.9(2).

GENERAL NOTE

Subs. (1)

Any sum paid to a local education authority under para. 7 of Schedule 1 to the Education Act 1946 is deemed, for the purposes of s.14 of the School Sites Act 1841, to be a sum applied in a purchase of a site for a school. S.6(2) of this Act provides that where a school site is sold by charity trustees under s.14 of the 1841 Act a trust for sale under s.1 does not attach to the original land, nor to any land acquired with the proceeds of sale. Consequently, if the Secretary of State determines (under para. 7 of Schedule 1 to the 1946 Act) that the proceeds of sale of a voluntary school are to be paid to the local education authority the rights of the revertee will be overridden.

This subsection requires that before a determination under para. 7 is made steps are taken to protect the interests of the revertee. If adequate steps are not taken, under general administrative law principles, a determination made by the Secretary of State may be quashed by the court on an application for judicial review by the revertee.

Subs. (4)

The third proviso to s.2 of the School Sites Act 1841 provides for the reverter of a school site on cesser of the specified purposes.

Under s.2(3) of the Education Act 1973 (as originally enacted) on making an order under s.2(1) of the 1973 Act the Secretary of State could exclude the operation of the third proviso contained in s.2 of the School Sites Act 1841 (thereby extinguishing the revertee's rights) if he was satisfied either that the revertee could not be found, or (if the revertee could be found) that he consented to relinquish his rights to the land (with or without compensation).

Although as a result of ss.5 and 8 changes have been made to the conditions which must be satisfied before the Secretary of State may make an order under s.2(1) of the 1973 Act, these amendments do not affect the operation of any order made prior to the commencement of this Act.

Short title, commencement and extent

9.—(1) This Act may be cited as the Reverter of Sites Act 1987.

(2) This Act shall come into force on such day as the Lord Chancellor may by order made by statutory instrument appoint.

(3) This Act shall extend to England and Wales only.

GENERAL NOTE

Subs. (3)

In the working party report it was suggested that any legislation in this area could be confined to England and Wales, since the Places of Worship Sites Act 1873 only applies in England and Wales, the School Sites Act 1841, although extended to Scotland, has been infrequently resorted to in that jurisdiction, and the Literary and Scientific Institutions Act 1854, which was apparently extended only to Ireland, has seldom been used in Northern Ireland (Law Com. No. 111, para. 119).

Section 8   SCHEDULE

REPEALS

Chapter	Short title	Extent of repeal
15 & 16 Geo. 5. c.20.	The Law of Property Act 1925.	In section 3(3), the words "of a statutory or other right of reverter, or". In section 7(1), the words "the School Sites Acts".
1973 c.16.	The Education Act 1973.	In section 2(3) the words from "and in the case of" onwards.

FINANCE ACT 1987*

(1987 c.16)

---

* Annotations by Christopher Cant, M.A., Barrister; Ian Ferrier, M.A., Barrister and David Goy, LL.M., Barrister.

PART IV

INHERITANCE TAX

PART V

OIL TAXATION

PART VI

MISCELLANEOUS AND SUPPLEMENTARY

An Act to grant certain duties, to alter other duties, and to amend the law relating to the National Debt and the Public Revenue, and to make further provision in connection with Finance.   [15th May 1987]

PARLIAMENTARY DEBATES
   Hansard: H.C. Vol. 113, col. 22; Vol. 114, col. 683; Vol. 115, cols. 319, 427; Vol. 116, col. 185; H.L. Vol. 487, cols. 726, 734.
   The Bill was considered in Standing Committee B on May 6 and 8, 1987.

Part I

Customs and Excise and Value Added Tax

Chapter I

Customs and Excise

Duties of excise

Unleaded petrol

1.—(1) After section 13 of the Hydrocarbon Oil Duties Act 1979 there shall be inserted the following section—

"Rebate on unleaded petrol

13A.—(1) On unleaded petrol charged with the excise duty on hydrocarbon oil and delivered for home use there shall be allowed at the time of delivery a rebate of duty at the rate of £0.0096 a litre.

(2) For the purposes of this section petrol is "unleaded" if it contains not more than 0.013 grams of lead per litre of petrol or, if the petrol is delivered for home use before 1st April 1990, not more than 0.020 grams of lead per litre of petrol.

(3) Rebate shall not be allowed under this section in any case where it is allowed under section 14 below."

(2) In section 24 of that Act (control of use of duty-free and rebated oil) in subsection (1) (power of Commissioners to make regulations) after the words "section 12" there shall be inserted "section 13A".

(3) In section 27 of that Act (interpretation) in the definition of "rebate" after the words "section 11" there shall be inserted "13A".

(4) This section shall be deemed to have come into force at 6 o'clock in the evening of 17th March 1987.

General Note

To encourage the use of unleaded petrol and compensate the oil companies for the higher cost of producing and marketing it, the duty on such petrol is reduced from 19.38p. per litre to 18.42p. per litre as compared with other petrol. The effect is a differential in tax of 5p. per gallon in favour of unleaded petrol and should ensure that it costs the consumer no more than four-star leaded petrol.

Vehicles excise duty

2.—(1) The Vehicles (Excise) Act 1971 and the Vehicles (Excise) Act (Northern Ireland) 1972 shall be amended in accordance with this section.

(2) In Schedule 4 to each of the Acts of 1971 and 1972 (annual rates of duty on goods vehicles)—

(a) in Part I, in sub-paragraph (2) of paragraph 6 (farmer's goods vehicle or showman's goods vehicle having a plated gross weight or a plated train weight) in paragraph (b) (weight exceeding 7·5 tonnes but not exceeding 12 tonnes) for "£155" (which applies to farmers' goods vehicles only) there shall be substituted "£175"; and

(b) in Part II, for Tables A(1), C(1) and D(1) (rates for farmers' goods vehicles having plated weight exceeding 12 tonnes) there shall be substituted the Tables set out in Part I of Schedule 1 to this Act.

(3) In section 16 of the Act of 1971, in subsection (5) (annual rates of duty for trade licences), including that subsection as set out in paragraph 12 of Part I of Schedule 7 to that Act, for "£70" and "£14" there shall be substituted respectively "£85" and "£17".

(4) In section 16 of the Act of 1972, in subsection (6) (annual rates of duty for trade licences), including that subsection as set out in paragraph

12 of Part I of Schedule 9 to that Act, for "£70" and "£14" there shall be substituted respectively "£85" and "£17".

(5) The amendments of the Acts of 1971 and 1972 set out in Part II of Schedule 1 to this Act shall have effect for the purpose of, and in connection with, establishing recovery vehicles as a class of vehicles chargeable with a specific duty of excise.

(6) The Acts of 1971 and 1972 and section 102 of the Customs and Excise Management Act 1979, as it applies in relation to licences under the Act of 1971, shall have effect subject to the further amendments in Part III of Schedule 1 to this Act.

(7) Subsection (2) above applies in relation to licences taken out after 17th March 1987; and subsections (3) to (5) above apply in relation to licences taken out after 31st December 1987.

(8) In Part III of Schedule 1 to this Act—

(a) paragraphs 8 to 11 shall not affect any amount payable in respect of any day before the day on which this Act is passed,

(b) paragraphs 12 and 13 shall not affect any amount payable in respect of, or any part of, the calendar month in which this Act is passed or in respect of, or any part of, any previous calendar month, and

(c) paragraphs 20 and 21 shall not affect the penalty for an offence committed before the passing of this Act,

but, subject to that, that Part of that Schedule shall come into force on the passing of this Act.

GENERAL NOTE

There is once again no increase in the duty on cars and vans. Following on the increase last year, the rates for trade licences are raised by subss. (3) and (4) from 70 to 85 per cent. of those for private cars and motorcycles. For other changes in the law on vehicle excise duty see the Note to Sched. 1.

Abolition of general betting duty on on-course bets

3.—(1) General betting duty shall not be chargeable on any bet made on or after 29th March 1987 which is an on-course bet within the meaning of Part I of the Betting and Gaming Duties Act 1981 (in this section referred to as "the 1981 Act") and, accordingly, with respect to bets made on or after that date, section 1 of the 1981 Act (charge to, and rates of, duty) shall be amended as follows—

(a) in subsection (1) after the words "on any bet" there shall be inserted "which is not an on-course bet and"; and

(b) in subsection (2) the words from the beginning of paragraph (a) to "bet" in paragraph (b) shall be omitted.

(2) With respect to bets made on or after 29th March 1987 but before the betting commencement date within the meaning of section 6 of the Finance Act 1986, Part III of the Miscellaneous Transferred Excise Duties Act (Northern Ireland) 1972 (in this section referred to as "the 1972 Act") (which made separate provision for Northern Ireland corresponding to that made by the 1981 Act and which ceased to have effect on the betting commencement date except in relation to bets made before that date) shall be deemed to have been amended as follows—

(a) in section 16(1) (charge of duty) after the words "on any bet" there shall be inserted "which is not an on-course bet and"; and

(b) in section 17 (rates of duty) in subsection (1) paragraph (a) and, in paragraph (b), the words from the beginning to "bet" shall be omitted.

(3) In Schedule 1 to the 1981 Act (supplementary provisions)—

(a) in paragraph 1 (definitions) at the end of the definition of "general betting business" there shall be added the words "or

16–5

would or might involve such sums becoming so payable if on-course bets were not excluded from that duty"; and

    (b) in paragraph 2 (power to make regulations for administration of general betting duty) in sub-paragraph (4)(a) after the words "liable for duty" there shall be inserted "or would be or might be or become liable for duty if on-course bets were not excluded from duty".

(4) The amendments made by subsection (3) above shall be deemed to have come into force on 29th March 1987.

(5) During the period beginning with 29th March 1987 and ending with the betting commencement date within the meaning of section 6 of the Finance Act 1986, in Schedule 2 to the 1972 Act (supplementary provisions) the references to a business which involves, or may involve, general betting duty becoming payable by any person and the references to an activity by reason of which a person is or may be or become liable for that duty shall be deemed to have included respectively references to a business which would or might involve that duty becoming payable, and to an activity by reason of which a person would be or might be or become liable for that duty, if on-course bets were not excluded from that duty.

GENERAL NOTE

    The duty on bets made at horse and greyhound racing tracks, first introduced by Winston Churchill in 1926, is abolished. The cost to the revenue, £20m, is recouped by the increase in gaming machine duty (see s.4). On-course betting had declined by half in real terms since 1974 and competition from betting shops controlled by major bookmakers using sophisticated technology was increasing. The measure is designed to support the racing and bloodstock industries, which are significant employers.

Gaming machine licence duty: rates

4. With respect to licences for any period beginning on or after 1st June 1987, for the Tables set out in section 23(1) of the Betting and Gaming Duties Act 1981 there shall be substituted the following Tables—

TABLE A

Small-prize machines

Description of machines authorised by the licence	Duty on whole-year licence
	£
Chargeable at the lower rate	150 per machine
Chargeable at the higher rate	375 per machine

TABLE B

Other machines

Description of machines authorised by the licence	Duty on whole-year licence
	£
Chargeable at the lower rate	375 per machine
Chargeable at the higher rate	960 per machine

GENERAL NOTE
The duty on gaming machines, last increased in 1982, is adjusted to recoup the revenue lost by the abolition of on-course betting duty (see s.3). Table A relates to amusement-with prizes machines in public houses, cafes, and arcades and Table B to jackpot machines in private clubs. The increase, 28 per cent. in the case of 10p. and 20p. jackpot machines, and 25 per cent. in the other three categories roughly compensates for inflation since the last increase.

Gaming machine licence duty: other amendments

5.—(1) With respect to licences for any period beginning on or after 1st October 1987, in the Betting and Gaming Duties Act 1981 (in this section referred to as "the 1981 Act") for subsection (3) of section 21 (which specifies the periods for which licences may be granted) there shall be substituted the following subsection—

"(3) A gaming machine licence may be a whole-year, a half-year or a quarter-year licence and shall be granted for a period of twelve, six or three months beginning with the first day of any month."

(2) In subsection (3) of section 26 of the 1981 Act (which provides that if one or more gaming machines are made available on any premises in such a way that they can be played, any gaming machine anywhere on the premises shall be treated as provided for gaming) after the word "and" there shall be inserted "subject to subsection (3A) below".

(3) After subsection (3) of the said section 26 there shall be inserted the following subsection—

"(3A) The Commissioners may by regulations make provision for the purpose of enabling spare gaming machines to be kept on premises for use in the case of the breakdown of other gaming machines on those premises; and such regulations may provide that, in such circumstances and subject to such conditions as may be specified in the regulations, a gaming machine on any premises which is not made available as mentioned in subsection (3) above, or is not in a state in which it can be played, shall not be treated by virtue of that subsection as provided for gaming on those premises."

(4) With effect from 1st October 1987, in Schedule 4 to the 1981 Act at the beginning of paragraph 4 (months preceding and following licences for summer months) there shall be inserted the words "Subject to sub-paragraph (2) below" and at the end of that paragraph there shall be added the following sub-paragraph—

"(2) Sub-paragraph (1) above shall not apply in relation to the provision of a machine on any premises—
(a) during March of any year, if any person has become entitled to a repayment of duty under paragraph 11 below on the surrender of a licence in respect of those premises or any machine on those premises during the preceding February,
(b) during October of any year, if any person has become entitled to such a repayment on the surrender of such a licence during the preceding March, June or September."

(5) With respect to the surrender of licences on or after 1st October 1987, in Schedule 4 to the 1981 Act, in sub-paragraph (1) of paragraph 11 (surrender of licences) for the words from "be entitled" onwards there shall be substituted "be entitled to a repayment of duty, in respect of each complete month in the unexpired period of the licence, of an amount equal—
(a) in the case of a whole-year licence, to one-twelfth of the duty paid on the grant of the licence, and
(b) in the case of a half-year licence, to one-twelfth of the duty that would have been payable on the grant of the licence if it had been a whole-year licence."

GENERAL NOTE
GENERAL NOTE
Various changes are made in the administration of gaming machine licence duty.

Subs. (1) abolishes the present system of separate commencement dates for different regions. All licences will be available from the first day of any month. Quarter-year special licences are introduced for the first time.

Subss. (2) and (3) authorise the keeping of spare machines on premises without licence under regulations to be made.

Subss. (4) and (5) provide that where a licence is surrendered duty will be refunded for each complete unexpired calendar month at the whole year rate of duty, if the surrendered licence has at least three months still to run and is not to be immediately replaced by a summer licence.

Amendments of the Management Act

Access to approved wharves and transit sheds

6.—(1) At the end of section 20 of the Customs and Excise Management Act 1979 (approved wharves) there shall be added the following subsection—

"(4) An officer may at any time enter an approved wharf and inspect it and any goods for the time being at the wharf."

(2) At the end of section 25 of that Act (approval of transit sheds) there shall be added the following subsection—

"(5) An officer may at any time enter a transit shed and inspect it and any goods for the time being in the transit shed."

GENERAL NOTE
Although Customs and Excise officers already have a general power under the writ of assistance issued at the beginning of every monarch's reign to carry out any search in order to further the collection of duties, the Keith Committee on the enforcement powers of the revenue departments found it unsatisfactory that entry to wharves and transit sheds should not rest on a statutory basis. The statutory provision now made is modelled on Customs and Excise Management Act 1979, s.33, which applies to airports.

Powers of search and access etc. in respect of vehicles

7.—(1) In section 27 of the Customs and Excise Management Act 1970 (officers' power of boarding) in subsection (1) for the words from "a vehicle" to "any officer" there shall be substituted "a vehicle is—

(a) entering, leaving or about to leave the United Kingdom,
(b) within the prescribed area,
(c) within the limits of or entering or leaving a port or any land adjacent to a port and occupied wholly or mainly for the purpose of activities carried on at the port,
(d) at, entering or leaving an aerodrome,
(e) at, entering or leaving an approved wharf, transit shed, customs warehouse or free zone, or
(f) at, entering or leaving any such premises as are mentioned in subsection (1) of section 112 below,
any officer".

(2) In section 28 of that Act (officers' powers of access, etc.) in subsection (1) after the words "any vehicle" there shall be inserted "which falls within paragraphs (a) to (f) of subsection (1) of section 27 above or is".

GENERAL NOTE
The Keith Committee did not consider the power in Customs and Excise Management Act 1979, s.163(1), which relates to searches in connection with suspected criminal offences such as smuggling, adequate for the general control of vehicles operating in and around ports and airports. Customs officers have had to work in conjunction with port and airport

authorities to exercise controls to prevent possible smuggling activities. They are now given power to act independently.

Local export control

8.—(1) In section 58A of the Customs and Excise Management Act 1979 (local export control) at the end of subsection (1) there shall be inserted "and, subject to and to such modifications as may be specified in the directions, this section and section 58D below shall apply in relation to goods which, for the purposes of any Community regulation relating to export refunds or monetary compensatory amounts, are treated as exports as if the supply of the goods were their exportation or, as the case may require, their shipping for exportation".

(2) In subsection (3)(b) of that section (conditions for the application of local export control) after the word "shipped" there shall be inserted "for exportation or exported by land".

(3) After subsection (7) of that section (power of Commissioners to relax requirements) there shall be inserted—

"(7A) Without prejudice to the powers of the Commissioners under subsection (7) above, they may direct that, in relation to goods of a description specified in the directions which are shipped for exportation or exported by land by an exporter of a description so specified, paragraph (a) of subsection (3) above shall have effect as if—
  (a) in sub-paragraph (i) the words "time and" were omitted; and
  (b) for sub-paragraph (ii) there were substituted—
        "(ii) at the time that notice is delivered or immediately thereafter, the exporter enters such particulars of the goods and of such other matters as may be required by the directions in a record maintained by him at such place as the proper officer may require; and
        (iii) the proper officer informs the exporter that he consents to the removal of the goods; and"."

(4) In section 58D of that Act (operative date for Community purposes) in subsection (2)(b) for the words following "above" there shall be substituted "as set out in section 58A(7A)(b) above, the day entry is made".

GENERAL NOTE
  The provisions for local export control introduced by F.A. 1981, Sched. 7, are extended. The amendments are made at the request of the Food and Drink Federation to assist exporters to obtain their entitlements under the common agricultural policy of the EEC.

Records relating to importation and exportation

9. After section 75 of the Customs and Excise Management Act 1979 there shall be inserted the following—

"Keeping and preservation of records

Records relating to importation and exportation

75A.—(1) Every person who is concerned (in whatever capacity) in the importation or exportation of goods of which an entry or specification is required for that purpose by or under this Act shall keep such records as the Commissioners may require.

(2) The Commissioners may require any records kept in pursuance of this section to be preserved for such period not exceeding four years as they may require.

(3) The duty under this section to preserve records may be discharged by the preservation of the information contained therein by such means as the Commissioners may approve; and where that

information is so preserved a copy of any document forming part of the records shall, subject to the following provisions of this section, be admissible in evidence in any proceedings, whether civil or criminal, to the same extent as the records themselves.

(4) The Commissioners may, as a condition of an approval under subsection (3) above of any means of preserving information, impose such reasonable requirements as appear to them necessary for securing that the information will be as readily available to them as if the records themselves had been preserved.

(5) The Commissioners may at any time for reasonable cause revoke or vary the conditions of any approval given under subsection (3) above.

(6) A statement contained in a document produced by a computer shall not by virtue of subsection (3) above be admissible in evidence—

(a) in civil proceedings in England and Wales, except in accordance with sections 5 and 6 of the Civil Evidence Act 1968;

(b) in criminal proceedings in England and Wales, except in accordance with sections 68 to 70 of the Police and Criminal Evidence Act 1984;

(c) in civil proceedings in Northern Ireland, except in accordance with sections 2 and 3 of the Civil Evidence Act (Northern Ireland) 1971; and

(d) in criminal proceedings in Northern Ireland, except in accordance with the said sections 2 and 3, which shall, for the purposes of this section, apply with the necessary modifications to such proceedings."

GENERAL NOTE

The purpose of the new section 75A is to permit the acceptance in certain circumstances of electronically transmitted customs freight declarations without any additional paper declarations, provided importers and exporters retain the necessary supporting documents.

Subs. (6)

The admissibility of computer-produced documents for customs purposes will be determined in Scotland by the courts.

Information powers

10. In section 77 of the Customs and Excise Management Act 1979 (information in relation to goods imported, exported or shipped for carriage coastwise) in subsection (1)(a) the words "importation, exportation or" shall be omitted, and after that section there shall be inserted the following section—

"Information powers

77A.—(1) Every person who is concerned (in whatever capacity) in the importation or exportation of goods for which an entry or specification is required for that purpose by or under this Act shall—

(a) furnish to the Commissioners, within such time and in such form as they may reasonably require, such information relating to the goods or to the importation or exportation as the Commissioners may reasonably specify; and

(b) if so required by an officer, produce or cause to be produced for inspection by the officer—

(i) at the principal place of business of the person upon whom the demand is made or at such other place as the officer may reasonably require, and

(ii) at such time as the officer may reasonably require,

any documents relating to the goods or to the importation or exportation.

(2) Where, by virtue of subsection (1) above, an officer has power to require the production of any documents from any such person as is referred to in that subsection, he shall have the like power to require production of the documents concerned from any other person who appears to the officer to be in possession of them; but where any such other person claims a lien on any document produced by him, the production shall be without prejudice to the lien.

(3) An officer may take copies of, or make extracts from, any document produced under subsection (1) or subsection (2) above.

(4) If it appears to him to be necessary to do so, an officer may, at a reasonable time and for a reasonable period, remove any document produced under subsection (1) or subsection (2) above and shall, on request, provide a receipt for any document so removed; and where a lien is claimed on a document produced under subsection (2) above, the removal of the document under this subsection shall not be regarded as breaking the lien.

(5) Where a document removed by an officer under subsection (4) above is reasonably required for the proper conduct of a business, the officer shall, as soon as practicable, provide a copy of the document, free of charge, to the person by whom it was produced or caused to be produced.

(6) Where any documents removed under the powers conferred by this section are lost or damaged, the Commissioners shall be liable to compensate their owner for any expenses reasonably incurred by him in replacing or repairing the documents.

(7) If any person fails to comply with a requirement under this section, he shall be liable on summary conviction to a penalty of level 3 on the standard scale."

GENERAL NOTE

The new section 77A widens the powers of the Customs and Excise in relation to obtaining information regarding goods imported or exported. In particular they may now remove documents in addition to inspecting or copying them. This power is subject to safeguards requiring the provision of copies and the payment of compensation in cases of damage or loss.

CHAPTER II

VALUE ADDED TAX

Accounting for and payment of tax

11.—(1) At the end of section 14(1) of the principal Act (which provides for tax to be accounted for and paid in accordance with regulations) there shall be added the words ", and regulations may make different provision for different circumstances".

(2) In Schedule 7 to that Act (administration, collection and enforcement) after sub-paragraph (3) of paragraph 2 there shall be inserted—

"(3A) Regulations under this paragraph may make provision whereby, in such cases and subject to such conditions as may be determined by or under the regulations, tax in respect of a supply may be accounted for and paid by reference to the time when consideration for the supply is received; and any such regulations may make such modifications of the provisions of this Act (including in particular, but without prejudice to the generality of the power, the provisions as to the time when, and the circumstances in which, credit for input tax is to be allowed) as appear to the Commissioners necessary or expedient.".

GENERAL NOTE
This section provides the necessary powers to introduce cash accounting and annual accounting for small businesses with turnover under £250,000. Such businesses will be given the option of accounting for VAT when they receive payment rather than when they issue a tax invoice. Similarly, they will be able to reclaim the VAT incurred on their purchases only when they make payment rather than when they receive a tax invoice. They will have the further option of making one VAT return a year rather than four as at present. Businesses choosing to use that option would make nine payments by direct debit on account and a tenth balancing payment with their annual return.
   Subject to the necessary derogation from EEC regulations being obtained, cash accounting will start on October 1, 1987, and annual accounting in the summer of 1988.
   These proposals arise from a wide-ranging review of VAT policy towards small businesses announced in the White Paper entitled "Building Businesses . . . not Barriers."

Credit for input tax

12.—(1) In section 15 of the principal Act, for subsections (1) to (3) there shall be substituted—

"(1) The amount of input tax for which a taxable person is entitled to credit at the end of any period shall be so much of the input tax for the period (that is input tax on supplies and importations in the period) as is allowable by or under regulations as being attributable to supplies within subsection (2) below.

(2) The supplies within this subsection are the following supplies made or to be made by the taxable person in the course or furtherance of his business—

(a) taxable supplies;

(b) supplies outside the United Kingdom which would be taxable supplies if made in the United Kingdom;

(c) supplies which section 35 below provides are to be disregarded for the purposes of this Act and which would otherwise be taxable supplies.

(3) The Commissioners shall make regulations for securing a fair and reasonable attribution of input tax to supplies within subsection (2) above, and any such regulations may provide for—

(a) determining a proportion by reference to which input tax for any prescribed accounting period is to be provisionally attributed to those supplies;

(b) adjusting, in accordance with a proportion determined in like manner for any longer period comprising two or more prescribed accounting periods or parts thereof, the provisional attribution for any of those periods; and

(c) the making of payments in respect of input tax, by the Commissioners to a taxable person (or a person who has been a taxable person) or by a taxable person (or a person who has been a taxable person) to the Commissioners, in cases where events prove inaccurate an estimate on the basis of which an attribution was made.".

(2) In section 6(1) of that Act, for the words "the charge to tax" there shall be substituted the words "this Act".

(3) In section 35(1) and (2) of that Act, for the words "shall be disregarded" there shall be substituted the words "shall, except where the contrary intention appears, be disregarded".

(4) This section shall have effect in relation to supplies and importations made on or after 1st April 1987, and shall be deemed to have come into force on 23rd March 1987.

GENERAL NOTE
Where a business makes both taxable and exempt supplies the basic principle in the EEC's Sixth Directive and in U.K. law is that it should be able to recover input tax only to the extent that it makes taxable supplies. The existing rules for determining the amount of input tax that can be deducted have been subject to manipulation. There has been an excessively generous *de minimis* limit for ignoring exempt supplies; also, the apportionment of input tax has been calculated by reference to the amounts of exempt and taxable sales, which may not correlate with purchases. The change to a stricter system, together with the related measures in ss.15, 17 and 18, is expected to increase the tax yield by £400m per annum.

Supplies abroad etc.

13.—(1) The principal Act shall be amended as follows.

(2) In section 2(5), at the end there shall be added the words ", and a person who is registered under paragraph 11A of that Schedule is a taxable person (notwithstanding that he does not make and does not intend to make taxable supplies)".

(3) In section 48(1), for the definition of "taxable person" there shall be substituted—

"'taxable person' means a person who is a taxable person under section 2(2) or (5) above;".

(4) In Schedule 1, after paragraph 11 there shall be inserted—

"11A.—(1) Where a person satisfies the Commissioners that he is within sub-paragraph (2) below, they may, if he so requests and they think fit, register him from such date and subject to such conditions as they think fit.

(2) A person is within this sub-paragraph if—

(a) he has a business establishment in the United Kingdom or his usual place of residence is in the United Kingdom;

(b) he does not make and does not intend to make taxable supplies; and

(c) he makes or intends to make in the course or furtherance of his business supplies within sub-paragraph (3) below.

(3) A supply is within this sub-paragraph if—

(a) it is made outside the United Kingdom but it would be a taxable supply if made in the United Kingdom; or

(b) section 35 of this Act provides that it is to be disregarded for the purposes of this Act, and it would otherwise be a taxable supply.

(4) The Commissioners may at any time, if they think fit, cancel as from that time the registration of a person who is not liable to be registered and whose registration was effected under this paragraph.

(5) A registered person whose registration was effected under this paragraph shall, if he makes or forms the intention of making taxable supplies, notify the Commissioners within thirty days that he has done so or formed the intention of doing so.

(6) Conditions under sub-paragraph (1) above—

(a) may be imposed wholly or partly by reference to, or without reference to, any conditions prescribed for the purposes of this paragraph; and

(b) may (whenever imposed) be subsequently varied by the Commissioners.

(7) Where the Commissioners refuse to act on a request made by a person under sub-paragraph (1) above, or where they cancel a person's registration under sub-paragraph (4) above, they shall give him written notice of their decision and of the grounds on which it was made.

(8) For the purposes of this paragraph—

(a) a person carrying on a business through a branch or agency in the United Kingdom shall be treated as having a business establishment in the United Kingdom; and

(b) 'usual place of residence', in relation to a body corporate, means the place where it is legally constituted.".

(5) In Schedule 5, item 2 of and Note (1) to Group 15 shall cease to have effect.

GENERAL NOTE

This section permits the registration for VAT of overseas businesses that make no taxable supplies in the U.K. but maintain a buying establishment or have a registered office here. It also provides for the registration of businesses that make supplies only of warehoused goods, even though they are disregarded under the Value Added Tax Act 1983, s.35. Such businesses will accordingly be enabled to reclaim some input tax on their purchases.

Registration

14.—(1) Schedule 1 to the principal Act shall be amended as follows.

(2) For paragraph 1 there shall be substituted—

"1.—(1) Subject to sub-paragraphs (2) to (5) below, a person who makes taxable supplies but is not registered is liable to be registered—

(a) after the end of any quarter, if the value of his taxable supplies—

(i) in that quarter has exceeded £7,250; or

(ii) in the four quarters then ending has exceeded £21,300; or

(b) at any time, if there are reasonable grounds for believing that the value of his taxable supplies in the period of one year then beginning will exceed £21,300.

(2) A person is not liable to be registered by virtue of sub-paragraph (1)(a)(i) above after the end of any quarter if the Commissioners are satisfied that the value of his taxable supplies in that quarter and the next three quarters will not exceed £21,300.

(3) A person is not liable to be registered by virtue of sub-paragraph (1)(a)(ii) above after the end of any quarter if the Commissioners are satisfied that the value of his taxable supplies in the next four quarters will not exceed £20,300.

(4) In determining the value of a person's supplies for the purposes of sub-paragraph (1)(a) above, supplies made at a time when he was previously registered shall be disregarded if—

(a) his registration was cancelled otherwise than under paragraph 10 below, and

(b) the Commissioners are satisfied that before his registration was cancelled he had given them all the information they needed in order to determine whether to cancel the registration.

(5) In determining the value of a person's supplies for the purposes of sub-paragraph (1) above, supplies of goods that are capital assets of the business in the course or furtherance of which they are supplied shall be disregarded.".

(3) For paragraph 2 there shall be substituted—

"2.—(1) Subject to sub-paragraph (2) below, a registered person who makes taxable supplies shall cease to be liable to be registered at any time if the Commissioners are satisfied that the value of his taxable supplies in the period of one year then beginning will not exceed £20,300.

(2) A person shall not cease to be liable to be registered by virtue of sub-paragraph (1) above if the Commissioners are satisfied that the reason the value of his taxable supplies will not exceed £20,300 is that

in the period in question he will cease making taxable supplies, or will suspend making them for a period of thirty days or more.

(3) In determining the value of a person's supplies for the purposes of sub-paragraph (1) above, supplies of goods that are capital assets of the business in the course or furtherance of which they are supplied shall be disregarded.".

(4) For paragraph 3 there shall be substituted—

"3.—(1) A person who by virtue of paragraph 1(1)(a) above is liable to be registered after the end of any quarter shall notify the Commissioners of that liability within thirty days of the end of that quarter.

(2) The Commissioners shall register any such person (whether or not he so notifies them) with effect from the end of the month in which the thirtieth day falls or from such earlier date as may be agreed between them and him.".

(5) For paragraph 4 there shall be substituted—

"4.—(1) A person who by virtue of paragraph 1(1)(b) above is liable to be registered by reason of the value of his taxable supplies in any period shall notify the Commissioners of that liability within thirty days of the beginning of that period.

(2) Subject to sub-paragraph (3) below, the Commissioners shall register any such person (whether or not he so notifies them) with effect from the end of the thirty days or from such earlier date as may be agreed between them and him.

(3) Where there are reasonable grounds for believing that the value of such a person's taxable supplies in the first thirty days of the period will exceed £21,300, the Commissioners may, if they think fit, register him with effect from the beginning of the period.".

(6) Paragraph 6 shall cease to have effect.

(7) For paragraph 7 there shall be substituted—

"7.—(1) A registered person who ceases to make taxable supplies shall notify the Commissioners of that fact within thirty days of the day on which he does so.

(2) Subject to sub-paragraph (3) below, the Commissioners shall cancel the registration of a registered person who ceases to make taxable supplies with effect from the day on which he so ceases or from such later date as may be agreed between them and him.

(3) The Commissioners shall not be under a duty to cancel the registration of such a person (although they may cancel it if they think fit) if they are satisfied that he is (on ceasing to make taxable supplies) within paragraph 11A(2) below.".

(8) In paragraph 9, for the words "paragraph 2(b)" there shall be substituted the words "paragraph 2".

(9) In paragraph 11, for sub-paragraph (2) there shall be substituted—

"(2) Where there is a material change in the nature of the supplies made by a person exempted from registration under sub-paragraph (1)(a) above he shall notify the Commissioners of the change—

(a) within thirty days of the day on which it occurred; or
(b) if no particular day is identifiable as the day on which it occurred, within thirty days of the end of the quarter in which it occurred.

(2AA) Where there is a material alteration in any quarter in the proportion of taxable supplies of such a person that are zero-rated, he shall notify the Commissioners of the alteration within thirty days of the end of the quarter.".

(10) For paragraph 13 there shall be substituted—

"13. The value of a supply of goods or services shall be determined for the purposes of this Schedule on the basis that no tax is chargeable on the supply.".

GENERAL NOTE

Normally the registration limits for VAT are altered by statutory instrument. This year they are included in the Finance Act because of a number of other amendments to Value Added Tax 1983, Sched. 1. The annual and quarterly taxable turnover limits which determine whether a person is required to be registered are increased from £20,500 to £21,300 and from £7,000 to £7,250 respectively. The turnover limit below which a registered person may apply to be deregistered is increased from £19,500 to £20,300 (inclusive of VAT). These limits are the highest thresholds permissible under EEC law. A proposal for the compulsory deregistration of traders below the threshold was not proceeded with.

The most material changes made by the other amendments to Sched. 1 are an increase in the grace periods allowed under paras. 3, 4 and 7 from ten days, nil and ten days respectively to a uniform limit of thirty days.

Supplies to groups

15.—(1) In the principal Act, after section 29 there shall be inserted—

"Supplies to groups

29A.—(1) Subject to subsections (2) and (3) below, subsection (4) below applies where—

(a) a business, or part of a business, carried on by a taxable person is transferred as a going concern to a body corporate treated as a member of a group under section 29 above;

(b) on the transfer of the business or part, chargeable assets of the business are transferred to the body corporate; and

(c) the transfer of the assets is treated by virtue of section 3(3)(c) above as neither a supply of goods nor a supply of services.

(2) Subsection (4) below shall not apply if the representative member of the group is entitled to credit for the whole of the input tax on supplies to it and importations by it—

(a) during the prescribed accounting period in which the assets are transferred, and

(b) during any longer period to which regulations under section 15(3)(b) above relate and in which the assets are transferred.

(3) Subsection (4) below shall not apply if the Commissioners are satisfied that the assets were acquired by the taxable person transferring them more than three years before the day on which they are transferred.

(4) The chargeable assets shall be treated for the purposes of this Act as being, on the day on which they are transferred, both supplied to the representative member of the group for the purpose of its business and supplied by that member in the course or furtherance of its business.

(5) A supply treated under subsection (4) above as made by a representative member shall not be taken into account as a supply made by him when determining the allowance of input tax in his case under section 15 above.

(6) The value of a supply treated under subsection (4) above as made to or by a representative member shall be taken to be the open market value of the chargeable assets.

(7) For the purposes of this section, the open market value of any chargeable assets shall be taken to be the price that would be paid on a sale (on which no tax is payable) between a buyer and a seller who are not in such a relationship as to affect the price.

(8) The Commissioners may reduce the tax chargeable by virtue of subsection (4) above in a case where they are satisfied that the person by whom the chargeable assets are transferred has not received credit for the full amount of input tax arising on the acquisition by him of the chargeable assets.

(9) For the purposes of this section, assets are chargeable assets if their supply in the United Kingdom by a taxable person in the course or furtherance of his business would be a taxable supply (and not a zero-rated supply).".

(2) This section shall have effect in relation to transfers of assets made on or after 1st April 1987, and shall be deemed to have come into force on 23rd March 1987.

GENERAL NOTE
The new s.29A is designed to prevent a practice by which an exempt trader such as a financial institution could recover VAT on purchases of capital equipment. The practice depended on the ability to choose whether to group or not to group subsidiaries for VAT purposes. Typically, a non-grouped subsidiary would be set up to carry on a business of buying and leasing equipment. The subsidiary would buy the equipment and lease it to its parent. After reclaiming the VAT on the purchase the subsidiary would join the VAT group and would thereafter not have to charge VAT on the lease rentals. To counter this device the parent will be treated as having made a notional supply to itself, on which VAT will be chargeable, at the time the subsidiary joins the VAT group.

Tour operators

16.—(1) After section 37 of the principal Act there shall be added—

"Tour operators
37A.—(1) The Treasury may by order modify the application of this Act in relation to supplies of goods or services by tour operators or in relation to such of those supplies as may be determined by or under the order.

(2) Without prejudice to the generality of subsection (1) above, an order under this section may make provision—

(a) for two or more supplies of goods or services by a tour operator to be treated as a single supply of services;

(b) for the value of that supply to be ascertained, in such manner as may be determined by or under the order, by reference to the difference between sums paid or payable to and sums paid or payable by the tour operator;

(c) for account to be taken, in determining the tax chargeable on that supply, of the different rates of tax that would have been applicable apart from this section;

(d) excluding any body corporate from the application of section 29 above;

(e) as to the time when a supply is to be treated as taking place.

(3) In this section 'tour operator' includes a travel agent acting as principal and any other person providing for the benefit of travellers services of any kind commonly provided by tour operators or travel agents.

(4) Section 45(3) below shall not apply to an order under this section, notwithstanding that it makes provision for excluding any tax from credit under section 14 above.".

(2) In section 45 of that Act, at the beginning of subsection (4) there shall be inserted the words "Subject to section 37A(4) above".

GENERAL NOTE
The new s.37A implements Art. 26 of the Sixth Council Directive of the EEC. Tour operators' margins in respect of standard-rated supplies included in package holidays within

the EEC will be brought within charge to VAT. The margin is the difference between the tax-inclusive cost of the relevant supplies and the price at which they are sold to the customer. Additionally, tour operators will not be able to recover any VAT which may be charged by their suppliers for such services. The Treasury order indicating precisely the goods and services covered by the margin scheme will be subject to the negative procedure (subs. (4)).

Valuation of supplies at less than market value

17.—(1) In Schedule 4 to the principal Act, at the beginning of paragraph 1(1)(c) there shall be inserted the words "if the supply is a taxable supply,".

(2) This section shall have effect in relation to supplies made on or after 1st April 1987, and shall be deemed to have come into force on 23rd March 1987.

GENERAL NOTE

The purpose of the amendment to Value Added Tax Act 1983, Sched. 4, para. 1(1)(c) is to permit the Commissioners of Customs and Excise to direct that exempt supplies made between connected persons shall be valued at the open market value. Previously, the special valuation provisions in Sched. 4 did not apply to exempt supplies. The change in the law is to prevent distortion of partial exemption calculations through artificial valuation of supplies.

Issue of securities

18.—(1) In Schedule 6 to the principal Act (exemptions), in Group 5 (finance)—

(a) at the end of item 5 there shall be added the words "or the underwriting of an issue within item 1"; and

(b) after item 6 there shall be inserted the following item—
  "6A. The making of arrangements for, or the underwriting of, an issue within item 6.".

(2) This section shall have effect in relation to supplies made on or after 1st April 1987, and shall be deemed to have come into force on 23rd March 1987.

GENERAL NOTE

The exemption from VAT of the making of arrangements for and the underwriting of capital issues is part of the package of measures designed to prevent the exploitation of the rules for deduction of input tax in the case of businesses making taxable and exempt supplies (see also ss.12, 15 and 17).

Interpretation and miscellaneous further amendments

19.—(1) In this Chapter "the principal Act" means the Value Added Tax Act 1983.

(2) The principal Act shall have effect subject to the further amendments in Schedule 2 to this Act; and the amendment in that Schedule of section 7 of the principal Act shall have effect with respect to services supplied on or after 1st April 1987.

GENERAL NOTE

Sched. 2 makes four relatively minor amendments to V.A.T.A. 1983. See further the Note to the Schedule.

PART II

INCOME TAX, CORPORATION TAX AND CAPITAL GAINS TAX

CHAPTER I

GENERAL

Tax rates

Charge of income tax for 1987–88

20.—(1) Income tax for the year 1987–88 shall be charged at the basic rate of 27 per cent.; and in respect of so much of an individual's total income as exceeds the basic rate limit (£17,900) at such higher rates as are specified in the Table below:

TABLE

Higher rate bands	*Higher rate*
The first £2,500	40 per cent.
The next £5,000	45 per cent.
The next £7,900	50 per cent.
The next £7,900	55 per cent.
The remainder	60 per cent.

and paragraphs (a) and (b) of subsection (1) of section 32 of the Finance Act 1971 (charge of tax at the basic and higher rates) shall have effect accordingly.

(2) Section 24(4) of the Finance Act 1980 (indexation of thresholds) shall not, so far as it relates to the higher rate bands, apply for the year 1987–88.

GENERAL NOTE

This section gives effect to the reduction in the basic rate by 2 per cent. Modest changes are made to the basic rate limit which is increased by £700 and to the threshold for the 45 per cent. rate which is increased by £200. The other thresholds remain constant.

Charge of corporation tax for financial year 1987

21. Corporation tax shall be charged for the financial year 1987 at the rate of 35 per cent.

GENERAL NOTE

The rate of corporation tax remains constant.

Corporation tax: small companies

22.—(1) For the financial year 1987 the small companies rate shall be 27 per cent.

(2) For the financial year 1987, the fraction mentioned in section 95(2) of the Finance Act 1972 (marginal relief for small companies) shall be one fiftieth.

GENERAL NOTE

In line with the reduction in the basic rate of income tax the small companies' rate of corporation tax is likewise reduced to 27 per cent. The upper and lower limits of profits between which marginal relief is available remain constant at £500,000 and £100,000 respectively with the result that the marginal reliefs fraction is altered from three two-hundredths to one-fiftieth.

Deduction rate for sub-contractors in construction industry

23. Section 69(4) of the Finance (No. 2) Act 1975 (which requires deductions to be made from payments to certain sub-contractors in the construction industry) shall have effect in relation to payments made on or after 2nd November 1987 with the substitution for the words "29 per cent." of the words "27 per cent.".

GENERAL NOTE
  The reduction in the rate at which deductions must be made from payments to certain contractors in the construction industry is in line with the reduction in the basic rate of income tax.

Personal reliefs etc.

Personal reliefs: operative date for PAYE

24. For the year 1987–88, in subsection (7) of section 24 of the Finance Act 1980 (which specifies the date from which indexed changes in income tax thresholds and allowances are to be brought into account for the purposes of PAYE) for "5th May" there shall be substituted "18th May".

GENERAL NOTE
  Changes in tax thresholds and allowances are only to be brought into account for the purposes of PAYE on and after May 18 as opposed to May 5, as provided for in F.A. 1980, s.24. This is a purely administrative measure.

Relief for interest

25. For the year 1987–88 the qualifying maximum referred to in paragraphs 5(1) and 24(3) of Schedule 1 to the Finance Act 1974 (limit on relief for interest on certain loans for the purchase or improvement of land) shall be £30,000.

GENERAL NOTE
  Mortgage interest relief continues to be limited to loans of £30,000 and below.

Increased personal relief for those aged eighty and over

26.—(1) Subject to the provisions of this section, subsection (1) of section 8 of the Taxes Act (personal reliefs) shall have effect—
  (a) in relation to a claim by a person who proves that he or his wife was at any time within the year of assessment of the age of eighty or upwards, as if the sum specified in paragraph (a) (married) were £4,845; and
  (b) in relation to a claim by a person who proves that he was at any time within the year of assessment of the age of eighty or upwards, as if the sum specified in paragraph (b) (single) were £3,070.

(2) For the purposes of subsection (1) above, a person who would have been of the age of eighty or upwards within the year of assessment if he had not died in the course of it shall be treated as having been of that age within that year.

(3) For any year of assessment for which a person is entitled to increased personal relief by virtue of this section, he shall not be entitled to increased relief under subsection (1A) of section 8 of the Taxes Act (increased relief for persons of sixty-five and upwards).

(4) For the purpose of any enactment which refers to Part I of the Taxes Act or to Chapter II of that Part, subsections (1) and (2) above shall be taken to be included in that Chapter.

(5) In the following enactments—
  (a) subsection (1B) of section 8 of the Taxes Act (tapering of relief under subsection (1A)),

(b) subsection (2) of section 14 of that Act (which, as applied by
    section 15A of that Act, determines the amount of widow's
    bereavement allowances), and

(c) paragraph 3(3) of Schedule 4 to the Finance Act 1971 (exclusion
    of certain reliefs where there is separate taxation of wife's
    earnings),

any reference to subsection (1A) of section 8 of the Taxes Act includes a
reference to subsection (1) above.

(6) In subsection (8) of section 36 of the Finance Act 1976 (application
of provisions relating to transfer of balance of certain reliefs between
spouses) the reference in paragraph (b) to section 8(1A)(b) of the Taxes
Act includes a reference to subsection (1)(b) above.

(7) In section 24 of the Finance Act 1980 (indexation of income tax
thresholds and allowances), any reference to section 8 of the Taxes Act
includes a reference to subsection (1) above.

(8) This section has effect for the year 1987–88 and subsequent years of
assessment.

<small>GENERAL NOTE</small>

The normal personal allowances have been increased automatically under the indexation
provisions of F.A. 1980, s.24(5). This section introduces a special age allowance for persons
over 80 (or married to persons over 80) over and above the additional allowance available
to persons over 65. The position for married persons is now that the married man's allowance
is £3,795, the age allowance for married couples over 65 is £4,465 and for couples over 80
is £4,845. The single person allowances are respectively £2,425, £2,960 and £3,070.

The income limit for age allowance has been increased from £9,400 to £9,800 and this
limit applies to both the higher and lower age allowances (see subs. (5)).

Invalid care allowance and unemployment benefit

27.—(1) In section 8 of the Taxes Act (personal reliefs) in paragraph
(b) of subsection (2) (wife's earned income relief) after sub-paragraph
(iii) there shall be inserted the words "and

> (iv) invalid care allowance".

(2) In Schedule 4 to the Finance Act 1971 (separate taxation of wife's
earnings) in paragraph 1 (meaning of wife's earnings) at the end of
paragraph (b) there shall be inserted the words "unemployment benefit or
invalid care allowance".

(3) This section—

(a) so far as it relates to invalid care allowance, has effect for the
    year 1984–85 and subsequent years of assessment, and

(b) so far as it relates to unemployment benefit, has effect for the
    year 1987–88 and subsequent years of assessment;

and all such adjustments (whether by repayment of tax or otherwise) shall
be made as are appropriate to give effect to this section.

<small>GENERAL NOTE</small>

A wife's earned income relief is limited to the extent that her earned income is less than
the relief given (now £2,425)—see I.C.T.A. 1970, s.8(2). This section provides that an
invalid care allowance is not to be treated as earned income for this purpose. Such an
allowance, together with unemployment benefit is also not to be treated as earned income
for the purposes of the wife's earned income election in F.A. 1971, s.23 (see Sched. 4).

Increased relief for blind persons

28. For the year 1987–88 and subsequent years of assessment, in section
18 of the Taxes Act—

(a) in subsection (1) (single blind persons and married couples of
    whom one is blind) for "£360" there shall be substituted "£540";
    and

(b) in subsection (2) (married couples, both of whom are blind) for "£720" there shall be substituted "£1,080".

GENERAL NOTE
This section increases the reliefs available for state registered blind persons or to persons married to such blind persons.

Income support etc.

29.—(1) For subsection (2) of section 219 of the Taxes Act (which specifies certain social security benefits which are not to be treated as income for the purposes of the Income Tax Acts) there shall be substituted the following subsection—

"(2) The following payments shall not be treated as income for any purpose of the Income Tax Acts—

   (a) payments of income support, family credit or housing benefit under the Social Security Act 1986 or the Social Security (Northern Ireland) Order 1986 other than payments of income support which are taxable by virtue of section 29 of the Finance Act 1987;

   (b) payments of child benefit; and

   (c) payments excepted by subsection (1) above from the charge to tax imposed by that subsection.";

and, accordingly, paragraph 101(b) of Schedule 10 to the Social Security Act 1986 shall cease to have effect.

(2) Subject to the following provisions of this section, payments to any person of income support under the Social Security Act 1986 in respect of any period shall be charged to income tax under Schedule E if during that period—

   (a) his right to income support is subject to the condition specified in section 20(3)(d)(i) of that Act (availability for employment); or

   (b) he is one of a married or unmarried couple and section 23 of that Act (trade disputes) applies to him but not to the other person;

and in paragraph (b) above "married couple" and "unmarried couple" have the same meaning as in Part II of the Social Security Act 1986.

(3) Where the amount of income support paid to any person in respect of any week or part of a week exceeds the taxable maximum for that period as defined in Part I of Schedule 3 to this Act the excess shall not be taxable.

(4) Where payments of unemployment benefit and payments of income support are made to any person in respect of the same week or part of a week, the amount taxable in respect of that period in respect of those payments shall not exceed the taxable maximum for that period within the meaning of subsection (3) above.

(5) In their application to Northern Ireland subsections (2) to (4) above and Part I of Schedule 3 to this Act shall have effect as if—

   (a) for the references to the Social Security Act 1986, to Part II of that Act and to sections 20(3)(d)(i) and 23 of that Act there were substituted respectively references to the Social Security (Northern Ireland) Order 1986, Part III of that Order and Articles 21(3)(d)(i) and 24 of that Order; and

   (b) for the references to paragraph 1 of Part I of Schedule 4 to the Social Security Act 1975 and paragraph 1(a) of Part IV of that Schedule there were substituted respectively references to paragraph 1 of Part I of Schedule 4 to the Social Security (Northern Ireland) Act 1975 and paragraph 1(a) of Part IV of that Schedule.

(6) The consequential amendments in Part II of Schedule 3 to this Act shall have effect.

(7) Except as provided by subsection (8) below, this section and Schedule 3 to this Act shall have effect in relation to payments in respect of periods beginning on or after the income support date.

(8) Subsection (1) above, so far as it relates to family credit or housing benefit, shall have effect in relation to payments in respect of periods beginning on or after the family credit date and the housing benefit date respectively; and nothing in that subsection shall affect payments of family income supplement in respect of periods before the family credit date.

(9) In subsections (7) and (8) above, the "income support date", the "family credit date" and the "housing benefit date" mean the days on which regulations containing the first schemes under section 20 of the Social Security Act 1986 and Article 21 of the Social Security (Northern Ireland) Order 1986 providing respectively for income support, for family credit and for housing benefit come into force.

GENERAL NOTE

I.C.T.A. 1970, s. 219(2) exempts from charge to income tax certain social security benefits. The new subsection (2), introduced by this section, takes account of the revision in social security benefits provided for by the Social Security Act 1986.

The payments referred to in paragraph (a) of the new subsection are income related and may in certain circumstances be subject to tax (see subs. (2)). This is where the right to income support depends on a person being available for employment or where the claimant is one of a married or unmarried couple involved in a trade dispute as a result of which reduced income support is payable, the other spouse or other person not being so involved. In so far as the amount of income support and/or unemployment benefit exceeds the taxable maximum as defined in Sched. 3 to this Act the excess is not taxable.

Friendly societies, trade unions and charities

Registered friendly societies

30.—(1) In so far as the profits of a registered friendly society from life or endowment business relate to contracts made on or after 1st September 1987, section 332 of the Taxes Act (registered friendly societies: tax exempt limits etc.) shall be amended in accordance with subsections (2) and (3) below.

(2) In paragraph (a) of subsection (2) for the words from "the assurance" onwards there shall be substituted—

"(i) the assurance of gross sums under contracts under which the total premiums payable in any period of twelve months exceed £100; or

(ii) the granting of annuities of annual amounts exceeding £156; and".

(3) For subsection (3) there shall be substituted the following subsection—

"(3) In determining for the purposes of subsection (2)(a)(i) above the total premiums payable in any period of twelve months—

(a) where those premiums are payable more frequently than annually, there shall be disregarded an amount equal to 10 per cent. of those premiums; and

(b) so much of any premium as is charged on the ground that an exceptional risk of death is involved shall be disregarded;

and in applying the limit of £156 in subsection (2)(a)(ii) above, any bonus or addition declared upon an annuity shall be disregarded."

(4) In section 64 of the Friendly Societies Act 1974 (which relates to the maximum contractual benefits a person may have with friendly societies and is in the following provisions of this section referred to as "section 64"), paragraph (a) of subsection (1) shall not apply as respects sums assured under contracts made on or after 1st September 1987; and after that subsection there shall be inserted the following subsections—

"(1A) With respect to contracts for the assurance of gross sums under tax exempt life or endowment business, a member of a

16–23

registered friendly society or branch shall not be entitled to have outstanding with any one or more such societies or branches (taking together all such societies or branches throughout the United Kingdom) contracts under which the total premiums payable in any period of twelve months exceed £100 unless all those contracts were entered into before 1st September 1987.

(1B) In applying the limit in subsection (1A) above, the premiums under any contract for an annuity which was made before 1st June 1984 by a new society, shall be brought into account as if the contract were for the assurance of a gross sum."

(5) At the end of subsection (2) of section 64 (provisions disregarded in applying limits) there shall be added the following "and

(d) so far as concerns the total premiums payable in any period of twelve months,—

    (i) 10 per cent. of the premiums payable under any contract under which the premiums are payable more frequently than annually; and

    (ii) £10 of the premiums payable under any contract made before 1st September 1987 by a society which is not a new society; and

    (iii) so much of any premium as is charged on the ground that an exceptional risk of death is involved."

(6) In subsection (2B) of section 64 (contracts not to be qualifying policies where limits are exceeded)—

(a) in paragraph (a) after the words "sums assured" there shall be inserted "or premiums payable"; and

(b) in paragraph (b) after the words "sums assured by" there shall be inserted "or, as the case may be, the premiums payable under".

(7) At the end of subsection (6) of section 64 (declaration that limits are not exceeded) there shall be added the words "and that the total premiums under those contracts do not exceed those limits".

(8) At the end of section 41(9) of the Finance Act 1985 (gains on non-qualifying policies issued by friendly societies in the course of tax exempt business to be chargeable under section 399 of the Taxes Act at basic rate as well as at higher rates) there shall be added the words "but any relief under section 400 of that Act shall be computed as if this subsection had not been enacted".

GENERAL NOTE

This section has the effect of increasing the limit on tax exempt life assurance business carried on by friendly societies. Previously such societies could not issue and would enjoy no tax exemption for policies insuring a gross sum of more than £750. The new rule, as regards policies taken out after September 1, 1987, is that the premiums under the policies must not exceed £100 per annum. The limit applicable to annuity contracts remains unchanged.

In determining the total of annual premiums for these purposes certain amounts fall to be disregarded namely 10 per cent. of premiuns paid more frequently than annually and so much of any premium charged on the ground that an exceptional risk of death is involved.

Relief in respect of certain income of trade unions

31.—(1) In section 338 of the Taxes Act (which, as amended by section 36 of the Finance Act 1982, provides for exemption for certain income and gains of a trade union precluded by Act or rules from assuring to any person a sum exceeding £2,400 by way of gross sum or £500 a year by way of annuity) for "£2,400" and "£500" there shall be substituted respectively "£3,000" and "£625".

(2) This section has effect in relation to income or gains which are applicable and applied as mentioned in the said section 338 on or after 17th March 1987.

GENERAL NOTE
This section increases the tax-exempt limits relating to provident benefits provided by trade unions for their members. To qualify for relief under section 338 the benefits must not exceed certain limits and these are now increased from £2,400 to £3,000 in the case of lump sums and from £500 to £626 in the case of annuities.

Charities: payroll deduction scheme

32.—(1) In section 27(7) of the Finance Act 1986 (which limits to £100 the deductions attracting relief) for "£100" there shall be substituted "£120".

(2) This section has effect for the year 1987–88 and subsequent years of assessment.

GENERAL NOTE
F.A. 1986, s.27, introduced a scheme to allow charitable contributions to be withheld from emoluments and be deductible in computing liability to income tax under Schedule E. The original limit to the annual contributions that would be made under the scheme was £100. This section increases the limit to £120.

Employees etc.

Employee share schemes, etc.

33.—(1) Schedule 10 to the Finance Act 1980 (savings-related share option schemes) and Schedule 10 to the Finance Act 1984 (approved share option schemes) shall have effect subject to the amendments in Part I of Schedule 4 to this Act (which enable schemes to allow rights acquired under them to be exchanged for other rights in certain circumstances); and the transitional provisions in Part II of that Schedule and the consequential provisions relating to capital gains tax in Part III thereof shall have effect.

(2) Subject to subsection (3) below, the provisions of Part IV of Schedule 4 to this Act shall have effect for the purpose only of determining whether an individual has a material interest in a company for the purposes of the employee share scheme legislation.

(3) Paragraph 8 of Schedule 4 to this Act shall also have effect for the purpose of determining whether interest on a loan made on or after 6th April 1987 is eligible for relief under section 75 of the Finance Act 1972 by virtue of paragraph 9 of Schedule 1 to the Finance Act 1974.

(4) In this section "the employee share scheme legislation" means—
(a) Schedule 9 to the Finance Act 1978,
(b) Schedule 10 to the Finance Act 1980, and
(c) Schedule 10 to the Finance Act 1984.

GENERAL NOTE
This section introduces Sched. 4 which makes various amendments to employee share scheme legislation.

Employees seconded to educational bodies

34.—(1) With respect to expenditure attributable to the employment of a person on or after 26th November 1986 and before 1st April 1997, section 28 of the Finance Act 1983 (employees seconded to charities) shall have effect as if the references in subsections (1) and (2A) of that section to a charity included references to any of the bodies specified in subsection (2) below.

(2) The bodies referred to in subsection (1) above are—
(a) in England and Wales, any local education authority and any educational institution maintained by such an authority;
(b) in Scotland, any education authority, any educational estab-

lishment maintained by such an authority, and any college of education or central institution within the meaning of the Education (Scotland) Act 1980;

(c) in Northern Ireland, any education and library board, college of education or controlled school within the meaning of the Education and Libraries (Northern Ireland) Order 1986 and any institution of further education which is under the management of an education and library board by virtue of Article 28 of that Order; and

(d) any other educational body which is for the time being approved for the purposes of this section by the Secretary of State or, in Northern Ireland, the Department of Education for Northern Ireland.

(3) Any approval granted by the Secretary of State or the Department of Education for Northern Ireland under subsection (2)(d) above before 1st September 1987 may be expressed to have effect for any period before that date.

GENERAL NOTE
  F.A. 1983, s.28, permits trading and investment companies to deduct expenditure attributable to the employment of a person albeit that person has been seconded temporarily to work for a charity. This section extends the operator of s.28 to secondment to specified educational bodies.

Relief for costs of training etc.

35.—(1) Where, on or after 6th April 1987, a person (in this section referred to as the "employer") incurs expenditure in paying or reimbursing relevant expenses incurred in connection with a qualifying course of training which—

(a) is undertaken by a person (in this section referred to as the "employee") who is the holder or past holder of any office or employment under the employer, and

(b) is undertaken with a view to retraining the employee,

the employee shall not thereby be regarded as receiving any emolument which forms part of his income for any purpose of Schedule E.

(2) Schedule 5 to this Act shall have effect to determine for the purposes of this section—

(a) what is a qualifying course of training;

(b) whether such a course is undertaken by an employee with a view to retraining; and

(c) what are relevant expenses in relation to such a course.

(3) Subject to subsection (4) below, where—

(a) an employer incurs expenditure in paying or reimbursing relevant expenses as mentioned in subsection (1) above, and

(b) that subsection has effect in relation to the income of the employee for the purposes of Schedule E,

then, if and so far as that expenditure would not, apart from this subsection, be so deductible, it shall be deductible in computing for the purposes of Schedule D the profits or gains of the trade, profession or vocation of the employer for the purposes of which the employee is or was employed.

(4) If the employer carries on a business, the expenses of management of which are eligible for relief under section 304 of the Taxes Act, subsection (3) above shall have effect as if for the words from "in computing" onwards there were substituted "as expenses of management for the purposes of section 304 of the Taxes Act".

(5) In any case where—

(a) an employee's liability to tax for any year of assessment is determined (by assessment or otherwise) on the assumption that subsection (1) above applies in his case and, subsequently, there is a failure to comply with any provision of paragraph 4 of Schedule 5 to this Act, or

(b) an employer's liability to tax for any year is determined (by assessment or otherwise) on the assumption that, by virtue only of subsection (3) above (or subsections (3) and (4) above), he is entitled to a deduction on account of any expenditure and, subsequently, there is such a failure as is referred to in paragraph (a) above,

an assessment under section 29(3) of the Taxes Management Act 1970 of an amount due in consequence of the failure referred to above may be made at any time not later than six years after the end of the chargeable period in which the failure occurred.

(6) Where an event occurs by reason of which there is a failure to comply with any provision of paragraph 4 of Schedule 5 to this Act, the employer of the employee concerned shall within sixty days of coming to know of the event give a notice in writing to the inspector containing particulars of the event.

(7) If the inspector has reason to believe that an employer has not given a notice which he is required to give under subsection (6) above in respect of any event, the inspector may by notice in writing require the employer to furnish him within such time (not being less than sixty days) as may be specified in the notice with such information relating to the event as the inspector may reasonably require for the purposes of this section.

(8) The Table in section 98 of the Taxes Management Act 1970 (penalties) shall be amended as follows—

(a) at the end of the first column there shall be inserted—
    "Section 35(7) of the Finance Act 1987"; and
(b) at the end of the second column there shall be inserted—
    "Section 35(6) of the Finance Act 1987".

GENERAL NOTE

This section gives tax reliefs for expenditure incurred with a view to retraining present or past employees. First the employee or past employee will not be taxable under Schedule E in respect of any costs of training him for a new job or business incurred by his employer or past employer, Secondly the employer or past employer will be able to deduct the cost of the training in computing his profits, if he is not already able to do so.

The reliefs given by this section depend upon the expenses being incurred in respect of a "qualifying course of training" and "with a view to retraining." Sched. 6 has effect to determine whether these requirements are satisfied.

The reliefs go hand in hand with an extra statutory concession (August 1986) under which an employee is not charged to income tax on expenses incurred by his employer on sending him on a training course related to his employment or on certain courses of general education intended to enable him to perform the duties of his employment better.

Companies

Time for payment of corporation tax by certain long-established companies and building societies

36.—(1) Section 244 of the Taxes Act (which, in the case of certain companies trading before the financial year 1965, provides that the interval within which corporation tax is to be paid in respect of any accounting period shall be longer than the period of nine months provided for, in relation to companies generally, by section 243(4) of that Act) shall not apply with respect to any accounting period of a company beginning on or after 17th March 1987.

(2) Section 344 of the Taxes Act (which, in the case of certain building societies carrying on business in the year 1965–66, makes special provision as to the time for payment of corporation tax) shall not apply with respect to any accounting period of a building society ending on or after 6th April 1990.

(3) In Schedule 6 to this Act—

(a) Part I has effect with respect to and in connection with the payment of corporation tax for certain accounting periods by a company to which, by virtue of section 244 of the Taxes Act, section 243(4) of that Act did not apply as respects the last accounting period ending before 17th March 1987; and

(b) Part II has effect with respect to and in connection with the payment by a building society to which section 344 of the Taxes Act applies of corporation tax for accounting periods ending in the year 1989–90.

GENERAL NOTE

The aim of this section is to standardise the time for payment of corporation tax to nine months after the end of an accounting period. Previously companies trading before 1965 paid tax after a like interval from the end of their accounting period as existed between the end of the basic period of the trade for 1965–66 and January 1 1966. This could be as long as 21 months.

The change to the new payment date is phased in over three years commencing with the company's first accounting period starting on or after March 17, 1987.

In certain cases building societies have had to pay tax after a payment interval of less than nine months after the end of an accounting date and in some cases even before the accounting period ended. The nine-month rule is also to be applied to these cases after a phasing in period.

Sched. 6 contains provisions dealing with the transitional arrangements applying to the introduction of the changes made.

Close companies: meaning of "associate"

37.—(1) In subsection (3) of section 303 of the Taxes Act (close companies: meaning of "associate")—

(a) in paragraph (c) for the words "any other person interested therein" there shall be substituted—

"(i) the trustee or trustees of the settlement concerned or, as the case may be, the personal representatives of the deceased, and

(ii) if the participator is a company, any other company interested in those shares or obligations"; and

(b) the proviso shall be omitted.

(2) In determining whether, by virtue of paragraph 9 of Schedule 1 to the Finance Act 1974, interest on a loan is eligible for relief under section 75 of the Finance Act 1972, the amendments made by subsection (1) above shall have effect with respect to loans made after 13th November 1986.

(3) Subject to subsection (2) above, the amendments made by subsection (1) above shall be deemed to have come into force on 6th April 1986.

GENERAL NOTE

This section limits the definition of "associate" in s.303(3) of the Taxes Act. Previously if a participator was interested in any shares in a company subject to a trust or which were part of the estate of a deceased person any other person interested in those shares, whether as trustee, personal representative or beneficiary was an associate. The amended definition has the effect that only trustees or personal representatives will be "associates" in such circumstances and not other beneficiaries. Whereas previously individuals interested in trusts relating exclusively to exempt approved schemes or for the benefit of employees and dependents could not be associates, this is no longer the case. Similarly charitable trusts can no longer be disregarded.

Unit trusts and investment companies

Authorised unit trusts

38.—(1) For section 354 of the Taxes Act there shall be substituted—

"**Authorised unit trusts**

354.—(1) In respect of income arising to the trustees of an author-ised unit trust, and for the purposes of the provisions relating to relief for capital expenditure, the Tax Acts shall have effect as if—

(a) the trustees were a company resident in the United Kingdom, and

(b) the rights of the unit holders were shares in the company.

(2) The Tax Acts shall also have effect as if the aggregate amount shown in the accounts of the trust as income available for payment to unit holders or for investment were dividends on the shares referred to in subsection (1) above paid to them in proportion to their rights, the date of payment, in the case of income not paid to unit holders, being taken to be—

(a) the date or latest date provided by the terms of the authorised unit trust for any distribution in respect of the distribution period in question;

(b) if no date is so provided, the last day of the distribution period.

(3) References in the Corporation Tax Acts to a body corporate shall be construed in accordance with the preceding provisions of this section, and section 242 of this Act shall apply with any necessary modifications.

(4) Section 304 of this Act shall apply in relation to an authorised unit trust whether or not it falls within the definition of "investment company" in subsection (5) of that section; and sums periodically appropriated for managers' remuneration shall be treated for the purposes of that section as sums disbursed as expenses of management.

(5) In this section 'distribution period' means a period over which income from the investments subject to the trusts is aggregated for the purposes of ascertaining the amount available for distribution to unit holders.".

(2) This section shall have effect in relation to distribution periods (within the meaning of section 354 of the Taxes Act) beginning on or after 1st April 1987.

GENERAL NOTE

This and the following two sections contain modifications to the tax rules applicable to unit trusts to take account of the changes in the law made by the Financial Services Act 1986. The basic position of these bodies remains constant.

This section applies to authorised unit trusts and takes account of their new found ability to invest in a wider range of securities than previously. Under the original s.354 a unit trust, in order to qualify as an authorised unit trust had to have a business consisting "mainly in the making of investments and the principal part of whose income is derived therefrom." This requirement no longer exists.

Authorised unit trusts are treated for tax purposes in the following way:

(i)   the trustees are regarded now as a company resident in the U.K. (previously as an investment company);

(ii) the unit holders as shareholders;

(iii) income distributable by the trustees as dividends on shares.

Other unit trusts

39.—(1) After section 354 of the Taxes Act there shall be inserted—

"**Other unit trusts**

354A.—(1) This section applies to—

(a) any unit trust scheme that is not an authorised unit trust, and

(b) any authorised unit trust to which, by virtue of section 60 of the Finance Act 1980, section 354 of this Act does not apply,

except where the trustees of the scheme are not resident in the United Kingdom.

(2) Income arising to the trustees of the scheme shall be regarded for the purposes of the Tax Acts as income of the trustees (and not as income of the unit holders); and the trustees (and not the unit holders) shall be regarded as the persons to or on whom allowances or charges are to be made under the provisions of those Acts relating to relief for capital expenditure.

(3) For the purposes of the Tax Acts the unit holders shall be treated as receiving annual payments (made by the trustees under deduction of tax) in proportion to their rights.

(4) The total amount of those annual payments in respect of any distribution period shall be the amount which, after deducting income tax at the basic rate in force for the year of assessment in which the payments are treated as made, is equal to the aggregate amount shown in the accounts of the scheme as income available for payment to unit holders or for investment.

(5) The date on which the annual payments are treated as made shall be the date or latest date provided by the terms of the scheme for any distribution in respect of the distribution period in question, except that, if—

(a) the date so provided is more than twelve months after the end of the period, or

(b) no date is so provided,

the date on which the payments are treated as made shall be the last day of the period.

(6) In this section 'distribution period' has the same meaning as in section 354 of this Act, but—

(a) if the scheme does not make provision for distribution periods, then for the purposes of this section its distribution periods shall be taken to be successive periods of twelve months, the first of which began with the day on which the scheme took effect, and

(b) if the scheme makes provision for distribution periods of more than twelve months, then for the purposes of this section each of those periods shall be taken to be divided into two (or more) distribution periods, the second succeeding the first after twelve months (and so on for any further periods).

(7) In this section 'unit trust scheme' has the same meaning as in the Financial Services Act 1986, except that the Treasury may by regulations provide that any scheme of a description specified in the regulations shall be treated as not being a unit trust scheme for the purposes of this section.

(8) Regulations under this section—

(a) may contain such supplementary and transitional provisions as appear to the Treasury to be necessary or expedient, and

(b) shall be made by statutory instrument, which shall be subject to annulment in pursuance of a resolution of the House of Commons.

(9) Sections 16 and 17 of the Finance Act 1973 (which make provision for charging tax at the additional rate on certain trust income) shall not apply to a scheme to which this section applies.

(10) Paragraph 8(1) of Schedule 23 to the Finance Act 1985 (which charges tax at the additional rate on certain sums treated as received by trustees in respect of accrued interest) shall not apply in relation to profits or gains treated as received by the trustees of a scheme to

which this section applies if or to the extent that those profits or gains represent accruals of interest (within the meaning of Chapter IV of Part II of that Act) which are treated as income in the accounts of the scheme.".

(2) This section shall have effect in relation to distribution periods (within the meaning of section 354A of the Taxes Act) beginning on or after 6th April 1987.

GENERAL NOTE

This section introduces a new framework to govern the position of:
  (i) unauthorised unit trusts
  (ii) authorised unit trusts which can only invest in such a way that any income arising will only be chargeable under Schedule C as profits from U.K. public revenue dividends and Case III of Schedule D (*i.e.* gilts and fixed interest investments).

It is possible for certain unit trusts to be excluded from the operation of the tax rules. This will be governed by regulations to be issued.

The tax position of unit trusts within this framework is:
  (i) any income arising is regarded as the trustees' income and any capital allowances or charges under the Capital Allowances Act 1968 are to be made to or on the trustees;
  (ii) the trustees will not be subject to the charge to additional rate tax under F.A. 1973, ss.16 and 17, nor will the charge to additional rate tax applicable to accrued interest schemes cover such unit trusts;
  (iii) the unit holders will be treated as receiving annual payments in proportion to their rights.

Unit trusts: miscellaneous amendments

40.—(1) For section 358 of the Taxes Act there shall be substituted—

"Definitions: unit trusts
358. In this Act—
  'authorised unit trust' means, as respects an accounting period, a unit trust scheme in the case of which an order under section 78 of the Financial Services Act 1986 is in force during the whole or part of the accounting period;
  'unit holder' means a person entitled to a share of the investments subject to the trusts of a unit trust scheme;
  'unit trust scheme' has the same meaning as in section 354A of this Act.".

(2) In section 526(5) of the Taxes Act the following definitions shall be inserted at the appropriate places in alphabetical order—
  "'authorised unit trust' has the meaning given by section 358 of this Act";
  "'unit holder', in relation to a unit trust scheme, has the meaning given by section 358 of this Act";
  "'unit trust scheme' has the same meaning as in section 354A of this Act".

(3) In section 92 of the Capital Gains Tax Act 1979, for the words from the beginning of the section to the end of paragraph (a) there shall be substituted—
  "(1) Subject to subsection (2) below, in this Act—
    (a) 'unit trust scheme' has the same meaning as in the Financial Services Act 1986".

(4) At the end of section 92 of the Capital Gains Tax Act 1979 there shall be added—
  "(2) The Treasury may by regulations provide that any scheme of a description specified in the regulations shall be treated as not being a unit trust scheme for the purposes of this Act.
  (3) Regulations under this section—

     (a) may contain such supplementary and transitional provisions as appear to the Treasury to be necessary or expedient, and

     (b) shall be made by statutory instrument, which shall be subject to annulment in pursuance of a resolution of the House of Commons.".

(5) This section, and the repeals effected by section 72 below and Part VI of Schedule 16 to this Act, shall come into force on such day as the Board may by order appoint; and different days may be appointed for different purposes.

(6) An order under subsection (5) above—

     (a) may contain such transitional provisions as appear to the Board to be necessary or expedient, and

     (b) shall be made by statutory instrument.

Investment companies, etc.

41.—(1) In section 304(1) of the Taxes Act, for the words "income for the purposes of Schedule A" there shall be substituted the words "profits apart from this section".

(2) This section shall have effect in relation to sums disbursed on or after 1st April 1987.

GENERAL NOTE

S.304 of the Taxes Act permits the expenses of management of an investment company to be deducted in computing profits save where such expenses are deductible in computing Schedule A income. This section amends s.304(1) to preclude the deduction where the expenses are allowable other than under the section itself in computing any form of profits.

This change applies to sums disbursed after March 31, 1987.

Business expansion scheme

Carry-back of relief

42.—(1) In paragraph 2 of Schedule 5 to the Finance Act 1983, at the beginning of sub-paragraph (3) (which provides that relief is to be given as a deduction from income for the year in which the relevant shares are issued) there shall be inserted the words "Subject to sub-paragraph (4A) below"; and after sub-paragraph (4) there shall be inserted—

     "(4A) If—

       (a) the shares are issued before 6th October in a year of assessment, and

       (b) the claimant so requests in his claim for relief,

the relief shall be given partly by way of deduction from the claimant's total income for the year of assessment in which the shares are issued and partly by way of deduction from his total income for the preceding year of assessment.

     (4B) A deduction from the claimant's total income for the year of assessment preceding that in which the shares are issued shall be of such amount as may be specified in the claim, but—

       (a) that amount shall not exceed one half of the total relief in respect of the shares, and

       (b) the aggregate of that amount and the amounts of any other deductions made by virtue of sub-paragraph (4A) above from the claimant's total income for the year of assessment preceding that in which the shares are issued shall not exceed £5,000.".

(2) For sub-paragraph (9) of paragraph 2 of that Schedule there shall be substituted—

"(9) Section 52(7) of Chapter II shall apply, but with the deletion of the reference to section 204(3) of the Taxes Act (pay as you earn).

(10) Where effect is given to a claim for relief by repayment of tax, section 47 of the Finance (No. 2) Act 1975 (repayment supplement) shall have effect in relation to the repayment as if the time from which the twelve months mentioned in subsections (1)(a) and (4)(a) of that section are to be calculated were the end of the year of assessment in which the shares are issued or, if the period mentioned in sub-paragraph (4)(a) above ends in a later year, the end of that later year.".

(3) For sub-paragraph (2) of paragraph 3 of that Schedule there shall be substituted—

"(2) No more than £40,000 may be deducted by way of relief under paragraph 2 above from the total income of an individual for a year of assessment.".

(4) In paragraph 12 of that Schedule, after sub-paragraph (2) there shall be added—

"(3) Section 60(4) and (5) of Chapter II shall apply in relation to the limit of £5,000 imposed by paragraph 2(4B) above as it applies in relation to the limit of £40,000 imposed by paragraph 3(2) above; and for this purpose the reference in section 60(5) to a division in proportion to the amounts subscribed by the husband and the wife shall be construed as a reference to a division in proportion to the aggregate amounts of the relevant deductions sought by each of them in their claims under paragraph 2(4A) above.".

(5) In paragraph 14 of that Schedule, after sub-paragraph (1) there shall be inserted—

"(1A) Where by virtue of paragraph 2(4A) above relief has been given for each of two consecutive years of assessment, any withdrawal of relief shall be made for the first of those years before being made for the second.".

(6) This section shall have effect in relation to shares issued on or after 6th April 1987.

GENERAL NOTE

This section provides for a carryback of BES relief in respect of shares issued before October 6 in a year. The carryback is to the immediately preceding year of assessment but is subject to a limit of one half of the total relief in respect of the shares purchased. In addition the carryback for all BES investments cannot exceed £5,000.

The limit of £5,000 applies to spouses jointly if they are living together and the husband is assessed on the wife's income. If an election for separate assessment has been made then the limit is divided between them in proportion to the amounts claimed to be carried back by them.

Films

43.—(1) In paragraph 6 of Schedule 5 to the Finance Act 1983 (qualifying trades), for paragraphs (a) and (b) of sub-paragraph (2A) there shall be substituted—

"(a) the company carrying on the trade is engaged throughout the relevant period in—
  (i) the production of films, or
  (ii) the production of films and the distribution of films produced by it in the relevant period; and
(b) all royalties and licence fees received by it in that period are in respect of films produced by it in that period or sound recordings in relation to such films or other products arising from such films.".

(2) This section shall have effect in relation to shares issued on or after 17th March 1987.

GENERAL NOTE
Previously a film production company in order to qualify for BES investment was required to operate as such for an entire three-year period. In future it will be sufficient if for part of the period it merely distributes films made by it earlier in that period.

Oil industry: advance corporation tax

Limited right to carry back surrendered ACT

44.—(1) In any case where,—
  (a) on a date not earlier than 17th March 1987, a company which is the surrendering company for the purposes of section 92 of the Finance Act 1972 (setting of company's advance corporation tax against subsidiary's liability) paid a dividend, and
  (b) at no time in the accounting period of the surrendering company in which that dividend was paid was the surrendering company under the control of a company resident in the United Kingdom (construing "control" in accordance with section 302 of the Taxes Act), and
  (c) under subsection (1) of the said section 92 the benefit of the advance corporation tax (in this section referred to as "ACT") paid in respect of that dividend was surrendered to a subsidiary of the surrendering company, and
  (d) that ACT is not such that the restriction in paragraph (a) or paragraph (b) of subsection (2) of section 16 of the Oil Taxation Act 1975 (ACT on distributions to associated companies etc.) applies with respect to it, and
  (e) in one or more of the accounting periods of the subsidiary beginning in the six years preceding the accounting period in which falls the date referred to in paragraph (a) above, the subsidiary has a liability to corporation tax in respect of income which consists of or includes income arising from oil extraction activities or oil rights, within the meaning of Part II of the Oil Taxation Act 1975 (in this section referred to as "ring fence income"),
sections 85 and 92 of the Finance Act 1972 shall have effect subject to subsections (3) to (7) below.
  (2) Where the conditions in subsection (1) above are fulfilled, the subsidiary to which the benefit of the ACT is surrendered is in the following provisions of this section referred to as a "qualifying subsidiary"; and in those provisions—
  (a) "section 85" means section 85 of the Finance Act 1972 (payments of ACT to be set against company's liability to corporation tax on its profits) and "section 92" means section 92 of that Act;
  (b) "the surrendering company" has the same meaning as in section 92;
  (c) "surrendered ACT" means ACT which, by virtue of subsection (2) of section 92, a qualifying subsidiary is treated as having paid in respect of a distribution made on a particular date; and
  (d) "the principal accounting period" means the accounting period of the qualifying subsidiary in which that date falls.
  (3) So much of subsection (3A) of section 92 as would prevent surrendered ACT being set against a qualifying subsidiary's liability to corporation tax under subsection (3) of section 85 (carry back to earlier periods) shall not apply; but the said subsection (3) shall have effect subject to the following provisions of this section.
  (4) Surrendered ACT may not under subsection (3) of section 85 be set against a qualifying subsidiary's liability to corporation tax for an account-

ing period earlier than the principal accounting period unless throughout—

(a) that period,

(b) the principal accounting period, and

(c) any intervening accounting period,

the qualifying subsidiary was carrying on activities which, under and for the purposes specified in section 13 of the Oil Taxation Act 1975, constitute a separate trade (oil extraction activities etc.).

(5) Subject to subsection (6) below, for each accounting period of the surrendering company in which is paid a dividend, the ACT on which gives rise, under section 92, to surrendered ACT, the total amount of that surrendered ACT in respect of which claims may be made under subsection (3) of section 85 (whether by one qualifying subsidiary of the surrendering company or by two or more taken together) shall not exceed whichever of the following limits is appropriate to the accounting period of the surrendering company—

(a) for periods ending on or after 17th March 1987 and before 1st April 1989, £10 million;

(b) for periods ending on or after 1st April 1989 and before 1st April 1991, £15 million;

(c) for later periods, £20 million.

(6) In any case where an accounting period of the surrendering company is less than twelve months, the amount which is appropriate to it under paragraphs (a) to (c) of subsection (5) above shall be proportionately reduced.

(7) The amount of surrendered ACT of the principal accounting period which, on a claim under subsection (3) of section 85, may be treated as if it were ACT paid in respect of distributions made by the qualifying subsidiary concerned in any earlier accounting period shall not exceed the amount of ACT that would have been payable in respect of a distribution made at the end of that earlier period of an amount which, together with the ACT so payable in respect of it, would equal the qualifying subsidiary's ring fence income of that period.

(8) In determining the amount (if any) of ACT which may be repayable—

(a) under section 17(3) of the Oil Taxation Act 1975, or

(b) under section 127(5) of the Finance Act 1981,

any ACT in respect of a distribution actually made on or after 17th March 1987 shall be left out of account.

GENERAL NOTE

The normal rule is that a subsidiary company to whom ACT is surrendered cannot carry back that ACT to set against corporation tax on earlier accounting periods, as is possible as regards the company which itself pays the ACT. This section allows a carryback in the case of companies with oil extraction activities in the U.K. or on the U.K. continental shelf. The carry back is subject to the monetary limits specified in subs. (5) and only permits a set-off against the ring fence liability to corporation tax of the subsidiary in the previous six years.

Surrender of ACT where oil extraction company etc. owned by a consortium

45.—(1) In any case where—

(a) a company (in this section referred to as "the consortium company") is owned by a consortium consisting of two members only, each of which owns 50 per cent. of the issued share capital of the company, and

(b) the consortium company carries on a trade consisting of or including activities falling within paragraphs (a) to (c) of subsection (1) of section 13 of the Oil Taxation Act 1975 (oil extraction etc.), and

(c) all of the issued share capital of the consortium company is of the same class and carries the same rights as to voting, dividends and distribution of assets on a winding up,

section 92 of the Finance Act 1972 (setting of company's advance corporation tax against subsidiary's liability) shall have effect, subject to the following provisions of this section, as if the company were a subsidiary of each member of the consortium.

(2) This section has effect with respect to advance corporation tax paid by either member of the consortium in respect of a dividend paid by it on or after 17th March 1987; and, in relation to a surrender under the said section 92 of the benefit of the advance corporation tax paid in respect of such a dividend,—

(a) "surrendered ACT" means advance corporation tax which, by virtue of subsection (2) of that section, the consortium company is treated as having paid; and

(b) "the notional distribution date" means the date of the distribution in respect of which the surrendered ACT is treated as paid.

(3) No surrender under subsection (1) of section 92 of the Finance Act 1972 of the benefit of advance corporation tax may be made by virtue of this section—

(a) unless the conditions in paragraphs (a) to (c) of subsection (1) above are fulfilled throughout that accounting period of the consortium company in which falls the notional distribution date; or

(b) if arrangements are in existence by virtue of which any person could cause one or more of those conditions to cease to be fulfilled at some time during that or any later accounting period.

(4) In the application of section 85 of the Finance Act 1972 (payments of ACT to be set against company's liability to corporation tax on its income) in relation to surrendered ACT resulting from a surrender by either one of the consortium members under section 92 of that Act, the reference in subsection (2) of section 85 (the limit on the amount to be set against corporation tax) to the consortium company's income charged to corporation tax shall be construed as a reference to one half of so much of that income as consists of income arising from oil extraction activities or oil rights, within the meaning of Part II of the Oil Taxation Act 1975.

(5) So much of any surplus advance corporation tax as consists of or includes surrendered ACT shall not be treated under section 85(4) of the Finance Act 1972 as if it were advance corporation tax paid in respect of distributions made by the consortium company in a later accounting period unless the conditions in paragraphs (a) to (c) of subsection (1) above are fulfilled throughout that later period.

(6) In any case where—

(a) as a result of a surrender by one of the consortium members, the consortium company is treated as paying an amount of surrendered ACT which exceeds the limit applicable under subsection (2) of section 85 of the Finance Act 1972 (as modified by subsection (4) above), and

(b) that excess falls to be treated under subsection (4) of that section as advance corporation tax paid by the consortium company in respect of distributions made in a later accounting period,

then, for the purposes of the application of subsection (2) of that section (as modified by subsection (4) above) in relation to that later accounting period, the excess of the surrendered ACT shall be treated as resulting from a surrender by that one of the consortium members referred to in paragraph (a) above.

(7) Where section 92 of the Finance Act 1972 has effect as mentioned in subsection (2) above, subsection (9) of that section shall have effect with the omission of paragraph (b) (and the word "and" immediately preceding it).

(8) Notwithstanding the provisions of subsection (1) above the consortium company shall not be regarded as a subsidiary for the purposes of section 44 above.

GENERAL NOTE

This section enables a member of a 50/50 consortium to surrender ACT to a trader owned by the consortium which has ring fence liabilities.

ACT on redeemable preference shares

46.—(1) In section 16 of the Oil Taxation Act 1975 (oil extraction activities etc.: restriction on setting advance corporation tax against profits therefrom) in subsection (2), after the words "United Kingdom" there shall be inserted "or, where subsection (2A) below applies, in respect of any distribution consisting of a dividend on a redeemable preference share".

(2) At the end of subsection (2) of the said section 16 there shall be inserted the following subsections—

"(2A) Subject to subsection (2B) below, this subsection applies in relation to the payment of a dividend on redeemable preference shares if the dividend is paid on or after 17th March 1987 and—

(a) at the time the shares are issued, or

(b) at the time the dividend is paid,

the company paying the dividend is under the control of a company resident in the United Kingdom, and in this subsection "control" shall be construed in accordance with section 302 of the Taxes Act.

(2B) Subsection (2A) above does not apply if or to the extent that it is shown that the proceeds of the issue of the redeemable preference shares—

(a) were used to meet expenditure incurred by the company issuing them in carrying on oil extraction activities or in acquiring oil rights otherwise than from a connected person; or

(b) were appropriated to meeting expenditure to be so incurred by that company;

and section 533 of the Taxes Act (connected persons) applies for the purposes of this subsection."

(3) At the end of the said section 16 there shall be added the following subsections—

"(4) For the purposes of subsections (2) to (2B) above, shares in a company are redeemable preference shares either if they are so described in the terms of their issue or if, however they are described, they fulfil the condition in paragraph (a) below and either or both of the conditions in paragraphs (b) and (c) below—

(a) that, as against other shares in the company, they carry a preferential entitlement to a dividend or to any assets in a winding up or both;

(b) that, by virtue of the terms of their issue, the exercise of a right by any person or the existence of any arrangements, they are liable to be redeemed, cancelled or repaid, in whole or in part;

(c) that, by virtue of any material arrangements, the holder has a right to require another person to acquire the shares or is obliged in any circumstances to dispose of them or another person has a right or is in any circumstances obliged to acquire them.

(5) For the purposes of paragraph (a) of subsection (4) above, shares are to be treated as carrying a preferential entitlement to a dividend as against other shares if, by virtue of any arrangements, there are circumstances in which a minimum dividend will be payable on those shares but not on others; and for the purposes of paragraph (c) of that subsection arrangements relating to shares are material arrangements if the company which issued the shares or a company associated with that company is a party to the arrangements."

GENERAL NOTE
This section is aimed at companies raising capital through an issue of preference shares, setting off losses against the resulting income and settling the ACT on the preference dividends against the corporation tax as their ring fence income, and eroding the ring fence principle. To avoid this result the section prevents ACT paid as preference share dividends paid by a company under the control of another U.K. resident company being available for offset against ring fence corporation tax under the capital raised by the issue of preference shares has been applied by the company in its ring fence activities.

CHAPTER II

CAPITAL GAINS

Retirement relief

47.—(1) In Schedule 20 to the Finance Act 1985 (relief for certain disposals associated with retirement) in paragraphs 13(1) (the amount available for relief) and 16(4)(b) (aggregation of spouse's interest in the business) for "£100,000" there shall be substituted "£125,000".

(2) Subsection (1) above has effect with respect to qualifying disposals (within the meaning of the said Schedule 20) occurring on or after 6th April 1987.

GENERAL NOTE
The maximum limit on the amount of relief available in respect of disposals connected with retirement and qualifying for relief under F.A. 1985, ss.69 to 70, is increased from £100,000 to £125,000.

PART III

STAMP DUTY AND STAMP DUTY RESERVE TAX

Stamp duty

Unit trusts

48. In section 57 of the Finance Act 1946 and in section 28 of the Finance (No. 2) Act (Northern Ireland) 1946—
   (a) for the definition in subsection (1) of "unit trust scheme" there shall be substituted—
      "'unit trust scheme' has the same meaning as in the Financial Services Act 1986 (but subject to subsection (1A) of this section)";
   (b) in the definition in subsection (1) of "trust instrument", for the words from "by virtue" to "aforesaid" there shall be substituted the words "on which the property in question is held";
   (c) after subsection (1) there shall be inserted—
      "(1A) The Treasury may by regulations provide that any scheme of a description specified in the regulations shall be treated as not being a unit trust scheme for the purposes of this Part of this Act.

(1B) Regulations under this section—
  (a) may contain such supplementary and transitional pro-
      visions as appear to the Treasury to be necessary or
      expedient, and
  (b) shall be made by statutory instrument, which shall be
      subject to annulment in pursuance of a resolution of the
      House of Commons.".

GENERAL NOTE
  The definition of "unit trust scheme" for stamp duty purposes in F.A. 1946, s.57(1) is
replaced by the rather simpler definition in Financial Services Act 1986, s.75(8), but subject
to the power of the Treasury to exclude by regulation any particular description of scheme.
For a parallel provision relating to corporation tax, see I.C.T.A. s.354A(7) and (8), as
inserted by s.39, *supra*.

Contract notes

49.—(1) Sections 77 to 79 of the Finance (1909–10) Act 1910, so far as
unrepealed, shall cease to have effect.
  (2) Subsection (1) above shall come into force on such day as the
Treasury may appoint by order made by statutory instrument.

GENERAL NOTE
  When the stamp duty on contract notes was abolished by F.A. 1985, s.86, the requirement
to issue such notes was retained. This will be covered by a code provided for in Financial
Services Act 1986, and when it comes into force the surviving requirement under the stamp
duty legislation will become unnecessary.

Warrants to purchase Government stock, etc.

50.—(1) Where an interest in, a right to an allotment of or to subscribe
for, or an option to acquire, exempt securities is transferred to or vested
in any person by any instrument, no stamp duty shall be chargeable on
the instrument by virtue of either of the following headings in Schedule
1 to the Stamp Act 1891—
  (a) "Conveyance or Transfer on Sale";
  (b) "Conveyance or Transfer of any kind not hereinbefore described".
  (2) No stamp duty under the heading "Bearer Instrument" in Schedule
1 to the Stamp Act 1891 shall be chargeable—
  (a) on the issue of an instrument which relates to such an interest,
      right or option as is mentioned in subsection (1) above, or
  (b) on the transfer of the interest, right or option constituted by, or
      transferable by means of, such an instrument.
  (3) For the purposes of this section, "exempt securities" means—
  (a) securities the transfer of which is exempt from all stamp duties,
  (b) securities constituted by or transferable by means of an instrument
      the issue of which is by virtue of section 30 of the Finance Act 1967
      or section 7 of the Finance Act (Northern Ireland) 1967 exempt
      from stamp duty under the heading "Bearer Instrument" in Sched-
      ule 1 to the Stamp Act 1891, or
  (c) securities the transfer of which is exempt by virtue of section 30 of
      the Finance Act 1967 or section 7 of the Finance Act (Northern
      Ireland) 1967 from stamp duty under that heading;
and "securities" means stock or marketable securities and includes loan
capital as defined in section 78(7) of the Finance Act 1986.
  (4) Subsection (1) above applies to any instrument executed on or after
1st August 1987.
  (5) Subsection (2) above applies—
  (a) to any instrument which falls within section 60(1) of the Finance
      Act 1963, or section 9(1)(a) of the Finance Act (Northern Ireland)
      1963, and is issued on or after 1st August 1987, and

(b) to any instrument which falls within section 60(2) of the Finance Act 1963, or section 9(1)(b) of the Finance Act (Northern Ireland) 1963, if the interest, right or option constituted by or transferable by means of it is transferred on or after 1st August 1987.

GENERAL NOTE

The exemptions from stamp duty applying to gilt-edged securities and most categories of loan stock (see F.A. 1986, s.79) are extended to options to acquire such stock.

Bearer instruments relating to stock in foreign currencies

51.—(1) With respect to the issue of instruments and the transfer of stock on or after the day on which this Act is passed, section 30 of the Finance Act 1967 (stamp duty exemption for bearer instruments relating to stock in foreign currencies) and section 7 of the Finance Act (Northern Ireland) 1967 (the equivalent provision for Northern Ireland) shall have effect subject to the amendments in subsections (2) to (4) below.

(2) In subsection (1) for the words "in the currency of a territory outside the scheduled territories" there shall be substituted "in any currency other than sterling or in any units of account defined by reference to more than one currency (whether or not including sterling)".

(3) In subsection (2) for the words from "between" to "other currencies" there shall be substituted "between sterling and one or more other currencies".

(4) Subsection (4) and, in subsection (5), the definition of "the scheduled territories" shall cease to have effect.

GENERAL NOTE

The exemption from stamp duty for bearer instruments relating to stock in foreign currencies in F.A. 1967, s.30 utilised the definition of "the scheduled territories" in Exchange Control Act 1947, Sched. 1. This statute is repealed by s.68 *infra,* and accordingly a new definition of foreign currencies is provided by subs. (2).

Clearance services

52.—(1) In section 70(6) of the Finance Act 1986 (transfer of securities to clearance system), for the word "relevant" (in each place where it occurs) there shall be substituted the words "shares, stock or other marketable".

(2) The amendments made by this section have effect in relation to instruments executed on or after 1st August 1987.

GENERAL NOTE

F.A. 1986, s.70 imposed a higher rate of duty on transfers of company shares or stock to nominee companies acting for settlement systems such as Euroclear, since successive dealings without liability to stamp duty could then take place. The amendment extends the charge to nominee companies holding any kind of marketable securities rather than exclusively those to which the charge itself applies.

Borrowing of stock by market makers

53. In section 82(6) of the Finance Act 1986, for the words "subsection (3)" there shall be substituted the words "subsection (4)".

GENERAL NOTE

The amendment corrects a slip in F.A. 1986, s.82. The provision in question relates to the power of the Treasury to substitute a different definition of "market maker" for that in F.A. 1986, s.82(4).

Shared ownership transactions

54.—(1) In section 97 of the Finance Act 1980 (which provides for certain leases to be stamped as conveyances) in subsection (3)(b)—

(a) for the words "registered under" there shall be substituted the words "within the meaning of", and

(b) for the words "Article 124" there shall be substituted the words "Part VII".

(2) Section 97 of the Finance Act 1980 and section 108(5) and (6) of the Finance Act 1981 shall apply to a lease within subsection (3) below as they apply to a lease granted by a body mentioned in section 97(3) of the Finance Act 1980.

(3) A lease is within this subsection if it is granted—

(a) by a person against whom the right to buy under Part V of the Housing Act 1985 is exercisable by virtue of section 171A of that Act (preservation of right to buy on disposal to private sector landlord), and

(b) to a person who is the qualifying person for the purposes of the preserved right to buy and in relation to whom that dwelling-house is the qualifying dwelling-house.

(4) This section applies to leases granted on or after 1st August 1987.

GENERAL NOTE

F.A. 1980, s.97, as amended and extended by F.A. 1981, s.108, applied to restrict multiple charges to stamp duty in cases of shared ownership schemes. These were developed by a number of local authorities and housing associations to allow people of limited means to acquire, say, half the equity in a dwelling coupled with a lease and option to acquire the other half. Following on amendments made by Housing and Planning Act 1986, the stamp duty relief is extended to leases granted by unregistered as well as registered housing associations and by private landlords taking over public housing estates.

Crown exemption

55.—(1) Where any conveyance, transfer or lease is made or agreed to be made to a Minister of the Crown or to the Solicitor for the affairs of Her Majesty's Treasury, no stamp duty shall be chargeable by virtue of any of the following headings in Schedule 1 to the Stamp Act 1891—

(a) "Conveyance or Transfer on Sale",

(b) "Conveyance or Transfer of any kind not hereinbefore described",

(c) "Lease or Tack",

on the instrument by which the conveyance, transfer or lease, or the agreement for it, is effected.

(2) In this section "Minister of the Crown" has the same meaning as in the Ministers of the Crown Act 1975.

(3) Article 3(6) of the Secretary of State for the Environment Order 1970 and Article 4(5) of the Secretary of State for Transport Order 1976 (which exempt transfers by, to or with those Ministers) shall cease to have effect.

(4) This section applies to instruments executed on or after 1st August 1987.

GENERAL NOTE

The exemptions from stamp duty enjoyed hitherto by the Departments of the Environment and of Transport are extended to all government departments.

Stamp duty reserve tax

Stamp duty reserve tax

56. Schedule 7 to this Act (which contains miscellaneous amendments of Part IV of the Finance Act 1986) shall have effect.

GENERAL NOTE
Stamp duty reserve tax ("S.D.R.T.") was introduced by F.A. 1986, ss.86 to 99, to underpin stamp duty by charging transactions which escaped duty because they were never evidenced in documentary transfers. Sched. 7 is generally designed to give relief by retrospectively rectifying anomalies in the S.D.R.T. code. The only other change is to advance the time of charge to S.D.R.T. on transfers of renounceable letter of allotment. See further the Note to Sched. 7.

PART IV

INHERITANCE TAX

Reduced rates of tax

57.—(1) In the Inheritance Tax Act 1984 (in this Part of this Act referred to as "the 1984 Act") section 8(1) (indexation of rate bands) shall not apply to chargeable transfers made in the year beginning 6th April 1987.

(2) For the Table in Schedule 1 to that Act there shall be substituted the Table set out below:

TABLE OF RATES OF TAX

Portion of value		Rate of tax
Lower limit £	*Upper limit* £	*Per cent.*
0	90,000	Nil
90,000	140,000	30
140,000	220,000	40
220,000	330,000	50
330,000	—	60

(3) Subsection (2) above applies to any chargeable transfer (within the meaning of the 1984 Act) made on or after 17th March 1987.

GENERAL NOTE
The threshold for inheritance tax is raised by more than 25 per cent., from £71,000 to £90,000. Above that level the rate bands are simplified, with the elimination of the 35, 45 and 55 per cent. bands. The effect is that the tax at death rates on an estate of £330,000, at which the maximum rate of 60 per cent. becomes applicable, is reduced from £118,300 to £102,000.

Securities, other business property and agricultural property

58.—(1) The 1984 Act and Schedule 20 to the Finance Act 1986 (gifts with reservation) shall have effect subject to the amendments in Schedule 8 to this Act, being amendments—

(a) making provision with respect to the treatment for the purposes of the 1984 Act of shares and securities dealt in on the Unlisted Securities Market;

(b) making other amendments of Chapter I of Part V of the 1984 Act (business property);

(c) making provision with respect to the application to certain transfers of relief under that Chapter and under Chapter II of that Part (agricultural property); and

(d) making provision with respect to the payment of tax by instalments.

(2) Subject to subsection (3) below, Schedule 8 to this Act shall have effect in relation to transfers of value made, and other events occurring, on or after 17th March 1987.

(3) The amendments of the 1984 Act made by Schedule 8 to this Act shall be disregarded in determining under section 113A(3) or section 113B(3) of the 1984 Act whether any property acquired by the transferee before 17th March 1987 would be relevant business property in relation to a notional transfer of value made on or after that date.

GENERAL NOTE
This section introduces various amendments to the provisions for business and agricultural property relief under I.H.T.A. 1984. The most important is an increase from 30 per cent. to 50 per cent. in the relief available to substantial minority shareholdings (defined as shareholdings over 25 per cent. held for at least two years) in unquoted companies. On the other hand, to reflect the growth in the unlisted securities market ("USM"), shares dealt with on the USM will be treated in the same way as shares with a full listing on the Stock Exchange. For further details of the amendment see the commentary to Sched. 8.

Maintenance funds for historic buildings, etc.

59. Schedule 9 to this Act shall have effect.

GENERAL NOTE
Sched. 9 makes two changes in relation to the regime for maintenance funds for historic buildings in I.H.T.A. 1984, s.27, and Sched. 4. See further the commentary to Sched. 9.

Acceptance in lieu: waiver of interest

60.—(1) In section 233 of the 1984 Act (interest on unpaid tax) in subsection (1), at the beginning of the words following paragraph (c) there shall be inserted the words "then, subject to subsection (1A) below".

(2) After subsection (1) of that section there shall be inserted the following subsection—

"(1A) If, under section 230 above, the Board agree to accept property in satisfaction of any tax on terms that the value to be attributed to the property for the purposes of that acceptance is determined as at a date earlier than that on which the property is actually accepted, the terms may provide that the amount of tax which is satisfied by the acceptance of the property shall not carry interest under this section from that date."

(3) This section applies in any case where the acceptance referred to in section 230 of the 1984 Act occurs on or after 17th March 1987.

GENERAL NOTE
Where heritage property is offered in lieu of I.H.T., interest continues to run until the offer is accepted by the authorities and the property is valued as at the date of acceptance. Now, at the offeror's option, the value of the property can be determined as at the date of offer, and interest will cease to run from that date.

PART V

OIL TAXATION

Nomination of disposals and appropriations

61.—(1) The provisions of Schedule 10 to this Act shall have effect, being provisions for and in connection with the establishment of a scheme of nominations by participators in oil fields of certain proposed sales, supplies and appropriations of oil.

(2) Nothing in this section or Schedule 10 to this Act applies—

(a) to oil which is gaseous at a temperature of 15 degrees centigrade and pressure of one atmosphere; or

(b) to oil of a kind which is normally disposed of crude by deliveries in quantities of 25,000 metric tonnes or less; or

(c) to oil which is excluded from this section by regulations under subsection (8) below;

and references to oil in this section and Schedule 10 to this Act shall be construed accordingly.

(3) As respects each participator in an oil field, it shall be determined, for each calendar month in a chargeable period beginning with the month of March 1987, whether his aggregate nominated proceeds, as defined in Schedule 10 to this Act, exceed the proceeds of his disposals and appropriations in that month, as defined in subsection (6) below and, if they do, that excess shall be brought into account in accordance with subsection (5) below.

(4) For each chargeable period of an oil field, "the excess of nominated proceeds for the period", in relation to a participator in that field, means the sum of the excess (if any) of each of the months in that chargeable period, as determined in his case under subsection (3) above.

(5) In subsection (5) of section 2 of the principal Act (amounts to be taken into account in determining whether a gross profit or loss accrues to a participator in any chargeable period) at the end of paragraph (d) there shall be added "and

(e) the excess of the nominated proceeds for that period, as defined in section 61 of the Finance Act 1987".

(6) In relation to any calendar month, the proceeds of a participator's disposals and appropriations from an oil field means the total of—

(a) the price received or receivable for so much of any oil forming part of his equity production from the field in that month as was disposed of by him crude in sales at arm's length; and

(b) the market value, ascertained in accordance with Schedule 3 to the principal Act, of the rest of his equity production from the field in that month;

and in this subsection any reference to a participator's equity production from an oil field in any month shall be construed in accordance with paragraph 1(2) of Schedule 10 to this Act.

(7) The Treasury may by regulations made by statutory instrument make provision for any purpose for which regulations described as "Treasury regulations" may be made under Schedule 10 to this Act.

(8) The Board may by regulations made by statutory instrument make provision, including provision having effect with respect to things done on or after 9th February 1987,—

(a) as to oil which is excluded from this section, as mentioned in subsection (2) above; and

(b) for any purpose for which regulations, other than those described as "Treasury regulations", may be made under Schedule 10 to this Act;

and regulations made by virtue of paragraph (a) above may amend paragraphs (a) and (b) of subsection (2) above.

(9) A statutory instrument made in the exercise of the power conferred by subsection (7) or subsection (8) above shall be subject to annulment in pursuance of a resolution of the Commons House of Parliament.

GENERAL NOTE

This section, together with Sched. 10, provides for the establishment and operation of a crude oil nomination scheme for petroleum revenue tax ("P.R.T."). The existing system had become unsatisfactory as a result of developments in the oil market which enabled participators to pick and choose with hindsight which of a range of contracts and prices should form the basis of their P.R.T. liabilities. Under the new scheme, a participator in an oilfield may nominate proposed sales at arm's length of crude oil that he has produced himself and proposed appropriations or transfers of such oil to associates for refining purposes. Where such a nomination is made, and the deal actually transacted as nominated, the price taken for P.R.T. will be as under the present rules. The details of the scheme are set out in Sched. 10.

Subss. (3) to (6) provide that where the proceeds of nominated disposals as determined under Sched. 10 exceed the proceeds of actual disposals during any month, the excess is taken into account in determining the participator's gross profit under Oil Taxation Act 1975, s.2(5).

Subss. (7) to (9) provide for regulations to be made on various matters by the Treasury and the Inland Revenue, subject to annulment by the House of Commons.

Market value of oil to be determined on a monthly basis

62.—(1) In the following provisions of the principal Act (which refer to the market value of oil at the material time in a particular calendar month) the words "at the material time" shall be omitted—

(a) in section 2 (assessable profits and allowable losses), in subsection (9), paragraphs (a)(i) and (a)(ii);

(b) in section 5A (allowance of exploration and appraisal expenditure), subsection (5B);

(c) in section 14 (valuation of oil disposed of or appropriated in certain circumstances), subsections (4) and (4A)(b); and

(d) in paragraph 2 of Schedule 2 (returns by participators), sub-paragraphs (2)(a)(iii) and (2)(b)(ii).

(2) In the following provisions of the principal Act (which refer to the market value of stocks of oil at the end of a chargeable period) for the words "at the end" there shall be substituted "in the last calendar month"—

(a) section 2(4)(b);

(b) section 2(5)(d); and

(c) in Schedule 2, paragraph 2(2)(d)(ii);

and in the provisions specified in paragraphs (a) and (b) above for the word "then" there shall be substituted "at the end of that period".

(3) In Schedule 3 to the principal Act (miscellaneous provisions relating to petroleum revenue tax) paragraphs 2, 2A and 3 (market value of oil) shall be amended in accordance with Part I of Schedule 11 to this Act; and the consequential amendments of the principal Act in Part II of that Schedule shall have effect.

(4) A participator in an oil field who is required by paragraph 2 of Schedule 2 to the principal Act to deliver to the Board a return for a chargeable period shall, not later than the end of the second month after the end of that period, deliver to the Board an additional return of all relevant sales of oil (as defined in subsection (6) below) stating—

(a) the date of the contract of sale;

(b) the name of the seller;

(c) the name of the buyer;

(d) the quantity of oil actually sold and, if it is different, the quantity of oil contracted to be sold;

(e) the price receivable for that oil;

(f) the date which, under the contract, was the date or, as the case may be, the latest date for delivery of the oil and the date on which the oil was actually delivered; and

(g) such other particulars as the Board may prescribe.

(5) Where two or more companies which are participators in the same oil field are members of the same group of companies, within the meaning of section 258 of the Taxes Act, a return made for the purposes of subsection (4) above by one of them and expressed also to be made on

behalf of the other or others shall be treated for the purposes of this section as a return made by each of them.

(6) For the purposes of the return required by subsection (4) above from a participator in an oil field, a relevant sale of oil is a contract for the sale of oil to which the participator or any company which is resident in the United Kingdom and associated with the participator for the purposes of section 115(2) of the Finance Act 1984 is a party (as seller, buyer or otherwise), being a sale of oil—

    (a) for delivery at any time during the chargeable period referred to in subsection (4) above; and

    (b) details of which are not included in the return made for the period under paragraph 2 of Schedule 2 to the principal Act (by virtue of sub-paragraph (3A) thereof); and

    (c) which is for the delivery of at least 500 metric tonnes of oil; and

    (d) which is not a contract for the sale of oil consisting of gas of which the largest component by volume over the chargeable period concerned is methane or ethane or a combination of those gases.

(7) A return under subsection (4) above shall be in such form as the Board may prescribe and shall include a declaration that the return is correct and complete; and if a participator fails to deliver a return under that subsection he shall be liable—

    (a) to a penalty not exceeding £500; and

    (b) if the failure continues after it has been declared by the court or the Commissioners before whom proceedings for the penalty have been commenced, to a further penalty not exceeding £100 for each day on which the failure so continues;

except that a participator shall not be liable to a penalty under this subsection if the failure is remedied before proceedings for the recovery of the penalty are commenced.

(8) Where a participator fraudulently or negligently delivers an incorrect return under subsection (4) above, he shall be liable to a penalty not exceeding £2,500 or, in the case of fraud, £5,000.

(9) This section has effect with respect to chargeable periods ending after 31st December 1986.

GENERAL NOTE

When oil or gas is disposed of other than by way of a sale at arm's length P.R.T. is charged on the market value of that oil or gas, in accordance with the valuation rules in Oil Taxation Act 1975, Sched. 3. These rules in some respects fail to reflect the market conditions which prevail today. Under the amendments to the rules made by this section and Sched. 11, such oil will continue to be valued on a monthly basis, but this value will be calculated by reference to an evidential base consisting primarily of prices obtained in arm's length sales of oil of the same kind made by participators and their associates. The time-frame of the deals to be taken into account includes all contracts for delivery in the valuation month which had been made in the period starting on the first day of the month preceding delivery and ending on the middle day of the month of delivery. To guard against this rule itself becoming out of line with market practice, this time-frame may be changed in future by Treasury order.

Blends of oil from two or more fields

63.—(1) If, at any time prior to its disposal or relevant appropriation, oil won from an oil field is mixed with oil won from another oil field, the provisions of this section shall have effect to determine what is the share of a participator in one of those fields of the oil won from that field in any chargeable period ending after 1st January 1987; and in the following provisions of this section—

    (a) "blended oil" means oil which has been so mixed; and

    (b) "the originating fields" means the oil fields from which the blended oil is derived.

(2) If, for the purposes of commerce, blended oil is allocated to the participators in the originating fields in accordance with an agreed method, then, subject to the following provisions of this section, for the purposes of the oil taxation legislation, the blended oil which, in accordance with that method, is allocated to a participator in one of the originating fields in respect of any chargeable period shall be taken to be that participator's share of the oil won from that field in that period.

(3) With respect to any blended oil, each of the participators in the originating fields (either jointly or individually) shall, not later than 1st August 1987 or, if it is later, not later than thirty days after the date on which the first allocation is made in accordance with a particular method falling within subsection (2) above, furnish to the Board for the purposes of this section such details as may be prescribed with respect to that method and to the blended oil concerned; and if any participator fails to comply with this subsection he shall be liable—

  (a) to a penalty not exceeding £500; and

  (b) if the failure continues after it has been declared by the court or the Commissioners before whom proceedings for the penalty have been commenced, to a further penalty not exceeding £100 for each day on which the failure so continues;

except that a participator shall not be liable to a penalty under this subsection if the failure is remedied before proceedings for the recovery of the penalty are commenced.

(4) Where a participator in an oil field fraudulently or negligently furnishes any incorrect details for the purposes of this section, he shall be liable to a penalty not exceeding £2,500 or, in the case of fraud, £5,000.

(5) If, at any time after details with respect to a method of allocation have been furnished to the Board in accordance with subsection (3) above,—

  (a) that method is in any respect changed, or

  (b) there is a material change of any kind in the quantity or quality of any of the oil which makes up the blended oil,

any allocation made after that change shall be taken to be made in accordance with a new method of allocation.

(6) The provisions of Schedule 12 to this Act shall have effect for supplementing this section.

(7) In this section—

  (a) "the oil taxation legislation" means Part I of the principal Act and any enactment construed as one with that Part; and

  (b) "prescribed" means prescribed by the Board, whether before or after the passing of this Act.

GENERAL NOTE

    Under Sched. 10, para. 12 *infra*, a participator in two or more fields may nominate blended oil for the purposes of the system set up by s.61 and Sched. 10. This section, supplemented by Sched. 12, provides for the allocation of such oil to participators and reporting of such allocation to the Revenue.

Relief for research expenditure

    64.—(1) The section set out in Part I of Schedule 13 to this Act shall be inserted in the principal Act after section 5A for the purpose of setting up a new allowance by virtue of which a participator in an oil field may obtain relief for certain research expenditure which is incurred otherwise than in connection with that field.

    (2) For the purpose of giving effect to, and in consequence of, the new allowance, the enactments specified in Part II of Schedule 13 to this Act shall have effect subject to the amendments there specified.

(3) Part III of Schedule 13 to this Act shall have effect with respect to sums falling to be set off against expenditure which would otherwise be allowable under the new section set out in Part I of that Schedule.

GENERAL NOTE
The North Sea oil industry had been hard hit by the oil price collapse in 1986. The Advance Petroleum Revenue Tax Act 1986 brought forward the repayment of over £300m. of A.P.R.T. This section, together with s.65 and Scheds. 13 and 14, introduces two further reliefs which are expected in due course to benefit the industry by over £100m. a year. The provisions of this section and Sched. 13 bring the scope of P.R.T. relief for research expenditure more closely into line with that for corporation tax. It is designed to encourage general research into ways of reducing the cost of developments, and so make it more likely that new projects will be undertaken.

Cross-field allowance of certain expenditure incurred on new fields

65.—(1) Where an election is made by a participator in an oil field (in this section referred to as "the receiving field"), up to 10 per cent. of certain expenditure incurred on or after 17th March 1987 in connection with another field, being a field which is for the purposes of this section a relevant new field, shall be allowable in accordance with this section in respect of the receiving field; and in the following provisions of this section the relevant new field in connection with which the expenditure was incurred is referred to as "the field of origin".

(2) An election under this section may be made only in respect of expenditure which—

(a) was incurred by the participator making the election or, if that participator is a body corporate, by an associated company; and

(b) as regards the field of origin, is allowable under section 3 or section 4 of the principal Act or section 3 of the Oil Taxation Act 1983; and

(c) as regards the field of origin, has been allowed as qualifying for supplement under section 2(9)(b)(ii) or (c)(ii) of the principal Act (in the following provisions of this section referred to as "supplement"); and

(d) is not expenditure falling within subsection (1) of section 5A of the principal Act (allowance of exploration and appraisal expenditure);

and Part I of Schedule 14 to this Act shall have effect with respect to elections under this section.

(3) A participator may not make an election under this section in respect of expenditure which was incurred before the date which is his qualifying date, within the meaning of section 113 of the Finance Act 1984 (restriction of PRT reliefs), in relation to the receiving field unless that date falls before the end of the first chargeable period in relation to that field.

(4) Where, by virtue of an election by a participator under this section, an amount of expenditure is allowable in respect of the receiving field, it shall be allowable as follows—

(a) it shall be taken into account in that assessment to tax or determination relating to a chargeable period of the receiving field which is specified in Part II of Schedule 14 to this Act; and

(b) it shall be so taken into account under subsection (8) of section 2 of the principal Act (allowable expenditure etc.) as if, for the chargeable period in question, it were an addition to the sum mentioned in paragraph (a) of that subsection; and

(c) it shall be excluded in determining for the purposes of section 111(2) of the Finance Act 1981 (restriction of expenditure supplement) whether any, and if so what, assessable profit or allowable loss accrues to the participator in any chargeable period of the receiving field.

(5) Where, by virtue of an election by a participator under this section, an amount of expenditure is allowable in respect of the receiving field, that amount shall be disregarded in determining, as regards the field of origin, the amounts referred to (in relation to the participator or the associated company, as the case may be) in paragraph (b) or paragraph (c) of subsection (9) of section 2 of the principal Act (allowable expenditure and supplement thereon).

(6) In Schedule 14 to this Act—

(a) Part III has effect to determine for the purposes of this section what is a relevant new field and who is an associated company of a participator making an election;

(b) Part IV contains provisions supplemental to and consequential upon the allowance of expenditure by virtue of an election under this section, including provisions applicable where a notice of variation is served in respect of expenditure which is already the subject of such an election;

(c) "the receiving field" and "the field of origin" have the meaning assigned by subsection (1) above;

(d) "the principal section" means this section;

(e) "election" means an election under this section; and

(f) "supplement" has the meaning assigned by subsection (2)(c) above.

GENERAL NOTE

The relief introduced by this section and Sched. 14 widens the scope for recovering expenditure on a new oil field. Normally such expenditure can be claimed against the P.R.T. liability only for that field itself. A participator will now be able to elect to set off up to 10 per cent. of his qualifying expenditure incurred after March 16, 1987, in developing a new offshore field outside the Southern Basin immediately against his P.R.T. liabilities in another field. Qualifying expenditure is broadly expenditure agreed as qualifying for supplement in the field for which it was incurred under Oil Taxation Act 1975. The relief will improve the post-tax economics of new developments and so encourage companies to proceed with projects which might otherwise be delayed.

Oil allowance: adjustment for final periods

66.—(1) For the purposes of this section—

(a) "the final allocation period", in relation to an oil field, means the chargeable period of that field in which section 8(6)(b) of the principal Act applies (the earliest chargeable period in which oil allowance is subject to "the necessary restriction" in order to confine it within the overall maximum); and

(b) "the penultimate period", in relation to an oil field, means the chargeable period of that field which immediately precedes the final allocation period;

and any reference in this section to the two final periods is a reference to the final allocation period and the penultimate period.

(2) The following provisions of this section apply if the responsible person gives notice to the Board (in this section referred to as an "apportionment notice") specifying the manner in which the oil allowance for the field is to be apportioned between the participators in each of the two final periods, being a manner designed—

(a) to produce, so far as practicable, the result specified in subsection (4) below, being a result which, in the circumstances of the case, could not be achieved under section 8(6)(b) of the principal Act; and

   (b) to secure that adjustments in a participator's share of the oil allowance are made in the final allocation period in preference to the penultimate period.

(3) An apportionment notice shall be of no effect unless—

   (a) it is given not later than six months after the expiry of the final allocation period; and

   (b) not later than the date of the notice the responsible person notifies the Board in accordance with paragraph (b) of subsection (6) of section 8 of the principal Act of the manner in which the necessary restriction, as defined in that subsection, is to be apportioned between the participators; and

   (c) it specifies a period for each of paragraphs (a) and (b) of subsection (4) below; and

   (d) it contains such information as the Board may prescribe for the purpose of showing how, or to what extent, the apportionment of the oil allowance achieves the result specified in subsection (4) below.

(4) The result referred to in subsection (2) above is that the respective shares of the oil allowance utilised by each of two or more participators specified in the apportionment notice bear to each other the same proportion as their respective shares in oil won and saved from the field and, for this purpose—

   (a) a participator's share of the oil allowance means the total amount of the allowance utilised by him over the period specified for the purpose of this paragraph in the apportionment notice; and

   (b) a participator's share in oil won and saved from the field means the total of the oil included in his share of oil won and saved from the field (as specified in returns under Schedule 2 to the principal Act) over the period specified for the purposes of this paragraph in the apportionment notice, being a period which includes that specified for the purposes of paragraph (a) above.

(5) If the Board are satisfied that an apportionment notice complies with subsections (2) to (4) above, they shall give notice to the responsible person accepting the apportionment notice and, on the giving of that notice—

   (a) the apportionment specified in the apportionment notice shall, as respects the two final periods, have effect as if it were the apportionment resulting from section 8(2) of the principal Act; and

   (b) all such amendments of assessments to tax and determinations shall be made as may be necessary in consequence of paragraph (a) above.

(6) If the Board are not satisfied that an apportionment notice complies with subsections (2) to (4) above, they shall give notice to the responsible person rejecting the apportionment notice and, where the Board give such a notice, the responsible person may, by notice in writing given to the Board within thirty days after the date of the notice of rejection, appeal to the Special Commissioners against the notice.

(7) Where notice of appeal is given under subsection (6) above—

   (a) if, at any time after the giving of the notice and before the determination of the appeal by the Commissioners, the Board and the appellant agree that the apportionment notice should be accepted or withdrawn or varied, the same consequences shall ensue as if the Commissioners had determined the appeal to that effect;

   (b) if, on the hearing of the appeal, it appears to the majority of the Commissioners present at the hearing that the apportionment notice should be accepted, with or without modifications, they shall allow the appeal and, where appropriate, make such modifications of the apportionment specified in the notice as they think fit; and

(c) where the appeal is allowed, subsection (5) above shall apply as if the apportionment notice (subject to any modifications made by the Commissioners) had been accepted by the Board.

(8) Sub-paragraphs (2), (8) and (11) of paragraph 14 of Schedule 2 to the principal Act shall apply in relation to an appeal against a notice of rejection under subsection (6) above as they apply in relation to an appeal against an assessment or determination made under that Act, construing any reference in those provisions to the participator as a reference to the responsible person by whom notice of appeal is given.

(9) This section applies where the final allocation period ends on or after 30th June 1987.

GENERAL NOTE

The oil allowance rules exempt from P.R.T. the first 250,000 tonnes of oil produced each half-yearly period, up to a cumulative total of 5 million tonnes per field. These amounts were doubled for developments after March 31, 1982, outside the Southern Basin. In each period, the allowance is shared between the participators in the ratio of their shares of oil, but it is possible, over time, for the participators' cumulative shares of allowances to get out of step with their cumulative shares of oil. There was scope to rectify this imbalance in the last period for which any allowance was due, but the margin for adjustment was not always sufficient. Accordingly participators are now given further scope to balance their shares of oil allowance through reallocation in the last two periods of oil allowance utilisation.

Variation of decisions on claims for allowable expenditure

67. In Schedule 7 to the principal Act (claim for allowance of certain exploration expenditure etc.) at the end of the Table set out in paragraph 1(3) (which applies the provisions of Schedule 5 specified in the first column of the Table with the modifications specified in the second column) there shall be added—

"9	... ...	In sub-paragraph (2) omit paragraphs (b) and (c), in sub-paragraph (8) for the reference to all or any of the participators substitute a reference to the participator by whom the claim is made and in sub-paragraph (11) for "after 15th March 1983" substitute "on or after 17th March 1987"."

GENERAL NOTE

This section remedies a technical defect in the rules for putting matters right where either too little or too much expenditure on such items as exploration and appraisal has been allowed.

PART VI

MISCELLANEOUS AND SUPPLEMENTARY

Abolition of enactments relating to exchange control

68.—(1) The Exchange Control Act 1947 shall cease to have effect.

(2) Nothing in subsection (1) above affects the power of the Treasury to issue a certificate under subsection (2) of section 18 of that Act (including that subsection as applied by section 28(3) or section 29(3) of that Act) with respect to acts done before 13th December 1979.

(3) In section 150 of the Capital Gains Tax Act 1979 (general rules as to valuation), subsection (5) (assets of a kind the sale of which is subject to restrictions imposed under the Exchange Control Act 1947) shall cease

to have effect except in relation to the determination of the market value of any assets at a time before 13th December 1979.

(4) Subsections (1) and (2) above extend to the Channel Islands and the Isle of Man.

GENERAL NOTE

The system of exchange control introduced on the outbreak of war in 1939, and codified in Exchange Control Act 1947, was abolished by government action in 1979, but the enabling legislation remained in place. Its repeal recognises that with the development of a sophisticated worldwide money market such protectionist measures are outmoded for the foreseeable future.

Regulation of financial dealings

69. In section 2 of the Banking and Financial Dealings Act 1971 (power of Treasury to suspend financial dealings)—

(a) at the end of paragraph (c) of subsection (1) (power to suspend dealings in gold) there shall be added "or, according as may be specified in the order, gold of such kind as may be so specified"; and

(b) in subsection (6) for the definition beginning "foreign currency" there shall be substituted—

""foreign currency" means any currency other than sterling and any units of account defined by reference to more than one currency (whether or not including sterling); and

"gold" includes gold coin, gold bullion and gold wafers."

GENERAL NOTE

The amendments to Banking and Financial Dealings Act 1971 are made necessary by the repeal of Exchange Control Act 1947, which provided definitions of "foreign currency" and "gold."

Arrangements specified in Orders in Council relating to double taxation relief etc.

70.—(1) In section 497 of the Taxes Act (relief by agreement with other countries) after subsection (1) there shall be inserted the following subsection—

"(1A) Without prejudice to the generality of subsection (1) above, if it appears to Her Majesty to be appropriate, the arrangements specified in an Order in Council under this section may include provisions with respect to the exchange of information necessary for carrying out the domestic laws of the United Kingdom and the laws of the territory to which the arrangements relate concerning taxes covered by the arrangements including, in particular, provisions about the prevention of fiscal evasion with respect to those taxes; and where arrangements do include any such provisions, the declaration in the Order in Council shall state that fact."

(2) In section 158 of the Inheritance Tax Act 1984 (double taxation conventions) after subsection (1) there shall be inserted the following subsection—

"(1A) Without prejudice to the generality of subsection (1) above, if it appears to Her Majesty to be appropriate, the arrangements specified in an Order in Council under this section may include provisions with respect to the exchange of information necessary for carrying out the domestic laws of the United Kingdom and the laws of the territory to which the arrangements relate concerning taxes covered by the arrangements including, in particular, provisions about the prevention of fiscal evasion with respect to those taxes; and where arrangements do include any such provisions, the declaration in the Order in Council shall state that fact."

GENERAL NOTE

These amendments open the way for implementation of the draft Convention on Mutual Administrative Assistance in Tax Matters in relation to exchange of information with fellow-members of the Council of Europe and the Organisation for Economic Co-operation and Development.

Pre-consolidation amendments

71. The enactments specified in Schedule 15 to this Act shall have effect subject to the amendments specified in that Schedule, being amendments designed to facilitate, or otherwise desirable in connection with, the consolidation of the Income Tax Acts and the Corporation Tax Acts.

GENERAL NOTE

The law relating to income tax and corporation tax was consolidated in the Income and Corporation Taxes Act 1970. Many of the provisions of that Act have been replaced by amending legislation and successive Finance Acts have introduced numerous fiscal innovations, so that a further consolidation is desirable. The amendments in Sched. 15 correct anomalies, but make no substantive changes to the law.

Short title, interpretation, construction and repeals

72.—(1) This Act may be cited as the Finance Act 1987.

(2) In this Act "the Taxes Act" means the Income and Corporation Taxes Act 1970.

(3) Part II of this Act, so far as it relates to income tax, shall be construed as one with the Income Tax Acts, so far as it relates to corporation tax, shall be construed as one with the Corporation Tax Acts and, so far as it relates to capital gains tax, shall be construed as one with the Capital Gains Tax Act 1979.

(4) Part III of this Act, except section 56 and Schedule 7, shall be construed as one with the Stamp Act 1891.

(5) In Part IV of this Act "the 1984 Act" means the Inheritance Tax Act 1984.

(6) Part V of this Act shall be construed as one with Part I of the Oil Taxation Act 1975 and in that Part "the principal Act" means that Act.

(7) The enactments specified in Schedule 16 to this Act (which include enactments which are spent or otherwise unnecessary) are hereby repealed to the extent specified in the third column of that Schedule, but subject to any provision at the end of any Part of that Schedule.

Finance Act 1987

SCHEDULES

SCHEDULE 1

VEHICLES EXCISE DUTY

PART I

TABLES SUBSTITUTED IN PART II OF SCHEDULE 4 TO THE ACTS OF 1971 AND 1972

TABLE A(1)

RATES OF DUTY ON RIGID GOODS VEHICLES EXCEEDING 12 TONNES PLATED GROSS WEIGHT

RATES FOR FARMERS' GOODS VEHICLES

Plated gross weight of vehicle		Rate of duty		
1. Exceeding	2. Not exceeding	3. Two axle vehicle	4. Three axle vehicle	5. Four or more axle vehicle
tonnes	tonnes	£	£	£
12	13	245	190	190
13	14	340	205	205
14	15	445	205	205
15	17	620	205	205
17	19	—	295	205
19	21	—	395	205
21	23	—	540	295
23	25	—	965	415
25	27	—	—	600
27	29	—	—	880
29	30.49	—	—	1,450

TABLE C(1)

RATES OF DUTY ON TRACTOR UNITS EXCEEDING 12 TONNES PLATED TRAIN WEIGHT AND HAVING ONLY 2 AXLES

RATES FOR FARMERS' GOODS VEHICLES

Plated train weight of tractor unit		Rate of duty		
1. Exceeding	2. Not exceeding	3. For a tractor unit to be used with semi-trailers with any number of axles	4. For a tractor unit to be used only with semi-trailers with not less than two axles	5. For a tractor unit to be used only with semi-trailers with not less than three axles
tonnes	tonnes	£	£	£
12	14	280	250	250
14	16	355	265	265
16	18	415	265	265
18	20	485	265	265
20	22	565	330	265
22	23	600	370	265
23	25	690	470	265
25	26	690	520	320
26	28	690	655	430
28	29	725	725	490
29	31	1,010	1,010	630
31	33	1,470	1,470	1,010
33	34	1,470	1,470	1,350
34	36	1,650	1,650	1,650
36	38	1,860	1,860	1,860

TABLE D(1)

RATES OF DUTY ON TRACTOR UNITS EXCEEDING 12 TONNES PLATED TRAIN WEIGHT AND HAVING THREE OR MORE AXLES

RATES FOR FARMERS' GOODS VEHICLES

Plated train weight of tractor unit		Rate of duty		
1. Exceeding	2. Not exceeding	3. For a tractor unit to be used with semi-trailers with any number of axles	4. For a tractor unit to be used only with semi-trailers with not less than two axles	5. For a tractor unit to be used only with semi-trailers with not less than three axles
tonnes	tonnes	£	£	£
12	14	250	250	250
14	20	265	265	265
20	22	330	265	265
22	23	370	265	265
23	25	470	265	265
25	26	520	265	265
26	28	655	265	265
28	29	725	310	265
29	31	1,010	385	265
31	33	1,470	580	265
33	34	1,470	850	330
34	36	1,470	1,220	500
36	38	1,640	1,640	745

PART II

RECOVERY VEHICLES

Interpretation

1. In this Part of this Schedule—
  "the 1971 Act" means the Vehicles (Excise) Act 1971; and
  "the 1972 Act" means the Vehicles (Excise) Act (Northern Ireland) 1972.
2. At the end of Part I of Schedule 3 to each of the 1971 Act and the 1972 Act there shall be added—

  "8.—(1) In this Schedule "recovery vehicle" means, subject to the provisions of this paragraph, a vehicle which is either constructed or permanently adapted primarily for the purposes of lifting, towing and transporting a disabled vehicle or for any one or more of those purposes.

  (2) Subject to sub-paragraph (3) below, a vehicle which is constructed or permanently adapted as mentioned in sub-paragraph (1) above shall not be a recovery vehicle if at any time it is used for any purpose other than—
  (a) the recovery of a disabled vehicle;
  (b) the removal of a disabled vehicle from the place where it became disabled to premises at which it is to be repaired or scrapped;
  (c) the removal of a disabled vehicle from premises to which it was taken for repair to other premises at which it is to be repaired or scrapped; and
  (d) carrying any load other than fuel and other liquids required for its propulsion and tools and other articles required for the operation of or in connection with apparatus designed to lift, tow or transport a disabled vehicle.

(3) At any time when a vehicle is being used for purposes specified in paragraphs (a) and (b) of sub-paragraph (2) above, the following uses shall be disregarded in determining whether the vehicle is a recovery vehicle—

    (a) use for the carriage of any person who immediately before a vehicle became disabled, was the driver of or a passenger in that vehicle;

    (b) use for the carriage of any goods which, immediately before a vehicle became disabled, were being carried in the disabled vehicle; and

    (c) use for any purpose prescribed for the purposes of this paragraph."

The charge of duty

3. At the end of the Table in Part II of Schedule 3 to each of the 1971 Act and the 1972 Act there shall be added—

    "4. Recovery vehicles — — 50 — ".

Recovery vehicles not chargeable as goods vehicles

4.—(1) In Part I of Schedule 4 to each of the 1971 Act and the 1972 Act (goods vehicles), in paragraph 11 (exempted vehicles) in paragraph (c) for the words "or fisherman's tractor" there shall be substituted "fisherman's tractor or recovery vehicle".

(2) In paragraph 15(1) of that Schedule (interpretation) after the definition beginning "mobile crane" there shall be inserted—

    ""recovery vehicle" has the same meaning as in Schedule 3 to this Act".

Exclusion of recovery vehicles from trade licences

5. In section 16 of the 1971 Act (trade licences)—

    (a) in subsection (1)(i) the words from "and all recovery vehicles" to "that business" shall be omitted.

    (b) in paragraph (a) of the proviso to subsection (1) the words from "except" to "disabled vehicle" shall be omitted;

    (c) in subsection (3) paragraph (b) shall be omitted and at the end of paragraph (e) there shall be added the words "other than a trailer which is for the time being a disabled vehicle"; and

    (d) in subsection (8) the definition of "recovery vehicle" shall be omitted.

6. In section 16 of the 1972 Act (trade licences)—

    (a) in subsection (1)(a) the words from "and all recovery vehicles" to "that business" shall be omitted;

    (b) in subsection (2)(a) the words from "except" to "disabled vehicle" shall be omitted;

    (c) in subsection (4) paragraph (b) shall be omitted and at the end of paragraph (e) there shall be added the words "other than a trailer which is for the time being a disabled vehicle"; and

    (d) in subsection (10) the definition of "recovery vehicle" shall be omitted.

PART III

MISCELLANEOUS AMENDMENTS

Introductory

7. In this Part of this Schedule—

    "the 1971 Act" means the Vehicles (Excise) Act 1971; and

    "the 1972 Act" means the Vehicles (Excise) Act (Northern Ireland) 1972.

Additional liability for evasion of duty

8. In section 9(3) of the 1971 Act (circumstances in which additional liability for keeping unlicensed vehicle not to be payable) paragraphs (b) and (c) (vehicles not used or kept on a public road and vehicles not chargeable with duty) shall be omitted.

9. In section 9(4) of the 1972 Act (circumstances in which additional liability for keeping unlicensed vehicle not to be payable) paragraphs (b) and (c) (vehicles not used or kept on a public road and vehicles not chargeable with duty) shall be omitted.

10. In section 18A(7) of the 1971 Act (circumstances in which additional liability in relation to alteration of vehicle or its use not to be payable)—
   (a) for paragraph (b) (vehicle neither used nor kept on public road) there shall be substituted the word "or"; and
   (b) paragraph (d) (vehicle not chargeable with duty) and the word "or" immediately preceding it shall be omitted.

11. In section 18A(7) of the 1972 Act (circumstances in which additional liability in relation to alteration of vehicle or its use not to be payable)—
   (a) for paragraph (b) (vehicle neither used nor kept on public road) there shall be substituted the word "or"; and
   (b) paragraph (d) (vehicle not chargeable with duty) and the word "or" immediately preceding it shall be omitted.

12. In Part I of Schedule 7 to the 1971 Act (transitional modifications)—
   (a) in paragraph 7, paragraph (b)(ii) shall be omitted and in paragraph (b)(iii) for the words "paragraphs (c) and (d)" there shall be substituted the words "paragraph (d)"; and
   (b) in paragraph 17A, paragraph (b)(ii) shall be omitted and in paragraph (b)(iii) for the words "paragraphs (c) and (d)" and "paragraph (d)" there shall be substituted respectively the words "paragraph (c)" and "that paragraph".

13. In Part I of Schedule 9 to the 1972 Act (transitional modifications)—
   (a) in paragraph 7, paragraph (b)(ii) shall be omitted and in paragraph (b)(iii) for the words "paragraphs (c) and (d)" there shall be substituted the words "paragraph (d)"; and
   (b) in paragraph 17A, paragraph (b)(ii) shall be omitted and in paragraph (b)(iii) for the words "paragraphs (c) and (d)" and "paragraph (d)" there shall be substituted respectively the words "paragraph (c)" and "that paragraph".

Offences relating to trade licences

14. In section 16(7) of the 1971 Act (offences relating to trade licences) after the words "keeping on a road" there shall be inserted "in any circumstances other than such circumstances as may have been prescribed under paragraph (c) of the proviso to subsection (1) above".

15. In section 16(8) of the 1972 Act (offences relating to trade licences) after the words "keeping on a road" there shall be inserted "in any circumstances other than such circumstances as may have been prescribed under subsection (2)(c)".

Regulations concerning transfer etc. of vehicles

16.—(1) Section 23 of the 1971 Act (regulations with respect to the transfer and identification of vehicles) shall be amended as follows.
   (2) In paragraph (e) (inspection and surrender of registration documents) after the word "inspection" there shall be inserted the word ", transfer".
   (3) In that section as set out in paragraph 20 of Part I of Schedule 7 to the Act—
      (a) in subsection (1)(c) (requirements on person to whom vehicle transferred to furnish particulars) after the word "person" there shall be inserted the words "by whom or"; and
      (b) in subsection (1)(d) (issue, surrender etc. of registration books) before the word "surrender" there shall be inserted the word "transfer".
   (4) Regulation 12(1) of the Road Vehicles (Registration and Licensing) Regulations 1971 shall have effect on and after the day on which this paragraph comes into force as if subparagraph (3) above had been in force when that regulation was made.

17.—(1) Section 23(1) of the 1972 Act (regulations with respect to transfer and identification of vehicles) shall be amended as follows.
   (2) In paragraph (e) (inspection and surrender of registration documents) after the word "inspection" there shall be inserted the word "transfer".
   (3) In that section as set out in paragraph 20 of Part I of Schedule 9 to the Act—
      (a) in paragraph (c) (requirements on person to whom vehicle transferred to furnish particulars) after the word "person" there shall be inserted the words "by whom or"; and
      (b) in paragraph (d) (issue, surrender etc of registration books) before the word "surrender" there shall be inserted the word "transfer".

(4) Regulation 13(1) of the Road Vehicles (Registration and Licensing) Regulations (Northern Ireland) 1973 shall have effect on and after the day on which this paragraph comes into force as if sub-paragraph (3) above had been in force when that regulation was made.

Increase of certain penalties for offences under regulations

18.—(1) Section 37 of the 1971 Act (regulations) shall be amended as follows.

(2) For paragraph (a) of subsection (3) (fine of level 3 on the standard scale on conviction for offences against certain regulations) there shall be substituted—

"(a) in the case of regulations prescribed for the purposes of this paragraph, of regulations made under section 24 or of a contravention or failure to comply with requirements imposed in pursuance of section 23(a) above, level 3 on the standard scale;";

(3) After that subsection there shall be inserted—

"(3A) The prescribing of regulations for the purposes of subsection (3)(a) above shall not affect the punishment for a contravention of or a failure to comply with those regulations before they were so prescribed.".

(4) For subsection (3) of that section as set out in paragraph 24 of Part I of Schedule 7 to the Act there shall be substituted—

"(3) Any person who contravenes or fails to comply with any regulations under this Act (other than regulations under section 2(5), 11(3), 14, 20 or 24) shall be guilty of an offence and liable on summary conviction—

(a) in the case of regulations prescribed for the purposes of this paragraph, to a fine not exceeding level 3 on the standard scale; and

(b) in any other case, to a fine not exceeding level 2 on the standard scale.

(3A) Regulations under section 14, 20 or 24 above may provide that a person who contravenes or fails to comply with any specified provision of the regulations shall be guilty of an offence and a person guilty of such an offence shall be liable on summary conviction—

(a) in the case of regulations under section 14 or 20, to a fine not exceeding level 1 on the standard scale; and

(b) in the case of regulations under section 24, to a fine not exceeding level 3 on the standard scale.

(3B) The prescribing of regulations for the purposes of subsection (3)(a) above shall not affect the punishment for a contravention of or failure to comply with those regulations before they were so prescribed."

19.—(1) Section 34 of the 1972 Act (regulations) shall be amended as follows.

(2) For paragraph (a) of subsection (3) (fine of level 3 on the standard scale on conviction of offences against certain regulations) there shall be substituted—

"(a) in the case of regulations prescribed for the purposes of this paragraph, of regulations made under section 24 or of a contravention or failure to comply with requirements imposed in pursuance of section 23(1)(a), level 3 on the standard scale;";

(3) After that subsection there shall be inserted—

"(3A) The prescribing of regulations for the purposes of subsection (3)(a) shall not affect the punishment for a contravention of or failure to comply with those regulations before they were so prescribed.".

(4) For subsection (3) of that section as set out in paragraph 24 of Part I of Schedule 9 to the Act there shall be substituted—

"(3) Any person who contravenes or fails to comply with any regulations under this Act (other than regulations under section 2(6), 11(3), 14, 20 or 24) shall be guilty of an offence and liable on summary conviction—

(a) in the case of regulations prescribed for the purposes of this paragraph, to a fine not exceeding level 3 on the standard scale; and

(b) in the other case, to a fine not exceeding level 2 on the standard scale.

(3A) Regulations under section 14, 20 or 24 may provide that a person who contravenes or fails to comply with any specified provision of the regulations shall be guilty of an offence and a person guilty of such an offence shall be liable on summary conviction—

(a) in the case of regulations under section 14 or 20, to a fine not exceeding level 1 on the standard scale; and

(b) in the case of regulations under section 24, to a fine not exceeding level 3 on the standard scale.

(3B) The prescribing of regulations for the purposes of subsection (3)(a) shall not affect the punishment for a contravention of or failure to comply with those regulations before they were so prescribed."

Dishonoured cheques

20. In subsection (3) of section 102 of the Customs and Excise Management Act 1979 (penalty for failure to deliver up excise licence following dishonour of cheque) after paragraph (a) there shall be inserted the following paragraph—

"(aa) where the licence is a licence under the Vehicles (Excise) Act 1971, a penalty of whichever is the greater of—

(i) level 3 on the standard scale, or

(ii) an amount equal to five times the annual rate of duty that was payable on the grant of the licence or would have been so payable if it had been taken out for a period of twelve months."

21. After paragraph 2 of Part II of Schedule 6 to the 1972 Act (modified application of certain provisions of the Miscellaneous Transferred Excise Duties Act (Northern Ireland) 1972) there shall be added the following paragraph—

"3. Section 10(2) of the Transferred Excise Duties Act shall apply as if for the words from "in the case of" onwards there were substituted the words "whichever is the greater of—

(a) level 3 on the standard scale, or

(b) an amount equal to five times the annual rate of duty that was payable on the grant of the licence or would have been so payable if it had been taken out for a period of twelve months.""

GENERAL NOTE

Pt. I completes a three year programme to bring the rates for farmers' goods vehicles up to a level broadly proportionate to the mileage which they cover on the roads by comparison with the average lorry, estimated at 60 per cent. The increases this year vary from 5 to 34 per cent. Over the three year period rates for lighter vehicles have approximately doubled, with higher increases at the top of the scale.

Pt. II rationalises the taxation of recovery vehicles. A new definition is introduced which allows associated carriage of passengers and goods and prevents abuse of the concessionary rate by excluding unadapted vehicles which carry loose equipment designed to raise disabled vehicles from the ground. It is proposed to issue regulations under the new para. 8(3)(c) to provide for any other valid uses of a recovery vehicle.

Pt. III makes various minor amendments to the Vehicles (Excise) Act 1971 and the corresponding Northern Ireland legislation, and to associated legislation and regulations, primarily in relation to the tariff of penalties for various offences.

Section 19(2)   SCHEDULE 2

AMENDMENTS OF VALUE ADDED TAX ACT 1983

Supplies received from abroad

1. Section 7 of the principal Act (reverse charge on supplies received from abroad) shall be amended as follows—

(a) in paragraph (b) of subsection (1), for the words "taxable person" there shall be substituted "person (in this section referred to as 'the recipient')";

(b) in subsection (1), in the words following paragraph (b) for the words "as if the taxable person" there shall be substituted "as if the recipient";

(c) in subsections (3) and (4) for the words "taxable person" there shall be substituted "recipient"; and

(d) in subsection (3) for the words "the allowance" there shall be substituted "any allowance".

Repayment of tax on importation to those in business overseas

2. In subsection (1) of section 23 of the principal Act (which enables the Commissioners to provide by regulations for the repayment to persons carrying on business in other member States and certain other countries of tax on supplies to them in the United Kingdom) after

the words "United Kingdom", where they first occur, there shall be inserted "or on the importation of goods by them into the United Kingdom".

Transfers of going concerns

3. In section 33 of the principal Act (transfers of going concerns), after subsection (1) there shall be inserted—

"(1A) Where the transferee is liable to be registered by virtue of paragraph 1(1)(b) of Schedule 1 to this Act at the time the business is transferred, paragraph 4(2) of that Schedule shall not apply but the Commissioners shall register him with effect from that time.".

Appeals

4. In section 40(1) of the principal Act (appeals) for paragraph (d) there shall be substituted—

"(d) the proportion of input tax allowable under section 15 above".

GENERAL NOTE
Para. 1. Because of a loophole in V.A.T.A. 1983, s.7, exempt businesses were able to import certain services free of VAT and avoid the tax they would have had to pay on identical services bought from U.K. registered traders. An example was newspaper advertising ordered through agencies in the Channel Islands. This loophole is now closed for an estimated annual saving to the revenue of £5m. The services concerned are listed in V.A.T.A. 1983, Sched. 3.

Para. 2 widens the ambit of refunds under the EEC's Eighth Directive to VAT suffered on goods imported into the U.K. The relevant regulations are Value Added Tax (Repayment to Community Traders) Regulations (S.I. 1980 No. 1537).

Para. 3 provides that where a going concern with turnover over the taxable threshold is transferred the transferee shall be registered for VAT forthwith and not at the later date available under V.A.T.A. 1983, Sched. 1, para. 4(2), as substituted by s.14 *supra*.

Para. 4 makes a minor amendment to V.A.T.A. 1983, s.40 to clarify the subject-matter of appeals to tribunals against the refusal of a deduction of input tax.

Section 29   SCHEDULE 3

INCOME SUPPORT

PART I

THE TAXABLE MAXIMUM

1.—(1) For the purposes of subsections (3) and (4) of the principal section, the taxable maximum in respect of a week shall be determined in accordance with paragraphs 2 to 4 below and the taxable maximum in respect of part of a week shall be equal to one-sixth of the taxable maximum in respect of a week multiplied by the number of days in the part.

(2) In this Part of this Schedule—
  (a) "married couple" and "unmarried couple" have the same meaning as in Part II of the Social Security Act 1986; and
  (b) "the principal section" means section 29 of this Act.

2. Where the income support is paid to one of a married or unmarried couple in a case not falling within subsection (2)(b) of the principal section, the taxable maximum in respect of a week shall be equal to the aggregate of—
  (a) the weekly rate specified for the week in question in relation to unemployment benefit in paragraph 1 of Part I of Schedule 4 to the Social Security Act 1975; and
  (b) the increase for an adult dependant specified for that week in paragraph 1(a) of Part IV of that Schedule.

3. Where the income support is paid to one of a married or unmarried couple in a case falling within subsection (2)(b) of the principal section, the taxable maximum in respect of a week shall—
  (a) if the applicable amount (within the meaning of Part II of the Social Security Act 1986) consists only of an amount in respect of them, be equal to one half of that amount; and

(b) if the applicable amount includes other amounts, be equal to one half of the portion of it which is included in respect of them.

4. Where the income support is paid to a person who is not one of a married or unmarried couple, the taxable maximum in respect of a week shall be equal to the weekly rate referred to in paragraph 2(a) above.

Part II

Consequential Amendments

The Income and Corporation Taxes Act 1970

5. In subsection (2) of section 530 of the Taxes Act (meaning of "earned income" in the Income Tax Acts) in paragraph (c) for the words "or section 27 of the Finance Act 1981" there shall be substituted "or section 29 of the Finance Act 1987".

The Finance Act 1981

6. In section 28(1) of the Finance Act 1981 (notification of amount of benefit which is taxable) for the words "under section 27 above" there shall be substituted "in respect of any unemployment benefit or income support".

7. In section 29 of the Finance Act 1981 (pay as you earn repayments) for paragraph (b) there shall be substituted the following—
   "(b) he has claimed a payment of income support under the Social Security Act 1986 or the Social Security (Northern Ireland) Order 1986 in respect of a period including that time and his right to that income support is subject to the condition specified in section 20(3)(d)(i) of that Act or, in Northern Ireland, Article 21(3)(d)(i) of that Order (availability for employment);"

General Note
   Pt. I of the Schedule supplements s.29 by providing rules for determining the maximum amount of social security benefits which can be brought into charge to income tax under Schedule E.
   Pt. II makes consequential amendments to other statutes.

Section 33   SCHEDULE 4

Employee Share Schemes, etc.

Part I

Amendments of Schedule 10 to the Finance Act 1980 and Schedule 10 to the Finance Act 1984

1.—(1) In Schedule 10 to the Finance Act 1980 (savings-related share option schemes) after paragraph 10 there shall be inserted the following paragraph—
   "10A.—(1) The scheme may also provide that if any company (in this paragraph referred to as "the acquiring company")—
      (a) obtains control of a company whose shares are scheme shares as a result of making a general offer falling within sub-paragraph (i) or sub-paragraph (ii) of paragraph 10(1)(a) above, or
      (b) obtains control of a company whose shares are scheme shares in pursuance of a compromise or arrangement sanctioned by the court under section 425 of the Companies Act 1985 or Article 418 of the Companies (Northern Ireland) Order 1986, or
      (c) becomes bound or entitled to acquire shares in a company whose shares are scheme shares under sections 428 to 430 of the said Act of 1985 or Articles 421 to 423 of the said Order of 1986,
   any participant in the scheme may at any time within the appropriate period, by agreement with the acquiring company, transfer to the acquiring company his rights under the scheme (in this paragraph referred to as "the old rights") in consideration of the grant to him of rights (in this paragraph referred to as "the new rights") which are equivalent to the old rights but relate to shares in a different company (whether the

acquiring company itself or some other company falling within paragraph (b) or paragraph (c) of paragraph 15 below).

(2) In sub-paragraph (1) above "the appropriate period" means—

    (a) in a case falling within paragraph (a), the period of six months beginning with the time when the person making the offer has obtained control of the company and any condition subject to which the offer is made is satisfied,

    (b) in a case falling within paragraph (b), the period of six months beginning with the time when the court sanctions the compromise or arrangement, and

    (c) in a case falling within paragraph (c), the period during which the acquiring company remains bound or entitled as mentioned in that paragraph.

(3) The new rights shall not be regarded for the purposes of this paragraph as equivalent to the old rights unless—

    (a) the shares to which they relate satisfy the conditions specified, in relation to scheme shares, in paragraphs 15 to 19 below; and

    (b) the new rights will be exercisable in the same manner as the old rights and subject to the provisions of the scheme as it had effect immediately before the exchange; and

    (c) the total market value, immediately before the exchange, of the shares which were subject to the participant's old rights is equal to the total market value, immediately after the exchange, of the shares in respect of which the new rights are granted to the participant; and

    (d) the total amount payable by the participant for the acquisition of shares in pursuance of the new rights is equal to the total amount that would have been payable for the acquisition of shares in pursuance of the old rights.

(4) Where any new rights are granted pursuant to a provision included in a scheme by virtue of this paragraph they shall be regarded—

    (a) for the purposes of section 47 of this Act and this Schedule, and

    (b) for the purposes of the subsequent application (by virtue of a condition complying with sub-paragraph (3)(b) above) of the provisions of the scheme,

as having been granted at the time when the corresponding old rights were granted."

(2) In paragraph 11 of the said Schedule 10 (rights not to be capable of being transferred) after the words "paragraph 7" there shall be inserted "or paragraph 10A".

2.—(1) In Schedule 10 of the Finance Act 1984 (approved share option schemes) after paragraph 4 there shall be inserted the following paragraph—

    "4A.—(1) The scheme may provide that if any company (in this paragraph referred to as "the acquiring company")—

    (a) obtains control of a company whose shares are scheme shares as a result of making—

        (i) a general offer to acquire the whole of the issued share capital of the company which is made on a condition such that if it is satisfied the person making the offer will have control of the company, or

        (ii) a general offer to acquire all the shares in the company which are of the same class as the scheme shares, or

    (b) obtains control of a company whose shares are scheme shares in pursuance of a compromise or arrangement sanctioned by the court under section 425 of the Companies Act 1985 or Article 418 of the Companies (Northern Ireland) Order 1986, or

    (c) becomes bound or entitled to acquire shares in a company whose shares are scheme shares under sections 428 to 430 of the said Act of 1985 or Articles 421 to 423 of the said Order of 1986,

any participant in the scheme may at any time within the appropriate period, by agreement with the acquiring company, transfer to the acquiring company his rights under the scheme (in this paragraph referred to as "the old rights") in consideration of the grant to him of rights (in this paragraph referred to as "the new rights") which are equivalent to the old rights but relate to shares in a different company (whether the acquiring company itself or some other company falling within paragraph (b) or paragraph (c) of paragraph 7 below).

(2) In sub-paragraph (1) above "the appropriate period" means—

   (a) in a case falling within paragraph (a), the period of six months beginning with the time when the person making the offer has obtained control of the company and any condition subject to which the offer is made is satisfied,

   (b) in a case falling within paragraph (b), the period of six months beginning with the time when the court sanctions the compromise or arrangement, and

   (c) in a case falling within paragraph (c), the period during which the acquiring company remains bound or entitled as mentioned in that paragraph.

(3) The new rights shall not be regarded for the purposes of this paragraph as equivalent to the old rights unless—

   (a) the shares to which they relate satisfy the conditions specified, in relation to scheme shares, in paragraphs 7 to 11 below; and

   (b) the new rights will be exercisable in the same manner as the old rights and subject to the provisions of the scheme as it had effect immediately before the exchange; and

   (c) the total market value, immediately before the exchange, of the shares which were subject to the participant's old rights is equal to the total market value, immediately after the exchange, of the shares in respect of which the new rights are granted to the participant; and

   (d) the total amount payable by the participant for the acquisition of shares in pursuance of the new rights is equal to the total amount that would have been payable for the acquisition of shares in pursuance of the old rights.

(4) Where any new rights are granted pursuant to a provision included in a scheme by virtue of this paragraph they shall be regarded—

   (a) for the purposes of section 38 of this Act and this Schedule, and

   (b) for the purposes of the subsequent application (by virtue of a condition complying with sub-paragraph (3)(b) above) of the provisions of the scheme,

as having been granted at the time when the corresponding old rights were granted."

(2) In paragraph 12 of the said Schedule 10 (transfer of rights) after the words "any of them" there shall be inserted "(except pursuant to a provision included in the scheme by virtue of paragraph 4A above)".

PART II

TRANSITIONAL PROVISIONS

3.—(1) Where an existing scheme is altered before 1st August 1989 so as to include such a provision as is mentioned in paragraph 10A of Schedule 10 to the Finance Act 1980 or, as the case may be, paragraph 4A of Schedule 10 to the Finance Act 1984 (in this paragraph referred to as "an exchange provision"), the scheme as altered may by virtue of this paragraph apply that provision to rights obtained under the scheme before the date on which the alteration takes effect.

(2) If an exchange provision is applied as mentioned in sub-paragraph (1) above in a case where, on or after 17th March 1987 but before the date on which the alteration takes effect, an event has occurred by reason of which a person holding rights under the scheme would be able to take advantage of the exchange provision—

   (a) the scheme may permit a person who held rights under the scheme immediately before that event to take advantage of the exchange provision, and

   (b) in a case where rights then held would otherwise, by reason of the event, have ceased to be exercisable, the scheme may provide that the exchange provision shall apply as if the rights were still exercisable.

(3) The application of an exchange provision as mentioned in sub-paragraph (1) or sub-paragraph (2) above shall not itself be regarded for the purposes of Schedule 10 to the Finance Act 1980 or, as the case may be, Schedule 10 to the Finance Act 1984 as the acquisition of a right.

(4) In sub-paragraph (1) above "an existing scheme" means a scheme approved under Schedule 10 to the Finance Act 1980 or Schedule 10 to the Finance Act 1984 before 1st August 1987.

(5) This paragraph has effect subject to paragraph 3(2) of Schedule 10 to the said Act of 1980 or, as the case may be, paragraph 2(2) of Schedule 10 to the said Act of 1984 (which require the approval of the Board for any alteration in a scheme).

Part III

Consequential Provisions Relating to Capital Gains Tax

4. In section 47 of the Finance Act 1980 (savings-related share option schemes) after subsection (2) there shall be inserted the following subsection—

"(2A) Where a right to acquire shares in a body corporate which was obtained as mentioned in subsection (1) above is exchanged for a right to acquire shares in another body corporate in accordance with a provision included in a scheme pursuant to paragraph 10A of Schedule 10 to this Act, the exchange shall not be treated for the purposes of the Capital Gains Tax Act 1979 as involving any disposal of the first-mentioned right or any acquisition of the other right, but for those purposes the other right shall be treated as the same asset acquired as the first-mentioned right was acquired."

5. In section 38 of the Finance Act 1984 (approved share option schemes) after subsection (6) there shall be inserted the following subsection—

"(6A) Where a right to acquire shares in a body corporate is exchanged for a right to acquire shares in another body corporate in accordance with a provision included in a scheme pursuant to paragraph 4A of Schedule 10 to this Act, the exchange shall not be treated for the purposes of the Capital Gains Tax Act 1979 as involving any disposal of the first-mentioned right or any acquisition of the other right, but for those purposes the other right shall be treated as the same asset acquired as the first-mentioned right was acquired.".

Part IV

Material Interest Test

Interests under trusts

6.—(1) This paragraph applies in a case where—
  (a) the individual (in this paragraph referred to as "the beneficiary") was one of the objects of a discretionary trust, and
  (b) the property subject to the trust at any time consisted of or included any shares or obligations of the company.

(2) If neither the beneficiary nor any relevant associate of his had received any benefit under the discretionary trust before 14th November 1986, then, as respects any time before that date, the trustees of the settlement concerned shall not be regarded, by reason only of the matters referred to in sub-paragraph (1) above, as having been associates (as defined in section 303(3) of the Taxes Act) of the beneficiary.

(3) If, on or after 14th November 1986,—
  (a) the beneficiary ceases to be eligible to benefit under the discretionary trust by reason of—
    (i) an irrevocable disclaimer or release executed by him under seal, or
    (ii) the irrevocable exercise by the trustees of a power to exclude him from the objects of the trust, and
  (b) immediately after he so ceases, no relevant associate of his is interested in the shares or obligations of the company which are subject to the trust, and
  (c) during the period of twelve months ending with the date when the beneficiary so ceases, neither the beneficiary nor any relevant associate of his received any benefit under the trust,

the beneficiary shall not be regarded, by reason only of the matters referred to in sub-paragraph (1) above, as having been interested in the shares or obligations of the company as mentioned in section 303(3)(c) of the Taxes Act at any time during the period of twelve months referred to in paragraph (c) above.

(4) In sub-paragraphs (2) and (3) above "relevant associate" has the meaning given to "associate" by section (3) of section 303 of the Taxes Act, but with the omission of paragraph (c) of that subsection.

(5) Sub-paragraph 3(a)(i) above, in its application to Scotland, shall be construed as if the words "under seal" were omitted.

Options etc.

7.—(1) For the purposes of paragraph (a) of subsection (6) of section 285 of the Taxes Act (cases in which a person has a material interest in a company) a right to acquire any shares (however arising) shall be taken to be a right to control them.

(2) Any reference in sub-paragraph (3) below to the shares attributed to an individual is a reference to the shares which, in accordance with section 285(6)(a) of the Taxes Act, fall to be brought into account in his case to determine whether their number exceeds a particular percentage of the company's ordinary share capital.

(3) In any case where—

    (a) the shares attributed to an individual consist of or include shares which he or any other person has a right to acquire, and

    (b) the circumstances are such that, if that right were to be exercised, the shares acquired would be shares which were previously unissued and which the company is contractually bound to issue in the event of the exercise of the right,

then, in determining at any time prior to the exercise of that right whether the number of shares attributed to the individual exceeds a particular percentage of the ordinary share capital of the company, that ordinary share capital shall be taken to be increased by the number of unissued shares referred to in paragraph (b) above.

(4) This paragraph has effect as respects any time on or after 6th April 1987.

Shares held by trustees of approved profit sharing schemes

8. In applying section 285(6) of the Taxes Act (cases in which a person has a material interest in a company), as respects any time before or after the passing of this Act, there shall be disregarded—

    (a) the interest of the trustees of a profit sharing scheme approved under Part I of Schedule 9 to the Finance Act 1978 in any shares which are held by them in accordance with the scheme and have not yet been appropriated to an individual; and

    (b) any rights exercisable by those trustees by virtue of that interest.

GENERAL NOTE

Pts. I and II of the Schedule are designed to permit holders of share options under savings related or approved share option schemes where the options are to acquire shares in companies which are taken over, to exchange their options for options to acquire shares in the taking-over company. Provisions in the schemes to permit this will no longer preclude approval. All that is permitted however is an exchange of rights in the original company for "equivalent" rights in the new company.

Pt. III of the Schedule makes minor changes in the rules for deciding whether an employee or director has a "material interest" in a close company. If he has a material interest he is unable to participate in an approved scheme.

Section 35   SCHEDULE 5

SUPPLEMENTARY PROVISIONS AS TO TRAINING COSTS

Interpretation

1.—(1) In this Schedule—

    "the principal section" means section 35 of this Act; and

    "employer" and "employee" have the same meaning as in the principal section.

(2) Any reference in this Schedule to an employee being employed by an employer is a reference to the employee holding office or employment under the employer.

Qualifying courses of training

2. Subject to paragraph 3 below, a course is a qualifying course of training if—

    (a) it provides a course of training designed to impart or improve skills or knowledge relevant to, and intended to be used in the course of, gainful employment (including self-employment) of any description; and

(b) the course is entirely devoted to the teaching or practical application of the skills or knowledge (or to both such teaching and practical application); and

(c) the duration of the course does not exceed one year; and

(d) all teaching and practical application forming part of the course takes place within the United Kingdom.

3. A course shall not be regarded as a qualifying course of training in relation to a particular employee unless—

(a) he attends the course on a full-time or substantially full-time basis; and

(b) he is employed by the employer full-time throughout the period of two years ending at the time when he begins to undertake the course or, if it is earlier, at the time he ceases to be employed by him; and

(c) the opportunity to undertake the course, on similar terms as to payment or reimbursement of relevant expenses, is available either generally to holders or past holders of offices or employment under the employer or to a particular class or classes of such holders or past holders.

Courses undertaken with a view to retraining

4.—(1) An employee shall not be regarded as undertaking a course with a view to retraining unless—

(a) he begins to undertake the course of training while he is employed by the employer or within the period of one year after he ceases to be so employed; and

(b) he ceases to be employed by the employer not later than the end of the period of two years beginning at the end of the qualifying course of training.

(2) An employee shall not be regarded as having undertaken a course with a view to retraining if, any time within the period of two years beginning at the time when he ceased to be employed as mentioned in sub-paragraph (1)(b) above, he is again employed by the employer.

Relevant expenses

5.—(1) Where an employee undertakes a qualifying course of training, the relevant expenses consist of—

(a) Fees for attendance at the course;

(b) fees for any examination which is taken during or at the conclusion of the course;

(c) the cost of any books which are essential for a person attending the course; and

(d) travelling expenses falling within sub-paragraph (2) below.

(2) The travelling expenses referred to in sub-paragraph (1)(d) above are those which would be deductible under section 189 of the Taxes Act (relief for necessary expenses)—

(a) on the assumption that attendance at the course is one of the duties of the employee's office or employment; and

(b) if the employee has in fact ceased to be employed by the employer, on the assumption that he continues to be employed by him.

GENERAL NOTE

Under s.35 expenditure incurred by an employer on a "qualifying course of training" for an employee "with a view to retraining him" and in reimbursing "relevant expenses" is not taxable on the employee as a Schedule E benefit and is deductible by the employer as a business expense. The Schedule provides definitions for the three phrases in inverted commas.

Section 36   SCHEDULE 6

TRANSITIONAL PROVISIONS AS TO CORPORATION TAX
PAYMENT DATES

PART I

COMPANIES

Interpretation

1.—(1) In this Part of this Schedule an "old company" means a company to which section 244 of the Taxes Act applied in respect of the last accounting period ending before 17th March 1987.

(2) In relation to an old company—
    (a) "the company's section 244 interval" means the interval after the end of an accounting period of the company which, in accordance with section 244 of the Taxes Act, was the period within which corporation tax assessed for that period was required to be paid; and
    (b) "the period of reduction" means the number of whole days which are comprised in a period equal to one-third of the difference between nine months and the company's section 244 interval.

General rules

2. Subject to paragraph 5 below, with respect to the first accounting period of an old company beginning on or after 17th March 1987, section 243(4) of the Taxes Act (time for payment of corporation tax) shall have effect as if for the reference to nine months there were substituted a reference to a period which is equal to the company's section 244 interval less the period of reduction.

3. Subject to paragraph 5 below, with respect to any accounting period of an old company which begins—
    (a) after the accounting period referred to in paragraph 2 above, but
    (b) before the second anniversary of the beginning of that period,
section 243(4) of the Taxes Act shall have effect as if for the reference to nine months there were substituted a reference to a period equal to the previous payment interval less the period of reduction.

4. In relation to any accounting period of an old company falling within paragraph 3 above, "the previous payment interval" means the interval after the end of the immediately preceding accounting period within which corporation tax for that preceding period is required to be paid by virtue of section 243(4) of the Taxes Act, as modified by this Part of this Schedule.

5. If the accounting period referred to in paragraph 2 above or any accounting period falling within paragraph 3 above is less than twelve months, the paragraph in question shall have effect in relation to that accounting period as if for the reference in that paragraph to the period of reduction there were substituted a reference to the number of whole days comprised in a period which bears to the period of reduction the same proportion as that accounting period bears to twelve months.

Consequential provisions

6. With respect to any accounting period of an old company which falls within paragraph 2 or paragraph 3 above, section 86 of the Taxes Management Act 1970 (interest on overdue tax) shall have effect as if, in paragraph 5(a) of the Table in subsection (4) (the reckonable date in relation to corporation tax), the reference into the nine months mentioned in section 243(4) of the Taxes Act were a reference to the period which, under the preceding provisions of this Part of this Schedule, is substituted for those nine months.

7. In section 88 of the Taxes Management Act 1970 (interest on tax recovered to make good loss due to taxpayer's fault) in paragraph (e) of subsection (5) (the date when corporation tax ought to have been paid) for the words from "where section 244(1)" to "the interval" there shall be substituted "in the case of an accounting period in respect of which subsection (4) of section 243 of the principal Act applies as modified by paragraph 2 or paragraph 3 of Schedule 6 to the Finance Act 1987, at the end of the period which, under that paragraph, is substituted for the period of nine months".

8. With respect to any accounting period of an old company which falls within paragraph 2 or paragraph 3 above, section 48 of the Finance (No. 2) Act 1975 (repayment supplement in respect of delayed repayments of certain taxes to companies) shall have effect as if, in subsection (9) in paragraph (a) of the definition of "the material date", the reference to the nine months mentioned in section 243(4) of the Taxes Act were a reference to the period which, under the preceding provisions of this Part of this Schedule, is substituted for those nine months.

PART II

BUILDING SOCIETIES

9. In this Part of this Schedule a "1989 accounting period" means an accounting period ending in the year 1989–90.

10. Where, by virtue of section 344(2)(a) of the Taxes Act, corporation tax assessed on a building society in respect of a 1989 accounting period would, apart from this paragraph, be payable by a date which is earlier than the end of the period of two months from the end of that accounting period, the tax shall be payable within that period of two months.

11. If, apart from this paragraph, the date on which, under section 344(2)(b) of the Taxes Act, a building society would be required to make a provisional payment of corporation tax for a 1989 accounting period would fall before the end of the period of two months from the end of that accounting period, that date shall be postponed until the end of that period of two months.

12. With respect to a 1989 accounting period of a building society to which paragraph 10 above applies, in the following enactments—
   (a) in section 86(4) of the Taxes Management Act 1970, paragraph 5(c) in the second column of the Table (the reckonable date for interest on overdue tax); and
   (b) in section 48(9) of the Finance (No. 2) Act 1975, paragraph (c) of the definition of "the material date" (for repayment supplement),
the reference to the time limit imposed by subsection (2)(a) of section 344 of the Taxes Act shall be construed as a reference to the limit imposed by paragraph 10 above.

GENERAL NOTE
   This Schedule provides for the phasing in of the new date for payment of corporation tax for companies that have previously paid tax more than nine months after the end of their accounting period. The new rule will only apply to accounting periods beginning on or after March 17, 1987, and payment after nine months will only fall to be made in respect of the third accounting period commenced thereafter.
   As regards building societies who pay tax less than nine months after the end of an accounting period, the introduction of the nine month rule will be spread normally over two years starting with accounting periods ending in the 1989–90 tax year.

Section 56   SCHEDULE 7

STAMP DUTY RESERVE TAX

1. Part IV of the Finance Act 1986 shall be amended in accordance with the following provisions of this Schedule.

Principal charge

2.—(1) In section 87, after subsection (7) there shall be inserted—
   "(7A) Where there would be no charge to tax under this section in relation to some of the chargeable securities to which the agreement between A and B relates if separate agreements had been made between them for the transfer of those securities and for the transfer of the remainder, this section shall have effect as if such separate agreements had been made.
   (7B) This section shall have effect in relation to a person to whom the chargeable securities are transferred by way of security for a loan to B as it has effect in relation to a nominee of B.".
   (2) This paragraph shall be deemed always to have had effect.

Renounceable letters of allotment, etc.

3.—(1) In section 88(3)(a), after the words "Subsection (2)" there shall be inserted the words "the words 'the expiry of the period of two months beginning with' and".
   (2) This paragraph shall have effect in relation to agreements made on or after 1st August 1987.

Market makers in options

4.—(1) In section 89, after subsection (1) there shall be inserted—
   "(1A) Section 87 above shall not apply as regards an agreement to transfer securities to B or his nominee if the agreement is made by B in the ordinary course of his business as a market maker in securities consisting of related quoted options; and in this subsection—
      (a) 'quoted options' means options quoted on The Stock Exchange, and
      (b) 'related quoted options' means quoted options to buy or sell securities of the kind transferred.".

(2) This paragraph shall be deemed always to have had effect.

Clearance services

5.—(1) In section 90, for subsection (5) there shall be substituted—

"(5) Section 87 above shall not apply as regards an agreement to transfer securities which the Board are satisfied are held, when the agreement is made, by a person within subsection (6) below.

(6) A person is within this subsection if his business is exclusively that of holding shares, stock or other marketable securities—

(a) as nominee or agent for a person whose business is or includes the provision of clearance services for the purchase and sale of shares, stock or other marketable securities, and

(b) for the purpose of such part of the business mentioned in paragraph (a) above as consists of the provision of such clearance services (in a case where the business does not consist exclusively of that);

and in this subsection, 'marketable securities' shall be construed in accordance with section 122(1) of the Stamp Act 1891.".

(2) This paragraph shall be deemed always to have had effect.

Charities, etc.

6.—(1) In section 90, at the end there shall be added—

"(7) Section 87 above shall not apply as regards an agreement to transfer securities to—

(a) a body of persons established for charitable purposes only, or

(b) the trustees of a trust so established, or

(c) the Trustees of the National Heritage Memorial Fund, or

(d) the Historic Buildings and Monuments Commission for England.".

(2) This paragraph shall be deemed always to have had effect.

Interest on tax repayments

7.—(1) In section 92, after subsection (4) there shall be inserted—

"(4A) Interest paid under subsection (2) above shall not constitute income for any tax purposes.".

(2) This paragraph shall be deemed always to have had effect.

GENERAL NOTE

Six specific amendments are made to Stamp Duty Reserve Tax ("S.D.R.T.") in paras. 2 to 7.

Para. 2 rectifies retrospectively two anomalies in the original provision for the charge to S.D.R.T. The new subs. (7A) makes it clear that where there is a sale of a parcel of shares from A to B, a resale by B to C of part of the parcel and transfers charged to stamp duty by A to B and C, B's liability to S.D.R.T. extends only to the shares resold. The new subs. (7B) extends the exemption where stamp duty is paid within the prescribed period of two months on a transfer to B or his nominee to cases where a financial institution holding the shares as security is the transferee.

Para. 3. Sales of renounceable letters of allotment are subject only to S.D.R.T. and there is therefore no need for a two month grace period to allow for the payment of stamp duty on the transaction. Accordingly S.D.R.T. is made payable when the sale is made.

Para. 4 extends retrospectively the exemption from S.D.R.T. for market makers in securities to market makers in both traded and traditional options.

Para. 5 exempts retrospectively from charge to S.D.R.T. under F.A. 1986, s.87 agreements to transfer securities to clearance services which in any case attract a charge to stamp duty or S.D.R.T. at 1.5 per cent. under F.A. 1986, s.70 or s.96.

Para. 6. The exemptions from stamp duty accorded under F.A. 1982, s.129 and F.A. 1983, s.46(3) to the persons listed in sub.-para. (1) are retrospectively extended to S.D.R.T.

Para. 7 exempts retrospectively from tax interest paid on repayments of S.D.R.T. Such an exemption already applies in relation to interest on repayments of income tax, capital gains tax, corporation tax (F.(No. 2)A. 1975, ss.47 and 48) and Inheritance Tax (I.H.T.A., s.235).

SECURITIES, OTHER BUSINESS PROPERTY AND AGRICULTURAL PROPERTY

1. In section 10 of the 1984 Act (dispositions not intended to confer gratuitous benefit) in subsection (2) for the words from "shares" to "stock exchange" there shall be substituted "unquoted shares or unquoted debentures".

2. In section 98 of the 1984 Act (effect of alterations of capital, etc.) in subsection (1)—
  (a) in paragraph (a) for the words from "shares" onwards there shall be substituted "quoted shares or quoted securities";
  (b) in paragraph (b) for the words from "shares" onwards there shall be substituted "unquoted shares in or unquoted debentures of a close company"; and
  (c) for the words "shares or debentures not so quoted" there shall be substituted "unquoted shares or unquoted debentures".

3. In section 100 of the 1984 Act (alterations of capital where participators are trustees) in subsection (1)(c) for the words from "shares" onwards there shall be substituted "unquoted shares in or unquoted securities of the close company".

4. In section 104 of the 1984 Act (relief for business property) in subsection (1)(a) for the words "or (b)" there shall be substituted "(b) or (bb)".

5.—(1) Section 105 of the 1984 Act (relevant business property) shall be amended as follows.

(2) In subsection (1) after the words "sections 106, 108," there shall be inserted "109A" and for paragraph (c) there shall be substituted the following paragraphs—
  "(bb) unquoted shares in a company which do not fall within paragraph (b) above and which immediately before the transfer satisfied the condition specified in subsection (1A) below;
  (c) unquoted shares in a company which do not fall within paragraph (b) or paragraph (bb) above".

(3) After subsection (1) there shall be inserted the following subsections—
  "(1A) The condition referred to in subsection (1)(bb) above is that the shares (either by themselves or together with other shares or securities owned by the transferor) gave the transferor control of powers of voting on all questions affecting the company as a whole which if exercised would have yielded more than 25 per cent. of the votes capable of being exercised on them; and shares shall be taken to satisfy this condition if, together with any shares which are related property within the meaning of section 161 below, they would have been sufficient to give the transferor such control.
  (1B) Subsections (3) and (4) of section 269 below have effect in relation to subsection (1A) above as they have effect in relation to subsection (1) of that section."

(4) After subsection (2) there shall be inserted the following subsection—
  "(2A) Shares of a company do not fall within subsection (1)(bb) above if—
      (a) they would not have been sufficient, without other property, to satisfy the condition specified in subsection (1A) above immediately before the transfer; and
      (b) their value is taken by virtue of section 176 below to be less than the value previously determined."

6. In section 107 of the 1984 Act (replacements) in subsection (4)—
  (a) for the words "section 105(1)(c)" there shall be substituted "section 105(1)(bb) or (c)"; and
  (b) after the words "section 106 above" there shall be inserted "and section 109A below".

7. After section 109 of the 1984 Act there shall be inserted the following section—

"Additional requirement in case of minority shareholdings
  109A. Shares in a company do not fall within subsection (1)(bb) of section 105 above unless the condition specified in subsection (1A) of that section was satisfied—
      (a) throughout the two years immediately preceding the transfer, or
      (b) where section 108 or section 109 above applies and the transferor owned the shares for a period of less than two years immediately preceding the transfer, throughout that lesser period."

8.—(1) In section 113A of the 1984 Act (application of relief for business property to transfers made within seven years before death of transferor) in subsection (3) at the beginning of paragraph (b) there shall be inserted the words "except to the extent that the original property consists of shares or securities to which subsection (3A) below applies".

(2) After subsection (3) of that section there shall be inserted the following subsection—

"(3A) This subsection applies to shares or securities—
    (a) which were quoted at the time of the chargeable transfer referred to in subsection (1) or subsection (2) above; or
    (b) which fell within paragraph (b) of section 105(1) above in relation to that transfer and were unquoted throughout the period referred to in subsection (3)(a) above."

9. In section 124A of the 1984 Act (application of agricultural relief to transfers within seven years before death of transferor) in subsection (6) for the words following paragraph (b) there shall be substituted "his period of ownership of the original property shall be treated as including his period of ownership of the shares."

10. In section 136 of the 1984 Act (transactions of close companies) in subsection (1)(b) for the words "shares quoted on a recognised stock exchange" there shall be substituted "quoted shares" and for the words "shares in or debentures of the company which are not so quoted" there shall be substituted "unquoted shares in or unquoted debentures of the company".

11. In section 140(2) of the 1984 Act (market value for purposes of Chapter IV of Part IV) in paragraph (b) for the words from "shares" to "exchange" there shall be substituted "unquoted shares".

12.—(1) In section 168 of the 1984 Act (unquoted shares and securities) in subsection (1) before the word "securities" where it first occurs, there shall be inserted "unquoted".

(2) Subsection (2) of that section shall be omitted.

13.—(1) In section 178 of the 1984 Act (sale of shares etc. from deceased's estate) in subsection (1), in the definition of "qualifying investments", for the words from "at the date" to "exchange" there shall be substituted "are quoted at the date of the death in question".

(2) In subsection (2) of that section—
    (a) after the words "quotation on a recognised stock exchange" there shall be inserted "or dealing on the Unlisted Securities Market"; and
    (b) the words "on a recognised stock exchange", in the second place where they occur, shall be omitted.

14. In section 180 of the 1984 Act (effect of purchases) in subsection (3) after the word "exchange" there shall be inserted "or separately dealt in on the Unlisted Securities Market".

15.—(1) In section 227 of the 1984 Act (payment by instalments) for subsection (1A) there shall be substituted the following subsection—
"(1A) Subsection (1) above does not apply to—
    (a) tax payable on the value transferred by a potentially exempt transfer which proves to be a chargeable transfer, or
    (b) additional tax becoming payable on the value transferred by any chargeable transfer by reason of the transferor's death within seven years of the transfer,
except to the extent that the tax is attributable to the value of property which satisfies one of the conditions specified in subsection (1C) below and, in the case of property consisting of unquoted shares or unquoted securities, the further condition specified in section 228(3A) below."

(2) In subsection (1B) of that section for the words "subsection (1A) above" there shall be substituted "this section".

(3) After subsection (1B) of that section there shall be inserted the following subsection—
"(1C) The conditions referred to in subsection (1A) above are—
    (a) that the property was owned by the transferee throughout the period beginning with the date of the chargeable transfer and ending with the death of the transferor (or, if earlier, the death of the transferee), or
    (b) that for the purposes of determining the tax, or additional tax, due by reason of the death of the transferor, the value of the property is reduced in accordance with the provisions of Chapter I or Chapter II of Part V of this Act by virtue of section 113B or section 124B above."

16.—(1) In section 228 of the 1984 Act (shares etc. within section 227) in subsection (1) for the words "not falling under paragraph (a) above and not quoted on a recognised stock exchange", in each place where they occur, there shall be substituted "which do not fall under paragraph (a) above and are unquoted".

(2) After subsection (3) of that section there shall be inserted the following subsection—
"(3A) The further condition referred to in section 227(1A) above is that the shares or securities remained unquoted throughout the period beginning with the date of the

chargeable transfer and ending with the death of the transferor (or, if earlier, the death of the transferee)."

17. In section 272 of the 1984 Act (general interpretation) after the definition of "purchaser" there shall be inserted—

""quoted", in relation to any shares or securities, means quoted on a recognised stock exchange or dealt in on the Unlisted Securities Market and "unquoted", in relation to any shares or securities, means neither so quoted nor so dealt in".

18.—(1) In Schedule 20 to the Finance Act 1986 (gifts with reservation) paragraph 8 (agricultural and business property) shall be amended as follows.

(2) In sub-paragraph (1) for the word "Where" there shall be substituted "This paragraph applies where" and the words from "then" onwards shall be omitted.

(3) After sub-paragraph (1) there shall be inserted the following sub-paragraph—

"(1A) Where this paragraph applies—

(a) any question whether, on the material transfer of value, any shares or securities fall within paragraph (b) or paragraph (bb) of section 105(1) of the 1984 Act (which specify shares and securities qualifying for 50 per cent. relief) shall be determined, subject to the following provisions of this paragraph, as if the shares or securities were owned by the donor and had been owned by him since the disposal by way of gift; and

(b) subject to paragraph (a) above, any question whether, on the material transfer of value, relief is available by virtue of Chapter I or Chapter II of Part V of the 1984 Act and, if relief is available by virtue of Chapter II, what is the appropriate percentage for that relief, shall be determined, subject to the following provisions of this paragraph, as if, so far as it is attributable to the property comprised in the gift, that transfer were a transfer of value by the donee."

(4) In sub-paragraph (2) for the words "sub-paragraph (1)" there shall be substituted "sub-paragraph (1A)(b)".

(5) In sub-paragraph (3)—

(a) for the words "that sub-paragraph shall not apply" there shall be substituted "relief shall not be available by virtue of Chapter II of Part V of the 1984 Act on the material transfer of value"; and

(b) for the words "by virtue of sub-paragraph (1) above" there shall be substituted "by virtue of sub-paragraph (1A)(b) above".

GENERAL NOTE

Most of the amendments made to I.H.T.A. 1984 and F.A. 1986, Sched. 20 by this Schedule relate to two matters, the assimilation of the treatment of shares dealt in on the unlisted securities market ("USM") with that accorded to shares quoted on the Stock Exchange itself, and the increase in the rate of business property relief on minority shareholdings in excess of 25 per cent. in companies not so quoted or dealt in from 30 per cent. to 50 per cent.

Para. 1, together with paras. 2, 3, 10–14 and 16, is concerned with the first matter mentioned above.

Paras. 4 to 8 are concerned with the second matter.

Para. 9 corrects an anomaly in the legislation in relation to the position where agricultural land which is the subject of a potentially exempt transfer is exchanged for shares in a company.

Para. 15 amplifies and clarifies the provisions relating to instalment relief on potentially exempt transfers of property qualifying for business or agricultural relief which become chargeable.

Para. 17 adds a new definition to I.H.T.A. 1984, s.272. A "quoted" share now includes one dealt in on the USM.

Para. 18 modifies the provisions applying the gifts with reservation of benefit rules to business and agricultural property.

Section 59   SCHEDULE 9

MAINTENANCE FUNDS FOR HISTORIC BUILDINGS ETC.

1. The following section shall be inserted after section 57 of the Inheritance Tax Act 1984—

"Relief where property enters maintenance fund

57A.—(1) Subject to the following provisions, subsection (2) below applies where—

    (a)   a person dies who immediately before his death was beneficially entitled to an interest in possession in property comprised in a settlement, and

    (b)   within two years after his death the property becomes held on trusts (whether of that or another settlement) by virtue of which a direction under paragraph 1 of Schedule 4 to this Act is given in respect of the property.

(2) Where this subsection applies, this Act shall have effect as if the property had on the death of the deceased become subject to the trusts referred to in subsection (1)(b) above; and accordingly no disposition or other event occurring between the date of the death and the date on which the property becomes subject to those trusts shall, so far as it relates to the property, be a transfer of value or otherwise constitute an occasion for a charge to tax.

(3) Where property becomes held on trusts of the kind specified in paragraph (b) of subsection (1) above as the result of proceedings before a court and could not have become so held without such proceedings, that paragraph shall have effect as if it referred to three years instead of two.

(4) Subsection (2) above shall not apply if—

    (a)   the disposition by which the property becomes held on the trusts referred to in subsection (1)(b) above depends on a condition or is defeasible; or

    (b)   the property which becomes held on those trusts is itself an interest in settled property; or

    (c)   the trustees who hold the property on those trusts have, for a consideration in money or money's worth, acquired an interest under a settlement in which the property was comprised immediately before the death of the person referred to in subsection (1)(a) above or at any time thereafter; or

    (d)   the property which becomes held on those trusts does so for a consideration in money or money's worth, or is acquired by the trustees for such a consideration, or has at any time since the death of the person referred to in subsection (1)(a) above been acquired by any other person for such consideration.

(5) If the value of the property when it becomes held on the trusts referred to in subsection (1)(b) above is lower than so much of the value transferred on the death of the person referred to in subsection (1)(a) as is attributable to the property, subsection (2) above shall apply to the property only to the extent of the lower value.

(6) For the purposes of this section, a person shall be treated as acquiring property for a consideration in money or money's worth if he becomes entitled to it as a result of transactions which include a disposition for such consideration (whether to him or another) of that or other property.".

2. At the end of paragraph 3 of Schedule 4 to the 1984 Act there shall be added—

"(5A) In the case of property which, if a direction is given under paragraph 1 above, will be property to which paragraph 15A below applies, sub-paragraph (1)(b) above shall have effect as if for the reference to the settlor there were substituted a reference to either the settlor or the person referred to in paragraph 15A(2).".

3. After paragraph 15 of that Schedule there shall be inserted—

"Maintenance fund following interest in possession

15A.—(1) In relation to settled property to which this paragraph applies, the provisions of this Part of this Schedule shall have effect with the modifications set out in the following sub-paragraphs.

(2) This paragraph applies to property which became property to which paragraph 8 above applies on the occasion of a transfer of value which was made by a person beneficially entitled to an interest in possession in the property, and which (so far as the value transferred by it was attributable to the property)—

    (a)   was an exempt transfer by virtue of the combined effect of either—

        (i)   sections 27 and 57(5) of this Act, or

        (ii)   sections 27 and 57A of this Act, and

    (b)   would but for those sections have been a chargeable transfer;

and in the following sub-paragraphs "the person entitled to the interest in possession" means the person above referred to.

(3) Paragraph 9(2) shall have effect as if for the reference to the settlor there were substituted a reference to either the settlor or the person entitled to the interest in possession.

(4) Paragraph 10 shall not apply if the person entitled to the interest in possession had died at or before the time when the property became property to which paragraph 8 above applies; and in any other case shall have effect with the substitution in sub-paragraph (1) of the following words for the words from "on becoming" onwards—

"(a) on becoming property to which the person entitled to the interest in possession is beneficially entitled, or

(b) on becoming—

    (i) property to which that person's spouse is beneficially entitled, or

    (ii) property to which that person's widow or widower is beneficially entitled if that person has died in the two years preceding the time when it becomes such property;

but paragraph (b) above applies only where the spouse, widow or widower would have become beneficially entitled to the property on the termination of the interest in possession had the property not then become property to which paragraph 8 above applies.".

(5) Paragraph 11 shall not apply.

(6) Sub-paragraphs (1) to (3) of paragraph 14 shall have effect as if for the references to the settlor there were substituted references to the person entitled to the interest in possession.

(7) Sub-paragraph (4) of paragraph 14 shall have effect with the insertion after paragraph (b) of the words "and

(c) was, in relation to either of those settlements, property to which paragraph 15A below applied,",

and with the substitution for the words from "settlor shall" onwards of the words "person entitled to the interest in possession shall, if the Board so determine, be construed as references to the person who was the settlor in relation to the current settlement.".

(8) Sub-paragraph (5) of paragraph 14 shall have effect with the insertion after paragraph (b) of the words "and

(c) was, in relation to any of those settlements, property to which paragraph 15A below applied,",

and with the substitution for the words from "settlor shall" onwards of the words "person entitled to the interest in possession shall, if the Board so determine, be construed as references to any person selected by them who was the settlor in relation to any of the previous settlements or the current settlement."

(9) Except in a case where the board have made a determination under sub-paragraph (4) or (5) of paragraph 14, sub-paragraphs (6) and (7) of that paragraph shall have effect as if for the references to the settlor there were substituted references to the person entitled to the interest in possession.

(10) Sub-paragraph (9) of paragraph 14 shall have effect with the substitution for the words "(if the settlement was made on death)" of the words "(if the person entitled to the interest in possession had died at or before the time when the property became property to which paragraph 8 above applies)".

4. Paragraph 1 above shall have effect in relation to deaths occurring on or after 17th March 1987.

5. Paragraph 2 above shall have effect in relation to directions given on or after 17th March 1987.

6. Paragraph 3 above shall have effect where the occasion of the charge or potential charge to tax under paragraph 8 of Schedule 4 to the 1984 Act falls on or after 17th March 1987.

GENERAL NOTE

This Schedule makes two modifications to the rules regarding maintenance funds for historic buildings.

Para. 1 extends the exemption from charge on property entering such funds to cases where settled property does so within two years of the death of a life tenant. If the value of the property is lower on entry into the fund than it was on the death of the life tenant, the exemption will apply to the lower value. The period is extended to three years where a court order is necessary, for example where children or unborn persons are included in the class of beneficiaries under the settlement.

Paras. 2 and 3 make it clear that the charge when settled property leaves a maintenance fund for non-heritage purposes will be based on the cumulated chargeable transfers made by the former life tenant rather than the original settlor. This charge will also apply to property which formerly had an interest in possession and entered the fund on the termination of that interest with the benefit of the existing maintenance fund exemption.

Paras. 4 to 6 apply these changes to events occurring on or after Budget Day.

Section 61

SCHEDULE 10

Nomination Scheme for Disposals and Appropriations

Interpretation

1.—(1) In this Schedule—

"month" means calendar month;

"nominal volume" shall be construed in accordance with paragraph 7 below;

"nominated price" shall be construed in accordance with paragraph 6 below;

"nomination" means a nomination made in such manner as may be prescribed by regulations made by the Board;

"proposed sale", "proposed supply" and "proposed appropriation" shall be construed in accordance with paragraphs (a) to (c) of sub-paragraph (1) of paragraph 2 below;

"proposed delivery month" shall be construed in accordance with paragraph 3 below;

"proposed transaction" means one falling within paragraph 2(1) below;

"regulations made by the Board" means regulations under section 61(8) of this Act; and

"Treasury regulations" means regulations under section 61(7) of this Act.

(2) For the purposes of this Schedule, a participator's equity production from an oil field in any month is his share of the oil won from the field which, in that month, is either delivered or relevantly appropriated, other than oil which is delivered to the Secretary of State pursuant to a notice served by him.

Transactions which may be nominated

2.—(1) The proposed transactions which may be nominated by a participator in an oil field for the purposes of this Schedule are—

(a) proposed sales at arm's length by the participator of specified quantities of oil for delivery from that oil field; and

(b) proposed supplies by the participator (being a company) to another company which is associated with the participator of specified quantities of oil for delivery from that oil field for use for refining either by that other company or by a third company associated with the participator; and

(c) proposed relevant appropriations by the participator of specified quantities of oil won from that field; and

(d) any other proposed transactions specified for the purposes of this sub-paragraph by Treasury regulations;

and two companies are associated with each other for the purposes of paragraph (b) above if they would be so associated for the purposes of section 115(2) of the Finance Act 1984.

(2) Where a proposed sale is nominated before a contract of sale comes into being, any reference in this Schedule to the contract of sale is a reference to the subsequent contract for the sale of oil in accordance with the terms of the nomination; and, accordingly, if no such contract of sale comes into being, the nomination of the proposed sale shall be of no effect.

(3) A participator may not nominate a proposed sale if—

(a) under the terms of the contract of sale as originally entered into, the party undertaking to sell the oil is someone other than the participator; or

(b) it is of a description prescribed for the purposes of this sub-paragraph by regulations made by the Board.

Period for which nomination has effect

3.—(1) Subject to sub-paragraph (3) below, a nomination shall have effect with respect to proposed deliveries and appropriations of oil in one month only and, accordingly, where a nomination is of a proposed sale and the contract of sale provides for the supply of oil in more than one month, the nomination shall be effective only in relation to oil proposed to be delivered in the month for which the nomination has effect.

(2) Subject to sub-paragraph (3) below, in relation to a nomination, "the proposed delivery month" means the month for which the nomination has effect in accordance with sub-paragraph (1) above.

(3) In relation to a contract of sale of a description specified in the regulations, regulations made by the Board may permit a nomination to have effect as a nomination of a proposed sale for each of a number of months and, in relation to such a nomination, this Schedule shall have effect subject to such modifications as may be prescribed in the regulations.

Timing of nominations

4.—(1) Subject to sub-paragraph (2) below, a nomination shall be effective only if it is made not later than five o'clock in the afternoon of the second business day following the date which, in relation to a proposed transaction of that description, is prescribed as the transaction base date.

(2) Sub-paragraph (1) above does not apply to a nomination made on or before 16th February 1987 which specified a proposed transaction having a transaction base date earlier than 12th February 1987.

(3) The transaction base date prescribed for a proposed sale may be a date earlier than the date on which a legally binding agreement for the sale of the oil in question comes into being but may not be later than the date on which there is an agreed price at which any oil which is to be delivered pursuant to the contract of sale will be sold.

(4) In this paragraph—
    (a) "business day" has the same meaning as in the Bills of Exchange Act 1882;
    (b) "prescribed" means prescribed by regulations made by the Board.

Content of nomination

5.—(1) A nomination of a proposed transaction shall not be effective unless it specifies, with respect to that transaction,—
    (a) the name of the participator;
    (b) except in the case of a proposed appropriation, the name of the person to whom the oil is to be delivered;
    (c) the field from which the oil is to be delivered or relevantly appropriated;
    (d) the nominated price of the oil to be supplied or relevantly appropriated;
    (e) the nominated volume of that oil;
    (f) the proposed delivery month;
    (g) the transaction base date; and
    (h) such other information as may be prescribed by the Board.

(2) A nomination shall include a declaration that it is correct and complete and, in the case of a nomination of a proposed sale which is made before the contract of sale comes into being, shall also include a declaration that, to the best of the knowledge and belief of the participator making the nomination, a contract of sale will come into being in accordance with the terms of the nomination.

(3) Where a participator fraudulently or negligently furnishes any incorrect information or makes any incorrect declaration in or in connection with a nomination he shall be liable to a penalty not exceeding £50,000 or, in the case of fraud, £100,000.

Nominated price

6.—(1) Subject to sub-paragraph (3) below, in the case of a proposed sale, the "nominated price", in relation to the oil which is to be delivered pursuant to the sale, is the price specified in the contract of sale (expressed as a unit price) or, as the case may be, the formula under which, in accordance with the contract, the price for that oil (as so expressed) is to be determined.

(2) Subject to sub-paragraph (3) below, in the case of a proposed supply or proposed appropriation, the "nominated price" of the oil concerned means the market value of that oil, ascertained in accordance with Schedule 3 to the principal Act and expressed as a unit price; and for the purposes of paragraph 5(d) above a statement that the nominated price of oil is its "market value" shall be sufficient.

(3) Treasury regulations may—
    (a) vary the meaning of "nominated price" in relation to a proposed sale, supply or appropriation and, for that purpose, amend sub-paragraph (1) or sub-paragraph (2) above; and

(b) make provision as to the meaning of "nominated price" in relation to a proposed transaction falling within paragraph 2(1)(d) above.

Nominal volume

7.—(1) Subject to sub-paragraph (3) below, in the case of a proposed sale, the nominal volume means the quantity of oil which it is proposed should be delivered under the contract of sale in the proposed delivery month.

(2) Subject to sub-paragraph (3) below, in the case of a proposed supply or proposed appropriation, the nominal volume means the quantity of oil which the participator making the nomination proposes to supply or relevantly appropriate (as the case may be) in the proposed delivery month.

(3) In the case of any proposed transaction, the nominal volume means the quantity of oil expressed in such manner as may be prescribed by regulations made by the Board.

(4) In any case where—

(a) apart from this sub-paragraph, the nominal volume in any proposed transaction would be expressed as a specific volume of oil, plus or minus a particular tolerance, and

(b) that tolerance exceeds the limits prescribed for the purposes of this Schedule by regulations made by the Board,

the nominal volume shall for those purposes be taken to be the specific volume referred to in paragraph (a) above, plus or minus the maximum tolerance permitted by the regulations.

(5) Where a nominal volume is expressed as a specific volume of oil, plus or minus a tolerance, any reference in paragraph 9 below to the maximum nominal volume or the minimum nominal volume is a reference to that specific volume of oil, plus or minus the tolerance respectively.

Revision of nominations

8.—(1) Except as provided by this paragraph, a nomination may not be amended or withdrawn.

(2) If a participator who has made a nomination of a proposed sale does not, in whole or in part, fulfil his obligations under the contract of sale by the delivery of oil forming part of his equity production for the proposed delivery month, then, in accordance with regulations made by the Board, he may amend or withdraw the nomination if in his opinion—

(a) there were good commercial reasons for the failure to fulfil those obligations; or

(b) the failure was occasioned by circumstances over which neither he nor any person connected or associated with him had control.

(3) An amendment or withdrawal of a nomination by a participator in accordance with sub-paragraph (2) above shall not be effective unless the Board give notice to the participator that the amendment or withdrawal is accepted, and the Board shall not give such a notice unless they are satisfied—

(a) as to the matters mentioned in either paragraph (a) or paragraph (b) of sub-paragraph (2) above; and

(b) if sub-paragraph (2)(a) above applies, that the failure was not part of a scheme or arrangement the main purpose of which was the avoidance of tax.

(4) For the purposes of sub-paragraph (2)(b) above,—

(a) section 533 of the Taxes Act (connected persons) applies; and

(b) two companies of which one is a participator in an oil field are associated with each other if one has control over the other or both are under the control of the same person or persons;

and in paragraph (b) above "control" shall be construed in accordance with section 302 of the Taxes Act.

(5) Where a nomination is amended in accordance with this paragraph, the preceding provisions of this Schedule shall apply in relation to it subject to such modifications as may be specified in regulations made by the Board.

Effective volume for nominated transactions

9.—(1) The provisions of this paragraph have effect to determine, in relation to each nominated transaction, what is the effective volume of oil.

(2) In relation to a proposed sale where the nominal volume is expressed as mentioned in paragraph 7(5) above and oil is in fact delivered under the contract of sale, the effective volume is whichever is the greater of—

(a) the minimum nominal volume; and

(b) so much of the total volume of oil actually delivered under the contract as does not exceed the maximum nominal volume.

(3) In relation to any proposed sale which does not fall within sub-paragraph (2) above, the effective volume shall be taken to be the nominal volume.

(4) In relation to a proposed supply or proposed appropriation, the effective volume is the nominal volume.

Aggregate effective volume for a month

10.—(1) Subject to the provisions of this paragraph, for each month the aggregate effective volume of a participator's nominated transactions is the sum of the effective volumes of all of the proposed transactions nominated by him for that month.

(2) If a participator's aggregate effective volume for any month, as determined under sub-paragraph (1) above, would exceed his equity production for that month—

(a) his nominated transactions for that month shall be taken to be reduced by cancelling later nominations in priority to earlier ones until the cancellation of the next nominated transaction would produce an aggregate effective volume less than the participator's equity production; and

(b) the effective volume of the latest remaining nominated transaction shall be taken to be reduced so far as necessary to secure that the aggregate effective volume is equal to the participator's equity production.

Aggregate nominated proceeds for a month

11.—(1) For each month, a participator's aggregate nominated proceeds for the purposes of section 61 of this Act is the sum of—

(a) the proceeds of each nominated transaction falling within sub-paragraph (2) below; and

(b) the market value of any excess falling within sub-paragraph (3) below.

(2) For each nominated transaction, the effective volume of which forms part of the participator's aggregate effective volume for the month, as defined in paragraph 10 above, the proceeds of the transaction means the effective volume multiplied by the nominated price.

(3) If the participator's equity production for a month exceeds his aggregate effective volume for that month, as defined in paragraph 10 above, the market value of the excess shall be determined in accordance with Schedule 3 to the principal Act.

(4) The reference in sub-paragraph (2) above to the nominated price is a reference to that price expressed in sterling; and regulations made by the Board shall make provision with respect to the conversion into sterling of any nominated price which is expressed in a currency other than sterling.

Blended oil

12. In accordance with regulations made by the Board, a person who is a participator in two or more fields may nominate a proposed sale, supply or appropriation of oil which is blended oil, within the meaning of section 63 of this Act; and the preceding provisions of this Schedule shall have effect in relation to such a nomination subject to such modifications as may be prescribed by regulations made by the Board.

Returns

13. In paragraph 2 of Schedule 2 to the principal Act (returns by participators) at the end of sub-paragraph (3) there shall be inserted the following sub-paragraph—

"(3A) A return under this paragraph for a chargeable period shall—

(a) state the amount (if any) which, in the case of the participator, is to be brought into account for that period in accordance with section 2(5)(e) of this Act;

(b) contain such particulars as the Board may prescribe (whether before or after the passing of the Finance Act 1987) with respect to any nominated transaction under Schedule 10 to that Act—

(i) the effective volume of which forms part of the participator's aggregate effective volume (construing those terms in accordance with that Schedule) for any calendar month comprised in that chargeable period; and

(ii) which has not led to deliveries of oil or relevant appropriations of which particulars are included in the return by virtue of sub-paragraph (2) above; and

(c) contain such other particulars as the Board may prescribe (as mentioned above) in connection with the application of section 61 of and Schedule 10 to the Finance Act 1987."

GENERAL NOTE

Detailed provision is made for the new crude oil nomination scheme for petroleum revenue tax ("P.R.T."). For a summary of the scheme, see the Note to s.61 *supra*.

Para. 1 provides general definitions.

Para. 2 specifies the transactions which may be nominated.

Para. 3 limits nominations to one month's deliveries and appropriations, subject to extension under Revenue regulations.

Para. 4. Nominations must be made within two business days of a base date to be prescribed by Revenue regulations, not later than the date on which the price is agreed.

Para. 5 prescribes the particulars which must be given in a nomination and sets a penalty not exceeding £50,000 for negligence and £100,000 for fraud in relation to incorrect information or declarations.

Para. 6 defines "nominated price", subject to Treasury regulation.

Para. 7 gives the Revenue power to prescribe by regulation the manner in which the volume of oil in any transaction is to be expressed, within permitted tolerances.

Para. 8. Nominations are generally irrevocable, unless the Revenue are satisfied that there were good commercial reasons for the participator failing to fulfil his obligations and the failure was due to circumstances beyond the control of the participator or his associates. In such a case, provided a tax avoidance scheme is not involved, nominations may be amended or withdrawn under Revenue regulations.

Para. 9 provides that the effective volume for a nominated transaction which is carried through shall be the nominal volume under para. 7, subject to the tolerances allowed under that paragraph.

Para. 10. The aggregate effective volume for the month is the total of all the nominated transactions for that month. Where that total exceeds the participator's equity production (defined in para. 1(2)) the nominations are cancelled or reduced on a LIFO basis.

Para. 11. In the converse situation where equity production exceeds the aggregate effective volume the balance is valued in accordance with the market value rules in Oil Taxation Act 1975, Sched. 3.

Para. 12 permits the nomination of blended oil, within the meaning of s.63 and Sched. 12.

Para. 13 authorises the Revenue to prescribe returns by participators for the purposes of the scheme.

Section 62

SCHEDULE 11

MARKET VALUE OF OIL

PART I

AMENDMENTS OF PARAGRAPHS 2, 2A AND 3 OF SCHEDULE 3 TO PRINCIPAL ACT

1.—(1) Paragraph 2 of Schedule 3 (definition of market value of oil) shall be amended in accordance with this paragraph.

(2) For sub-paragraph (1) there shall be substituted—

"(1) The market value of any oil in any calendar month shall be determined for the purposes of this Part of this Act in accordance with this paragraph."

(3) In sub-paragraph (2) for the words from the beginning to "to be delivered" in paragraph (b) there shall be substituted—

"(2) Subject to the following provisions of this paragraph, the market value of any oil in a calendar month (in this paragraph referred to as "the relevant month") is the price at which oil of that kind might reasonably have been expected to be sold under a contract of sale satisfying the following conditions—

(a) the contract is for the sale of the oil at arm's length to a willing buyer;

(b) the contract is for the delivery of the oil at a time in the relevant month;

(c) the contract is entered into within the period beginning at the beginning of the month preceding the relevant month and ending on the middle day of the

relevant month or, if the Treasury by order so direct, within such other period as may be specified in the order; .
  (d) the contract requires the oil to have been subjected to appropriate initial treatment before delivery;
  (e) the contract requires the oil to be delivered".
  (4) In sub-paragraph (2), paragraph (c) shall become paragraph (f) and shall be amended as follows—
  (a) for the words "as at a particular time" there shall be substituted "as in a particular month"; and
  (b) for the words "as at that time" there shall be substituted "as in that month".
  (5) At the end of sub-paragraph (2) there shall be added the words "and, for the purposes of paragraph (c) above, the middle day of a month containing an even number of days shall be taken to be the last day of the first half of the month, and the power to make an order under that paragraph shall be exercisable by statutory instrument which shall be subject to annulment in pursuance of a resolution of the Commons House of Parliament."
  (6) After sub-paragraph (2) there shall be inserted the following sub-paragraphs—
    "(2A) For the purpose of sub-paragraph (2) above, the price of any oil in a calendar month shall be determined, subject to sub-paragraphs (2B) and (2C) below, by taking the average of the prices under actual contracts for the sale of oil of that kind—
  (a) which are contracts for the sale of oil by a participator in an oil field or by a company which, for the purposes of section 115(2) of the Finance Act 1984, is associated with such a participator; and
  (b) which, subject to sub-paragraph (2B) below, satisfy the conditions in paragraphs (a) to (e) of sub-paragraph (2) above; and
  (c) which do not contain terms as to payment which differ from those customarily contained in contracts for the sale at arm's length of oil of the kind in question.
    (2B) For the purposes of sub-paragraph (2A)(b) above, a contract shall be treated as fulfilling the condition in paragraph (c) of sub-paragraph (2) above if it contains provisions under which the price for oil to be delivered in the relevant month either is determined or subject to review in the period relevant for the purposes of that paragraph or is determined by reference to other prices which are themselves determined in that period, being prices for oil to be delivered in the relevant month.
    (2C) The average referred to in sub-paragraph (2A) above shall be determined—
  (a) by establishing an average price for oil of the kind in question for each business day within the period relevant for the purposes of sub-paragraph (2)(c) above; and
  (b) by taking the arithmetic mean of the average prices so established;
and in this sub-paragraph "business day" has the same meaning as in the Bills of Exchange Act 1882.
    (2D) If or in so far as the Board are satisfied that it is impracticable or inappropriate to determine for the purposes of sub-paragraph (2) above the price of any oil in a calendar month as mentioned in sub-paragraph (2A) above (whether by virtue of an insufficiency of contracts satisfying the conditions or of information relating to such contracts or by virtue of the nature of the market for oil of the kind in question or for any other reason), that price shall be determined,—
  (a) so far as it is practicable and appropriate to do so by reference to such other contracts (whether or not relating to oil of the same kind) and in accordance with the principles in sub-paragraph (2C) above; and
  (b) so far as it is not practicable or appropriate to determine it as mentioned in paragraph (a) above, in such other manner as appears to the Board to be appropriate in the circumstances."
  (7) In sub-paragraph (3)—
  (a) for the words "as at a particular time" there shall be substituted "as in a particular month";
  (b) the words "at that time", where they first occur, shall be omitted;
  (c) after the words "was disposed of" there shall be inserted "in that month";
  (d) for the words "and (2)" there shall be substituted "to (2D)";
  (e) for the words "as at that time" there shall be substituted "as in that month"; and
  (f) for "(2)(b)" there shall be substituted "(2)(e)".
2. In paragraph 2A of that Schedule (modifications in the case of oil consisting of gas)—
  (a) in sub-paragraphs (1) and (3) for "(1) and (2)" there shall be substituted "(1) to (2D)";
  (b) in sub-paragraph (2) for "(2)(a)" in each place where it occurs, there shall be substituted "(2)(d)"; and

(c) in sub-paragraph (3) for "(2)(b)" there shall be substituted "(2)(e)".

3. In paragraph 3 of that Schedule (aggregate market value of oil for purposes of section 2(5))—
   (a) in sub-paragraph (1) the words "at the material time" shall be omitted; and
   (b) in sub-paragraph (2) the words from "and 'the material time'" onwards shall be omitted.

PART II

CONSEQUENTIAL AMENDMENTS OF PRINCIPAL ACT

4. In section 5A (allowance of exploration and appraisal expenditure) in subsection (5C)(a) for "(c)" there shall be substituted "(f)".

5. In section 12 (interpretation) in subsection (1) in the definition beginning "calendar month" for the words from "and" to "have" there shall be substituted "has".

6. In section 14 (valuation of oil disposed of or appropriated in certain circumstances)—
   (a) in subsections (1) and (2) for the words "at a particular time" there shall be substituted "in a particular month";
   (b) in subsection (5) for the words from the beginning to "this Act", in the first place where those words occur, there shall be substituted "In subsections (4) and (4A) above "calendar month" means a month of the calendar year"; and
   (c) in paragraph (a) of subsection (5) for "(2)(c)" there shall be substituted "(2)(f)" and for "(c)" there shall be substituted "(f)".

7. In Schedule 9 (sales etc. at undervalue or overvalue) in paragraph 6 (determination of arm's length price) for sub-paragraph (2) there shall be substituted—
   "(2) In this paragraph "calendar month" means a month of the calendar year and "material time", in relation to a calendar month, means noon on the middle day of the month which, in the case of a month containing an even number of days, shall be taken to be the last day of the first half of the month."

GENERAL NOTE

This Schedule makes detailed provision for and consequential amendments arising from the new system for establishing the market value of oil or gas under Oil Taxation Act 1975, Sched. 3. See further the Note to s.62 *supra*.

Section 63

SCHEDULE 12

SUPPLEMENTARY PROVISIONS AS TO BLENDED OIL

Interpretation

1. In this Schedule—
   (a) "the principal section" means section 63 of this Act;
   (b) "blended oil" and "the originating fields" have the same meaning as in the principal section;
   (c) a "method of allocation" means such a method as is referred to in subsection (2) of the principal section; and
   (d) "the oil taxation legislation" means Part I of the principal Act and any enactment construed as one with that Part.

Amendments of allocation by the Board

2. If at any time it appears to the Board that a method of allocation of blended oil of which details have been furnished to them in accordance with subsection (3) of the principal section is not just and reasonable for the purposes of the oil taxation legislation, having regard to the quantity and quality of the oil derived from each of the originating fields,—
   (a) they shall give notice in writing to each of the participators in those fields informing them of that fact and proposing amendments which would render the method acceptable to the Board; and
   (b) subject to the following provisions of this Schedule, for any chargeable period beginning after the date of a notice under paragraph (a) above, the method of allocation shall be treated for the purposes of the oil taxation legislation as amended in accordance with the Board's proposals.

16–82

Appeals

3.—(1) Where the Board give notice to the participators in the originating fields under paragraph 2(a) above, any of those participators may appeal to the Special Commissioners against the notice by giving notice in writing to the Board within thirty days after the date of the notice given by the Board.

(2) Where notice of appeal is given under sub-paragraph (1) above—

(a) the Board shall give notice in writing to all those participators in the originating fields who have not given notice of appeal and they shall, by virtue of that notice, become parties to the appeal and be entitled to appear accordingly;

(b) if, before the determination of the appeal by the Special Commissioners, the Board and the participators in the originating fields agree that the method of allocation concerned should not be amended or should have effect with particular amendments, the same consequences shall ensue as if the Commissioners had determined the appeal to that effect;

(c) if, on the hearing of the appeal, it appears to the majority of the Commissioners present that the method of allocation concerned is satisfactory, with or without modifications, for the purposes of the oil taxation legislation they shall allow the appeal and, where appropriate, shall amend the method of allocation accordingly for those purposes; and

(d) sub-paragraphs (2), (8) and (11) of paragraph 14 of Schedule 2 to the principal Act shall apply in relation to the appeal as they apply in relation to an appeal against an assessment or determination made under that Act.

4. Any method or amended method of allocation having effect by virtue of paragraph 3(2) above shall have effect with respect to any such chargeable period as is referred to in paragraph 2(b) above.

GENERAL NOTE

If the Revenue are unhappy with a method of allocating blended oil to participants under s.63, they may amend the method to make it acceptable to them, subject to a right of appeal to the Special Commissioners.

Section 64

SCHEDULE 13

RELIEF FOR RESEARCH EXPENDITURE

PART I

SECTION TO BE INSERTED AFTER SECTION 5A OF THE PRINCIPAL ACT

"Allowance of research expenditure

5B.—(1) Subject to the following provisions of this section and Schedule 7 to this Act, the research expenditure which is allowable in the case of a person who is a participator in an oil field is any expenditure (whether or not of a capital nature) which—

(a) is incurred by him on or after 17th March 1987; and

(b) at the expiry of the period of three years from the time at which it was incurred, has not become allowable under section 3 or section 4 of this Act or section 3 of the Oil Taxation Act 1983; and

(c) was not incurred for purposes relating to a particular oil field; and

(d) was not incurred wholly and exclusively for one or more of the purposes which, subject to subsection (2) below, are specified in section 5A(2) of this Act; and

(e) was incurred for the purpose of research of such a description that, if it had been incurred by the participator in relation to a particular field, it would have been allowable for that field under section 3 or section 4 of this Act or section 3 of the Oil Taxation Act 1983; and

(f) was incurred wholly or partly for United Kingdom purposes.

(2) For the purposes only of subsection (1)(d) above, any reference in section 5A(2) of this Act to the territorial sea of the United Kingdom shall be taken to include a reference to the United Kingdom itself.

(3) Where expenditure falling within paragraphs (a) to (e) of subsection (1) above is incurred partly for United Kingdom purposes and partly for other purposes, only such

part of the expenditure as it is just and reasonable to apportion to United Kingdom purposes shall be allowable by virtue of this section.

(4) In subsections (1)(f) and (3) above, "United Kingdom purposes" means purposes relating to the United Kingdom, the territorial sea thereof or designated areas, excluding any sector which, by virtue of subsection (3)(b) of section 107 of the Finance Act 1980 (transmedian fields), is deemed to be a designated area.

(5) Expenditure is not allowable under this section if, or to the extent that, it has been allowed under Schedule 5, Schedule 6 or Schedule 7 to this Act for or in connection with an oil field.

(6) To the extent that it is reasonable to assume that expenditure which, apart from this subsection would be allowable under this section has been incurred for purposes relating to excluded oil, within the meaning of section 10(1) of this Act, that expenditure is not allowable under this section.

(7) Subject to subsection (3) above, subsections (2) and (6) of section 5 of this Act apply for the purposes of this section as they apply for the purposes of that section except that—

(a) any reference in subsection (2) of section 5 to the purpose mentioned in subsection (1)(b) of that section shall be construed as a reference to the purpose referred to in subsection (1)(e) of this section;

(b) the reference in paragraph (a) of subsection (2) to subsection (1) of that section shall be construed as a reference to subsection (1) of this section; and

(c) where any expenditure falls to be apportioned under subsection (3) of this section, any receipt to which it gives rise shall be similarly apportioned in the application of subsection (6) of section 5.

(8) Paragraph 2 of Schedule 4 to this Act applies in relation to this section as it applies in relation to sections 3 and 4 of this Act."

PART II

AMENDMENTS RELATING TO THE NEW ALLOWANCE

The principal Act

1. In section 2(9) of the principal Act (amounts to be taken into account in respect of expenditure) at the end of paragraph (f) there shall be added "and

(g) any research expenditure allowable in the case of the participator under section 5B of this Act which, on a claim made by him under Schedule 7 to this Act, has been allowed under that Schedule before the Board have made an assessment to tax or a determination on or in relation to him for the period in respect of the field, so far as that expenditure has not been taken into account in any previous assessment to tax or determination."

2. In section 3 of that Act, in subsection (3) (expenditure not allowable under that section if already allowed under other provisions) after the words "section 5A" there shall be inserted "or section 5B".

3. In section 9 of that Act (limit on amount of tax payable) in subsection (2)(a)(ii) for the words "and (f)" there shall be substituted "(f) and (g)".

4. In paragraph 2 of Schedule 2 to that Act (returns by participators) in sub-paragraph (2A) (initial return to include particulars of certain expenditure already claimed) for the words "exploration and appraisal expenditure to which section 5A" there shall be substituted "expenditure to which section 5A or section 5B".

5.—(1) In Schedule 7 to that Act (claim for allowance of certain exploration expenditure etc.) at the end of paragraph 1(1)(b) there shall be added "or

(c) of any research expenditure allowable under section 5B of this Act".

(2) In paragraph 1(3) of that Schedule after the words "section 5A" there shall be inserted "or section 5B".

The Petroleum Revenue Tax Act 1980

6. In the Schedule to the Petroleum Revenue Tax Act 1980 (computation of payment on account) in paragraph 2(4) for the words "or (f)" there shall be substituted "(f) or (g)".

The Finance Act 1980

7. In Schedule 17 to the Finance Act 1980 (transfers of interests in oil fields) after paragraph 16A (exploration and appraisal expenditure) there shall be inserted—

"Research expenditure

16B. In relation to research expenditure to which section 5B applies, paragraph 16 above has effect as if any reference therein to section 5 were a reference to section 5B."

The Finance Act 1981

8. In section 111 of the Finance Act 1981 (restriction of expenditure supplement) in subsection (3)(a) the words following "the principal Act" (which specify certain types of expenditure and losses) shall be omitted.

The Finance Act 1984

9.—(1) In section 113 of the Finance Act 1984 (restriction on PRT reliefs), in subsection (1)—

    (a) the words "abortive exploration expenditure or exploration and appraisal" shall be omitted; and

    (b) after the words "section 5A" there shall be inserted "or section 5B".

(2) In subsection (6) of that section—

    (a) after the words "section 5A" there shall be inserted "or section 5B"; and

    (b) for the words "paragraph 16 or paragraph 16A" there shall be substituted "paragraphs 16 to 16B".

PART III

RECEIPTS TO BE SET AGAINST ALLOWABLE EXPENDITURE

10. In this Part of this Schedule—

"allowable expenditure" means expenditure which, in accordance with section 5B of the principal Act, is allowable on a claim made by a participator under Schedule 7 to that Act; and

"qualifying receipt" means a sum the amount of which falls, by virtue of subsection (6) of section 5 of the principal Act, to be applied by way of reduction in the amount of expenditure which would otherwise be allowable expenditure.

11.—(1) A return made by a participator for a chargeable period under paragraph 2 of Schedule 2 to the principal Act shall give details of any qualifying receipt (whether received by him or by a person connected with him) of which details have not been given in a return made by him for an earlier chargeable period.

(2) Section 533 of the Taxes Act (connected persons) applies for the purposes of this paragraph.

12.—(1) This paragraph applies where—

    (a) a claim for allowable expenditure has been made by a participator under Schedule 7 to the principal Act; and

    (b) as a result of the receipt (whether before or after the making of the claim) of a qualifying receipt, the amount allowed by way of allowable expenditure on the claim exceeds what it should have been.

(2) In determining, in a case where this paragraph applies, the assessable profit or allowable loss accruing to the participator in the chargeable period in which the qualifying receipt is received, the amount of the excess referred to in sub-paragraph (1)(b) above shall be taken into account under section 2 of the principal Act as an amount which is to be included among the positive amounts referred to in subsection (3)(a) of that section.

(3) In the application of section 9 of the principal Act (limit on amount of tax payable) to a chargeable period in respect of which sub-paragraph (2) above applies, the amount of the excess referred to in sub-paragraph (1)(b) above shall be deducted from the amount which would otherwise be the total ascertained under subsection (2)(a)(ii) of that section and, if the amount of that excess is greater than the amount which would otherwise be that total, that total shall be a negative amount equal to the difference.

GENERAL NOTE

Expenditure on oil-related research which has not become allowable in a particular field within three years of being incurred will be allowed against a participator's P.R.T. liability in any field. Expenditure on exploration and appraisal, whether offshore or onshore, is specifically excluded from this relief.

SCHEDULE 14

CROSS-FIELD ALLOWANCE

PART I

ELECTIONS

General

1.—(1) An election shall be made in such form as may be prescribed by the Board.

(2) Without prejudice to sub-paragraph (1) above, an election shall specify—
    (a) the expenditure in respect of which it is made and the amount of that expenditure (in this Part of this Schedule referred to as "the elected amount"), which shall not exceed 10 per cent., which is to be allowable under the principal section;
    (b) the field of origin and the receiving field;
    (c) the notice, agreement or determination which, under paragraph 2 below, determines the earliest date on which the election could be made;
    (d) in a case where the elected amount is to be allowable in respect of more than one receiving field, the proportions in which that amount is to be apportioned between those fields; and
    (e) in the case of expenditure incurred by a company which is an associated company of the participator for the purposes of the principal section, the name of that company.

(3) An election shall be irrevocable.

Earliest date for an election

2.—(1) No election may be made in respect of an amount of expenditure until a final decision as to supplement has been made on a claim in respect of that amount under Schedule 5 or Schedule 6 to the principal Act.

(2) For the purposes of this paragraph, a final decision as to supplement is made in relation to an amount of expenditure when—
    (a) the Board give to the responsible person or, as the case may be, the participator notice under paragraph 3 of Schedule 5 to the principal Act stating that amount of expenditure as an amount qualifying for supplement; or
    (b) after notice of appeal has been given against a decision on a claim, an agreement is made as mentioned in sub-paragraph (1) of paragraph 6 of Schedule 5 to the principal Act and that amount of expenditure is, for the purposes of that sub-paragraph, the appropriate amount of the expenditure claimed as qualifying for supplement; or
    (c) on an appeal against a decision on a claim, there is a determination by the Special Commissioners or the court by virtue of which that amount of expenditure falls (under paragraph 7(2) or paragraph 8(2) of Schedule 5 to the principal Act) to be treated for the purposes of Part I of that Act as qualifying for supplement.

(3) Nothing in Schedule 5 to the principal Act relating to the date on which an amount of expenditure is to be treated as having been allowed as qualifying for supplement applies for the purposes of sub-paragraph (2) above.

Latest date for election

3.—(1) Subject to sub-paragraph (2) below, an election by a participator in respect of a particular amount of expenditure may be made at any time before—
    (a) the Board make, for a chargeable period of the field of origin, an assessment or determination which takes account of that amount of expenditure as qualifying for supplement; and
    (b) notice of that assessment or determination is given to the participator or, as the case may be, the associated company, under paragraph 10 of Schedule 2 to the principal Act.

(2) When the earliest date for the making of an election in respect of a particular amount of expenditure is a date determined under paragraph 2(2)(b) or paragraph 2(2)(c) above, such an election may be made at any time before notice is given as mentioned in sub-paragraph (1)(b) above or, if it is later, before the expiry of the period of thirty days beginning on the day following that earliest date.

Two or more elections relating to same expenditure

4. Where more than one election is made in respect of the same amount of expenditure—

    (a) the maximum of 10 per cent. specified in paragraph 1(2)(a) above shall be cumulative; and

    (b) if the elected amount specified in a second or subsequent election is such that, when aggregated with the elected amount or amounts specified in the earlier election or elections, it would exceed 10 per cent., that second or subsequent election shall have effect as if it specified such an elected amount as would, when so aggregated, be equal to 10 per cent. of the expenditure concerned; and

    (c) an election shall be of no effect if it is made after one or more earlier elections have specified (or been treated by paragraph (b) above as having specified) an elected amount or an aggregate of elected amounts equal to 10 per cent.

Part II

Effect on Receiving Field

5.—(1) In relation to an election, the assessment to tax or determination referred to in subsection (4)(a) of the principal section is that which is first made after the relevant date on or in relation to the participator by whom the election is made.

(2) Subject to paragraphs 6 and 7 below, the relevant date for the purposes of sub-paragraph (1) above is the date of the election.

6. In any case where—

    (a) an election is made in the period of thirty days beginning on the day following that on which the Board give notice under paragraph 3 of Schedule 5 to the principal Act stating the expenditure in respect of which the election is made as expenditure qualifying for supplement, and

    (b) after the date of that notice but on or before the date of the election, an assessment to tax or determination for the receiving field is made on or in relation to the participator making the election,

the relevant date for the purposes of paragraph 5(1) above is the date of the notice referred to in paragraph (a) above; and the assessment or determination referred to in paragraph (b) above shall be amended accordingly.

7. In any case where, following the giving of a notice of appeal, an election is made in respect of expenditure which (under paragraph 6(1), paragraph 7(2) or paragraph 8(2) of Schedule 5 to the principal Act) is treated for the purposes of Part I of that Act as having been allowed as qualifying for supplement on the date on which the notice of appeal was given, the relevant date for the purposes of paragraph 5(1) above is the date on which that notice was given; and in any assessment to tax or determination (relating to the field of origin or the receiving field) all such adjustments or further adjustments shall be made as are necessary in consequence of the election.

Part III

Relevant New Fields and Associated Companies

Relevant new fields

8.—(1) For the purposes of the principal section "relevant new field" means, subject to sub-paragraph (2) below, an oil field—

    (a) no part of which lies in a landward area, within the meaning of the Petroleum (Production) Regulations 1982 or in an area to the East of the United Kingdom and between latitudes 52° and 55° North; and

    (b) for no part of which consent for development has been granted to the licensee by the Secretary of State before 17th March 1987; and

    (c) for no part of which a programme of development had been served on the licensee or approved by the Secretary of State before that date.

(2) In determining, in accordance with sub-paragraph (1) above, whether an oil field (in this sub-paragraph referred to as "the new field") is a relevant new field, no account shall be taken of a consent for development granted before 17th March 1987 or a programme of development served on the licensee or approved by the Secretary of State before that date if—

    (a) in whole or in part that consent or programme related to another oil field for which a determination under Schedule 1 to the principal Act was made before the determination under that Schedule for the new field; and

(b) on or after 17th March 1987 a consent for development is or was granted or a programme of development is or was served on the licensee or approved by the Secretary of State and that consent or programme relates, in whole or in part, to the new field.

9.—(1) In paragraph 8 above "development" means—

(a) the erection or carrying out of permanent works for the purpose of getting oil from the field or for the purpose of conveying oil won from the field to a place on land; or

(b) winning oil from the field otherwise than in the course of searching for oil or drilling wells;

and consent for development does not include consent which is limited to the purpose of testing the characteristics of an oil-bearing area and does not relate to the erection or carrying out of permanent works.

(2) In sub-paragraph (1) above "permanent works" means any structures or other works whatsoever which are intended by the licensee to be permanent and are neither designed to be moved from place to place without major dismantling nor intended by the licensee to be used only for searching for oil.

Associated companies

10.—(1) For the purposes of the principal section, a company is an associated company of a participator (being itself a company) making an election under that section if—

(a) throughout that part of the relevant period in which both were in existence one was a 51 per cent. subsidiary of the other and the other was not a 51 per cent. subsidiary of any company; or

(b) each of them was, throughout that part of the relevant period in which it was in existence, a 51 per cent. subsidiary of a third company which was not itself a 51 per cent. subsidiary of any company.

(2) In this paragraph "company" means any body corporate and section 532 of the Taxes Act (subsidiaries) applies for the purposes of this paragraph.

(3) For the purposes of this paragraph the relevant period ends on the date on which the election in question is made and begins—

(a) in the case of an election relating to expenditure incurred in the first claim period of the field of origin, on the date on which any part of that field was first determined under Schedule 1 to the principal Act; and

(b) in the case of an election relating to expenditure incurred in any other claim period of the field of origin, at the beginning of that claim period.

Part IV

Supplemental and Consequential Provisions

Notice of variation reducing expenditure qualifying for supplement

11.—(1) This paragraph applies in any case where—

(a) an amount of expenditure is allowed as qualifying for supplement as regards the field of origin; and

(b) one or more elections is made in respect of that expenditure; and

(c) a notice of variation is served under paragraph 9 of Schedule 5 to the principal Act; and

(d) on that notice of variation becoming effective for the purposes of the said paragraph 9, the amount of the expenditure referred to in paragraph (a) above is taken for the purposes of Part I of the principal Act as having been reduced.

(2) In sub-paragraph (3) below—

(a) "the original expenditure" means the amount of expenditure referred to in sub-paragraph (1)(a) above, disregarding the effect of the notice of variation;

(b) "the reduced expenditure" means the amount of that expenditure after the notice of variation became effective for the purposes of paragraph 9 of Schedule 5 to the principal Act; and

(c) "the expenditure originally allowable" means the amount of the original expenditure which, having regard to the election or elections in respect of that expenditure but disregarding the effect of the notice of variation, was allowable in accordance with the principal section.

(3) If the expenditure originally allowable exceeds 10 per cent. of the reduced expenditure, the principal section shall have effect as if the election or elections had specified an amount of that expenditure equal (or equal in the aggregate) to 10 per cent. of the reduced expenditure and, where there was more than one election, paragraph 4 above shall be taken to have applied accordingly.

(4) Such amendments of assessments to tax or determinations (relating to the field of origin or the receiving field) shall be made as may be necessary in consequence of the preceding provisions of this paragraph.

Elections following variation increasing expenditure qualifying for supplement

12.—(1) In any case where—
- (a) an amount of expenditure is allowed as qualifying for supplement as regards the field of origin, and
- (b) one or more elections is made in respect of that expenditure, and
- (c) a notice of variation is served under paragraph 9 of Schedule 5 to the principal Act, and
- (d) on that notice of variation becoming effective for the purposes of the said paragraph 9, the amount of the expenditure referred to in paragraph (a) above is taken for the purposes of Part I of the principal Act as having been increased,

an election may be made in respect of the amount of the increase as if it were a separate amount of expenditure.

(2) In the circumstances referred to in sub-paragraph (1) above an election may be made by the participator in question at any time before—
- (a) notice is given to the participator or, as the case may be, the associated company of the making of that assessment or determination or that amendment of an assessment or determination which takes account of the increase resulting from the notice of variation; or
- (b) if it is later, the expiry of the period of thirty days beginning on the date on which the notice of variation becomes effective for the purposes of paragraph 9 of Schedule 5 to the principal Act.

(3) Where an election is made by a participator in the circumstances referred to in sub-paragraph (1) above—
- (a) paragraph 1(2)(c) above shall have effect as if it referred to the notice of variation;
- (b) subsection (4)(a) of the principal section shall not apply; and
- (c) the expenditure allowable as a result of the election shall be taken into account in the first assessment to tax or determination relating to a chargeable period of the receiving field which is made on or in relation to the participator after the date of the decision to which the notice of variation relates.

(4) Such amendments of assessments to tax or determinations (relating to the field of origin or the receiving field) shall be made as may be necessary in consequence of the preceding provisions of this paragraph.

Limit on amount of tax payable in respect of receiving field

13.—(1) Where an election has been made by a participator, this paragraph has effect with respect to the determination under section 9 of the principal Act (limit on amount of tax payable) of the adjusted profit of the participator in respect of the receiving field.

(2) For the chargeable period in which the amount of expenditure allowable by virtue of the election is taken into account as mentioned in subsection (4) of the principal section, that amount shall also be taken into account as if it were an addition to the total amount mentioned in section 9(2)(a)(ii) of the principal Act.

GENERAL NOTE
Procedural and consequential provisions are made in relation to the new 10 per cent. cross-field allowance introduced by s.65, including time limits for elections under the section. The allowance is only available for fields outside the Southern Basin, as defined in para. 8(1)(a).

PRE-CONSOLIDATION AMENDMENTS: INCOME TAX AND CORPORATION TAX

The Capital Allowances Act 1968 (c.3)

1. In section 34(4) of the Capital Allowances Act 1968 for the words "Part VIII of the principal Act" there shall be substituted the words "Part III of the Finance Act 1976".

The Income and Corporation Taxes Act 1970 (c.10)

2.—(1) The Income and Corporation Taxes Act 1970 shall have effect subject to the following provisions of this paragraph.

(2) In section 14(7) for all the words following "the Board may consult" there shall be substituted the words "the Secretary of State or the Department of Education for Northern Ireland".

(3) In section 18(6) for all the words following "1948" there shall be substituted the words "or, in the case of a person ordinarily resident in Scotland or in Northern Ireland, a person who is a blind person within the meaning of section 64(1) of the National Assistance Act 1948.".

(4) In section 20 in subsection (1) for "the appropriate rate" there shall be substituted "the basic rate" and subsections (3) to (5) shall cease to have effect.

(5) In section 21(4)(b) for "has the same meaning as in the said section 20" there shall be substituted "means the basic rate".

(6) In section 73(3) for "feu" there shall be substituted "fee".

(7) At the end of section 103 there shall be added—

"For the avoidance of doubt it is hereby declared that interest to which section 18 of the Taxes Management Act 1970 applies does not include interest to which this section applies."

(8) In section 117(3)(i) and (ii) for "legal representatives" there shall be substituted "personal representatives", and in subsection (4) of that section for "executors or administrators" there shall be substituted "personal representatives".

(9) In section 130(c) for "trade or profession" there shall be substituted "trade, profession or vocation".

(10) In section 133—

(a) in subsection (1) the words "for Education and Science" shall cease to have effect; and

(b) the following shall be substituted for subsection (3)—

"(3) In relation to technical colleges or other institutions in Northern Ireland, subsection (1) above shall have effect as if for the reference to the Secretary of State there were substituted a reference to the Department of Education for Northern Ireland.".

(11) In section 168(7) after "trade", in both places, there shall be inserted "profession or vocation" and after "Case I" there shall be inserted "or II".

(12) In section 194(1) for "This section" there shall be substituted "Subsection (2) below".

(13) At the end of sections 213(1), 216(2) and 217(2) there shall be added—

"A claim for relief under this subsection shall be made to the Board."

(14) In section 214(6) for all the words following "do not include" there shall be substituted the words "Australia, Canada, New Zealand, India, Sri Lanka and Cyprus".

(15) In section 433—

(a) in paragraph (a) after "payable" there shall be inserted "prior rights of surviving spouse on intestacy"; and

(b) in paragraph (d) after "in respect of" there shall be inserted "prior rights by surviving spouse or in respect of".

(16) In section 434 for subsection (1A) there shall be substituted the following—

"(1A) Subsection (1) above shall not apply in relation to income which is payable as a covenanted payment to charity.".

(17) In section 438(2)(b) for "that section" substitute "section 437 above".

(18) In section 503(1) the reference to corporation tax shall cease to have effect and accordingly section 100(1) of the Finance Act 1972 shall cease to apply to that subsection.

(19) In section 516(1) for "country" there shall be substituted "territory".

(20) Section 526 shall have effect and shall be deemed always to have had effect with the addition, at the end of subsection (5), of the words—

"and 'industrial assurance business' means industrial assurance business within the meaning of the Industrial Assurance Act 1923 or the Industrial Assurance (Northern Ireland) Order 1979."

(21) In section 526 the following subsection shall be inserted after subsection (5)—

"(5A) In the Tax Acts any reference to a child, however expressed, shall be construed as including a reference to an adopted child.

This subsection does not apply for the purposes of paragraph 18 of Schedule 14 to this Act."

(22) In paragraph 16(1) of Schedule 10 for the definition of "premiums trust fund" there shall be substituted the following—

"'premiums trust fund' means such a trust fund as is referred to in section 83 of the Insurance Companies Act 1982;"

(23) In paragraph 6 of Part III of Schedule 12 there shall be added at the end—

"(5) This paragraph shall apply to—

    (a) any banker or other person in the United Kingdom who obtains payment of any such interest, dividends or other annual payments as is or are mentioned in sub-paragraph (1) above; and

    (b) to any person who would, apart from this paragraph, be obliged to pay income tax in respect of the proceeds of the sale or other realisation of any coupon for any such interest, dividends or other annual payments,

as it applies to any person entrusted with the payment of any such interest, dividends or other annual payments, with the substitution in a case falling within paragraph (b) above, of references to the proceeds of the sale or other realisation for references to such interest, dividends or other annual payments.

In this sub-paragraph 'coupon' has the same meaning as in section 159 of this Act."

The Finance Act 1970 (c.24)

3. In section 20(3) of the Finance Act 1970 for "an existing scheme" there shall be substituted "a scheme which was in existence on 6th April 1980".

The Finance Act 1972 (c.41)

4. In paragraph 10(9) of Schedule 16 to the Finance Act 1972—

    (a) for "paragraphs (b) and (c)" there shall be substituted "paragraph (b)";

    (b) the paragraph lettered (c) shall become paragraph (bb); and

    (c) at the end there shall be added the words—

"and in paragraph (c) for 'thirdly' there shall be substituted 'fourthly' and for '(a) or (b)' there shall be substituted '(a), (b) or (bb)'".

The Finance Act 1973 (c.51)

5. In paragraph 1(6)(b) of Schedule 12 to the Finance Act 1973 for the words from "any of" to "partnership)" there shall be substituted—

"(i) a first-year allowance within the meaning of Chapter I of Part III of the Finance Act 1971 ("the 1971 Act") in respect of expenditure incurred by the company on the provision of machinery or plant;

(ii) a writing-down allowance within the meaning of Chapter II of Part I of the Capital Allowances Act 1968 ("the 1968 Act") or, as the case may require, Chapter I of Part III of the 1971 Act in respect of expenditure incurred by the company on the provision of machinery or plant; or

(iii) an allowance under section 91 of the 1968 Act in respect of expenditure incurred by the company on scientific research;".

The Finance Act 1974 (c.30)

6. In section 27(5) of the Finance Act 1974 for "specified in" there shall be substituted "of".

The Finance Act 1975 (c.7)

7.—(1) In section 12 of the Finance Act 1975 for the words from "in section" to "1958" there shall be substituted "below" and at the end of that section there shall be added—

"In this section "statutory corporation" means—

    (a) a corporation incorporated by an Act of Parliament of the United Kingdom or the Parliament of Northern Ireland or by a Measure of the

Northern Ireland Assembly or by an Order made under paragraph 1 of Schedule 1 to the Northern Ireland Act 1974; or

(b) any other corporation, being a corporation to which functions in respect of the carrying on of an undertaking are entrusted by such an Act, Measure or Order, or by an order made under or confirmed by such an Act or Measure;

but, save as is provided by paragraph (b) above, does not include any company within the meaning of the Companies Act 1985 or the Companies (Northern Ireland) Order 1986."

(2) It is hereby declared for the avoidance of doubt that the reference in paragraph 1(4) of Schedule 2 to the Finance Act 1975 to paragraph 3 of Schedule 1 to the 1970 Act includes a reference both to paragraph 3 of that Schedule as enacted and to paragraphs 3 and 3A of that Schedule as substituted by Part I of Schedule 10 to the Finance Act 1985.

The Finance (No. 2) Act 1975 (c.45)

8.—(1) In section 42(11) of the Finance (No. 2) Act 1975 for the definitions of "financial year", "insurance company" and "long term business" there shall be substituted the following definitions—

"financial year" has the meaning given by section 96 of the Insurance Companies Act 1982;

"insurance company" means an insurance company to which Part II of that Act applies;

"long term business" has the meaning given by section 1(1) of that Act.

(2) In paragraph 6(1) of Part IV of Schedule 12 to that Act (as amended by Schedule 2 to the Companies Consolidation (Consequential Provisions) Act 1985) before sub-paragraph (a) there shall be inserted the following sub-paragraph—

"(aa) sections 227 and 241 (contents, laying and delivery of annual accounts;"

The Finance Act 1976 (c.40)

9. In paragraph 13(4) of Schedule 4 to the Finance Act 1976 after paragraph (d) there shall be inserted—

"(e) section 64 of the Friendly Societies Act 1974;".

The Finance Act 1977 (c.36)

10. In section 38(2)(b) of the Finance Act 1977 for "subsection (3)(a)(i) of the said section 84" substitute "paragraph 3(1)(a)(i) of Schedule 4 to the Inheritance Tax Act 1984".

The Finance Act 1978 (c.42)

11.—(1) Section 30(7)(c) of the Finance Act 1978 shall have effect and shall be deemed always to have had effect with the addition after "1975" of the words "and paragraph 3(1) of Schedule 2 to the Social Security (Northern Ireland) Act 1975".

(2) For the purposes of section 31 of that Act "commodity futures" has the same meaning as it has for the purposes of section 72(1) of the Finance Act 1985.

(3) In section 59(7) of that Act for the words "excess shares" there shall be substituted the words "excess or unauthorised shares".

The Interpretation Act 1978 (c.30)

12. In Schedule 1 to the Interpretation Act 1978 for the definitions of "the Corporation Tax Acts" and "the Tax Acts" there shall be substituted the following definitions—

"The Corporation Tax Acts" means the enactments relating to the taxation of the income and chargeable gains of companies and of company distributions (including provisions relating to income tax);

"The Tax Acts" means the Income Tax Acts and the Corporation Tax Acts.

The Finance Act 1980 (c.48)

13.—(1) At the end of section 53 of the Finance Act 1980 there shall be added the following subsection—

"(6) In sections 77, 79 and 80 of the Taxes Act references to section 72 of that Act shall be read as including references to this section."

(2) In Schedule 10 to that Act—

(a) at the end of paragraph 1(1)(b) there shall be added the words—

"and the matters as to which the Board are required to be so satisfied are referred to below as 'the relevant requirements'"; and

(b) in paragraph 3(1) for "they cease to be satisfied as mentioned in paragraph 1 above" there shall be substituted "any of the relevant requirements cease to be satisfied".

The Finance Act 1981 (c.35)

14.—(1) In section 48(10) of the Finance Act 1981 for the words from "subscription" to "funds" there shall be substituted the words "payment made, out of public funds or by shares subscribed for, whether for money or money's worth,".

(2) In section 58(8) of that Act after "goods" there shall be inserted "or services".

The Finance Act 1983 (c.28)

15.—(1) At the end of paragraph 10(4) of Schedule 5 to the Finance Act 1983 there shall be added the words—

"In relation to companies incorporated under the law of Northern Ireland references in this sub-paragraph to the Companies Act 1985 and to section 117 of that Act shall have effect as references to the Companies (Northern Ireland) Order 1986 and to Article 127 of that Order respectively."

(2) In paragraph 17(1A)(b) of that Schedule for "more than" there shall be substituted "not less than".

The Finance Act 1984 (c.43)

16.—(1) For section 96(6) of the Finance Act 1984 there shall be substituted—

"(6) A charity shall be exempt from tax in respect of an offshore income gain if the gain is applicable and applied for charitable purposes; but if property held on charitable trusts ceases to be subject to charitable trusts and that property represents directly or indirectly an offshore income gain, the trustees shall be treated as if they had disposed of and immediately reacquired that property for a consideration equal to its market value, any gain (calculated in accordance with Schedule 20 to this Act) accruing being treated as an offshore income gain not accruing to a charity.

In this subsection "charity" has the same meaning as in section 360 of the Taxes Act and "market value" has the same meaning as in the Capital Gains Tax Act 1979."

(2) For paragraph 2(1)(d) of Schedule 8 to that Act there shall be substituted the following paragraph—

"(d) any company to which property and rights belonging to a trustee savings bank were transferred by section 3 of the Trustee Savings Bank Act 1985;".

(3) For paragraph 12 of Schedule 9 to that Act there shall be substituted—

"12. A charity shall be exempt from income tax in respect of an amount which (apart from this paragraph) is chargeable to income tax by virtue of this Schedule or Schedule 11 to the Finance Act 1985 if the amount is applicable and applied for charitable purposes.

In this paragraph "charity" has the same meaning as in section 360 of the Taxes Act."

The Finance Act 1986 (c.41)

17. At the end of paragraph 21(3) of Schedule 9 to the Finance Act 1986 there shall be added the words—

"and paragraph 20(4) shall have effect in relation to shares whenever issued".

Section 72

SCHEDULE 16

REPEALS

PART I

VEHICLES EXCISE DUTY

Chapter	Short title	Extent of repeal
1971 c.10.	The Vehicles (Excise) Act 1971.	Section 9(3)(b) and (c). In section 16, in subsection (1) in paragraph (i) the words from "and all recovery vehicles" to "that business" and in paragraph (a) of the proviso the words from "except" to "disabled vehicle", subsection (3)(b) and in subsection (8) the definition of "recovery vehicle". In section 18A(7), paragraph (d) and the word "or" immediately preceding it. In Part I of Schedule 7, paragraphs 7(b)(ii) and 17A(b)(ii).
1972 c.10 (N.I.).	The Vehicles (Excise) Act (Northern Ireland) 1972.	Section 9(4)(b) and (c). In section 16, in subsection (1)(a) the words from "and all recovery vehicles" to "that business", in subsection (2)(a) the words from "except" to "disabled vehicle", subsection (4)(b) and in subsection (10) the definition of "recovery vehicle". In section 18A(7) paragraph (d) and the word "or" immediately preceding it. In Part I of Schedule 9, paragraphs 7(b)(ii) and 17A(b)(ii).

1. The repeals in section 16 of each of the Vehicles (Excise) Act 1971 and the Vehicles (Excise) Act (Northern Ireland) Act 1972 have effect in relation to licences taken out after 31st December 1987.

2. The remaining repeals have effect in accordance with section 2(8)(a) and (b) of this Act.

PART II

BETTING AND GAMING DUTIES

Chapter	Short title	Extent of repeal
1981 c.63.	The Betting and Gaming Duties Act 1981.	In section 1(2) the words from the beginning of paragraph (a) to "bet" in paragraph (b). Section 3. Section 21(4). In Schedule 4, in paragraph 9(a), the words from "or" to "this Act)".
1982 c.39.	The Finance Act 1982.	In Schedule 6, paragraph 10.
1984 c.43.	The Finance Act 1984.	In Schedule 3, paragraph 7(5)(b).
1985 c.54.	The Finance Act 1985.	In Schedule 5, paragraph 1(2).

1. The repeal in section 1 of the Betting and Gaming Duties Act 1981 and the repeal of section 3 of that Act have effect with respect to bets made on or after 29th March 1987.

2. The repeal in the Finance Act 1982 has effect with respect to gaming machine licences for any period beginning on or after 1st June 1987.

3. The remaining repeals have effect with respect to gaming machine licences for any period beginning on or after 1st October 1987.

Part III

Management of Customs and Excise

Chapter	Short title	Extent of repeal
1979 c.2.	The Customs and Excise Management Act 1979.	In section 77(1)(a) the words "importation, exportation or".
1983 c.28.	The Finance Act 1983.	Section 7(4).

Part IV

Value Added Tax

Chapter	Short title	Extent of repeal
1983 c.55.	The Value Added Tax Act 1983.	In Schedule 1, paragraphs 6 and 8. In Schedule 5, item 2 of and Note (1) to Group 15.

Part V

Income Tax and Corporation Tax: General

Chapter	Short title	Extent of repeal
1970 c.9.	The Taxes Management Act 1970.	In section 86(4), in the second column of the Table, paragraph 5(b).
1970 c.10.	The Income and Corporation Taxes Act 1970.	In section 243, the words "section 244 below and". Section 244. In section 303, in subsection (3), the proviso and, in subsection (6), the words from "and in" onwards.
1975 c.45.	The Finance (No. 2) Act 1975.	In section 44(2), the words from "section 244(1)" to "1965)". In section 48(9), in the definition of "the material date", paragraph (b).
1978 c.42.	The Finance Act 1978.	In Schedule 9, paragraph 11(3)(c).
1980 c.48.	The Finance Act 1980.	Section 46(12). In Schedule 10, paragraph 26(3).
1981 c.35.	The Finance Act 1981.	Section 27.
1982 c.39.	The Finance Act 1982.	Section 32.
1984 c.43.	The Finance Act 1984.	In Schedule 10, in paragraph 4(4), the words from "and paragraph" to "associate")".
1986 c.50.	The Social Security Act 1986.	In Schedule 10, paragraph 101(b).

1. The repeals in section 86 of the Taxes Management Act 1970, sections 243 and 244 of the Income and Corporation Taxes Act 1970 and sections 44 and 48 of the Finance (No. 2) Act 1975 have effect with respect to accounting periods beginning on or after 17th March 1987.

2. Subject to section 37(2) of this Act, the repeals in section 303 of the Income and Corporation Taxes Act shall be deemed to have come into force on 6th April 1986.

3. The repeals in Schedule 9 to the Finance Act 1978, section 46 of and Schedule 10 to the Finance Act 1980 and Schedule 10 to the Finance Act 1984 shall be deemed to have come into force on 6th April 1986.

4. The repeals of section 27 of the Finance Act 1981 and section 32 of the Finance Act 1982 do not apply in relation to payments of supplementary allowance in respect of periods before the day on which regulations containing the first schemes under section 20(1)(a) of the Social Security Act 1986 and Article 21(1)(a) of the Social Security (Northern Ireland) Order 1986 come into force.

PART VI

UNIT TRUSTS

Chapter	Short title	Extent of repeal
1970 c.10.	The Income and Corporation Taxes Act 1970.	In section 248(6)(c), the word "scheme". In section 533(8), the words from "(as defined" to "1940)".
1980 c.48.	The Finance Act 1980.	In section 60, the words from "(Tax Acts" to "shareholders)".
1984 c.43.	The Finance Act 1984.	In section 92(7)(a), the words from "as defined" to "1958". In section 94(1)(b), the words from "as defined" to "1958".

These repeals have effect in accordance with an order under section 40 of this Act.

PART VII

INCOME TAX AND CORPORATION TAX: PRE-CONSOLIDATION AMENDMENTS

Chapter	Short title	Extent of repeal
1970 c.10.	The Income and Corporation Taxes Act 1970.	Section 20(3) to (5). Section 34(3) and in section 34(4) the words "given after 6th April 1948 and". Section 105. Section 122(1)(c). Section 175(2)(d). Section 212(2). In section 214(1)(b) the words from "by virtue" to "1956". In section 226(9)(c) the words "Schedule A". In section 227, in subsection (5)(b) the words following "husband", in subsection (9) the words "for chargeable periods after the year 1955–56" and subsection (12). Section 229(2). In section 312(2)(c) the words "not earlier than the year 1923–24".

Chapter	Short title	Extent of repeal
1970 c.10— *cont.*	The Income and Corporation Taxes Act 1970— *cont.*	Section 325. Section 345(1) and (2)(c). Section 352(10). Section 362(4). Section 375(3). In section 388(4) the words from "on or" to "Act 1952". Sections 403 and 404. Section 420(3)(b)(i). Sections 422 to 424. In section 460(1), the proviso. In section 467(3), the proviso. Section 468. In section 495 in subsection (1) the words from "and which is" to the end and subsection (3). Section 514. Section 519(3). In Schedule 10 the words, in paragraph 1, "or any approved association of underwriters", in paragraph 7(3)(a), "or the association in question" and, in paragraph 14, from "or the managing" to "in question"; and in paragraph 16(1) the definition of "approved association of underwriters", in the definition of "business" the words from "or of whatever" to "in question" and in the definition of "underwriting year" all the words following "calendar year".
1972 c.41.	The Finance Act 1972.	In Schedule 15, paragraph 1. Section 76. In Schedule 16, in paragraph 12(1)(a) the words from "otherwise" to "1914".
1973 c.51.	The Finance Act 1973.	Section 31(6) to (8). Section 44.
1975 c.44.	The Finance (No. 2) Act 1975.	Section 41. In section 47, in subsection (1) in paragraph (a), the words "surtax" and the last "or" and paragraph (b) and subsections (2), (3)(b) and (4)(b).
1976 c.46.	The Finance Act 1976.	In section 33(1) the words from "Until" to "appoint".
1980 c.48.	The Finance Act 1980.	In section 36(1)(a) the words "and is not being considered for approval".
1982 c.39.	The Finance Act 1982.	Section 142(3) and (4).
1985 c.54.	The Finance Act 1985.	In Schedule 11, paragraph 2(8). In Schedule 23 the words, in paragraph 21, "approved association of underwriters" and, in paragraphs 22(1), 27(1) and 28(1) and (5), "or of an approved association of underwriters" and "or the association in question".

The repeal of section 514 of the Taxes Act shall not have effect in relation to the Relief from Double Income Tax on Shipping Profits (Iceland) Declaration 1928.

PART VIII

STAMP DUTY

Chapter	Short title	Extent of repeal
1910 c.8.	The Finance (1909–10) Act 1910.	Sections 77 to 79.
1946 c.64.	The Finance Act 1946.	Section 54(6).
1946 c.17 (N.I.).	The Finance (No. 2) Act (Northern Ireland) 1946.	Section 25(6).
1967 c.54.	The Finance Act 1967.	In section 30, subsection (4) and, in subsection (5), the definition of "the scheduled territories".
1967 c.20 (N.I.).	The Finance Act (Northern Ireland) 1967.	In section 7, subsection (4) and, in subsection (5), the definition of "the scheduled territories".
1970 c.24.	The Finance Act 1970.	In Schedule 7, paragraph 9.
1970 c.21 (N.I.).	The Finance Act (Northern Ireland) 1970.	In Schedule 2, paragraph 9.

1. The repeals in section 30 of the Finance Act 1967 and section 7 of the Finance Act (Northern Ireland) 1967 have effect with respect to the issue of instruments and the transfer of stock on or after the day on which this Act is passed.

2. The remaining repeals shall come into force on the day on which section 49(1) of this Act comes into force.

PART IX

INHERITANCE TAX

Chapter	Short title	Extent of repeal
1984 c.51.	The Inheritance Tax Act 1984.	Section 168(2). In section 178(2), the words "on a recognised stock exchange" in the second place where they occur.
1986 c.41.	The Finance Act 1986.	In Schedule 20, in paragraph 8(1) the words from "then" onwards.

These repeals have effect in relation to transfers of value made, and other events occurring, on or after 17th March 1987.

Part X

Oil Taxation

Chapter	Short title	Extent of repeal
1975 c.22.	The Oil Taxation Act 1975.	In section 2(9)(a)(i) and (ii), the words "at the material time".
		In section 5A(5B), the words "at the material time".
		In section 14, in subsection (4) and (4A)(b), the words "at the material time".
		In Schedule 2, in paragraph 2(2)(a)(iii) and (b)(ii), the words "at the material time".
		In Schedule 3, in paragraph 2(3), the words "at that time", where they first occur, and in paragraph 3, in sub-paragraph (1) the words "at the material time" and in sub-paragraph (2) the words from "and 'the material time'" onwards.
1981 c.35.	The Finance Act 1981.	In section 111(3)(a), the words following "the principal Act".
1983 c.28.	The Finance Act 1983.	In Schedule 8, in Part II, paragraph 9.
1984 c.43.	The Finance Act 1984.	In section 113(1), the words "abortive exploration expenditure or exploration and appraisal".

The repeals in the Oil Taxation Act 1975 have effect with respect to chargeable periods ending after 31st December 1986.

Part XI

Exchange Control

Chapter	Short title	Extent of repeal
10 & 11 Geo. 6 c.14.	The Exchange Control Act 1947.	The whole Act.
1 & 2 Eliz. 2 c.136.	The Post Office Act 1953.	Section 16(4).
8 & 9 Eliz. 2 c.52.	The Cyprus Act 1960.	In the Schedule, paragraph 2.
1963 c.25.	The Finance Act 1963.	In section 71(1) the words "section 10 of the Exchange Control Act 1947, and to".
1965 c.2.	The Administration of Justice Act 1965.	In Schedule 1, the entry relating to the Exchange Control Act 1947.
1968 c.39.	The Gas and Electricity Act 1968.	In section 2(5) the words from "or from" onwards.
1970 c.lxix.	The City of London (Various Powers) Act 1970.	In section 8(4) the words "with the Exchange Control Act 1947 and".
1977 c.36.	The Finance Act 1977.	Section 58.
1978 c.23.	The Judicature (Northern Ireland) Act 1978.	In Schedule 5, in Part II, the entry relating to the Exchange Control Act 1947.
1979 c.2.	The Customs and Excise Management Act 1979.	In Schedule 4, in Part I of the Table, the entry relating to the Exchange Control Act 1947.

Chapter	Short title	Extent of repeal
1979 c.11.	The Electricity (Scotland) Act 1979.	In section 27(9)(b) the words "or from" onwards.
1979 c.14.	The Capital Gains Tax Act 1979.	Section 150(5).
1979 c.43.	The Crown Agents Act 1979.	In section 8(5) paragraph (i) and, in paragraph (ii), the words "in relation to any time on or after that date".
1981 c.35.	The Finance Act 1981.	In section 136, subsections (1) and (3). Schedule 18.
1981 c.54.	The Supreme Court Act 1981.	In Schedule 5, the entry relating to the Exchange Control Act 1947.
1982 c.41.	The Stock Transfer Act 1982.	In section 6(3) the words from "and" onwards. In Schedule 2, paragraph 3.
1985 c.65.	The Insolvency Act 1985.	In Schedule 8, paragraph 8.
1985 c.66.	The Bankruptcy (Scotland) Act 1985.	In Schedule 7, paragraph 7.
1986 c.45.	The Insolvency Act 1986.	In Schedule 14, the entry relating to the Exchange Control Act 1947.

1. The repeal of the Exchange Control Act 1947 does not affect the power of the Treasury to issue a certificate under subsection (2) of section 18 of that Act (including that subsection as applied by section 28(3) or section 29(3) of that Act) with respect to Acts done before 13th December 1979.

2. The repeal of section 150(5) of the Capital Gains Tax Act 1979 does not affect the determination of the market value of any assets at a time before 13th December 1979.

APPROPRIATION ACT 1987

(1987 c. 17)

An Act to apply a sum out of the Consolidated Fund to the service of the year ending on 31st March 1988, to appropriate the supplies granted in this Session of Parliament, and to repeal certain Consolidated Fund and Appropriation Acts.   [15th May 1987]

PARLIAMENTARY DEBATES
Hansard: H.C. Vol. 116, cols. 243, 344; H.L. Vol. 487, col. 726.

GRANT OUT OF THE CONSOLIDATED FUND

Issue out of the Consolidated Fund for the year ending 31st March 1988

1. The Treasury may issue out of the Consolidated Fund of the United Kingdom and apply towards making good the supply granted to Her Majesty for the service of the year ending on 31st March 1988 the sum of £59,571,457,000.

APPROPRIATION OF GRANTS

Appropriation of sums voted for supply services

2. All sums granted by this Act and the other Acts mentioned in Schedule (A) annexed to this Act out of the said Consolidated Fund towards making good the supply granted to Her Majesty amounting, as appears by the said schedule, in the aggregate, to the sum of £108,355,119,629·84 are appropriated, and shall be deemed to have been appropriated as from the date of the passing of the Acts mentioned in the said Schedule (A), for the services and purposes expressed in Schedule (B) annexed hereto.

The abstract of schedules and schedules annexed hereto, with the notes (if any) to such schedules, shall be deemed to be part of this Act in the same manner as if they had been contained in the body thereof.

In addition to the said sums granted out of the Consolidated Fund, there may be applied out of any money directed, under section 2 of the Public Accounts and Charges Act 1891, to be applied as appropriations in aid of the grants for the services and purposes specified in Schedule (B) annexed hereto the sums respectively set forth in the last column of the said schedule.

Repeals

3. The enactments mentioned in Schedule (C) annexed to this Act are hereby repealed.

Short title

4. This Act may be cited as the Appropriation Act 1987.

ABSTRACT
OF
SCHEDULES (A) and (B) to which this Act refers

Section 2   SCHEDULE (A)

Grants out of the Consolidated Fund - - - - - - - £108,355,119,629·84

Section 2   SCHEDULE (B)—Appropriation of Grants

	Supply Grants	Appropriations in Aid
1985–86 and 1986–87	£	£
Part 1. Defence and Civil (Excesses), 1985–86	392,730,629·84	3,214,798·66
Part 2. Supplementary, 1986–87 - - - -	3,483,899,000·00	403,383,000·00
	3,876,629,629·84	406,597,798·66

	Supply Grants	Appropriations in Aid
1987–88	£	£
Part 3. Class I - - - - - - -	18,785,745,000·00	1,999,140,000·00
Part 4. Class II - - - - - - -	1,940,924,000·00	153,743,000·00
Part 5. Class IV - - - - - - -	982,846,000·00	451,165,000·00
Part 6. Class V - - - - - - -	1,408,341,000·00	1,590,055,000·00
Part 7. Class VI - - - - - - -	1,172,148,000·00	487,510,000·00
Part 8. Class VII - - - - - -	3,563,210,000·00	653,184,000·00
Part 9. Class VIII - - - - - -	2,749,667,000·00	145,400,000·00
Part 10. Class IX - - - - - -	2,064,284,000·00	46,713,000·00
Part 11. Class X - - - - - -	10,997,831,000·00	37,666,000·00
Part 12. Class XI - - - - - -	4,809,531,000·00	249,798,000·00
Part 13. Class XII - - - - - -	3,672,688,000·00	1,153,735,000·00
Part 14. Class XIII - - - - - -	292,693,000·00	3,000·00
Part 15. Class XIV - - - - - -	13,805,167,000·00	3,601,720,000·00
Part 16. Class XV - - - - - -	24,043,852,000·00	811,678,000·00
Part 17. Class XVI - - - - - -	5,743,944,000·00	580,759,000·00
Part 18. Class XVII - - - - - -	2,607,686,000·00	150,582,000·00
Part 19. Class XVIII - - - - - -	1,474,405,000·00	4,087,000·00
Part 20. Class XIX - - - - - -	2,255,592,000·00	343,144,000·00
Part 21. Class XX - - - - - -	2,059,721,000·00	1,318,391,000·00
Part 22. Class XXA - - - - - -	24,538,000·00	215,000·00
Part 23. Class XXB - - - - - -	23,677,000·00	3,800,000·00
TOTAL - - - - - - - -	104,478,490,000·00	13,782,488,000·00
GRAND TOTAL - - - - - -	108,355,119,629·84	14,189,085,798·66

SCHEDULE (A)

GRANTS OUT OF THE CONSOLIDATED FUND

	£
For the service of the year ended 31st March 1986—	
Under Act 1987 c. 8 - - - - - - -	392,730,629·84
For the service of the year ended 31st March 1987—	
Under Act 1986 c. 67 - - - - - -	2,206,135,000·00
Under Act 1987 c. 8 - - - - - - -	1,277,764,000·00
For the service of the year ending on 31st March 1988—	
Under Act 1986 c. 67 - - - - - -	44,907,033,000·00
Under this Act - - - - - - - -	59,571,457,000·00
TOTAL - - - - - - - -	108,355,119,629·84

Defence and Civil (Excesses)   SCHEDULE (B)—PART 1
1985–86

DEFENCE AND CIVIL (EXCESSES), 1985–86

SUMS granted, and sums which may be applied as appropriations in aid in addition thereto, to make good excesses on certain grants for defence and civil services for the year ended 31st March 1986, viz.:—

	Supply Grants	Surplus receipts available to be applied as Appropriations in Aid
	£	£
Vote		
CLASS II		
8. OVERSEAS AID ADMINISTRATION - - - -	109,831·07	460·14
9. BUDGET OF THE EUROPEAN COMMUNITIES - - -	189,248·51	—
CLASS III		
1. AGRICULTURAL SUPPORT (INTERVENTION BOARD FOR AGRICULTURAL PRODUCE) - - - - -	59,384,975·88	—
CLASS XII		
2. SUPPLEMENTARY BENEFITS - - - - -	309,767,447·12	3,214,338·52
4. HOUSING BENEFITS - - - - - - -	22,995,535·37	—
CLASS XV		
16. STUDENT AWARDS, SCOTLAND - - - - -	11,910·48	—
CLASS XVI		
3. REGIONAL ASSISTANCE, WALES - - - -	46,523·73	—
CLASS XVIII		
7. RATE REBATE GRANTS TO LOCAL REVENUE, WALES	225,157·68	—
TOTAL, DEFENCE AND CIVIL (EXCESSES) 1985–86 £	392,730,629·84	3,214,798·66

SUPPLEMENTARY, 1986–87

SCHEDULE OF SUPPLEMENTARY SUMS granted, and of the sums which may be applied as appropriations in aid in addition thereto, to defray the charges for the Services herein particularly mentioned, for the year ended 31st March 1987, viz.:—

	Supply Grants	Appropriations in Aid
Vote	£	£
CLASS I		
1. For expenditure by the Ministry of Defence on personnel costs etc., of the Armed Forces and their Reserves and Cadet Forces etc.; personnel costs etc., of Defence Ministers and of certain civilian staff employed by the Ministry of Defence; on movements; certain stores; supplies and services; plant and machinery; charter and contract repair of ships; certain research; lands and buildings; sundry grants; payments abroad including contributions and subscriptions to international organisations; and grants in aid - - -	1,000	*–10,888,000
2. For expenditure by the Procurement Executive of the Ministry of Defence in operating its Headquarters and Establishments and for its other common services; for research etc., by contract; lands and buildings; for development by contract, production, repair etc. and purchases for sale abroad of sea systems, land systems, air systems and associated equipment; for certain contingent liabilities, and for sundry other Procurement Executive services including those on repayment terms to non-exchequer customers - - -	242,219,000	*–5,516,000
4. For expenditure including loans by the Property Services Agency of the Department of the Environment on public building work and certain accommodation services etc., for defence purposes	15,000,000	10,062,000
5. For operating the Royal Dockyards and for the repair of ships by contract including work undertaken on repayment terms for exchequer and non-exchequer customers - - - -	1,000	1,280,000
6. For expenditure by the Ministry of Defence in connection with the sale of Government shares in Royal Ordnance plc. - - - - - -	1,000	798,000
CLASS II		
1. For expenditure by the Foreign and Commonwealth Office on its salaries, building and other accommodation services, and administration, and those of HM Diplomatic Service official information services, sundry services and loans and a grant in aid for catering services - - -	11,430,000	2,984,000
2. For expenditure by the Foreign and Commonwealth Office on grants and subscriptions, etc., to certain international organisations, certain grants in aid, special payments and assistance, military aid and sundry other grants and services -	4,061,000	—
3. For expenditure by the Foreign and Commonwealth Office on grants in aid of the British Broadcasting Corporation for external broadcasting and monitoring services - - - - -	1,000	—

* Deficit

	Supply Grants	Appropriations in Aid
CLASS II—*continued*	£	£
Vote		
4. For expenditure by the Foreign and Commonwealth Office on a grant in aid of the British Council - - - - - - -	2,060,000	—
5. For expenditure by the Foreign and Commonwealth Office (Overseas Development Administration) on the official United Kingdom Aid Programme including capital subscriptions and other contributions and payments under guarantees to certain multilateral development banks and other bodies; subscriptions and grants in aid to certain international and regional organisations; bilateral capital aid and technical co-operation; refugee and other relief assistance; the cost of in-house Scientific Units; assistance, including grants in aid, to certain UK-based institutions and voluntary agencies; loans to the Commonwealth Development Corporation; and pensions and allowances in respect of overseas service - -	7,509,000	*−1,833,000
6. For expenditure by the Foreign and Commonwealth Office (Overseas Development Administration) on administration - - -	50,000	—
CLASS IV		
1. For expenditure by the Intervention Board for Agricultural Produce in giving effect in the United Kingdom to the agricultural support provisions of the Common Agricultural Policy of the European Community and to Community food aid measures and for certain other services - - -	2,000	—
3. For expenditure by the Ministry of Agriculture, Fisheries and Food on market support, grants and loans for capital and other improvements, support for agriculture in special areas and compensation to sheep producers, animal health, arterial drainage, flood and coast protection, and certain other services - - - - - - -	23,986,000	925,000
4. For expenditure by the Ministry of Agriculture, Fisheries and Food on commissioned research and development and advice, education and training services, botanical services, assistance to production, marketing and processing, support for the fishing industry, emergency and strategic food services, protective, agency and other services, including grants in aid and international subscriptions - - - - - - -	477,000	—
5. For expenditure by the Ministry of Agriculture, Fisheries and Food on departmental research, advisory services and administration and certain other services - - - - - -	4,388,000	100,000
CLASS V		
1. For expenditure by the Department of Trade and Industry on regional development grants, regional selective assistance, selective assistance to individual industries, certain other services including UK contributions to the funding of buffer stock operations and administrative costs of		

* *Deficit*

	Supply Grants	Appropriations in Aid
	£	£
CLASS V—*continued*		
Vote		
international commodity agreements, a strategic mineral stockpile, and the film industry, and support for the aerospace, shipbuilding and steel industries, including loans, grants and the purchase of assets and assistance to redundant steel workers	62,869,000	*31,378,000
2. For expenditure by the Department of Trade and Industry at its research establishments and on the running costs of certain of its headquarters divisions, radio regulatory division and the Patent Office, support for innovation (including industrial research and development, aircraft and aeroengine research and development, and space technology programmes), promotion of standards, export promotion and trade co-operation, miscellaneous support services, grants in aid, international subscriptions, provision of land and buildings, loans, grants and other payments - -	459,000	—
3. For expenditure by the Department of Trade and Industry on the regulation of trading practices, on consumer protection, and on central and miscellaneous services including grants in aid, international subscriptions, and grants to the fund for sub-postmasters - - - - -	1,000	1,721,000
4. For Government investment in British Ship-builders, grants from the shipbuilding intervention fund to assist public sector yards and assistance to redundant shipyard workers - - - - -	138,060,000	1,304,000
8. For expenditure by the Department of Trade and Industry in connection with the sale of shares in British Telecommunications plc - - - -	1,000	3,187,000
11. For expenditure by the Department of Trade and Industry in support of restructuring of Rover Group's commercial vehicle businesses - - -	680,000,000	—
CLASS VI		
1. For expenditure by the Department of Energy on assistance to the coal industry including grants to British Coal and payments to redundant workers	241,300,000	29,700,000
3. For expenditure by the Department of Energy on salaries and other services - - - - -	1,000	199,000
6. For expenditure by the Department of Energy in connection with the sale of Government shares in British Gas - - - - - - - -	1,000	207,999,000
CLASS VII		
1. For expenditure by the Department of Employment on the promotion of tourism including grants in aid, general labour market services including grants in aid, services for seriously disabled people, and an international subscription - - - -	1,000	—
3. For expenditure by the Department of Employment on the administration of benefit services and on central and miscellaneous services - - -	10,500,000	7,650,000
CLASS VIII		
1. For expenditure by the Department of Transport on essential additional maintenance of all-purpose trunk roads - - - - - - -	680,000	—

* *Deficit*

	Supply Grants	Appropriations in Aid
CLASS VIII—*continued*	£	£

Vote

2. For expenditure by the Department of Transport on assistance to shipping; civil aviation; central administration; certain licensing and testing schemes; research and development; road safety; and certain other transport services including civil defence; and international subscriptions, including grants in aid   -   -   -   -   -   - | 6,810,000 | — |

5. For expenditure by the Department of Transport on transport supplementary grants to county councils and some district councils in England, and certain other grants and payments in support of local roads and transport expenditure   -   - | 2,711,000 | *–1,110,000 |

6. For expenditure by the Department of Transport in connection with the sale of shares in British Airways   -   -   -   -   -   -   - | 1,000 | 35,322,000 |

8. For expenditure by the Department of Transport in connection with the sale of National Bus Company Operations -   -   -   -   -   - | 1,000 | 99,000 |

CLASS IX

1. For expenditure by the Department of the Environment on subsidies, improvements and investment, grants to housing associations and the Housing Corporation and other sundry services | 149,164,000 | 7,400,000 |

2. For expenditure by the Department of the Environment on housing administration, including rent officers, rent assessment panels, and grant in aid to the Housing Corporation; housing research; housing management and mobility; grants to voluntary organisations concerned with homelessness; and contributions towards the work of the National Federation of Housing Associations | 1,000 | — |

CLASS X

1. For expenditure by the Department of the Environment on other water supply, conservation and sewerage, local authority and other environmental services (including recreation), town and country planning (including compensation) and assistance to the construction industry -   -   - | 11,301,000 | — |

2. For expenditure by the Department of Environment on other environmental services including grants in aid and international subscriptions, on grants in aid to the Development Commission and British Waterways Board, on bridgeworks on developing Civil Defence water services and grants to New Towns   -   -   - | 1,250,000 | — |

3. For expenditure by the Department of the Environment on derelict land reclamation, grants in aid for Urban Development Corporations, transitional grants for voluntary bodies, Urban Programme and urban regeneration   -   -   - | 22,664,000 | — |

4. For expenditure by the Department of the Environment on royal palaces, etc., royal parks, etc., historic buildings, ancient monuments and certain public buildings, the national heritage, on

* *Deficit*

	Supply Grants	Appropriations in Aid
CLASS X—*continued*	£	£
Vote		
grants in aid, other grants and on payments to Inland Revenue covering assets accepted in lieu of tax, on an international subscription and on the administration of those activities - - -	1,165,000	*–1,000,000
5. For expenditure by the Department of the Environment on central administration, including royal commissions, committees, etc.; payments in connection with licence fees and environmental research and surveys including building and civil engineering research - - - - - -	1,000	18,992,000
6. For expenditure by the Department of the Environment for rate support grants to local authorities in England - - - - -	31,500,000	3,500,000
8. For expenditure by the Department of the Environment for rate rebate grants to local authorities in England - - - - - -	16,800,000	—
CLASS XI		
1. For expenditure by the Home Office on court services, compensation for criminal injuries, including a grant in aid, probation, police, community services, and superannuation payments for police and fire services - - - - - -	73,424,000	552,000
2. For expenditure by the Home Office on prisons (including central administration staff) and associated stores in England and Wales and the Parole Board - - - - - - - - -	2,916,000	—
3. For expenditure by the Home Office on court services, other services related to crime, probation and aftercare, police, fire, civil defence, control of immigration and nationality, issue of passports etc., other protective services and community services and other miscellaneous services including grants in aid and international subscriptions; and on administrative and operational staff (excluding prisons) and central services - - - -	1,000	—
4. For expenditure by the Home Office on grants to the British Broadcasting Corporation for home broadcasting and sundry other services - -	25,061,000	—
5. For expenditure by the Lord Chancellor's Department on the Court Service, the Law Commission, the Office of the Special Commissioners for Income Tax, the Office of the Social Security Commissioners, the VAT tribunals, the Public Trustee Office and certain other legal services, including grants in aid to the Council for Licensed Conveyancers and for administration of legal aid	1,000	1,999,000
6. For grants to the Legal Aid Fund and for expenditure by the Lord Chancellor's Department on legal aid in criminal cases, court services, and costs paid from central funds - - - -	23,000,000	—
CLASS XII		
1. For expenditure by the Department of Education and Science on schools, further education,		

* *Deficit*

	Supply Grants	Appropriations in Aid
Class XII—*continued*	£	£
Vote		
teacher training, adult education, miscellaneous educational services and research, including grants in aid and international subscriptions - -	2,000,000	—
2. For expenditure by the Department of Education and Science on the assisted places scheme, student awards, reimbursement of fees for qualifying students from other European Community countries (EC students), education support grants and compensation payments to redundant teachers and staff of certain institutions - - - -	1,000	—
4. For expenditure by the Department of Education and Science and the University Grants Committee on administration - - - - - -	1,032,000	15,000
5. For grants in aid of the Agricultural and Food Research Council - - - - - -	4,470,000	—
8. For grants in aid of the Science and Engineering Research Council including subscriptions to certain international organisations - - - -	658,000	—
9. For a grant in aid of the Economic and Social Research Council - - - - - -	186,000	—
Class XIII		
10. For certain grants and services for the benefit of the arts, for grants in aid to the Arts Council and certain other institutions, for a grant in aid to the National Heritage Memorial Fund and for payments to the Inland Revenue covering assets accepted in lieu of tax, for international subscriptions and for expenditure on the Government Art Collection - - - - - - -	2,565,000	—
Class XIV		
1. For expenditure by the Department of Health and Social Security on the provision of services under the national health service in England, on other health services including a grant in aid and on certain other services including research - -	2,000	40,000,000
2. For expenditure by the Department of Health and Social Security on the provision of services under the national health service in England, on other health and personal social services, on welfare food and certain other services including grants under section 8 of the Industrial Development Act 1982 - - - - - - -	2,367,000	31,283,000
3. For expenditure by the Department of Health and Social Security on the provision of services under the national health service in England, on other health and personal social services including certain services in relation to the United Kingdom, and on research, exports, services for the disabled and certain other services including grants in aid and international subscriptions - - - - -	1,165,000	3,142,000
Class XV		
1. For expenditure by the Department of Health and Social Security on non-contributory retirement pensions, Christmas bonus payments to pensioners,		

	Supply Grants	Appropriations in Aid
CLASS XV—*continued*	£	£

Vote

pensions etc., for disablement or death arising out of war or service in the armed forces after 2 September 1939 and on sundry other services, on attendance allowances, invalid care allowance, severe disablement allowance and mobility allowance - - - - - - - - — **232,700,000** — —

2. For expenditure by the Department of Health and Social Security on supplementary pensions and allowances and mobility allowance - - - **780,001,000** —

3. For expenditure by the Department of Health and Social Security on child benefit, one parent benefit, family benefit income supplements and non-contributory maternity grants - - - - **79,000,000** —

4. For expenditure by the Department of Health and Social Security on rent rebate, rent allowance and rate rebate subsidies, to housing, rating, and local authorities, on expenditure and subsidies towards the administrative costs incurred by these authorities in operating the housing benefit scheme - **190,300,000** —

5. For expenditure by the Department of Health and Social Security on administration and certain other services including grants to voluntary organisations and an international subscription - - - - **5,766,000** **1,880,000**

6. For sums payable out of the Consolidated Fund to the National Insurance Fund - - - - **18,000,000** —

CLASS XVI

1. For expenditure by the Department of Agriculture and Fisheries for Scotland on price guarantees, production grants and subsidies, grants and loans for capital and other improvements, support for agriculture in special areas and compensation to sheep producers and certain other services including services relating to livestock diseases - **5,958,000** —

2. For expenditure by the Department of Agriculture and Fisheries for Scotland on educational and advisory services, botanical services, assistance to marketing and processing, administration, land management and land settlement, livestock services, assistance to crofters, assistance to the Scottish fishing industry, protective and certain other services including research and development, special services and a grant in aid - - - **2,677,000** —

5. For expenditure by the Industry Department for Scotland on regional development grants and regional selective assistance - - - - - **41,478,000** ** –2,049,000*

6. For expenditure by the Scottish Development Department in connection with acquisition of land and related services, on roads and certain associated services, including lighting and road safety, on assistance to local transport, on support for transport services in the Highlands and Islands, piers and harbours and on certain other transport services and grants, on housing subsidies, Royal Palaces and Royal Parks, historic buildings and ancient monuments, other central environmental services and grants in aid - - - - - **1,784,000** **4,000**

* Deficit

	Supply Grants	Appropriations in Aid
CLASS XVI—*continued*	£	£

Vote

8. For expenditure by the Scottish Development Department on subsidies, the option mortgage scheme, improvements and investment, housing defects grants, certain rent registration expenses, capital grants to housing associations, loans and grants to first time purchasers and sundry other housing services - - - - - - - | 14,623,000 | 104,000 |

9. For expenditure by the Industry Department for Scotland on grants to New Town Development Corporations in connection with housing and other services - - - - - - - - | 637,000 | — |

10. For expenditure by the Scottish Development Department in connection with water supply and sewerage, flood prevention, town and country planning (including compensation), recreation, land reclamation, coast protection, urban programme and other local environmental services - | 5,318,000 | — |

12. For expenditure by the Scottish Home and Health Department on legal aid and criminal injuries compensation (excluding administration), on police and fire services superannuation and police grant | 2,700,000 | — |

13. For expenditure by the Scottish Courts Administration on costs and fees in connection with legal proceedings - - - - - - - | 400,000 | — |

14. For expenditure by the Scottish Home and Health Department on legal aid administration, certain services relating to crime, prisons, treatment of offenders, civil defence (including grants) and on fire and police services (excluding grants and superannuation), on the provision of services under the national health service, on other health services, on research, services for the disabled and certain other services including a grant in aid | 2,220,000 | — |

15. For expenditure by the Scottish Education Department on schools and certain grants to the local authorities, higher and further education, libraries, miscellaneous educational services including compensation payments for redundant staff at colleges of education, research and administration, grant in aid to the National Museums of Scotland, the National Galleries of Scotland and the National Library of Scotland including purchase grants in aid, certain grants for the arts, sport, social work, other grants in aid and certain payments on behalf of the European Community - - - - | 1,000 | 187,000 |

16. For expenditure by the Scottish Education Department on awards to students receiving higher and further education - - - - - - - | 963,000 | 37,000 |

17. For expenditure by the Scottish Home and Health Department on the provision of services under the National Health Service in Scotland, on welfare food and certain other services - - - | 1,000 | 6,000,000 |

21. For expenditure by the Scottish Office on administration, Royal Commissions and certain other services - - - - - - - | 56,000 | 100,000 |

	Supply Grants	Appropriations in Aid
CLASS XVI—*continued*	£	£
Vote		
23. For expenditure by the Scottish Office for rate rebate grants to local authorities in Scotland- -	280,000	—
CLASS XVII		
1. For expenditure by the Welsh Office on market support, grants and loans for capital and other improvements, support for agriculture in special areas, compensation to sheep producers, animal health and support services, arterial drainage, flood and coast protection and certain other services- - - - - - - - -	4,693,000	245,000
2. For expenditure by the Welsh Office on assistance to agricultural production, food processing and marketing, certain other services including research, land management, assistance to the Welsh fishing industry including protective and other services, special assistance for rural and highland areas, on the Welsh Development Agency and some special and other services including grants in aid- - - - - - - -	1,000	—
3. For expenditure by the Welsh Office on regional development grants, regional selective assistance and housing subsidy - - - - -	22,500,000	—
5. For expenditure by the Welsh Office on tourism, roads and certain associated services including road safety, housing administration, historic buildings and ancient monuments, other environmental services, civil defence (including grants), education, libraries and museums, centrally funded health services and personal social services, grants in aid, EC agency payments, other grants and certain other services, including research - -	2,000	—
6. For expenditure by the Welsh Office on housing subsidies, improvements and investment, the option mortgage scheme, grants to housing associations, water, sewerage, town and country planning (including compensation), recreation, other local services, including clean air grants, urban programme (including urban development grant), welfare food, EC medical costs, certain EC agency payments and other services - -	39,136,000	11,000
7. For expenditure by the Welsh Office on family practitioner services under the National Health Service - - - - - - -	13,793,000	2,097,000
10. For expenditure by the Welsh Office for rate support grants to local authorities in Wales and on adjustments between England and Wales in respect of pooled education expenditure - -	5,000,000	—
12. For expenditure by the Welsh Office for grants in respect of rate rebates for the disabled in Wales -	735,000	—
CLASS XVIII		
1. For expenditure by the Northern Ireland Office on central and miscellaneous services, services related to crime, police, prisons, training schools, probation and after-care etc., compensation		

	Supply Grants	Appropriations in Aid
Class XVIII—*continued*	£	£

Vote

schemes, Crown prosecutions, and other legal services, grants in aid to Co-operation North and the Police Complaints Board and certain other grants - - - - - - - | 7,411,000 | —

	Supply Grants	Appropriations in Aid
CLASS XIX		
1. For expenditure by the Central Office of Information on home and overseas publicity - - -	81,023,000	—
2. For expenditure by the Customs and Excise Department including an international subscription	1,971,000	—
6. For expenditure by the Controller of Her Majesty's Stationery Office on the reimbursement of the HMSO trading fund in respect of goods and services supplied to the Houses of Parliament and to United Kingdom members of the European Assembly - - - - - -	950,000	50,000
7. For the expenditure of the Inland Revenue Department - - - - - - -	2,900,000	—
8. For the expenditure of the Inland Revenue Department on life assurance premium relief and mortgage interest relief - - - -	74,000,000	—
13. For expenditure by the Treasury in connection with the manufacture, storage and distribution of coinage for use in the United Kingdom- - -	1,500,000	—
14. For expenditure by the Central Computer and Telecommunications Agency (Treasury) in connection with computers and general telecommunications including an international subscription - -	624,000	—
16. For rates and contributions in lieu of rates paid by the Rating of Government Property Department in respect of property occupied by the Crown and premises occupied by representatives of commonwealth and foreign countries and international organisations - - - - -	4,100,000	1,300,000
CLASS XX		
1. For the expenditure by the Management and Personnel Office on the central management of the civil service on the Office of the Parliamentary Counsel and certain other services including grants in aid - - - - - - - -	1,000	75,000
2. For the expenditure by the Cabinet Office, including the Central Statistical Office and grants in aid to international organisations - -	260,000	—
4. For the expenditure of the Charity Commission for England and Wales - - - -	187,000	—
6. For a grant in aid of the Commonwealth War Graves Commission - - - - -	1,176,000	—
8. For the expenditure of the House of Commons on members' salaries, allowances, pensions, etc., financial assistance to opposition parties and a grant in aid - - - - - - -	3,400,000	—
9. For the expenditure of the House of Lords - -	230,000	32,000
10. For the expenditure of the Land Registry - -	1,000	2,031,000
11. For expenditure by the Ordnance Survey on the survey of Great Britain and other mapping services	450,000	—
18. For expenditure (partly recoverable), including loans, by the Property Services Agency of the		

	Supply Grants	Appropriations in Aid
Class XX—*continued*	£	£
Vote		
Department of the Environment on acquisitions, public building work, accommodation services, administration and certain other services for civil purposes in the United Kingdom and on certain defence services the costs of which are recovered from clients - - - - - - -	3,426,000	31,971,000
19. For the expenditure of the Office of Population Censuses and Surveys, including a grant in aid -	1,000	93,000
20. For expenditure by the Lord Advocate's Departments on central and miscellaneous services including grants in aid - - - - -	180,000	20,000
21. For expenditure by the Crown Office on crown prosecutions and certain other legal services - -	150,000	—
22. For expenditure by the Northern Ireland Court Service on court services and certain other legal services including grants in aid - - - -	34,000	100,000
23. For expenditure by the Northern Ireland Court Service on legal aid and court services - - -	600,000	—
24. For expenditure by the Departments of the Law Officers and the Procurator General and Treasury Solicitor on central and certain other services -	495,000	366,000
25. For expenditure by the Department of the Procurator General and Treasury Solicitor on other legal services - - - - - -	250,000	203,000
Class XXa		
1. For expenditure by the House of Commons Commission - - - - - - - -	579,000	38,000
Total Supplementary 1986–87 - - £	3,483,899,000	403,383,000

Class I, 1987–88   SCHEDULE (B).—Part 3

Class I

Schedule of Sums granted, and of the sums which may be applied as appropriations in aid in addition thereto, to defray the charges of the several Services herein particularly mentioned, which will come in course of payment during the year ending on 31st March 1988, including provision for numbers of personnel as set out hereunder, viz.:—

	Sums not exceeding	
	Supply Grants	Appropriations in Aid
	£	£
Vote		
1. For expenditure by the Ministry of Defence on personnel costs etc., of the Armed Forces and their Reserves and Cadet Forces etc., (including provision for Naval Service to a number not exceeding 69,950, provision for Army Service to a number not exceeding 178,400, for the Individual Reserves to a number not exceeding		

	Supply Grants	Appropriations in Aid
CLASS I—*continued*	£	£
Vote		
96,000, for the Territorial Army to a number not exceeding 87,350, for the Home Service Force to a number not exceeding 5,000, and for the Ulster Defence Regiment to a number not exceeding 7,800, and provision for Air Force Service to a number not exceeding 96,700, for RAF Reserves to a number not exceeding 5,650, and for the Royal Auxiliary Air Force to a number not exceeding 2,370); personnel costs etc., of Defence Ministers and of certain civilian staff employed by the Ministry of Defence; on movements; certain stores; supplies and services; plant and machinery; charter of ships; certain research; lands and buildings; sundry grants; payments abroad including contributions and subscriptions to international organisations; and grants in aid - - - - - -	7,255,411,000	1,052,582,000
2. For expenditure by the Procurement Executive of the Ministry of Defence in operating its Headquarters and Establishments and for its other common services; for research etc., by contract; for lands and buildings; for development by contract, production, repair etc., and purchases for sale abroad of sea systems, land systems, air systems and associated equipment; for certain contingent liabilities, and for sundry other Procurement Executive services including those on repayment terms to non-exchequer customers	8,551,837,000	618,287,000
3. For expenditure by the Ministry of Defence on retired pay, pensions etc. - - - - -	1,049,853,000	1,059,000
4. For expenditure including loans by the Property Services Agency of the Department of the Environment on public building work and certain accommodation services etc., for defence purposes - - - - - - -	1,480,330,000	288,588,000
5. For expenditure by the Ministry of Defence on the refit and repair of ships and related expenditure on administrative and operational costs - - - - - - - -	448,312,000	35,225,000
6. For expenditure by the Ministry of Defence in connection with the sale of Government shares in Royal Ordnance plc. (including a supplementary sum of £1,000) - - - - - - -	2,000	3,399,000
TOTAL, CLASS I - - - - - - £	18,785,745,000	1,999,140,000

Class II, 1987–88   SCHEDULE (B).—Part 4

CLASS II

SCHEDULE OF SUMS granted, and of the sums which may be applied as appropriations in aid in addition thereto, to defray the charges of the several Services herein particularly mentioned, which will come in course of payment during the year ending on 31st March 1988, viz.:—

	Sums not exceeding	
	Supply Grants	Appropriations in Aid
	£	£
Vote		
1. For expenditure by the Foreign and Commonwealth Office on its salaries, building and other accommodation services, and administration, and those of HM Diplomatic Service, official information services, sundry services and loans and a grant in aid for catering services	424,360,000	46,082,000
2. For expenditure by the Foreign and Commonwealth Office on grants and subscriptions, etc., to certain international organisations, certain grants in aid, special payments and assistance, scholarships, military aid and sundry other grants and services - - - - - -	112,511,000	26,052,000
3. For expenditure by the Foreign and Commonwealth Office on grants in aid of the British Broadcasting Corporation for external broadcasting and monitoring services and for contractual services in connection with FCO relay stations - - - - - -	116,500,000	2,850,000
4. For expenditure by the Foreign and Commonwealth Office on a grant in aid of the British Council - - - - - - -	55,658,000	—
5. For expenditure by the Foreign and Commonwealth Office (Overseas Development Administration) on the official United Kingdom Aid Programme including bilateral financial aid, grants in aid and technical co-operation; the cost of in-house Scientific Units; grants and grants in aid to UK institutions, voluntary agencies and individuals, and other expenditure in support of the programme; capital and other subscriptions, other contributions including grants in aid and payments under guarantee, to multilateral development banks and other international and regional bodies; emergency, refugee and other relief assistance; loans to the Commonwealth Development Corporation; and pensions and allowances in respect of overseas service - -	1,083,750,000	76,430,000
6. For expenditure by the Foreign and Commonwealth Office (Overseas Development Administration) on administration - - -	27,791,000	189,000
7. For expenditure by the Foreign and Commonwealth Office (Overseas Development Administration) on pensions and superannuation payments etc., in respect of overseas service and sundry other services and expenses - - -	120,354,000	2,140,000
TOTAL, CLASS II - - - - - £	1,940,924,000	153,743,000

     SCHEDULE (B).—Part 5

CLASS IV

SCHEDULE OF SUMS granted, and of the sums which may be applied as appropriations in aid in addition thereto, to defray the charges of the several Services herein particularly mentioned, which will come in course of payment during the year ending on 31st March 1988, viz.:—

	Sums not exceeding	
	Supply Grants	Appropriations in Aid
	£	£
Vote		
1. For expenditure by the Intervention Board for Agricultural Produce in giving effect in the United Kingdom to the agricultural support provisions of the Common Agricultural Policy of the European Community and to Community food aid measures and for certain other services	423,979,000	402,552,000
2. For expenditure by the Intervention Board for Agricultural Produce on central administration and miscellaneous services - - - -	30,070,000	706,000
3. For expenditure by the Ministry of Agriculture, Fisheries and Food on market support, grants and loans for capital and other improvements, support for agriculture in special areas and compensation to sheep producers, animal health, arterial drainage, flood and coast protection, and certain other services - - - -	126,987,000	14,266,000
4. For expenditure by the Ministry of Agriculture, Fisheries and Food on commissioned research and development and advice, education and training services, botanical services, assistance to production, marketing and processing, support for the fishing industry, emergency and strategic food services, protective, agency and other services including grants in aid and international subscriptions - - - - - -	141,801,000	12,126,000
5. For expenditure by the Ministry of Agriculture, Fisheries and Food on departmental research, advisory services and administration and certain other services - - - - - -	206,219,000	21,515,000
6. For a grant in aid of the Forestry Fund - -	53,790,000	—
TOTAL, CLASS IV - - - - - £	982,846,000	451,165,000

Class V

Schedule of Sums granted, and of the sums which may be applied as appropriations in aid in addition thereto, to defray the charges of the several Services herein particularly mentioned, which will come in course of payment during the year ending on 31st March 1988, viz.:—

	Sums not exceeding	
	Supply Grants	Appropriations in Aid
	£	£
Vote		
1. For expenditure by the Department of Trade and Industry on regional development grants, regional selective assistance, selective assistance to individual industries, certain other services including UK contributions to the funding of buffer stock operations of international commodity agreements, a strategic mineral stockpile, and the film industry, and support for the aerospace, shipbuilding and steel industries, including loans, grants and the purchase of assets and assistance to redundant steel workers - -	308,712,000	83,783,000
2. For expenditure by the Department of Trade and Industry at its research establishments and on the running costs of certain of its headquarters divisions, radiocommunications division and the Patent Office, support for innovation (including industrial research and development, aircraft and aeroengine research and development, and space technology programmes), promotion of standards, export promotion and trade co-operation, miscellaneous support services, grants in aid, international subscriptions, provision of land and buildings, loans, grants and other payments - - - - - - -	462,124,000	115,219,000
3. For expenditure by the Department of Trade and Industry on the regulation of trading practices, on consumer protection, and on central and miscellaneous services including grants in aid, international subscriptions, grants to the fund for sub-postmasters and residual expenses arising from the sale of shares in British Telecommunications plc. - - - - -	150,083,000	53,536,000
4. For Government investment in British Shipbuilders and grants from the shipbuilding intervention fund to assist public sector yards - -	49,000,000	1,000
5. For expenditure by the Export Credits Guarantee Department on administration - - - -	38,075,000	967,000
6. For expenditure by the Export Credits Guarantee Department in connection with interest support to banks and other lenders providing fixed rate export finance, cost escalation cover, grants towards financing of exports to match foreign competition and cover under the tender to contract/forward exchange supplement scheme	164,817,000	80,150,000

	Supply Grants	Appropriations in Aid
CLASS V—*continued*	£	£
Vote		
7. For expenditure by the Export Credits Guarantee Department in connection with export credits guarantees including an international subscription, guarantees given in the national interest and overseas investment insurance - - -	235,528,000	932,809,000
8. For expenditure by the Department of Trade and Industry in connection with the purchase and sale of Government shares in Rolls-Royce plc (including a supplementary sum of £1,000)	2,000	323,590,000
TOTAL, CLASS V - - - - - - £	1,408,341,000	1,590,055,000

Class VI, 1987–88   SCHEDULE (B).—PART 7

CLASS VI

SCHEDULE OF SUMS granted, and of the sums which may be applied as appropriations in aid in addition thereto, to defray the charges of the several Services herein particularly mentioned, which will come in course of payment during the year ending on 31st March 1988, viz.:—

	Sums not exceeding	
	Supply Grants	Appropriations in Aid
	£	£
Vote		
1. For expenditure by the Department of Energy on assistance to the coal industry including grants to the British Coal Corporation and payments to redundant workers - - -	898,000,000	44,000,000
2. For expenditure by the Department of Energy in connection with the energy industries including related research and development, energy efficiency, oil storage and pipelines, selective assistance to industry, promotion and security of oil and gas supplies, grants and certain other services, including payments to the Oil and Pipelines Agency, subscriptions and contributions to international organisations - - - -	251,272,000	28,021,000
3. For expenditure by the Department of Energy on salaries and other administrative costs - -	22,873,000	4,441,000
4. For expenditure by the Department of Energy on refunds and repayments of petroleum licensing proceeds, and other payments in connection with such proceeds - - - - - - -	1,000	267,500,000
5. For payment of pensions, etc., to members of the United Kingdom Atomic Energy Authority's superannuation schemes and other related expenditure- - - - - - - - -	1,000	58,549,000
6. For expenditure by the Department of Energy in connection with the sale of shares in British Gas - - - - - - - - -	1,000	84,999,000
TOTAL, CLASS VI - - - - - £	1,172,148,000	487,510,000

CLASS VII

SCHEDULE OF SUMS granted, and of the sums which may be applied as appropriations in aid in addition thereto, to defray the charges of the several Services herein particularly mentioned, which will come in course of payment during the year ending on 31st March 1988, viz.:—

	Sums not exceeding	
	Supply Grants	Appropriations in Aid
	£	£
Vote		
1. For expenditure by the Department of Employment on the promotion of enterprise, tourism and general labour market services including grants in aid, measures to promote and preserve employment opportunities, services for seriously disabled people, publicity, compensation for persons disabled by pneumoconiosis, byssinosis and diffuse mesothelioma, payments towards expenses of trade union ballots and an international subscription - - - - -	1,397,636,000	6,944,000
2. For expenditure by the Department of Employment on the administration of benefit services and on central and miscellaneous services - -	63,860,000	348,499,000
3. For expenditure by the Department of Employment on a grant in aid to the Advisory, Conciliation and Arbitration Service - - -	15,851,000	—
4. For expenditure by the Department of Employment on a grant in aid to the Health and Safety Commission - - - - - - -	93,735,000	35,000
5. For expenditure by the Department of Employment on a grant in aid to the Manpower Services Commission - - - - - - -	1,992,128,000	297,706,000
TOTAL, CLASS VII - - - - £	3,563,210,000	653,184,000

       SCHEDULE (B).—PART 9

CLASS VIII

SCHEDULE OF SUMS granted, and of the sums which may be applied as appropriations in aid in addition thereto, to defray the charges of the several Services herein particularly mentioned, which will come in course of payment during the year ending on 31st March 1988, viz.:—

	Sums not exceeding	
	Supply Grants	Appropriations in Aid
	£	£
Vote		
1. For expenditure by the Department of Transport on the construction, improvement and maintenance of motorways and trunk roads, including the acquisition of land, scheme design and preparation, compensation, the purchase of maintenance vehicles and equipment and the maintenance and operation of Woolwich Ferry -	910,829,000	62,246,000
2. For expenditure by the Department of Transport on assistance to shipping; civil aviation; central administration; certain licensing and testing schemes; research and development; road safety; and certain other transport services including civil defence; and international subscriptions, including grants in aid - - - - -	190,446,000	58,055,000
3. For expenditure by the Department of Transport on support to nationalised transport industries and to ports; rebate of fuel duty to bus operators; and costs of the driver testing and training organisation - - - - - -	1,324,916,000	832,000
4. For expenditure by the Department of Transport in connection with driver and motor vehicle registration and licensing; the collection of revenue and the development of information technology projects for other licensing and testing activities - - - - - -	114,179,000	9,595,000
5. For expenditure by the Department of Transport on transport supplementary grants to Highway Authorities in England, and certain other grants and payments in support of local roads and transport expenditure - - - - -	205,095,000	13,063,000
6. For residual expenditure by the Department of Transport in connection with the sale of shares in British Airways and for the costs of the second instalment - - - - - -	1,000	1,249,000
7. For expenditure by the Department of Transport in connection with the sale of shares in BAA plc (including a supplementary sum of £4,199,000) - - - - - - -	4,200,000	1,000
8. For expenditure by the Department of Transport in connection with the sale of National Bus Company operations - - - - - -	1,000	359,000
TOTAL, CLASS VIII - - - - £	2,749,667,000	145,400,000

Class IX, 1987–88   SCHEDULE (B).—Part 10

Class IX

Schedule of Sums granted, and of the sums which may be applied as appropriations in aid in addition thereto, to defray the charges of the several Services herein particularly mentioned, which will come in course of payment during the year ending on 31st March 1988, viz.:—

	Sums not exceeding	
	Supply Grants	Appropriations in Aid
	£	£
Vote		
1. For expenditure by the Department of the Environment on subsidies, improvements and investment, grants to housing associations and the Housing Corporation and sundry other services - - - - - - - -	2,020,329,000	46,615,000
2. For expenditure by the Department of the Environment on housing administration, including rent officers, rent assessment panels, and grant in aid to the Housing Corporation; housing research; housing management and mobility; grants to voluntary organisations concerned with homelessness; and contributions towards the work of the National Federation of Housing Associations - - - - - - -	43,955,000	98,000
Total, Class IX - - - - - - £	2,064,284,000	46,713,000

Class X, 1987–88   SCHEDULE (B).—Part 11

Class X

Schedule of Sums granted, and of the sums which may be applied as appropriations in aid in addition thereto, to defray the charges of the several Services herein particularly mentioned, which will come in course of payment during the year ending on 31st March 1988, viz.:—

	Sums not exceeding	
	Supply Grants	Appropriations in Aid
	£	£
Vote		
1. For expenditure by the Department of the Environment on other water supply, conservation and sewerage, local authority and other environmental services (including recreation), town and country planning (including compensation) and assistance to the construction and environmental protection industries - - - - - -	68,133,000	92,000

	Supply Grants	Appropriations in Aid
CLASS X—*continued*	£	£
Vote		
2. For expenditure by the Department of the Environment on other environmental services including grants in aid and international subscriptions, on grants in aid to the Development Commission and British Waterways Board, on bridgeworks and on developing Civil Defence water services and grants to New Towns - -	195,909,000	—
3. For expenditure by the Department of the Environment on derelict land reclamation, grants and other assistance to the private sector for urban regeneration, grants in aid for existing and newly constituted Urban Development Corporations, the Urban Programme and transitional grants for voluntary bodies - - -	434,440,000	—
4. For expenditure by the Department of the Environment on royal palaces, etc., (including administration), royal parks, etc., (including administration), historic buildings, ancient monuments and certain public buildings, the national heritage, on grants in aid and other grants, on payments to the Inland Revenue covering assets accepted in lieu of tax, on an international subscription and on the resurvey of listed buildings - - - - - - - -	85,876,000	10,073,000
5. For expenditure by the Department of the Environment on central administration, including royal commissions, committees etc., payments in connection with research, surveys and licence fees - - - - - - - -	154,489,000	27,501,000
6. For expenditure by the Department of the Environment for rate support grants to local authorities in England - - - - -	9,927,000,000	—
7. For expenditure by the Department of the Environment for national parks supplementary grants to local authorities in England - - -	7,284,000	—
8. For expenditure by the Department of the Environment on rate rebate grants to local authorities in England - - - - -	122,700,000	—
9. For expenditure by the Department of the Environment for expenses incurred in connection with the sale of shares in the water services public limited companies - - - - -	2,000,000	—
TOTAL, CLASS X - - - - - £	10,997,831,000	37,666,000

CLASS XI

SCHEDULE OF SUMS granted, and of the sums which may be applied as appropriations in aid in addition thereto, to defray the charges of the several Services herein particularly mentioned, which will come in course of payment during the year ending on 31st March 1988, viz.:—

	Sums not exceeding	
	Supply Grants	Appropriations in Aid
	£	£
Vote		
1. For expenditure by the Home Office on court services, compensation for criminal injuries, including a grant in aid, probation, police, community services, and superannuation payments for police and fire services - - -	2,099,395,000	16,443,000
2. For expenditure by the Home Office on prisons (including central administrative staff) and associated stores in England and Wales, and on the Parole Board - - - - - - -	677,904,000	35,719,000
3. For expenditure by the Home Office on court services, other services related to crime, probation and aftercare, police, fire, civil defence, control of immigration and nationality, issue of passports etc., other protective services and community services and other miscellaneous services including grants in aid and international subscriptions; and on administrative and operational staff (excluding prisons) and central services - - - - - - - -	406,319,000	49,928,000
4. For expenditure by the Home Office on grants to the British Broadcasting Corporation for home broadcasting and payments in respect of the collection and enforcement of licence fees -	1,035,020,000	—
5. For expenditure by the Lord Chancellor's Department on the Court Service, the Law Commission, the Office of the Special Commissioners for Income Tax, the Office of the Social Security Commissioners, the VAT tribunals, the Public Trustee Office and certain other legal services, including grants in aid to the Council for Licensed Conveyancers and for administration of legal aid - - - - - - -	127,528,000	146,788,000
6. For grants to the Legal Aid Fund and for expenditure by the Lord Chancellor's Department on legal aid in criminal cases and costs paid from central funds - - - - -	463,365,000	920,000
TOTAL, CLASS XI - - - - - £	4,809,531,000	249,798,000

CLASS XII

SCHEDULE OF SUMS granted, and of the sums which may be applied as appropriations in aid in addition thereto, to defray the charges of the several Services herein particularly mentioned, which will come in course of payment during the year ending on 31st March 1988, viz.:—

	Sums not exceeding	
	Supply Grants	Appropriations in Aid
Vote	£	£
1. For expenditure by the Department of Education and Science on schools, further education, teacher training, adult education, miscellaneous educational services and research, including grants in aid and international subscriptions -	376,982,000	10,232,000
2. For expenditure by the Department of Education and Science on the assisted places scheme, student awards, reimbursement of fees for qualifying European Community students and compensation payments to redundant teachers and staff of certain institutions - - - -	729,600,000	8,000
3. For expenditure by the Department of Education and Science on universities and certain other institutions, grants for higher and further education, payment of certain licence fees to the Home Office, grants in aid and a subscription to an international organisation - - - -	1,664,683,000	1,549,000
4. For expenditure by the Department of Education and Science and the University Grants Committee on administration - - - - -	58,309,000	1,502,000
5. For a grant in aid of the Agricultural and Food Research Council, and for the payment of certain licence fees to the Home Office - - -	52,927,000	—
6. For a grant in aid of the Medical Research Council including subscriptions to certain international organisations, and for payment of certain licence fees to the Home Office - - -	133,530,000	—
7. For a grant in aid of the Natural Environment Research Council, and for payment of certain licence fees to the Home Office - - - -	71,270,000	—
8. For a grant in aid of the Science and Engineering Research Council including subscriptions to certain international organisations - - -	350,252,000	—
9. For a grant in aid of the Economic and Social Research Council - - - - - -	24,045,000	—
10. For a grant in aid of the British Museum (Natural History) - - - - -	17,558,000	—
11. For grants in aid of the Royal Society and the Fellowship of Engineering, and the science policy studies programme of the Advisory Board for the Research Councils - - - -	7,667,000	—
12. For expenditure by the Department of Education and Science on superannuation allowances and gratutities, etc., in respect of teachers, and the widows, children and dependants of deceased teachers - - - - - - - -	185,864,000	1,140,044,000

	Supply Grants	Appropriations in Aid
Class XII—*continued*	£	£
Vote		
13. For expenditure by the Department of Education and Science in connection with the sale of the National Seed Development Organisation Ltd. and assets of the Plant Breeding Institute - -	1,000	400,000
Total, Class XII - - - - £	3,672,688,000	1,153,735,000

Class XIII, 1987–88   SCHEDULE (B).—Part 14

Class XIII

Schedule of Sums granted, and of the sums which may be applied as appropriations in aid in addition thereto, to defray the charges of the several Services herein particularly mentioned, which will come in course of payment during the year ending on 31st March 1988, viz.:—

	Sums not exceeding	
	Supply Grants	Appropriations in Aid
	£	£
Vote		
1. For expenditure by the Office of Arts and Libraries on a grant in aid to the British Museum	13,938,000	—
2. For expenditure by the Office of Arts and Libraries on a grant in aid to the Imperial War Museum - - - - - -	4,727,000	—
3. For expenditure by the Office of Arts and Libraries on a grant in aid to the National Gallery - - - - - -	7,017,000	—
4. For expenditure by the Office of Arts and Libraries on a grant in aid to the National Maritime Museum - - - -	4,677,000	—
5. For expenditure by the Office of Arts and Libraries on a grant in aid to the National Portrait Gallery - - - - -	1,899,000	—
6. For expenditure by the Office of Arts and Libraries on a grant in aid to the Science Museum - - - - - -	9,589,000	—
7. For expenditure by the Office of Arts and Libraries on a grant in aid to the Tate Gallery	6,497,000	—
8. For expenditure by the Office of Arts and Libraries on a grant in aid to the Victoria and Albert Museum - - - - -	11,680,000	—
9. For expenditure by the Office of Arts and Libraries on a grant in aid to the Wallace Collection - - - - - -	939,000	—
10. For expenditure by the Office of Arts and Libraries on grants in aid to the Arts Council and other bodies; on grants to museums and other institutions; on payments to the Inland Revenue for assets accepted in lieu of tax; on the Government Art Collection; and on international subscriptions and certain other services for the benefit of the arts - - -	176,126,000	2,000

	Supply Grants	Appropriations in Aid
CLASS XIII—*continued*	£	£
Vote		
11. For grants in aid to the British Library and the Royal Geographical Society; for the expenses of the Royal Commission on Historical Manuscripts; and for payments in respect of Public Lending Right - - - - - - -	54,337,000	—
12. For expenditure by the Office of Arts and Libraries on administration - - -	1,267,000	1,000
TOTAL, CLASS XIII - - - - £	292,693,000	3,000

Class XIV, 1987–88   SCHEDULE (B).—PART 15

CLASS XIV

SCHEDULE OF SUMS granted, and of the sums which may be applied as appropriations in aid in addition thereto, to defray the charge of the several Services herein particularly mentioned, which will come in course of payment during the year ending on 31st March 1988, viz.:—

	Sums not exceeding	
	Supply Grants	Appropriations in Aid
	£	£
Vote		
1. For expenditure by the Department of Health and Social Security on the provision of services under the national health service in England, on other health services including grant in aid and on certain other services including research -	10,078,558,000	1,983,060,000
2. For expenditure by the Department of Health and Social Security on the provision of services under the national health service in England, on other health and personal social services, on welfare food and certain other services - -	3,309,323,000	588,126,000
3. For expenditure by the Department of Health and Social Security on the national health service in England and on miscellaneous health, personal social and other services (some of which are administered on a United Kingdom basis), including Family Practitioner Committee administration, mental health, medical, scientific and technical services, services for disabled persons, grants to voluntary organisations, etc., grants in aid and subscriptions to international organisations - - - - - - - -	397,724,000	29,065,000
4. For expenditure by the Department of Health and Social Security on pensions, allowances, gratuities, etc., to or in respect of persons engaged in health services or in other approved employment - - - - - - -	19,562,000	1,001,469,000
TOTAL, CLASS XIV - - - - £	13,805,167,000	3,601,720,000

CLASS XV

SCHEDULE OF SUMS granted, and of the sums which may be applied as appropriations in aid in addition thereto, to defray the charges of the several Services herein particularly mentioned, which will come in course of payment during the year ending on 31st March 1988, viz.:—

	Sums not exceeding	
	Supply Grants	Appropriations in Aid
	£	£
Vote		
1. For expenditure by the Department of Health and Social Security on non-contributory retirement pensions, Christmas bonus payments to pensioners, pensions etc., for disablement or death arising out of war or service in the armed forces after 2 September 1939 and on sundry other services, on attendance allowances, invalid care allowance, severe disablement allowance, and mobility allowance - - - - - -	2,395,000,000	—
2. For expenditure by the Department of Health and Social Security on supplementary pensions and allowances - - - - - - -	8,188,000,000	112,000,000
3. For expenditure by the Department of Health and Social Security on child benefit, one parent benefit, family income supplement and non-contributory maternity grant - - - -	4,918,300,000	—
4. For expenditure by the Department of Health and Social Security on rent rebate, rent allowance and rate rebate subsidies, to housing, rating, and local authorities, and expenditure on subsidies towards the administrative costs incurred by these authorities in operating the housing benefit scheme - - - - - - -	5,105,600,000	—
5. For expenditure by the Department of Health and Social Security on administration, for agency payments, and for certain other services including grants to local authorities, voluntary organisations, and an international subscription - -	1,347,252,000	699,678,000
6. For sums payable into the social fund for expenditure on maternity expenses and funeral expenses - - - - - - -	32,700,000	—
7. For sums payable out of the Consolidated Fund by way of supplement to the National Insurance Fund - - - - - - - -	2,032,000,000	—
8. For expenditure by the Department of Health and Social Security on subsidies to housing, rating and local authorities towards the administrative costs incurred in preparing for the revised housing benefit scheme - - -	25,000,000	—
TOTAL, CLASS XV - - - - £	24,043,852,000	811,678,000

CLASS XVI

SCHEDULE OF SUMS granted, and of the sums which may be applied as appropriations in aid in addition thereto, to defray the charges of the several Services herein particularly mentioned, which will come in course of payment during the year ending on 31st March 1988, viz.:—

	Sums not exceeding	
	Supply Grants	Appropriations in Aid
	£	£
Vote		
1. For expenditure by the Department of Agriculture and Fisheries for Scotland on price guarantees, production grants and subsidies, grants and loans for capital and other improvements, support for agriculture in special areas, compensation to sheep producers and certain other services including services relating to livestock diseases	54,661,000	14,268,000
2. For expenditure by the Department of Agriculture and Fisheries for Scotland on educational and advisory services, botanical services, assistance to marketing and processing, administration, land management and land settlement, livestock services, assistance to crofters, assistance to the Scottish fishing industry, protective and certain other services including research and development, special services and a grant in aid	69,832,000	5,478,000
3. For expenditure by the Industry Department for Scotland on grants in aid to the Scottish Development Agency and to the Highlands and Islands Development Board; on the promotion of tourism, including a grant in aid; on financial assistance to nationalised industries; on employment services in Scotland; on consumer protection; and on sundry other services in connection with trade and industry - - -	124,787,000	4,913,000
4. For expenditure by the Industry Department for Scotland on a contribution to the Department of Employment towards the grant in aid to the Manpower Services Commission in relation to activities in Scotland - - - - -	180,754,000	—
5. For expenditure by the Industry Department for Scotland on regional development grants and regional selective assistance - - - -	105,957,000	17,832,000
6. For expenditure by the Scottish Development Department on roads and certain associated services, including the acquisition of land, lighting, road safety and related services, on assistance to local transport, on support for transport services in the Highlands and Islands, piers and harbours and on certain other transport services and grants, on housing subsidies. Royal Palaces and Royal Parks, historic buildings and ancient monuments, other central environmental services and grants in aid - - - - -	165,061,000	3,313,000
7. For expenditure by the Scottish Development Department on assistance to local transport, and on piers and harbours - - - - -	17,156,000	—

	Supply Grants	Appropriations in Aid
CLASS XVI—*continued*	£	£

Vote
8. For expenditure by the Scottish Development Department on housing subsidies, capital grants to housing associations and a range of other Exchequer contributions and grants relating to housing (including home improvements) and sundry other housing services including sites for travelling people - - - - - - | 268,155,000 | 1,656,000 |

9. For expenditure by the Industry Department for Scotland on grants to New Town Development Corporations in connection with housing and other services - - - - - - - | 41,537,000 | — |

10. For expenditure by the Scottish Development Department in connection with water supply and sewerage, flood prevention, land reclamation, coast protection, the urban programme and other local environmental services - - - | 29,814,000 | — |

11. For expenditure by the Scottish Courts Administration on court services, the Scottish Law Commission and certain legal services, including a grant in aid - - - - - - | 13,121,000 | 7,424,000 |

12. For expenditure by the Scottish Home and Health Department on legal aid and criminal injuries compensation (excluding administration), on police and fire services superannuation and police grant - - - - - - | 227,682,000 | 116,000 |

13. For expenditure by the Scottish Courts Administration on costs and fees in connection with legal proceedings - - - - - | 3,155,000 | — |

14. For expenditure by the Scottish Home and Health Department on legal aid administration, certain services relating to crime, prisons, treatment of offenders, civil defence (including grants) and on fire and police services (excluding grants and superannuation), on the provision of services under the national health service, on other health services, on research, services for the disabled and certain other services including a grant in aid - - - - - - | 1,678,483,000 | 212,770,000 |

15. For expenditure by the Scottish Education Department on schools, higher and further education, miscellaneous educational services including compensation payments for redundant staff at colleges of education, community education, curriculum development, research and administration, grant in aid to the Scottish Sports Council, grant in aid to the National Library of Scotland, the National Museums of Scotland and the National Galleries of Scotland including purchase grants, certain grants for the arts, social work, other grants in aid, certain payments on behalf of the European Community and certain grants to local authorities - - - | 177,134,000 | 1,331,000 |

16. For expenditure by the Scottish Education Department on awards to students receiving higher and further education and reimbursement of fees for qualifying European Community students - - - - - - - | 108,189,000 | 10,000 |

	Supply Grants	Appropriations in Aid
Class XVI—*continued*	£	£
Vote		
17. For expenditure by the Scottish Home and Health Department on the provision of services under the National Health Service in Scotland, on welfare food and certain other services - -	396,921,000	51,551,000
18. For the expenditure of the Scottish Record Office on administrative costs and grant in aid	1,852,000	476,000
19. For the expenditure of the General Register Office for Scotland on administrative and operational costs - - - - - -	3,411,000	870,000
20. For the expenditure of the Department of the Registers of Scotland on administrative costs	1,000	11,860,000
21. For expenditure by the Scottish Office on administrative costs, the Royal Commission on the Ancient and Historical Monuments of Scotland and a grant to the Commission for Local Authority Accounts - - - - -	114,584,000	3,051,000
22. For expenditure by the Scottish Office for rate support grants in Scotland - - - - -	1,896,760,000	—
23. For expenditure by the Scottish Office on rate rebate grants to local authorities in Scotland	32,400,000	—
24. For expenditure by the Scottish Home and Health Department on superannuation allowances and gratuities, etc., in respect of teachers, and the widows and dependants of deceased teachers	32,536,000	114,837,000
25. For expenditure by the Scottish Home and Health Department on pensions, allowances, gratuities, etc., to or in respect of persons engaged in health service or in other approved employment - - - - - - -	1,000	129,003,000
Total, Class XVI - - - - - £	5,743,944,000	580,759,000

Class XVII, 1987–88   SCHEDULE (B).—Part 18

Class XVII

Schedule of Sums granted, and of the sums which may be applied as appropriations in aid in addition thereto, to defray the charges of the several Services herein particularly mentioned, which will come in course of payment during the year ending on 31st March 1988, viz.:—

	Sums not exceeding	
	Supply Grants	Appropriations in Aid
	£	£
Vote		
1. For expenditure by the Welsh Office on market support, grants and loans for capital and other improvements, support for agriculture in special areas and compensation to sheep producers, animal health and support services, arterial drainage, flood and coast protection and certain other services - - - - - - -	42,710,000	9,301,000

	Supply Grants	Appropriations in Aid
CLASS XVII—*continued*	£	£
Vote		
2. For expenditure by the Welsh Office on assistance to agricultural production, food processing and marketing, certain other services including research, land management, assistance to the Welsh fishing industry including protective and other services, special assistance for rural and highland areas, on the Welsh Development Agency and some special and other services including grants in aid - - - - -	53,887,000	65,000
3. For expenditure by the Welsh Office on regional development grants, regional selective assistance and housing subsidy - - - - - -	75,647,000	5,672,000
4. For expenditure by the Welsh Office on a contribution to the Department of Employment towards the grant in aid to the Manpower Services Commission in relation to activities in Wales - - - - - - - -	113,158,000	—
5. For expenditure by the Welsh Office on tourism, roads and certain associated services including road safety, housing, historic buildings and ancient monuments, other environmental services, civil defence (including grants), education, libraries and museums, health and personal social services, grants in aid, EC agency payments, other grants and certain other services, including research - - - - -	214,298,000	4,907,000
6. For expenditure by the Welsh Office on housing subsidies, grants to housing associations, and a range of other Exchequer contributions and grants relating to housing (including home improvements); urban programme grants (including urban development grant) grants for urban regeneration, and grant in aid to the Urban Development Corporation; grants in respect of water, sewerage, town and country planning, gypsy sites, recreation and other local services including clean air grants; welfare food payments, EC medical costs, certain EC agency payments; and other services - - - - - -	187,817,000	2,174,000
7. For expenditure by the Welsh Office on family practitioner services under the National Health Service - - - - - - -	220,703,000	31,001,000
8. For expenditure by the Welsh Office on Hospital and Community Health Services, supporting health services, family practitioner services administration and related services, and services for the disabled - - - - - -	699,106,000	96,521,000
9. For expenditure by the Welsh Office on central administration - - - - - - -	38,595,000	941,000
10. For expenditure by the Welsh Office on rate support grants to local authorities in Wales -	930,614,000	—
11. For expenditure by the Welsh Office for national parks supplementary grants to county councils in Wales - - - - - - - -	2,517,000	—
12. For expenditure by the Welsh Office on rate rebate grants to local authorities in Wales - -	7,268,000	—

	Supply Grants	Appropriations in Aid
CLASS XVII—*continued*	£	£
Vote		
13. For expenditure by the Welsh Office on supplementary grants for transport purposes to county councils in Wales - - - - -	21,366,000	—
TOTAL, CLASS XVII - - - - £	2,607,686,000	150,582,000

Class XVIII, 1987–88   SCHEDULE (B).—PART 19

CLASS XVIII

SCHEDULE OF SUMS granted, and of the sums which may be applied as appropriations in aid in addition thereto, to defray the charges of the several Services herein particularly mentioned, which will come in course of payment during the year ending on 31st March 1988, viz.:—

	Sums not exceeding	
	Supply Grants	Appropriations in Aid
	£	£
Vote		
1. For expenditure by the Northern Ireland Office on central and miscellaneous services, services related to crime, police, prisons, training schools, probation and after-care etc., compensation schemes, crown prosecutions and other legal services, grants in aid, certain other grants and an international subscription - - - -	512,405,000	4,087,000
2. For expenditure by the Northern Ireland Office on a grant in aid of the Northern Ireland Consolidated Fund and other transfers - -	962,000,000	—
TOTAL, CLASS XVIII - - - - £	1,474,405,000	4,087,000

Class XIX, 1987–88   SCHEDULE (B).—PART 20

CLASS XIX

SCHEDULE OF SUMS granted, and of the sums which may be applied as appropriations in aid in addition thereto, to defray the charges of the several Services herein particularly mentioned, which will come in course of payment during the year ending on 31st March 1988, viz.:—

	Sums not exceeding	
	Supply Grants	Appropriations in Aid
	£	£
1. For expenditure by the Central Office of Information on home and overseas publicity -	111,127,000	—

	Supply Grants	Appropriations in Aid
CLASS XIX—*continued*	£	£
Vote		
2. For expenditure by the Customs and Excise Department on administrative costs, both capital and current, including an international subscription - - - - - - - -	441,125,000	9,616,000
3. For expenditure on administrative costs by the Registry of Friendly Societies on behalf of the Building Societies Commission and the Central Office of the Registry- - - - - -	1,290,000	2,250,000
4. For expenditure of the Department of the Government Actuary on administrative costs	1,429,000	631,000
5. For expenditure by the Controller of Her Majesty's Stationery Office to compensate the HMSO Trading Fund for the provision of reports of Parliamentary debates at less than full cost, and for the price concessions to public libraries -	4,254,000	—
6. For expenditure by the Controller of Her Majesty's Stationery Office on the reimbursement of the HMSO trading fund in respect of goods and services supplied to the Houses of Parliament and to United Kingdom members of the European Assembly - - - - - -	14,899,000	180,000
7. For expenditure of the Inland Revenue Department on administrative costs, both capital and current - - - - - - - -	1,013,831,000	50,770,000
8. For expenditure of the Inland Revenue Department on life assurance premium relief and mortgage interest relief - - - - -	248,000,000	—
9. For expenditure by the National Debt Office and Public Works Loan Commission on administrative costs - - - - - -	1,000	1,200,000
10. For expenditure of the Department for National Savings on administrative and publicity costs -	159,229,000	977,000
11. For expenditure by the Treasury on economic and financial administration, and for certain other services including grants in aid to certain parliamentary bodies and others - - -	51,708,000	3,635,000
12. For expenditure by the Treasury in connection with the manufacture, storage and distribution of coinage for use in the United Kingdom - -	14,600,000	2,500,000
13. For expenditure by the Central Computer and Telecommunications Agency (Treasury) in connection with computers and general telecommunications including an international subscription - - - - - - -	17,096,000	25,584,000
14. For expenditure of the Civil Service Catering Organisation (Treasury) in connection with the provision of catering services - - - -	3,000	—
15. For rates and contributions in lieu of rates paid by the Rating of Government Property Department in respect of property occupied by the Crown and premises occupied by representatives of Commonwealth and foreign countries and international organisations - -	175,500,000	245,800,000
16. For expenditure by the Treasury in connection with the sale of shares in BP plc - - -	1,500,000	1,000
TOTAL, CLASS XIX - - - - £	2,255,592,000	343,144,000

CLASS XX

SCHEDULE OF SUMS granted, and of the sums which may be applied as appropriations in aid in addition thereto, to defray the charges of the several Services herein particularly mentioned, which will come in course of payment during the year ending on 31st March 1988, viz.:—

	Sums not exceeding	
	Supply Grants	Appropriations in Aid
	£	£
Vote		
1. For the expenditure by the Management and Personnel Office on the central management of the civil service, on the Office of the Parliamentary Counsel and certain other services including grants in aid - - - - - - -	33,602,000	3,784,000
2. For the expenditure by the Cabinet Office, including the Central Statistical Office, on administrative costs and grants in aid to international organisations - - - -	15,163,000	4,727,000
3. For Her Majesty's foreign and other secret services - - - - - - -	104,200,000	—
4. For the expenditure of the Charity Commission for England and Wales on administrative costs -	6,204,000	1,000
5. For a grant in aid of the Commonwealth War Graves Commission - - - - -	13,916,000	—
6. For the salaries of the Crown Estate Commissioners and the expenses of their office - -	765,000	—
7. For the expenditure of the House of Commons on members' salaries, allowances, pensions, etc., financial assistance to opposition parties and a grant in aid - - - - - -	40,770,000	—
8. For the expenditure of the House of Lords on Peers' expenses, administrative costs, staff pensions and security - - - - -	11,697,000	280,000
9. For expenditure by the Land Registry on administrative costs - - - - -	1,000	98,259,000
10. For expenditure by the Ordnance Survey on the survey of Great Britain and other mapping services - - - - - -	20,403,000	36,117,000
11. For the expenditure of the Office of the Parliamentary Commissioner for Administration and the Health Service Commissioners for England, Scotland and Wales on administrative costs, including an international subscription	1,931,000	—
12. For expenditure by the Paymaster General's Office on administrative costs - - -	16,688,000	546,000
13. For expenditure by the Paymaster General's Office on the superannuation of civil servants, pensions, etc., in respect of former members of the Royal Irish Constabulary and other pensions and non-recurrent payments; and for certain other services - - - - -	1,304,873,000	282,000,000
14. For the expenditure of the Department of Her Majesty's Most Honourable Privy Council on administrative costs - - - - -	1,138,000	20,000
15. For the expenditure of the Public Record Office on administrative and operational costs - -	11,020,000	479,000

	Supply Grants	Appropriations in Aid
CLASS XX—*continued*	£	£
Vote		
16. For expenditure by the Office of Fair Trading on administrative and operational costs - -	9,362,000	3,000
17. For expenditure by the Office of Gas Supply on administrative costs - - - - - -	1,000	1,850,000
18. For expenditure by the Office of Telecommunications on administrative and operational costs -	1,000	3,942,000
19. For expenditure (partly recoverable), including loans, by the Property Services Agency of the Department of the Environment on acquisitions, public building work, accommodation services, administration and certain other services for civil purposes in the United Kingdom; and on certain defence services the costs of which are recovered from clients - - - - - -	228,075,000	865,053,000
20. For the expenditure of the Office of Population Censuses and Surveys on administrative and operational costs, including a grant in aid - -	30,664,000	7,960,000
21. For expenditure by the Lord Advocate's Departments on administrative costs including grants in aid - - - - - - - -	17,706,000	56,000
22. For expenditure by the Crown Office on witnesses' expenses and other costs associated with crown prosecutions - - - -	3,586,000	3,000
23. For expenditure by the Northern Ireland Court Service on court services and certain other legal services including grants in aid - - - -	13,143,000	4,064,000
24. For expenditure by the Northern Ireland Court Service on legal aid and court services - -	7,493,000	—
25. For expenditure by the Crown Prosecution Service on administrative costs - - - -	107,009,000	100,000
26. For expenditure by the Director of Public Prosecutions on crown prosecutions - - -	44,900,000	7,100,000
27. For expenditure by the Serious Fraud Office on administrative costs - - - - - -	2,000,000	—
28. For expenditure by the Serious Fraud Office on investigations and prosecutions - - -	1,000,000	—
29. For expenditure by the Departments of the Law Officers and the Procurator General and Treasury Solicitor on administrative costs - - -	9,813,000	1,247,000
30. For expenditure by the Department of the Procurator General and Treasury Solicitor on costs and fees for legal services - - - -	2,597,000	8,000,000
TOTAL, CLASS XX - - - - £	2,059,721,000	1,318,391,000

Class XXA, 1987–88   SCHEDULE (B).—PART 22

CLASS XXA

SCHEDULE OF SUMS granted, and of the sums which may be applied as appropriations in aid in addition thereto, to defray the charges of the several Services herein particularly mentioned, which will come in course of payment during the year ending on 31st March 1988, viz.:—

	Sums not exceeding	
	Supply Grants	Appropriations in Aid
	£	£
Vote		
1. For expenditure by the House of Commons Commission - - - - - - -	24,538,000	215,000
TOTAL, CLASS XXA - - - - £	24,538,000	215,000

Class XXB, 1987–88   SCHEDULE (B).—PART 23

CLASS XXB

SCHEDULES OF SUMS granted, and of the sums which may be applied as appropriations in aid in addition thereto, to defray the charges of the several Services herein particularly mentioned, which will come in course of payment during the year ending on 31st March 1988, viz:—

	Sums not exceeding	
	Supply Grants	Appropriations in Aid
	£	£
Vote		
1. For the expenditure of the National Audit Office including an international subscription - -	23,677,000	3,800,000
TOTAL, CLASS XXB - - - - £	23,677,000	3,800,000

SCHEDULE (C)

ENACTMENTS REPEALED

Chapter	Short title
1985 c.1	Consolidated Fund Act 1985.
1985 c.11	Consolidated Fund (No. 2) Act 1985.
1985 c.55	Appropriation Act 1985.
1985 c.74	Consolidated Fund (No. 3) Act 1985.

DEBTORS (SCOTLAND) ACT 1987*

(1987 c. 18)

ARRANGEMENT OF SECTIONS

PART I

EXTENSION OF TIME TO PAY DEBTS

Time to pay directions on granting decree

PART II

POINDINGS AND WARRANT SALES

Poinding

---

* Annotations by Dr. D. I. Nichols, M.A., Ph.D., W.S. The opinions expressed are those of the annotator alone and should not be taken to represent the views of any government department or body.

PART III

DILIGENCE AGAINST EARNINGS

Introduction

PART IV

RECOVERY OF RATES AND TAXES ETC.

An Act to make new provision with regard to Scotland for an extension of time for payment of debts; to amend the law relating to certain diligences; to make provision in respect of messengers-at-arms and sheriff officers; and for connected purposes. [15th May 1987]

PARLIAMENTARY DEBATES
  Hansard, H.L. Vol. 483, cols. 484, 504; Vol. 484, cols. 334, 360, 1028; Vol. 485, col. 64; Vol. 487, col. 12; H.C. Vol. 114, col. 484.
  The Bill was considered in the Scottish Grand Committee on March 10, 1987, and in the First Scottish Standing Committee on March 17 and 24, 1987.

GENERAL NOTE
  The Act is closely based upon the Scottish Law Commission's Report on Diligence and Debtor Protection which was published in November 1985 (Scot. Law Com. No. 95). However, the recommendations relating to debt arrangement schemes were not implemented, and the provisions giving debtors time to pay have been disapplied from local authority rates, central government taxes and similar debts.
  Pt. I (ss.1–15) introduces into Scots law two sets of provisions giving debtors time to pay their debts. First, the court in granting decree for payment of money may (with some exceptions) attach a time to pay direction to the decree. Secondly, after diligence has commenced to enforce a decree for payment of money but before the diligence has got to its final stages, the debtor may apply for a time to pay order.
  Pt. II (ss.16–45) contains various reforms of the existing diligence of poinding and sale designed to remove its harsher aspects.
  Pt. III (ss.46–73) abolishes arrestment of wages and replaces it by three new diligences: (1) an earnings arrestment to enforce a lump sum debt; (2) a current maintenance arrestment to enforce maintenance; and (3) a conjoined arrestment order to enable two or more creditors to do diligence simultaneously against a debtor's earnings.
  Pt. IV (s.74 and Scheds. 4 and 5) makes changes in the diligences available for enforcement of central and local government debts.
  Pt. V (ss.75–86) deals with messengers-at-arms and sheriff officers whose functions include the execution of diligence. The provisions relate mainly to the appointment, control of officers and the regulation of their functions.
  Pt. VI (ss.87–91) states the effect of warrants for execution in decrees and other documents, abolishes letters of poinding and deals with charges for payment of money.
  Pt. VII (ss.92–109) contain miscellaneous and general provisions, including liability of debtors for the expenses of diligence done against them.

COMMENCEMENT
  The Act received Royal Assent on May 15, 1987. It will come into force on such date or dates as the Lord Advocate may appoint (s.109(2)).

EXTENT
  The Act applies to Scotland only (s.109(3)).

PART I

EXTENSION OF TIME TO PAY DEBTS

Time to pay directions on granting decree

Time to pay directions

1.—(1) Subject to subsections (3) to (5) below and to section 14 of this Act, the court, on granting decree for payment of any principal sum of money may, on an application by the debtor, direct that any sum decerned for in the decree (including any interest claimed in pursuance of subsections (6) and (7) below) or any expenses in relation to which the decree contains a finding as to liability or both such sum and such expenses shall be paid—

  (a) by such instalments, commencing at such time after the date of intimation by the creditor to the debtor of an extract of the decree containing the direction, payable at such intervals; or

  (b) as a lump sum at the end of such period following intimation as mentioned in paragraph (a) above,

as the court may specify in the direction.

(2) A direction under subsection (1) above shall be known as a "time to pay direction".

(3) Where a court grants a decree which contains a finding as to liability for expenses but does not at the same time make a time to pay direction, then (whether or not the decree also decerns for payment of the expenses), it shall not at any time thereafter be competent for the court to make a time to pay direction in relation to those expenses.

(4) Where a court grants a decree which contains a finding as to liability for expenses and makes a time to pay direction in relation to those expenses but—

(a) does not decern for payment of the expenses; or
(b) decerns for payment of the expenses as taxed by the auditor of court but does not specify the amount of those expenses,

in relation to so much of the time to pay direction as relates to the expenses, the reference in subsection (1) above to the date of intimation of an extract of the decree containing the direction shall be treated as a reference to the date of intimation of an extract of a decree decerning for payment of the expenses, being an extract specifying their amount.

(5) It shall not be competent for the court to make a time to pay direction—

(a) where the sum of money (exclusive of any interest and expenses) decerned for exceeds £10,000 or such amount as may be prescribed in regulations made by the Lord Advocate;
(b) where the decree contains an award of a capital sum on divorce or on the granting of a declarator of nullity of marriage;
(c) in connection with a maintenance order;
(d) in an action by or on behalf of the Inland Revenue for payment of any sum recoverable in respect of tax or as if it were tax;
(e) in an action by or on behalf of a rating authority for payment of rates; or
(f) in an action for payment of—
    (i) any duty due under the Betting and Gaming Duties Act 1981;
    (ii) car tax due under the Car Tax Act 1983; or
    (iii) value added tax due under the Value Added Tax Act 1983 or any sum recoverable as if it were value added tax.

(6) Without prejudice to section 2(5) of this Act, interest payable under a decree containing a time to pay direction (other than interest awarded as a specific sum in the decree) shall not be recoverable by the creditor except in accordance with subsection (7) below.

(7) A creditor who wishes to recover interest to which subsection (6) above applies shall serve a notice on the debtor, not later than the date prescribed by Act of Sederunt occurring—

(a) in the case of a direction under subsection (1)(a) above, before the date when the last instalment of the debt concerned (other than such interest) is payable under the direction;
(b) in the case of a direction under subsection (1)(b) above, before the end of the period specified in the direction,

stating that he is claiming such interest and specifying the amount of the interest claimed.

(8) Any sum paid by a debtor under a time to pay direction shall not be ascribed to interest claimed in pursuance of subsections (6) and (7) above until the debt concerned (other than such interest) has been discharged.

DEFINITIONS
"court": s.15(2).
"the debt concerned": s.15(2).
"maintenance order": s.106.

GENERAL NOTE
This section empowers the court, on an application by the debtor, to allow some or all of the sums due in terms of the decree to be paid either by specified regular instalments or in

a lump sum at the end of a specified period, by attaching a time to pay direction to the decree. Such directions are competent only in relation to debtors who are individuals and for debts not exceeding £10,000. Instalment decrees were available in the sheriff court for summary causes. The Act's time to pay directions supersede instalment decrees and extend the principle of time to pay to the Court of Session and the sheriff's ordinary court. Both the Court of Session and the sheriff courts have power to "supersede extract"—delay the issuing of an extract of the decree and hence its enforceability. The new statutory power to defer the time for payment could prove useful since the extent of the power to supersede extract is ill-defined.

Subss. (1)–(4)

On an application by an individual debtor (see s.14) the court has a discretionary power to attach a time to pay direction to any principal sum of money ordered to be paid by a decree. The application must be made before the court grants decree. If the decree contains several sums of money a direction can be attached to one, some or all of them. "Principal sum" includes pre-decree interest provided it is quantified as a specific sum. Unquantified or post-decree interest is dealt with by subss. (6) and (7) although the time to pay direction still governs the terms of payment of such interest.

Unless some principal sum of money is decerned for a time to pay direction is not competent. Time to pay the expenses awarded in non-monetary proceedings (such as interdicts, declarators, petitions or special cases) can be obtained by means of time to pay orders (see ss.5–14).

Probably the most common type of direction will be that in subs. (1)(a) allowing payment by instalments. Most instalments will be at regular intervals (weekly or monthly) but this need not necessarily be so. Subs. (1)(b)—a deferred period—could be useful where the debtor needs time to realise assets or is already paying off another decree by instalments and cannot afford any increase.

The instalments start to run only after the expiry of an interval (specified by the court in the direction) following intimation of an extract of the decree to the debtor. Creditors should not overlook intimation as the decree is not enforceable until then, although interest will be accruing. Intimation is a useful innovation. Summary cause instalment decrees used to provide for payment of instalments immediately. Often they lapsed because by the time the debtor got to know of the decree the first two instalments were in arrears and default had occurred. A certain number of days (eight for a Court of Session decree and 14 for a sheriff court decree) must normally elapse after the granting of a decree before it can be extracted and hence intimated. The debtor therefore has this time in addition to the period given by the direction to get ready to pay the first instalment.

The deferment period specified in a subs. (1)(b) direction similarly starts to run only after intimation.

The position regarding expenses is complex. In sheriff court summary causes or undefended ordinary causes the expenses are quantified before decree is granted so that the decree specifies the principal sum and the amount of expenses for which the debtor is liable. The court may, but is not bound to, include such expenses in the time to pay direction. If they are not included a later application is incompetent and a time to pay order is the appropriate remedy. In the Court of Session or in defended ordinary causes in the sheriff court decree is granted for the principal sum and a finding of liability for expenses as they shall be later taxed is made. Such unquantified expenses may be included in the direction, but the court will probably decline to do so if a reasonable estimate of their amount cannot be made. It is not possible to seek to have a time to pay direction attached to the later decree quantifying the taxed expenses. The time for such an application was when decree in the action was being granted. If future expenses are included in the time to pay direction the extract of the later decree quantifying the taxed amount has to be intimated to the debtor before the liability to pay such expenses by instalments or otherwise arises.

Example

In a reparation action the court granted decree on February 1, for £5,000 plus pre-decree interest of £500 with a finding of liability for expenses. The time to pay direction requires the sums and expenses to be paid by monthly instalments of £250 commencing 14 days after intimation. The creditor intimates on February 15, so that the first payment is due on March 1. On October 1, the expenses are taxed at £1,000 and decree granted accordingly. The creditor intimates the expenses decree on October 17. By October 31, the debtor has paid eight instalments totalling £2,000. The remaining £4,500 is paid over the following 18 months at the rate of £250 per month.

Subs. (5)

This subsection excludes the attachment of time to pay directions from certain classes of debt.

A monetary limit of £10,000 is imposed since time to pay orders are designed for ordinary debtors. Persons owing very large sums of money which they cannot pay should be liable to be sequestrated rather than allowed to pay over many years. The limit is very much greater than that for previous instalment decrees (£1,000). It should be noted that the limit is exclusive of interest (pre- and post-decree) and expenses (whether quantified in the decree or not).

Maintenance and capital sums on termination of marriage are excluded; the former because the decree already takes the form of regular instalments, the latter because the court has power under ss.12 and 17 of the Family Law (Scotland) Act 1985 to order payment by instalments.

Central and local government give debtors time to pay as a matter of practice although this assertion has been treated with scepticism. A time to pay direction cannot be attached to a summary warrant for arrears of rates or taxes since the warrant is not a decree. The same reasoning excludes fines since a criminal court imposing a fine makes a finding of liability.

Subss. (6), (7), (8)

These subsections deal with the collection of interest, other than pre-decree interest quantified and awarded in the decree. For small debts the interest is usually not worth the bother of calculating it and creditors will probably continue not to claim. Interest will however be substantial on larger debts particularly if the rate of interest is high and the time to pay period long.

Subs. (7) lays down the procedure for recovery of interest. Should the creditor fail to follow this the interest becomes irrecoverable by any legal means unless s.2(5) applies. The creditor must intimate timeously to the debtor that interest is being charged and specify the amount due. Where the time to pay direction is for payment by instalments, the debtor pays off the interest by instalments after satisfying the debt. Where the direction takes the form of a deferred period, the debt and interest become payable at the expiry of that period.

Subs. (8) reverses the normal rule that payments are ascribed to interest before capital. This reversal is necessary to tie in with the rule that interest can only be recovered under subs. (7).

Example

1. Debt of £2,400 payable by monthly instalments of £100. Interest rate 15 per cent. Just before the end of the second year the creditor claims interest of £360. This is paid off in the first four months of the third year by 3 instalments of £100 and a final instalment of £60.

2. Debt and interest as above, but payment deferred for one year. Creditor claims interest of £360 just before end of the year. £2,760 due on first day of next year.

Effect of time to pay direction on diligence

2.—(1) While a time to pay direction is in effect, it shall not be competent—

    (a) to serve a charge for payment; or

    (b) to commence or execute any of the following diligences—

        (i) an arrestment and action of furthcoming or sale;

        (ii) a poinding and sale;

        (iii) an earnings arrestment;

        (iv) an adjudication for debt,

to enforce payment of the debt concerned.

(2) While a time to pay direction is in effect an arrestment used on the dependence of the action or in security of the debt concerned shall remain in effect—

    (a) if it has not been recalled; and

    (b) to the extent that it has not been restricted under subsection (3) below,

but, while the direction is in effect, it shall not be competent to commence an action of furthcoming or sale following on such an arrestment.

(3) The court may, on making a time to pay direction, recall or restrict an arrestment of the kind described in subsection (2) above.

(4) If an arrestment of the kind described in subsection (2) above is in effect, the court may order that the making of a time to pay direction and the recall or restriction of the arrestment shall be subject to the fulfilment by the debtor of such conditions within such period as the court thinks fit; and, where the court so orders, it shall postpone granting decree until such fulfilment or the end of that period, whichever is the earlier.

(5) Where a time to pay direction is recalled or ceases to have effect, otherwise than—

(a) under section 12(2)(a) of this Act; or

(b) by reason of the debt concerned being paid or otherwise extinguished,

the debt in so far as it remains outstanding and interest thereon, whether or not awarded as a specific sum in the decree, shall, subject to any enactment or rule of law to the contrary, become enforceable by any diligence mentioned in subsection (1)(b) above.

DEFINITIONS

"adjudication for debt": s.15(1).
"court": s.15(2).
"the debt concerned": s.15(2).
"poinding": s.15(1).

GENERAL NOTE

This section prevents the execution of diligence to enforce payment of a debt by the creditor while the debt is subject to a time to pay direction. Only the ordinary diligences available to unsecured creditors are affected; the special remedies of sequestration for rent, poinding of the ground, maills and duties, repossession, or sale remain available to creditors entitled to use them (s.13(1)). Furthermore inhibition remains competent; the reason being that it merely creates a preference rather than leading to loss of assets by the debtor.

Subs. (1)

Current maintenance orders are not mentioned in the list of incompetent diligences since maintenance orders cannot have a time to pay direction attached to them (s.1(5)(c)). The inability to charge prevents the creditor from applying for a conjoined arrestment order. It also prevents the creditor from petitioning for the debtor's sequestration at least in relation to the debt in question.

Subss. (2)–(4)

On granting decree an arrestment on the dependence of the action becomes an arrestment in execution. But where the decree contains a time to pay direction no action of furthcoming or sale is competent.

The court may recall or restrict the arrestment and impose conditions. For example the court may order the debtor to pay one half of the debt immediately out of the arrested fund, restrict the arrestment to the remaining half and grant time to pay for that half provided the debtor does pay the first half immediately. Creditors should urge the court not to recall an arrestment since otherwise they will lose the preference over other unsecured creditors created by the arrestment.

Subs. (5)

The creditor's normal rights to use diligence in execution of the debt revive if the time to pay direction is recalled or it lapses on default by the debtor. S.12(2)(a) relates to sequestration of the debtor which, although resulting in a direction ceasing to have effect, prevents creditors doing diligence.

Variation and recall of time to pay direction and arrestment

3.—(1) The court which granted a decree containing a time to pay direction may, on an application by the debtor or the creditor—

(a) vary or recall the direction if it is satisfied that it is reasonable to do so; or

(b) if an arrestment in respect of the debt concerned is in effect, recall or restrict the arrestment.

(2) If an arrestment in respect of the debt concerned is in effect, the court may order that any variation, recall or restriction under subsection (1) above shall be subject to the fulfilment by the debtor of such conditions as the court thinks fit.

(3) The clerk of court or sheriff clerk shall as soon as is reasonably practicable intimate a variation under subsection (1) above to the debtor and to the creditor, and the variation shall come into effect on the date of such intimation.

DEFINITIONS
"court": s.15(2).
"the debt concerned": s.15(2).

GENERAL NOTE
Either the debtor or the creditor may apply to the court for a recall or variation of the time to pay direction on a change of circumstances. For example, the debtor may be unable to keep up the level of instalments and seek a lower rate, or the creditor may aver non-disclosure or acquisition of funds by the debtor sufficient to pay the debt, or the creditor may be in pressing need of immediate payment.

An arrestment in subss. (1) and (2) refers to an arrestment on the dependence which was converted into an arrestment in execution on granting the decree, since post-decree arrestment is incompetent under s.2(1)(b)(i) and (iii).

Lapse of time to pay direction

4.—(1) If, on the day on which an instalment payable under a time to pay direction becomes due, there remains unpaid a sum, due under previous instalments, of not less than the aggregate of 2 instalments, the direction shall cease to have effect.

(2) If at the end of the period of 3 weeks immediately following the day on which the last instalment payable under a time to pay direction becomes due, any part of the debt concerned remains outstanding, the direction shall cease to have effect.

(3) If any sum payable under a time to pay direction under section 1(1)(b) of this Act remains unpaid 24 hours after the end of the period specified in the direction, the direction shall cease to have effect.

(4) Where—
    (a) a decree for payment of a principal sum of money contains a finding as to liability for expenses and decree for payment of the expenses is subsequently granted; and
    (b) a time to pay direction is made in relation to both the principal sum and the expenses,
if under subsections (1) to (3) above the direction ceases to have effect in relation to the sum payable under either of the decrees, the direction shall also cease to have effect in relation to the sum payable under the other decree.

DEFINITION
"the debt concerned": s.15(2).

GENERAL NOTE
This section provides for the automatic lapse of a time to pay direction on default by the debtor. There is no need to go to court for a recall. Lapse results in the creditor's right to do diligence reviving (s.2(5)).

Subss. (1), (2)
These subsections deal with the case where the time to pay direction allows payment by instalments. During the period allowed for payment lapse occurs if the debtor is two

instalments in arrears when a third becomes due. A debtor who cannot pay the instalments should consider applying for a downward variation or even a suspension of the instalments under s.3(1). At the end of the instalment period the debtor has three weeks to pay off the balance of the debt on pain of lapse of the direction.

Subs. (3)
The subsection deals with deferred period directions. Lapse occurs if payment is more than a day late.

Subs. (4)
Where the debtor defaults in relation to the principal sum in the decree any time to pay direction in relation to a separate decree for expenses flies off.

Time to pay orders following charge or diligence
Time to pay orders

5.—(1) Subject to section 14 of this Act, this section applies to a debt due under a decree or other document in respect of which—
   (a) a charge for payment has been served on the debtor;
   (b) an arrestment has been executed; or
   (c) an action of adjudication for debt has been commenced.
(2) Subject to subsections (4) and (5) below, the sheriff may, on an application by the debtor, make an order that a debt to which this section applies (including any interest claimed in pursuance of subsections (6) and (7) below) so far as outstanding, shall be paid—
   (a) by such instalments, commencing at such time after the date of intimation in accordance with section 7(4) of this Act by the sheriff clerk to the debtor of the order under this subsection, payable at such intervals; or
   (b) as a lump sum at the end of such period following intimation as mentioned in paragraph (a) above,
as the sheriff may specify in the order.
(3) An order under subsection (2) above shall be known as a "time to pay order".
(4) It shall not be competent for the sheriff to make a time to pay order—
   (a) where the amount of the debt outstanding at the date of the making of the application under subsection (2) above (exclusive of any interest) exceeds £10,000 or such amount as may be prescribed in regulations made by the Lord Advocate;
   (b) where, in relation to the debt, a time to pay direction or a time to pay order has previously been made (whether such direction or order is in effect or not);
   (c) where, in relation to the debt, a summary warrant has been granted;
   (d) in relation to a debt including any sum recoverable by or on behalf of the Inland Revenue in respect of tax or as if it were tax;
   (e) in relation to a debt including rates payable to a rating authority; or
   (f) in relation to a debt including—
       (i) any duty due under the Betting and Gaming Duties Act 1981;
       (ii) car tax due under the Car Tax Act 1983; or
       (iii) value added tax due under the Value Added Tax Act 1983 or any sum recoverable as if it were value added tax.
(5) Where in respect of a debt to which this section applies—
   (a) there has been a poinding of articles belonging to the debtor and a warrant of sale has been granted in respect of them but has not been executed;
   (b) moveable property of the debtor has been arrested and in respect of the arrested property—

      (i) a decree in an action of furthcoming has been granted
          but has not been enforced; or
      (ii) a warrant of sale has been granted but the warrant has
          not been executed; or
  (c) a decree in an action of adjudication for debt has been granted
      and the creditor has, with the debtor's consent or acquiescence,
      entered into possession of any property adjudged by the decree
      or has obtained a decree of maills and duties, or a decree of
      removing or ejection, in relation to any such property,
it shall not be competent for the sheriff to make a time to pay order in
respect of that debt until the diligence has been completed or has
otherwise ceased to have effect.

(6) Without prejudice to section 9(12) of this Act, interest payable
under a decree for payment of a debt in respect of which a time to pay
order has been made (other than interest awarded as a specific sum in the
decree) shall not be recoverable by the creditor except in accordance with
subsection (7) below.

(7) A creditor who wishes to recover interest to which subsection (6)
above applies shall serve a notice on the debtor not later than the date
prescribed by Act of Sederunt occurring—

  (a) in the case of an order under subsection (2)(a) above, before the
      date when the last instalment of the debt (other than such interest)
      is payable under the order;
  (b) in the case of an order under subsection (2)(b) above, before the
      end of the period specified in the order,
stating that he is claiming such interest and specifying the amount of the
interest claimed.

(8) Any sum paid by a debtor under a time to pay order shall not be
ascribed to interest claimed in pursuance of subsections (6) and (7) above
until the debt concerned (other than such interest) has been discharged.

DEFINITIONS
  "adjudication for debt": s.15(1).
  "debt": s.15(3).
  "decree or other document": s.15(3).
  "poinding": s.15(1).
  "sheriff": s.15(3).
  "summary warrant": s.106.
  "warrant of sale": ss.30, 106.

GENERAL NOTE
  Time to pay orders, like time to pay directions in decrees (see ss.1–4), are discretionary
remedies allowing debtors who are individuals either to pay their debts by specified
instalments or in a lump sum at the end of a specified period. The main differences are that
time to pay orders are a post-decree, indeed a post-commencement of diligence remedy,
and are within the exclusive jurisdiction of the sheriff. They are incompetent if diligence has
reached an advanced stage.

Subs. (1)
  In order to prevent the granting of time to pay orders where the debtor is able to pay the
debt immediately an application can be made only after diligence has commenced. Para. (b)
applies to arrestments generally although an arrestment of earnings requires the prior
execution of a charge which is a "trigger" under para. (a).

Subs. (2)
  Two types of time to pay order may be made. The first (para. (a)) permits the debtor to
pay the balance of the debt due at the date of the application for the order by instalments
of amounts and at intervals specified in the order. The second allows the debtor to defer
payment of the debt (in a lump sum) until the end of the period specified in the order. It

does not seem competent to have a mixed order—part of the debt deferred and part paid by instalments.

The instalments become payable only after a certain interval has elapsed since the time to pay order was intimated to the debtor by the sheriff clerk. This delayed effect should prove helpful in preventing inadvertent default through ignorance of the terms of the order. The deferred period similarly starts to run after intimation.

The definition of "debt" (s.15(3)) results in the exclusion of time to pay orders in respect of criminal fines and similar amounts, maintenance, and capital sums awarded on divorce or nullity of marriage. Provisions already exist for time to pay in relation to fines (Criminal Procedure (Scotland) Act 1975, ss.396–401) and capital sums on termination of marriage (Family Law (Scotland) Act 1985, ss.12 and 17), while maintenance consists of periodic payments.

Subs. (4)

In addition to the restrictions mentioned in the last paragraph above this subsection contains further restrictions on the court's powers.

Para. (a)

Time to pay orders are designed to help ordinary "consumer" debtors. People owing large sums of money should be sequestrated rather than have to pay by instalments over many years. The limit of £10,000 relates to the balance due at the date of application not the amount originally contained in the decree. For the purpose of calculating the balance, payments made prior to the application would be ascribed first to expenses of diligence already done, then to interest accrued and finally to the principal sum specified in the decree (s.94).

Para. (b)

This provision prevents debtors having more than one bite at the cherry. If they have defaulted on an earlier time to pay direction or order an application for an order or a further order is incompetent. Somewhat unfairly perhaps a debtor who was granted a time to pay direction or order which was recalled when financial circumstances improved is unable to reapply if they deteriorate again and there appears to be no way of recalling the recall.

Paras. (c)–(f)

Time to pay orders would be incompatible with the summary nature of summary warrant diligence. Exclusion of central and local government debts may be justified on the grounds that people often defer paying such debts for a far longer period than for other debts and that the authorities do in general allow time to pay in cases of genuine financial difficulty.

Subs. (5)

A time to pay order would seriously interfere with the progress of a diligence if made on the eve of its completion. So once judicial authority has been granted to complete the diligence an application for a time to pay order is incompetent. The debtor must then wait until the diligence is completed or abandoned. If any balance still remains due an application can be made in respect of that balance.

Subss. (6)–(8)

These provisions are the same as those for time to pay directions (see notes on s.1(6)–(8)).

Application for time to pay order

6.—(1) An application for a time to pay order shall specify, to the best of the debtor's knowledge, the amount of the debt outstanding as at the date of the making of the application and shall include an offer to pay it—

(a) by specified instalments, payable at specified intervals; or

(b) as a lump sum at the end of a specified period.

(2) The sheriff clerk's duty under section 96(2)(b) of this Act to assist the debtor in the completion of certain forms shall, in relation to a form of application for a time to pay order, consist of a duty to assist him in the completion of the form in accordance with proposals for payment made by the debtor.

(3) On receipt of an application for a time to pay order, the sheriff shall, if the application is properly made and unless it appears to him that the making of a time to pay order would not be competent, make an interim order sisting diligence as provided for in section 8(1) of this Act.

(4) The sheriff may, where the debtor is unable to furnish the necessary information, make an order requiring the creditor, within such period as may be specified therein, to furnish to the sheriff such particulars of the decree or other document under which the debt is payable as may be prescribed by Act of Sederunt.

(5) If a creditor fails to comply with an order under subsection (4) above the sheriff may, after giving the creditor an opportunity to make representations, make an order recalling or extinguishing any existing diligence, and interdicting the creditor from executing diligence, for the recovery of the debt.

(6) Where the sheriff makes an interim order under subsection (3) above, the sheriff clerk shall as soon as is reasonably practicable—

    (a) serve a copy of the application for the time to pay order on the creditor informing him that he may object to the granting of the application within a period of 14 days after the date of service; and

    (b) serve on the creditor a copy of the interim order and of any order under subsection (4) above.

DEFINITIONS
    "debt": s.15(3).
    "decree or other document": s.15(3).
    "sheriff": s.15(3).

GENERAL NOTE
Subss. (1), (2)
    The debtor in the application for a time to pay order is required to specify the outstanding balance of the debt and set out proposals for payment. The prescribed form of application will no doubt contain space for the debtor to give brief details of his or her financial circumstances, but such disclosure will be voluntary. The sheriff clerk's duty to assist debtors in completing their application forms does not extend to advising them what proposals to make for paying their debts. Debtors can obtain help from a Citizens Advice Bureau or similar organisation on this aspect.

Subs. (3)
    If the debtor's application is in order (*i.e.* for an allowed debt, complies with subs. (1) above, and is presented to the correct court) the sheriff is under a duty to grant an order sisting diligence until the application is determined. The granting of such interim orders could be delegated to sheriff clerks.

Subss. (4), (5)
    The debtor ought to be able to state the outstanding balance of the debt since this will be contained in the diligence documents already served on him or her. This balance may have been reduced by subsequent payments to account. The creditor has an opportunity to dispute the balance as shown by the debtor later.
    Where the debtor is unable to supply the necessary information the creditor is required to do so on pain of the debt being made unenforceable.

Subs. (6)
    The interim order sisting diligence is served on the creditor together with a copy of the application by the sheriff clerk. If no objection is received from the creditor within 14 days a time to pay order in the terms proposed by the debtor will be made. Creditors who forget or delay will be faced with the expense of an application for recall which might not be successful.

Disposal of application

7.—(1) If no objection is made in pursuance of section 6(6)(a) of this Act, the sheriff shall make a time to pay order in accordance with the application.

(2) If such an objection is made, the sheriff shall not dispose of the application without first—

(a) giving the debtor an opportunity to make representations; and

(b) if agreement is not reached as to whether a time to pay order should be made or as to its terms, giving the parties an opportunity to be heard.

(3) Where the sheriff refuses to make a time to pay order, he shall recall any interim order under section 6(3) of this Act.

(4) The sheriff clerk shall as soon as is reasonably practicable—

(a) intimate the decision of the sheriff on an application for a time to pay order (including any recall of an interim order under subsection (3) above) to the debtor and the creditor; and

(b) if the sheriff has made a time to pay order, inform the creditor of the date when he intimated that fact to the debtor.

DEFINITION
"sheriff": s.15(3).

GENERAL NOTE
This section sets out the sheriff's powers in dealing with an application for a time to pay order. Where the creditor does not object the sheriff will simply make the order in the terms proposed by the debtor. In the absence of full information about the debtor's means and the reason for the creditor's failure to object the sheriff is unable to make any other disposal.

It is envisaged that an objection by the creditor could be dealt with informally if the debtor agreed with the creditor's counter-proposal or objection. Only in the event of disagreement should a hearing be necessary at which the debtor could give evidence of his or her financial circumstances and the creditor the reasons for requiring immediate payment.

The sheriff clerk intimates the sheriff's decision to the creditor and debtor. The date of intimation to the debtor is important since it regulates the starting of the instalments or the deferred period. The creditor needs to know the date in order to determine whether the debtor is in default and when the claim for interest accrued (see s.5(7)) should be served.

Effect of interim order on diligence

8.—(1) While an interim order under section 6(3) of this Act is in effect it shall not be competent in respect of the debt—

(a) to grant a warrant of sale of articles which, before or after the making of the interim order, have been poinded, and any application for such warrant of sale (other than an application for an order under section 21(1)(b) of this Act) which is pending when the interim order comes into effect shall fall;

(b) to execute an earnings arrestment;

(c) where an arrestment of property belonging to the debtor (other than an arrestment of earnings in the hands of his employer) has been executed before or after the making of the interim order, to commence an action of furthcoming or sale, or to grant decree in any such action which has already been commenced, in pursuance of that arrestment;

(d) to commence an action of adjudication for debt or, if such an action has already been commenced, to take any steps other than the registration of a notice of litigiosity in connection with the action, the obtaining and extracting of a decree in the action, the registration of an abbreviate of adjudication and the completion of title to property adjudged by the decree.

(2) An interim order under section 6(3) of this Act shall come into effect on intimation to the creditor under section 6(6)(b) of this Act and shall remain in effect until intimation of the sheriff's decision on the application for a time to pay order is made to the debtor and the creditor under section 7(4)(a) of this Act.

(3) For the purposes of section 27 of this Act, the period during which such an interim order is in effect shall be disregarded in calculating the period during which a poinding to which the interim order applies remains in effect.

"adjudication for debt": s.15(1).
"debt": s.15(3).
"earnings": ss.73(2) and 106.
"employer": ss.73(1) and 106.
"poinded": s.15(1).
"sheriff": s.15(3).
"warrant of sale": ss.30 and 106.

GENERAL NOTE
An interim order affects the diligences available to ordinary unsecured creditors. It comes into force on being intimated by the sheriff clerk to the creditor in question and lasts until the sheriff's decision granting or refusing a time to pay order is likewise intimated (subs. (2)).

An interim order prevents a diligence being completed by warrant sale, furthcoming or gaining possession. The execution of an earnings arrestment is prohibited as this is a self-executing diligence requiring no further steps for its completion (see Pt. III). However, the creditor can still serve a charge, execute a poinding, report a poinding, and even apply for a warrant of sale of perishable goods, execute an arrestment of funds other than earnings, serve an inhibition, proceed with a pending adjudication to the stage of completing title, and petition for the debtor's sequestration.

Subs. (3)
See note on s.27.

Effect of time to pay order on diligence

9.—(1) While a time to pay order is in effect, it shall not be competent—
    (a) to serve a charge for payment; or
    (b) to commence or execute any of the following diligences—
        (i) an arrestment and action of furthcoming or sale;
        (ii) a poinding and sale;
        (iii) an earnings arrestment;
        (iv) an adjudication for debt,
to enforce payment of the debt concerned.
  (2) On making a time to pay order, the sheriff in respect of the debt—
    (a) shall make an order recalling any existing earnings arrestment;
    (b) where the debt is being enforced by a conjoined arrestment order, shall—
        (i) if he, or another sheriff sitting in the same sheriff court, made the conjoined arrestment order, vary it so as to exclude the debt or, where no other debt or maintenance is being enforced by the order, recall the order;
        (ii) if a sheriff sitting in another sheriff court made the conjoined arrestment order, require intimation of the time to pay order to be made to a sheriff sitting there who shall so vary or, as the case may be, recall the conjoined arrestment order;
    (c) where an action of adjudication for debt has been commenced, shall make an order prohibiting the taking of any steps other than the registration of a notice of litigiosity in connection with the action, the obtaining and extracting of a decree in the action, the registration of an abbreviate of adjudication and the completion of title to property adjudged by the decree;

    (d) may make an order recalling a poinding;

    (e) may make an order recalling or restricting any arrestment other than an arrestment of the debtor's earnings in the hands of his employer.

(3) If a poinding or such an arrestment as is mentioned in subsection (2)(e) above is in effect, the sheriff may order that the making of a time to pay order or the recall of the poinding or the recall or restriction of the arrestment shall be subject to the fulfilment by the debtor of such conditions as the sheriff thinks fit.

(4) Where the sheriff does not exercise the powers conferred on him by subsection (2)(d) or (e) above to recall a diligence, he shall order that no further steps shall be taken by the creditor in the diligence concerned other than, in the case of a poinding, applying for an order under section 21(1) of this Act or making a report of the execution of the poinding under section 22 of this Act.

(5) Any order made under subsection (2) or (4) above shall specify the diligence in relation to which it is made.

(6) The sheriff shall not make an order under subsection (2)(d) or (e) above without first giving the creditor an opportunity to make representations.

(7) The sheriff clerk shall, at the same time as he makes intimation under section 7(4)(a) of this Act—

    (a) intimate any order under subsection (2) or (4) above to the debtor and the creditor and the order shall come into effect on such intimation being made to the creditor;

    (b) intimate any order under subsection (2)(a) or (b) above to the employer.

(8) While an order under subsection (4) above is in effect it shall not be competent to grant—

    (a) a warrant (other than an order under section 21(1)(b) of this Act) to sell articles which have been poinded;

    (b) a decree of furthcoming or sale of arrested property.

(9) For the purposes of section 27 of this Act, the period during which an order under subsection (4) above is in effect shall be disregarded in calculating the period during which a poinding to which the order applies remains in effect.

(10) Where, before the making of a time to pay order in respect of a debt, a charge to pay that debt has been served—

    (a) if the period for payment specified in the charge has not expired, the charge shall lapse on the making of the order;

    (b) if that period has expired, nothing in the time to pay order nor in any order under this section shall affect retrospectively the effect of the charge in the constitution of apparent insolvency within the meaning of section 7 of the Bankruptcy (Scotland) Act 1985.

(11) If, when a time to pay order in relation to a debt is made, any diligence enforcing it is in effect which is not specified in an order under subsection (2) or (4) above, the diligence shall remain in effect unless and until it is recalled under section 10(4) of this Act.

(12) Where a time to pay order is recalled or ceases to have effect, otherwise than—

    (a) under section 12(2)(a) of this Act; or

    (b) by the debt payable under the order being paid or otherwise extinguished,

the debt in so far as it remains outstanding (including interest thereon, whether or not awarded as a specific sum in the decree) shall, subject to any enactment or rule of law to the contrary, become enforceable by any diligence mentioned in subsection (1)(b) above; and, notwithstanding section 25 of this Act, in this subsection "diligence" includes, where the debt was, immediately before the time to pay order was made, being enforced by a poinding in any premises, another poinding in those premises.

DEFINITIONS
"adjudication for debt": s.15(1).
"debt": s.15(3).
"earnings": ss.73(2) and 106.
"employer": ss.73(1) and 106.
"maintenance": s.106.
"sheriff": s.15(3).

GENERAL NOTE
The effect of a time to pay order on existing diligence and the creditor's entitlement to execute new diligence to enforce the debt concerned is best seen by considering each possible diligence in turn.

(a)	an adjudication for debt	—a new action is incompetent (subs. (1)(b)(iv)).
		—an existing action may proceed as far as completion of title (subs. (2)(c)).
(b)	an arrestment	—a new arrestment is incompetent (subs. (1)(b)(i)).
		—an existing arrestment may be restricted or recalled (subs. (2)(e)).
		—where an arrestment remains in effect (wholly or partly) no further steps can be taken (sub. (4)), and if an action of furthcoming is pending no decree can be granted (subs. (8)(b)).
(c)	a charge	—a new charge is incompetent (subs. (1)(a)).
		—an existing unexpired charge lapses (subs. (10)(a)).
		—an existing expired charge remains effective for the constitution of apparent insolvency (subs. (10)(b)).
(d)	a conjoined arrestment order	—a new order is incompetent since any existing earnings arrestment is recalled (subs. 2(a)).
		—the debt is taken out of any existing order resulting in its variation or recall as the case may be (subs. (2)(b)).
(e)	an earnings arrestment	—a new arrestment is incompetent (subs. (1)(b)(iii)).
		—an existing arrestment is recalled (subs. (2)(a)).
(f)	an inhibition	—a new inhibition is competent.
		—an existing inhibition is unaffected.
(g)	a poinding	—a new poinding is incompetent (subs. (1)(b)(ii)).
		—an existing poinding may be recalled (subs. (2)(d)).
		—where an existing poinding is not recalled no steps may be taken other than reporting it or applying for perishables to be sold immediately (subs. (4)), and no warrant of sale other than of perishables may be granted (subs. (8)(a)).

The special diligences of sequestration for rent, poinding of the ground, maills and duties, and repossession available to certain creditors are unaffected and may be commenced or completed while a time to pay order is in force.

Existing diligences not expressly recalled or frozen remain in full force and effect (subs. (11)). This should happen only if the sheriff is unaware of a diligence or inadvertently fails to recall it, since subs. 4 imposes a duty to freeze an unrecalled diligence.

Subss. (3), (6)
The sheriff on granting a time to pay order may impose conditions for the recall of an existing poinding or the recall or restriction of an existing arrestment. For example the debtor may be required to sell some of the poinded goods and hand over the proceeds to the creditor, or to undertake not to dispose of the goods, or to pay over part of the arrested fund to the creditor.

No order recalling or restricting an arrestment or recalling a poinding may be made without the creditor having an opportunity to make representations opposing it or suggesting suitable conditions.

Sub. (12)
The creditor's rights to enforce the debt by diligence revive if the time to pay order lapses on default by the debtor or is recalled. Sequestration, although resulting in an order ceasing to have effect, prevents the creditor from doing diligence (s.12(2)(a)).

Variation and recall of time to pay order and arrestment

10.—(1) The sheriff may, on an application by the debtor or the creditor—

(a) vary or recall a time to pay order if he is satisfied that it is reasonable to do so; or

(b) if a poinding or an arrestment in respect of the debt is in effect, recall the poinding or recall or restrict the arrestment.

(2) If a poinding or an arrestment in respect of the debt is in effect, the sheriff may order that any variation, recall or restriction under subsection (1) above shall be subject to the fulfilment by the debtor of such conditions as the sheriff thinks fit.

(3) The sheriff clerk shall as soon as is reasonably practicable intimate a variation under subsection (1) above to the debtor and to the creditor, and the variation shall come into effect on the date of such intimation.

(4) Where, after a time to pay order has been made, it comes to the knowledge of the sheriff that the debt to which the order applies is being enforced by any of the diligences mentioned in section 9(1)(b) of this Act which was in effect when the time to pay order was made, the sheriff, after giving all interested parties an opportunity to be heard, may make—

(a) an order recalling the time to pay order; or

(b) any of the orders mentioned in subsection (2) or (4) or section 9 of this Act; and that section shall, subject to any necessary modifications, apply for the purposes of an order made under this paragraph as it applies for the purposes of an order made under either of those subsections.

DEFINITIONS
"debt": s.15(3).
"poinding": s.15(1).
"sheriff": s.15(3).

GENERAL NOTE
This section empowers the sheriff, on application, to vary or recall a time to pay order. For example, the debtor may apply for smaller instalments because of loss of earnings or the creditor may seek recall on the basis of the debtor's improved financial circumstances or the debtor's incurring of new credit. In exercising these powers the sheriff may also exercise the recall and restriction powers in relation to existing arrestments and poindings (see notes on s.9).

Where through ignorance of the existence of a diligence or inadvertence the sheriff failed when granting a time to pay order to recall, restrict or freeze the diligence, the sheriff may take any of these steps when the diligence comes to light. But the sheriff may recall the time to pay order instead and let the diligence continue.

Lapse of time to pay order

11.—(1) If, on the day on which an instalment payable under a time to pay order becomes due, there remains unpaid a sum, due under previous instalments, of not less than the aggregate of 2 instalments, the order shall cease to have effect.

(2) If at the end of the period of 3 weeks immediately following the day on which the last instalment payable under a time to pay order becomes due, any part of the debt payable under the order remains outstanding, the order shall cease to have effect.

(3) If any sum payable under a time to pay order under section 5(2)(b) of this Act remains unpaid 24 hours after the end of the period specified in the order, the order shall cease to have effect.

DEFINITION
"debt": s.15(3).

   This section provides that a time to pay order lapses automatically on default by the debtor in complying with the terms for payment. The provisions are identical to those for time to pay directions; see notes on s.4.

Miscellaneous

Sequestration and insolvency

   12.—(1) While a time to pay direction or a time to pay order is in effect, the creditor shall not be entitled to found on the debt concerned in presenting, or in concurring in the presentation of, a petition for the sequestration of the debtor's estate.
   (2) A time to pay direction or a time to pay order shall cease to have effect—
   (a) on the granting of an award of sequestration of the debtor's estate;
   (b) on the granting by the debtor of a voluntary trust deed whereby his estate is conveyed to a trustee for the benefit of his creditors generally; or
   (c) on the entering by the debtor into a composition contract with his creditors.

DEFINITION
   "debt": s.15(3).

GENERAL NOTE
   This section deals with the relationship between time to pay directions and orders and the various insolvency processes.
   A creditor who wishes to present or concur in a petition for the debtor's sequestration but whose debt is subject to a time to pay direction or order has first to apply to the court for recall of the direction or order. More commonly perhaps other creditors will petition.
   Any of the insolvency processes automatically terminate any existing time to pay direction or order relating to the debtor.

Saving of creditor's rights and remedies

   13.—(1) No right or remedy of a creditor to enforce his debt shall be affected by—
   (a) a time to pay direction;
   (b) a time to pay order; or
   (c) an interim order under section 6(3) of this Act,
except as expressly provided in this Part of this Act.
   (2) The recall—
   (a) on the making of a time to pay direction or an order under section 3(1) of this Act, of an arrestment; or
   (b) on the making of a time to pay order or an order under section 10(1) of this Act, of an arrestment or a poinding,
shall not prevent the creditor therein from being ranked by virtue of that arrestment of poinding pari passu under paragraph 24 of Schedule 7 to the Bankruptcy (Scotland) Act 1985 on the proceeds of any other arrestment or poinding.

DEFINITIONS
   "debt": s.15(3).
   "poinding": s.15(1).

GENERAL NOTE
Subs. (1)
   A time to pay direction or order affects only the entitlement of the creditor to enforce the debt by the ordinary diligences of charge, poinding and sale, arrestment and furthcoming, earnings arrestment, conjoined arrestment order and sequestration. Secured creditors may continue to call up their securities, exercise their liens or use the special diligences (if entitled

to do so) of poinding of the ground, or maills and duties. A landlord may bring an action for recovery of possession even though the debtor has been given time to pay the arrears of rent due and may sequestrate for rent (see Sched. 6, para. 26, for Rent Act tenancies). The fuel boards may also exercise their powers of disconnection.

Furthermore the creditor may plead set-off or compensation in respect of the debt, or pursue a guarantor or cautioner. The creditor may also execute an inhibition.

Subs. (2)

Para. 24 of Sched. 7 to the Bankruptcy (Scotland) Act 1985 entitles a creditor executing a poinding or an arrestment to claim a share of the proceeds of another creditor's poinding or arrestment. This subsection provides that the recall on granting a time to pay direction or order of the claiming creditor's diligence shall not affect that creditor's entitlement to share.

Circumstances where direction or order not competent or no longer effective

14.—(1) It shall be competent to make a time to pay direction or a time to pay order only in relation to a debtor who is an individual and only if, and to the extent that, the debtor is liable for payment of the debt concerned in either or both of the following capacities—

(a) personally;

(b) as a tutor of an individual or as a judicial factor loco tutoris, curator bonis or judicial factor loco absentis on an individual's estate.

(2) A time to pay direction or a time to pay order shall cease to have effect on the death of the debtor or on the transmission of the obligation to pay the debt concerned during his lifetime to another person.

(3) Where a time order for the payment by instalments of a sum owed under a regulated agreement or a security has been made under section 129(2)(a) of the Consumer Credit Act 1974 it shall not thereafter be competent to make a time to pay direction or a time to pay order in relation to that sum.

DEFINITION

"debt": s.15(3).

GENERAL NOTE

Subs. (1)

This subsection restricts time to pay directions and orders to individuals owing money either personally or in a representative capacity on behalf of some other individual.

A decree against a partnership usually takes the form of a decree against the firm and the partners as individuals and as trustees for the firm. Diligence can then be done against the firm's assets and the assets of the partners as individuals. A time to pay direction or order could be sought by the partners as individuals but not by the firm. The creditor would therefore still be entitled to do diligence against the firm's assets and against the assets held by the partners as trustees for the firm.

Subs. (2)

Time to pay is a privilege which is personal to the debtor and which is not transmissible by assignation or death along with the obligation to pay the debt. The assignee or beneficiary could however apply for a (new) time to pay order if the conditions of competency (including those in subs. (1) above) were met.

Subs. (3)

Time orders under the 1974 Act are rather similar to time to pay orders. It would be confusing if both remedies could be in operation concurrently and unfair for the debtor to get two bites at the cherry by defaulting on one and then applying for the other. Paras. 16 and 17 of Sched. 6 (amending the 1974 Act) similarly exclude the granting of a time order where a time to pay direction or order has been made.

Interpretation of Part I

15.—(1) In this Part of this Act—
"adjudication for debt" does not include—
(a) an adjudication on a debitum fundi; or
(b) an adjudication under section 23 of the Conveyancing
(Scotland) Act 1924 (adjudication to recover arrears of
ground annual);
"poinding" does not include poinding of the ground, and "poinded"
shall be construed accordingly.
(2) In sections 1 to 4 of this Act—
"the court" means the Court of Session or the sheriff;
"the debt concerned" means the sum or expenses in respect of which
a time to pay direction is made.
(3) In sections 5 to 14 of this Act—
"debt" means the sum due by a debtor under a decree or other
document (including any interest thereon and any expenses
decerned for), and any expenses of diligence used to recover
such sum which are chargeable against the debtor, but does
not include—
(a) any sum due under an order of court in criminal
proceedings;
(b) maintenance, whether due at the date of application for
the time to pay order or not, or any capital sum awarded
on divorce or on the granting of a declarator of nullity of
marriage or any other sum due under a decree awarding
maintenance or such a capital sum; or
(c) any fine imposed—
(i) for contempt of court;
(ii) under any enactment, for professional misconduct;
or
(iii) for failure to implement an order under section 91
of the Court of Session Act 1868 (orders for
specific performance of statutory duty);
"decree or other document" means—
(a) a decree of the Court of Session or the sheriff;
(b) an extract of a document which is registered for execution
in the Books of Council and Session or the sheriff court
books;
(c) an order or determination which by virtue of any enactment is enforceable as if it were an extract registered
decree arbitral bearing a warrant for execution issued by
the sheriff;
(d) a civil judgment granted outside Scotland by a court,
tribunal or arbiter which by virtue of any enactment or
rule of law is enforceable in Scotland; and
(e) a document or settlement which by virtue of an Order in
Council made under section 13 of the Civil Jurisdiction
and Judgments Act 1982 is enforceable in Scotland,
but does not include a maintenance order or a summary
warrant;
"sheriff"—
(a) in relation to a debt constituted by decree granted by a
sheriff, means that sheriff or another sheriff sitting in the
same sheriff court;
(b) in any other case, means the sheriff having
jurisdiction—
(i) in the place where the debtor is domiciled;

    (ii) if the debtor is not domiciled in Scotland, in a place in Scotland where he carries on business; or

    (iii) if the debtor does not carry on business in Scotland, in a place where he has property which is not exempt from diligence;

and, for the purposes of sub-paragraphs (i) and (ii) above, the debtor's domicile shall be determined in accordance with section 41 of the Civil Jurisdiction and Judgments Act 1982.

DEFINITIONS

"maintenance": s.106.
"maintenance order": s.106.
"summary warrant": s.106.

GENERAL NOTE

Subs. (1)

Adjudication for debt. The exceptions are special diligences competent to enforce a heritable debt or arrears of a ground annual respectively.

Poinding of the ground. This is a remedy available to a heritable creditor. Moveables belonging to the debtor (and the debtor's tenants in so far as their rent is in arrears) on the security subjects may be poinded and sold. Such a poinding is not prohibited or affected by any time to pay direction or order.

Subs. (2)

The court. The court hearing the action in which decree is granted has exclusive jurisdiction to grant, vary or recall a time to pay direction attached to the decree. Time to pay becomes available in the Court of Session, although the number of non-Revenue decrees for sums under £10,000 is limited.

Subs. (3)

Debt. Fines and similar sums imposed by a criminal court cannot be the subject of a time to pay order. They are also excluded from time to pay directions (see note on s.1(5)).

Decree or other document. Debts enforceable by diligence on extracts of writs registered for execution or their equivalents may be subject to time to pay orders. Time to pay directions, however, are limited to decrees actually (rather than notionally) pronounced by either the Court of Session or the sheriff court.

PART II

POINDINGS AND WARRANT SALES

Poinding

Articles exempt from poinding

  16.—(1) The following articles belonging to a debtor shall be exempt from poinding at the instance of a creditor in respect of a debt due to him by the debtor—

    (a) clothing reasonably required for the use of the debtor or any member of his household;

    (b) implements, tools of trade, books or other equipment reasonably required for the use of the debtor or any member of his household in the practice of the debtor's or such member's profession, trade or business, not exceeding in aggregate value £500 or such amount as may be prescribed in regulations made by the Lord Advocate;

    (c) medical aids or medical equipment reasonably required for the use of the debtor or any member of his household;

    (d) books or other articles reasonably required for the education or training of the debtor or any member of his household not exceed-

ing in aggregate value £500 or such amount as may be prescribed in regulations made by the Lord Advocate;
  (e) toys for the use of any child who is a member of the debtor's household;
  (f) articles reasonably required for the care or upbringing of a child who is a member of the debtor's household.

(2) The following articles belonging to a debtor shall be exempt from poinding if they are at the time of the poinding in a dwellinghouse and are reasonably required for the use in the dwellinghouse of the person residing there or a member of his household—
  (a) beds or bedding;
  (b) household linen;
  (c) chairs or settees;
  (d) tables;
  (e) food;
  (f) lights or light fittings;
  (g) heating appliances;
  (h) curtains;
  (j) floor coverings;
  (k) furniture, equipment or utensils used for cooking, storing or eating food;
  (l) refrigerators;
  (m) articles used for cleaning, mending, or pressing clothes;
  (n) articles used for cleaning the dwellinghouse;
  (o) furniture used for storing—
      (i) clothing, bedding or household linen;
      (ii) articles used for cleaning the dwellinghouse; or
      (iii) utensils used for cooking or eating food;
  (p) articles used for safety in the dwellinghouse;
  (q) tools used for maintenance or repair of the dwellinghouse or of household articles.

(3) The Lord Advocate may by regulations add to the list set out in subsection (2) above, or delete or vary any of the items contained in that list.

(4) If, on an application made within 14 days after the date of the execution of the poinding—
  (a) by the debtor or any person who owns a poinded article in common with the debtor; or
  (b) by any person in possession of a poinded article,
the sheriff is satisfied that the article is exempt from poinding under this section, he shall make an order releasing the article from the poinding.

DEFINITION
  "dwellinghouse": s.45.

GENERAL NOTE
  This section sets out the main exemptions from poinding. It is not exhaustive. It is doubtful whether money and negotiable instruments can be poinded (*Alexander* v. *McLay* (1826) 4S. 439) but in practice they never are. Carriages and other stock of a private railway company cannot be poinded (Railway Companies (Scotland) Act 1867, s.4).
  The range of household items exempt from poinding is very considerably larger than those exempt by the Law Reform (Diligence) (Scotland) Act 1973 and the common law. This extension might make a substantial difference to domestic poindings.

Subs. (1)
  This subsection exempts specified articles belonging to the debtor wherever they are situated.

Para. (a)
  This paragraph restates the previous common law exemption.

Para. (b)

The common law exemption for "tools of trade" applied to modest items only. The statutory reformulation continues this policy by imposing a £500 limit but extends it to members of the debtor's household as well as the debtor. However the limit applies to the debtor and any member of the household; each person does not have an individual £500 exemption. It is thought that a car or a van is neither an implement, a tool or other equipment, however necessary it might be to the debtor's business.

Para. (c)

This is a new exemption although such items were never poinded in practice because they are not readily saleable.

Para. (d)

This paragraph contains another new exemption. It would cover tools of an apprentice car mechanic, a student's books, and perhaps even a cassette player needed for Open University course tapes. It could be argued that almost any book was educational; whether it is reasonably required is another matter.

Para. (e)

This new exemption is not qualified either by a monetary limit or by the test of the items being reasonably required. The effect is that not only teddies, Lego and dolls' houses are exempt but also BMX bikes, electric train sets, computers and possibly even micro computers and snooker tables.

Para. (f)

The intention is to cover articles such as prams, buggies, and playpens. "Upbringing" however extends the scope considerably. A piano might be reasonably required for the upbringing of a musically gifted child as might the more expensive items for teenage children's hobbies.

Subs. (2)

This subsection is restricted to articles situated in a dwellinghouse at the time when the officer proposes to poind them. The exemptions go a great deal further than those contained in the Law Reform (Diligence) (Scotland) Act 1973. First, the list of exempt items is much greater; secondly, an article qualifies for exemption if it is reasonably required rather than reasonably necessary to avoid undue hardship. The continued efficiency of poinding as a method of debt enforcement will depend on the attitude taken by the courts to the words "reasonably required." It is suggested that the debtor's financial circumstances should not be ignored, so that the test should be reasonably required by debtors unable to pay their debts rather than by people in better financial circumstances.

Items that could be poinded include a television set, a video, a record player, a piano, spare beds, fires and other surplus furniture, a car in the garage and perhaps garden tools, but see para. (q). The debtor's family circumstances will also have a bearing on what is reasonably required. A washing machine could be exempt under "articles used for cleaning . . . clothes" (para. (m)) if there were young children in the house. A microwave oven would be exempt if it was the only oven but not if it was an additional one. Officers executing a poinding may have to ask more questions before being able to decide whether an article is reasonably required.

The debtor may have a freezer exempt as well as a refrigerator if living in an area remote from shops on the ground that the freezer is necessary for storing food (para. (k)). It appeared from the Lords Committee stage that several peers used their freezers to cool down bottles of champagne for unexpected guests but this use could hardly constitute a reasonable requirement!

It should be noted that although the articles have to be owned by the debtor, they do not have to be situated in the debtor's dwellinghouse or be used by the debtor and family in order to qualify for exemption. So creditors of a landlord could not poind listed items situated in a furnished flat which were reasonably required by the tenant or members of the tenant's household.

Subs. (4)

The decision whether to poind or exempt is at first instance for the officer executing the poinding. However, the debtor or possessor can appeal to the sheriff within 14 days (lengthened from the seven days allowed under the Law Reform (Diligence) (Scotland) Act

1973). Since there is no right of appeal by the creditor nor can a second poinding be executed to cover articles not poinded on the first visit, officers will no doubt err on the side of caution and poind articles unless it is clear they are exempt.

Restrictions on times when poinding may be executed

17.—(1) No poinding shall be executed on Sunday, Christmas Day, New Year's Day, Good Friday or such other day as may be prescribed by Act of Sederunt.

(2) The execution of a poinding shall not—
  (a) be commenced before 8 a.m. or after 8 p.m.; or
  (b) be continued after 8 p.m.,
unless the officer of court has obtained prior authority from the sheriff for such commencement or continuation; and any rule of law which prohibits poindings outwith the hours of daylight shall cease to have effect.

DEFINITION
  "officer of court": s.106.

GENERAL NOTE
Subs. (1)
  This subsection clarifies and alters the previous law. Poindings executed in contravention of its provisions are null.

Subs. (2)
  The common law rule prohibiting a poinding from starting or being continued during the hours of darkness is replaced by a more flexible and certain system. A car may well have to be poinded in the evening if the debtor is away at work all day. The officer has to seek prior authority to poind outwith the prescribed hours but there is no express requirement that such an application has to be intimated to the debtor. Indeed it might defeat the purpose if it were to be intimated.

Power of entry for execution of poinding

18.—(1) Subject to subsection (2) below, notwithstanding any warrant authorising him to open shut and lockfast places, an officer of court shall not enter a dwellinghouse to execute a poinding if, at the time of his intended entry, there appears to him to be nobody, or only children under the age of 16 years, present there unless, at least 4 days before the date of his intended entry, he has served notice on the debtor specifying that date.

(2) If it appears to the sheriff, on an application made to him by the officer of court (which shall not require to be intimated to the debtor), that the requirement of service under this section would be likely to prejudice the execution of the poinding he may dispense with such service.

DEFINITIONS
  "dwellinghouse": s.45.
  "officer of court": s.106.

GENERAL NOTE
  The warrant of execution contained in an extract decree authorised the officer in executing a poinding to open shut and lockfast places (see s.87(2)(a)). This allowed the officer to get a locksmith to open empty premises, although officers generally left a notice of when they intended to return in order to allow the debtor to be present and open the premises. Only if the premises were still empty on the second visit would a locksmith be engaged.
  The previous law (summarised above) regarding commercial premises is unchanged. But subs. (1) prohibits an officer from entering an empty dwellinghouse or one in which only children under 16 are present, unless at least four days notice has been given or the sheriff has granted authority under subs. (2). There is a danger that some debtors will use the four days notice to move any exempt items round to their friends' houses. In order to prevent this officers may seek authority to enter houses without giving notice and such an application

need not be intimated to the debtor. But if officers were to apply for, and sheriffs were to grant, authority to enter without notice as a matter of course in every case the protection afforded to debtors by this section would be nugatory.

Value of articles which may be poinded and presumption as to ownership

19.—(1) The officer of court shall be entitled to poind articles only to the extent necessary to ensure that the sum recoverable at the time of the sale would be realised if they were sold at the values fixed under section 20(4) of this Act.

(2) In executing a poinding, an officer of court shall be entitled to proceed on the assumption that any article in the possession of the debtor is owned by him unless the officer of court knows or ought to know that the contrary is the case.

(3) The officer of court shall not be precluded from relying on the assumption mentioned in subsection (2) above by reason only of one or both of the following circumstances—

   (a) that the article belongs to a class which is commonly held under a hire, hire-purchase or conditional sale agreement or on some other limited title of possession;

   (b) that an assertion has been made that the article is not owned by the debtor.

DEFINITIONS
   "officer of court": s.106.
   "sum recoverable": s.45.

GENERAL NOTE
Subs. (1)
   This restates the previous common law (*McKinnon* v. *Hamilton* (1866) 4M. 852). An officer is entitled to poind to cover the debt and expenses already incurred and expenses that are likely to be incurred in carrying through the diligence to a conclusion. Sched. 1 details the expenses that are chargeable against the debtor and recoverable out of the proceeds of sale.

Subss. (2), (3)
   These subsections replace somewhat uncertain common law rules and provisions of doubtful vires contained in Practice Notes of the sheriffs principal. All articles situated in premises owned or occupied by the debtor are now presumed to be possessed by the debtor and hence poindable for his or her debts unless the officer of court knows or ought to know that this is not the case. The officer ought to know that articles in an auctioneer's premises or a laundry are far more likely to belong to customers than to the owner of the business. Again the officer might be told that an article does not belong to the debtor. While the officer need not believe an unsupported assertion, evidence such as a hire purchase agreement or a notice on the back of a television set stating that it belongs to the hiring company would corroborate the assertion and fix the officer with knowledge. Officers are under a duty to make inquiries before poinding as to ownership from any person present in the premises (see s.20(2)(c)).

   When it is clear that an article does not belong to the debtor the officer should refrain from poinding it. In a doubtful case the officer should err on the side of caution and poind but mention in the report of poinding any assertion made as to ownership. Debtors or others present at the poinding should speak out; failure to raise the issue of ownership at the poinding when given an opportunity to do so may lead the sheriff to regard a later assertion as a fabrication.

Poinding procedure

20.—(1) The procedure in a poinding shall be in accordance with this section and section 21 of this Act.

(2) Before executing the poinding, the officer of court shall—

   (a) exhibit to any person present the warrant to poind and the certificate of execution of the charge relating thereto;

18–26

(b) demand payment of the sum recoverable from the debtor, if he is present, or any person present appearing to the officer of court to be authorised to act for the debtor; and

(c) make enquiry of any person present as to the ownership of the articles proposed to be poinded, and in particular whether there are any persons who own any articles in common with the debtor,

but it shall not be necessary for the officer of court to make public proclamation of the poinding or to read publicly the extract decree containing the warrant to poind and the execution of the charge relating thereto.

(3) The officer of court shall be accompanied at the poinding by one witness.

(4) The poinded articles shall be valued by the officer of court according to the price which they would be likely to fetch if sold on the open market unless he considers that the articles are such that a valuation by a professional valuer or other suitably skilled person is advisable, in which case he may arrange for such a valuation.

(5) The officer of court shall prepare a schedule (referred to in this Part of this Act as "the poinding schedule"), in the form prescribed by Act of Sederunt, which shall specify—

(a) the identity of the creditor and of the debtor;

(b) the articles poinded, and their respective values;

(c) the sum recoverable; and

(d) the place where the poinding was executed.

(6) On completion of the valuation the officer of court shall—

(a) along with the witness sign the poinding schedule;

(b) deliver the poinding schedule to any person in possession of the articles or—

    (i) where the poinding was executed in a dwellinghouse or other premises, leave it in the premises; or

    (ii) in any other case, deliver it to premises occupied by that person;

(c) if the person in possession of the articles is not the debtor and it is reasonably practicable, serve a copy of it by post on the debtor;

(d) inform the debtor (if present) of his right to redeem poinded articles under section 21(4) of this Act;

(e) inform any person present who owns any poinded article in common with the debtor of his right to redeem poinded articles under section 41(2) and (3)(a) of this Act; and

(f) inform the debtor (if present) and any person present who owns any poinded article in common with the debtor, or who is in possession of any poinded article, of his right to apply for an order releasing articles from poinding under section 16(4), 23(1) or 41(3)(b) of this Act.

(7) The officer of court shall leave poinded articles at the place where they were poinded, except that where that place is not a dwellinghouse or other premises, if he considers it necessary for their security or the preservation of their value and there is insufficient time to obtain an order under section 21(1)(a) of this Act, he shall remove them at the creditor's expense—

(a) to the nearest convenient premises belonging to the debtor or to the person in possession of the articles; or

(b) if no such premises are available, to the nearest suitable secure premises.

DEFINITIONS
"dwellinghouse": s.45.
"officer of court": s.106.
"poinding schedule": ss.20(5), 45.
"sum recoverable": s.45.

GENERAL NOTE
This section restates the existing procedure for executing a poinding with modifications, some of which serve to bring the law into line with previous practice. The major changes are:—
(a) The opening ceremony of 3 oyezes and reading the extract decree is expressly abolished (subs. (2)). There was some doubt whether this was an essential part of the procedure and it had fallen into disuse.
(b) The number of witnesses is reduced from 2 to 1 (subs. (3)).
(c) The articles are valued by the officer (or a specialist valuator). This reflects previous practice—the two valuators required by the Debtors (Scotland) Act 1838 had become mere witnesses to the officer's valuation. Valuation of poinded goods has long been a controversial issue. Debtors feel their goods are undervalued while officers tend to err on the low side to avoid claims by creditors whose debts are reduced by the appraised value of unsold goods. The officer is now required to value at open market value at the time of poinding (subs. (5)). Loss due to subsequent deterioration through normal wear and tear or passage of time is borne by the creditor (see note on s.21(6)). It has to be recognised that even the open market value of second hand furniture is normally only a fraction of its price when new.
(d) The "offer back" in terms of which the officer at the end of the poinding offered the goods back to the debtor at their appraised values is replaced by an entitlement of the debtor to redeem all or any of the goods at their appraised values within 14 days of the execution of the poinding (subs. 6(d)).
(e) The officer along with the witness must sign the poinding schedule (subs. (6)(a)).

Poinding procedure—further provisions

21.—(1) The sheriff, on an application by the creditor, the officer of court or the debtor intimated in accordance with subsection (2) below, may at any time after the execution of a poinding make an order—
(a) for the security of any of the poinded articles; or
(b) in relation to any of the articles which are of a perishable nature or which are likely to deteriorate substantially and rapidly in condition or value, for their immediate disposal and, in the event of their disposal by sale, for payment of the proceeds of sale to the creditor or for consignation of the proceeds in court until the diligence is completed or otherwise ceases to have effect,
and a decision of the sheriff under paragraph (b) above for the immediate disposal of articles shall not be subject to appeal.
(2) An application for an order under subsection (1)(b) above—
(a) by the creditor or the officer of court, shall be intimated by him to the debtor;
(b) by the debtor, shall be intimated to the creditor or the officer of court,
at the time when it is made.
(3) It shall not be competent for an officer of court in executing a poinding to examine a person on oath as to the ownership of any article.
(4) Subject to subsection (1)(b) above, the debtor shall be entitled, within 14 days after the date of execution of the poinding, to redeem any poinded article at the value fixed under section 20(4) of this Act; and the officer of court shall mention any such redemption in his report under section 22 of this Act or, if he has already made that report, shall report the redemption as soon as is reasonably practicable to the sheriff.
(5) The officer of court shall, on receiving payment from the debtor for the redemption under subsection (4) above of a poinded article, grant a

receipt in the form prescribed by Act of Sederunt to the debtor; and the receipt shall operate as a release of the article from the poinding.

(6) Subject to section 29(2)(b) of this Act, the revaluation in the same poinding of an article which has been valued under section 20(4) of this Act shall not be competent.

(7) A poinding shall be deemed to have been executed on the date when the poinding schedule has been delivered, or left on the premises, in pursuance of section 20(6)(b) of this Act.

(8) Subject to subsection (9) below, at any time before the execution of a poinding on behalf of a creditor, an officer of court shall, if requested to do so by any other creditor who has delivered to him a warrant to poind, conjoin that creditor in the poinding.

(9) It shall not be competent for an officer of court to conjoin a creditor in a poinding in respect of a debt for which the creditor holds a summary warrant.

DEFINITIONS
   "officer of court": s.106.
   "poinding schedule": ss.20(5) and 45.

GENERAL NOTE
Subss. (1), (2)
   These subsections restate the previous law with some amendments. The type of articles which can be sold immediately is widened. As well as perishables (fish for example) articles which retain their structure but deteriorate in value rapidly such as Christmas cards or computer software may be sold immediately. Either the debtor or creditor may apply. Officers of court are mentioned here (and elsewhere in the Act) in order to give them standing to make applications on behalf of their instructing creditors. It is not intended that officers should have an independent right to apply. Because of the need for finality the sheriff's decision is not appealable.

Subs. (3)
   This subsection abolishes the common law requirement for an officer to examine on oath a person present at the poinding who claimed to own the goods proposed to be poinded. See also the note on s.19.

Subs. (4)
   The entitlement to redeem replaces the "offer back" (see note on s.20). Redemption will be more useful since debtors rarely had money available when the poinding took place to repurchase their goods at the "offer back," but now they have 14 days in which to act and find the money. Redemption will also serve as a check to undervaluation. It is suggested that goods redeemed cannot be repoinded by the same creditor for the same debt in line with a similar rule in relation to the "offer back" (*Fiddes* v. *Fyfe* (1791) Bell's Octavo Cases 355).
   The officer is required to report any such redemption to the sheriff either in the report of poinding, or if the report has already been lodged, then in a separate document as soon as reasonably practicable.

Subs. (6)
   Unless the articles have been damaged or destroyed (in which case the sheriff may authorise a revaluation under s.29(2)(b)) revaluation is incompetent. The risk of deterioration by normal wear and tear or the passage of time is therefore borne by the creditor. This is reasonable since the interval between poinding and sale is usually at the discretion of the creditor. However the creditor could be seriously prejudiced if the interval is lengthened by a time to pay order. A creditor who anticipates a considerable loss of value of the poinded articles over the period of a time to pay order should request the sheriff to recall the poinding. If default occurs later the articles may be repoinded and valued at that date.

Subs. (7)
   This subsection settles a centuries old controversy. It applies not only for the purposes of the Act but also for the purposes of equalisation or striking down of diligences under the Bankruptcy (Scotland) Act 1985.

Subss. (8), (9)

These subsections restate the previous law (Debtors (Scotland) Act 1838, s.23). Conjoining is mainly of use where two or more creditors instruct the same officer or firm of officers to execute a poinding. If there are insufficient poindable goods available to satisfy all the debts, the creditors rank rateably on the proceeds of sale of what goods there are. The need for a creditor to deliver to the officer a warrant to poind means the creditor must have served a charge which has expired without payment.

Ordinary poindings cannot be conjoined with summary warrant poindings because of the many differences in procedure.

Report of execution of poinding

22.—(1) The officer of court shall, within a period of 14 days after the date of execution of the poinding (or such longer period as the sheriff on cause shown may allow on an application by the officer of court) make to the sheriff in the form prescribed by Act of Sederunt a report of the execution of the poinding which shall be signed by the officer of court and the witness who attended the poinding.

(2) The officer of court shall note in the report under subsection (1) above any assertion made before the submission of the report that any poinded article does not belong to the debtor.

(3) The sheriff may refuse to receive a report on the ground that it has not been made and signed in accordance with subsection (1) above, and if the sheriff refuses to receive a report on that ground the poinding shall cease to have effect.

(4) The sheriff clerk shall intimate a refusal under subsection (3) above—

    (a) to the debtor; and

    (b) if he is a different person from the debtor, to the person in possession of the poinded articles.

(5) Any rule of law whereby the sheriff may refuse to receive a report of the execution of a poinding on a ground other than one specified in subsection (3) above shall cease to have effect.

DEFINITION

"officer of court": s.106.

GENERAL NOTE

This section regulates the report of the execution of the poinding (report of poinding for short) which the officer has to make to the sheriff. The report to the court enables the sheriff to supervise the diligence and provides a formal record of what was poinded and what the officer did for the purposes of further procedure such as applying for a warrant of sale.

Subs. (1)

The normal period for lodging the report is extended from the eight days allowed under the Debtors (Scotland) Act 1838 s.25 to 14 days. The form of report is to be prescribed as uniformity will help the sheriff court staff to check that reports are in order.

Subs. (2)

Breach of the duty to report an assertion may lead to disciplinary action against the officer. It may also make the poinding invalid, but this point is not clear. Failure to record an assertion may seriously prejudice a third party owner (see note on s.19(3)).

Subs. (3), (5)

Previously a report which revealed a fundamental defect in the way the poinding was executed was not received with the result that the poinding terminated. Now the sheriff can refuse to receive a report only because it is not signed or not submitted in time without good cause. Presumably the sheriff would allow the officer an opportunity to remedy the lack of signature before refusing to receive a report. Where the defect was incurable (the witness was dead, for example) the report could still be accepted since the sheriff has a power rather than a duty to refuse to receive a report. Fundamental defects in the execution of a poinding are now dealt with under s.24(1).

Release of poinded article on ground of undue harshness

23.—(1) The sheriff may, on an application made within 14 days after the date of execution of a poinding by the debtor or any person in possession of a poinded article, make an order releasing an article from the poinding if it appears to the sheriff that its continued inclusion in the poinding or its sale under warrant of sale would be unduly harsh in the circumstances.

(2) Where the sheriff has made an order under subsection (1) above he may, notwithstanding section 25 of this Act, on an application by the creditor or by an officer of court on his behalf, authorise the poinding of other articles belonging to the debtor on the same premises.

DEFINITIONS
  "officer of court": s.106.
  "warrant of sale": ss.30, 106.

GENERAL NOTE
  This section introduces a new protection for debtors. The sheriff may release articles from the poinding on the ground of harshness but may couple release with an order authorising a further poinding in the same premises. The availability of other goods which could be so poinded might be a factor in deciding whether to release.
  Articles of sentimental value such as a wedding or engagement ring, or a family photograph album could be released under this section and the sheriff is likely to order release whether or not other non-exempt goods are available to restore the value of the poinding. The power could also be used for high value articles which were essential to the debtor and which had been poinded although other non-exempt articles had been available. A farmer's tractor (the Diligence Act 1503 prohibiting poinding of ploughs during the ploughing season is repealed by Sched. 8) or a joiner's power saw (if over £500-tools of trade exemption, see s.16(1)(b)) are possible examples of articles that might be released on condition that other poindable articles were available.

Invalidity, cessation and recall of poinding

24.—(1) If, at any time before the sale of the poinded articles, the sheriff is satisfied that the poinding is invalid or has ceased to have effect he shall, on his own initiative or on an application by the debtor, make an order declaring that to be the case, and may make such consequential order as appears to him to be necessary in the circumstances.

(2) Without prejudice to section 16(4) of this Act, it shall not be competent for the sheriff to make an order under subsection (1) above on the ground that any poinded article is exempt from poinding under that section.

(3) At any time before an application is made under section 30 of this Act for a warrant of sale, the sheriff may, on an application by the debtor, recall a poinding on any of the following grounds—

  (a) that it would be unduly harsh in the circumstances for a warrant of sale of the poinded articles to be granted;

  (b) that the aggregate of the values of the poinded articles fixed under section 20(4) of this Act was substantially below the aggregate of the prices which they would have been likely to fetch if sold on the open market; or

  (c) that the likely aggregate proceeds of sale of the poinded articles would not exceed the expenses likely to be incurred in the application for warrant of sale and in any steps required to be taken under this Part of this Act in execution of such a warrant, on the assumption that that application and such steps are unopposed.

(4) The sheriff shall not grant an application on the ground mentioned in subsection (3)(c) above if an order for further poinding of articles belonging to the debtor has been authorised under section 23(2), 28(6) or 29(2), or has become competent by reason of section 9(12), 28(2), 40(5) or 41(6), of this Act.

(5) The sheriff shall not make an order under subsection (1) above, recall a poinding or refuse an application under this section without first giving the debtor and the creditor—
(a) an opportunity to make representations; and
(b) if either party wishes to be heard, an opportunity to be heard.
(6) The sheriff clerk shall intimate to the debtor any order made under subsection (1) above by the sheriff on his own initiative.

DEFINITION
"warrant of sale": ss.30, 106.

GENERAL NOTE
Subss. (1), (2), (5), (6)
These subsections enable the sheriff to deal with any fundamental irregularity in the poinding. For example the days of charge might not have expired before the poinding was executed, the officer might have entered an empty dwellinghouse without giving notice or obtaining authorisation as required by s.18, or a poinding on a Court of Session decree might have been executed by an officer who was not a messenger-at-arms. An initially valid poinding may cease to have effect, by payment of the debt and expenses, or by not being timeously extended under s.27 for example.

A poinding is not void simply because it contains articles which are exempt from poinding. If the debtor fails to apply for exemption within the 14 days period set out in s.16(4) the inclusion of the articles cannot be challenged later by means of an application under s.24(1).

Sheriffs may declare poindings to be void on their own initiative or on application by the debtor. In both cases the sheriff must give the creditor and debtor an opportunity to make representations, at a hearing if necessary.

Subs. (3)
This subsection provides for a poinding to be recalled on application by the debtor before the creditor applies for a warrant of sale. It enables debtors to take the initiative to free themselves from the threat of diligence.

Para. (a)
This is a new ground. The undue harshness must be due to the personal circumstances of the debtor (seriously ill in hospital for example) since undue harshness arising out of the particular nature of the goods is covered by s.23. It is envisaged that the power to recall on this ground will be used very sparingly because diligence by its very nature is harsh.

Para. (b)
This restates an existing ground for terminating the diligence (*Scottish Gas Board* v. *Johnstone* 1974 S.L.T. (Sh. Ct.) 65). Not valuing the articles properly, for example lumped together instead of separately (*Le Conte* v. *Douglas* (1880) 8R. 175), is a ground for invalidating the poinding under subs. (1).

Para. (c)
This restates the criterion for refusing warrant of sale introduced by *S.S.E.B.* v. *Carlyle* 1980 S.L.T. (Sh. Ct.) 98. A sale should be carried out only where it is going to produce a pecuniary benefit to the creditor. Creditors are not entitled to carry out a fruitless sale against one debtor in order to frighten other debtors into paying. The likely aggregate proceeds will in the vast majority of cases simply be taken as the value placed on the goods by the officer (or specialist valuator) in executing the poinding since there is not likely to be any other evidence as to value before the court. The likely expenses of sale are calculated according to the officer's fees and the provisions of Sched. 1.

Subs. (4)
Where a further poinding for the same debt is possible the sheriff is prevented from recalling an existing poinding on the grounds that a sale of the poinded goods would not be

worth it since the creditor may wish to conjoin the further poinding (s.43). For example suppose there was one poinding with goods to the value of £100 and a second poinding with goods to the value of £75. Neither poinding separately would be worth it if the expenses of sale were £110, but if the poindings were conjoined into a single poinding of £175 a sale would then be likely to produce £65.

Second poinding in same premises

25. Subject to sections 9(12), 23(2), 28(2) and (6), 29(2), 40(5) and 41(6) of this Act, where articles are poinded in any premises (whether or not the poinding is valid), another poinding in those premises to enforce the same debt shall not be competent except in relation to articles which have been brought on to the premises since the execution of the first poinding.

GENERAL NOTE
The validity of second poindings was previously regulated by Practice Notes of the sheriffs principal in four of the six sheriffdoms. This section restates the position but provides for exceptions to the general rule. The exemptions generally relate to circumstances where the value of the poinding has been reduced by partial recall or damage, or where the poinding was recalled on granting a time to pay order and the right to diligence revives on subsequent default by the debtor.

Sist of proceedings in poinding of mobile homes

26.—(1) Where a caravan, houseboat or other moveable structure which is the only or principal residence of the debtor or another person has been poinded the sheriff, on an application by the debtor or that other person made at any time after the execution of the poinding and before the granting of a warrant of sale, may order that for such period as he shall specify no further steps shall be taken in the poinding.

(2) In calculating under section 27(1) or (2) of this Act the period during which a poinding in respect of which an order has been made under subsection (1) above shall remain effective, there shall be disregarded the period specified in the order.

DEFINITION
"warrant of sale": ss.30, 106.

GENERAL NOTE
A caravan, etc., which is not so attached to the ground as to be heritable is moveable and therefore capable of being poinded. This could result in debtors losing their homes within a week or so, whereas the sale of a heritable dwelling under an adjudication requires a period of ten years (the legal) to expire. To give the debtor time to find alternative accommodation, to pay the debt by instalments, or to offer other goods for poinding the sheriff may sist or freeze the diligence for an appropriate period. An application for a sist must be made before warrant of sale is granted. On expiry of the period of the sist an application may be made for an extension, since if a statutory power is given it may be exercised on one or more occasions.
The reference to another person is to cater for the situation where the mobile home is tenanted and is poinded for a debt of the landlord.

Duration of poinding

27.—(1) Subject to subsections (2), (3) and (5)(a) below, a poinding shall cease to have effect on the expiry of a period of one year after the date of execution of the poinding, unless before such expiry an application has been made under section 30(1) of this Act for a warrant of sale in relation to the poinded articles.

(2) The sheriff, on an application by the creditor or by an officer of court on his behalf made before the expiry of the period mentioned in

subsection (1) above and before an application has been made under section 30(1) of this Act, may extend that period—

    (a) where he considers that, if the said period is extended, the debtor is likely to comply with an agreement between the creditor and the debtor for the payment of the sum recoverable by instalments or otherwise; or

    (b) to enable further proceedings to be taken in the diligence where the termination of the poinding would prejudice the creditor and the creditor cannot be held responsible for the circumstances giving rise to the need for the extension,

for such further period as he considers reasonable in the circumstances.

(3) The sheriff may grant further extensions under subsection (2) above, on application being made to him before the expiry of the previously extended period.

(4) The decision of the sheriff under subsection (2) above shall not be subject to appeal, and shall be intimated to the debtor by the sheriff clerk.

(5) Where, within the period mentioned in subsection (1) above or within that period as extended under subsection (2) above, an application is made—

    (a) under subsection (2) above—

        (i) if the application is made on the ground referred to in paragraph (a) of that subsection, the poinding shall, if the date of disposal of the application is later than 14 days before the poinding is due to expire, continue to have effect until 14 days after that disposal;

        (ii) in any other case, the poinding shall continue to have effect until the disposal of the application;

    (b) under section 30 of this Act for a warrant of sale, the poinding shall, if the sheriff refuses to grant a warrant of sale, continue to have effect—

        (i) until the period for leave to appeal has expired without an application for leave having been made;

        (ii) where an application for leave to appeal is made, until leave has been refused or the application has been abandoned;

        (iii) where leave to appeal has been granted, until the period for an appeal has expired without an appeal being made; or

        (iv) where an appeal against the decision is made, until the matter has been finally determined or the appeal has been abandoned; or

    (c) under section 30 of this Act for a warrant of sale, the poinding shall, if the sheriff grants a warrant of sale, continue to have effect—

        (i) if the articles are sold, or ownership passes to the creditor under section 37(6) of this Act, until the date of such sale or such ownership passing; or

        (ii) if the articles are not sold, or ownership does not pass to the creditor, until the expiry of the period specified for the warrant sale in the warrant of sale.

(6) Without prejudice to subsection (7) below, if a report has been made to the sheriff under section 36(2) of this Act, the poinding shall continue to have effect for a period of 6 months after the date when the latest such report was made.

(7) Where, within the period specified for the warrant sale in the warrant of sale, or within the period mentioned in subsection (6) above, an application is made under section 35 of this Act for a variation of the warrant of sale, the poinding shall cease to have effect—

    (a) if the sheriff refuses to grant a variation—

(i) when the period for leave to appeal has expired without an application for leave having been made;

(ii) where an application for leave to appeal is made, when leave has been refused or the application has been abandoned;

(iii) where leave to appeal has been granted, when the period for an appeal has expired without an appeal being made; or

(iv) where an appeal against the decision is made, when the matter has been finally determined in favour of the sheriff's decision or the appeal has been abandoned,

or on such later date as the sheriff may direct;

(b) if the sheriff grants a variation—

(i) where the articles are sold, or ownership passes to the creditor under section 37(6) of this Act in the period specified for the warrant sale in the warrant of sale as so varied, on the date of the warrant sale or of ownership so passing;

(ii) where the articles are not sold and ownership does not pass to the creditor within that period, on the expiry of that period.

DEFINITIONS
"officer of court": s.106.
"sum recoverable": s.45.
"warrant of sale": ss.30, 106.

GENERAL NOTE
Subs. (1)
A poinding lasts for one year unless extended by order of the sheriff or unless a warrant of sale is applied for. In the latter case the duration of the poinding is governed by subs. (5)(b) and (c). The period of one year does not include any time during which an interim order in a time to pay application (s.8(3)), a time to pay order (s.9(9)), or a sist of poinding (s.26) is in effect.

Subss. (2), (3)
The sheriff may, on application, extend the poinding in order for the creditor to allow the debtor time to pay while retaining the security afforded by the poinding and the threat of warrant sale on default. The application has to be made by or on behalf of the creditor and an officer of court has a right of audience on behalf of the creditor. Before an application is made there must be an antecedent agreement between debtor and creditor about time to pay. In the absence of agreement the debtor may apply for a time to pay order under s.5.

Para. (b) is a long-stop provision designed to ensure that an "innocent" creditor is not penalised by an unforeseen train of events.

Further extensions are competent on the same ground. An application for an extension must be made while the poinding is still in existence. A poinding which lapses by passage of time cannot be revived.

Subs. (5)
Para. (a)
This para. extends the duration of the poinding until the determination of an application for extension. Its purpose is to prevent a poinding from lapsing while an application is pending. If the application is granted the poinding is extended accordingly; if the application is refused the poinding continues until the expiry of the unextended period or ceases to have effect if that period expired pending the determination of the application. Fourteen days allows time for the creditor to apply for a warrant of sale.

Para. (b)
Where a warrant of sale is refused the poinding remains in existence for at least a certain period to allow the creditor time to lodge an application for leave to appeal against the sheriff's refusal. The period will be specified in rules of court as it is not set out in the Act.

Para. (c)
This paragraph deals with the case where warrant of sale is granted. The poinding then lasts until the goods are exposed for sale within the period specified in the warrant or until the expiry of that period if no exposure for sale has occurred.

Subs. (6)

After a warrant of sale has been granted the creditor and debtor may agree that the debtor should be allowed time to pay. The effect of making a report under s.36(2) to the court on such an agreement is to extend by six months the period specified in the warrant of sale within which a sale must be held.

Removal, damage or destruction of poinded articles

Removal of poinded articles

28.—(1) The debtor or the person in possession of poinded articles may move them to another location if—

    (a) the creditor or an officer of court on behalf of the creditor has consented in writing to their removal; or

    (b) the sheriff, on an application by the debtor or the person in possession, has authorised their removal.

(2) Where poinded articles have been removed under subsection (1) above, an officer of court may, under the same warrant to poind, again poind any of the articles so removed and, notwithstanding section 25 of this Act, any articles which were not so removed, whether or not they were previously poinded; and, on the execution of any such further poinding, the original poinding shall be deemed to have been abandoned.

(3) The removal, except in accordance with this Part of this Act, from any premises of poinded articles by—

    (a) the debtor; or

    (b) any person, other than the creditor or an officer of court, who knows that the articles have been poinded,

shall be a breach of the poinding and may be dealt with as a contempt of court.

(4) Where articles have been removed from premises otherwise than in accordance with this Part of this Act, the sheriff, on an application by the creditor—

    (a) may, subject to subsection (5) below, make an order requiring the person in possession of the articles to restore them to the premises from which they were removed within a period specified in the order; and

    (b) if an order under paragraph (a) above is not complied with, and it appears to the sheriff that the articles are likely to be found in premises specified in the application, may grant a warrant to officers of court—

        (i) to search for the articles in those premises; and

        (ii) to restore the articles to the premises from which they were removed or to make such other arrangements for their security as the sheriff may direct,

and such a warrant shall be authority to open shut and lockfast places for the purpose of its execution.

(5) Where it appears to the sheriff, on an application made to him by any person having an interest, that any article which has been removed from premises otherwise than in accordance with this Part of this Act has been acquired for value and without knowledge of the poinding, he shall—

    (a) refuse an order under subsection (4)(a) above relating to that article;

    (b) recall any such order which he has already made; and

    (c) make an order releasing the article from the poinding.

(6) Where articles have been removed from premises otherwise than in accordance with this Part of this Act in circumstances in which the debtor is at fault the sheriff, on an application by the creditor or by an officer of court on his behalf, may, notwithstanding section 25 of this Act, authorise the poinding of other articles belonging to the debtor in the same premises.

(7) The removal of poinded articles to another location shall not have the effect of releasing the articles from the poinding.

DEFINITION
  "officer of court": s.106.

GENERAL NOTE
Subss. (1), (3)
  On being poinded the articles are deemed to be in the hands of the court and wilful unauthorised removal constitutes a breach of poinding which is punishable as a contempt of court. Previously creditors often allowed debtors to remove the poinded goods to another location, although strictly speaking an application should have been presented to the sheriff for authorisation. This useful but informal procedure is given statutory recognition in subs. (1)(a). If the creditor will not agree to the removal, the debtor can apply to the sheriff under subs. (1)(b) for authority.

Subss. (2), (7)
  Where articles have been removed the creditor has a choice, either to do nothing and rely on the fact that they remain poinded by virtue of subs. (7), or to repoind them in their new location. Where the goods remain within the sheriff court district it would usually be sensible not to repoind. Practical difficulties arise if the goods are removed to a different sheriff court district and in this case repoinding is preferable. In the case of partial removal the creditor may repoind the removed articles in their new location and repoind the other articles in their original location. The danger of thus splitting the poinding into two is that each poinding may then fail to pass the "not worth it" test (s.24(3)(c)), although they can be conjoined (s.43) if in the same sheriffdom. On the execution of a repoinding of all or part of the poinded articles the original poinding automatically ceases to have effect.
  The debtor is liable for the expenses of the new poinding(s) but ceases to be liable for those of the original poinding, unless the creditor in consenting to, or the sheriff authorising, removal has made it a condition that the debtor remains liable (Sched. 1, paras. 5 and 6). Creditors are very likely to impose such a condition.

Subs. (4)
  This subsection makes new provision for unauthorised removal of poinded goods in place of s.30 of the Debtors (Scotland) Act 1838 (repealed by Sched. 8) which rendered an unauthorised remover liable to imprisonment unless the goods were restored or double the appraised value paid to the creditor.
  Now the primary remedy is restoration of the poinded goods. If the goods are not restored officers of court can be authorised to search for them and restore them by force if necessary. It is not clear whether the sheriff can grant a search warrant under subs. (4)(b) at the same time as granting an order for restoration under subs. (4)(a), or whether the creditor must wait for the restoration order not to be complied with before applying for a search warrant. The former would be the more sensible practice.
  The search warrant covers only premises specified in the application and hence the warrant. Officers of court have no general licence to search wherever they think fit.

Subs. (5)
  In order to protect a good faith purchaser from having to restore poinded articles, no order of restoration can be made and any such order made must, on application, be recalled.

Subs. (6)
  Where restoration is impossible (for example because the goods have been sold to a good faith purchaser or they cannot be found) a further poinding may be authorised to restore the value of the creditor's security. In most cases this remedy will be worthless since few debtors have sufficient poindable goods to leave enough for a further poinding.
  A further poinding is competent only where the removal is due to some fault of the debtor. For example, the debtor would be at fault if he or she connived at the removal but would not be at fault if the goods were stolen.

Unlawful acts relating to poinded articles

  29.—(1) The wilful damage or destruction of poinded articles by—
      (a) the debtor; or

    (b) any person, other than the creditor or an officer of court, who knows that the articles have been poinded,
shall be a breach of the poinding and may be dealt with as a contempt of court.

(2) Where poinded articles have been damaged or destroyed the sheriff, on an application by the creditor or by the officer of court on his behalf, may—

    (a) where the debtor has been at fault, authorise the poinding of other articles belonging to the debtor in the premises in which the original poinding took place; and

    (b) in any case, authorise the revaluation of any damaged article in accordance with section 20(4) of this Act.

(3) Where a third party, knowing that an article has been poinded—

    (a) wilfully damages or destroys it; or

    (b) removes it from premises in breach of a poinding, and—

        (i) it is damaged, destroyed, lost or stolen; or

        (ii) it is acquired from or through him by another person without knowledge of the poinding and for value,

the sheriff may order the third party to consign the sum mentioned in subsection (4) below in court until the completion of the sale or until the poinding otherwise ceases to have effect.

(4) The sum to be consigned in court under subsection (3) above shall be—

    (a) where the article has been damaged but not so damaged as to make it worthless, a sum equal to the difference between the value of the article fixed under section 20(4) of this Act and the value of the article as so damaged;

    (b) in any other case, a sum equal to the value fixed under that section.

(5) Any sum consigned in court under subsection (3) above shall, on the completion of the sale or on the poinding otherwise ceasing to have effect, be paid to the creditor to the extent necessary to meet the sum recoverable, any surplus thereof being paid to the debtor.

DEFINITIONS
    "officer of court": s.106.
    "sum recoverable": s.45.

GENERAL NOTE
    This section deals with damage or destruction of poinded goods as opposed to their removal.
    First (subs. (1)), wilful damage or destruction is punishable as a contempt of court. Secondly (subs. (2)), the sheriff may authorise a further poinding to restore the value of the creditor's security and/or order a revaluation so that the debtor does not remain credited with the original appraised value. Thirdly (subss. (3) and (4)), if the person who wilfully damaged or destroyed the articles can be traced the sheriff can order that person to consign the difference between the original appraised values and the value (if any) of the articles in their present state. The consigned sum is treated as proceeds of sale (subs. (5)).

Warrant sales

Application for warrant of sale

30.—(1) A creditor shall not be entitled to sell articles poinded by him unless, on an application by him or by an officer of court on his behalf, the sheriff has granted a warrant under this section (referred to in this Act as a "warrant of sale").

(2) The sheriff may refuse to grant a warrant of sale—

    (a) on his own initiative or on an objection by the debtor—

        (i) on the ground that the poinding is invalid or has ceased to have effect;

(ii) on a ground mentioned in section 24(3)(b) or (c) of this Act;
(b) on an objection by the debtor, on the ground that the granting of the application would be unduly harsh in the circumstances.

(3) The creditor or officer of court, when making an application under subsection (1) above, shall serve a copy thereof on the debtor together with a notice in the form prescribed by Act of Sederunt informing him—
(a) that he may object to the application within 14 days after the date when it was made; and
(b) of his right to redeem poinded articles under section 33(2) of this Act.

(4) The sheriff shall not—
(a) refuse to grant a warrant of sale on his own initiative; or
(b) dispose of an application under subsection (1) above where the debtor has objected thereto in accordance with subsection (3)(a) above,
without first giving the parties an opportunity to be heard.

(5) It shall not be competent for the sheriff to refuse to grant a warrant of sale on the ground that any poinded article is exempt from poinding under section 16 of this Act.

(6) Where the sheriff refuses to grant a warrant of sale, the sheriff clerk shall intimate that refusal to the debtor and, if he is a different person from the debtor, to the person in possession of the poinded articles.

(7) A sale under a warrant of sale shall be known as a "warrant sale".

DEFINITIONS
"officer of court": s.106.
"warrant of sale": s.30(1).

GENERAL NOTE
Subss. (1), (3)
As under the previous law a warrant of sale is required before the creditor is authorised to sell goods poinded by virtue of a decree or other similar document. For summary warrants see s.74 and Scheds. 4 and 5.

The application for a warrant to sell however now becomes one which is intimated to the debtor and which he or she thus has an opportunity to object to. A period of 14 days is allowed for objections.

The debtor also has a further opportunity to redeem some or all of the poinded goods at their appraised values within seven days from the date of intimation of the application (s.33(2)).

Subs. (2)
This subsection sets out the grounds of objection. They are the same as for recall (see note on s.24). A danger must exist that a debtor will redeem so many of the poinded goods that the sale of the rest will not meet the expenses of selling them with the result that warrant of sale will be refused. In remote areas the cost of transporting household goods to an auction room will be prohibitive. If household poindings are to retain their effectiveness creditors will have to find (or be provided with) nearby premises from which the goods can be sold (see s.32(3)).

Subs. (5)
A poinding is not invalid because it contains exempt goods which should not have been poinded. The debtor's remedy is to apply for their exclusion under s.16(4) within 14 days of the execution of the poinding.

Subs. (6)
Intimation of refusal of warrant of sale informs the debtor that the goods are no longer poinded. Previously debtors were often left in the dark.

Provisions of warrant of sale

31.—(1) Every warrant of sale shall provide that the warrant sale shall be by public auction and shall specify the location of the sale in accordance with section 32 of this Act.

(2) A warrant of sale shall—

    (a) appoint an officer of court to make arrangements for the warrant sale in accordance with the warrant;

    (b) specify a period within which the warrant sale shall take place; and

    (c) empower the officer of court to open shut and lockfast places for the purpose of executing the warrant.

(3) Where the warrant of sale provides for the sale to be held in premises other than an auction room, it shall appoint to conduct the warrant sale—

    (a) if the aggregate of the values of the poinded articles fixed under section 20(4) of this Act exceeds £1,000 or such other sum as may be prescribed by Act of Sederunt and a person who carries on business as an auctioneer is available, that person;

    (b) in any other case, the officer of court appointed under subsection (2) above or another suitable person.

(4) A warrant of sale which provides for the warrant sale to be held in premises other than where the poinded articles are situated shall also empower the officer of court appointed by the warrant to remove the poinded articles to such premises for the sale.

DEFINITIONS
    "officer of court": s.106.
    "warrant of sale": ss.30, 106.

GENERAL NOTE
    The warrant of sale specifies the arrangements for sale. First, as under the previous law, the sale must be by public auction. A private sale (which might be advantageous) requires the creditor to abandon the poinding. Secondly, an officer is appointed to arrange the sale and supervise it. Where the goods are valued at not more than £1,000 this officer may also act as auctioneer; otherwise a person who carries on business as an auctioneer must, if possible, be appointed. The auctioneer should not be an employee of the officer (*Cantors* v. *Hardie*, 1974 S.L.T.(Sh.Ct.) 26). Thirdly, the warrant specifies a period within which the sale has to be held. This is different from the previous law where the date and time of sale were inserted in the warrant. Flexibility is desirable where goods are to be sold in auction rooms.

Location of sale

32.—(1) The warrant of sale shall not provide for the warrant sale to be held in a dwellinghouse except with the consent in writing, in a form to be prescribed by Act of Sederunt, of the occupier thereof and, if he is not the occupier, of the debtor.

(2) Subject to subsection (3) below, where articles are poinded in a dwellinghouse and any consent required under subsection (1) above is not given, the warrant of sale shall provide for the warrant sale to be held in an auction room specified in the warrant.

(3) Where—

    (a) articles are poinded in a dwellinghouse and any consent required under subsection (1) above is not given; and

    (b) it appears to the sheriff that, if the sale were to be held in an auction room, the likely proceeds of the warrant sale would not exceed the expenses of the application for warrant of sale and the expenses likely to be incurred in any steps required to be taken under this Part of this Act in the execution of the

　　　　　warrant on the assumption that that application and any such
　　　　　steps are unopposed,
if the creditor is able to offer suitable premises in which the warrant sale
could be held, the warrant of sale shall, subject to subsection (1) above
and subsections (4) and (5) below, provide for the sale to be held in those
premises, but otherwise the sheriff shall refuse to grant a warrant of sale.

　　(4) Subject to subsection (5) below, the warrant of sale shall not provide
for the sale to be held in premises (other than a dwellinghouse or an
auction room) which are occupied by a person other than the debtor or
the creditor except with the consent in writing, in a form to be prescribed
by Act of Sederunt, of the occupier thereof.

　　(5) Where the occupier of premises (other than a dwellinghouse or an
auction room) where poinded articles are situated does not give his
consent under subsection (4) above to the holding of the warrant sale in
those premises, the warrant of sale may, if the sheriff considers that it
would be unduly costly to require the removal of the poinded articles to
other premises for sale, nevertheless provide that the warrant sale shall
be held in the premises where they are situated.

　　(6) In this section "occupier", in relation to premises where there are
2 or more occupiers, means each of them.

DEFINITIONS
　"dwellinghouse": s.45.
　"occupier": s.32(6).
　"warrant of sale": ss.30, 106.

GENERAL NOTE
Subss. (1)–(3)
　　Under the previous law the debtor's consent was not required to a sale in his or her
dwellinghouse and most sales of goods poinded in dwellinghouses were conducted there.
Such sales were widely regarded as humiliating for debtors, because of the invasion of
domestic privacy and the public advertisement of the sale which necessarily mentioned the
debtor's name and address.
　　Now, unless the debtor consents in writing, goods poinded in a dwellinghouse must be
removed to other premises for sale. Furthermore, where the debtor is not the sole occupier
of the dwellinghouse the consent of all the other occupiers must be obtained. Thus where
a couple own or rent their home in common the debtor's spouse will also be required to
consent and it may be that a spouse who is not a co-owner or co-tenant also counts as an
occupier by virtue of his or her occupancy rights under the Matrimonial Homes (Family
Protection) (Scotland) Act 1981. The effect of these requirements will probably be to make
domestic sales a relic of the past.
　　If the debtor and/or the occupier refuses to consent, the goods have to be removed to an
auction room. Where the cost of removal is such that the likely expenses of sale exceed the
likely proceeds of sale, other nearer premises have to be available otherwise warrant of sale
will be refused. There is a danger that in remote areas warrant sales cannot be held and so
poinding will become useless as a method of enforcement against debtors living in such
areas. Debtors cannot object to their non-domestic premises (such as a shop or an office)
being used as a place of sale.

Subss. (4), (5)
　　The subsections deal with the holding of warrant sales in premises (other than a
dwellinghouse or an auction room) occupied by a person other than the creditor or debtor.
Dwellinghouses are dealt with by subss. (1)–(3) above. It is unnecessary to regulate use of
auction rooms since proprietors have the choice of accepting or refusing goods.
　　A third party's premises may be involved in two ways. First, the goods may have been
poinded there (a car in a neighbour's garage, for example) and it is desired to sell them
there. Second, it may be desired to remove goods to the third party's premises for sale. In
the first case the third party occupier may refuse consent to the goods being sold there. This
is an innovation. Under the previous law the occupier of premises in which the goods were
poinded had no right to object (*McNaught and Co.* v. *Lewis* (1935) 51 Sh.Ct.Rep. 138). The
third party's refusal can be overridden by the sheriff (under subs. (6) if removal would be

unduly costly (heavy machinery for example)). In the second case, the third party occupier must consent and his or her lack of consent cannot be overridden by the court.

Release or redemption of poinded articles after warrant

33.—(1) Where a warrant sale is to be held in premises other than where the poinded articles are situated, the officer of court may, in pursuance of section 31(4) of this Act, remove to those premises only such poinded articles as, if sold at their values fixed under section 20(4) of this Act, would realise in total the sum recoverable at the time of the sale; and shall release the remaining poinded articles from the poinding.

(2) Subject to section 21(1) of this Act, the debtor may, within 7 days after the date when a copy of an application for warrant of sale has been served on him, redeem any poinded article by paying to the officer of court a sum equal to its value fixed under section 20(4) of this Act.

(3) The officer of court shall, on receiving payment from the debtor under subsection (2) above, grant a receipt in the form prescribed by Act of Sederunt to the debtor; and the receipt shall operate as a release of the article from the poinding.

(4) The creditor and the debtor may by agreement release articles from the poinding.

(5) Any release or redemption of poinded articles under this section—

    (a) shall be mentioned in the next subsequent application (if any) which is made for warrant of sale or for variation of warrant of sale; or

    (b) if it takes place after an application for warrant of sale (or variation thereof) has been made and before it has been disposed of, shall be reported as soon as is reasonably practicable by the officer of court to the sheriff; or

    (c) in any other case, shall be mentioned in any report of sale.

DEFINITIONS
    "officer of court": s.106.
    "report of sale": s.45.
    "sum recoverable": s.45.
    "warrant of sale": ss.30, 106

GENERAL NOTE
This section deals with release or redemption of goods from the poinding.

Subs. (1)
Under the previous law it was not clear whether officers were entitled to remove for sale only sufficient goods to meet the amount due and future expenses or whether their duty was to remove all the poinded goods. This subsection provides that the first course is to be followed.

Subss. (2), (3), (5)
On being served with a copy of the creditor's application for warrant of sale, the debtor has a new opportunity within seven days to redeem some or all of the goods at their appraised values. The exception relates to an application for the immediate sale of perishables under s.21(1). The officer accepting redemption must give a receipt and inform the court as soon as is reasonably practicable so that the sheriff considering the application for warrant of sale knows what goods remain in the poinding. This information may affect the decision whether or not to grant a warrant (see note on s.30(2)).

Subs. (4)
This section preserves the right of creditors and debtors to agree a release of articles from the poinding. Release can be done at any time although the debtor has only two statutory opportunities to redeem.

Intimation and publication of sale

34.—(1) The officer of court appointed under section 31(2)(a) of this Act to make arrangements for the warrant sale shall—

(a) as soon as is reasonably practicable intimate to the debtor and, if the person in possession of the poinded articles is not the debtor, to that person, the date arranged for the warrant sale; and

(b) not later than the date of intimation under paragraph (a) above, serve a copy of the warrant of sale on the debtor and any such person.

(2) Where the warrant sale is not to be held in the premises where the poinded articles are situated, the officer of court referred to in subsection (1) above shall, not less than 7 days before the date arranged for the removal of the poinded articles from those premises, intimate to the debtor and, if he is not the debtor, to the person in possession of the poinded articles—

(a) the place where the sale is to be held; and

(b) the date arranged for the removal.

(3) The sheriff clerk shall arrange for such particulars of the warrant of sale as are prescribed by Act of Sederunt to be displayed on the walls of court.

(4) The warrant sale shall be advertised by public notice and, where the sale is to be held otherwise than in an auction room, the public notice shall be as directed by the warrant of sale.

(5) Where the warrant sale is to be held in premises not belonging to the debtor, the public notice under subsection (4) above shall not name him or disclose that the articles for sale are poinded articles.

(6) Where the warrant sale is to be held in premises other than the debtor's premises or an auction room, any public notice of the sale shall state that the articles to be sold do not belong to the occupier of the premises where the sale is to be held.

DEFINITIONS
"officer of court": s.106.
"warrant of sale": ss.30, 106.

GENERAL NOTE
Subss. (1), (2)
These subsections lay upon the officer appointed to make arrangements for the sale a duty of intimating the warrant of sale and the arrangements that have been made. The copy of the warrant of sale may be served before intimation of the arrangements in order to introduce another step in the diligence and hence put further pressure on the debtor to pay. On the other hand it is competent to serve the copy warrant and intimate the arrangements simultaneously as soon as the arrangements have been made.

The debtor (or possessor) must have at least seven days' notice of removal of the goods for sale. There is no minimum period of notice of the impending sale where the goods are to be sold on the premises in which they are situated.

Subs. (3)
Since few public advertisements of sale will now mention the debtor's name and address, hire-purchase companies and other third party owners will not be alerted to a sale of their goods in this way. This subsection provides a less public way of informing such owners.

Subss. (4), (5), (6)
In the case of sales in an auction room no specific public notice is required, the auction room's general notice of sale suffices. Neither the names and addresses of debtors whose goods are to be sold there must be mentioned, nor the fact that the goods are poinded. The public advertisement of the sale was one of the most resented aspects of the previous practice.

Where the goods are to be sold in third party premises other than an auction room, the public notice required is specified in the warrant of sale. The notice must not name the debtor or disclose that the goods are poinded, but it must state that the goods are not those of the third party occupier. The notice may take the form of an advertisement in the local newspaper (if the paper will accept it), handbills, posters on the premises or perhaps simply the subs. (3) notice in the sheriff court.

Where the goods are to be sold on the debtor's premises the public notice has to name the debtor and give the place of sale so that intending purchasers go to the correct place. The notice may state that the sale is one of poinded goods.

Alteration of arrangements for sale

35.—(1) Where, for any reason for which neither the creditor nor the officer of court is responsible, the arrangements made for the warrant sale cannot be implemented in accordance with the provisions of the warrant of sale, the sheriff may, on an application by the creditor or by the officer of court on his behalf, grant a variation of the warrant of sale.

(2) Subject to subsection (3) below, the sheriff may, on his own initiative or on an objection by the debtor, refuse to grant an application under subsection (1) above on the ground that—

(a) the poinding is invalid or has ceased to have effect; or

(b) the proposed variation is unsuitable.

(3) It shall not be competent for the sheriff to refuse to grant an application under subsection (1) above on the ground that any poinded article is exempt from poinding under section 16 of this Act.

(4) Section 32 of this Act shall apply to a warrant of sale as varied under this section.

(5) A creditor or officer of court who makes an application under subsection (1) above shall at the same time—

(a) serve on the debtor a copy thereof together with a notice in the form prescribed by Act of Sederunt, informing him that he may object to the application within 7 days after the date of such service; and

(b) serve on any other person in possession of the poinded articles a copy of the application.

(6) The sheriff shall not—

(a) refuse to grant a variation under subsection (1) above on his own initiative; or

(b) dispose of an application under that subsection where the debtor has objected thereto in accordance with subsection (5) above,

without first giving the parties an opportunity to be heard.

(7) On granting a variation under subsection (1) above, the sheriff may make such consequential orders as he thinks fit including, where appropriate—

(a) an order requiring service on the debtor, and on any other person in possession of the poinded articles, of the warrant of sale as varied;

(b) the retaking of any steps in the diligence which have already been taken.

(8) Where the sheriff refuses to grant a variation under subsection (1) above, the sheriff clerk shall intimate that refusal to the debtor and to any other person in possession of the poinded articles.

(9) Subject to subsection (10) below and without prejudice to section 36(3) of this Act, after intimation has been given under section 34 of this Act to the debtor of the date arranged for the warrant sale or for the removal for sale of the poinded articles from the premises where they are situated, the creditor or officer of court shall not be entitled to arrange a new date for the sale or for such removal.

(10) Where, for any reason for which neither the creditor nor the officer of court is responsible, it is not possible for the warrant sale or, as the

case may be, the removal for sale of the poinded articles from the premises where they are situated, to take place on the date arranged for it, the creditor may instruct the officer of court to arrange a new date in accordance with subsection (11) below, and the officer of court shall intimate the new date to the debtor and to any other person in possession of the poinded articles.

(11) The new date arranged under subsection (10) above—
  (a) shall not in any case be less than 7 days after the date of intimation under that subsection; and
  (b) in the case of a new date arranged for a warrant sale, shall be a date within the period specified in the warrant of sale as the period within which the sale is required to be held.

DEFINITIONS
  "officer of court": s.106.
  "warrant sale": ss.30, 106.

GENERAL NOTE
  This section contains provisions for variation of the arrangements made for sale. Since the officer now makes the arrangements for sale within the confines of the warrant the officer can alter the arrangements made at any time before such arrangements have been intimated to the debtor. Thereafter the officer is entitled to make new arrangements only if the arrangements made for sale need to be altered due to circumstances outwith the control of the creditor or officer (subss. (9)–(11)).
  The officer may find that arrangements cannot be made which comply with the terms of the warrant. For example, the auction room may be able to take the goods only after the period specified for holding the sale in expires, or the named auctioneer is no longer available. In these cases an application for variation of the warrant must be made to the sheriff. The provisions applicable to an application for a warrant of sale generally apply to an application for a variation except that the debtor does not have a new opportunity to redeem or object on the grounds of substantial undervaluation, sale not worth it or undue harshness (see s.30(2)).

Payment agreements after warrant of sale

36.—(1) Without prejudice to section 35(1) and (10) of this Act, in order to enable the sum recoverable to be paid by instalments or otherwise in accordance with an agreement between the creditor and the debtor, the creditor may, after the granting of a warrant of sale, cancel the arrangements for the warrant sale on not more than 2 occasions.

(2) The creditor or the officer of court on his behalf shall as soon as is reasonably practicable after any agreement of the kind referred to in subsection (1) above has been entered into make a report of the agreement to the sheriff.

(3) Where, following cancellation of the warrant sale in pursuance of subsection (1) above, the debtor is in breach of the agreement—
  (a) if the provisions of the original warrant of sale still allow, the creditor may instruct the officer of court to make arrangements for the warrant sale in accordance with those provisions;
  (b) if, for any reason for which neither the creditor nor the officer of court is responsible, arrangements for the warrant sale cannot be implemented in accordance with the provisions of the original warrant of sale, the sheriff may, on an application by the creditor or by the officer of court on his behalf made within 6 months after the date when the report was made under subsection (2) above, grant a variation of the warrant of sale under section 35(1) of this Act.

(4) For the purposes of subsection (3) above, the original warrant of sale shall be deemed to have specified that the sale is required to be held

within the period of 6 months after the date when the latest report was made under subsection (2) above.

DEFINITIONS
DEFINITIONS
  "officer of court": s.106.
  "sum recoverable": s.45.
  "warrant of sale": ss.30, 106.

GENERAL NOTE
  The effect of *City Bakeries* v. *S and S Snack Bars and Restaurants* 1979 S.L.T. (Sh.Ct.) 28 was that a creditor could not abandon a warrant of sale in order to give the debtor time to pay and later apply for a new warrant when the debtor defaulted. Creditors were faced with a choice; to abandon the diligence and rely on the debtor's undertaking to pay or to execute the sale in terms of the warrant.
  This section allows the creditor and debtor to agree to cancel the arrangements made for sale on not more than two occasions for the purpose of giving the debtor time to pay. The creditor cannot be made to give time to pay since a time to pay order is incompetent after warrant of sale has been granted (s.5(5)(a)). A report of this agreement on being lodged in court has the effect of extending by six months the period specified in the warrant of sale within which the sale has to be carried out. Failure to lodge the report may mean that the poinding lapses and the creditor loses the diligence.

Subs. (3)
  This subsection deals with subsequent default by the debtor. If the original warrant of sale (as extended by the six month period) can still be implemented arrangements for a new sale can simply be made and intimated to the debtor; if not, an application for variation of the warrant has to be made. This application must be made within the period as extended.

The warrant sale

  37.—(1) Where the warrant of sale does not appoint as auctioneer the officer of court appointed under section 31(2)(a) of this Act to conduct the warrant sale, that officer—

  (a) shall attend the sale and keep a record of any articles which are sold and the amount for which they are sold and of any articles whose ownership passes to the creditor under subsection (6) below; and

  (b) if the sale is to be held in premises other than an auction room, shall supervise the sale.

  (2) Where the officer of court appointed under section 31(2)(a) of this Act is appointed as auctioneer to conduct the sale, he shall be attended at the sale by one witness.

  (3) In the warrant sale there shall be no reserve price unless the creditor chooses to have one and, if he does so choose, it shall not exceed the value of the article fixed under section 20(4) of this Act.

  (4) The value of a poinded article fixed under section 20(4) of this Act and the reserve price, if any, fixed by the creditor under subsection (3) above need not be disclosed to any person bidding for the article.

  (5) In the warrant sale any poinded article exposed for sale may be purchased by—

  (a) any creditor, including the creditor on whose behalf the poinding was executed; or

  (b) a person who owns the article in common with the debtor.

  (6) Subject to subsection (7) below and without prejudice to the rights of any third party, where the sum recoverable has not been realised by the warrant sale, ownership of a poinded article which remains unsold after being exposed for sale shall pass to the creditor.

  (7) Without prejudice to the rights of any third party, where the warrant sale is held in premises belonging to the debtor, the ownership of a poinded article which has passed to the creditor under subsection (6)

above shall revert to the debtor unless the creditor uplifts the article by 8 p.m. (or such other time as may be prescribed by Act of Sederunt)—

    (a) if the premises are a dwellinghouse in which the debtor is residing, on the day when the sale is completed;

    (b) in any other case, on the third working day following that day,

and the officer of court may remain on or re-enter any premises (whether open, shut or lockfast) for the purpose of enabling the creditor to uplift any such article.

(8) For the purposes of subsection (7) above "working day" means a day which is not—

    Saturday;
    Sunday;
    1st or 2nd January;
    Good Friday;
    Easter Monday;
    25th or 26th December;
    a public holiday in the area in which the premises are situated.

(9) Subject to subsection (10) below, where at the warrant sale any article is unsold or is sold at a price below the value fixed under section 20(4) of this Act, the debtor shall be credited with an amount equal to that valuation.

(10) Where—

    (a) any damaged article has been revalued under section 20(4) of this Act on the authority of the sheriff given under section 29(2) of this Act;

    (b) the damage was not caused by the fault of the debtor; and

    (c) no order has been made under section 29(3) of this Act requiring a third party to consign a sum in respect of the article, or such an order has been made but has not been complied with,

the amount credited to the debtor under subsection (9) above shall be an amount equal to the original valuation and not the revaluation referred to in paragraph (a) above.

DEFINITIONS
    "dwellinghouse": s.45.
    "officer of court": s.106.
    "sum recoverable": s.45.
    "warrant of sale": ss.30, 106.

GENERAL NOTE
Subss. (1), (2)

Where the officer acts as auctioneer a witness (usually a member of the officer's staff) is required to be in attendance, but there is no need for any other person to be present. The officer combines the roles of auctioneer and supervisor.

Where the goods are to be sold by an auctioneer (whether in an auction room or on other premises) the officer attends the sale to note the proceedings. The officer also has the duty of supervising the sale (previously termed acting as judge of the roup) in non-auction room sales.

Subss. (3), (4), (9)

Under the Debtors (Scotland) Act 1838 s.27 the appraised value was an upset value. No bid below that value could be accepted and the upset was disclosed to potential bidders. This is at variance with the normal practice of auctioneers who start off bids at a moderate level with a view to working them up.

Now an article may be sold at any price unless the creditor chooses to place a reserve (which may be less than the appraised value) on it. The creditor also has a choice whether or not to disclose the existence of a reserve to potential bidders. If the article is not sold because no bid reaches the reserve it becomes the property of the creditor. Creditors will probably not bother with reserves in order to avoid becoming the owners of unwanted goods. The debtor is protected by being credited with the greater of the amount for which the article is sold or the appraised value.

Subs. (5)
Para. (a)
This restates the previous law (Debtors (Scotland) Act 1838, s.29) allowing the creditor to bid for the goods.

Para. (b)
This permits a co-owner to bid. The debtor may not bid, such a practice being termed "whitebonneting," but there is nothing to stop others (such as relatives or friends) acquiring the goods with the intention of returning them to the debtor.

Subss. (6), (7), (8)
Where no bid is made for an article or any bid does not reach the reserve put on the article by the creditor, the article becomes the property of the creditor, and the debtor is credited with the appraised value.

The officer or auctioneer ought to stop the sale once sufficient goods have been sold to satisfy the debt and expenses. Where the sale inadvertently continues goods which thereafter are not sold remain the property of the debtor and do not become the property of the creditor.

The creditor who becomes the owner of unsold goods must, when the sale takes place on the debtor's premises, uplift them within the period specified. Failure to do so results in the ownership reverting to the debtor. Creditors may well abandon low value goods rather than incur yet more expense in removing them. Goods which revert to the debtor become poindable by other creditors of the debtor, but the prohibition against second poindings (s.25) prevents the abandoning creditor repoinding them in the same premises.

These provisions as to passing of ownership are without prejudice to the rights of any third party. A third party owner whose goods are inadvertently exposed for sale may recover them from the creditor (*George Hopkinson* v. *Napier & Son,* 1953 S.C. 139) or a purchaser (*Carlton* v. *Miller,* 1978 S.L.T.(Sh.Ct.) 36).

Disposal of proceeds of sale

38. The officer of court appointed under section 31(2)(a) of this Act shall dispose of the proceeds of the warrant sale—
 (a) by paying to the creditor the proceeds so far as necessary to meet the sum recoverable (subject to any agreement between the officer of court and the creditor relating to the fees or outlays of the officer of court) or, if the sheriff so directs, by consigning such proceeds in court; and
 (b) by paying to the debtor any surplus remaining after the sum recoverable has been paid or, if the debtor cannot be found, by consigning such surplus in court.

DEFINITIONS
 "officer of court": s.106.
 "sum recoverable": s.45.

GENERAL NOTE
This section restates the previous law and practice. The officer pays over the proceeds of sale to the creditor after deducting fees and outlays. Officers may prefer to wait until the report of sale is approved just in case any adjustments are made at that stage. In the rare event of a surplus being produced by the sale it is handed over to the debtor.

Consignation is very unusual but it might be ordered where another creditor claims a share under the equalisation provisions, or the trustee in sequestration claims that the diligence had been rendered ineffectual (Bankruptcy (Scotland) Act 1985, Sched. 7, para. 24 and s.37(4) respectively).

Report of warrant sale

39.—(1) The officer of court appointed under section 31(2)(a) of this Act shall within a period of 14 days after the date of completion of the warrant sale make to the sheriff a report in the form prescribed by Act of Sederunt (referred to in this Part of this Act as "the report of sale") setting out—

(a) any articles which have been sold and the amount for which they have been sold;

(b) any articles which remain unsold;

(c) the expenses chargeable against the debtor under Schedule 1 to this Act;

(d) any surplus paid to the debtor; and

(e) any balance due by or to the debtor.

(2) The report of sale shall be signed by the officer of court and, if a witness was required to attend at the sale under section 37(2) of this Act, by that witness.

(3) If an officer of court—

(a) without reasonable excuse makes a report of sale after the expiry of the period mentioned in subsection (1) above; or

(b) wilfully refuses or delays to make a report of sale after the expiry of that period,

the sheriff may, without prejudice to his right to report the matter to the Court of Session or the sheriff principal under section 79(1)(b) of this Act, make an order that the officer of court shall be liable for the expenses chargeable against the debtor under Schedule 1 to this Act, either in whole or in part.

(4) The report of sale shall be remitted by the sheriff to the auditor of court who shall—

(a) tax the expenses chargeable against the debtor under Schedule 1 to this Act;

(b) certify the balance due by or to the debtor following the poinding and sale; and

(c) make a report to the sheriff,

but shall not alter the amount of the expenses or of the balance referred to in paragraph (b) above without first giving all interested persons an opportunity to make representations.

(5) On receipt of the auditor's report, the sheriff may make an order—

(a) declaring the balance due by or to the debtor, as certified by the auditor;

(b) declaring such a balance after making modifications to the balance as so certified; or

(c) if he is satisfied that there has been a substantial irregularity in the poinding and sale (other than the making of the report of sale after the expiry of the period mentioned in subsection (1) above), declaring the poinding and sale to be void, in which case (subject to subsection (9) below) he may make such consequential order as appears to him to be necessary in the circumstances,

and the sheriff clerk shall intimate the sheriff's order under this subsection to the debtor.

(6) The sheriff shall not make an order under subsection (5)(b) or (c) above without first giving all interested persons an opportunity to be heard.

(7) The auditor of court shall not be entitled to charge a fee in respect of his report.

(8) The report of sale and the auditor's report shall be retained by the sheriff clerk for the period prescribed by Act of Sederunt and during that period they shall be open for inspection in the sheriff clerk's office by any interested person on payment of such fee as may be prescribed in an order made under section 2 of the Courts of Law Fees (Scotland) Act 1895.

(9) An order under subsection (5)(c) above shall not affect the title of a person to any article acquired by him at the warrant sale, or subsequently, in good faith and for value.

(10) Any rule of law whereby the sheriff may refuse to receive the report of sale shall cease to have effect.

DEFINITIONS

"officer of court": s.106.
"report of sale": ss.39(1), 45.

GENERAL NOTE

This section by and large restates the previous law and practice including the regulations contained in the Practice Notes of the sheriffs principal.

Subss. (1)–(3)

The officer charged with the duty of reporting the sale to the court is the officer appointed in the warrant of sale to make arrangements for the sale. Failure to make a report within the 14 days allowed without reasonable excuse renders the officer liable to be reported to the authorities with a view to disciplinary action being taken and to forfeit all or part of the diligence fees and outlays. A report must be received however late it is made.

The purpose of the report is to provide an independent accounting between debtor and creditor and to check that the warrant of sale has been properly carried out. The previous multiplicity of styles of report made checking difficult; a standardised prescribed form should help the auditor and staff at the sheriff court.

In making out the balance due to or by the debtor, the debtor has to be credited with payments to account, sums paid to redeem articles, and for each item the greater of the appraised value or the amount for which it was sold. All poinded goods not earlier redeemed must be exposed for sale, unless there are more than sufficient to satisfy the sum recoverable (*Cantors* v. *Hardie*, 1974 S.L.T.(Sh.Ct.) 26 at p.30).

Subs. (4)

After receipt of the report the sheriff remits it to the auditor of court for checking. The auditor not only checks the expenses and balance but should also note any matter (such as a patent irregularity) which ought to be drawn to the sheriff's attention (*Lombard North Central* v. *Wilson* (unreported), Glasgow Sheriff Court, October 1980). The debtor, creditor and officer have an opportunity to make representations to the auditor if any changes are to be made.

Subss. (5), (6), (9), (10)

The next step is the sheriff's consideration of the report of sale together with the auditor's report. In the majority of cases the auditor will have made no adverse comments and the sheriff will simply declare the balance as brought out in the report. Where changes are proposed the debtor, creditor and officer are entitled to be heard first. Where a substantial irregularity is disclosed (the sale executed outwith the permitted period for example) the diligence may be declared null. The consequential orders that might be made include relieving the debtor of any liability for expenses and ordering the creditor to refund the proceeds of sale already received to the debtor. Where goods have been acquired by a purchaser in good faith restoration cannot be ordered. It is suggested that goods cannot be recovered from a creditor who was unaware of the irregularity and to whom the goods have been passed in default of sale. Such a creditor is in good faith and acquires for value in that he or she is debited with the appraised value of the goods.

Finally the sheriff clerk informs the debtor what the result of the sale was. This will be useful as most sales will not take place on the debtor's premises or in the presence of the debtor.

Articles belonging to third parties or in common ownership

Release from poinding of articles belonging to third party

40.—(1) An officer of court may, at any time after the execution of a poinding and before the warrant sale, release an article from the poinding if—

(a) he is satisfied that the article belongs to a third party; and

(b) the debtor or other person in possession of the article does not deny that it belongs to the third party.

(2) Where, on an application made to him by a third party, at any time after the execution of a poinding and before the warrant sale, the sheriff is satisfied that a poinded article belongs to that third party, he shall make an order releasing it from the poinding.

(3) The making of an application under subsection (2) above shall not prejudice the taking of any other proceedings by the third party for the recovery of a poinded article belonging to him, and an order of the sheriff under that subsection shall not be binding in any other proceedings.

(4) The release of a poinded article under subsection (1) above—

(a) shall be mentioned in the next subsequent application (if any) which is made for warrant of sale or for variation of warrant of sale; or

(b) if it takes place after an application for warrant of sale (or variation thereof) has been made and before it has been disposed of, shall be reported as soon as is reasonably practicable by the officer of court to the sheriff; or

(c) in any other case, shall be mentioned in any report of sale.

(5) Where an article has been released from a poinding under this section, an officer of court may, notwithstanding section 25 of this Act, poind other articles belonging to the debtor in the same premises.

DEFINITIONS
"officer of court": s.106.
"report of sale": s.45.
"warrant of sale": ss.30, 106.

GENERAL NOTE
This section deals with the remedies available to a third party whose goods have been included in a poinding.

The third party owner would probably first approach the officer or creditor to see if they will agree to release the articles. Although subs. (1) confers a discretion to release on the officer, a prudent officer would ensure that the instructing creditor agreed to the release.

If the informal method in subs. (1) failed the third party's next step would be to apply to the sheriff under subs. (2). If that fails the third party may appeal or try some other remedy such as interdicting the creditor from applying for a warrant of sale or carrying out a sale (*Jack* v. *Waddell's Trs.*, 1918 S.C. 73), or recovering goods from purchasers (*Carlton* v. *Miller*, 1978 S.L.T.(Sh.Ct.) 36) or the creditor to whom unsold goods have been delivered (*George Hopkinson* v. *Napier and Son* 1953 S.C. 139). The fact that the sheriff in an application under subs. (2) was not satisfied as to the third party's ownership is not *res judicata* in other proceedings raising the same question.

Where an article is released either by the officer of court or the sheriff on an application under subs. (2), the creditor may poind further articles to restore the value of the poinding (subs. (5)). This right does not arise in connection with other methods of obtaining release.

Poinding and sale of articles in common ownership

41.—(1) Articles which are owned in common by a debtor and a third party may be poinded and disposed of in accordance with this Part of this Act in satisfaction of the debts of that debtor.

(2) Where, at any time after the execution of a poinding and before the warrant sale, a third party—

(a) claims that a poinded article is owned in common by the debtor and himself; and

(b) pays to the officer of court a sum equal to the value of the debtor's interest in the article,

the officer of court may, unless the debtor (or the person in possession of the article, if not the debtor) denies the claim, release the article from the poinding.

(3) If, on an application made by a third party, at any time after the execution of a poinding and before the warrant sale, the sheriff is satisfied that a poinded article is owned in common by the debtor and that third party and either—

(a) the third party undertakes to pay to the officer of court a sum equal to the value of the debtor's interest in the article; or

(b) the sheriff is satisfied that the continued poinding of that article or its sale under warrant of sale would be unduly harsh to the third party in the circumstances,

he shall make an order releasing the article from the poinding.

(4) A release under subsection (2) above or where subsection (3)(a) above applies shall not become effective until the granting by the officer of court of a receipt for payment in accordance therewith, when the debtor's interest in the released article shall be transferred to the third party.

(5) A release of a poinded article under subsection (2) above—

(a) shall be mentioned in the next subsequent application (if any) which is made for warrant of sale or for variation of warrant of sale; or

(b) if it takes place after an application for warrant of sale (or variation thereof) has been made and before it has been disposed of, shall be reported as soon as is reasonably practicable by the officer of court to the sheriff; or

(c) in any other case, shall be mentioned in any report of sale.

(6) Where an article is released in pursuance of subsection (3)(b) above from a poinding, an officer of court may, notwithstanding section 25 of this Act, poind other articles belonging to the debtor in the same premises.

(7) This subsection applies where, at any time after the execution of a poinding, a third party claims that any of the poinded articles is owned in common by the debtor and himself but does not seek release of the article from the poinding, and either—

(a) the claim is admitted by the creditor and the debtor; or

(b) the claim is not admitted by both the creditor and the debtor, but the sheriff, on an application made to him, is satisfied that the claim is valid.

(8) Where subsection (7) above applies, the creditor shall pay to the third party—

(a) if the article is sold, the fraction of the proceeds of sale (or of the value of that article fixed under section 20(4) of this Act, whichever is the greater) which corresponds to the third party's interest in the article;

(b) if ownership of the article passes to the creditor in default of sale, the fraction of the value of the article fixed under section 20(4) of this Act which corresponds to the third party's interest in the article.

DEFINITIONS

"officer of court": s.106.

"report of sale": s.45.

"warrant of sale": ss.30 and 106.

GENERAL NOTE

Goods owned in common by the debtor and a third party are not poindable for the debts of the debtor. (*Fleming* v. *Twaddle* (1828) 7 S. 92). The increasing incidence of co-ownership amongst spouses and cohabitants forced a re-appraisal of the rule. This section allows co-owned goods to be poinded for the debts of any co-owner while protecting the interest of the other co-owner(s). Joint property remains unpoindable for the debts of any joint owner since he or she has no separate interest.

The remedies of the co-owner are:—

(a) to buy out the debtor's interest in the article, subs. (2). The officer will require good evidence of co-ownership and the extent of the debtor's interest. The officer of court has a discretion whether to release and a prudent officer would ensure that the poinding creditor agreed with the proposed course of action. Where co-ownership is disputed by the debtor (or possessor) the officer cannot release the article. The money received from the co-owner is applied towards reduction of the debtor's debt, and the co-owner becomes sole owner of the article.
(b) to apply to the sheriff to buy out the debtor's interest in the article if the officer refuses to allow this (subs. 3(a)).
(c) to apply to the sheriff for release on grounds of undue harshness, (subs. (3)(b)). See note on s.23.
(d) to allow the article to be sold but to require the creditor to pay back a share of the price (or value) corresponding to his or her (the third party's) interest (subs. (7) and (8)). The claim may be made after the sale has been carried out.
(e) to arrange that the debtor redeems his or her (the debtor's) own interest so releasing the article from the poinding, (ss.21(4) and 33(2)).
(f) to arrange that the debtor exercises any other competent remedy which results in the recall/or termination of the poinding of the article.

Supplementary

Certain proceedings under Part II to postpone further steps in the diligence

42.—(1) Where an application under any of the provisions of this Act listed in subsection (3) below has been made, it shall not be competent during a relevant period to grant a warrant of sale in respect of the poinded articles, to remove them for sale or to hold a warrant sale.

(2) Where subsection (1) above applies, a relevant period shall be disregarded in calculating—
(a) the period within which a warrant sale is required to be held under section 31(2)(b) of this Act; or
(b) the period on the expiry of which the poinding ceases to have effect under section 27 of this Act.

(3) The provisions referred to in subsection (1) above are—
(a) section 16(4), 23(1), 40(2) or 41(3) (release of poinded articles);
(b) section 24(1) or (3) (invalidity, cessation or recall of poinding);
(c) section 26(1) (sist of proceedings in poinding of mobile homes);
(d) section 28(4) (restoration of articles removed without consent or authority);
(e) section 28(5) (recall of order under section 28(4)).

(4) In subsections (1) and (2) above "a relevant period" means—
(a) the period while the application is pending;
(b) where the application has been disposed of by the sheriff—
  (i) the period during which an application for leave to appeal may be made;
  (ii) where an application for leave to appeal is made, the period until leave has been refused or the application has been abandoned;
  (iii) where leave to appeal has been granted, the period during which an appeal may be made; or
  (iv) where an appeal against the decision is made, the period until the matter has been finally determined or the appeal has been abandoned.

DEFINITION
"warrant of sale" ss.30, 106.

GENERAL NOTE
The primary purpose of this section is to prevent the diligence proceeding while certain applications are pending or appealable. For example, it would be pointless for the debtor to

apply for release of articles from the poinding if the creditor could have them sold while the application was pending. Also the period during which an application is pending or appealable does not count for the purposes of working out the duration of a poinding or the period specified in a warrant of sale within which the sale is to be held.

Conjoining of further poinding with original poinding

43.—(1) Subject to subsection (2) below, where a report of a further poinding by the same creditor to enforce the same debt executed in pursuance of section 9(12), 23(2), 28(2) or (6), 29(2), 40(5) or 41(6) of this Act has been received under section 22 of this Act, the sheriff shall, on an application made to him by the creditor or by an officer of court on his behalf, make an order conjoining the further poinding with the original poinding.

(2) It shall not be competent for the sheriff to make an order under subsection (1) above—

(a) where a warrant of sale has been granted in respect of the original poinding or the further poinding;

(b) until 14 days after the date of execution of the further poinding; or

(c) while an application under this Part of this Act in relation to the further poinding is pending or, where such an application has been disposed of by the sheriff—

(i) until the period for leave to appeal has expired without an application for leave having been made;

(ii) where an application for leave to appeal is made, until leave has been refused or the application has been abandoned;

(iii) where leave to appeal has been granted, until the period for an appeal has expired without an appeal being made; or

(iv) where an appeal against the decision is made, until the matter has been finally determined or the appeal has been abandoned.

(3) Where the sheriff makes an order under subsection (1) above, it shall not thereafter be competent for him to grant any application for warrant of sale relating to the original poinding which is pending when the order is made.

(4) The effect of an order under subsection (1) above shall be that thereafter the further poinding shall be treated for all purposes as if it were part of the original poinding, except that the references to a poinding being invalid or having ceased to have effect in sections 24(1), 30(2)(a)(i) and 35(2)(a) of this Act shall be construed as references to either poinding being invalid or having ceased to have effect.

(5) The decision of the sheriff under subsection (1) above shall not be subject to appeal.

DEFINITIONS
"officer of court": s.106.
"warrant of sale": ss.30, 106.

GENERAL NOTE
Conjoining two or more poindings may be of assistance to the creditor. Separate applications for warrants of sale, the execution of separate sales and the submission of separate reports of sale would thereby be avoided. Furthermore, each separate poinding may be liable to recall or warrant of sale refused on the ground that the likely proceeds of sale would not exceed the likely expenses of sale. Conjoining the poindings might render this ground inapplicable. (See example in notes on s.24(4).)

An application for conjunction cannot be made once a warrant of sale has been granted in respect of either poinding. The 14 day delay after execution of the further poinding is designed to allow the debtor to apply for release of the articles under ss.16(4) or 23(1).

A possible disadvantage to conjoining is that the further poinding becomes part of the original poinding. An irregularity or defect in either poinding therefore renders the conjoined poinding liable to recall, leading to a complete loss of both diligences.

Expenses of poinding and sale

44. Schedule 1 to this Act shall have effect for the purposes of determining the liability, as between the creditor and the debtor, for expenses incurred in serving a charge and in the process of poinding and warrant sale.

Interpretation of Part II

45. In this Part of this Act—

"dwellinghouse" includes a caravan, a houseboat and any structure adapted for use as a residence;

"the poinding schedule" means the schedule provided for in section 20(5) of this Act;

"the report of sale" means the report provided for in section 39(1) of this Act;

"the sum recoverable" means the total of—

(a) the amount outstanding of the sum due by the debtor under the decree or other document on which the diligence proceeds (including any interest thereon and any expenses decerned for);

(b) any sum due under section 93(5) of this Act; and

(c) any expenses which have been incurred in serving a charge and in the process of poinding and sale which are chargeable against the debtor under Schedule 1 to this Act.

Part III

Diligence Against Earnings

Introduction

New diligences against earnings

46.—(1) The following diligences against earnings of a debtor in the hands of his employer shall replace the diligence of arrestment and action of furthcoming against such earnings—

(a) a diligence, to be known as an "earnings arrestment", to enforce the payment of any ordinary debt which is due as at the date of execution of the diligence;

(b) a diligence, to be known as a "current maintenance arrestment", to enforce the payment of current maintenance;

(c) an order, to be known as a "conjoined arrestment order", to enforce the payment of two or more debts owed to different creditors against the same earnings.

(2) Any rule of law whereby there is exempted from arrestment of earnings of a debtor in the hands of his employer a reasonable amount for the subsistence of the debtor and his dependants shall cease to have effect.

Definitions

"creditor": s.73(1).
"current maintenance": s.73(1).
"earnings": s.73(2).
"employer": s.73(1).
"maintenance": s.106.
"ordinary debt": s.73(1).

GENERAL NOTE

This section introduces three new diligences against earnings to replace the diligence of arrestment and furthcoming of wages. These new diligences apply to debtors who are individuals. They are capable of attaching only earnings in the hands of the debtor's employer. "Earnings" and "employer" have extended meanings and include pensions and the payer of pensions respectively. It is important to note the scope of the new diligences, since they and the existing diligence of arrestment and furthcoming are mutually exclusive. So if one of the new diligences is competent, arrestment and furthcoming is incompetent; likewise if none of the new diligences is appropriate, then the existing diligence of arrestment and furthcoming remains competent, unless the funds are protected from any diligence (the pay of a member of the armed forces for example). Thus the self-employed and those remunerated under a contract for services remain liable to arrestment and furthcoming and do not get the benefit of the subsistence exemptions built into the new diligences.

Diligence against assets such as bank or building society accounts, shares, debts or moveable goods continues to take the form of arrestment and furthcoming, and neither a prior charge nor default is a pre-requisite for execution of that diligence.

Subs. (1)(a)

Earnings arrestments are designed to enforce ordinary debts—debts other than current maintenance. Typical examples are fuel bills, sums due in respect of goods or services, or damages awarded. Arrears of maintenance and the expenses previously incurred in executing a current maintenance arrestment are also ordinary debts and recoverable via an earnings arrestment. The debt to be enforced must be due at the date of service of the schedule of arrestment on the employer since the schedule has to set out the debt due, and the arrestment is only effective to the extent that this is done (s.48(3)). Earnings arrestments can therefore not be used in security of payment of future or contingent debts or on the dependence (arrestment of wages on the dependence is already incompetent: Law Reform (Miscellaneous Provisions) (Scotland) Act 1966, s.1).

More than one ordinary debt due to the same creditor may be enforced by a single earnings arrestment provided the schedule served on the employer sets out the total amount due.

Subs. (1)(b)

The primary purpose of a current maintenance arrestment is to enforce and collect payment of maintenance falling due after the date of execution of the arrestment—the date on which the schedule is served on the maintenance debtor's employer (s.51(2)(a)). Maintenance means aliment, periodical allowance and sums due at regular intervals under contribution orders and non-Scottish orders of similar type.

Subs. (1)(c)

A conjoined arrestment order allows two or more creditors to share in the sums deducted from their debtor's earnings by virtue of the order. Sharing by means of a claim to equalise diligence under para. 24 of Sched. 7 to the Bankruptcy (Scotland) Act 1985 is prohibited by s.67 of this Act. A conjoined arrestment order requires at least two different creditors and at least two different debts, but it is possible for one of the creditors in the order to be conjoined in respect of more than one debt. For example, an ex-wife may be enforcing arrears of maintenance and current maintenance while at the same time British Telecom is enforcing an unpaid telephone bill.

Subs. (2)

The rule of law referred to is the centuries-old *beneficium competentiae (Shanks* v. *Thomson* (1838) 16S. 1353). This rule protected wages required by debtors for their own subsistence from arrestment, with only the surplus being capable of attachment. The rule was to a large extent superseded by the Wages Arrestment Limitation (Scotland) Act 1870 as amended. It is now abolished as far as the new diligences are concerned since the methods of calculating deductions used in this Act achieve the same result.

Earnings arrestments

General effect of earnings arrestment

47.—(1) Subject to section 69 of this Act, an earnings arrestment shall have the effect of requiring the employer of a debtor, while the arrestment is in effect, to deduct a sum calculated in accordance with section 49 of this Act from the debtor's net earnings on every pay-day and, as soon as is reasonably practicable, to pay any sum so deducted to the creditor.

(2) Subject to sections 59 (priority among arrestments), 62 (relationship of conjoined arrestment order with certain other arrestments) and 90 (provisions relating to charges for payment) of this Act, an earnings arrestment—

(a) shall come into effect on the date of its execution, being the date on which a schedule in the form prescribed by Act of Sederunt (to be known as an "earnings arrestment schedule") is served on the employer; and

(b) shall remain in effect until the debt recoverable has been paid or otherwise extinguished, the debtor has ceased to be employed by the employer, or the arrestment has been recalled or abandoned by the creditor or has for any other reason ceased to have effect.

DEFINITIONS
"creditor": s.73(1).
"debt recoverable": ss.48(1) and 73(1).
"decree or other document": s.73(1).
"employer": s.73(1).
"net earnings": s.73(1), (2).
"pay-day": s.73(1).

GENERAL NOTE
This section describes the general scheme of earnings arrestments. First, the debtor is served with a charge to pay within either 14 or 28 days depending on the circumstances (see s.90(3)). On expiry of the charge without payment a schedule of arrestment can be served on a debtor's employer which requires the employer to deduct a sum from the debtor's net earnings on each pay-day occurring after service and to pay it to the arresting creditor. The main differences from an arrestment of wages are that an earnings arrestment requires a prior charge, it operates as a completed diligence in that no further step is required for the creditor to obtain payment, and, unless it for some reason ceases to have effect, it continues until the debt is paid.

Subs. (1)
S.69 allows employers a seven-day period of grace after service of the schedule before they are obliged to make deductions. Subject to this, while the arrestment is "in effect" (see subs. (2)) deductions must be calculated every pay-day—which means every day on which earnings are actually paid. The name of the arresting creditor or collecting agent to whom the deductions are to be sent should clearly appear on the schedule of arrestment. See s.57(2) and (3) for the methods of payment employers may use to remit to creditors.

Subs. (2)
This subsection sets out when an arrestment is in effect. It is important to note the distinction between being in effect and being operated by the employer. An arrestment may be in effect and hence render ineffective another earnings arrestment schedule served later (s.59(1)), although the employer has not yet got round to putting the first schedule into operation since a pay-day has not yet arrived. Moreover, an arrestment may have ceased to be in effect and yet the employer may quite correctly continue to operate it until the proper notice of cessation is received (see s.69(1)).

Ss. 59 and 62 render incompetent an earnings arrestment served during the period when a prior earnings arrestment or conjoined arrestment order is in effect.

Earnings paid after the debtor ceases to be employed are not subject to an earnings arrestment. The correct diligence to attach such earnings would be an arrestment and furthcoming.

Another reason for an arrestment ceasing to have effect (para. (b)) is the debtor's sequestration (see s.72(2)).

Debt recoverable by earnings arrestment

48.—(1) Subject to subsections (2) and (3) below, the debt recoverable by an earnings arrestment shall consist of the following sums, in so far as outstanding—

(a) any ordinary debt and any expenses due under the decree or other document on which the earnings arrestment proceeds;

(b) any interest on those sums which has accrued at the date of execution of the earnings arrestment; and

(c) the expenses incurred in executing the earnings arrestment and the charge which preceded it.

(2) In relation to arrears of maintenance, the ordinary debt referred to in subsection (1)(a) above shall be the amount of those arrears less any sum which the debtor is entitled to deduct from that amount under any enactment in respect of income tax.

(3) Any sum mentioned in subsection (1) above shall be included in the debt recoverable only if, and to the extent that, it is specified in the earnings arrestment schedule.

(4) It shall be competent for a creditor to enforce payment of more than one debt payable to him by the same debtor by means of a single earnings arrestment, whether the arrestment is executed in pursuance of the same warrant or of 2 or more different warrants authorising diligence.

DEFINITIONS
"creditor": s.73(1).
"debt recoverable": ss.48(1), 73(1).
"decree or other document": s.73(1).
"ordinary debt": s.73(1).

GENERAL NOTE
This section defines the sums enforceable by means of an earnings arrestment.

Subs. (1)
Para. (a)
Expenses. This means the judicial expenses of the proceedings leading to the decree or other document and which are specified therein. A finding of liability for expenses is not a sufficient warrant for diligence; there must be an extract decree for or including expenses as a specified sum.

Para. (b)
Pre-execution interest must be calculated and specified in order to be recoverable by the arrestment. Interest which continues to run on the sum during the currency of the arrestment is not recoverable by the arrestment and will have to be recovered by further diligence (including a further earnings arrestment). In most cases creditors will probably waive this interest, but in the case of a bank or other lending institution where the arrestment was for a substantial sum the interest could be well worth enforcing.

Para. (c)
These expenses are the officer's and witness's fees in connection with service of the charge, schedule of arrestment and intimation of a copy of the arrestment to the debtor (see s.70(1)) and the fees of the solicitor (if any) instructing the officer.

Subs. (2)
A debtor paying maintenance out of taxable income is entitled to deduct tax at the basic rate from sums paid to the creditor, except where the maintenance is due under a court order and the amount is not in excess of the small maintenance payment limits (Income and Corporation Taxes Act 1970, s.65(1A) as amended). See *Finnie* v. *Finnie* 1984 S.L.T. 439 for the appropriate limit where a pupil child is the creditor but the maintenance is paid to the parent as tutor.

Previously where an arrestment of wages was executed for arrears of maintenance the employer was not entitled to deduct tax and consequently paid the full gross amount to the creditor (*Fletcher* v. *Young* 1936 S.L.T. 572). This remains the position for arrestments of funds other than earnings in the hands of the debtor's employer—a bank or building society account, for example. For earnings arrestments if the debtor is entitled to deduct tax the figure to be inserted in the schedule is the arrears of maintenance net of tax at the basic rate for the tax year in which the arrestment is executed. The arresting creditor or his or her solicitors will be responsible for telling the officer the correct figure to insert. For example where gross arrears of £1,000 have accrued over several years the net figure to be inserted for an arrestment served in the period from April 6, 1987, to April 5, 1988, would be £730 (basic rate 1987/88 27 per cent.).

Subs. (3)

It will be important to include the diligence expenses otherwise they will be irrecoverable by virtue of the rule (s.93) that save in exceptional cases such expenses can only be recovered by the diligence in question.

Subs. (4)

This subsection makes it clear that a single schedule of arrestment can enforce more than one ordinary debt due to the same creditor. Where the debts are due to different creditors a conjoined arrestment order must be used. Where both debts are constituted about the same time it would be sensible for the creditor to charge for and then serve a schedule of arrestment specifying both debts. Where one debt was constituted much later the creditor would probably charge and serve an earnings arrestment for the first debt and when the second debt was constituted abandon the first arrestment and serve a new arrestment for both debts (remembering to give credit for payments received under the abandoned arrestment). The charge grounding the new arrestment would need to specify only the second debt, since unless more than two years had elapsed since the first debt was charged for (see s.90(5)) that charge remains effective.

Deductions from net earnings to be made by employer

49.—(1) The sum to be deducted under section 47 of this Act on any pay-day shall be—

(a) where the debtor's earnings are payable weekly, the sum specified in column 2 of Table A in Schedule 2 to this Act opposite the band in column 1 of that Table within which his net earnings payable on that pay-day fall;

(b) where his earnings are payable monthly, the sum specified in column 2 of Table B in that Schedule opposite the band in column 1 of that Table within which his net earnings payable on that pay-day fall;

(c) where his earnings are payable at regular intervals of a whole number of weeks or months, the sum arrived at by—

(i) calculating what would be his weekly or monthly net earnings by dividing the net earnings payable to him on the pay-day by that whole number (of weeks or months, as the case may be);

(ii) ascertaining the sum specified in column 2 of Table A (if the whole number is of weeks) or of Table B (if the whole number is of months) in Schedule 2 to this Act opposite the band in column 1 of that Table within which the notional net earnings calculated under sub-paragraph (i) above fall; and

(iii) multiplying that sum by the whole number (of weeks or months, as the case may be).

(2) Where the debtor's earnings are payable at regular intervals other than at intervals to which subsection (1) above applies, the sum to be deducted on any pay-day under section 47 of this Act shall be arrived at by—

(a) calculating what would be his daily net earnings by dividing the net earnings payable to him on the pay-day by the number of days in the interval;

(b) ascertaining the sum specified in column 2 of Table C in Schedule 2 to this Act opposite the band in column 1 of that Table within which the notional net earnings calculated under paragraph (a) above fall; and

(c) multiplying that sum by the number of days in the interval.

(3) Where the debtor's earnings are payable at irregular intervals, the sum to be deducted on any pay-day under section 47 of this Act shall be arrived at by—

(a) calculating what would be his daily net earnings by dividing the net earnings payable to him on the pay-day—

    (i) by the number of days since earnings were last paid to him; or

    (ii) if the earnings are the first earnings to be paid to him by the employer, by the number of days since he commenced his employment with the employer;

(b) taking the sum specified in column 2 of Table C in Schedule 2 to this Act opposite the band in column 1 of that Table within which the notional net earnings calculated under paragraph (a) above fall; and

(c) multiplying that sum by the number of days mentioned in paragraph (a) above.

(4) Where on the same pay-day there are paid to the debtor both earnings payable at regular intervals and earnings which are not payable at regular intervals, for the purpose of arriving at the sum to be deducted on that pay-day under section 47 of this Act, all those earnings shall be aggregated and treated as earnings payable at the regular interval.

(5) Where earnings payable to a debtor at regular intervals are paid to him on one pay-day and earnings which are not payable at regular intervals are paid to him on a different pay-day, the sum to be deducted on each of those pay-days under section 47 of this Act in respect of those earnings which are not paid at regular intervals shall be 20 per cent. of the net earnings paid to him on that pay-day.

(6) Where earnings are paid to a debtor by 2 or more series of payments at regular intervals—

(a) if the intervals are of different lengths—

    (i) for the purpose of arriving at the sum to be deducted under section 47 of this Act, whichever of subsections (1) and (2) above is appropriate shall apply to the series with the shortest interval; and

    (ii) in relation to the earnings paid in any other series, the said sum shall be 20 per cent. of the net earnings;

(b) if the intervals are of the same length and payments in more than one series are payable on the same day—

    (i) the payments in those series shall be aggregated and whichever of subsections (1) and (2) above is appropriate shall apply to the aggregate; and

    (ii) paragraph (a)(ii) above shall apply to every other series;

(c) if the intervals are of the same length and no 2 payments are payable on the same day paragraph (a)(i) above shall apply to such series as the employer may choose, and paragraph (a)(ii) above shall apply to every other series.

(7) The Lord Advocate may, by regulations, vary—

(a) Tables A, B and C of Schedule 2 to this Act;

(b) the percentage specified in subsections (5) and (6)(a)(ii) above, and such regulations may make different provision for different cases.

(8) Subject to section 69(1) and (2) of this Act, regulations under subsection (7) above shall not apply in relation to an existing earnings arrestment unless and until the creditor or the debtor intimates the making of the regulations to the employer in the form prescribed by Act of Sederunt.

DEFINITIONS
"creditor": s.73(1).
"earnings": s.73(1).
"employer": s.73(1).
"net earnings": s.73(1).
"pay-day": s.73(1).

GENERAL NOTE
This section sets out the way in which the employer calculates the sum to be deducted under an earnings arrestment on a pay-day from the debtor's net earnings. The provisions are inevitably complex since earnings may be paid in many different ways. The vast majority of employees however are paid weekly or monthly so that most employers will only need to refer to the appropriate statutory deduction tables (Tables A and B in Sched. 2).

Deductions are to be made from cash earnings only. The value of benefits such as a car, clothing allowance, free accommodation or free coal is ignored for the purposes of diligence even though they are included for income tax purposes.

Debtors, who find the statutory deductions too burdensome in their particular circumstances can apply to the court for a time to pay order with lower instalments (see ss.5–11).

Subs. (1)
Probably well over 90 per cent. of the cases will be covered by the provisions of this subsection. Para. (a) applies to weekly paid employees, para. (b) to monthly paid employees and para. (c) to payments in multiples of weeks or months—a quarterly pension for example. The Tables in Sched. 2 provide for a certain basic non-arrestable amount for subsistence and the proportion of the earnings above this figure deducted increases with increasing earnings until the 50 per cent. level is reached at just over £300 net per week (£15,600 net per year). It should be noted that the Tables, which the Lord Advocate may vary by regulation (subs. (7)), apply to the net earnings of debtors.

Examples
1. A weekly paid shop assistant earns £110 net per week: £17 per week is deducted (Table A) leaving him with £93 "take home" pay.
2. A monthly paid computer programmer earns £850 net per month: £180 is deducted (Table B) leaving her with £680 "take home" pay.
3. A pension of £3,720 net per year is payable in quarterly instalments of £930.
The notional monthly pension is 930 ÷ 3, *i.e.* £310.
The deduction for £310 is £34 (Table B).
The quarterly deduction is £34 × 3 (*i.e.* £102) so that the pensioner receives £828 per quarter.

Subs. (2)
This subsection applies to the unusual case where the debtor is paid at regular intervals which are not a whole number of weeks or months—every 17 days for example. The principle is to evaluate the daily rate of earnings, apply Table C to that daily rate and then multiply the daily deduction by the number of days in the interval in order to find the total deduction to be applied each pay-day.

Subs. (3)
In the case of payment at irregular intervals each pay-day has to be treated as a one-off situation. The normal calculation will involve steps (a)(i), (b) and (c); (a)(ii) applies where the earnings arrestment is served before the debtor has received any pay in that employment.

Subss. (4), (5)
In addition to regular payments the employee may receive bonus, commission or other payments at irregular intervals. Where the sums are paid on the same pay-day as the regular earnings they are aggregated and treated as earnings; where the irregular payments are paid separately a 20 per cent. deduction is made from them and Table A, B or C as the case may be is applied to the regular earnings.

Example
A car salesman gets a basic salary of £100 per week net. His commission is paid whenever it amounts to £500. If the employer pays the commission with the basic pay then every so often he will have net earnings of £600 for that week. The appropriate deduction is £183.

(Table A). If the employer pays the commission two days before the basic pay, £100 is deducted from the £500 commission (*i.e.* 20 per cent. of £500) and £13 is deducted from the basic pay (Table A) giving a total deduction of £113. It is clearly advantageous to employees not to have large bonuses, etc., paid with their regular pay.

Subs. (6)

This subsection deals with two or more series of regular payments. Para. (a) applies where the periods are of different lengths—such as weekly basic pay and monthly commission, while paras. (b) and (c) apply to situations where the periods are the same but not all the series are paid on the same day—weekly earnings paid on Friday and weekly bonus paid on Tuesday for example.

Subs. (8)

From time to time the tables or the percentages will be altered by regulations made by the Lord Advocate under subs. (7). Where an arrestment is served after the regulations have come into force the employer is bound to make deductions in accordance with the new regulations. Where the employer is operating a subsisting arrestment when the regulations come into force the employer is not bound to give effect to the new figures until either the creditor or the debtor intimates the regulations. Even then there is a seven-day period of grace under s.69. The employer may however choose to implement the regulations if aware of their existence from another source—another arrestment for example—without waiting for intimation from the debtor or creditor concerned.

Review of earnings arrestment

50.—(1) If the sheriff is satisfied that an earnings arrestment is invalid or has ceased to have effect he shall, on an application by the debtor or the person on whom the earnings arrestment schedule was served, make an order declaring that to be the case, and may make such consequential order as appears to him to be necessary in the circumstances; and the sheriff clerk shall intimate any order under this subsection to the debtor, the creditor and the person on whom the earnings arrestment schedule was served.

(2) An order under subsection (1) above declaring that an arrestment is invalid or has ceased to have effect shall not be subject to appeal.

(3) The sheriff, on an application by the debtor, the creditor or the employer, may make an order determining any dispute as to the operation of an earnings arrestment.

(4) Without prejudice to section 57(5) of this Act, the sheriff, when making an order under subsection (3) above, may order—

(a) the reimbursement of any payment made in the operation of the arrestment which ought not to have been made; or

(b) the payment of any sum which ought to have been paid in the operation of the arrestment but which has not been paid.

(5) An order under subsection (4) above shall require the person against whom it is made to pay interest on the sum to be paid by him under the order at the specified rate from such date as the sheriff shall specify in the order.

DEFINITIONS
"creditor": s.73(1).
"employer": s.73(1).
"sheriff": s.73(1).
"specified rate": s.73(1).

GENERAL NOTE
Provision is made for judicial control of earnings arrestments and the way in which they are operated. Subs. (1) deals with arrestments which were invalid from the start (not properly served for example) and those that have become invalid (such as where the debtor ceases to be employed under a contract of service and becomes employed under a contract for services).

Subss. (3) and (4) deal with a valid arrestment which one party avers is not being operated correctly. In addition to directing how the arrestment is to be operated in future, past errors can be corrected by the appropriate order for payment, the sums awarded bearing interest at the specified rate from a date to be decided by the sheriff. This remedy is an alternative to the common law duty on the creditor to repay sums received to which he or she is not entitled, and any remedy the debtor has against the employer on the ground of breach of contract to pay earnings. S.57(5) relates to the situation where the debt has been paid or extinguished or has ceased to be enforceable by diligence so that the arrestment has ceased to have effect. The debtor is automatically due reimbursement without an order from the sheriff.

Under s.69(4) the employer is not liable for mistakes made in the operation of an arrestment more than a year before proceedings are brought. The debtor can however claim repayment from the creditor of vice versa within a five-year period (Prescription and Limitation (Scotland) Act 1973, s.6 and Sched. 1).

Current maintenance arrestments

General effect of current maintenance arrestment

51.—(1) Subject to sections 58(2) and 69 of this Act, a current maintenance arrestment shall have the effect of requiring the employer of the debtor while the arrestment is in effect to deduct a sum calculated in accordance with section 53 of this Act from the debtor's net earnings on every pay-day and as soon as is reasonably practicable to pay any sum so deducted to the creditor.

(2) Subject to sections 59 and 62 of this Act, a current maintenance arrestment—

(a) shall come into effect on the date of its execution, being the date on which a schedule in the form prescribed by Act of Sederunt (to be known as a "current maintenance arrestment schedule") is served on the employer of the debtor; and

(b) shall remain in effect until the debtor has ceased to be employed by the employer concerned, or the arrestment has been recalled or abandoned by the creditor or has ceased to have effect under section 55(8) of this Act or for any other reason.

(3) The expenses incurred in executing a current maintenance arrestment shall be recoverable from the debtor as an ordinary debt.

(4) Subject to section 52(2)(b) of this Act, a current maintenance arrestment schedule shall specify the maintenance payable by the debtor expressed as a daily rate.

(5) For the purposes of subsection (4) above the daily rate shall be arrived at—

(a) where the maintenance is paid monthly, by multiplying the monthly rate by 12 and dividing it by 365;

(b) where it is paid quarterly, by multiplying the quarterly rate by 4 and dividing it by 365.

(6) No interest shall accrue on any arrears of the maintenance which arise while a current maintenance arrestment is in effect.

DEFINITIONS
   "creditor": s.73(1).
   "employer": s.73(1).
   "maintenance": s.106.
   "maintenance order": s.106.
   "net earnings": s.73(1).
   "ordinary debt": s.73(1).
   "pay-day": s.73(1).

GENERAL NOTE
   This section describes the general scheme of current maintenance arrestments. Every pay-day the employer is required to deduct from the debtor's net earnings the maintenance due for the period since the last pay-day and pay it to the arresting creditor.

Other diligences such as arrestment, earnings arrestment or poinding enforce arrears of maintenance only, although the threat of such diligence may ensure more regular payments in future. Current maintenance arrestment being a continuing diligence is particularly appropriate to enforce a continuing obligation such as maintenance.

Subs. (1)

This subsection requires the employer to make deductions for maintenance due and pay them to the maintenance creditor. See s.57(2) and (3) for the methods of payment employers may use. S.58(2) deals with the case where the employer is operating an earnings arrestment for an ordinary debt as well as a current maintenance arrestment for maintenance while s.69 allows the employer a period of seven days from the date of service of the current maintenance arrestment schedule before being required to make a deduction in order to give time to make the necessary internal arrangements. The name of the arresting creditor or collecting agent to whom the deductions are to be sent should clearly appear on the current maintenance arrestment schedule served on the employer.

Subs. (2)

This is the equivalent for current maintenance arrestments of s.47(2). The reasons for cessation are wider than for earnings arrestments since s.55(8) provides that a current maintenance arrestment ceases to have effect if the maintenance order is varied or recalled or the obligation ceases to be enforceable.

Subs. (3)

The unpaid expenses of a current maintenance arrestment cannot be recovered by that arrestment. They may be enforced by other diligence including a simultaneous earnings arrestment.

Subss. (4), (5)

For the purposes of calculating the deduction the maintenance obligation has to be expressed as a daily rate. The officer of court will insert the daily rate in the schedule, but the responsibility for converting the obligation as expressed in the maintenance order to a daily rate should be that of the instructing solicitor or creditor.

Subs. (6)

Arrears may arise during the operation of an arrestment due to insufficiency of income. To avoid very complex calculations no interest on such arrears is due. Interest on arrears due at the date of execution of the arrestment however accrues at the rate specified in the maintenance order, and is enforceable by other diligence.

Enforcement of 2 or more obligations to pay maintenance

52.—(1) This section applies where one or more maintenance orders are in effect which provide for the payment by the same debtor to the same person (whether for his own benefit or for another person's) of maintenance in respect of more than one individual.

(2) Where this section applies—

    (a) all or any of the obligations to pay maintenance may be enforced by a single current maintenance arrestment against the same earnings; and

    (b) in that case, the current maintenance arrestment schedule shall specify one daily rate of maintenance, being the aggregate of the daily rates calculated in accordance with section 51(5) of this Act.

DEFINITIONS
"earnings": s.73(1).
"maintenance": s.106.
"maintenance order": s.106.

GENERAL NOTE
Normally when two or more creditors seek to enforce their obligations against the same debtor's earnings a conjoined arrestment order is necessary. However, if the payee in each

obligation is the same a single current maintenance arrestment may be used. The paradigm case is the order on separation or divorce providing for periodical allowance for the (ex-) wife payable to her and aliment for the children payable to her as their tutor. The payee— the ex-wife—is the same in each obligation. Whether these maintenance obligations are contained in a single decree or in separate decrees they may be enforced by a single current maintenance arrestment which sets out the aggregate daily rate of the various obligations.

The section is permissive; the creditor is not obliged to enforce all the obligations in which he or she is the payee. However, the creditor cannot use separate current maintenance arrestments (s.59(2)) or a conjoined arrestment order (s.60(4)).

Subs. (1) distinguishes between "person" and "individual." Maintenance enforceable by a current maintenance arrestment is confined to sums due in respect of an individual. The payee however may be a person, such as the local authority, the Secretary of State or other similar official body or person.

Deductions from net earnings to be made by employer

53.—(1) The sum to be deducted from a debtor's net earnings on a pay-day under section 51 of this Act shall be whichever is the lesser of the amounts mentioned in paragraphs (a) and (b) of subsection (2) below, less any sum which the debtor is entitled to deduct under any enactment in respect of income tax.

(2) The amounts referred to in subsection (1) above are—

(a) subject to subsections (3) and (5) below, a sum arrived at by multiplying the daily rate of maintenance (as specified in the current maintenance arrestment schedule) by the number of days—

(i) since the last pay-day when a deduction was made in respect of the arrestment; or

(ii) if there was no such pay-day, since the date of execution of the arrestment; or

(b) any net earnings in so far as they exceed the sum of £5 per day for the number of days mentioned in paragraph (a) above.

(3) The sum specified in subsection (2)(b) above may be varied by regulations made by the Lord Advocate and such regulations may make different provision for different cases.

(4) Subject to section 69(1) and (2) of this Act, regulations under subsection (3) above shall not apply to an existing current maintenance arrestment unless and until the creditor or the debtor intimates the making of the regulations to the employer in the form prescribed by Act of Sederunt.

(5) An employer operating a current maintenance arrestment shall be entitled, but shall not be required, to apply a change in the small maintenance payments limits before the creditor or the debtor intimates the change to the employer in the form prescribed by Act of Sederunt.

(6) For the purposes of subsection (5) above, the small maintenance payments limits are the rates mentioned in section 65(1A) of the Income and Corporation Taxes Act 1970.

DEFINITIONS
  "creditor": s.73(1).
  "employer": s.73(1).
  "maintenance": s.106.
  "net earnings": s.73(1).
  "pay-day": s.73(1)

GENERAL NOTE
Subss. (1), (2)
  These subsections set out the rules for calculating the deductions from the debtor's net earnings to be made by the employer operating a current maintenance arrestment.
  A debtor paying maintenance out of taxable income is entitled to deduct tax at the basic rate from sums paid to the creditor, except where the maintenance is due under a court

order and the amount due is not in excess of the small maintenance payment limits (Income and Corporation Taxes Act 1970, s.65(1A) as amended). See *Finnie* v. *Finnie* 1984 S.L.T. 439 for the appropriate limit where a pupil child is the creditor but the maintenance is paid to the parent as tutor.

Where the debtor is entitled to deduct tax the employer operating a current maintenance arrestment is under a duty to deduct tax (at the basic rate in force at the time of making the deduction) from the maintenance due. Only the net maintenance is deducted from the debtor's pay and remitted to the creditor. Presumably the schedule of arrestment served on the employer will indicate whether or not tax falls to be deducted. The officer will have to be given this information (along with details of the maintenance obligation sought to be enforced) by the arresting creditor or his or her solicitors.

Example

Maintenance of £140 per week (not a small maintenance payment) is due under a court order.

The schedule specifies a daily rate of £20 and indicates that tax is to be deducted.

The employer in 1987/88 deducts £20 × 7 × ·73, *i.e.* £102·20 per week from the debtor's pay and remits this to the creditor (basic rate 1987/88 27 per cent.).

Where the employer fails to deduct tax the debtor could raise this with the employer. If an informal approach fails the debtor could apply to the court under s.55(5) for an order directing the employer to deduct.

See subss. (5) and (6) for changes in the small maintenance payment limits.

Para. (a)(ii) applies to the first deduction under the arrestment and para. (a)(i) to all the subsequent deductions. Para. (b) introduces a subsistence exemption for maintenance debtors of £5 per day. Earnings below this amount are exempt in contrast to an arrestment of wages for maintenance which under the previous law arrested the whole wage (Wages Arrestment Limitation (Scotland) Act 1870, s.4).

Example

An arrestment is executed to enforce payment of maintenance of £304·17 per month net of basic rate tax (£10 per day). The debtor normally receives net monthly earnings of £750.

5th January	Arrestment executed.
31st January	Employer deducts £260 (26 days maintenance at £10 per day).
28th February	Employer deducts £280 (28 days maintenance at £10 per day).
31st March	Employer deducts £310 (31 days maintenance at £10 per day).

In April the debtor is sick and earns £400 net. The employer should deduct £300 on the 30th April (30 days maintenance at £10 per day) but can deduct only £250 (£400—(£5 × 30)).

See the note on s.69(3) for the situation where the schedule is served within seven days of a pay-day.

Subs. (4)

This is the equivalent for current maintenance arrestments of s.49(8).

Subss. (5), (6)

Where the maintenance is paid under a court order and is not in excess of the small maintenance payments limits, the employer uses the gross daily rate specified in the schedule. In other cases the employer deducts tax at the basic rate. A change in the limits may require a change of practice by the employer.

Either the creditor or the debtor may give notice in prescribed form to the employer of a change in the limits if such a change will affect the operation of the arrestment. It will be in the creditor's interest to intimate any increase in the limits where this increase results in him or her receiving the full gross maintenance instead of a net sum. If employers get to know of a change in the limits otherwise than by intimation from the debtor or creditor in question (from another creditor for example) they are entitled (but not bound) to give effect to it themselves.

Current maintenance arrestment to be preceded by default

54.—(1) Subject to subsections (2) and (3) below, a current maintenance arrestment schedule may be served in pursuance of a maintenance order which is subsisting at the date of such service only if—

(a) the creditor has intimated to the debtor in the manner prescribed by Act of Sederunt—
   (i) in the case of an order mentioned in paragraph (a) or (b) of the definition of "maintenance order" in section 106 of this Act, the making of the order;
   (ii) in the case of an order mentioned in paragraph (c), (e), (f), (g) or (h) thereof, the registration mentioned in the paragraph concerned;
   (iii) in the case of an order mentioned in paragraph (d) thereof, the confirmation of the order mentioned in that paragraph;
(b) at least 4 weeks have elapsed since the date of intimation under paragraph (a) above; and
(c) except where section 56 of this Act applies, at the time when it is proposed to serve the schedule, a sum not less than the aggregate of 3 instalments of maintenance remains unpaid.
(2) Subsection (1) above shall not apply where—
   (a) the maintenance order is one that has been registered in Scotland as mentioned in paragraph (c), (e), (f) or (g) of the said definition; and
   (b) a certificate of arrears (within the meaning of section 21 of the Maintenance Orders (Reciprocal Enforcement) Act 1972) was produced to the court in Scotland which registered the order to the effect that at the time at which the certificate was issued the debtor was in arrears in his payment of instalments under the order.
(3) Where a current maintenance arrestment which was validly executed has ceased to have effect otherwise than by virtue of its recall under section 55(2) of this Act, the creditor may within 3 months after the date when the arrestment ceased to have effect execute another current maintenance arrestment without complying with subsection (1) above.

DEFINITIONS
"creditor": s.73(1).
"maintenance": s.106.
"maintenance order": s.106.

GENERAL NOTE
To prevent current maintenance arrestments being served unnecessarily the maintenance order must in general first be intimated to the debtor and arrears be due under it.

Subss. (1), (2)
Scottish orders
The creditor intimates the making of the order and can execute a current maintenance arrestment at any time after four weeks have elapsed provided that a sum representing at least three instalments of maintenance are due at the date of service. Creditors whose maintenance is payable in quarterly or annual instalments will be at a severe disadvantage. These default provisions apply equally to creditors with pre-commencement maintenance orders, however large the accrued arrears are.

Non-Scottish orders
The creditor intimates the registration for enforcement in Scotland or, as the case may be, the confirmation of the provisional order by a Scottish court, to the debtor. If a certificate of arrears is produced at the time of registration (subs. (2)(b)) a current maintenance arrestment can be executed forthwith; if not at least four weeks must elapse and three instalments of maintenance remain unpaid at the date of service of the schedule before an arrestment is competent.

Subs. (3)
This subsection permits a creditor whose current maintenance arrestment has ceased to have effect because of a variation of the underlying maintenance obligation to serve a fresh

current maintenance arrestment to enforce the varied obligation without re-intimation and waiting for arrears to accrue under it.

Review and termination of current maintenance arrestment

55.—(1) If the sheriff is satisfied, on an application by the debtor or the person on whom the current maintenance arrestment schedule was served, that a current maintenance arrestment is invalid or has ceased to have effect, he shall make an order declaring that to be the case, and may make such consequential order as appears to him to be necessary in the circumstances.

(2) If the sheriff is satisfied, on an application by the debtor, that the debtor is unlikely to default again in paying maintenance, he may make an order recalling a current maintenance arrestment.

(3) The sheriff clerk shall intimate any order made under subsection (1) or (2) above to the debtor, the creditor and the person on whom the current maintenance arrestment schedule was served.

(4) An order under subsection (1) above declaring that an arrestment is invalid or has ceased to have effect or under subsection (2) above shall not be subject to appeal.

(5) The sheriff, on an application by the debtor, the creditor or the employer, may make an order determining any dispute as to the operation of a current maintenance arrestment.

(6) Without prejudice to section 57(5) of this Act, the sheriff, when making an order under subsection (5) above, may order—

> (a) the reimbursement of any payment made in the operation of the arrestment which ought not to have been made;
>
> (b) the payment of any sum which ought to have been paid in the operation of the arrestment but which has not been paid.

(7) An order under subsection (6) above shall require the person against whom it is made to pay interest on the sum to be paid by him under the order at the specified rate, and such interest shall be payable as from such date as the sheriff shall specify in the order.

(8) A current maintenance arrestment shall cease to have effect—

> (a) on the coming into effect of an order or decree which varies, supersedes or recalls a maintenance order which is being enforced by the arrestment;
>
> (b) on an obligation to pay maintenance under a maintenance order being so enforced ceasing or ceasing to be enforceable in Scotland.

(9) In the case of an order mentioned in paragraph (c), (e), (f) or (g) of the definition of "maintenance order" in section 106 of this Act, the reference in subsection (8)(a) above to the coming into effect of an order or decree shall be construed as a reference to the registration of the order in Scotland.

DEFINITIONS
    "creditor": s.73(1).
    "maintenance": s.106.
    "maintenance order": s.106.
    "sheriff": s.73(1).

GENERAL NOTE
    This section empowers the sheriff to control current maintenance arrestments and the way in which they are operated.

Subs. (1)
    This subsection deals with arrestments which were invalid from the start (not properly served for example) and those which were valid but have subsequently ceased to have effect (some circumstances are listed in subs. (8)).

Subs. (2)

This subsection deals with the recall of a valid arrestment. The debtor's circumstances may have changed for the better and make arrestment unnecessary. The creditor would be wise to ask for a banker's order to be granted or some similar scheme to secure payment before he or she agrees not to oppose the application.

Subss. (5), (6), (7)

These deal with a valid arrestment which one party avers is not being properly operated. The sheriff may give directions as to the proper future operation and correct past over- or under- payments by directing reimbursement with interest from a date to be decided. This remedy is an alternative to the common law duty on the creditor to repay sums to which he or she is not entitled and any remedy the debtor has based on the employer's breach of contract to pay earnings. S.57(5) is concerned with the situation where the maintenance order is varied or recalled or the maintenance obligation ceases or ceases to be enforceable by diligence. There the debtor is automatically due reimbursement by the creditor of sums overpaid without the need for an order from the sheriff.

Subs. (8)

This subsection sets out the circumstances in which a current maintenance arrestment ceases to have effect. It is not an exhaustive list; an arrestment ceases to have effect for example on being abandoned by the creditor. On variation of a maintenance order the current maintenance arrestment enforcing the obligation falls, so that if the creditor wishes to enforce the varied order by means of a current maintenance arrestment he or she must serve a new schedule setting out the new daily rate of maintenance.

Examples of the cessation of maintenance obligations include:—

(a) the death of the alimentary creditor,

(b) the death or remarriage of the recipient of periodical allowance, Family Law (Scotland) Act 1985, s.13(7)(b), and

(c) the expiry of the period for which aliment or periodical allowance was granted or the occurrence of a specified event, 1985 Act, ss.3(1)(a) and 13(3).

Subs. (9)

Where a non-Scottish court pronounces an order recalling, varying or superseding a maintenance order (whether Scottish or non-Scottish) being enforced by a current mainten-ance arrestment, the arrestment ceases to have effect only when the recalling, etc., order is registered in Scotland.

Effect of new maintenance order on current maintenance arrestment

56.—(1) Where a maintenance order (referred to in this section as "the earlier order") which is being enforced by a current maintenance arrest-ment is varied or superseded by an order or decree granted by a court in Scotland (referred to in this section as "the later order"), the later order may include a condition that it shall not come into effect until the earlier of—

(a) the expiry of such period specified in the later order as the court considers necessary to allow notice to be given to the employer that the earlier order has been varied or superseded; or

(b) the service of a new current maintenance arrestment schedule in pursuance of the later order.

(2) Subsection (1) above shall not apply where the earlier order includes an order for the payment of aliment for the benefit of a spouse and the later order includes an order for the payment of a periodical allowance on divorce or on the granting of a declarator of nullity of marriage for the benefit of that spouse.

DEFINITIONS
"employer": s.73(1).
"maintenance order": s.106.

GENERAL NOTE
The purpose of this provision is to facilitate the transition from one current maintenance arrestment to the next. Where the maintenance obligation or one of the maintenance obligations being enforced is varied the arrestment immediately ceases to have effect and a new arrestment has to be served to enforce the varied obligation. Unless the variation had delayed effect the creditor would, on pain of wrongful diligence, have to intimate the cessation of the original arrestment forthwith, but would not be in a position to serve a new maintenance arrestment schedule until the variation decree was extractable. A decree is usually extractable after eight days in the Court of Session and after 14 days in the sheriff court. Delaying the effect of variation for say three weeks should give the creditor sufficient time.

Subs. (2) contains an exception to the above provision because a decree of divorce ends the alimentary relationship between the spouses and hence the legal basis of the decree of aliment. It would not be right to allow a decree to remain in effect for the purpose of diligence when its legal basis had been destroyed.

General

Failure to comply with arrestment, manner of payment and creditor's duty when arrestment ceases to have effect

57.—(1) Subject to section 69(4) of this Act, where an employer fails to comply with an earnings arrestment or a current maintenance arrestment—

(a) he shall be liable to pay to the creditor any sum which he would have paid to him under section 47(1) or 51(1) of this Act if he had so complied; and

(b) he shall not be entitled to recover any sum which he has paid to the debtor in contravention of the arrestment.

(2) Subject to subsection (3) below, a creditor shall not be entitled to refuse to accept payment under section 47(1) or 51(1) of this Act which is tendered by cheque or by such other method as may be prescribed by Act of Sederunt.

(3) If a cheque tendered in payment under section 47(1) or 51(1) of this Act is dishonoured or for any other reason the method of payment used by the employer is ineffectual, the creditor may insist that the payment concerned and any future payment under that provision shall be tendered in cash.

(4) Where—

(a) the debt recoverable under an earnings arrestment is paid or otherwise extinguished;

(b) a current maintenance arrestment ceases to have effect under section 55(8) above; or

(c) the debt being enforced by an earnings arrestment ceases to be enforceable by diligence,

the creditor shall, as soon as is reasonably practicable, intimate that fact to the employer.

(5) Where an event mentioned in subsection (4) above occurs, any sum paid by an employer—

(a) under an earnings arrestment, in excess of the debt recoverable; or

(b) under a current maintenance arrestment, in excess of the sum to be deducted under section 51(1) of this Act,

shall be recoverable by the debtor from the creditor with interest on that sum at the specified rate.

(6) Without prejudice to subsection (5) above, where a creditor has failed to comply with subsection (4) above the sheriff, on an application by the debtor, may make an order requiring the creditor to pay to the

debtor an amount not exceeding twice the amount recoverable by the debtor under the said subsection (5).

DEFINITIONS
"creditor": s.73(1).
"debt recoverable": ss.48(1) and 73(1).
"employer": s.73(1).
"sheriff": s.73(1).
"specified rate": s.73(1).

GENERAL NOTE
Civil rather than criminal proceedings are the sanction used to enforce duties arising in connection with arrestments of earnings, although in exceptional cases a flagrant breach of arrestment may be punishable as contempt of court (Graham Stewart, *Diligence* (1898), pp. 222–223).

Subs. (1)
This subsection deals with the case where the employer knowingly fails to make proper deductions under an earnings or current maintenance arrestment and pays the debtor the net earnings without the proper deduction. The employer has to pay the creditor and in law has to stand the loss, although few employees would refuse to reimburse their employer when the failure to operate was inadvertent. S.69(4) provides that no recovery can be made against the employer in respect of a failure occurring more than one year beforehand.
The case where the employer operates an arrestment in good faith but fails to do so properly is covered by s.50(4) or 55(6). The court on application may order reimbursement to correct under- or over-payments.

Subss. (2), (3)
Since there is no judicial monitoring of sums paid in pursuance of an arrestment, it is important that each party has a record of what was deducted. The use of cheques provides the creditor with a written record and the employer with a receipt since a cashed cheque is a receipt (Cheques Act 1957, s.3). Creditors are entitled to be paid in cash only if a cheque is dishonoured. Other methods which may be evolved in future for transmission of funds could be authorised by regulations.

Subss. (4)–(6)
The onus is on the creditor to tell the employer that the arrestment has ceased to have effect. If the creditor fails to do so, he or she is liable to reimburse the debtor for the deductions wrongly made, with interest. In addition the sheriff, on application, may impose a penalty, payable by the creditor to the debtor, of up to twice the total of the wrongful deductions. The imposition of such penalties will probably be confined to cases of wilful failure to intimate.

Simultaneous operation of earnings and current maintenance arrestment

58.—(1) Subject to subsection (2) below, one earnings arrestment and one current maintenance arrestment may be in effect simultaneously against earnings payable to the same debtor by the same employer.
(2) If on any pay-day the net earnings of the debtor are less than the total of the sums required to be paid under sections 47(1) and 51(1) of this Act, the employer shall—
(a) first operate the earnings arrestment; and
(b) secondly operate the current maintenance arrestment against the balance of the net earnings in accordance with section 53(1) of this Act.

DEFINITIONS
"earnings": s.73(1).
"employer": s.73(1).
"net earnings": s.73(1).
"pay-day": s.73(1).

GENERAL NOTE
As a general rule an employer is not required to operate more than one arrestment in respect of the same debtor's earnings at the same time (s.59(1) and (2)). The exception is where one of the arrestments is an earnings arrestment and the other is a current maintenance arrestment. This exception will assist a maintenance creditor since he or she will be able to collect and enforce current maintenance, and at the same time recover the arrears of maintenance due by the defaulting debtor.

Subs. (2) provides for priority to be given to the earnings arrestment if there are insufficient net earnings to enable the employer to deduct what is due under the earnings arrestment and the current maintenance arrestment and still leave the debtor with £5 per day exempt earnings for subsistence.

Example
A weekly paid debtor earning £80 net is subject to an earnings arrestment and a current maintenance arrestment for £40 per week. The employer deducts £9 under the earnings arrestment (Sched. 2 Table A) but only £36 for maintenance as the debtor has to be left with £35 (s.53(1)(b)).

Priority among arrestments

59.—(1) While an earnings arrestment is in effect, any other earnings arrestment against the earnings of the same debtor payable by the same employer shall not be competent.

(2) While a current maintenance arrestment is in effect, any other current maintenance arrestment against the earnings of the same debtor payable by the same employer shall not be competent.

(3) Where an employer receives on the same day 2 or more earnings arrestment schedules or 2 or more current maintenance arrestment schedules relating to earnings payable by him to the same debtor—

(a) if the employer receives the schedules at different times and he is aware of the respective times of receipt, only the earnings arrestment or, as the case may be, the current maintenance arrestment to which the first schedule he received relates shall have effect;

(b) in any other case, only such one of the earnings arrestments or, as the case may be, current maintenance arrestments as he shall choose shall have effect.

(4) Where a creditor (referred to in this section as "the second creditor") serves on an employer an earnings arrestment schedule or, as the case may be, a current maintenance arrestment schedule and, by virtue of this section, the arrestment to which that schedule relates does not come into effect, the employer shall as soon as is reasonably practicable give the following information to the second creditor regarding any other earnings arrestment or current maintenance arrestment in effect against the earnings of the same debtor payable by the same employer—

(a) the name and address of the creditor;

(b) the date and place of execution; and

(c) the debt recoverable specified in the earnings arrestment schedule or, as the case may be, the daily rate of maintenance specified in the current maintenance arrestment schedule.

(5) If the employer fails without reasonable excuse to give information to the second creditor under subsection (4) above, the sheriff, on an application by the second creditor, may order the employer to give the required information to the second creditor.

DEFINITIONS
"creditor": s.73(1).
"debt recoverable": ss.48(1) and 73(1).
"earnings": s.73(1).
"employer": s.73(1).
"sheriff": s.73(1).

GENERAL NOTE
Subss. (1), (2)
   An employer is not required to operate more than one arrestment of the same kind against
the same debtor's earnings at any one time. Once the first arrestment has been served and
is therefore in effect (s.47(3)(a) or s.51(2)(a)) a later arrestment of the same kind is
incompetent. The "shut out" second creditor's remedy is to apply for a conjoined arrestment
order (see ss.60 to 66).

Subs. (3)
   This subsection sets out the rules for determining priority between arrestments served on
the same day. Para. (a) restates the rule of priority applicable to arrestments under the
previous law—priority according to time of service (Graham Stewart, *Diligence* (1898), pp.
137–138). It would be helpful if in the case of hand served arrestments the officer noted on
the schedule the time of service. Para. (b) allows employers to choose which arrestment is
to receive effect if they are not aware of the different times of receipt of the arrestments, or
(and this is more likely) they arrive in the same post.

Subs. (4)
   The employer must furnish to a creditor who serves a later incompetent arrestment the
details of the existing arrestment set out in paras. (a) to (c). This will enable the disappointed
creditor to apply to the court for a conjoined arrestment order and so share with the first
creditor in the deductions from the debtor's earnings.

Subs. (5)
   An employer who failed to obey the sheriff's order would be liable to be punished for
contempt of court.

Conjoined arrestment orders

   60.—(1) This section applies where at the date of an application under
subsection (2) below—
   (a) there is in effect against the earnings of a debtor in the hands of a
       single employer an earnings arrestment or a current maintenance
       arrestment or (under section 58 of this Act) both; and
   (b) a creditor, who may be a creditor already enforcing a debt by an
       arrestment mentioned above, (referred to in this section as "a
       qualified creditor") would be entitled, but for section 59(1) or (2)
       of this Act, to enforce his debt by executing an earnings arrestment
       or a current maintenance arrestment.
   (2) Subject to subsection (4) below, where this section applies the
sheriff, on an application made by a qualified creditor, shall make a
conjoined arrestment order.
   (3) A conjoined arrestment order shall—
   (a) recall any arrestment mentioned in subsection (1)(a) above so
       that it shall cease to have effect on the coming into effect of
       the order; and
   (b) require the employer concerned, while the order is in effect, to
       deduct a sum calculated in accordance with section 63 of this
       Act from the debtor's net earnings on any pay-day and to pay
       it as soon as is reasonably practicable to the sheriff clerk.
   (4) It shall not be competent to make a conjoined arrestment order—
   (a) where all the debts concerned are maintenance payable by the
       same debtor to the same person (whether for his own benefit
       or for another person's) so that, if the existing current main-
       tenance arrestment were abandoned, they could all be enforced
       under section 52(2)(a) of this Act; or
   (b) where there are only 2 debts, one an ordinary debt and one
       maintenance, so that they could be enforced under section
       58(1) of this Act (one earnings arrestment and one current
       maintenance arrestment); or

    (c) where the same person is the creditor or person to whom any maintenance is payable (as described in paragraph (a) above) in relation to all the debts sought to be enforced by the order.

(5) A conjoined arrestment order—

    (a) shall come into effect 7 days after a copy of it has been served on the employer under subsection (7) below; and

    (b) shall remain in effect until a copy of an order recalling the conjoined arrestment order has been served on the employer under section 66(7) of this Act or the debtor ceases to be employed by him.

(6) A conjoined arrestment order shall be in the form prescribed by Act of Sederunt, and—

    (a) where an ordinary debt is to be enforced, the order shall specify the amount recoverable in respect of the debt under the order; and

    (b) where current maintenance is to be enforced, the order shall specify the maintenance expressed as a daily rate or, as the case may be, as an aggregate of the daily rates; and subsection (5) of section 51 of this Act shall apply for the purposes of this paragraph as it applies for the purposes of subsection (4) of that section.

(7) The sheriff clerk shall as soon as is reasonably practicable serve a copy of the conjoined arrestment order on the employer and the debtor, and on the creditor in every arrestment mentioned in subsection (1)(a) above.

(8) A decision of the sheriff making a conjoined arrestment order shall not be subject to appeal.

(9) Subject to section 69(4) of this Act, where an employer fails to comply with a conjoined arrestment order—

    (a) the employer shall be liable to pay to the sheriff clerk any sum which he would have paid if he had so complied;

    (b) the employer shall not be entitled to recover any sum which he has paid to the debtor in contravention of the order; and

    (c) the sheriff, on an application by the sheriff clerk, may grant warrant for diligence against the employer for recovery of the sums which appear to the sheriff to be due.

DEFINITIONS
  "creditor": s.73(1).
  "earnings": s.73(2).
  "employer": s.73(1).
  "maintenance": s.106.
  "net earnings": s.73(1).
  "ordinary debt": s.73(1).
  "pay-day": s.73(1).
  "sheriff": s.73(1).

GENERAL NOTE

This section introduces conjoined arrestment orders. In general an employer is not required to operate more than one arrestment at any one time against the same debtor's earnings. Therefore some method has to be found of sharing the fruits of diligence, otherwise a prior creditor will shut out later creditors for years perhaps and a race of diligence may ensue. Sharing under the equalisation of diligence provisions of the Bankruptcy (Scotland) Act 1985 (Sched. 7, para. 24) is expressly disapplied in relation to arrestments against earnings as it would require the first creditor to act as a unremunerated debt collector for the others. The chosen method of sharing the fruits of diligence is a conjoined arrestment order in terms of which the employer remits the deductions made from the debtor's earnings to the court which in turn apportions them between the conjoined creditors.

Subss. (1), (4)

These two subsections set out the circumstances in which a conjoined arrestment order is competent. Their effect may be summarised in the following way:

First creditor (A)	Second creditor (B)	
2 or more current maintenance debts	—	Order incompetent: s.60(4)(a). A can abandon existing arrestment and serve a new arrestment for aggregate amount: s.52(2)(a).
2 or more ordinary debts	—	Order competent except for arrears of maintenance: s.60(4)(a). But A can abandon existing arrestment and serve a new one for the combined amount: s.48(3).
2 or more ordinary and current maintenance debts	—	Order incompetent. A can abandon existing arrestment(s) and serve new arrestments (1 for the combined ordinary debts and 1 for the aggregate amount of maintenance).
1 ordinary debt	1 current maintenance debt	Order incompetent. Both creditors' arrestments can operate simultaneously: s.60(4)(b).
1 ordinary debt	1 ordinary debt	B may apply for an order as arrestment incompetent: s.59(1).
1 current maintenance debt	1 current maintenance debt	B may apply for an order as arrestment incompetent: s.59(2).
1 ordinary debt and 1 current maintenance debt	1 ordinary debt or 1 current maintenance debt	B may apply for an order as arrestment incompetent: s.59(1) or (2).

Where the employer is already operating an earnings arrestment for creditor A and a current maintenance arrestment for creditor B, then if a third creditor wishes to enforce either an ordinary debt or current maintenance, or creditor A wishes to enforce current maintenance or creditor B wishes to enforce an ordinary debt an arrestment to enforce the third debt will be incompetent and an order could be applied for.

Also if creditor A wishes to enforce an additional ordinary debt or creditor B wishes to enforce an additional maintenance obligation he or she may do so by way of a conjoined arrestment order since an additional arrestment would be incompetent. Alternatively A or B may abandon the existing arrestment and serve a new arrestment in respect of the total of the original and the additional debt.

A creditor applying for a conjoined arrestment order must be in a position to enforce the debt by arrestment. He or she must therefore be in possession of a decree or other document containing a warrant of execution and have charged and waited for the period of charge to expire without payment (ordinary debt), or have intimated the maintenance order, waited four weeks and still be due three instalments of maintenance (current maintenance). But the creditor need not have served an abortive arrestment first, although in many cases this will be the only way of finding out about the existence of a previous arrestment or arrestments which render the applicant creditor's arrestment incompetent.

Subs. (2)

Provided the application is in order the sheriff is directed to make a conjoined arrestment order. The making is thus an administrative act which could be delegated to sheriff clerks.

Subs. (3)

As soon as the conjoined arrestment order comes into effect—seven days after service on the employer (subs. (5))—the employer ceases to deduct under the existing arrestment(s) and deducts under the order. Future deductions are sent to the sheriff clerk rather than the arresting creditor(s).

Subss. (5), (7)
Unlike an earnings arrestment or a current maintenance arrestment, the employer is not entitled to operate a conjoined arrestment order until seven days have elapsed from the date of service. Service is effected by the sheriff clerk.
With the exception of termination of the debtor's employment, the employer is bound to carry on deducting under a conjoined arrestment order until served with a recall by the sheriff clerk. A conjoined arrestment order does not lapse and is not recallable simply because only one creditor remains in it after the others have been satisfied.

Subs. (6)
To enable the sheriff clerk to prepare the conjoined arrestment order the applicant creditor must furnish details of his or her own debt and the debts of creditors with existing arrestments. The latter information may be obtained from the employer by serving an abortive arrestment or otherwise.

Para. (a)
The amount recoverable is set out in s.61. If more than one ordinary debt is being enforced the order must set out the amount recoverable in respect of each.

Para. (b)
S.51(5) contains the rules for converting a weekly, monthly, etc. maintenance obligation into a daily rate. If there is more than one obligation being enforced the daily rates are aggregated.

Subs. (8)
Although the making of an order is not appealable it may be recalled later on application by an interested person under s.66(1).

Subs. (9)
Paras. (a) and (b) are the equivalent of s.57(1). Para. (c) provides for direct enforcement without the need for constitution of the debt against the employer by a separate action.

Amount recoverable under conjoined arrestment order

61.—(1) Subject to subsection (2) below, the amount recoverable under any conjoined arrestment order in respect of an ordinary debt shall consist of the following sums, in so far as outstanding—
    (a) any sum (including expenses) due under the decree or other document on which the creditor founds or, as the case may be, under section 51(3) of this Act;
    (b) any interest on that sum which had accrued at the date of execution of the arrestment or, where no arrestment was executed, at the date of the making of the conjoined arrestment order; and
    (c) where an earnings arrestment has been executed, the expenses of executing it and the charge which preceded it.
    (2) Any sum mentioned in subsection (1) above shall be recoverable only if and to the extent that—
    (a) it was specified in an earnings arrestment schedule in respect of an arrestment which is recalled under subsection (3)(a) of section 60 of this Act; or
    (b) it is specified in the application under subsection (2) of that section.
    (3) Where an obligation to pay maintenance is enforced by a conjoined arrestment order, no interest shall accrue on any arrears of maintenance which arise while the order is in effect.
    (4) Subject to subsection (5) below, a creditor who makes an application under section 60(2) of this Act shall be entitled to recover as an ordinary debt under any conjoined arrestment order which is made his expenses in connection with the application to the extent that they are specified in the application.
    (5) There shall not be recoverable under subsection (4) above any expenses incurred in serving an earnings arrestment schedule or a current

maintenance arrestment schedule on the employer after the date of the application.

DEFINITIONS
"creditor": s.73(1).
"decree or other document": s.73(1).
"employer": s.73(1).
"maintenance": s.106.
"ordinary debt": s.73(1).

GENERAL NOTE
Subss. (1), (2)
These subsections set out what a creditor with an ordinary debt can recover under a conjoined arrestment order. In the case of the first creditor—the creditor whose earnings arrestment was recalled by the order, these sums will already have been specified in that earnings arrestment schedule (see s.48) and will be repeated in the order. In the case of the second creditor—the creditor who applied for the conjoined arrestment order—these sums are recoverable only to the extent that they are specified in the application. S.51(3) provides that the expenses of executing a current maintenance arrestment may be recovered as an ordinary debt.

Subs. (3)
This is the equivalent of s.51(6).

Subss. (4), (5)
Subs. (4) is straightforward. The creditor who applies for a conjoined arrestment order is entitled to recover the expenses of application for the order under it. Since the order is served by the sheriff clerk there will be no other expenses.
Subs. (5) presents difficulties. If the theory is that an incompetent arrestment does not give rise to any expenses chargeable against the debtor, then the subsection is without content. If, on the other hand, expenses of abortive arrestments are recoverable then it is hard to see why the subsection is confined to arrestments served after the application, since it is inconceivable that a creditor applying for a conjoined arrestment order would serve a further arrestment which is bound to be incompetent.

Relationship of conjoined arrestment order with earnings and current maintenance arrestments

62.—(1) While a conjoined arrestment order is in effect, it shall not be competent to execute any earnings arrestment or current maintenance arrestment or for the sheriff to grant any other conjoined arrestment order against the earnings of the same debtor payable by the same employer.

(2) If, while a conjoined arrestment order is in effect, a creditor whose debt is not being enforced by it serves an earnings arrestment schedule or a current maintenance arrestment schedule, against earnings payable to the debtor, on the employer, the employer shall as soon as is reasonably practicable inform that creditor which court made the order.

(3) If, after an application is made under section 60(2) of this Act for a conjoined arrestment order and before any such order comes into effect, an earnings arrestment or a current maintenance arrestment against earnings payable by the employer to the debtor comes into effect under section 58(1) of this Act—

    (a) the arrestment shall cease to have effect when the conjoined arrestment order comes into effect; and

    (b) the employer shall, as soon as is reasonably practicable after the service of a copy of the conjoined arrestment order on him under section 60(7) of this Act, inform the creditor on whose behalf the arrestment was executed which court made the order.

(4) If an employer fails without reasonable excuse to give information to a creditor under subsection (2) or (3) above, the sheriff, on an

application by the creditor, may order the employer to give the required information to the creditor.

(5) Where a conjoined arrestment order is in effect, the sheriff, on an application made by a creditor whose debt is not being enforced by the order and who, but for the order, would be entitled to enforce his debt by an earnings arrestment or a current maintenance arrestment, shall make an order varying the conjoined arrestment order so that the creditor's debt is included among the debts enforced by the conjoined arrestment order; and section 61(1), (2), (4) and (5) of this Act shall apply in relation to an application under this subsection as it applies in relation to an application under section 60 of this Act.

(6) The sheriff clerk shall as soon as is reasonably practicable serve a copy of an order under subsection (5) above on the debtor, the employer and the other creditors whose debts are being enforced by the conjoined arrestment order.

(7) Subject to section 69(2) of this Act, an order under subsection (5) above shall come into effect 7 days after a copy of it has been served on the employer under subsection (6) above.

(8) Section 60(6) of this Act shall apply to a conjoined arrestment order as varied under subsection (5) above as it applies to a conjoined arrestment order mentioned in that section.

(9) A decision of the sheriff under subsection (5) above shall not be subject to appeal.

DEFINITIONS
  "creditor": s.73(1).
  "earnings": s.73(1).
  "employer": s.73(1).
  "sheriff": s.73(1).

GENERAL NOTE
  This section renders incompetent any earnings arrestment or current maintenance arrestment served after a conjoined arrestment order is in effect. The disappointed creditor has to apply for inclusion in the existing conjoined arrestment order. The provisions are very similar to those set out in s.60 which apply to a creditor applying for a conjoined arrestment order. There is no limit to the number of creditors who may be conjoined in a conjoined arrestment order.

Subs. (3)
  This subsection deals with a rather unusual and complex situation and is best illustrated by an example:
    Creditor A serves an earnings arrestment for an ordinary debt.
    Creditor B attempts to serve another earnings arrestment which is incompetent and applies for a conjoined arrestment order which is made.
    Before the order is served on the employer creditor C serves a current maintenance arrestment.
    The employer must give effect to the arrestments of creditors A and C until the order is served. The employer is then required to cease and operate the order instead. C is not included in the order and the employer's duty is to inform C which court made the order so that C can apply to be conjoined in the order.

Sum payable by employer under conjoined arrestment order

63.—(1) Subject to section 69(3) of this Act, this section shall have effect for the purpose of determining the sum to be deducted on a pay-day and paid to the sheriff clerk under a conjoined arrestment order.

(2) Where all the debts are ordinary debts, the said sum shall be the sum which the employer would pay under section 47(1) of this Act if the debts were one debt being enforced on the pay-day by an earnings arrestment.

(3) Where all the debts are current maintenance, the sum shall be whichever is the lesser of the amounts mentioned in paragraphs (a) and (b) of subsection (4) below, less any sum which the debtor is entitled to deduct under any enactment in respect of income tax.

(4) The amounts referred to in subsection (3) above are—
  (a) the aggregate of the sums arrived at by multiplying each of the daily rates of maintenance (as specified in the conjoined arrestment order) by the number of days—
    (i) since the last pay-day when a deduction from earnings was made by the employer under section 51(1) or 60(3)(b) of this Act in respect of the maintenance obligation; or
    (ii) if there was no such previous pay-day, since the date when the conjoined arrestment order or any order under section 62(5) of this Act varying it came into effect; or
  (b) any net earnings in so far as they exceed the sum of £5 per day for the number of days mentioned in paragraph (a) above.

(5) Where one or more of the debts are ordinary debts, and one or more are current maintenance, the sum shall be the aggregate of the following—
  (a) the sum which the employer would pay under section 47(1) of this Act if the ordinary debt was being enforced on the pay-day by an earnings arrestment (where there is more than one ordinary debt, treating the aggregate amount of them as if it were one debt); and
  (b) in relation to the debts which are current maintenance, the sum which would be payable under subsection (3) above if all the debts were current maintenance and so much of the debtor's net earnings as are left after deduction of the sum provided for in paragraph (a) above were his whole net earnings.

(6) The sum specified in subsection (4)(b) above may be varied by regulations made by the Lord Advocate and such regulations may make different provision for different cases.

(7) The sheriff clerk shall intimate to the employer operating a conjoined arrestment order, in the form prescribed by Act of Sederunt, the making of regulations under section 49(7) of this Act or subsection (6) above; and, subject to section 69(1) and (2) of this Act, such regulations shall not apply to the conjoined arrestment order until such intimation.

(8) An employer operating a conjoined arrestment order in relation to current maintenance shall be entitled, but shall not be required, to apply a change in the small maintenance payments limits before the sheriff clerk intimates the change to the employer in the form prescribed by Act of Sederunt.

(9) For the purposes of subsection (8) above, the small maintenance payment limits are the rates mentioned in section 65(1A) of the Income and Corporation Taxes Act 1970.

(10) Subject to subsection (11) below, the sheriff clerk shall not be entitled to refuse to accept payment by the employer under section 60(3)(b) of this Act which is tendered by cheque or by such other method as may be prescribed by Act of Sederunt.

(11) If a cheque tendered in payment under section 60(3)(b) of this Act is dishonoured or for any other reason the method of payment used is ineffectual, the sheriff clerk may insist that the payment for which the cheque was tendered and any future payment by the employer under the conjoined arrestment order shall be tendered in cash.

DEFINITIONS
  "current maintenance": s.73(1).
  "earnings": s.73(2).
  "employer": s.73(1).

"maintenance": s.106.
"net earnings": s.73(1).
"ordinary debts": s.73(1).
"pay-day": s.73(1).

GENERAL NOTE
This section sets out the rules for calculating the deductions to be made from the debtor's net earnings in pursuance of a conjoined arrestment order.

Subs. (2)
Where all the debts being enforced by a conjoined arrestment order are ordinary debts the employer simply treats the order as if it were an earnings arrestment for the purposes of calculating the deductions and accordingly applies Tables A, B or C or the other provisions of s.49.

Subss. (3), (4)
Where all the debts are current maintenance the employer simply multiplies the aggregate daily rate of maintenance by the number of days since the last pay-day when a deduction was made either under the conjoined arrestment order, or a previous order, or a current maintenance arrestment superseded by the order to arrive at the gross maintenance. Tax may have to be deducted, see note on s.53(1) and (2). If there was no previous pay-day on which deductions were made (as might happen if the first current maintenance arrestment was swiftly superseded by a conjoined arrestment order) the number of days since the order came into effect (seven days after service on the employer, s.60(5)(a)) is used instead.
The above deductions are always subject to the subsistence exemption of £5 per day (see note on s.53(1) and (2) for how this works).

Subs. (5)
This subsection deals with a "mixed" conjoined arrestment order, where there is at least one of each kind of debt. The employer first operates subs. (2), *i.e.* the normal earnings arrestment rules, and then operates subs. (3) and (4) on the balance. This is the same rule as applies in the case of an earnings arrestment and a current maintenance arrestment being operated concurrently, see s.58(2).

Subss. (6), (7)
Regulations may be made altering the deductions under an earnings arrestment which will affect the deductions to be made in respect of ordinary debts contained in a conjoined arrestment order, s.49(7). Similar regulations may alter the subsistence level for deductions in respect of maintenance obligations (subs. (6)).
Where a conjoined arrestment order is served after intimation of the regulations the employer must deduct in accordance with the regulations.
Where an employer is already operating an order when the regulations are intimated the employer is entitled, but is not bound, to operate in accordance with the new regulations on a pay-day falling within seven days of such intimation. The purpose of this provision is to avoid last minute changes in pay having to be made. On later pay-days the employer must deduct in accordance with the regulations. The employer is similarly entitled, but not bound, to operate in accordance with the new regulations on becoming aware of them otherwise than by intimation. This is perhaps not very likely to happen as sheriff clerks are under a duty to intimate the regulations to all employers concerned as soon as they are made.

Subss. (8), (9)
These subsections are the equivalent of s.53(5) and (6) for current maintenance arrestments. An increase in the small maintenance payments limits may require the employer to switch from a net rate of maintenance to a (higher) gross rate of maintenance.

Subss. (10), (11)
These are the equivalent of s.57(2) and (3) for earnings arrestments and current maintenance arrestments.

Disbursement by sheriff clerk of sums received from employer

64. Sums paid to the sheriff clerk under section 60(3)(b) of this Act shall be disbursed by him to the creditors whose debts are being enforced by the conjoined arrestment order in accordance with Schedule 3 to this Act.

  "creditor": s.73(1).
  "current maintenance": s.73(1).
  "maintenance": s.106.
  "ordinary debt": s.73(1).

GENERAL NOTE

S.64 introduces Sched. 3 which directs the sheriff clerk how to distribute between the various creditors conjoined in the order the sums received from the employer. The provisions are inevitably complex since account has to be taken of the possibility that insufficient will be deducted on a pay-day to satisfy the claims of all the creditors. The complexity of the task was one of the main reasons for not imposing it on the employer but handing it instead to the court. (See further the annotations to Sched. 3.)

Operation of conjoined arrestment order

65.—(1) The sheriff may make an order determining any dispute as to the operation of a conjoined arrestment order, on an application by—
  (a) the debtor;
  (b) a creditor whose debt is being enforced by the order;
  (c) the employer; or
  (d) the sheriff clerk.
(2) Without prejudice to subsection (6) below, the sheriff, when making an order under subsection (1) above, may order—
  (a) the reimbursement of any payment made in the operation of the conjoined arrestment order which ought not to have been made; or
  (b) the payment of any sum which ought to have been paid in the operation of the conjoined arrestment order but which has not been paid.
(3) An order under subsection (2) above shall require the person against whom it is made to pay interest on the sum to be paid by him under the order at the specified rate from such date as the sheriff shall specify in the order.
(4) Where an ordinary debt is being enforced by a conjoined arrestment order, the creditor shall, as soon as is reasonably practicable after the debt recoverable has been paid or otherwise extinguished, or the debt has ceased to be enforceable by diligence, intimate that fact to the sheriff clerk.
(5) Where current maintenance is being enforced by a conjoined arrestment order, the creditor shall, as soon as is reasonably practicable after any obligation to pay such maintenance has ceased or has ceased to be enforceable by diligence, intimate that fact to the sheriff clerk.
(6) Any sum received by a creditor under a conjoined arrestment order in respect of—
  (a) an ordinary debt, after the debt has been paid or otherwise extinguished or has ceased to be enforceable by diligence; or
  (b) current maintenance after the obligation to pay such maintenance has ceased or has ceased to be enforceable by diligence;
shall be recoverable by the sheriff clerk from the creditor with interest on that sum at the specified rate.
(7) Without prejudice to subsection (6) above, where the creditor has failed to comply with subsection (4) or (5) above the sheriff may, on an application by the debtor, make an order requiring the creditor to pay to the debtor an amount not exceeding twice the amount recoverable by the sheriff clerk under subsection (6) above.

(8) Any amount recovered from a creditor by the sheriff clerk under subsection (6) above shall be disbursed by him to the creditors whose debts are being enforced by the conjoined arrestment order in accordance with Schedule 3 to this Act or, if there are no such creditors, shall be paid to the debtor.

DEFINITIONS
  "creditor": s.73(1).
  "current maintenance": s.73(1).
  "employer": s.73(1).
  "maintenance": s.106.
  "ordinary debt": s.73(1).
  "sheriff": s.73(1).
  "specified rate": s.73(1).

GENERAL NOTE
These provisions are, with minor changes due to the presence of the sheriff clerk, very similar to those applicable to earnings arrestments and current maintenance arrestments.
  Subs. (1) is the equivalent of ss.50(3) and 55(5).
  Subs. (2) is the equivalent of ss.50(4) and 55(6).
  Subs. (3) is the equivalent of ss.50(5) and 55(7).
  Subss. (4) and (5) are the equivalent of s.57(4). Variation of a maintenance obligation being enforced is dealt with by making a varied order under s.66(4).
  Subs. (6) is the equivalent of s.57(5).
  Subs. (7) is the equivalent of s.57(6).

Subs. (8)
  The overpayments recovered from a creditor under subs. (6) are (together with interest) distributed amongst the remaining creditors conjoined in the order or if none, paid to the debtor. The penalty imposed under subs. (7) however is not so distributed and becomes the property of the debtor as it is a kind of solatium for wrongful diligence. It could be attached in the hands of the liable creditor by another creditor using an arrestment and furthcoming.

Recall and variation of conjoined arrestment order

66.—(1) The sheriff shall make an order recalling a conjoined arrestment order—
  (a) on an application by any of the persons mentioned in subsection (2) below, if he is satisfied—
    (i) that the conjoined arrestment order is invalid;
    (ii) that all the ordinary debts enforced by the order have been paid or otherwise extinguished or have ceased to be enforceable by diligence and that all the obligations to pay current maintenance being so enforced have ceased or have ceased to be enforceable by diligence; or
    (iii) that the debtor's estate has been sequestrated; or
  (b) on an application for recall of the order by all the creditors whose debts are being enforced by the order.
  (2) The persons referred to in subsection (1)(a) above are—
    (a) the debtor;
    (b) any creditor whose debt is being enforced by the order;
    (c) the person on whom a copy of the order or an order varying the order was served under section 60(7) or 62(6) of this Act;
    (d) the sheriff clerk;
    (e) if the debtor's estate has been sequestrated, the interim trustee appointed under section 13 of the Bankruptcy (Scotland) Act 1985 or the permanent trustee in the sequestration.
  (3) Where the sheriff recalls a conjoined arrestment order under subsection (1) above, he may make such consequential order as appears to him to be necessary in the circumstances.
  (4) Where—

   (a) any ordinary debt being enforced by a conjoined arrestment order is paid or otherwise extinguished or ceases to be enforceable by diligence; or

   (b) current maintenance is being so enforced and—
      (i) an order or decree comes into effect which varies, supersedes or recalls the maintenance order which is being enforced; or
      (ii) the obligation to pay maintenance has ceased or has ceased to be enforceable in Scotland,

the sheriff, on an application by the debtor, any creditor whose debt is being enforced by the conjoined arrestment order, the employer or the sheriff clerk, may make an order varying the conjoined arrestment order appropriately.

(5) In the case of an order mentioned in paragraph (c), (e), (f) or (g) of the definition of "maintenance order" in section 106 of this Act, the reference in subsection (4)(b)(i) above to the coming into effect of an order shall be construed as a reference to the registration of the order in Scotland.

(6) The sheriff may vary a conjoined arrestment order to give effect to a request by a creditor whose debt is being enforced by the order that it should cease to be so enforced.

(7) The sheriff clerk shall as soon as is reasonably practicable serve a copy of any order under subsection (1), (3), (4) or (6) above on the debtor, the employer (or, where he is not the employer, the person mentioned in subsection (2)(c) above), any creditor whose debt is being enforced by the conjoined arrestment order and, if the conjoined arrestment order has been recalled on the ground of the sequestration of the debtor's estate, the interim trustee or the permanent trustee in the sequestration, if known to the sheriff clerk.

(8) Subject to section 103(6) of this Act, an order under subsection (3) above shall not come into effect until a copy of the order has been served on the employer under subsection (7) above.

(9) An order under subsection (1) above shall not come into effect until a copy of the order has been served on the employer under subsection (7) above and shall not be subject to appeal.

(10) An order under subsection (4) or (6) above shall come into effect 7 days after a copy of the order has been served on the employer under subsection (7) above.

DEFINITIONS
  "creditor": s.73(1).
  "current maintenance": s.73(1).
  "maintenance": s.106.
  "maintenance order": s.106.
  "ordinary debt": s.73(1).
  "sheriff": s.73(1).

GENERAL NOTE
Subs. (1)
  This subsection sets out the grounds of recall. It should be noted that a conjoined arrestment order does not terminate and is not recallable merely because only one creditor remains in it. The sheriff clerk continues to receive deductions from the employer and remits them to the creditor until the debt is paid or, in the case of maintenance, the obligation ceases. This may well result in sheriff clerks becoming maintenance collectors along the lines of magistrates' clerks in England and Wales.

Subs. (2)
  The person mentioned in para. (c) is usually the employer, but "person" is used to cover the case where the order was served on a person who was not in fact the employer.

Subs. (4)

This subsection deals with variation of a conjoined arrestment order. How the sheriff varies the order depends on the original order and the changes in the conjoined debts. For example, a variation of a maintenance obligation will require alteration of the daily rate, while payment of an ordinary debt will require deletion of that debt from the order.

Subs. (5)

Where the variation, supersession or recall order is made by a non-Scottish court it comes into effect on being registered in Scotland.

Subs. (6)

A creditor may "opt out" of having his or her debt enforced by a conjoined arrestment order.

Subs. (8)

S.103(6) provides that a consequential order made on recalling a conjoined arrestment order shall not take effect while it is appealable or subject to appeal.

Subs. (9)

An order recalling a conjoined arrestment order is final. Until a copy of the recall order is served (or the debtor ceases to be employed) the employer must continue to operate a conjoined arrestment order.

Supplementary provisions

Equalisation of diligences not to apply

67. Paragraph 24 of Schedule 7 to the Bankruptcy (Scotland) Act 1985 (equalisation of arrestments and poindings used within 60 days before, and 4 months after, apparent insolvency) shall not apply in relation to an earnings arrestment, a current maintenance arrestment or a conjoined arrestment order.

GENERAL NOTE

The equalisation of arrestments under para. 24 provides a means whereby creditors with decrees can share in a fund attached by another creditor who has executed an arrestment. This is disapplied for arrestments against earnings since creditors share outwith sequestration by means of a conjoined arrestment order.

Diversion of arrested earnings to Secretary of State

68. After section 25 of the Social Security Act 1986 there shall be inserted the following section—

"Diversion of arrested earnings to Secretary of State

25A.—(1) Where in Scotland a creditor who is enforcing a maintenance order or an alimentary bond or agreement by a current maintenance arrestment or a conjoined arrestment order is in receipt of income support, the creditor may in writing authorise the Secretary of State to receive any sums payable under the arrestment or order until the creditor ceases to be in receipt of income support or in writing withdraws the authorisation, whichever occurs first.

(2) On intimation by the Secretary of State—

    (a) to the employer operating the current maintenance arrestment; or

    (b) to the sheriff clerk operating the conjoined arrestment order;

of an authorisation under subsection (1) above, the employer or sheriff clerk shall, until notified by the Secretary of State that the authorisation has ceased to have effect, pay to the Secretary of State any sums which would otherwise be payable under the arrestment or order to the creditor.".

GENERAL NOTE
Where the Department of Health and Social Security pay supplementary benefit (or income support as it soon will be called) to a maintenance creditor they may seek to have payments due under the maintenance decree paid to them to reimburse them for benefit provided. At present this is not easy to accomplish since it involves the Department contacting the debtor and obtaining his or her consent. The purpose of this section is to allow the Department (with the creditor's consent) to receive maintenance due to the creditor out of deductions made by the employer. The debtor will not be aware that this diversion is taking place.

Restriction on liability of employer in operating diligence against earnings

69.—(1) An employer operating an earnings arrestment or a current maintenance arrestment or a conjoined arrestment order shall be entitled to apply regulations made under section 49(7), 53(3) or 63(6) of this Act before receiving intimation under section 49(8), 53(4) or 63(7) of this Act of the making of the regulations.

(2) Where a pay-day occurs within a period of 7 days after the date of—

(a) service on the employer of an earnings arrestment schedule or a current maintenance arrestment schedule or a copy of a conjoined arrestment order or of a variation thereof; or

(b) intimation under section 49(8), 53(4) or 63(7) of this Act to the employer of the making of regulations,

the employer shall be entitled, but shall not be required, on that day to operate the arrestment or order or, as the case may be, to give effect to the regulations.

(3) Where, in accordance with subsection (2) above, the employer on a pay-day (referred to below as "the previous pay-day")—

(a) does not operate an earnings arrestment, current maintenance arrestment or conjoined arrestment order; or

(b) does not give effect to regulations,

he shall not include in any sum deducted from the net earnings of the debtor on a subsequent pay-day under the arrestment or order any sum in respect of the debtor's net earnings on the previous pay-day.

(4) No claim may be made by—

(a) the debtor or the creditor against the employer in respect of any deduction which has, or ought to have, been made by the employer from the debtor's net earnings, or any payment which has been, or ought to have been, made by him, under an earnings arrestment or a current maintenance arrestment; or

(b) the debtor, the sheriff clerk or any creditor against the employer in respect of any such deduction or payment which has been, or ought to have been, made under a conjoined arrestment order,

more than one year after the date when the deduction or payment has, or ought to have, been made.

(5) The employer shall not be liable to the debtor for any deduction made by him from the debtor's net earnings—

(a) under an earnings arrestment unless and until he receives intimation—

(i) from the creditor under section 57(4) of this Act that the debt recoverable has been paid or otherwise extinguished or has ceased to be enforceable by diligence;

(ii) from the sheriff clerk under section 9(7)(b) or 50(1) of this Act that an order has been made recalling the arrestment or, as the case may be, declaring that it is invalid or has ceased to have effect;

(iii) that the debtor's estate has been sequestrated; or

  (iv) from the creditor that he has abandoned the arrestment;
 (b) under a current maintenance arrestment unless and until he receives intimation—
  (i) from the creditor under section 57(4) of this Act that the arrestment has ceased to have effect;
  (ii) from the sheriff clerk under section 55(3) of this Act that an order has been made recalling the arrestment or declaring that the arrestment is invalid or has ceased to have effect;
  (iii) that the debtor's estate has been sequestrated; or
  (iv) from the creditor that he has abandoned the arrestment.

DEFINITIONS
  "creditor": s.73(1).
  "employer": s.73(1).
  "net earnings": s.73(1).
  "pay-day": s.73(1).

GENERAL NOTE
Subs. (1)
  This subsection provides that an employer may give effect to regulations altering the amounts to be deducted in pursuance of an earnings arrestment, current maintenance arrestment or conjoined arrestment order before the regulations have been intimated by the creditor or sheriff clerk. The employer is, however, not bound to do so until intimation.

Subs. (2)
  Para. (a) allows employers a seven-day period after service in order to make the necessary administrative arrangements for processing the arrestment order. They are not bound (although they are entitled) to make deductions on any pay-day occurring within the seven-day period. They must make deductions on later pay-days.
  Para. (b) gives a similar period of grace to employers in respect of the intimation of regulations altering the amounts to be deducted in pursuance of an arrestment or order.

Subs. (3)
  The working of this subsection is best illustrated by an example:
  A debtor with weekly net earnings of £100 is subject to an earnings arrestment. He is paid on a Friday.

Monday 12th January	Arrestment served.
Friday 16th January	Employer chooses not to deduct.
Friday 23rd January	Employer applies Table A to one week's earnings only and deducts £13.

Subs. (4)
  This subsection protects employers against claims arising out of wrongful operation of an earnings arrestment, a current maintenance arrestment or a conjoined arrestment order occurring more than a year prior to the claim. It does not affect the rights of debtors or creditors to claim against each other in respect of under- or over-payments made. The debtor's claim for restitution of an over-payment is subject to a five years prescriptive period (Prescription and Limitation (Scotland) Act 1973, s.6 and Sched. 1, para. 1). A creditor's claim based on non-satisfaction of a decree prescribes after 20 years (1973 Act, s.7 and Sched. 1, para. 2).

Subs. (5)
  The employer is entitled to continue making deductions under an earnings arrestment or current maintenance arrestment until in receipt of intimation of one of the events mentioned. Intimation of sequestration may be made by any interested person—the interim or permanent trustee in sequestration, a sheriff clerk, a non-arresting creditor or the debtor for example.
  Employers are not bound to continue until intimation. They may stop earlier if they think the arrestment has ceased to have effect but they do so at their own risk. For example with an earnings arrestment the employer should be able to work out when the debt has been paid off and could then stop deducting without waiting for an intimation from the creditor.
  Where a creditor refuses or delays to intimate, the debtor may apply to the sheriff for the arrestment to be recalled. In addition to ordering reimbursement of overpayments the sheriff

can impose a penalty of up to twice the sum of the overpayments on a dilatory creditor (ss.57(6) and 65(7)).

The subsection is limited to earnings arrestments and current maintenance arrestments. Conjoined arrestment orders are court orders and the employer is obliged to continue deducting (under pain of contempt of court) until the order is recalled and the recall intimated or the debtor ceases to be employed.

Execution and intimation of copies

70.—(1) When an officer of court serves an earnings arrestment schedule or a current maintenance arrestment schedule on the employer of the debtor he shall, if reasonably practicable, intimate a copy of the schedule to the debtor.

(2) Failure to intimate a copy of the schedule to the debtor shall not by itself render the arrestment invalid.

(3) Service of any such schedule shall be by registered or recorded delivery letter or, if such a letter cannot be delivered, by any other competent mode of service.

(4) The certificate of execution of an earnings arrestment or a current maintenance arrestment shall be signed by the officer of court who effected the service.

(5) Section 17(1) of this Act shall apply to the service of an earnings arrestment schedule, a current maintenance arrestment schedule or a conjoined arrestment order as it applies to the execution of a poinding except where such service is by post.

DEFINITIONS
"employer": s.73(1).
"officer of court": s.106.

GENERAL NOTE
Subss. (1), (2)
The exclusive privilege of officers of court to execute arrestments is extended to the new diligences of earnings arrestments and current maintenance arrestments. Conjoined arrestment orders, and recalls and variations of such orders are, however, to be served by sheriff clerks, presumably by post.

Since failure to serve a copy of the schedule on the debtor does not invalidate the arrestment, the only sanction on the officer is the possibility of disciplinary proceedings.

Subss. (3), (5)
Earnings arrestment and current maintenance arrestment schedules are to be served postally. Only if the letter is returned as undelivered may the other methods of service be used. These are personal service, service on an employee or inmate, letterbox or "key-hole" service, or "affixing" service. These latter methods of service involve a personal visit by the officer together with a witness.

Postal service is competent on any day of the year and at any time of the day, but the other modes of service are not permitted on Sunday, Christmas Day, New Year's Day, Good Friday or any other day prescribed by Act of Sederunt under s.17(1).

Employer's fee for operating diligence against earnings

71. On any occasion on which an employer makes a payment to a creditor under an earnings arrestment or a current maintenance arrestment or to the sheriff clerk under a conjoined arrestment order, he may charge the debtor a fee of 50 pence or such other sum as may be prescribed in regulations made by the Lord Advocate which shall be deductible from the amount of the debtor's net earnings after any deduction has been made from them under section 47, 51 or 60 of this Act.

DEFINITIONS
"creditor": s.73(1).
"employer": s.73(1).

GENERAL NOTE
This section permits the employer to make a nominal charge for operating an earnings arrestment, current maintenance arrestment or a conjoined arrestment order. The fee is taken from the debtor's earnings left after the deduction has been made. It is recognised that the charge does not fully compensate the employer for the trouble involved in operating the diligence.

Effect of sequestration on diligence against earnings

72.—(1) This section shall have effect where a debtor's estate is sequestrated.

(2) Any existing earnings arrestment, current maintenance arrestment or, subject to subsection (3) below, conjoined arrestment order shall cease to have effect on the date of sequestration.

(3) Any sum paid by the employer to the sheriff clerk under a conjoined arrestment order on a pay-day occurring before the date of sequestration shall be disbursed by the sheriff clerk under section 64 of this Act notwithstanding that the date of disbursement is after the date of sequestration.

(4) The execution of an earnings arrestment or the making of a conjoined arrestment order shall not be competent after the date of sequestration to enforce a debt in respect of which the creditor is entitled to make a claim in the sequestration.

(5) In this section "date of sequestration" has the same meaning as in section 12(4) of the Bankruptcy (Scotland) Act 1985.

DEFINITIONS
 "employer": s.73(1).
 "pay-day": s.73(1).

GENERAL NOTE
Any existing diligence against earnings ceases to have effect on the date of sequestration, being the date when sequestration is awarded on a debtor's petition or the date when the court on a creditor's petition grants warrant to cite the debtor (Bankruptcy (Scotland) Act 1985 s.12(4)). The employer is entitled to continue deducting until the fact of sequestration is intimated. Payments received by a creditor in respect of deductions made after the date of sequestration are recoverable by the trustee for the benefit of the general body of creditors. Payments received by a creditor after the date of sequestration in respect of deductions made before such date are not recoverable by the trustee.

Interpretation of Part III

73.—(1) In this Part of this Act—
 "creditor", in relation to maintenance, means the payee specified in the maintenance order or orders or anyone deriving title from the payee;
 "current maintenance" means maintenance being deducted from earnings in accordance with section 53(1) or 63(3) or (5) of this Act;
 "debt recoverable" has the meaning given in section 48(1) of this Act;
 "decree or other document" means—
   (a) a decree of the Court of Session or the sheriff or a document registered for execution in the Books of Council and Session or the sheriff court books;
   (b) a summary warrant, a warrant for civil diligence or a bill protested for non-payment by a notary public;
   (c) an order or determination which by virtue of any enactment is enforceable as if it were an extract registered decree arbitral bearing a warrant for execution issued by the sheriff;

    (d) a civil judgment granted outside Scotland by a court, tribunal or arbiter which by virtue of any enactment or rule of law is enforceable in Scotland; or

    (e) a document or settlement which by virtue of an Order in Council made under section 13 of the Civil Jurisdiction and Judgments Act 1982 is enforceable in Scotland,

on which, or on an extract of which, an earnings arrestment, a current maintenance arrestment or a conjoined arrestment order is founded;

"earnings" has the meaning given in subsection (2) below;

"employer" means any person who pays earnings to a debtor under a contract of service or apprenticeship, but—

    (a) in relation to any sum payable as a pension within the meaning of subsection (2)(c) below, means the person paying that sum; and

    (b) where the employee is an officer of the Crown, means, subject to subsection (5) below, the chief officer in Scotland of the department or other body concerned,

and "employee", "employed" and "employment" shall be construed accordingly;

"net earnings" means the earnings which remain payable to the debtor after the employer has deducted any sum which he is required to deduct in respect of—

    (a) income tax;

    (b) primary class 1 contributions under Part I of the Social Security Act 1975;

    (c) amounts deductible under any enactment, or in pursuance of a request in writing by the debtor, for the purposes of a superannuation scheme within the meaning of the Wages Councils Act 1979;

"ordinary debt" means any debt (including a fine or any sum due under an order of court in criminal proceedings in respect of which a warrant for civil diligence has been issued, arrears of maintenance and the expenses of current maintenance arrestments) other than current maintenance;

"pay-day" means a day on which the employer of a debtor pays earnings to the debtor;

"sheriff", in relation to an application—

    (a) under section 50(1) or (3), 55(1), (2) or (5) or 57(6) of this Act, means the sheriff having jurisdiction—

        (i) over the place where the earnings arrestment or the current maintenance arrestment to which the application relates was executed; or

        (ii) if that place is unknown to the applicant, over an established place of business of the debtor's employer;

    (b) under section 59(5) or 62(4), means the sheriff having jurisdiction over the place where a creditor serves an earnings arrestment or a current maintenance arrestment schedule in relation to an arrestment which is not competent by reason of section 59 or 62 of this Act;

    (c) under section 60(2), means the sheriff having jurisdiction over the place where the existing earnings arrestment or current maintenance arrestment or either such arrestment was executed;

    (d) under section 60(9)(c), 62(5), 65 or 66 means the sheriff who made the conjoined arrestment order;

"specified rate", in relation to interest—

(a) included in a decree, order or extract, means the rate specified in such decree, order or extract (or deemed to be so specified by virtue of section 9 of the Sheriff Courts (Scotland) Extracts Act 1892);

(b) not included in a decree, order or extract, means the rate for the time being specified by virtue of that section.

(2) Subject to subsection (3) below, in this Part of this Act "earnings" means any sums payable to the debtor—

(a) as wages or salary;

(b) as fees, bonuses, commission or other emoluments payable under a contract of service or apprenticeship;

(c) as a pension, including a pension declared to be alimentary, an annuity in respect of past services, (whether or not the services were rendered to the person paying the annuity), and any periodical payments of compensation for the loss, abolition, relinquishment, or diminution in earnings of any office or employment; or

(d) as statutory sick pay.

(3) The following shall not be treated as earnings—

(a) a pension or allowance payable in respect of disablement or disability;

(b) any sum the assignation of which is precluded by section 203 of the Army Act 1955 or section 203 of the Air Force Act 1955, or any like sum payable to a member of the naval forces of the Crown, or to a member of any women's service administered by the Defence Council;

(c) in relation to the enforcement by an earnings arrestment of a debt other than maintenance, the wages of a seaman (other than a member of the crew of a fishing boat);

(d) any occupational pension payable under any enactment which precludes the assignation of the pension or exempts it from diligence;

(e) a pension, allowance or benefit payable under any enactment relating to social security;

(f) a guaranteed minimum pension within the meaning of the Social Security Pensions Act 1975;

(g) a redundancy payment within the meaning of section 81(1) of the Employment Protection (Consolidation) Act 1978.

(4) In subsection (3)(c) above—

(a) "seaman" has the same meaning as in section 742 of the Merchant Shipping Act 1894;

(b) "fishing boat" has the meaning given to it in section 370 of that Act as modified by section 744 thereof.

(5) Any question arising as to who is the chief officer in Scotland of a department or body referred to in paragraph (b) of the definition of "employer" in subsection (1) above shall be referred to and determined by the Minister for the Civil Service, and a document purporting to set out a determination of the Minister and signed by an official of the Minister shall be sufficient evidence of that determination.

DEFINITIONS
"maintenance": s.106.
"maintenance order": s.106.

GENERAL NOTE
Subs. (1)
Specified rate. The s.9 rate is currently 15 per cent., but the rate contained in decrees for repayment of bank or similar loans may be much higher.

Subs. (2)
Earnings. The use of the phrase "sums payable to the debtor" confines earnings to money payments. Moreover, payments by the employer to third parties for the benefit of the debtor are not caught (rent paid to the debtor's landlord for example). Earnings includes contractual sick pay, maternity pay, statutory sick pay, and guaranteed payments on lay off when work is not available. On the other hand credits paid to the managers of a holiday fund are excluded as are reimbursement of travelling and other expenses.

Although pensions, including alimentary pensions, are arrestable most public sector pensions are protected from diligence (see note on subs. (3)(d) below).

Subs. (3)
Para. (b)
Armed forces pay is excluded because the Defence Council operate a system by which deductions are made from pay roughly along the lines of an earnings arrestment or a current maintenance arrestment.

Para. (d)
Most public sector pensions (such as police pensions, teachers pensions, Civil Service pensions and local authority pensions) are protected from arrestment in terms of the statute or statutory instrument regulating them.

Para. (g)
A redundancy payment is a lump sum to compensate for loss of job security and lost earnings. The appropriate diligence to attach it is arrestment and furthcoming.

PART IV

RECOVERY OF RATES AND TAXES ETC.

Recovery of rates and taxes etc.

74.—(1) The enactments mentioned in Schedule 4 to this Act shall have effect subject to the amendments specified therein.

(2) A poinding and sale in pursuance of a summary warrant shall be proceeded with in accordance with Schedule 5 to this Act.

(3) No person shall be imprisoned for failure to pay rates or any tax.

(4) Section 248 of the Local Government (Scotland) Act 1947 (priority of claims for rates over other claims) is hereby repealed.

(5) The following provisions of the Exchequer Court (Scotland) Act 1856 are hereby repealed—

  (a) in section 28 (extracts of exchequer decrees), the words from "except that" to the end;
  (b) sections 29 to 34 (special modes of diligence for the enforcement of Crown debts);
  (c) section 36 (effects of deceased Crown debtor may be attached by arrestment or poinding);
  (d) section 42 (preference of Crown over other creditors).

DEFINITION
"summary warrant": s.106.

GENERAL NOTE
Central and local government debts have always been enforceable by a summary procedure authorised by a summary warrant. For historical reasons the various provisions relating to the enforcement of central and local government debts were all slightly different from each other. The summary procedure is retained with modifications, but so far as possible a uniform public debt enforcement regime has been created.

Subs. (1)
This subsection introduces Sched. 4 which sets out the procedure for obtaining a summary warrant and the diligences which such a warrant authorises.

Subs. (2)

This subsection introduces Sched. 5 which sets out a new uniform poinding procedure to enforce arrears of rates and taxes in place of the various different procedures that were used.

Subs. (3)

This subsection abolishes imprisonment for arrears of rates and taxes. Imprisonment of rates defaulters is virtually unknown in modern practice, nobody having been imprisoned since 1972. Imprisonment for arrears of tax was incompetent, and although imprisonment for non-payment of various tax penalties was competent it was never sought in practice by the Revenue. For civil debts imprisonment now has a very limited role. It remains competent to enforce arrears of aliment, fines for contempt of court in civil proceedings, and, under the Court of Session Act 1868, s.91, for breach of an order for restoration of possession or for specific performance of a statutory duty.

Subs. (4)

S.248 gave the rating authority a preference for one year's rates by providing that another creditor who executed diligence against the defaulter's moveables or a person who took them by assignation became liable to satisfy the arrears of rates. While this has been abolished, the analogous provision for Inland Revenue taxes (Taxes Management Act 1970, s.64) remains on the statute book. H.M. Customs and Excise do not enjoy a similar privilege in respect of arrears of their taxes and duties.

Subs. (5)

Ss. 28–32 of the Exchequer Court (Scotland) Act 1856 made special provision for enforcing debts due to the Crown which had been constituted by action in the Court of Session sitting as the Court of Exchequer. Exchequer diligence gave preferences to the Crown. For example an Exchequer arrestment prevailed over an ordinary arrestment which had not proceeded to a furthcoming. Imprisonment was also competent on Exchequer Court decrees under ss.33 and 34 by an administrative procedure after expiry of a charge without payment. The Crown obtained a preference over all moveable property vested in the debtor on giving a charge on an Exchequer decree. None of these preferences were used in modern practice.

Now an Exchequer decree will contain a warrant for execution of the normal diligences (s.87). To obtain the benefit of the summary diligences set out in Scheds. 4 and 5 the Inland Revenue and H.M. Customs and Excise will have to proceed by way of summary warrant in the sheriff court. Other Crown debts have to be enforced by ordinary diligence since summary warrants are confined to rates, taxes and duties.

PART V

MESSENGERS-AT-ARMS AND SHERIFF OFFICERS

Regulation of organisation, training, conduct and procedure

75.—(1) The Court of Session may, by Act of Sederunt, in respect of officers of court—

(a) regulate their organisation;

(b) regulate their training and the qualifications required to obtain a commission as messenger-at-arms or sheriff officer;

(c) regulate their conduct in exercising their official functions;

(d) regulate the scope of their official functions;

(e) make provision prohibiting the undertaking by them of activities other than their official functions (referred to in this Part of this Act as "extra-official activities") which appear to the Court to be incompatible with their official functions;

(f) make provision permitting the undertaking by them for remuneration of other extra-official activities, not appearing to the Court to be incompatible as aforesaid, and the Act of Sederunt may attach conditions to any such permission;

(g) prescribe the procedure in respect of applications for a commission as messenger-at-arms under section 77 of this Act or as sheriff officer;

(h) prescribe the procedure in disciplinary proceedings against them under section 79 of this Act, and provide for the remit of any such proceedings from the Court of Session to a sheriff principal, from one sheriff principal to another sheriff principal and from a sheriff principal to the Court of Session;

(j) make provision for the keeping of accounts by them and the auditing of those accounts;

(k) make provision for the keeping of records by them and the inspection of those records;

(l) make provision in respect of the finding of caution by them;

(m) make such other provision as may appear to the Court to be necessary or proper.

(2) No extra-official activity (not being an activity prohibited or regulated by an Act of Sederunt made under subsection (1)(e) or (f) above) may be undertaken by an officer of court for remuneration unless the officer of court obtains the permission of the sheriff principal from whom he holds a commission to his undertaking the activity, but the sheriff principal shall not withhold such permission unless it appears to him that the undertaking by the officer of court of the activity would be incompatible with the officer of court's official functions.

(3) The sheriff principal may attach conditions to any permission granted by him under subsection (2) above.

DEFINITIONS
"extra-official activities": s.75(1)(e).
"officer of court": s.106.

GENERAL NOTE
The Act continues the system of independent contractor enforcement officers remunerated by fees and controlled by sheriffs principal, the Lord Lyon, and the Court of Session rather than moving over to a system of salaried officers controlled by a new central authority. In order to provide some degree of centralisation this section empowers the Court of Session to make regulations covering almost every aspect of officers of court—messengers-at-arms and sheriff officers—not otherwise regulated by statute. The Court of Session in making any regulation will take into account any advice given by the Advisory Council (see s.76).
The effect of subs. (1)(e) and (f) and subss. (2) and (3) is that officers of court:—

(1) May carry out any extra-official activity not undertaken for remuneration as long as it is not on the list of activities prohibited by regulations made under subs. (1)(e).

(2) May carry out any extra-official activity undertaken for remuneration allowed by regulations made under subs. (1)(f). Possible examples are acting as enquiry agents or serving statutory notices.

(3) May not carry out any other extra-official activity undertaken for remuneration (for example collection of pre-decree debts in return for collection fees) save with the permission of the appropriate sheriff principal. Conditions may be attached to the permission—for example the activity is not to take up so much time the officer is unavailable to execute diligence when called on to do so. Local control by sheriffs principal ensures flexibility; what might be undesirable for city centre officers could be allowed in rural areas where the volume of official business is far less.

The Scottish Law Commission recommended (Recommendation 8.22) that debt collection after the debts had been constituted by decree should become part of the official functions of officers of court. This recommendation could be implemented by regulations made under para. 1(d).

Advisory Council

76.—(1) There shall be a body, (to be known as "the Advisory Council on Messengers-at-Arms and Sheriff Officers" and in this section referred to as "the Advisory Council") whose duties shall be to advise the Court of Session on the making of Acts of Sederunt under section 75 of this Act and generally to keep under review all matters relating to officers of court.

(2) The Advisory Council shall consist of—

    (a) the following persons appointed by the Lord President of the Court of Session—

        (i) a judge of the Court of Session who shall act as chairman;

        (ii) 2 sheriffs principal;

        (iii) 2 officers of court; and

        (iv) 2 solicitors;

    (b) one person appointed by the Lord Advocate; and

    (c) the Lord Lyon King of Arms.

(3) The secretary of the Advisory Council shall be appointed by the Secretary of State.

(4) Subject to subsections (5) and (6) below, the members of the Advisory Council appointed under paragraphs (a) and (b) of subsection (2) above shall hold office for 3 years and be eligible for reappointment.

(5) Subsection (4) above applies to members of the Advisory Council appointed under paragraph (a) of subsection (2) above only so long as they respectively retain the offices or, as the case may be, qualification specified in that paragraph.

(6) If the Lord President or, as the case may be, the Lord Advocate is satisfied that a person appointed by him under subsection (2) above has ceased to be a fit and proper person to hold the appointment, he may terminate that person's appointment.

(7) Where a member of the Advisory Council appointed under subsection (2)(a) or (b) above ceases to be a member (whether by resignation or otherwise) prior to the expiry of 3 years after the date of his appointment or reappointment, the vacancy shall be filled by appointment of another person holding the same office or, as the case may be, possessing the same qualification.

(8) Subject to subsection (6) above, any person appointed in pursuance of subsection (7) above to fill a vacancy shall remain a member of the Advisory Council only until the expiry of 3 years after the date of the appointment or reappointment of the member whom he succeeded, but shall be eligible for reappointment.

(9) The Advisory Council shall have power to regulate the summoning of its meetings and the procedure at such meetings; and at any such meetings 3 members shall be a quorum.

DEFINITION
  "officer of court": s.106.

GENERAL NOTE
  This section sets up an Advisory Council to advise the Court of Session in the execution of its rule-making powers under s.75 and to act as a forum in which matters relating to diligence may be discussed by all those involved in the process of enforcement. The provisions are modelled on s.33 of the Sheriff Courts (Scotland) Act 1971 which set up the Sheriff Court Rules Council.

  The person appointed by the Lord Advocate (subs. (2)(b)) could be a lay person who would be able to put forward the views of creditors and debtors, or a sheriff clerk.

Appointment of messenger-at-arms

77.—(1) The Court of Session, on an application made under this section by a sheriff officer, may find the applicant suitable to be appointed as a messenger-at-arms and recommend such appointment to the Lord Lyon King of Arms; and, on receipt of such a recommendation, the Lord

Lyon King of Arms may grant the applicant a commission as a messenger-at-arms.

(2) A messenger-at-arms shall not be authorised by his commission as messenger-at-arms to execute a warrant granted by a sheriff or sheriff clerk.

(3) A messenger-at-arms shall cease to be entitled to hold a commission as messenger-at-arms if he no longer holds a commission as a sheriff officer.

(4) Any rule of law and any other enactment regulating the appointment of messengers-at-arms shall cease to have effect.

GENERAL NOTE
    This section alters the way in which messengers-at-arms are to be appointed. Although the formal granting of a commission is left with the Lord Lyon, the applicant's fitness and the need for additional messengers are decided by the Court of Session. What the qualifications for appointment are to be and how they are to be established is left to be regulated by the Court of Session under s.75. One qualification however is essential—the applicant must be a sheriff officer (subs. (1)). Moreover, a messenger's commission lapses if he or she ceases to hold for whatever reason a commission as a sheriff officer.
    Subs. (2) excludes an officer acting as a messenger-at-arms from executing any sheriff court civil warrant (for criminal warrants see Criminal Procedure (Scotland) Act 1975, ss.70, 71 and 326). In order to execute a sheriff court civil warrant, the officer must either hold a commission in respect of the court which granted the warrant or the sheriff court district in which the warrant is to be executed (s.91(2)). The exclusion of messengers enables the sheriffs principal to retain local control over the number of officers available to execute warrants of their courts or in their sheriffdoms.

Inspection of work

78.—(1) The sheriff principal—
    (a) may from time to time in relation to any sheriff officer who holds a commission from him, and
    (b) shall, if directed to do so by the Court of Session in relation to any sheriff officer who is a messenger-at-arms,
appoint such a person as he thinks fit to inspect the work or particular aspects of the work of that officer.

(2) A person appointed under subsection (1) above may, and if the Court of Session directs the sheriff principal so to require shall, be required by the sheriff principal to make enquiry as to extra-official activities undertaken for remuneration by the officer of court concerned.

(3) A person appointed under subsection (1) above shall make a report of his inspection and of any enquiry under subsection (2) above to the sheriff principal and, if the report is concerned with the work or extra-official activities of any messenger-at-arms, shall send a copy thereof to the Court of Session.

(4) A person appointed under subsection (1) above shall be entitled—
    (a) to a fee, unless he is employed full-time in the civil service of the Crown; and
    (b) to payment of his outlays incurred,
in connection with an inspection, enquiry and report under this section.

DEFINITION
    "officer of court": s.106.

GENERAL NOTE
    In order to monitor the independent contractor officers of court their work may be inspected, either in response to a specific complaint or a spot check ordered by the sheriff principal or the Court of Session. A sheriff principal who wishes to investigate a firm of officers which includes messengers-at-arms should request a direction from the Court of Session so that the work of all the officers in their two capacities can be investigated.

Work means an officer's conduct or performance in relation to his or her official functions. Paid extra-official activities may be enquired into, but not inspected. The purpose of the enquiry is to establish whether such activities are authorised in terms of regulations made under s.75.

The type of people likely to be asked to undertake inspections are senior officers of court, sheriff clerks, solicitors or accountants depending on the sort of inspection required. An inspector's fees and outlays are a public expense in the first instance, although they may be recovered from an officer found guilty of misconduct.

Investigation of alleged misconduct

79.—(1) This section applies where—
   (a) a report under section 78(3) of this Act discloses that any officer of court may have been guilty of misconduct;
   (b) a report by a sheriff or a complaint by any other person is made—
      (i) to the Court of Session alleging misconduct by a messenger-at-arms;
      (ii) to the sheriff principal from whom a sheriff officer holds a commission alleging misconduct by the officer; or
   (c) any judge of the Court of Session, or a sheriff principal, has reason to believe that an officer of court may have been guilty of misconduct.

(2) Where this section applies, a judge nominated by the Lord President of the Court of Sesssion, or the sheriff principal, after giving the officer of court an opportunity to admit or deny the misconduct or to give an explanation of the matter, may appoint a solicitor to investigate the matter unless the officer of court—
   (a) admits the misconduct in writing, or
   (b) gives a satisfactory explanation of the matter.

(3) Where the solicitor after carrying out an investigation in pursuance of subsection (2) above is of the opinion—
   (a) that there is a probable case of misconduct and that there is evidence sufficient to justify proceedings, disciplinary proceedings shall be brought at his instance against the officer of court before the relevant court;
   (b) that there is not a probable case of misconduct or that there is insufficient evidence to justify proceedings, he shall report that fact to the relevant court.

(4) The solicitor shall be entitled to a fee, and to payment of his outlays incurred, in connection with an investigation, and any disciplinary proceedings brought by him, under this section.

(5) The relevant court may award expenses in any disciplinary proceedings brought under this section in favour of or against either party to the proceedings; and for the purposes of this subsection and section 45 of the Crown Proceedings Act 1947 the party bringing the proceedings shall be deemed to be the Lord Advocate.

(6) Where expenses are awarded under subsection (5) above in favour of—
   (a) the officer of court, the expenses shall be recoverable by him from the Lord Advocate;
   (b) the Lord Advocate, the expenses shall be recoverable from the officer of court by the Lord Advocate.

(7) If the person appointed under section 78(1) of this Act is a solicitor, that person may be appointed as solicitor under subsection (2) above.

(8) In this section "the relevant court" means whichever of the Court of Session or the sheriff principal made the appointment under subsection (2) above.

(9) In this section and section 80 of this Act "misconduct" includes conduct tending to bring the office of messenger-at-arms or sheriff officer into disrepute.

DEFINITIONS
"misconduct": s.79(9).
"officer of court": s.106.

GENERAL NOTE
One difficulty faced by sheriffs principal in investigating serious complaints against sheriff officers was the absence of any power to appoint a person to investigate the officer's conduct and prosecute any disciplinary proceedings. This section empowers the sheriff principal or the Court of Session to appoint such a person. The appointment of an investigator, unlike the appointment of an inspector under s.78, requires there to have been a complaint or suspicion of misconduct (subs. (1), paras. (a), (b) and (c)).

The sheriff principal (or Court of Session for messengers) may deal with the matter informally by giving the officer an opportunity to explain the situation or admit misconduct. If the officer gives a satisfactory explanation the matter may be dropped. Unless the officer admits misconduct in writing or is found guilty of misconduct in disciplinary proceedings, the sheriff principal or the Court of Session cannot impose any of the penalties set out in s.80 (censure, fine, suspension or dismissal) so their powers are limited to a "ticking off" as their common law powers, based on the officer's tenure during pleasure, are impliedly repealed.

The investigator is to be a solicitor (subs. (2)). Where a solicitor had previously inspected the work of the officer concerned and found it wanting, it would be sensible to appoint him or her to be the investigator and prosecutor (subs. (7)). Where the disciplinary proceedings are before a judge of the Court of Session the prosecutor would have to instruct counsel as subs. (3)(a) does not confer a right of audience.

Misconduct is not exhaustively defined. In addition to misconduct in relation to official functions it includes the carrying out of unauthorised extra-official activities and conduct, such as financial improbity, which would lower the officer's standing in the eyes of the community. Conviction of a criminal offence is dealt with separately under s.80.

Courts' powers in relation to offences or misconduct

80.—(1) Where the Court of Session becomes aware that a messenger-at-arms has been convicted by a court of any offence, it may make an order finding that the messenger-at-arms should be suspended from practice for such period as may be specified in the order, or deprived of office.

(2) Where the sheriff principal from whom a sheriff officer holds a commission becomes aware that the sheriff officer has been convicted by a court of any offence, the sheriff principal may make an order suspending the sheriff officer from practice for such period as may be specified in the order, or depriving him of office, in that sheriffdom.

(3) Subsections (1) and (2) above are without prejudice to section 4(3)(b) of the Rehabilitation of Offenders Act 1974; and in those subsections "offence" means any offence of which the officer of court has been convicted before or after he was granted a commission as an officer of court, other than any offence disclosed in his application for such a commission.

(4) Where—
  (a) a messenger-at-arms admits in writing that he is guilty of misconduct; or
  (b) the Court of Session at the end of disciplinary proceedings under section 79(3)(a) of this Act is satisfied that a messenger-at-arms is guilty of misconduct,
the Court of Session may make one or more of the orders specified in subsection (5) below.

(5) The orders referred to in subsection (4) above are—
  (a) an order finding that the messenger-at-arms should be sus-

pended from practice for such period as may be specified in the order, or deprived of office;

(b) an order imposing a fine on the messenger-at-arms not exceeding £2,500 or such sum as may be prescribed in regulations made by the Lord Advocate;

(c) an order censuring the messenger-at-arms;

(d) if the misconduct consists of, or includes, the charging of excessive fees or outlays, an order decerning for repayment by the messenger-at-arms of the fees or outlays, to the extent that they were excessive, to the person who paid them.

(6) Where—

    (a) a sheriff officer admits in writing that he is guilty of misconduct; or

(b) the sheriff principal at the end of disciplinary proceedings under section 79(3)(a) of this Act is satisfied that a sheriff officer is guilty of misconduct,

the sheriff principal may make one or more of the orders specified in subsection (7) below.

(7) The orders referred to in subsection (6) above are—

(a) an order suspending the sheriff officer from practice for such period as may be specified in the order, or depriving him of office, in that sheriffdom;

(b) an order in relation to the sheriff officer of a kind mentioned in subsection (5)(b), (c) or (d) above.

(8) Where an officer of court fails to comply with an order under this section imposing a fine on him, the Court of Session or, as the case may be, the sheriff principal may make an order—

(a) decerning for payment of the fine, and an extract of any such order shall contain a warrant in the form prescribed by Act of Sederunt which shall have the same effect as an extract of a decree for payment of money pronounced by the Court of Session; or

(b) of the kind specified in subsection (5)(a) or, as the case may be, (7)(a) above.

(9) Any fine imposed under this section shall be recoverable by the Lord Advocate.

DEFINITIONS
"misconduct": s.79(9).
"officer of court": s.106.

GENERAL NOTE
This section sets out the disciplinary powers of the courts over officers of court.

Subss. (1)–(3)
These subsections deal with the situation where an officer of court has been convicted of a criminal offence. Depending on the nature and gravity of the offence the appropriate disciplinary authority may take no further action or may suspend or dismiss the officer. There is no power to impose a fine.

In an application for a commission the officer should disclose any offence not spent in terms of the Rehabilitation of Offenders Act 1974, otherwise there is a risk of dismissal when it comes to light. An applicant is not obliged to disclose a spent conviction and would not be punished for failure to do so. Officers with a commission will no doubt be required by regulations made under s.75 to disclose the fact of having been convicted of a criminal offence as soon as conviction has occurred. The problem of post-commission convictions being spent is therefore unlikely to arise. Failure to disclose under any regulations would amount to misconduct.

Subss. (4), (5)
When a messenger-at-arms admits or is found guilty of misconduct in disciplinary proceedings the court may suspend the messenger for a period or dismiss him or her, and/or

impose a fine and/or censure the messenger and/or order repayment of excessive fees. These powers are exercisable only after an admission or conviction of misconduct. The existing disciplinary powers of the Lord Lyon over messengers-at-arms are expressly abolished (s.81(4)). The Court of Session's existing powers, which were in practice not exercised, are impliedly superseded by the statutory powers under the Act.

The Court of Session merely makes the finding that the messenger should be suspended or deprived of office; the actual suspension or deprivation is carried out by the Lord Lyon (s.81(3)(b)).

Subss. (6), (7)

These subsections confer on sheriffs principal in relation to sheriff officers very similar powers to those conferred by subss. (4) and (5) on the Court of Session in respect of messengers. The sheriff principal however suspends or deprives an officer directly since the officer holds his or her commission from the sheriff principal.

Subss. (8), (9)

An unpaid fine may either be enforced by civil diligence or the officer concerned may be suspended or deprived. It is thought that the provisions are alternative (compare the different formula in subss. (4) and (6)) so that if an officer is deprived for non-payment, the fine cannot thereafter be collected by civil diligence. As this is a civil fine, imprisonment cannot be imposed in the event of non-payment. Fines are recoverable by the Scottish Courts Administration on behalf of the Lord Advocate.

Provisions supplementary to section 80

81.—(1) The Court of Session shall cause intimation to be made of any order of the Court of Session under section 80(1), (4) or (8)(b) of this Act to—

(a) every sheriff principal from whom the messenger-at-arms holds a commission as a sheriff officer;

(b) the Lord Lyon King of Arms.

(2) The sheriff principal shall cause intimation to be made of any order made by him under section 80(2), (6) or (8)(b) of this Act—

(a) to every other sheriff principal from whom the sheriff officer holds a commission as a sheriff officer; and

(b) if the sheriff officer is a messenger-at-arms, to the Court of Session and the Lord Lyon King of Arms.

(3) On intimation under this section of an order under section 80(1), (2) or (8)(b) of this Act or of an order under subsection (4) or (6) of that section specified respectively in subsection (5)(a) or (7)(a) thereof—

(a) to a sheriff principal, he shall make an order suspending the sheriff officer concerned from practice until the expiry of the period for which he has been suspended by the order so intimated, or (as the case may be) depriving him of office, in the sheriffdom;

(b) to the Lord Lyon King of Arms, he shall—

(i) in the case of an order intimated under subsection (1) above, suspend the messenger-at-arms concerned from practice for the period specified in the order or (as the case may be) deprive him of office; or

(ii) in the case of an order intimated under subsection (2) above, suspend the messenger-at-arms from practice until the expiry of the period for which he has been suspended by the order so intimated or (as the case may be) deprive him of office.

(4) It shall not be competent for the Lord Lyon King of Arms to discipline a messenger-at-arms or suspend him from practice or deprive him of office except in accordance with subsection (3)(b) above.

GENERAL NOTE

Where one disciplinary authority suspends or deprives an officer, intimation is made to all other authorities from whom the officer holds a commission. The other authorities then either suspend or deprive the officer following the intimated order. Fines, censures, and orders for repayment of expenses are not intimated.

Subs. (3)(b) retains the Lord Lyon's power to suspend or deprive a messenger-at-arms of his or her commission, but it becomes a formal power only. Lyon must exercise it on intimation of a finding from the Court of Session or an intimation of suspension or deprivation by a sheriff principal, and may not exercise it otherwise, as subs. (4) terminates Lyon's powers to act independently.

Appeals from decisions under sections 79(5) and 80

82. An appeal to the Inner House of the Court of Session may be made against any decision of a Lord Ordinary or a sheriff principal under section 79(5) or section 80(1), (2), (4) or (6) of this Act, but the decision of the Inner House on any such appeal shall be final.

GENERAL NOTE

Appeals to the House of Lords are excluded. A similar restriction operates in connection with appeals from the Scottish Solicitors' Discipline Tribunal (Solicitors (Scotland) Act 1980, s.54).

Service of charge and execution of diligence or warrant void where officer of court has interest

83.—(1) The service of a charge for payment or the execution of diligence, or of a warrant in any proceedings, by an officer of court shall be void if the subject matter of the charge, diligence or proceedings—

(a) is one in which the officer of court has an interest as an individual; or

(b) consists of or includes a debt in respect of which any of the circumstances mentioned in subsection (2) below apply.

(2) The circumstances referred to in subsection (1)(b) above are where the debt is due to—

(a) a company or firm, and the officer of court—
  (i) is a director or partner of that company or firm or holds by himself, or along with a business associate or with a member of his family, a controlling interest therein; or
  (ii) has a pecuniary interest in that company or firm and the principal business of the company or firm is the purchase of debts for enforcement;

(b) a business associate of the officer of court, or to a member of the officer of court's family;

(c) a company or firm, and a business associate of the officer of court or a member of the officer of court's family—
  (i) is a director or partner of that company or firm or holds a controlling interest therein; or
  (ii) has a pecuniary interest in that company or firm and the principal business of the company or firm is the purchase of debts for enforcement.

(3) Any reference in subsection (2) above to—

(a) a business associate of an officer of court shall be construed as a reference to a co-director, partner, employer, employee, agent or principal of the officer of court;

(b) a member of an officer of court's family shall be construed as a reference to the wife or husband, a parent or child, a grandparent or grandchild, or a brother or sister of the officer of court (whether of the full blood or the half-blood or by affinity);

(c) a controlling interest in a company shall be construed in accordance with paragraph 13(7) of Schedule 4 to the Finance Act 1975.

(4) In subsection (3)(a) above "principal" does not include a principal in a contract for the service of a charge or the execution of diligence or of a warrant in relation to the debt concerned.

DEFINITIONS
   "business associate": s.83(3)(a).
   "controlling interest": s.83(3)(c).
   "member of his family": s.83(3)(b).
   "officer of court": s.106.

GENERAL NOTE
Subs. (1)
   The principle that officers of court cannot enforce debts due to themselves as individuals is a long-standing one (*Dalgleish* v. *Scott* (1822) 1 S. 506). It is based on their holding of a public office which must be discharged in an impartial independent manner.

Para. (a)
   This paragraph restates this principle and enlarges it to cover execution of warrants other than warrants for diligence (such as a warrant of citation, or for delivery of goods, but query whether interdicts are included). Interest means interest in the subject-matter or the debt and not an interest in the fees due for acting as an officer or commission for collecting the debt.

Para. (b)
   This paragraph taken with subss. (2) and (3) prevents officers evading the rule against enforcing their own debts by arranging for the debts to be due to their business, or a business associate or near relative. It does not prevent an officer serving a warrant of citation in a near relative's action where the action is not one of debt.
   The consequences of acting when prohibited from doing so are serious. The diligence, etc., is void, the creditor may claim damages for failure to carry out instructions, and the officer may be subject to disciplinary proceedings for misconduct.

Subs. (2)
Para. (a)
   An officer who is a director of a company or partner of a firm is prohibited from acting as an officer on behalf of that company or firm. An officer is also prohibited where, though not a director or partner, he or she has with business associates or relatives a controlling interest. A more stringent prohibition applies where the principal business of the company or firm is the purchase of debts for enforcement (a debt factoring business). Here any pecuniary interest (such as holding shares) of the officer is a disqualification.

Para. (b)
   Business associate is fairly widely drawn and includes persons so associated in businesses other than officers of court. An officer could not enforce a debt due to his or her gardener, partner in a firm of auctioneers, or part-time employer.

Para. (c)
   This paragraph extends the prohibitions still further by combining the elements of paras. (a) and (b). Where the principal business of the company or firm is the purchase of debts for enforcement the officer may unwittingly act when prohibited from doing unless he or she examines the share register first to see whether any relatives or business associates have an interest.

Subs. (3)(c)
   Controlling interest is defined in terms of the power to produce a majority of votes on any issue affecting the company.

Subs. (4)
   This subsection makes it clear that "principal" in the definition of business associate does not include the person instructing the officer to execute diligence, etc.; otherwise an officer could never act. "Principal" means principal in another agency.

Collection of statistics from officers of court

84.—(1) The Lord Advocate may require any officer of court to provide information, in such form and at such times as he may specify, regarding the officer of court's official functions.

(2) Subject to subsection (3) below, the Lord Advocate may publish, in such form as he thinks fit, information provided under subsection (1) above.

(3) Information published under subsection (2) above shall not be in a form which identifies or enables the identification of officers of court or persons against whom diligence has been executed.

DEFINITION
"officer of court": s.106.

GENERAL NOTE
The purpose of this section is to enable comprehensive but anonymous statistics on the use of diligence to be collected from officers. The present statistics are compiled from court records so that no information is available on the many steps in diligence (the execution of arrestments for example) which are not reported to the court. Such information can best be obtained from officers of court. The Scottish Law Commission's report recommended that officers of court should be remunerated for providing returns of diligence executed by them, but the present section is silent as to payment.

Measure of damages payable by officer of court for negligence or other fault

85. There shall cease to have effect any rule of law whereby, if an officer of court has been found liable to a creditor for negligent delay or failure to execute diligence, or for other fault in the execution of diligence, the damages payable by the officer of court are determined solely by reference to the amount of the debt.

DEFINITION
"officer of court": s.106.

GENERAL NOTE
Neglect or failure by an officer to carry out promptly instructions to execute a poinding or a warrant for civil imprisonment rendered the officer liable for the whole debt sought to be recovered by the diligence (Graham Stewart, *Diligence* (1898), p.823). This harsh rule is abolished by this section. The effect is to substitute the normal rule for quantifying damages for negligence or breach of contract.

Official identity card

86.—(1) An official identity card shall be issued to every officer of court by or on behalf of the person from whom he holds his commission.

(2) When carrying out his official functions an officer of court shall exhibit his identity card on being requested to do so.

DEFINITION
"officer of court": s.106.

GENERAL NOTE
Provision is made for official identity cards for officers of court to facilitate their dealings with debtors and others in the execution of their official functions. The Society of Messengers-at-Arms and Sheriff Officers issue identity cards to their members, but not all officers are members and the cards are not official documents.

Officers will have to carry their official identity card when carrying out their functions. They must also be able to exhibit on demand the warrant (or a certified copy, see Sched. 5, para. 5(2)(a)) authorising the diligence or function in question.

PART VI

WARRANTS FOR DILIGENCE AND CHARGES FOR PAYMENT

Effect of warrants for diligence in extract decrees and other documents

87.—(1) Every extract of a decree for the payment of money, or among other things for the payment of money, which is pronounced by—

    (a) the Court of Session;

    (b) the High Court of Justiciary; or

    (c) the Court of Teinds,

shall contain a warrant in the form prescribed by Act of Sederunt or, as the case may be, by Act of Adjournal.

(2) The warrant referred to in subsection (1) above shall have the effect of authorising—

    (a) in relation to an ordinary debt, the charging of the debtor to pay to the creditor within the period specified in the charge the sum specified in the extract and any interest accrued on the sum and, in the event of failure to make such payment within that period, the execution of an earnings arrestment and the poinding of articles belonging to the debtor and, if necessary for the purpose of executing the poinding, the opening of shut and lockfast places;

    (b) in relation to an ordinary debt, an arrestment other than an arrestment of the debtor's earnings in the hands of his employer; and

    (c) if the decree consists of or includes a maintenance order, a current maintenance arrestment in accordance with Part III of this Act.

(3) In section 7(1) of the Sheriff Courts (Scotland) Extracts Act 1892 (import of the warrant for execution), for the words from "it shall" to the end there shall be substituted the following words—

"the said warrant shall have the effect of authorising—

    (a) in relation to an ordinary debt within the meaning of the Debtors (Scotland) Act 1987, the charging of the debtor to pay to the creditor within the period specified in the charge the sum specified in the extract and any interest accrued on the sum and, in the event of failure to make such payment within that period, the execution of an earnings arrestment and the poinding of articles belonging to the debtor and, if necessary for the purpose of executing the poinding, the opening of shut and lockfast places;

    (b) in relation to an ordinary debt within the meaning of the Debtors (Scotland) Act 1987, an arrestment other than an arrestment of the debtor's earnings in the hands of his employer; and

    (c) if the decree consists of or includes a maintenance order within the meaning of the Debtors (Scotland) Act 1987, a current maintenance arrestment in accordance with Part III of that Act.".

(4) For section 3 of the Writs Execution (Scotland) Act 1877 there shall be substituted the following section—

"Power to execute diligence by virtue of warrant

3. The warrant inserted in an extract of a document registered in the Books of Council and Session or in sheriff court books which contains an obligation to pay a sum of money shall have the effect of authorising—

    (a) in relation to an ordinary debt within the meaning of the Debtors (Scotland) Act 1987, the charging of the debtor to pay to the creditor within the period specified in the charge the sum specified in the extract and any interest accrued on the sum and, in the event of failure to make such payment within that period, the execution of an earnings arrestment and the poinding of articles belonging to the debtor and, if necessary for the purpose of executing the poinding, the opening of shut and lockfast places;

(b) in relation to an ordinary debt within the meaning of the Debtors (Scotland) Act 1987, an arrestment other than an arrestment of the debtor's earnings in the hands of his employer; and

(c) if the document is a maintenance order within the meaning of the Debtors (Scotland) Act 1987, a current maintenance arrestment in accordance with Part III of that Act.".

(5) An extract of a decree in an action of poinding of the ground shall contain a warrant in the form prescribed by Act of Sederunt which shall have the effect of authorising a poinding of the ground.

DEFINITIONS
"earnings": s.73(2).
"employer": s.73(1).
"maintenance order": s.106.
"ordinary debt": s.73(1).

GENERAL NOTE
This section sets out the diligences which are authorised by extract decrees or their equivalents to enforce payment of the sums of money specified in such documents. It deals with diligence in execution; the warrants for diligence on the dependence or in security will continue to be granted according to the previous law and practice. Lyon Court warrants are also unaffected.

Subss. (1), (2)
These subsections deal with Supreme Court decrees. Extract decrees of the Court of Session sitting as the Court of Exchequer will bear the same warrant as Court of Session decrees (see note on s.74(5)). The new formulation authorises the two new diligences of earnings arrestment and current maintenance arrestment against the debtor's earnings in appropriate cases in addition to the existing diligences of charge and poinding and arrestment. It also replaces the long forms of warrant set out in the Debtors (Scotland) Act 1838 and slightly differently in Rules of Court 64, 65 and 170D(6) with a simple uniform style.

Subs. (3)
This subsection makes identical provisions for extracts of sheriff court decrees. Fines, compensation orders and the forfeiture of caution may be enforced by the sheriff granting a warrant for civil diligence (Criminal Procedure (Scotland) Act 1975, s.411). The effect of such a warrant is brought into line with civil warrants by the amendments made to the 1975 Act by Sched. 6, para. 18.

Subs. (4)
This subsection deals with the effect of a warrant for execution inserted in an extract of a writ registered for execution, or documents deemed to be so registered (an order by the comptroller for expenses under s.107(3) of the Patents Act 1977 for example). The warrant authorises the same diligences as are authorised by warrants in Supreme and sheriff court decrees.

Subs. (5)
Poinding of the ground is a little used form of diligence available to heritable creditors. The diligence takes the form of an action in the Court of Session or the sheriff court. An extract decree of poinding of the ground in the sheriff court contains a warrant to charge and poind; an extract of the decree in the Court of Session merely entitles the creditor to apply for letters of poinding which contain the warrant to charge and poind. This subsection paves the way for the abolition of letters of poinding in s.89.

Warrants for diligence: special cases

88.—(1) This section applies where a creditor has acquired by assignation intimated to the debtor, confirmation as executor, or otherwise a right to—

(a) a decree;

(b) an obligation contained in a document an extract of which, after the document has been registered in the Books of Council and Session or in sheriff court books, may be obtained containing warrant for execution;

(c) an order or determination which by virtue of any enactment is enforceable as if it were an extract registered decree arbitral bearing a warrant for execution issued by a sheriff,

either directly or through a third party from a person in whose favour the decree, order or determination was granted or who was the creditor in the obligation contained in the document.

(2) Where this section applies, the creditor who has acquired a right as mentioned in subsection (1) above may apply to the appropriate clerk for a warrant having the effect of authorising the execution at the instance of that creditor of any diligence authorised by an extract of the decree or document or by the order or determination, as the case may be.

(3) The applicant under subsection (2) above shall submit to the appropriate clerk—

(a) an extract of the decree or of the document registered as mentioned in subsection (1)(b) above or a certified copy of the order or determination; and

(b) the assignation (along with evidence of its intimation to the debtor), confirmation as executor or other document establishing the applicant's right.

(4) The appropriate clerk shall grant the warrant applied for under subsection (2) above if he is satisfied that the applicant's right is established.

(5) Where—

(a) a charge has already been served in pursuance of the decree, order, determination or registered document; and

(b) the applicant under subsection (2) above submits with his application the certificate of execution of the charge in addition to the documents mentioned in subsection (3) above,

a warrant granted under subsection (4) above shall authorise the execution at the instance of the applicant of diligence in pursuance of that charge.

(6) For the purposes of this section, "the appropriate clerk" shall be—

(a) in the case of a decree granted by the Court of Session or a document registered (whether before or after such acquisition) in the Books of Council and Session, a clerk of court of the Court of Session;

(b) in the case of a decree granted by the High Court of Justiciary, a clerk of Justiciary;

(c) in the case of a decree granted by a sheriff or a document registered (whether before or after such acquisition) in the books of a sheriff court, the sheriff clerk of that sheriff court;

(d) in the case of such an order or determination as is mentioned in subsection (1)(c) above, any sheriff clerk.

DEFINITION
"appropriate clerk": s.88(6).

GENERAL NOTE

Only the creditor in whose favour the extract decree or extract registered writ was granted is entitled to enforce it by diligence. Where a new creditor acquires right to the obligations in the extract decree or writ he or she needs to acquire a title to do diligence. In the case of a decree or writ which had been extracted before acquisition of right by the new creditor, the Debtors (Scotland) Act 1838, ss.7 and 12 provided an administrative procedure in terms of which the new creditor applied to a clerk of court.

This section reproduces the administrative procedure set out in the 1838 Act and extends it to the case where the decree was not extracted before acquisition of right by the new creditor. A warrant for diligence in the latter case had to be obtained by letters of horning or letters of horning and poinding. These are now abolished by s.89.

Abolition of letters of horning, horning and poinding, poinding, and caption

89. The granting of letters of horning, letters of horning and poinding, letters of poinding and letters of caption shall cease to be competent.

GENERAL NOTE

This section abolishes the almost obsolete methods of obtaining a warrant for diligence. The only cases of practical importance where such warrants remained necessary were acquisition of right to an unextracted decree or a Court of Session decree of poinding of the ground. These cases are now catered for by ss.88(1)(a) and 87(5) respectively.

Provisions relating to charges for payment

90.—(1) Subject to subsection (2) below, the execution of a poinding or an earnings arrestment shall not be competent unless a charge for payment has been served on the debtor and the period for payment specified in the charge has expired without payment being made.

(2) Subsection (1) above shall not apply to a poinding or an earnings arrestment executed in pursuance of a summary warrant.

(3) The period for payment specified in any charge for payment served in pursuance of a warrant for execution shall be 14 days if the person on whom it is served is within the United Kingdom and 28 days if he is outside the United Kingdom or his whereabouts are unknown.

(4) Any such charge shall be in the form prescribed by Act of Sederunt or Act of Adjournal.

(5) Subject to subsection (6) below, where any such charge has been served, it shall not be competent to execute a poinding or an earnings arrestment by virtue of that charge more than 2 years after the date of such service.

(6) A creditor may reconstitute his right to execute a poinding or an earnings arrestment by the service of a further charge for payment.

(7) No expenses incurred in the service of a further charge for payment within the period of 2 years after service of the first charge shall be chargeable against the debtor.

(8) Registration of certificates of execution of charges for payment in a register of hornings shall cease to be competent.

DEFINITION

"summary warrant": s.106.

GENERAL NOTE

This section deals with charges for the payment of money. Other types of charge such as charges to deliver goods or to remove from property are unaffected.

Subs. (1)

This subsection restates the previous position (under the Poinding Act 1669 repealed in Sched. 8) that a charge had to expire without payment before a poinding was competent. It extends this rule to an earnings arrestment and, as read with s.60(1), to an ordinary creditor applying for, or to join, a conjoined arrestment order. An arrestment of funds other than earnings (shares or bank accounts for example), however, remains competent without a prior charge since there is a greater danger that debtors if given warning would put such funds beyond the reach of their creditors.

Subs. (2)
This subsection also restates the previous law that a prior charge is not necessary for summary warrant poindings and extends this to earnings arrestments. A charge would be inconsistent with the summary nature of diligence on summary warrants.

Subs. (3)
The period of charge is standardised. Under the previous law there was a bewildering variety of periods ranging from 6 days (extract registered writs) to 60 days (Teind Court decrees where the debtor was furth of Scotland).

Subs. (5)
"Stale" charges cannot found further diligence. This subsection replaces r.91(2) of the Summary Cause Rules in terms of which a charge lasts for a year, and the uncertain period for Court of Session and sheriff court ordinary court decrees. A creditor may wish to serve a further charge for diligence or to render the debtor apparently insolvent as a prelude to sequestration.

Subs. (8)
Registration of the execution of a charge which had expired without payment entitled the creditor to apply to the clerk of court for a warrant to imprison the debtor. The procedure was virtually obsolete since for the few debts for which civil imprisonment remains competent the warrant for imprisonment is granted only after enquiry by a judge. Registration also had the effect of "rolling up" the interest with the principal sum (Debtors (Scotland) Act 1838, ss.5 and 10) but few creditors ever took advantage of this little known provision.

Enforcement of certain warrants and precepts of sheriff anywhere in Scotland

91.—(1) The following may be executed anywhere in Scotland—
  (a) a warrant for execution contained in an extract of a decree granted by a sheriff;
  (b) a warrant for execution inserted in an extract of a document registered in sheriff court books;
  (c) a summary warrant;
  (d) a warrant of a sheriff for arrestment on the dependence of an action or in security;
  (e) a precept (issued by a sheriff clerk) of arrestment in security of a liquid debt the term of payment of which has not arrived.

(2) A warrant or precept mentioned in subsection (1) above may be executed by a sheriff officer of—
  (a) the court which granted it; or
  (b) the sheriff court district in which it is to be executed.

DEFINITION
"summary warrant": s.106.

GENERAL NOTE
Under the Debtors (Scotland) Act 1838 execution of a sheriff court warrant in a different sheriffdom from that in which it was granted required a warrant of concurrence (s.13). This warrant had to be sought from the Court of Session or the clerk of the court within whose sheriffdom execution was sought. The Ordinary Cause Rules and Summary Cause Rules (rr.16 and 11 respectively) dispensed with the need for warrants of concurrence; these however remained necessary for summary warrants and extracts of writs registered in sheriff court books. Now warrants of concurrence are completely unnecessary.
  Subs. (2) makes it clear which sheriff officers are authorised to execute warrants.

PART VII

MISCELLANEOUS AND GENERAL

General provision relating to liability for expenses in court proceedings

92.—(1) Subject to subsection (2) below, a debtor shall not be liable to a creditor, nor a creditor to a debtor, for any expenses incurred by the other party in connection with an application, any objections to an application, or a hearing, under any provision of this Act.

(2) If—

(a) an application under any provision of this Act is frivolous;

(b) such an application is opposed on frivolous grounds; or

(c) a party requires a hearing under any provision of this Act to be held on frivolous grounds,

the sheriff may award a sum of expenses, not exceeding £25 or such amount as may be prescribed in regulations made by the Lord Advocate, against the party acting frivolously in favour of the other party.

(3) Subsections (1) and (2) above do not apply to—

(a) expenses of poinding and sale for which provision is made in Schedule 1 to this Act or paragraphs 25 to 34 of Schedule 5 to this Act; or

(b) expenses incurred—

(i) under section 1 of this Act;

(ii) in connection with an appeal under any provision of this Act; or

(iii) by or against a person other than the debtor or a creditor in connection with an application under any provision of this Act.

GENERAL NOTE

In order not to discourage debtors from making or defending applications under the provisions of the Act, the basic rule is that each side bears their own expenses. This rule does not apply to expenses of appeals, to persons other than debtors or creditors (for example a person attempting to recover his or her goods which had been wrongfully poinded, or an arrestee), or in relation to time to pay decrees. It also applies only to applications to a court (apart from an application for a warrant of sale and other necessary applications in connection with a poinding); the expenses of executing diligence against debtors remain chargeable against them.

Frivolous applications or defences can be penalised. The figure of £25 is set low so as not to deter debtors from seeking to take advantage of the protection provided by the Act.

Recovery from debtor of expenses of certain diligences

93.—(1) Subject to subsections (3) and (5) below, any expenses chargeable against the debtor which are incurred in—

(a) a poinding and sale (including the service of the charge preceding it);

(b) the service of an earnings arrestment schedule (including the service of the charge preceding it);

(c) an application for, or for inclusion in, a conjoined arrestment order under section 60(2) or 62(5) of this Act,

shall be recoverable from the debtor by the diligence concerned but not by any other legal process, and any such expenses which have not been recovered by the time the diligence is completed or otherwise ceases to have effect shall cease to be chargeable against the debtor.

(2) Subject to subsection (5) below, any expenses chargeable against the debtor which are incurred in the service of a schedule of arrestment and in an action of furthcoming or sale shall be recoverable from the debtor out of the arrested property; and the court shall grant a decree in

the action of furthcoming for payment of the balance of any expenses not so recovered.

(3) The sheriff shall grant decree for payment of—

(a) any expenses awarded by him against the debtor in favour of the creditor under paragraph 8 or 11 of Schedule 1 or paragraph 30 or 33 of Schedule 5 to this Act; or

(b) any additional sum of expenses awarded by him against the debtor in favour of the creditor under paragraph 9 of Schedule 1 or paragraph 31 of Schedule 5 to this Act.

(4) Subsection (5) below applies where any diligence mentioned in subsection (1) or (2) above is—

(a) recalled under section 9(2)(a), (d) or (e) of this Act in relation to a time to pay order;

(b) in effect immediately before the date of sequestration (within the meaning of the Bankruptcy (Scotland) Act 1985) of the debtor's estate;

(c) in effect immediately before the presentation of a petition for an administration order under Part II of the Insolvency Act 1986;

(d) in effect against property of the debtor immediately before a floating charge attaches to all or part of that property under section 53(7) or 54(6) of that Act;

(e) in effect immediately before the commencement of the winding up, under Part IV or V of that Act, of the debtor;

(f) rendered unenforceable by virtue of the creditor entering into a composition contract or acceding to a trust deed for creditors or by virtue of the subsistence of a protected trust deed within the meaning of Schedule 5 to the Bankruptcy (Scotland) Act 1985; or

(g) recalled by a conjoined arrestment order.

(5) Where this subsection applies—

(a) the expenses of the diligence which were chargeable against the debtor shall remain so chargeable; and

(b) if the debtor's obligation to pay the expenses is not discharged under or by virtue of the time to pay order, sequestration, administration order, receivership, winding up, composition contract, trust deed for creditors or conjoined arrestment order, those expenses shall be recoverable by further diligence in pursuance of the warrant which authorised the original diligence.

(6) The expenses incurred in the execution of a current maintenance arrestment shall be recoverable by any diligence other than a current maintenance arrestment, and shall be so recoverable in pursuance of the warrant which authorised the current maintenance arrestment.

GENERAL NOTE

The general principle is retained that debtors are liable for the expenses of diligence done against them. But there is an important change in that now the expenses of a particular diligence are normally recoverable only out of that diligence. Unrecovered expenses in general cease to be chargeable against the debtor. A creditor will therefore no longer be able to bring an action for recovery of unpaid diligence expenses, nor use another diligence to recover them, nor be able to set them off.

Subs. (2)

This subsection clarifies the law in relation to recovery of expenses of arrestments and furthcomings. The expenses are to be recoverable out of the arrested property and any balance will be the subject of a new decree which can be enforced by separate diligence.

Subs. (3)

This subsection provides the creditor with an alternative mode of recovery. If the expenses awarded in connection with an application in relation to a diligence are not recoverable under that diligence, the creditor may use the warrant in the decree for payment to enforce payment by further diligence.

Subss. (4), (5)

These subsections deal with the unusual case where a diligence is recalled by a time to pay order or other "diligence stopper" which is in turn recalled. Creditors are able to recover the expenses of the original diligence by new diligence under the original warrant of execution.

Subs. (6)

The expenses of executing a current maintenance arrestment have to be recovered by other diligence (such as a concurrent earnings arrestment) since such an arrestment recovers current maintenance only.

Ascription of sums recovered by diligence or while diligence is in effect

94.—(1) This section applies to any sums recovered by any of the following diligences—

(a) a poinding and sale;

(b) an earnings arrestment;

(c) an arrestment and action of furthcoming or sale; or

(d) a conjoined arrestment order in so far as it enforces an ordinary debt,

or paid to account of the sums recoverable by the diligence while the diligence is in effect.

(2) A sum to which this section applies shall be ascribed to the following in the order in which they are mentioned—

(a) the expenses already incurred in respect of—

(i) the diligence;

(ii) any previous diligence the expenses of which are chargeable against and recoverable from the debtor under section 93(5) of this Act;

(iii) the execution of a current maintenance arrestment;

(b) any interest, due under the decree or other document on which the diligence proceeds, which has accrued at the date of execution of the poinding, earnings arrestment or arrestment, or in the case of an ordinary debt included in a conjoined arrestment order which has accrued at the date of application under section 60(2) or 62(5) of this Act;

(c) any sum (including any expenses) due under the decree or other document, other than any expenses or interest mentioned in paragraphs (a) and (b) above.

GENERAL NOTE

This section lays down the order in which sums recovered by the diligences listed in subs. (1) are to be applied by the creditor. Broadly speaking the order is diligence expenses, post-decree interest and finally the debt (principal, expenses of the action and any pre-decree interest awarded in the decree).

Certain diligences terminated by payment or tender of full amount owing

95.—(1) Any of the following diligences—

(a) a poinding and sale;

(b) an earnings arrestment;

(c) an arrestment and action of furthcoming or sale,

shall cease to have effect if the full amount recoverable thereby is paid to the creditor, an officer of court, or any other person who has authority to receive payment on behalf of the creditor, or is tendered to any of those persons and the tender is not accepted within a reasonable time.

(2) Any rule of law whereby any diligence mentioned in subsection (1) above ceases to have effect on payment or tender of the sum due under the decree or other document is hereby abolished.

GENERAL NOTE
This subsection abolishes the common law rule that payment of the sum due under the decree plus interest stops any diligence used to enforce it. Unpaid diligence expenses used to have to be the subject of a new legal action. Now diligence expenses are recoverable by the diligence (s.93), so that a diligence is stopped only by payment or tender of the debt, interest and diligence expenses. The official functions of officers of court will include receiving money paid by debtors in settlement of the debts being enforced by diligence if regulations are made (see note on s.75). Then debtors will be able to stop diligence by paying the officers directly.

Provisions to assist debtor in proceedings under Act

96.—(1) No fees shall be payable by a debtor in connection with—
(a) any application by him;
(b) objections by him to an application by any other person; or
(c) a hearing held,
under any provision of this Act, to any officer of any office or department connected with the Court of Session or the sheriff court the expenses of which are paid wholly or partly out of the Consolidated Fund or out of money provided by Parliament.
(2) The sheriff clerk shall, if requested by the debtor—
(a) provide him with information as to the procedures available to him under this Act; and
(b) without prejudice to subsection (2) of section 6 of this Act, assist him in the completion of any form required in connection with any proceedings under this Act,
but the sheriff clerk shall not be liable for any error or omission by him in performing the duties imposed on him by this subsection or that subsection.

GENERAL NOTE
The purpose of this section is to encourage debtors to make use of the Act, principally the applications for time to pay orders or in connection with poindings.
Subs. (1) provides that no court dues are to be payable by debtors. Subs. (2) entitles debtors to request assistance from sheriff clerks as to what remedies there are, what they should do and filling in the appropriate forms. Sheriff clerks are not being turned into debt counsellors. Their duty is to assist in the completion of forms but not to advise debtors what terms to propose in any time to pay application under s.6(2).

97. In relation to any proceedings before the sheriff under any provision of this Act, the power conferred on the Court of Session by section 32 of the Sheriff Courts (Scotland) Act 1971 (power of Court of Session to regulate civil procedure in sheriff court) shall extend to the making of rules permitting a party to such proceedings, in such circumstances as may be specified in the rules, to be represented by a person who is neither an advocate nor a solicitor.

GENERAL NOTE
It is hoped that most of the issues raised in applications under the Act can be dealt with without legal representation. If regulations allow, debtors could be represented by debt counsellors, Citizens Advice Bureau workers and similar people while corporate creditors could be represented by one of their finance section employees.

98. At the end of Part II of Schedule 2 to the Legal Aid (Scotland) Act 1986 (proceedings for which civil legal aid shall not be available) there shall be added the following paragraphs—

"4. Subject to paragraph 5 below, civil legal aid shall not be available in relation to proceedings at first instance under the Debtors (Scotland) Act 1987, other than proceedings in connection with an application under section 1(1) or 3(1) of that Act to a Lord Ordinary or to the sheriff in an ordinary cause.

5. Nothing in paragraph 4 above shall preclude any third party to proceedings under the Debtors (Scotland) Act 1987 from obtaining legal aid in connection with those proceedings.".

GENERAL NOTE

This section prohibits legal aid being granted to either a debtor or a creditor in connection with proceedings under the Act other than appeals or applications for a time to pay decree in the Court of Session or the sheriff's ordinary court. Persons other than debtors or creditors, such as arrestees or persons whose goods have been mistakenly poinded, are not barred from obtaining legal aid if they meet the usual criteria.

99.—(1) Sections 16 to 18, 23 and 26 of this Act shall apply to a landlord's or superior's right of hypothec and its enforcement by a sequestration for rent or feuduty as they apply to a poinding.

(2) Section 16 of this Act shall apply to an arrestment other than an arrestment of a debtor's earnings in the hands of his employer as it applies to a poinding.

GENERAL NOTE
Subs. (1)

The new exemptions from poinding (s.16), restriction on times when poinding is allowed (s.17), powers of entry for executing a poinding (s.18), release of articles on ground of undue harshness (s.23), and sists where mobile homes are poinded (s.26) are to apply to the little-used remedy of sequestration for rent and the even rarer sequestration for unpaid feu-duty.

Subs. (2)

This subsection extends the exemptions from poinding of basic household furniture and other articles to arrestments. It will help the tenant of a furnished flat whose furnishings are threatened with arrestment by a creditor of the landlord.

100.—(1) An obligation ad factum praestandum which is contained in a document registered in the Books of Council and Session or in sheriff court books shall not by virtue of that registration be enforceable by imprisonment.

(2) A charge for the purpose of enforcing an obligation ad factum praestandum which is contained in an extract of a decree or of a document registered as aforesaid shall not be competent.

GENERAL NOTE

This section lays down new procedures for enforcing obligations *ad facta praestanda*. Imprisonment by an administrative process after the expiry of a charge to perform is prohibited. Poinding and arrestment are already incompetent to enforce a non-monetary obligation. Now the creditor will have to bring an action based on the registered obligation, obtain a decree (which the court has a discretion whether or not to grant), and in the event of non-compliance apply to the court for an order under s.1 of the Law Reform (Miscellaneous Provisions) (Scotland) Act 1940 (which empowers the court to impose imprisonment or to substitute damages or such other remedy as appears just).

101. It shall not be competent for a creditor to bring an action of adjudication for debt (other than an action under section 23(5) of the Conveyancing (Scotland) Act 1924) to enforce a debt payable under a liquid document of debt unless—

(a) the debt has been constituted by decree; or
(b) the debt is a debitum fundi; or

(c) the document of debt or, if the document is a bill of exchange or a promissory note, a protest of the bill or note, has been registered for execution in the Books of Council and Session or in sheriff court books.

GENERAL NOTE
The purpose of this section is to prevent a creditor holding a liquid document of debt (such as a bond, bill of exchange, or promissory note) bypassing the time to pay provision in ss.1–15 by raising an action of adjudication without having to constitute the debt in court proceedings. An action under s.23(5) of the 1924 Act is for forfeiture to the creditor of the subjects from which a ground-annual is payable if the payments are more than two years in arrears.

Para. (b)
An adjudication in respect of a *debitum fundi*—a special diligence available to heritable creditors—is not affected by a time to pay direction or order (s.15(1)).

Para. (c)
Since there are no court proceedings needed to constitute the debt the debtor will have no opportunity to apply for a time to pay direction. Once diligence has commenced, however, a time to pay order can be applied for.

Procedure in diligence proceeding on extract of registered document etc.

102.—(1) The Court of Session may by Act of Sederunt—
(a) regulate and prescribe the procedure and practice in; and
(b) prescribe the form of any document to be used in, or for the purposes of,
diligence of a kind specified in subsection (2) below.
(2) The diligences referred to in subsection (1) above are diligences proceeding—
(a) on an extract of a document which has been registered for execution in the Books of Council and Session or in sheriff court books; or
(b) on an order or a determination which by virtue of any enactment is to be treated as if it were so registered.

GENERAL NOTE
The Court of Session has power under the Administration of Justice (Scotland) Act 1933, s.16 and the Sheriff Courts (Scotland) Act 1971, s.32 to regulate forms relating to diligence on court decrees. This section extends its powers to regulate diligence forms in execution of extract registered writs or their equivalents (e.g. orders of the comptroller under the Patents Act 1977, s.107(3)).

Appeals

103.—(1) Subject to subsection (9) below and sections 21(1), 27(4), 43(5), 50(2), 55(4), 60(8), 62(9) and 66(9) of this Act and paragraphs 6(1), 11(4) and 14(5) of Schedule 5 thereto, an appeal may be made against any decision of the sheriff under this Act but only on a question of law and with the leave of the sheriff; and section 38 of the Sheriff Courts (Scotland) Act 1971 (appeal in summary causes) shall not apply to any appeal or any further appeal taken under this Act.
(2) Any appeal against a decision of the sheriff under subsection (1) above must be made within a period of 14 days from the date when leave to appeal against the decision was granted.
(3) An appeal may be made against any decision of the Lord Ordinary on an application under section 1(1) or 3(1) of this Act but only on a question of law and with the leave of the Lord Ordinary.
(4) Subject to subsections (6) and (7) below, any decision of the sheriff or of the Lord Ordinary under this Act shall take effect as soon as it is

made and shall remain in effect unless and until it is reversed on appeal and either—

    (a) the period allowed for further appeal has expired without an appeal being made; or

    (b) if such a further appeal has been made, the matter has been finally determined in favour of the reversal of the sheriff's or Lord Ordinary's decision.

(5) No decision reversing a decision of the sheriff or Lord Ordinary under this Act shall have retrospective effect.

(6) A decision or order of the sheriff under any provision of this Act mentioned in subsection (7) below shall not take effect—

    (a) until the period for leave to appeal specified in rules of court has expired without an application for leave having been made;

    (b) where an application for leave to appeal is made, until leave has been refused or the application has been abandoned;

    (c) where leave to appeal has been granted, until the period for an appeal has expired without an appeal being made; or

    (d) where an appeal against the decision is made, until the matter has been finally determined or the appeal has been abandoned.

(7) The provisions of this Act referred to in subsection (6) above are—

    (a) section 16(4);
    (b) section 23(1);
    (c) section 24(1) except in so far as it relates to orders declaring that a poinding is invalid or has ceased to have effect;
    (d) section 24(3);
    (e) section 30;
    (f) section 35(1);
    (g) section 39(5)(b) and (c);
    (h) section 40(2);
    (j) section 41(3);
    (k) section 50(1) except in so far as it relates to orders declaring that an arrestment is invalid or has ceased to have effect;
    (l) section 50(4);
    (m) section 55(1) except in so far as it relates to orders declaring that an arrestment is invalid or has ceased to have effect;
    (n) section 55(6);
    (o) section 65(2);
    (p) section 66(3);
    (q) paragraphs 1(4), 7(1), 8(1) and (3), 21(2) and 22(3) of Schedule 5.

(8) A court to which an appeal under this Act or a further appeal is made may—

    (a) before it disposes of the appeal, make such interim order; and

    (b) on determining the appeal, make such supplementary order,

as it thinks necessary or reasonable in the circumstances.

(9) This section does not apply to any decision of a court under Part V of this Act.

GENERAL NOTE

This section deals with appeals against determinations made under the provisions of the Act.

Subs. (1)

The general philosophy is to allow appeals on points of law only and to require the leave of the judge who made the decision under appeal.

The enumerated sections are exceptions to the general rule. They relate to situations where no appeals are allowed because of the need for finality. In addition subs. (9) prevents the decision of a sheriff principal of a Court of Session judge in connection with the appointment of officers of court from being appealed. Disposals following a finding or admission of misconduct are appealable on fact and/or law to the Inner House under the express provisions of s.82.

Subs. (2)

An appellant has 14 days in which to lodge an appeal after obtaining leave to appeal. Rules of court will set out the period after granting of decree within which leave to appeal must be applied for.

Subs. (3)

This relates to time to pay decrees in Court of Session actions.

Subss. (4), (6), (7)

Generally a first instance decision is to receive effect until it is reversed on appeal. But in certain cases (set out in subs. (7)) this rule would lead to consequences which could not be reversed on appeal. For example, the granting of a warrant of sale has to be suspended pending an appeal since the appeal court could not return to the debtor goods which had been sold.

Subs. (5)

Rights acquired by virtue of the decision in the interval between the granting of the decision and its reversal on appeal are not to be invalidated by the reversal.

Subs. (8)

This subsection empowers the court to make interim orders (such as for the custody of goods or the disposal of funds) pending appeal and consequential orders (such as remitting to the sheriff to grant a new warrant of sale) when confirming or reversing the decision under appeal.

Regulations

104.—(1) Regulations under this Act shall be made by statutory instrument and shall, except as provided in subsection (2) below, be subject to annulment in pursuance of a resolution of either House of Parliament.

(2) No regulation shall be made under paragraph 1(2) of Schedule 1 or paragraph 25(2) of Schedule 5 to this Act unless a draft of it has been laid before, and approved by a resolution of, each House of Parliament.

GENERAL NOTE

The tighter Parliamentary control afforded by the affirmative resolution procedure is appropriate for changes to the list of diligence expenses which are chargeable against the debtor (subs. (2)). Negative resolution procedure (subs. (1)) is used for other changes.

Application to Crown

105. Without prejudice to the Crown Proceedings Act 1947, this Act shall bind the Crown acting in its capacity as a creditor or employer.

GENERAL NOTE

Although the Crown is bound by the Act diligence against the Crown to enforce any order made under the Act remains incompetent (Crown Proceedings Act 1947, s.45).

Interpretation

106. In this Act—

"current maintenance" has the meaning given to it in section 73(1) of this Act;

"earnings" has the meaning given to it in section 73(2) of this Act;

"employer" has the meaning given to it in section 73(1) of this Act;

"maintenance" means periodical sums payable under a maintenance order;

"maintenance order" means—

(a) an order granted by a court in Scotland for payment of a periodical allowance on divorce or on the granting of a declarator of nullity of marriage, or for aliment;

(b) an order under section 43 or 44 of the National Assistance Act 1948, section 23 or 24 of the Ministry of Social Security Act 1966, section 80 or 81 of the Social Work (Scotland) Act 1968, section 11(3) of the Guardianship Act 1973, section 18 or 19 of the Supplementary Benefits Act 1976, section 50 or 51 of the Child Care Act 1980 or section 24 or 25 of the Social Security Act 1986;

(c) an order of a court in England and Wales or Northern Ireland registered in Scotland under Part II of the Maintenance Orders Act 1950;

(d) a provisional order of a reciprocating country which is confirmed by a court in Scotland under Part I of the Maintenance Orders (Reciprocal Enforcement) Act 1972;

(e) an order of a reciprocating country which is registered in Scotland under that Part of that Act;

(f) an order registered in Scotland under Part II, or under an Order in Council made in pursuance of Part III, of that Act;

(g) an order registered in Scotland under section 5 of the Civil Jurisdiction and Judgments Act 1982; or

(h) an alimentary bond or agreement (including a document providing for the maintenance of one party to a marriage by the other after the marriage has been dissolved or annulled)—

(i) registered for execution in the Books of Council and Session or sheriff court books; or

(ii) registered in Scotland under an Order in Council made under section 13 of the Civil Jurisdiction and Judgments Act 1982;

"net earnings" has the meaning given to it in section 73(1) of this Act;

"officer of court" means a messenger-at-arms or a sheriff officer;

"ordinary debt" has the meaning given to it in section 73(1) of this Act;

"summary warrant" means a summary warrant granted under or by virtue of any of the enactments mentioned in Schedule 4 to this Act;

"warrant of sale" has the meaning given in section 30 of this Act.

Financial provisions

107.—(1) Any sums recovered by the Lord Advocate under section 79(6)(b) or 80(9) of this Act shall be paid by him into the Consolidated Fund.

(2) There shall be paid out of money provided by Parliament—

(a) any fees or outlays payable under section 78(4) or 79(4) of this Act;

(b) any expenses payable by the Lord Advocate under section 79(6)(a) of this Act; and

(c) any increase attributable to this Act in the sums payable out of money so provided under any other Act.

Minor and consequential amendments, transitional provisions and repeals

108.—(1) The amendments specified in Schedule 6 to this Act, being minor amendments or amendments consequential on the provisions of this Act, shall have effect.

(2) The transitional provisions contained in Schedule 7 to this Act shall have effect.

(3) The enactments mentioned in columns 1 and 2 of Schedule 8 to this Act are repealed to the extent specified in column 3 thereof.

Short title, commencement and extent

109.—(1) This Act may be cited as the Debtors (Scotland) Act 1987.

(2) This Act (except this section) shall come into force on such day as the Lord Advocate may by order made by statutory instrument appoint, and different days may be so appointed for different purposes and for different provisions.

(3) This Act extends to Scotland only.

SCHEDULES

SCHEDULE 1

EXPENSES OF POINDING AND SALE

Expenses chargeable against the debtor

1.—(1) Subject to paragraphs 2, 3 and 5 to 7 below, there shall be chargeable against the debtor any expenses incurred—
  (a) subject to section 90(7) of this Act, in serving a charge;
  (b) in serving a notice under section 18 of this Act before entering a dwellinghouse for the purpose of executing a poinding;
  (c) in executing a poinding under section 20 of this Act;
  (d) in making a report under section 21(4) of this Act of the redemption by the debtor of any poinded article;
  (e) in granting a receipt under section 21(5) of this Act for payment for redemption under subsection (4) of that section;
  (f) in making a report under section 22 of this Act of the execution of a poinding, but not in applying for an extension of time for the making of such a report;
  (g) in applying for a warrant of sale under section 30(1) of this Act;
  (h) in granting a receipt under section 33(3) of this Act for payment for the redemption of any poinded article;
  (j) in making a report under section 33(5)(b) of this Act of the release or redemption of poinded articles;
  (k) in making intimation, serving a copy of the warrant of sale and giving public notice under section 34 of this Act;
  (l) in removing any articles for sale in pursuance of a warrant of sale;
  (m) in making arrangements for, conducting and supervising a warrant sale;
  (n) where the arrangements for a sale have been cancelled under section 36(1) of this Act, in returning poinded articles to any premises from which they have been removed for sale;
  (o) in making a report of an agreement under section 36(2) of this Act;
  (p) subject to section 39(3) of this Act, in making a report of sale under that section;
  (q) in granting a receipt under section 41(4) of this Act for payment for the release from a poinding of any article which is owned in common;
  (r) in making a report under section 41(5)(b) of this Act of the release of any such article;
  (s) in opening shut and lockfast places in the execution of the diligence;
  (t) by a solicitor in instructing an officer of court to take any of the steps specified in this sub-paragraph.

(2) The Lord Advocate may by regulations add to, delete or vary any of the steps specified in sub-paragraph (1) above.

2. Where a warrant of sale is varied under section 35 of this Act, there shall be chargeable against the debtor the expenses incurred in the application for the variation and the execution of the warrant of sale as varied but, subject to paragraph 4 below, not in the application for, and the execution of, the original warrant of sale.

3. Where arrangements for a sale are cancelled under subsection (1) of section 36 of this Act, if new arrangements are made for the sale in the circumstances mentioned in subsection (3)(a) of that section, there shall be chargeable against the debtor the expenses incurred in the making of the new arrangements but not in the making of the arrangements which have been cancelled.

4. Where a warrant of sale is varied under section 35 of this Act and the sheriff has awarded an additional sum of expenses under paragraph 9 below in the application for the original warrant of sale, that sum shall be chargeable against the debtor.

5. Subject to paragraph 6 below, where any such further poinding as is mentioned in section 28(2) of this Act has been executed, there shall be chargeable against the debtor the expenses incurred in that poinding but not the expenses incurred in the original poinding.

6. Where any such further poinding as is mentioned in subsection (2) of section 28 of this Act has been executed and—
   (a) the creditor has, as a condition of his consenting to the removal of the poinded articles under subsection (1)(a) of that section, required the debtor to undertake liability for the expenses incurred in the original poinding; or
   (b) the sheriff has, when authorising the removal of the poinded articles under subsection (1)(b) of that section, directed that the debtor shall be liable for those expenses,
there shall be chargeable against the debtor the expenses incurred in both poindings.

7. Where a new date is arranged under section 35(10) of this Act for the holding of a warrant sale or for the removal of poinded articles for sale, there shall be chargeable against the debtor the expenses incurred in connection with arranging the new date but not those incurred in connection with arranging the original date.

Circumstances where liability for expenses is at the discretion of the sheriff

8. The liability for any expenses incurred by the creditor or the debtor—
   (a) in an application by the creditor or an officer of court to the sheriff under any provision of Part II of this Act, other than an application for a warrant of sale under section 30(1) of this Act or an application for variation of a warrant of sale under section 35(1) of this Act; or
   (b) in implementing an order under—
      (i) section 21(1) of this Act (order for security or immediate disposal of poinded articles); or
      (ii) section 28(4) to (6) or 29 of this Act (orders dealing with unauthorised removal, damage or destruction of poinded articles),
shall be as determined by the sheriff.

Calculation of amount chargeable against debtor under the foregoing provisions

9. Expenses—
   (a) chargeable against the debtor by virtue of any of paragraphs 1 to 6 above in respect of an application under Part II of this Act; or
   (b) awarded by the sheriff against the debtor in favour of the creditor in a determination under paragraph 8 above in respect of an application other than an application under section 28(4) to (6) or 29 of this Act,
shall be calculated, whether or not the application is opposed by the debtor, as if it were unopposed, except that, if the debtor opposes the application on grounds which appear to the sheriff to be frivolous, the sheriff may award an additional sum of expenses, not exceeding £25 or such amount as may be prescribed in regulations made by the Lord Advocate, against the debtor.

Circumstances where no expenses are due to or by either party

10. Subject to paragraph 11 below, the debtor shall not be liable to the creditor nor the creditor to the debtor for any expenses incurred by the other party in connection with—
   (a) an application by the debtor to the sheriff under any provision of Part II of this Act;
   (b) any objections to such an application;
   (c) a hearing held by virtue of section 24(5), 30(4), 35(6) or 39(6) of this Act.
11. If—
   (a) an application mentioned in paragraph 10(a) above is frivolous;

(b) such an application is opposed on frivolous grounds; or

(c) a party requires a hearing held by virtue of any of the provisions mentioned in paragraph 10(c) above to be held on frivolous grounds,

the sheriff may award a sum of expenses, not exceeding £25 or such amount as may be prescribed in regulations made by the Lord Advocate, against the party acting frivolously in favour of the other party.

Supplementary

12. Any expenses chargeable against the debtor by virtue of any provision of this Schedule shall be recoverable out of the proceeds of sale.

Section 49   SCHEDULE 2

DEDUCTIONS TO BE MADE UNDER EARNINGS ARRESTMENT

TABLE A: DEDUCTIONS FROM WEEKLY EARNINGS

Net earnings	Deduction
Not exceeding £35	Nil
Exceeding £35 but not exceeding £40	£1
Exceeding £40 but not exceeding £45	£2
Exceeding £45 but not exceeding £50	£3
Exceeding £50 but not exceeding £55	£4
Exceeding £55 but not exceeding £60	£5
Exceeding £60 but not exceeding £65	£6
Exceeding £65 but not exceeding £70	£7
Exceeding £70 but not exceeding £75	£8
Exceeding £75 but not exceeding £80	£9
Exceeding £80 but not exceeding £85	£10
Exceeding £85 but not exceeding £90	£11
Exceeding £90 but not exceeding £95	£12
Exceeding £95 but not exceeding £100	£13
Exceeding £100 but not exceeding £110	£15
Exceeding £110 but not exceeding £120	£17
Exceeding £120 but not exceeding £130	£19
Exceeding £130 but not exceeding £140	£21
Exceeding £140 but not exceeding £150	£23
Exceeding £150 but not exceeding £160	£26
Exceeding £160 but not exceeding £170	£29
Exceeding £170 but not exceeding £180	£32
Exceeding £180 but not exceeding £190	£35
Exceeding £190 but not exceeding £200	£38
Exceeding £200 but not exceeding £220	£46
Exceeding £220 but not exceeding £240	£54
Exceeding £240 but not exceeding £260	£63
Exceeding £260 but not exceeding £280	£73
Exceeding £280 but not exceeding £300	£83
Exceeding £300	£83 in respect of the first £300 plus 50 per cent of the remainder

TABLE B: DEDUCTIONS FROM MONTHLY EARNINGS

Net earnings	Deduction
Not exceeding £152	Nil
Exceeding £152 but not exceeding £170	£5
Exceeding £170 but not exceeding £185	£8
Exceeding £185 but not exceeding £200	£11
Exceeding £200 but not exceeding £220	£14
Exceeding £220 but not exceeding £240	£18
Exceeding £240 but not exceeding £260	£22
Exceeding £260 but not exceeding £280	£26
Exceeding £280 but not exceeding £300	£30
Exceeding £300 but not exceeding £320	£34
Exceeding £320 but not exceeding £340	£38
Exceeding £340 but not exceeding £360	£42
Exceeding £360 but not exceeding £380	£46
Exceeding £380 but not exceeding £400	£50
Exceeding £400 but not exceeding £440	£58
Exceeding £440 but not exceeding £480	£66
Exceeding £480 but not exceeding £520	£74
Exceeding £520 but not exceeding £560	£82
Exceeding £560 but not exceeding £600	£90
Exceeding £600 but not exceeding £640	£98
Exceeding £640 but not exceeding £680	£109
Exceeding £680 but not exceeding £720	£121
Exceeding £720 but not exceeding £760	£133
Exceeding £760 but not exceeding £800	£145
Exceeding £800 but not exceeding £900	£180
Exceeding £900 but not exceeding £1000	£220
Exceeding £1000 but not exceeding £1100	£262
Exceeding £1100 but not exceeding £1200	£312
Exceeding £1200 but not exceeding £1300	£362
Exceeding £1300	£362 in respect of the first £1300 plus 50 per cent. of the remainder

TABLE C: DEDUCTIONS BASED ON DAILY EARNINGS

Net earnings	Deduction
Not exceeding £5	Nil
Exceeding £5 but not exceeding £6	£0.15
Exceeding £6 but not exceeding £7	£0.30
Exceeding £7 but not exceeding £8	£0.45
Exceeding £8 but not exceeding £9	£0.60
Exceeding £9 but not exceeding £10	£1.00
Exceeding £10 but not exceeding £11	£1.20
Exceeding £11 but not exceeding £12	£1.40
Exceeding £12 but not exceeding £13	£1.60
Exceeding £13 but not exceeding £14	£1.80
Exceeding £14 but not exceeding £15	£2.00
Exceeding £15 but not exceeding £17	£2.40
Exceeding £17 but not exceeding £19	£2.70
Exceeding £19 but not exceeding £21	£3.20
Exceeding £21 but not exceeding £23	£3.70
Exceeding £23 but not exceeding £25	£4.30
Exceeding £25 but not exceeding £27	£5.00
Exceeding £27 but not exceeding £30	£6.00
Exceeding £30 but not exceeding £33	£7.00
Exceeding £33 but not exceeding £36	£8.50

Net earnings	Deduction
Exceeding £36 but not exceeding £39	£10.00
Exceeding £39 but not exceeding £42	£11.50
Exceeding £42	£11.50 in respect of the first £42 plus 50 per cent. of the remainder

GENERAL NOTE
See General Note to s.49.

Section 64   SCHEDULE 3

DISBURSEMENTS BY SHERIFF CLERKS UNDER CONJOINED ARRESTMENT ORDER

1. Where all the debts are ordinary debts, in every disbursement by the sheriff clerk each creditor shall be paid the same proportion of the amount of his debt.

2. Where all the debts are current maintenance, then, in any such disbursement, if the sum available for disbursement is—
   (a) sufficient to satisfy every creditor in respect of the amount of maintenance to be deducted in respect of his debt on that pay-day, each creditor shall be paid that amount;
   (b) insufficient to satisfy every creditor in respect of the amount of maintenance specified in paragraph (a) above, each creditor shall be paid the same proportion of that amount.

3. Subject to paragraph 4 below, where the debts comprise both ordinary debts and current maintenance, then, in any such disbursement—
   (a) if only one of the debts is an ordinary debt, the creditor in that debt shall be paid the sum which would be payable to him if the debt were being enforced by an earnings arrestment;
   (b) if more than one of the debts is an ordinary debt, each of the creditors in those debts, out of the sum which would be payable to a creditor if the debt were a single debt being enforced by an earnings arrestment, shall be paid the same proportion of the amount of his debt;
   (c) if only one of the debts is current maintenance, the creditor in that debt shall be paid the sum which would be payable to him under section 51 of this Act if the debt were being enforced by a current maintenance arrestment;
   (d) if more than one of the debts is current maintenance, each of the creditors in those debts shall receive a payment in accordance with paragraph 2 of this Schedule.

4. If the sum available for any disbursement is insufficient to enable the provisions of paragraph 3 above to operate both in relation to the ordinary debts and the current maintenance, priority shall be given in the disbursement to the ordinary debts.

5. For the purposes of this Schedule, the amount of an ordinary debt—
   (a) of a creditor whose debt was being enforced by an earnings arrestment which was recalled under section 60(3) of this Act, shall be the amount specified in the earnings arrestment schedule;
   (b) of any other creditor, shall be the amount specified in the conjoined arrestment order or the order under section 62(5) of this Act.

GENERAL NOTE
Para. 1
   The ordinary creditors rank equally. Thus if creditor A has a debt of £700 and creditor B a debt of £300 a deduction of £50 received from the employer is split £35 to A and £15 to B.

Para. 2
   Maintenance creditors get their maintenance in full or abate equally. Suppose creditor A's daily rate of maintenance is £5 and creditor B's is £7. If the debtor's weekly net earnings are sufficient to deduct £84 (*i.e.* net earnings at least £35 more than this) A and B will get their maintenance in full, £35 and £49 respectively. If in one week only £48 is deducted:

creditor A gets $48 \times \dfrac{5}{5+7}$, *i.e.* £20 (4/7 of the amount due)

creditor B gets $48 \times \dfrac{7}{5+7}$, *i.e.* £28 (4/7 of the amount due).

Paras. 3, 4

In a "mixed" conjoined arrestment order each class of creditor (ordinary and maintenance), is dealt with separately. Where there is more than one creditor in each class the rules in paras. 1 and 2 operate, with priority being given to ordinary debts.

Example

Creditor A	ordinary debt of	£150
Creditor B	ordinary debt of	£200
Creditor C	maintenance debt of	£10 per week
Creditor D	maintenance debt of	£15 per week

Week 1   The debtor's net earnings are £160 and the sheriff clerk receives £60 from the employer.

The deduction in respect of ordinary debts is £35 (Table A). This is split between A and B in the ratio of 150:200. Creditor A gets £15. Creditor B gets £20. The sheriff clerk has £25 left which is sufficient to pay C and D in full. They get £10 and £15 respectively.

Week 2   The debtor's net earnings are £60 and the sheriff clerk receives £25. Note that the debtor is left with the basic subsistence of £35. Giving priority to the ordinary creditors the sheriff clerk first calculates their entitlement.

The deduction in respect of ordinary debts is £5 (Table A). This is split between A and B in the ratio of 150:200.

Creditor A gets $5 \times \dfrac{150}{150+200}$, *i.e.* £2.14

Creditor B gets $5 \times \dfrac{200}{150+200}$, *i.e.* £2.86.

The sheriff clerk has £20 left. This is split between C and D in the ratio 10:15.

Creditor C gets $20 \times \dfrac{10}{10+15}$, *i.e.* £8

Creditor D gets $20 \times \dfrac{15}{10+15}$, *i.e.* £12

Para. 5

The effect of this paragraph is to give a small measure of priority to an earlier creditor.

Example

A debtor earns £110 net per week. Creditor A whose debt is £150 executes an earnings arrestment and receives £15 per month. After 5 weeks A's debt has been reduced to £75. In that week creditor B with a debt of £75 applies for a conjoined arrestment order which is made. The deductions made by the employer and received by the sheriff clerk remain at £15 per week. This is split in the ratio of the initial debts, *i.e.* 150:75 so that A gets £10 and B gets £5 per week.

Section 74(1)   SCHEDULE 4

RECOVERY OF RATES AND TAXES ETC.

The Local Government (Scotland) Act 1947 (c. 43.)

1.—(1) For section 247 there shall be substituted the following sections—

"Recovery of rates

247.—(1) Subject to subsections (4) and (5) below, arrears of rates may be recovered by a rating authority by diligence—

    (a) authorised by a summary warrant granted under subsection (2) below; or

    (b) in pursuance of a decree granted in an action for payment.

(2) Subject to subsection (4) below, the sheriff, on an application by the rating authority accompanied by a certificate by the rating authority—

(a) stating that none of the persons specified in the application has paid the rates due by him;

(b) stating that the authority has given written notice to each such person requiring him to make payment of the amount due by him within a period of 14 days after the date of the giving of the notice;

(c) stating that the said period of 14 days has expired without payment of the said amount; and

(d) specifying the amount due and unpaid by each such person,

shall grant a summary warrant in a form prescribed by Act of Sederunt authorising the recovery by any of the diligences mentioned in subsection (3) below of the amount remaining due and unpaid along with a surcharge of 10 per cent. (or such percentage as may be prescribed) of that amount.

(3) The diligences referred to in subsection (2) above are—

(a) a poinding and sale in accordance with Schedule 5 to the Debtors (Scotland) Act 1987;

(b) an earnings arrestment;

(c) an arrestment and action of furthcoming or sale.

(4) It shall not be competent for the sheriff to grant a summary warrant under subsection (2) above in respect of rates due by a debtor if an action has already been commenced for the recovery of those rates; and, without prejudice to subsection (5) below, on the commencing of an action for the recovery of rates, any existing summary warrant in so far as it relates to the recovery of those rates shall cease to have effect.

(5) It shall not be competent to commence an action for the recovery of rates if, in pursuance of a summary warrant, any of the diligences mentioned in subsection (3) above for the recovery of those rates has been executed.

(6) In any proceedings for the recovery of rates, whether by summary warrant or otherwise, no person shall be entitled to found upon failure of the rating authority or any other authority to comply with any provision of this Part of this Act relating to the date by which something shall be done, not being a provision in this section or a provision regulating the diligence.

(7) Regulations under subsection (2) above shall be made by statutory instrument and shall be subject to annulment in pursuance of a resolution of either House of Parliament.

Sheriff officer's fees and outlays

247A.—(1) Subject to subsection (2) below and without prejudice to paragraphs 25 to 34 of Schedule 5 to the Debtors (Scotland) Act 1987 (expenses of poinding and sale), the sheriff officer's fees, together with the outlays necessarily incurred by him, in connection with the execution of a summary warrant shall be chargeable against the debtor.

(2) No fee shall be chargeable by the sheriff officer against the debtor for collecting, and accounting to the rating authority for, sums paid to him by the debtor in respect of the amount owing.".

(2) In section 250, for the words from "warrant" to "in payment" where third occurring there shall be substituted the words—

"a summary warrant in a form prescribed by Act of Sederunt authorising the recovery by any of the diligences mentioned in section 247(3) of this Act of the amount remaining due and unpaid".

The Taxes Management Act 1970 (c. 9.)

2. For section 63 there shall be substituted the following sections—

"Recovery of tax in Scotland

63.—(1) Subject to subsection (3) below, in Scotland, where any tax is due and has not been paid, the sheriff, on an application by the collector accompanied by a certificate by the collector—

(a) stating that none of the persons specified in the application has paid the tax due by him;

(b) stating that the collector has demanded payment under section 60 of this Act from each such person of the amount due by him;

(c) stating that 14 days have elapsed since the date of such demand without payment of the said amount; and

(d) specifying the amount due and unpaid by each such person,

shall grant a summary warrant in a form prescribed by Act of Sederunt authorising the recovery, by any of the diligences mentioned in subsection (2) below, of the amount remaining due and unpaid.

(2) The diligences referred to in subsection (1) above are—

(a) a poinding and sale in accordance with Schedule 5 to the Debtors (Scotland) Act 1987;

(b) an earnings arrestment;

(c) an arrestment and action of furthcoming or sale.

(3) Paragraph (c) of subsection (1) above shall not apply to an application under that subsection which relates to tax deducted from the emoluments of an office or employment by virtue of regulations under section 204 of the principal Act.

Sheriff officer's fees and outlays

63A.—(1) Subject to subsection (2) below and without prejudice to paragraphs 25 to 34 of Schedule 5 to the Debtors (Scotland) Act 1987 (expenses of poinding and sale), the sheriff officer's fees, together with the outlays necessarily incurred by him, in connection with the execution of a summary warrant shall be chargeable against the debtor.

(2) No fee shall be chargeable by the sheriff officer against the debtor for collecting, and accounting to the collector for, sums paid to him by the debtor in respect of the amount owing.".

The Car Tax Act 1983 (c. 53.)

3. In paragraph 3(2) of Schedule 1 (recovery of car tax), for the words from "and (b)" to the end there shall be substituted the following sub-paragraphs—

"(3) In respect of Scotland, where any tax is due and has not been paid, the sheriff, on an application by the Commissioners accompanied by a certificate by the Commissioners—

(a) stating that none of the persons specified in the application has paid the tax due from him;

(b) stating that payment of the amount due from each such person has been demanded from him; and

(c) specifying the amount due from and unpaid by each such person,

shall grant a summary warrant in a form prescribed by Act of Sederunt authorising the recovery, by any of the diligences mentioned in sub-paragraph (4) below, of the amount remaining due and unpaid.

(4) The diligences referred to in sub-paragraph (3) above are—

(a) a poinding and sale in accordance with Schedule 5 to the Debtors (Scotland) Act 1987;

(b) an earnings arrestment;

(c) an arrestment and action of furthcoming or sale.

(5) Subject to sub-paragraph (6) below and without prejudice to paragraphs 25 to 34 of Schedule 5 to the Debtors (Scotland) Act 1987 (expenses of poinding and sale), the sheriff officer's fees, together with the outlays necessarily incurred by him, in connection with the execution of a summary warrant shall be chargeable against the debtor.

(6) No fee shall be chargeable by the sheriff officer against the debtor for collecting, and accounting to the Commissioners for, sums paid to him by the debtor in respect of the amount owing.

(7) Regulations under this Schedule may make provision for anything which the Commissioners may do under sub-paragraphs (3) to (6) above to be done by an officer of the Commissioners holding such rank as the regulations may specify.".

The Value Added Tax Act 1983 (c. 55.)

4. In paragraph 6(4) of Schedule 7 (recovery of value added tax), for the words from "and (b)" to the end there shall be substituted the following sub-paragraphs—

"(5) In respect of Scotland, where any tax or any sum recoverable as if it were tax is due and has not been paid, the sheriff, on an application by the Commissioners accompanied by a certificate by the Commissioners—

(a) stating that none of the persons specified in the application has paid the tax or other sum due from him;

(b) stating that payment of the amount due from each such person has been demanded from him; and

(c) specifying the amount due from and unpaid by each such person,

shall grant a summary warrant in a form prescribed by Act of Sederunt authorising the recovery, by any of the diligences mentioned in sub-paragraph (6) below, of the amount remaining due and unpaid.

(6) The diligences referred to in sub-paragraph (5) above are—

(a) a poinding and sale in accordance with Schedule 5 to the Debtors (Scotland) Act 1987;

(b) an earnings arrestment;

(c) an arrestment and action of furthcoming or sale.

(7) Subject to sub-paragraph (8) below and without prejudice to paragraphs 25 to 34 of Schedule 5 to the Debtors (Scotland) Act 1987 (expenses of poinding and sale), the sheriff officer's fees, together with the outlays necessarily incurred by him, in connection with the execution of a summary warrant shall be chargeable against the debtor.

(8) No fee shall be chargeable by the sheriff officer against the debtor for collecting, and accounting to the Commissioners for, sums paid to him by the debtor in respect of the amount owing.

(9) The Commissioners may by regulations make provision for anything which the Commissioners may do under sub-paragraphs (5) to (8) above to be done by an officer of the Commissioners holding such rank as the regulations may specify.".

GENERAL NOTE

This schedule sets out the procedure for obtaining a summary warrant and the diligences which such a warrant authorises.

Local Government Rates

S.247(1) retains the existing law whereby the rating authority has a choice of proceeding by way of summary warrant or ordinary court action. Each method has its advantages and disadvantages. Subss. (4) and (5) fetter the freedom of the authority to change over to another method once one method of enforcement has commenced.

S.247(2) retains the previous method of obtaining a summary warrant and the 10 per cent. surcharge on unpaid rates. The surcharge percentage is alterable by statutory instrument.

S.247(3) sets out the diligences authorised by a summary warrant. The main differences from the previous law are that the new diligence of earnings arrestment replaces arrestment of wages (which for rates and taxes attached the whole wages), and the poinding procedure set out in Sched. 5 is materially different from that which used to be employed (see note on Sched. 5 for further details).

S.247(6). This subsection prevents a rates defaulter from challenging (on grounds of the authority's non-compliance with various time limits) the validity of the rate sought to be enforced in the process for enforcement. Any such challenge would have to take the form of a separate action for reduction of the determination of the rating authority.

S.247A. This subsection clarifies the law as to the expenses of enforcement payable by the debtor. Like diligence on a decree the debtor is liable for the officer's prescribed fees and outlays in addition to the arrears of rates and surcharge. Officers may negotiate with the rating authority for remuneration to cover the cost of collecting and accounting for the sums recovered from rates defaulters, but such remuneration would be payable by the authority, not by the rates defaulter.

The community charges introduced by the Abolition of Domestic Rates Etc. (Scotland) Act 1987 will be enforceable in the same way as rates.

Taxes

The main changes from the previous law are that:—

(1) Arrestment and furthcoming and the new diligences of earnings arrestment and conjoined arrestment orders become available to enforce arrears of tax.

(2) The officer's fee of 10 per cent. of the tax due for executing diligence under a summary warrant is replaced by the normal prescribed fees and outlays for diligence done.

(3) The poinding procedure in Sched. 5 (the same as that used to enforce arrears of rates) is nearer ordinary poinding procedure, although still summary in nature. (See notes on Sched. 5 for further details.)

           SCHEDULE 5

POINDINGS AND SALES IN PURSUANCE OF SUMMARY WARRANTS

Articles exempt from poinding

1.—(1) The following articles belonging to a debtor shall be exempt from poinding at the instance of a creditor in respect of a debt due to him by the debtor—

    (a) clothing reasonably required for the use of the debtor or any member of his household;

    (b) implements, tools of trade, books or other equipment reasonably required for the use of the debtor or any member of his household in the practice of the debtor's or such member's profession, trade or business, not exceeding in aggregate value £500 or such amount as may be prescribed in regulations made by the Lord Advocate;

    (c) medical aids or medical equipment reasonably required for the use of the debtor or any member of his household;

    (d) books or other articles reasonably required for the education or training of the debtor or any member of his household not exceeding in aggregate value £500 or such amount as may be prescribed in regulations made by the Lord Advocate;

    (e) toys for the use of any child who is a member of the debtor's household;

    (f) articles reasonably required for the care or upbringing of a child who is a member of the debtor's household.

(2) The following articles belonging to a debtor shall be exempt from poinding if they are at the time of the poinding in a dwellinghouse and are reasonably required for the use in the dwellinghouse of the person residing there or a member of his household—

    (a) beds or bedding;

    (b) household linen;

    (c) chairs or settees;

    (d) tables;

    (e) food;

    (f) lights or light fittings;

    (g) heating appliances;

    (h) curtains;

    (j) floor coverings;

    (k) furniture, equipment or utensils used for cooking, storing or eating food;

    (l) refrigerators;

    (m) articles used for cleaning, mending, or pressing clothes;

    (n) articles used for cleaning the dwellinghouse;

    (o) furniture used for storing—

        (i) clothing, bedding or household linen;

        (ii) articles used for cleaning the dwellinghouse; or

        (iii) utensils used for cooking or eating food;

    (p) articles used for safety in the dwellinghouse;

    (q) tools used for maintenance or repair of the dwellinghouse or of household articles.

(3) The Lord Advocate may by regulations add to the list set out in sub-paragraph (2) above, or delete or vary any of the items contained in that list.

(4) If, on an application made within 14 days after the date of the execution of the poinding—

    (a) by the debtor or any person who owns a poinded article in common with the debtor; or

    (b) by any person in possession of a poinded article,

the sheriff is satisfied that the article is exempt from poinding under this paragraph, he shall make an order releasing the article from the poinding.

Restrictions on time when poinding may be executed

2.—(1) No poinding shall be executed on Sunday, Christmas Day, New Year's Day, Good Friday or such other day as may be prescribed by Act of Sederunt.

(2) The execution of a poinding shall not—

    (a) be commenced before 8 a.m. or after 8 p.m.; or

    (b) be continued after 8 p.m.,

unless the sheriff officer has obtained prior authority from the sheriff for such commencement or continuation; and any rule of law which prohibits poindings outwith the hours of daylight shall cease to have effect.

Power of entry for execution of poinding

3.—(1) Subject to sub-paragraph (2) below, notwithstanding any warrant authorising him to open shut and lockfast places, a sheriff officer shall not enter a dwellinghouse to execute a poinding if, at the time of his intended entry, there appears to him to be nobody, or only children under the age of 16 years, present there unless, at least 4 days before the date of his intended entry, he has served notice on the debtor specifying that date.

(2) If it appears to the sheriff, on an application made to him by the sheriff officer (which shall not require to be intimated to the debtor), that the requirement of service under this paragraph would be likely to prejudice the execution of the poinding he may dispense with such service.

Value of articles which may be poinded and presumption as to ownership

4.—(1) The sheriff officer shall be entitled to poind articles only to the extent necessary to ensure that the sum recoverable and the likely expenses chargeable against the debtor under paragraphs 25 to 34 below would be realised if they were sold at the value fixed under paragraph 5(4) below.

(2) In executing a poinding, a sheriff officer shall be entitled to proceed on the assumption that any article in the possession of the debtor is owned by him unless the sheriff officer knows or ought to know that the contrary is the case.

(3) The sheriff officer shall not be precluded from relying on the assumption mentioned in sub-paragraph (2) above by reason only of one or both of the following circumstances—

   (a) that the article belongs to a class which is commonly held under a hire, hire-purchase or conditional sale agreement or on some other limited title of possession;

   (b) that an assertion has been made that the article is not owned by the debtor.

Poinding procedure

5.—(1) The procedure in a poinding shall be in accordance with this paragraph and paragraph 6 below.

(2) Before executing the poinding, the sheriff officer shall—

   (a) exhibit to any person present the summary warrant or, if the warrant does not identify the debtor, a certified copy of the warrant together with a statement certified by the creditor that the summary warrant applies to the debtor;

   (b) demand payment of the sum recoverable from the debtor, if he is present, or any person present appearing to the sheriff officer to be authorised to act for the debtor; and

   (c) make enquiry of any person present as to the ownership of the articles proposed to be poinded, and in particular whether there are any persons who own any articles in common with the debtor.

(3) The sheriff officer shall be accompanied at the poinding by one witness.

(4) The poinded articles shall be valued by the sheriff officer according to the price which they would be likely to fetch if sold on the open market unless he considers that the articles are such that a valuation by a professional valuer or other suitably skilled person is advisable, in which case he may arrange for such a valuation.

(5) The sheriff officer shall prepare a schedule (referred to in this Schedule as "the poinding schedule"), in the form prescribed by Act of Sederunt, which shall specify—

   (a) the identity of the creditor and of the debtor;

   (b) the articles poinded, and their respective values;

   (c) the sum recoverable; and

   (d) the place where the poinding was executed.

(6) On completion of the valuation the sheriff officer shall—

     (a) along with the witness sign the poinding schedule;

     (b) deliver the poinding schedule to any person in possession of the articles or—

        (i) where the poinding was executed in a dwellinghouse or other premises, leave it in the premises; or

        (ii) in any other case, deliver it to premises occupied by that person;

     (c) if the person in possession of the articles is not the debtor and it is reasonably practicable, serve a copy of it by post on the debtor;

     (d) inform the debtor (if present) of his right to redeem poinded articles under paragraph 6(4) below;

     (e) inform any person present who owns any poinded article in common with the debtor of his right to redeem poinded articles under paragraph 22(2) and (3) below; and

    (f) inform the debtor (if present) and any person present who owns any poinded article in common with the debtor, or who is in possession of any poinded article, of his right to apply for an order releasing articles from poinding under paragraph 1(4) above or paragraph 7(1) or 22(3)(b) below.

(7) The sheriff officer shall leave poinded articles at the place where they were poinded, except that where that place is not a dwellinghouse or other premises, if he considers it necessary for their security or the preservation of their value and there is insufficient time to obtain an order under paragraph 6(1)(a) below, he shall remove them at the creditor's expense—

    (a) to the nearest convenient premises belonging to the debtor or to the person in possession of the articles; or

    (b) if no such premises are available, to the nearest suitable secure premises.

6.—(1) The sheriff, on an application by the creditor, the sheriff officer or the debtor intimated in accordance with sub-paragraph (2) below, may at any time after the execution of a poinding make an order—

    (a) for the security of any of the poinded articles; or

    (b) in relation to any of the articles which are of a perishable nature or which are likely to deteriorate substantially and rapidly in condition or value, for their immediate disposal and, in the event of their disposal by sale, for payment of the proceeds of sale to the creditor or for consignation of the proceeds in court until the diligence is completed or otherwise ceases to have effect,

and a decision of the sheriff under paragraph (b) above for the immediate disposal of articles shall not be subject to appeal.

(2) An application for an order under sub-paragraph (1)(b) above—

    (a) by the creditor or the sheriff officer, shall be intimated by him to the debtor;

    (b) by the debtor, shall be intimated to the creditor or the officer of court,

at the time when it is made.

(3) It shall not be competent for a sheriff officer in executing a poinding to examine a person on oath as to the ownership of any article.

(4) Subject to sub-paragraph (1)(b) above, the debtor shall be entitled, within 14 days after the date of execution of the poinding, to redeem any poinded article at the value fixed under paragraph 5(4) above.

(5) The sheriff officer shall, on receiving payment from the debtor for the redemption under sub-paragraph (4) above of a poinded article, grant a receipt in the form prescribed by Act of Sederunt to the debtor; and the receipt shall operate as a release of the article from the poinding.

(6) Subject to paragraph 13(2)(b) below, the revaluation in the same poinding of an article which has been valued under paragraph 5(4) above shall not be competent.

(7) A poinding shall be deemed to have been executed on the date when the poinding schedule has been delivered, or left on the premises, in pursuance of paragraph 5(6)(b) above.

(8) At any time before the execution of a poinding on behalf of a creditor, a sheriff officer shall, if requested to do so by any other creditor who has exhibited to him a summary warrant authorising the poinding of articles belonging to the debtor, conjoin that creditor in the poinding.

Release of poinded article on ground of undue harshness

7.—(1) The sheriff may, on an application made within 14 days after the date of execution of a poinding by the debtor or any person in possession of a poinded article, make an order releasing an article from the poinding if it appears to the sheriff that its continued inclusion in the poinding or its sale under the summary warrant would be unduly harsh in the circumstances.

(2) Where the sheriff has made an order under subsection (1) above he may, notwithstanding paragraph 9 below, on an application by the creditor or by a sheriff officer on his behalf, authorise the poinding of other articles belonging to the debtor on the same premises.

Invalidity, cessation and recall of poinding

8.—(1) If, at any time before the sale of the poinded articles, the sheriff is satisfied that the poinding is invalid or has ceased to have effect he shall, on his own initiative or on an application by the debtor, make an order declaring the poinding to be void, and may make such consequential order as appears to him to be necessary in the circumstances.

(2) Without prejudice to paragraph 1(4) above, it shall not be competent for the sheriff to make an order under sub-paragraph (1) above on the ground that any poinded article is exempt from poinding under that paragraph.

(3) At any time before intimation is given to the debtor under paragraph 16 below of the date arranged for the removal of the poinded articles for sale or, if the articles are to be sold in the premises where they are situated, the date arranged for the sale, the sheriff may, on an application by the debtor, recall a poinding on any of the following grounds—

(a) that it would be unduly harsh in the circumstances for the poinded articles to be sold under the summary warrant;

(b) that the aggregate of the values of the poinded articles fixed under paragraph 5(4) above was substantially below the aggregate of the prices which they would have been likely to fetch if sold on the open market; or

(c) that the likely aggregate proceeds of sale of the poinded articles would not exceed the expenses likely to be incurred in the taking of further steps in the diligence, on the assumption that such steps are unopposed.

(4) The sheriff shall not grant an application on the ground mentioned in sub-paragraph (3)(c) above if an order for further poinding of articles belonging to the debtor has been authorised under paragraph 7(2) above or paragraphs 12(6) or 13(2) below, or has become competent by reason of paragraph 12(2), 21(4) or 22(5) below.

(5) The sheriff shall not make an order under sub-paragraph (1) above, recall a poinding or refuse an application under this paragraph without first giving the debtor and the creditor—

(a) an opportunity to make representations; and

(b) if either party wishes to be heard, an opportunity to be heard.

(6) The sheriff clerk shall intimate to the debtor any order made under sub-paragraph (1) above by the sheriff on his own initiative.

Second poinding in same premises

9. Subject to paragraph 7(2) above and paragraphs 12(2) and (6), 13(2), 21(4) and 22(5) below, where articles are poinded in any premises (whether or not the poinding is valid), another poinding in those premises to enforce the same debt shall not be competent except in relation to articles which have been brought on to the premises since the execution of the first poinding.

Sist of proceedings in poinding of mobile homes

10.—(1) Where a caravan, houseboat or other moveable structure which is the only or principal residence of the debtor or another person has been poinded the sheriff, on an application by the debtor or that other person made at any time after the execution of the poinding and before intimation is given to the debtor under paragraph 16 below of the date arranged for the removal of the poinded articles for sale or, if the articles are to be sold in the premises where they are situated, the date arranged for the sale, may order that for such period as he shall specify no further steps shall be taken in the poinding.

(2) In calculating under paragraph 11(1) or (2) below the period during which a poinding in respect of which an order has been made under sub-paragraph (1) above shall remain effective, there shall be disregarded the period specified in the order.

Duration of poinding

11.—(1) Subject to sub-paragraphs (2), (3) and (5) below, a poinding shall cease to have effect on the expiry of a period of one year after the date of execution of the poinding.

(2) The sheriff, on an application by the creditor or by a sheriff officer on his behalf made before the expiry of the period mentioned in sub-paragraph (1) above, may extend that period—

(a) where he considers that, if the said period is extended, the debtor is likely to comply with an agreement between the creditor and the debtor for the payment of the sum recoverable by instalments or otherwise; or

(b) to enable further proceedings to be taken in the diligence where the termination of the poinding would prejudice the creditor and the creditor cannot be held responsible for the circumstances giving rise to the need for the extension,

for such further period as he considers reasonable in the circumstances.

(3) The sheriff may grant further extensions under sub-paragraph (2) above, on application being made to him before the expiry of the previously extended period.

(4) The decision of the sheriff under sub-paragraph (2) above shall not be subject to appeal, and shall be intimated to the debtor by the sheriff clerk.

(5) Where, within the period mentioned in sub-paragraph (1) above or within that period as extended under sub-paragraph (2) above, an application is made under sub-paragraph (2) above, the poinding shall continue to have effect until the disposal of the application.

Removal, damage or destruction of poinded articles

12.—(1) The debtor or the person in possession of poinded articles may move them to another location if—
   (a) the creditor or a sheriff officer on behalf of the creditor has consented in writing to their removal; or
   (b) the sheriff, on an application by the debtor or the person in possession, has authorised their removal.

(2) Where poinded articles have been removed under sub-paragraph (1) above, a sheriff officer may, under the same warrant to poind, again poind any of the articles so removed and, notwithstanding paragraph 9 above, any articles which were not so removed, whether or not they were previously poinded; and, on the execution of any such further poinding, the original poinding shall be deemed to have been abandoned.

(3) The removal, except in accordance with this Schedule, from any premises of poinded articles by—
   (a) the debtor; or
   (b) any person, other than the creditor or a sheriff officer, who knows that the articles have been poinded,
shall be a breach of the poinding and may be dealt with as a contempt of court.

(4) Where articles have been removed from premises otherwise than in accordance with this Schedule, the sheriff, on an application by the creditor—
   (a) may, subject to sub-paragraph (5) below, make an order requiring the person in possession of the articles to restore them to the premises from which they were removed within a period specified in the order; and
   (b) if an order under paragraph (a) above is not complied with, and it appears to the sheriff that the articles are likely to be found in premises specified in the application, may grant a warrant to sheriff officers—
      (i) to search for the articles in those premises; and
      (ii) to restore the articles to the premises from which they were removed or to make such other arrangements for their security as the sheriff may direct,
      and such a warrant shall be authority to open shut and lockfast places for the purpose of its execution.

(5) Where it appears to the sheriff, on an application made to him by any person having an interest, that any article which has been removed from premises otherwise than in accordance with this Schedule has been acquired for value and without knowledge of the poinding, he shall—
   (a) refuse an order under sub-paragraph (4)(a) above relating to that article;
   (b) recall any such order which he has already made; and
   (c) make an order releasing the article from the poinding.

(6) Where articles have been removed from premises otherwise than in accordance with this Schedule in circumstances in which the debtor is at fault the sheriff, on an application by the creditor or by a sheriff officer on his behalf, may, notwithstanding paragraph 9 above, authorise the poinding of other articles belonging to the debtor in the same premises.

(7) The removal of poinded articles to another location shall not have the effect of releasing the articles from the poinding.

13.—(1) The wilful damage or destruction of poinded articles by—
   (a) the debtor; or
   (b) any person, other than the creditor or a sheriff officer, who knows that the articles have been poinded,
shall be a breach of the poinding and may be dealt with as a contempt of court.

(2) Where poinded articles have been damaged or destroyed the sheriff, on an application by the creditor or by the sheriff officer on his behalf, may—
   (a) where the debtor has been at fault, authorise the poinding of other articles belonging to the debtor in the premises in which the original poinding took place; and
   (b) in any case, authorise the revaluation of any damaged article in accordance with paragraph 5(4) above.

(3) Where a third party, knowing that an article has been poinded—
   (a) wilfully damages or destroys it; or
   (b) removes it from premises in breach of a poinding, and—

  (i) it is damaged, destroyed, lost or stolen; or
 (ii) it is acquired from or through him by another person without knowledge
        of the poinding and for value,
the sheriff may order the third party to consign the sum mentioned in sub-paragraph (4)
below in court until the completion of the sale or until the poinding otherwise ceases to have
effect.

(4) The sum to be consigned in court under sub-paragraph (3) above shall be—
  (a) where the article has been damaged but not so damaged as to make it worthless,
        a sum equal to the difference between the value of the article fixed under
        paragraph 5(4) above and the value of the article as so damaged;
  (b) in any other case, a sum equal to the value fixed under that paragraph.

(5) Any sum consigned in court under sub-paragraph (3) above shall, on the completion
of the sale or on the poinding otherwise ceasing to have effect, be paid to the creditor to the
extent necessary to meet the sum recoverable, any surplus thereof being paid to the debtor.

Arrangements for sale

14.—(1) A sale in pursuance of a summary warrant shall be by public auction.

(2) A sale in pursuance of a summary warrant shall not be held in a dwellinghouse except
with the consent in writing, in a form to be prescribed by Act of Sederunt, of the occupier
thereof and, if he is not the occupier, of the debtor.

(3) Subject to sub-paragraph (4) below, the sale shall not be held in premises (other than
a dwellinghouse or an auction room) which are occupied by a person other than the debtor
or the creditor except with the consent in writing, in a form to be prescribed by Act of
Sederunt, of the occupier thereof.

(4) Where the occupier of premises (other than a dwellinghouse or an auction room)
where poinded articles are situated does not give his consent under sub-paragraph (3) above
to the holding of the sale in those premises, the sheriff may, if on an application by the
creditor or the sheriff officer he considers that it would be unduly costly to require the
removal of the poinded articles to other premises for sale, nevertheless order that the sale
shall be held in the premises where they are situated.

(5) The decision of the sheriff under sub-paragraph (4) above shall not be subject to
appeal.

(6) In this paragraph "occupier", in relation to premises where there are 2 or more
occupiers, means each of them.

Release or redemption of poinded articles

15.—(1) Where a sale of poinded articles is to be held in premises other than where the
poinded articles are situated, the sheriff officer may remove to those premises only such
poinded articles as, if sold at their values fixed under paragraph 5(4) above, would realise
in total the sum recoverable and the likely expenses chargeable against the debtor under
paragraphs 25 to 34 below; and shall release the remaining poinded articles from the
poinding.

(2) Subject to paragraph 6(1) above, the debtor may, within 7 days after the date when
intimation is given to him under paragraph 16 below of the date arranged for the removal
of the poinded articles for sale or, if the articles are to be sold in the premises where they
are situated, the date arranged for the sale, redeem any poinded article by paying to the
officer of court a sum equal to its value fixed under paragraph 5(4) above.

(3) The sheriff officer shall, on receiving payment from the debtor under sub-paragraph
(2) above, grant a receipt in the form prescribed by Act of Sederunt to the debtor; and the
receipt shall operate as a release of the article from the poinding.

(4) The creditor and the debtor may by agreement release articles from the poinding.

Intimation and publication of sale

16.—(1) The sheriff officer who makes arrangements for the sale of the poinded articles
shall—
  (a) as soon as is reasonably practicable intimate to the debtor and, if the person in
        possession of the poinded articles is not the debtor, to that person, the date and place
        arranged for the sale; and
  (b) where the sale is not to be held in the premises where the poinded articles are
        situated, intimate to the debtor and, if he is not the debtor, to the person in possession

of the poinded articles, not less than 14 days before the date arranged for the removal of the poinded articles from those premises, the date arranged for the removal.

(2) The sheriff officer shall, at the same time as he intimates the date arranged for the sale under sub-paragraph (1) above, send such particulars of the arrangements for the sale as are prescribed by Act of Sederunt to the sheriff clerk of the sheriff court within whose jurisdiction the articles were poinded; and the sheriff clerk shall arrange for those particulars to be displayed on the walls of court.

(3) The sale shall be advertised by public notice.

(4) Where the sale is to be held in premises not belonging to the debtor, the public notice under sub-paragraph (3) above shall not name him or disclose that the articles for sale are poinded articles.

(5) Where the sale is to be held in premises other than the debtor's premises or an auction room, any public notice of the sale shall state that the articles to be sold do not belong to the occupier of the premises where the sale is to be held.

Alteration of arrangements for sale

17.—(1) Subject to sub-paragraph (2) below and without prejudice to sub-paragraph (5) below, after intimation has been given under paragraph 16(1) above to the debtor of the date arranged for the sale or for the removal for sale of the poinded articles from the premises where they are situated, the creditor or sheriff officer shall not be entitled to arrange a new date for the sale or for such removal.

(2) Where, for any reason for which neither the creditor nor the sheriff officer is responsible, it is not possible for the sale or, as the case may be, the removal for sale of the poinded articles from the premises where they are situated, to take place on the date arranged for it, the creditor may instruct the sheriff officer to arrange a new date in accordance with sub-paragraph (3) below, and the sheriff officer shall intimate the new date to the debtor and to any other person in possession of the poinded articles.

(3) The new date arranged under sub-paragraph (2) above shall not be less than 7 days after the date of intimation under that sub-paragraph.

(4) Without prejudice to sub-paragraph (2) above, in order to enable the sum recoverable to be paid by instalments or otherwise in accordance with an agreement between the creditor and the debtor, the creditor may, after intimation has been given under paragraph 16 above of the date arranged for the sale, cancel the arrangements for the sale on not more than 2 occasions.

(5) Where, following cancellation of the sale in pursuance of sub-paragraph (4) above, the debtor is in breach of the agreement, the creditor may instruct the sheriff officer to make arrangements for the sale of the poinded articles at any time while they remain poinded.

The sale

18.—(1) In the sale there shall be no reserve price unless the creditor chooses to have one and, if he does so choose, it shall not exceed the value of the article fixed under paragraph 5(4) above.

(2) The value of a poinded article fixed under paragraph 5(4) above and the reserve price, if any, fixed by the creditor under sub-paragraph (1) above need not be disclosed to any person bidding for the article.

(3) In the sale any poinded article exposed for sale may be purchased by—

    (a) any creditor, including the creditor on whose behalf the poinding was executed; or

    (b) a person who owns the article in common with the debtor.

(4) Subject to sub-paragraph (5) below and without prejudice to the rights of any third party, where the sum recoverable has not been realised by the sale, ownership of a poinded article which remains unsold after being exposed for sale shall pass to the creditor.

(5) Without prejudice to the rights of any third party, where the sale is held in premises belonging to the debtor, the ownership of a poinded article which has passed to the creditor under sub-paragraph (4) above shall revert to the debtor unless the creditor uplifts the article by 8 p.m. (or such other time as may be prescribed by Act of Sederunt)—

    (a) if the premises are a dwellinghouse in which the debtor is residing, on the day when the sale is completed;

    (b) in any other case, on the third working day following that day,

and the sheriff officer may remain on or re-enter any premises (whether open, shut or lockfast) for the purpose of enabling the creditor to uplift any such article.

(6) For the purposes of sub-paragraph (5) above "working day" means a day which is not—

Saturday;
Sunday;
1st or 2nd January;
Good Friday;
Easter Monday;
25th or 26th December;
a public holiday in the area in which the premises are situated.

(7) Subject to sub-paragraph (8) below, where at the sale any article is unsold or is sold at a price below the value fixed under paragraph 5(4) above, the debtor shall be credited with an amount equal to that valuation.

(8) Where—

    (a) any damaged article has been revalued under paragraph 5(4) above on the authority of the sheriff given under paragraph 13(2) above;

    (b) the damage was not caused by the fault of the debtor; and

    (c) no order has been made under paragraph 13(3) above requiring a third party to consign a sum in respect of the article, or such an order has been made but has not been complied with,

the amount credited to the debtor under sub-paragraph (7) above shall be an amount equal to the original valuation and not the revaluation referred to in paragraph (a) above.

Disposal of proceeds of sale

19. The sheriff officer who arranges the sale shall dispose of the proceeds of the sale—

    (a) by paying to the creditor the proceeds so far as necessary to meet the sum recoverable (subject to any agreement between the sheriff officer and the creditor relating to the fees or outlays of the officer of court); and

    (b) by paying to the debtor any surplus remaining after the sum recoverable has been paid or, if the debtor cannot be found, by consigning such surplus in court.

Report of sale

20.—(1) The sheriff officer who arranged the sale shall within a period of 14 days after the date of completion of the sale send to the creditor a report of the sale in the form prescribed by Act of Sederunt setting out—

    (a) any articles which have been sold and the amount for which they have been sold;

    (b) any articles which remain unsold;

    (c) the expenses of the diligence chargeable against the debtor;

    (d) any surplus paid to the debtor; and

    (e) any balance due by or to the debtor;

and the sheriff officer shall, within the same period, send a copy of the report to the debtor.

(2) The report of sale shall be signed by the sheriff officer.

(3) The creditor and the debtor may have the report of sale taxed by the auditor of court of the sheriff court within whose jurisdiction the articles were poinded.

Articles belonging to third parties or in common ownership

21.—(1) A sheriff officer may, at any time after the execution of a poinding and before the sale of the poinded articles, release an article from the poinding if—

    (a) he is satisfied that the article belongs to a third party; and

    (b) the debtor or other person in possession of the article does not deny that it belongs to the third party.

(2) Where, on an application made to him by a third party, at any time after the execution of a poinding and before the sale of the poinded articles, the sheriff is satisfied that a poinded article belongs to that third party, he shall make an order releasing it from the poinding.

(3) The making of an application under sub-paragraph (2) above shall not prejudice the taking of any other proceedings by the third party for the recovery of a poinded article belonging to him, and an order of the sheriff under that sub-paragraph shall not be binding in any other proceedings.

(4) Where an article has been released from a poinding under this paragraph, a sheriff officer may, notwithstanding paragraph 9 above, poind other articles belonging to the debtor in the same premises.

22.—(1) Articles which are owned in common by a debtor and a third party may be poinded and disposed of in accordance with this Schedule in satisfaction of the debts of that debtor.

(2) Where, at any time after the execution of a poinding and before the sale of the poinded articles, a third party—

(a) claims that a poinded article is owned in common by the debtor and himself; and

(b) pays to the sheriff officer a sum equal to the value of the debtor's interest in the article,

the sheriff officer may, unless the debtor (or the person in possession of the article, if not the debtor) denies the claim, release the article from the poinding.

(3) If, on an application made by a third party, at any time after the execution of a poinding and before the sale of the poinded articles, the sheriff is satisfied that a poinded article is owned in common by the debtor and that third party and either—

(a) the third party undertakes to pay to the sheriff officer a sum equal to the value of the debtor's interest in the article; or

(b) the sheriff is satisfied that the continued poinding of that article or its sale under summary warrant would be unduly harsh to the third party in the circumstances,

he shall make an order releasing the article from the poinding.

(4) A release under sub-paragraph (2) above or where sub-paragraph (3)(a) above applies shall not become effective until the granting by the sheriff officer of a receipt for payment in accordance therewith, when the debtor's interest in the released article shall be transferred to the third party.

(5) Where an article is released in pursuance of sub-paragraph (3)(b) above from a poinding, a sheriff officer may, notwithstanding paragraph 9 above, poind other articles belonging to the debtor in the same premises.

(6) This sub-paragraph applies where, at any time after the execution of a poinding, a third party claims that any of the poinded articles is owned in common by the debtor and himself but does not seek release of the article from the poinding, and either—

(a) the claim is admitted by the creditor and the debtor; or

(b) the claim is not admitted by both the creditor and the debtor, but the sheriff, on an application made to him, is satisfied that the claim is valid.

(7) Where sub-paragraph (6) above applies, the creditor shall pay to the third party—

(a) if the article is sold, the fraction of the proceeds of sale (or of the value of that article fixed under paragraph 5(4) above, whichever is the greater) which corresponds to the third party's interest in the article;

(b) if ownership of the article passes to the creditor in default of sale, the fraction of the value of the article fixed under paragraph 5(4) above which corresponds to the third party's interest in the article.

Certain proceedings under this Schedule to postpone further steps in the diligence

23.—(1) Where an application under any of the provisions of this Schedule listed in sub-paragraph (2) below has been made—

(a) it shall be not be competent during a relevant period to remove the poinded articles for sale or to hold a sale;

(b) a relevant period shall be disregarded in calculating the period on the expiry of which the poinding ceases to have effect under paragraph 11 above.

(2) The provisions referred to in sub-paragraph (1) above are—

(a) paragraph 1(4), 7(1), 21(2) or 22(3) (release of poinded articles);

(b) paragraph 8(1) or (3) (invalidity, cessation or recall of poinding);

(c) paragraph 10(1) (sist of proceedings in poinding of mobile homes);

(d) paragraph 12(4) (restoration of articles removed without consent or authority);

(e) paragraph 12(5) (recall of order under paragraph 12(4)).

(3) In sub-paragraph (1) above "a relevant period" means—

(a) the period while the application is pending;

(b) where the application has been disposed of by the sheriff—

(i) the period during which an application for leave to appeal may be made;

(ii) where an application for leave to appeal is made, the period until leave has been refused or the application has been abandoned;

(iii) where leave to appeal has been granted, the period during which an appeal may be made; or

(iv) where an appeal against the decision is made, the period until the matter has been finally determined or the appeal has been abandoned.

Power to enter premises and open shut and lockfast places

24. A summary warrant shall contain a warrant authorising a sheriff officer to enter premises in the occupancy of the debtor in order to execute the poinding or the sale, or the removal and sale of the poinded articles and, for any of those purposes, to open shut and lockfast places.

Expenses chargeable against the debtor

25.—(1) Subject to paragraphs 26 to 29 below, there shall be chargeable against the debtor any expenses incurred—
  (a) in serving a notice under paragraph 3 above before entering a dwellinghouse for the purpose of executing a poinding;
  (b) in executing a poinding under paragraph 5 above;
  (c) in granting a receipt under sub-paragraph (5) of paragraph 6 above for payment for redemption under sub-paragraph (4) thereof;
  (d) in granting a receipt under paragraph 15(3) above for payment for the redemption of any poinded article;
  (e) in making intimation, sending particulars of the arrangements for the sale to the sheriff clerk and giving public notice under paragraph 16 above;
  (f) in removing any poinded articles for sale;
  (g) in making arrangements for and conducting a sale;
  (h) where the arrangements for a sale have been cancelled under paragraph 17(4) above, in returning poinded articles to any premises from which they have been removed for sale;
  (j) in making a report of sale under paragraph 20 above;
  (k) in granting a receipt under paragraph 22(4) above for payment for the release from a poinding of any article which is owned in common;
  (l) in opening shut and lockfast places in the execution of the diligence;
  (m) by a solicitor in instructing a sheriff officer to take any of the steps specified in this sub-paragraph.
  (2) The Lord Advocate may by regulations add to, delete or vary any of the steps specified in sub-paragraph (1) above.
  26. Where arrangements for a sale are cancelled under sub-paragraph (4) of paragraph 17 above, if new arrangements are made for the sale in the circumstances mentioned in sub-paragraph (5) thereof, there shall be chargeable against the debtor the expenses incurred in the making of the new arrangements but not in the making of the arrangements which have been cancelled.
  27. Subject to paragraph 28 below, where any such further poinding as is mentioned in paragraph 12(2) above has been executed, there shall be chargeable against the debtor the expenses incurred in that poinding but not the expenses incurred in the original poinding.
  28. Where any such further poinding as is mentioned in sub-paragraph (2) of paragraph 12 above has been executed and—
  (a) the creditor has, as a condition of his consenting to the removal of the poinded articles under sub-paragraph (1)(a) of that paragraph, required the debtor to undertake liability for the expenses incurred in the original poinding; or
  (b) the sheriff has, when authorising the removal of the poinded articles under sub-paragraph (1)(b) of that paragraph, directed that the debtor shall be liable for those expenses,
there shall be chargeable against the debtor the expenses incurred in both poindings.
  29. Where a new date is arranged under paragraph 17(2) above for the holding of a sale or for the removal of poinded articles for sale, there shall be chargeable against the debtor the expenses incurred in connection with arranging the new date but not those incurred in connection with arranging the original date.

Circumstances where liability for expenses is at the discretion of the sheriff

30. The liability for any expenses incurred by the creditor or the debtor—
  (a) in an application by the creditor or a sheriff officer to the sheriff under any provision of this Schedule; or
  (b) in implementing an order under—
      (i) paragraph 6(1) above (order for security or immediate disposal of poinded articles); or
      (ii) paragraph 12(4) to (6) or 13 above (orders dealing with unauthorised removal, damage or destruction of poinded articles),
shall be as determined by the sheriff.

Calculation of amount chargeable against debtor under the foregoing provisions

31. Expenses awarded by the sheriff against the debtor in favour of the creditor in a determination under paragraph 30 above in respect of an application other than an application under paragraph 12(4) to (6) or 13 above shall be calculated, whether or not the application is opposed by the debtor, as if it were unopposed, except that, if the debtor opposes the application on grounds which appear to the sheriff to be frivolous, the sheriff may award an additional sum of expenses, not exceeding £25 or such amount as may be prescribed in regulations made by the Lord Advocate, against the debtor.

Circumstances where no expenses are due to or by either party

32. Subject to paragraph 33 below, the debtor shall not be liable to the creditor nor the creditor to the debtor for any expenses incurred by the other party in connection with—
(a) an application by the debtor to the sheriff under any provision of this Schedule;
(b) any objections to such an application;
(c) a hearing held by virtue of paragraph 8(5) above.
33. If—
(a) an application mentioned in paragraph 32(a) above is frivolous;
(b) such an application is opposed on frivolous grounds; or
(c) a party requires a hearing mentioned in paragraph 32(c) above to be held on frivolous grounds,
the sheriff may award a sum of expenses, not exceeding £25 or such amount as may be prescribed in regulations made by the Lord Advocate, against the party acting frivolously in favour of the other party.

Supplementary

34. Any expenses chargeable against the debtor by virtue of any provision of this Schedule shall be recoverable out of the proceeds of sale.
35. In this Schedule—
"creditor" means—
(a) for the purposes of section 247 of the Local Government (Scotland) Act 1947, a rating authority;
(b) for the purposes of section 63 of the Taxes Management Act 1970, any collector of taxes;
(c) for the purposes of paragraph 3 of Schedule 1 to the Car Tax Act 1983 and paragraph 6 of Schedule 7 to the Value Added Tax Act 1983, the Commissioners of Customs and Excise;
"dwellinghouse" includes a caravan, a houseboat and any structure adapted for use as a residence;
"the poinding schedule" means the schedule provided for in paragraph 5(5) above;
"the sum recoverable"—
(a) for the purposes of the said section 247, includes the surcharge recoverable thereunder but excludes interest;
(b) for the purposes of the said section 63, includes interest.

GENERAL NOTE
This schedule sets out a new uniform poinding procedure to enforce arrears of rates and taxes in place of the various different procedures that were used. The new procedure has become more like the ordinary poinding procedure although it is still summary in character. The main differences from ordinary procedure are:—
(1) No charge to pay is required, s.90(2).
(2) No report of poinding is made to the sheriff, no application for warrant of sale is necessary as the warrant is contained in the summary warrant, and no report of sale is made to the sheriff.
On the other hand many of the safeguards present in, or introduced by the Act into, ordinary poinding procedure now apply to summary warrant procedure. They include:—
(1) The debtor is credited with the value of goods as fixed by the officer or their sale price whichever is the higher (para. 18(7)).
(2) The range of household and other goods exempt from poinding is considerably extended (para. 1).

(3) The debtor has an opportunity to redeem goods at their appraised value (paras. 6(4) and 15(2)).
(4) The sheriff may release goods on ground of undue harshness (para. 7).
(5) Sales in dwellinghouses are competent only with the debtor's (and occupier's) consent (para. 14).
(6) The goods are valued at the time of poinding and only goods up to the value of the debt and likely future expenses may be poinded (paras. 5(4) and 4(1)).
(7) The sheriff may recall the poinding on the grounds of undue harshness, undervaluation, "not worth it", or the poinding being invalid or having ceased to have effect (para. 8).

Section 108(1)   SCHEDULE 6

MINOR AND CONSEQUENTIAL AMENDMENTS

General amendment

1. Any reference in any enactment to an order being enforceable in like manner as a recorded decree arbitral shall be construed as a reference to such an order being enforceable in like manner as an extract registered decree arbitral bearing a warrant for execution issued by the sheriff court of any sheriffdom in Scotland.

Specific amendments

The Bank Notes (Scotland) Act 1765 (c. 49)

2. In section 4 (summary execution on banker's notes), for the words from "letters of horning" to "the other" there shall be substituted the word "the".

The Debtors (Scotland) Act 1838 (c. 114)

3. At the end of section 22 (arrestment to prescribe in three years), there shall be added the following subsections—
    "(2) In the case of an arrestment which—
    (a) secures a debt which is subject to a time to pay direction or a time to pay order; or
    (b) is subject to an interim order under section 6(3) of the Debtors (Scotland) Act 1987 (order pending disposal of application for time to pay order),
    there shall be disregarded, in computing the period at the end of which the arrestment prescribes, the period during which the time to pay direction, time to pay order or interim order is in effect.
    (3) Nothing in this section shall apply to an earnings arrestment, a current maintenance arrestment or a conjoined arrestment order.".

The Harbours, Docks, and Piers Clauses Act 1847 (c. 27)

4. In section 57 (unserviceable vessels to be altogether removed from harbour), for the word "poinding" there shall be substituted the word "arrestment".

The Lyon King of Arms Act 1867 (c.17)

5. In section 2 (admittance to office of messengers-at-arms), for the words "according to the present law and practice" there shall be substituted the words "in accordance with Part V of the Debtors (Scotland) Act 1987 and any Act of Sederunt made thereunder".

The Court of Session Act 1868 (c. 100)

6. At the end of section 14 (induciae of summonses and other writs passing the signet), there shall be added the following subsection—
    "(2) Nothing in this section shall apply to a charge for payment.".

The Titles to Land Consolidation (Scotland) Act 1868 (c. 101)

7. In section 138 (import of short clauses of consent to registration), for the words from "letters of horning" to the end there shall be substituted the words ", upon the issue of an extract containing a warrant for execution, all lawful execution shall pass thereon".

The Debtors (Scotland) Act 1880 (c. 34)

8. In section 4 (abolition of imprisonment for debt, with certain exceptions), for paragraph 1 there shall be substituted the following paragraph—

"1. Fines imposed for contempt of court or under section 91 of the Court of Session Act 1868.".

The Sea Fisheries Act 1883 (c. 22)

9. In section 20(2) (masters of boats liable to fines imposed), for the word "poinding" there shall be substituted the word "arrestment".

The Merchant Shipping Act 1894 (c. 60)

10. In section 693 (sums ordered to be leviable by poinding and sale of ship), for the word "poinding" there shall be substituted the word "arrestment".

The Execution of Diligence (Scotland) Act 1926 (c. 16)

11. In section 1 (sheriff officer to have the powers of a messenger-at-arms in certain places), for the word "county" in both places where it occurs there shall be substituted the words "sheriff court district".

12. In section 2(1)(b) (execution of arrestment or charge by registered letter in certain cases), for the word "county" there shall be substituted the words "sheriff court district".

The Sea Fisheries Act 1968 (c. 77)

13. In section 12(2)(a) (recovery of fines imposed on master, etc. or crew), for the word "poinding" there shall be substituted the word "arrestment".

The Prevention of Oil Pollution Act 1971 (c. 60)

14. In section 20(1) (enforcement and application of fines), for the word "poinding" there shall be substituted the word "arrestment".

The Town and Country Planning (Scotland) Act 1972 (c. 52)

15. In section 267(8) (local inquiries), for the words "a recorded decree arbitral" there shall be substituted the words "an extract registered decree arbitral bearing a warrant for execution issued by the sheriff court of any sheriffdom in Scotland".

The Consumer Credit Act 1974 (c. 69)

16. After section 93 there shall be inserted the following section—

"Summary diligence not competent in Scotland
93A. Summary diligence shall not be competent in Scotland to enforce payment of a debt due under a regulated agreement or under any security related thereto.".

17. In section 129 (time orders)—
    (a) at the beginning of subsection (1) there shall be added the words "Subject to subsection (3) below,";
    (b) at the end there shall be added the following subsection—

        "(3) Where in Scotland a time to pay direction or a time to pay order has been made in relation to a debt, it shall not thereafter be competent to make a time order in relation to the same debt.".

The Criminal Procedure (Scotland) Act 1975 (c. 21)

18. In section 411 (recovery by civil diligence), in subsection (1) for the words from "the words" to "14 days" there shall be substituted the words "a warrant for civil diligence in a form prescribed by Act of Adjournal which shall have the effect of authorising—
    (a) the charging of the person who has been fined to pay the fine within the period specified in the charge and, in the event of failure to make such payment within that period, the execution of an earnings arrestment and the poinding of articles belonging to him and, if necessary for the purpose of executing the poinding, the opening of shut and lockfast places;
    (b) an arrestment other than an arrestment of earnings in the hands of his employer;".

The Crofting Reform (Scotland) Act 1976 (c. 21)

19. In section 17(1) (extension of powers of Land Court), for the words from "as if" to "to be enforced" there shall be substituted the words "in like manner as an extract registered decree arbitral bearing a warrant for execution issued by the sheriff court of any sheriffdom in Scotland".

The Patents Act 1977 (c. 37)

20. In section 93(b) and 107(3) (orders for expenses), for the words "a recorded decree arbitral" there shall be substituted the words "an extract registered decree arbitral bearing a warrant for execution issued by the sheriff court of any sheriffdom in Scotland.".

The Customs and Excise Management Act 1979 (c. 2)

21. In section 117 (execution and diligence against revenue traders), for subsection (9) there shall be substituted the following subsections—

"(9) This section shall apply to Scotland subject to the following modifications—
  (a) in subsection (3) for the words from "issue" to the end there shall be substituted the words "granting of a warrant for the recovery of a sum owing by the revenue trader, those goods shall not be liable to be taken in execution under this section.";
  (b) in subsection (4) for the word "seized" in both places where it occurs there shall be substituted the words "taken in execution";
  (c) subsection (10) below shall apply in place of subsection (5);
  (d) in subsection (6) for the word "distrained" in both places where it occurs there shall be substituted the words "taken into possession";
  (e) in subsection (7) for the words "of the distress and sale" there shall be substituted the words "incurred in the taking into possession and sale of the things under that subsection";
  (f) in subsection (7A) for the words "distress is levied" there shall be substituted the words "things are taken into possession" and for the word "distress" where second occurring there shall be substituted the words "taking into possession".

(10) The sheriff, on an application by the proper officer accompanied by a certificate by him that relevant excise duty payable by a revenue trader remains unpaid after the time within which it is payable, may grant a warrant authorising a sheriff officer—
  (a) to take into possession, by force if necessary, anything liable to be taken in execution under this section and for that purpose to open shut and lockfast places; and
  (b) to sell anything so taken into possession by public auction after giving 6 days notice of the sale.".

The Education (Scotland) Act 1980 (c. 44)

22. In paragraph 8 of Schedule 1 (local inquiries), for the words "a recorded decree arbitral" there shall be substituted the words "an extract registered decree arbitral bearing a warrant for execution issued by the sheriff court of any sheriffdom in Scotland.".

The Betting and Gaming Duties Act 1981 (c. 63)

23. Section 29 (recovery of duty in Scotland), shall have effect subject to the following modifications—
  (a) for subsection (1) there shall be substituted the following subsection—
      "(1) The sheriff, on an application by the proper officer accompanied by a certificate by him that a person, on written demand by the proper officer, has refused or neglected to pay any amount recoverable from him by way of general betting duty or bingo duty or by virtue of section 12(1) or 14 above or of Schedule 2 to this Act, may grant a warrant authorising a sheriff officer—
        (a) to take into possession, by force if necessary, any of that person's corporeal moveables which would not be exempted from poinding and for that purpose to open shut and lockfast places; and
        (b) to sell anything so taken into possession by public auction after giving 6 days' notice of the sale.";
  (b) in subsection (2) for the word "poinded" in both places where it occurs there shall be substituted the words "taken into possession";
  (c) in subsection (3)—

(i) for the words "of the poinding and" there shall be substituted the words "incurred in taking into possession the corporeal moveables and their";

(ii) in paragraph (a) for the word "poinded" there shall be substituted the words "taken into possession";

(iii) in paragraph (b) for the word "poinded" there shall be substituted the words "when they were taken into possession by the sheriff officer";

(d) in subsection (4) for the words "poinded" and "poinding" there shall be substituted respectively the words "taken into possession" and "taking into possession the corporeal moveables".

The British Fishing Boats Act 1983 (c. 8)

24. In section 5(2)(a) (recovery of fines), for the word "poinding" there shall be substituted the word "arrestment".

The Inshore Fishing (Scotland) Act 1984 (c. 26)

25. In section 8(2)(a) (recovery of fines), for the word "poinding" there shall be substituted the word "arrestment".

The Rent (Scotland) Act 1984 (c. 58)

26. For section 110 (restriction on diligence), there shall be substituted the following section—

"Restriction on sequestration for rent

110. At any stage before the grant of a warrant of sale in an action of sequestration for payment, or in security, of rent of any dwelling-house let on a protected tenancy or subject to a statutory tenancy, the sheriff may sist the proceedings or adjourn them for such period or periods as he thinks fit, in order to enable the tenant to pay the rent in such manner as the sheriff may determine (whether by instalments or otherwise).".

The Bankruptcy (Scotland) Act 1985 (c. 66)

27. In section 37 (effect of sequestration on diligence), after subsection (5) there shall be inserted the following subsection—

"(5A) Nothing in subsection (4) or (5) above shall apply to an earnings arrestment, a current maintenance arrestment or a conjoined arrestment order.".

28. In paragraph 24 of Schedule 7 (arrestments and poindings)—

(a) in sub-paragraph (3) after the words "a sale" there shall be inserted the words "or receives payment in respect of a poinded article upon its redemption";

(b) at the end there shall be added the following sub-paragraph—

"(8) Nothing in this paragraph shall apply to an earnings arrestment, a current maintenance arrestment or a conjoined arrestment order.".

Section 108(2)   SCHEDULE 7

TRANSITIONAL PROVISIONS

1. Notwithstanding the repeal by this Act of subsection (4) of section 36 of the Sheriff Courts (Scotland) Act 1971—

(a) any direction made under that subsection which is in force immediately before the commencement of that repeal shall continue in force; and

(b) any summary cause action for payment which is pending immediately before such commencement shall proceed and be disposed of,

as if this Act had not been passed.

2. The sheriff may refuse to make a time to pay order if, on an objection being duly made in pursuance of section 6(6)(a) of this Act, he is satisfied that a direction has been made under section 36(4) of the said Act of 1971 whereby the debt concerned was payable by instalments, but the right to pay by instalments has ceased by reason of failure to pay an instalment.

3. Without prejudice to paragraphs 4 to 6 of this Schedule, a warrant issued before the commencement of Part VI of this Act, for the enforcement by diligence of an obligation to pay money, contained in an extract of a decree of the Court of Session or the sheriff court or of a document which has been registered in the Books of Council and Session or in sheriff

court books shall be treated as if it were a warrant contained in such a decree granted after the commencement of that Part.

4. Nothing in Part II of this Act shall affect a poinding which is in effect immediately before the commencement of that Part; and further proceedings in such a poinding and in any warrant sale to follow thereon shall be in accordance with the law in force immediately before such commencement.

5. Nothing in this Act shall affect an arrestment of earnings in the hands of an employer which has been executed before the commencement of Part III of this Act nor preclude the bringing of an action of furthcoming in pursuance of such an arrestment or the granting of a decree in any such action.

6. Where an arrestment of a debtor's earnings in the hands of an employer which has been executed before the commencement of Part III of this Act has effect in relation to earnings payable on the first pay-day occurring after such commencement, the execution of an earnings arrestment or a current maintenance arrestment against earnings payable to the debtor by the employer shall not be competent until after that pay-day.

7.—(1) Subject to sub-paragraph (2) below, a summary warrant granted before the commencement of Schedules 4 and 5 to this Act under or by virtue of any of the enactments to which this paragraph applies shall be deemed to authorise only the following diligences—

    (a) a poinding and sale in accordance with the said Schedule 5;

    (b) an earnings arrestment; and

    (c) an arrestment other than an arrestment of the debtor's earnings in the hands of his employer.

(2) If at the commencement of those Schedules diligence executed in pursuance of a warrant referred to in sub-paragraph (1) above is in effect, that diligence shall proceed as if this Act had not been passed.

(3) This paragraph applies to the following enactments—

    (a) section 247 of the Local Government (Scotland) Act 1947;

    (b) section 63 of the Taxes Management Act 1970;

    (c) section 33 of the Finance Act 1972;

    (d) paragraph 16(2) of Schedule 7 to the Finance Act 1972;

    (e) paragraph 3 of Schedule 1 to the Car Tax Act 1983;

    (f) paragraph 6 of Schedule 7 to the Value Added Tax Act 1983.

8.—(1) Where before the commencement of paragraphs 21 and 23 of Schedule 6 to this Act—

    (a) a warrant has been granted under any of the enactments to which this paragraph applies; and

    (b) no diligence has been executed in pursuance of the warrant,

the warrant shall cease to have effect.

(2) Where before the commencement of the said paragraphs 21 and 23—

    (a) a warrant has been granted under any of the enactments to which this paragraph applies; and

    (b) diligence has been executed in pursuance of the warrant,

the diligence shall proceed as if this Act had not been passed.

(3) This paragraph applies to the following enactments—

    (a) section 253 of the Customs and Excise Act 1952;

    (b) paragraph 10 of Schedule 2 to the Betting and Gaming Duties Act 1972;

    (c) section 117 of the Customs and Excise Management Act 1979;

    (d) section 29 of the Betting and Gaming Duties Act 1981.

9.—(1) The provisions of this Act relating to the liability for the expenses of a diligence shall not apply in relation to a diligence to which this paragraph applies.

(2) Section 93(1) or (2) of this Act shall not prevent a creditor taking proceedings in court to recover any expenses of a diligence to which this paragraph applies which are chargeable against the debtor.

(3) Notwithstanding section 95 of this Act, a diligence to which this paragraph applies shall cease to have effect on payment or tender of the sum due under the decree or other document.

    (4) This paragraph applies to the following diligences—

    (a) a poinding and sale;

    (b) an arrestment and action of furthcoming or sale;

in effect at the commencement of sections 93 and 95 of this Act.

10. Until the commencement of the repeal of the Supplementary Benefits Act 1976 by Schedule 11 to the Social Security Act 1986 the said Act of 1976 shall have effect as if there

were inserted after section 18 of that Act the new section set out in section 68 of this Act with the following modifications—

(a) for "25A" there shall be substituted "18A"; and

(b) for references to income support there shall be substituted references to supplementary benefit.

| Section 108 | SCHEDULE 8 | |

REPEALS

Chapter	Short title	Extent of repeal
1503 c. 45.	The Diligence Act 1503.	The whole Act.
1579 c. 13.	The Registration Act 1579.	The whole Act.
1579 c. 45.	The Hornings Act 1579.	The whole Act.
1581 c. 26.	The Convention of Burghs Act 1581.	The whole Act.
1584 c. 15.	The Execution of Decrees Act 1584.	The whole Act.
1587 c. 30.	The Officers of Arms Act 1587.	The whole Act.
1592 c. 29.	The Lyon King of Arms Act 1592.	In section (3) the words "messingeris and", the words "and messingeris" and the words from "With power" to the end. In section (5) the words "and incarceratioun" and the words from "vnder the pane" to the end.
1593 c. 34.	The Hornings Act 1593.	The whole Act.
1600 c. 22.	The Hornings Act 1600.	The whole Act.
1607 c. 13.	The Convention of Burghs Act 1607.	The whole Act.
1621 c. 20.	The Hornings Act 1621.	The whole Act.
1661 c. 218.	The Poinding Act 1661.	The whole Act.
1669 c. 5.	The Poinding Act 1669.	The whole Act.
1669 c. 95.	The Lyon King of Arms Act 1669.	The words from "the fourtie sext" to "Together also with".
1672 c. 47.	The Lyon King of Arms Act 1672.	The words from "are judges" to "office and".
1681 c. 5.	The Subscription of Deeds Act 1681.	The word "hornings".
1681 c. 86.	The Bills of Exchange Act 1681.	The words from "Letters of horning" to "and other".
20 Geo. 2 c. 43.	The Heritable Jurisdictions (Scotland) Act 1746.	Section 28.
20 Geo. 2 c. 50.	The Tenures Abolition Act 1746.	Sections 12 and 13.
5 Geo. 3 c. 49.	The Bank Notes (Scotland) Act 1765.	In section 6 the words from "issuing" to "all other".
12 Geo. 3 c. 72.	The Bills of Exchange (Scotland) Act 1772.	In section 42 the words "by horning or other diligence". In section 43 the words "by horning or other diligence".
1 & 2 Vict. c. 114.	The Debtors (Scotland) Act 1838.	Sections 2 to 15. Sections 23 to 31. In section 32 the words "excepting in the case of poindings". Section 35. All the Schedules.
9 & 10 Vict. c. 67.	The Citations (Scotland) Act 1846.	In section 1 the words "excepting only in cases of poinding as aforesaid".

Chapter	Short title	Extent of repeal
19 & 20 Vict. c. 56.	The Exchequer Court (Scotland) Act 1856.	In section 28 the words from "except that" to the end. Sections 29 to 34. Section 36. Section 42. Schedules G to K.
19 & 20 Vict. c. 91.	The Debts Securities (Scotland) Act 1856.	In section 6 the words "of hornings".
33 & 34 Vict. c. 63.	The Wages Arrestment Limitation (Scotland) Act 1870.	The whole Act.
43 & 44 Vict. c. 34.	The Debtors (Scotland) Act 1880.	In section 4, the proviso, the words from "a warrant" to "or under" and the words "or obligation".
45 & 46 Vict. c. 42.	The Civil Imprisonment (Scotland) Act 1882.	Section 5.
55 & 56 Vict. c. 17.	The Sheriff Courts (Scotland) Extracts Act 1892.	Section 7(6).
10 & 11 Geo. 6 c. 43.	The Local Government (Scotland) Act 1947.	Sections 248 and 249. In section 250, the words from "together with" to "goods and effects" where second occurring. Sections 251 and 252.
10 & 11 Geo. 6 c. 44.	The Crown Proceedings Act 1947.	In section 46, proviso (a).
8 & 9 Eliz. 2 c. 21.	The Wages Arrestment Limitation Amendment (Scotland) Act 1960.	The whole Act.
1966 c. 19.	The Law Reform (Miscellaneous Provisions) (Scotland) Act 1966.	Sections 2 and 3.
1968 c. 49.	The Social Work (Scotland) Act 1968.	In section 80, subsections (2) and (3).
1970 c. 36.	The Merchant Shipping Act 1970.	In section 11(1)(a), the words "or arrestment".
1971 c. 58.	The Sheriff Courts (Scotland) Act 1971.	Section 36(4).
1973 c. 22.	The Law Reform (Diligence) (Scotland) Act 1973.	The whole Act.
1979 c. 39.	The Merchant Shipping Act 1979.	In section 39, subsection (2) and in subsection (3) the words "or arrestment" and the words from "and, as" to the end.
1979 c. 54.	The Sale of Goods Act 1979.	Section 40.
1984 c. 43.	The Finance Act 1984.	Section 16.

BILLIARDS (ABOLITION OF RESTRICTIONS) ACT 1987

(1987 c. 19)

An Act to abolish, as regards England and Wales, the restrictions by way of licensing or otherwise on the public playing of billiards, bagatelle and other games of the like kind, and a related power of entry.

[15th May 1987]

PARLIAMENTARY DEBATES

Hansard: H.L. Vol. 484, col. 650; Vol. 485, cols. 687, 1317; Vol. 486, col. 360; H.C. Vol. 113, col. 1399; Vol. 115, col. 552.

Repeal of enactments relating to billiard licences etc.

1. The enactments mentioned in the Schedule to this Act (which, so far as repealed by this Act, impose restrictions by way of licensing or otherwise on the public playing of billiards, bagatelle and other games of the like kind, and confer on constables power to enter places where public tables or boards are kept for playing at such games) are hereby repealed to the extent specified in the third column of that Schedule.

Short title and extent

2.—(1) This Act may be cited as the Billiards (Abolition of Restrictions) Act 1987.

(2) This Act extends to England and Wales only.

Section 1   SCHEDULE

REPEALS

Chapter	Short title	Extent of repeal
8 & 9 Vict. c.109.	Gaming Act 1845.	Sections 10 to 14. Schedule 3.
35 & 36 Vict. c.94.	Licensing Act 1872.	Section 75.
43 & 44 Vict. c.20.	Inland Revenue Act 1880.	Section 47.
12, 13 & 14 Geo. 6. c.101.	Justices of the Peace Act 1949.	In section 41— (a) in subsection (1), the words "billiard licence or"; (b) subsection (3); and (c) in subsection (4), the words from "the", where first occurring, to "1845 and"
1963 c.2.	Betting, Gaming and Lotteries Act 1963.	Section 56(1).
1964 c.26.	Licensing Act 1964.	Section 182(2).
1980 c.43.	Magistrates' Courts Act 1980.	In Schedule 6, paragraph 1 of Part III.
1982 c.22.	Gaming (Amendment) Act 1982.	Section 2. Schedule 2.

CHEVENING ESTATE ACT 1987

(1987 c. 20)

An Act to establish an incorporated board of trustees of the trusts contained in the trust instrument set out in the Schedule to the Chevening Estate Act 1959; to confer functions on, and to transfer property, rights and liabilities to, the board; to amend the trust instrument; and for purposes connected therewith.   [15th May 1987]

PARLIAMENTARY DEBATES
   Hansard, H.L. Vol. 482, col. 345; Vol. 483, col. 8; Vol. 484, col. 997; Vol. 485, col. 10; H.C. Vol. 114, col. 886, Vol. 115, col. 593.

Incorporation and functions of Board of Trustees

1.—(1) There shall be a body corporate known as the Board of Trustees of the Chevening Estate (in this Act referred to as "the Board").

(2) The Board shall be the trustee of the trusts contained in the trust instrument as amended by this Act and shall have the functions conferred by this Act and by that instrument as so amended.

(3) In this Act "the trust instrument" means the trust instrument set out in the Schedule to the Chevening Estate Act 1959.

(4) Schedule 1 to this Act shall have effect with respect to the Board.

Transfer of assets, liabilities etc. from trustees to the Board

2.—(1) On the appointed day there are hereby transferred to and vested in the Board, as trustee under the trust instrument as amended by this Act,—

(a) all the property and rights which, immediately before that day, are held by any of the Chevening trustees on the trusts contained in the trust instrument; and

(b) any liability or obligation to which, immediately before that day, any of the Chevening trustees are subject in their capacity as trustees under that instrument.

(2) In this section "the Chevening trustees" means the persons who, immediately before the appointed day, are "the Bank" or "the Administrative Trustees" for the purposes of the trust instrument.

(3) References in this section to property, rights, liabilities or obligations are references to any property, rights, liabilities or obligations whether or not capable of being transferred or assigned.

(4) Without prejudice to the generality of subsection (1) above, any legal proceedings or applications to any authority pending immediately before the appointed day by or against any of the Chevening trustees in

their capacity as trustees under the trust instrument shall be continued by or against the Board.

(5) Anything done before the appointed day in the exercise or performance of any power or duty conferred or imposed by the trust instrument shall, in so far as it relates or is capable of relating to any time on or after that day, have effect as if it had been done in the exercise or performance of the corresponding power or duty conferred or imposed by that instrument as amended by this Act.

Amendments of trust instrument

3.—(1) The trust instrument shall have effect on and after the appointed day subject to the amendments specified in Schedule 2 to this Act.

(2) Any reference to the trust instrument—
    (a) in the Chevening Estate Act 1959 or any other enactment, or
    (b) in any instrument or other document,
shall, in relation to any time on or after the appointed day, be construed as a reference to the trust instrument as so amended.

Amendments of 1959 Act

4. In consequence of the provisions of this Act, section 2 of the Chevening Estate Act 1959 (tax provisions) shall have effect on and after the appointed day with the following amendments—
    (a) in subsection (1)(a) (exemption from Schedule B income tax) for the words "the Bank or the administrative trustees in their capacity as trustees" there shall be substituted the words "the Board in its capacity as trustee";
    (b) in subsection (8) (relief from stamp duty) paragraph (b) is hereby repealed and in paragraph (c) for the words "the Bank or the administrative trustees" there shall be substituted the words "the Board"; and
    (c) in subsection (10) (definitions) for the words "'the Bank', 'the administrative trustees'" there shall be substituted the words "'the Board'".

Short title, citation and commencement

5.—(1) This Act may be cited as the Chevening Estate Act 1987 and this Act and the Chevening Estate Act 1959 may be cited together as the Chevening Estate Acts 1959 and 1987.

(2) This Act shall come into force on such day as the Lord Privy Seal may by order made by statutory instrument appoint (in this Act referred to as "the appointed day").

SCHEDULES

Section 1(4)   SCHEDULE 1

THE BOARD OF TRUSTEES OF THE CHEVENING ESTATE

Status

1.—(1) The Board shall not be regarded as the servant or agent of the Crown or as enjoying any status, immunity or privilege of the Crown.

(2) The members of the Board and any secretary or other staff employed by the Board shall not be regarded as civil servants and any property of the Board shall not be regarded as property of, or held on behalf of, the Crown.

Membership

2.—(1) The Board shall consist of the following members—
    (a)　the Lord Privy Seal;
    (b)　two persons appointed by the Prime Minister;
    (c)　a person appointed by the Secretary of State;
    (d)　the Director of the Victoria and Albert Museum; and
    (e)　such other persons as are from time to time appointed by the members holding office under paragraphs (a) to (d) above.

(2) At least one of the persons for the time being appointed under subparagraph (1)(b) above shall be a person experienced in estate management and forestry.

(3) The appointment of a member under sub-paragraph (1)(b) or (c) above shall be by an instrument signed by the Minister responsible.

(4) A member appointed under sub-paragraph (1)(b) or (c) above shall hold office for life unless—
    (a)　he is given written notice, signed by the Minister responsible, terminating his appointment; or
    (b)　he resigns his office by giving written notice to the Minister responsible.

(5) Any member appointed under sub-paragraph (1)(e) above shall hold office in accordance with the terms of his appointment.

(6) Any appointment or election of a person as an Administrative Trustee under—
    (a)　head (ii) or (iii) of paragraph (c) of clause 1 of the trust instrument, or
    (b)　the provision of that paragraph following head (iv),
which is in force immediately before the appointed day shall have effect on and after that day as an appointment under paragraph (b), (c) or (e), as the case may be, of sub-paragraph (1) above.

(7) In this paragraph "the Minister responsible" means—
    (a)　the Prime Minister, in relation to an appointment under paragraph (b) of sub-paragraph (1) above; and
    (b)　The Secretary of State, in relation to an appointment under paragraph (c) of that sub-paragraph.

Proceedings

3.—(1) The Lord Privy Seal shall be the chairman of the Board, but if he is absent from any meeting the members present may choose one of their number to be the chairman for the purposes of that meeting.

(2) Subject to sub-paragraphs (1) above and (4) below, the Board may regulate its own procedure.

(3) In doing so, the Board may make arrangements for any of its functions, other than the power to acquire or dispose of land, to be discharged by committees consisting of at least three members of the Board; and, if the arrangements so provide, anything done under them by a committee shall have effect as if done by the Board.

(4) The quorum for meetings of the Board or any committee shall be not less than three but neither the Board nor any committee shall reach a decision by correspondence unless all the members of the Board or, as the case may be, the committee have agreed in the correspondence to that decision.

(5) The validity of any proceedings shall not be affected by any vacancy among the members of the Board or by any defect in the appointment of a member.

Payments to members

4. Members of the Board shall be entitled to be paid out of the trust property—
    (a)　such expenses as they would be entitled to be so paid if they (and not the Board) were the trustees of the trusts contained in the trust instrument as amended by this Act; and
    (b)　in the case of members who are solicitors or engaged in any other profession or business, such professional or other charges as are for the time being authorised by that instrument.

Instruments

5.—(1) The fixing of the seal of the Board shall be authenticated by the signature of a member of the Board or the secretary to the Board.

(2) A document purporting to be duly executed under the seal of the Board, or to be signed on the Board's behalf, shall be received in evidence and, unless the contrary is proved, be deemed to be so executed or signed.

SCHEDULE 2

AMENDMENTS OF THE TRUST INSTRUMENT

Transfer to Board of certain functions of former trustees etc.

1.—(1) Subject to the provisions of this Schedule, the word "Board" shall be substituted for the words "Administrative Trustees", "Bank" and "Relevant Person" wherever occurring.

(2) In clause 1 (definitions)—

    (a) paragraph (b) ("the Bank") shall be omitted;

    (b) for paragraph (c) ("the Administrative Trustees") there shall be substituted the following paragraph—

        "(c) 'The Board' shall mean the Board of Trustees of the Chevening Estate (constituted by section 1(1) of the Chevening Estate Act 1987)";

    (c) in paragraph (g) ("the Chevening Trust Fund") for head (i) there shall be substituted the following head—

        "(i) so much of the property, rights, liabilities and obligations transferred to the Board by the Chevening Estate Act 1987 as constituted the Chevening Trust Fund immediately before that transfer",

    and in head (iii) for the words from "to the Bank" to "person" there shall be substituted the words "by or at the direction of any person whomsoever" and the words "with the concurrence of the Administrative Trustees" shall be omitted;

    (d) paragraph (k)(ii) ("the Lord Privy Seal", "the Minister of Works" and "the Director of the Victoria and Albert Museum in London") shall be omitted; and

    (e) paragraph (p) ("the Relevant Person") shall be omitted.

(3) In clause 4 (Settlor and Bank to hold Estate and Contents upon trusts there mentioned) for the words from the beginning to "set forth" there shall be substituted the following words—

    "The Board shall stand possessed of the Chevening Estate and of the Contents upon the trusts in this and the next five following Clauses set forth".

(4) In clause 9 (persons who may exercise the powers conferred by section 29 of the Settled Land Act 1925) the words from "so long" onwards shall be omitted.

(5) In clause 10 (Bank to hold land to order of Settled Land Act trustees) the words from "but so" onwards shall be omitted.

(6) In clause 16 (power to sell Contents) the words from the beginning to "then" shall be omitted.

(7) For clause 17 (duty to maintain inventory of contents and insurance) there shall be substituted the following clause—

    "17.—(1) An inventory of the Contents shall be maintained by the Board and the inventory as revised from time to time shall be signed by each member of the Board.

    (2) The Board shall arrange for such insurances and valuations of the Contents as it from time to time thinks fit.

    (3) The cost of maintaining the inventory and of the preservation and insurance of the Contents shall be paid out of the capital or income of the Chevening Trust Fund as the Board thinks fit.

    (4) The Board shall not be bound to see to the custody or preservation of the Contents or to interfere in any way in relation thereto (other than to maintain the inventory and have revisions thereof signed as aforesaid) and shall not be responsible for any omission neglect or default of the person entitled to the use or enjoyment thereof but shall nevertheless be at liberty at any time to interfere for the protection of the Contents or any of the Contents."

(8) In clause 21 (trusts of the Chevening Trust Fund)—

    (a) for the words preceding paragraph (i) there shall be substituted the words "The Board shall pay and apply the income of the Chevening Trust Fund for such one or more of the following purposes and in such manner as it thinks fit that is to say—";

    (b) in paragraph (i) the words from "of the acceptance" to "hereof and" shall be omitted;

    (c) at the end of paragraph (v) there shall be added the words "(or of members of the Board)"; and

    (d) in paragraph (viii) the words "paid to the Bank and" shall be omitted.";

(9) In clause 23 (application of capital money)—

    (a) in paragraph (a), in the paragraph substituted for paragraph (i) of section 73(1) of the Settled Land Act 1925, for the word "his" there shall be substituted the word "its"; and

    (b) paragraphs (d) and (e) shall be omitted.

(10) Clauses 24 to 28 and the heading relating to clause 24 (which relate to the appointment and proceedings of the administrative trustees) shall be omitted.

(11) In clause 30 (trustees for the purposes of the Settled Land Act 1925 to be successively the Bank, the Administrative Trustees and the Bank, and the Bank to be special executor)—

(a) For paragraphs (a) to (c) (the Settled Land Act trustees) there shall be substituted the following paragraph—

> "(aa) the Board shall be the trustee hereof for the purposes of the Settled Land Act 1925"; and

(b) in paragraph (d) (Bank deemed to have been special executor at Settlor's death) for the words "the Bank" there shall be substituted the words "Coutts & Company".

(12) Clause 35 (power of Bank to charge for its services as trustee) shall be omitted.

(13) In clause 36 (trustee charging provision) for the words "Any Trustee for the time being hereunder being" there shall be substituted the words "Any member of the Board for the time being who is".

(14) In the testimonium, for the words "the Bank has caused its Common Seal" there shall be substituted the words "Coutts & Company have caused their Common Seal".

Revival of trusts in favour of the Nominated Person

2.—(1) In clause 5 (which provides that in certain events the trusts in favour of the Nominated Person shall absolutely determine and trusts in favour of the Canadian High Commissioner shall arise) after the words "absolutely determine" there shall be inserted the words "(but without prejudice to Clauses 5A and 6A hereof)".

(2) Clause 6 (trusts in favour of the United States Ambassador to arise upon the determination of the trusts in favour of the Canadian High Commissioner) shall be re-numbered as clause 5A and for the words "United States Ambassador" in both places where they occur there shall be substituted the words "Nominated Person".

(3) After clause 5A there shall be inserted the following clause—

> "6. If at any time after the Nominated Person has become entitled to occupy use and enjoy the Chevening Estate under the provisions of Clause 5A hereof either—
>
> (a) there shall have been no Nominated Person during a continuous period of six years (such period beginning at a date after the determination of the trusts declared by Clause 5 hereof) or
>
> (b) during any continuous period of six years (such period beginning as aforesaid) no Nominated Person shall have occupied Chevening House or
>
> (c) the Prime Minister and the Leader of the Opposition notify the Board in writing that they desire to determine the trusts declared by Clause 5A hereof
>
> then and in any such event the trusts and provisions of Clause 5A hereof shall absolutely determine (but without prejudice to Clause 6A hereof) and the Chevening Estate and the Contents shall be held upon trust to permit the United States Ambassador to occupy use and enjoy the same as a furnished country residence and estate for such period or periods continuous or discontinuous as the United States Ambassador may think fit."

(4) Clause 7 (Chevening Estate, Contents and Trust Fund to be held for the National Trust absolutely upon the determination of the trusts in favour of the United States Ambassador) shall be re-numbered as clause 6A and in that clause for the words following "Contents" there shall be substituted the words "shall be held upon trust to permit the Nominated Person to occupy use and enjoy the same as a furnished country residence and estate for such period or periods continuous or discontinuous as the Nominated Person may think fit."

(5) After clause 6A there shall be inserted the following clause—

> "7. If at any time after the Nominated Person has become entitled to occupy use and enjoy the Chevening Estate under the Provisions of Clause 6A hereof either—
>
> (a) there shall have been no Nominated Person during a continuous period of six years (such period beginning at a date after the determination of the trusts declared by Clause 6 hereof) or
>
> (b) during any continuous period of six years (such period beginning as aforesaid) no Nominated Person shall have occupied Chevening House or
>
> (c) the Prime Minister and the Leader of the Opposition notify the Board in writing that they desire to determine the trusts declared by Clause 6A hereof

then and in any such event the trusts and provisions of Clause 6A hereof shall absolutely determine and the Chevening Estate and the Contents and the Chevening Trust Fund shall be held upon trust for the National Trust absolutely."

(6) In consequence of the amendments made by sub-paragraphs (1) to (5) above—

    (a) in clause 9 (trusts deemed public trusts for purposes of section 29 of the Settled Land Act 1925) for the words "Clauses 5 and 6" there shall be substituted the words "Clauses 5 to 6A";

    (b) in clause 10 (manner in which land to be held) for the words "Clauses 4 5 or 6" there shall be substituted the words "Clauses 4 to 6A";

    (c) in clause 32 (matters to be regarded in the exercise of certain powers of disposition and management) for the words "Clauses 4 5 and 6" there shall be substituted the words "Clauses 4 to 6A"; and

    (d) in clause 38 (construction of references to Chevening Estate) for the words "Clauses 4 5 6 and 7" there shall be substituted the words "Clauses 4 to 7".

Disposal and management: outlying parts of the specified land

3. In the Second Schedule (which describes those parts of the estate referred to as "the Specified Land", whose disposal the trust instrument prohibits) there shall be added at the end of the words "except so much thereof as lies to the south of Ovenden Road or to the south or east of Sundridge Road".

Power to grant leases of and easements over the specified land

4.—(1) For clause 12 (which provides that the powers to sell, lease, exchange or mortgage shall not apply to the specified land or Chevening House and shall not be exercisable in respect of any other part of the estate without the approval of the Prime Minister) there shall be substituted the following clause—

"12.—(1) The powers to sell, lease or exchange land or to raise money on the security of land (to the extent that their exercise is not prohibited by sub-paragraph (2) hereof) shall not be exercised in relation to any land comprised in the Chevening Estate unless the transaction has previously been approved by the person who, on the date of the contract of sale or other contract in question, is the Prime Minister.

(2) The prohibitions referred to in sub-paragraph (1) hereof are that—

    (a) the powers to lease land and grant easements shall not be exercisable in relation to Chevening House or so much of the Specified Land as consists of the pleasure gardens (for the purposes of this Clause being the land described in the Third Schedule hereto) and

    (b) the other powers to sell and exchange land and raise money on the security of land shall not be exercisable in relation to Chevening House or any of the Specified Land."

(2) In clause 32 (matters to be considered when exercising certain powers, including leasing) for the words "(other than Chevening House and the Specified Land)" there shall be substituted the words "(being land in relation to which the power is exercisable)".

(3) After the Second Schedule there shall be added the following Schedule—

"THE THIRD SCHEDULE

The lands tenements and hereditaments situate at Chevening aforesaid and shown edged red on the plan marked with the designation "Chevening House and Pleasure Gardens" and prepared in triplicate one copy of which has been deposited in each of the following offices—

    (a) the Office of the Clerk of the Parliaments

    (b) the Private Bill Office of the House of Commons and

    (c) the Chevening Estate Office."

Delegation of trustee investment functions

5.—(1) In clause 23 (application to the Chevening Trust Fund of the provisions of the Settled Land Act 1925 relating to capital money) for the words "subject to the last preceding Clause" there shall be substituted the words "subject to Clauses 22 and 23A hereof".

(2) After clause 23 there shall be inserted the following clause—

"23A.—(1) The Board may arrange for its powers, duties and discretions relating to the investment of capital money comprised in the Chevening Trust Fund (and to the retention, transposition and disposal of investments) to be exercised or performed, without any requirement of consultation with the Board, by agents appointed by the Board at such remuneration and upon such other terms and conditions as the Board thinks fit.

(2) Without prejudice to the generality of sub-paragraph (1) hereof, the Board may permit any investments for the time being subject to the trusts hereof to stand in the names of agents appointed under that sub-paragraph or in the names of any other nominees or trustees in any part of the world.

(3) Nothing in this Clause shall be taken to prejudice the generality of Clauses 19 and 29 thereof."

Omission of spent provisions and amendments in consequence

6.—(1) The following provisions (being covenants performed, interests determined, conditions satisfied and matters connected with the Settlor's death) shall be omitted—

(a) clause 2 and the heading immediately preceding it (Settlor's covenant to deliver Contents to the Bank);

(b) clause 3 and the heading immediately preceding it (Settlor's covenant to transfer investments to the Bank);

(c) clause 4(i) (Settlor's life interest, determined by his death on 15th August 1967);

(d) clause 18 (power of Settlor to make gifts or bequests of certain chattels comprised in the Contents);

(e) clause 20 (income of trust fund to be paid to Settlor during his life).

(2) In consequence of the omission of clause 4(i) the words "after the death of the Settlor" shall be substituted for the words from "after the determination" to "Clause 4(i) hereof"—

(a) in both places where such words occur in clause 5 (trusts in favour of the Canadian High Commissioner);

(b) in clause 9 (persons who may exercise the powers conferred by section 29 of the Settled Land Act 1925); and

(c) in clause 10 (person in whom land to be vested).

PILOTAGE ACT 1987*

(1987 c. 21)

---

* Annotations by F. D. Rose, M.A., B.C.L., Ph.D., Barrister, Senior Lecturer in Laws, University College, London.

An Act to make new provision in respect of pilotage.

[15th May 1987]

PARLIAMENTARY DEBATES
    Hansard: H.L. Vol. 482, cols. 23, 439, 457; Vol. 484, col. 744; Vol. 485, cols. 389, 776; Vol. 487, col. 291; H.C. Vol. 113, col. 831; Vol. 114, col. 502.
    The Bill was considered in Public Bill Committee from December 8 to January 15, 1987.
    Green Paper—*Marine Pilotage: A Consultative Document* (December 1985—but printed as December 1984).
    White Paper—*Marine Pilotage: Legislative Proposals* (November 1986).

ABBREVIATION
    CHA: Competent Harbour Authority (s.1(1)).

GENERAL NOTE
    The objectives of the Act have been expressed as the reform of the organisation of marine pilotage, simplification of its administration, and making it possible for changes to be made in pilotage services to meet modern requirements and to reflect changes in the patterns of shipping and trade. In particular, the Government's desire was to reduce the costs of pilotage and therefore of the ports being used and to enhance the competitiveness of ports, not only within the United Kingdom but in particular *vis-à-vis* Continental European ports.

The principal features of the legislation is the decentralisation of pilotage administration, putting control in the hands of local "competent harbour authorities," leaving the Secretary of State with a much reduced supervisory role, abolishing the Pilotage Commission, and considerably reducing any influence which Trinity House may have. Pilots have mainly occupied an individual position, operating mostly as independent contractors and classified by the Inland Revenue as self-employed. The legislation provides for the continuation of this position but with emphasis on pilots being employees, rather than independent contractors, of CHAs.

The Act contains a number of amendments to the more consciously commercially influenced original Bill, to meet criticisms: that there should be fair and equitable treatment for both pilots transferring to the new system and those leaving the profession; and that public safety and the environment should be protected. These considerations were also the subject of assurances by the Government on the operation of the new system, so it remains to be seen how the Act operates, and is operated, in practice to fulfil the various commercial, employment, safety and environmental expectations of it.

COMMENCEMENT

S.27 came into operation on the passing of the Act. Ss.15–26 and 28–29 come into force on such day or days as the Secretary of State may appoint. Ss.1–14 also come into effect on such day as the Secretary of State may appoint, but that day must not be less than nine months after the passing of the Act.

EXTENT

The Act extends to Northern Ireland.

PART I

PILOTAGE FUNCTIONS OF COMPETENT HARBOUR AUTHORITIES

Preliminary

Meaning of "competent harbour authority" and "harbour"

1.—(1) Subject to the following provisions of this section, in this Act "competent harbour authority" means any harbour authority—

(a) which has statutory powers in relation to the regulation of shipping movements and the safety of navigation within its harbour; and

(b) whose harbour falls wholly or partly within an active former pilotage district;

and references to a harbour authority's harbour are to the area or areas inside the limits of which its statutory powers and duties as a harbour authority are exercisable but, where there are two or more separate such areas, include only those areas which fall wholly or partly within an active former pilotage district.

(2) In this Act any reference to a former pilotage district is to a district which was a pilotage district within the meaning of the Pilotage Act 1983 immediately before the day appointed for the coming into force of this Part of this Act ("the appointed day") and for the purposes of subsection (1) above such a district is an active district if—

(a) at least one act of pilotage was performed there in 1984, 1985, 1986 or 1987 in respect of which information was given by the pilotage authority for the district in a return made by it under section 19 of that Act; or

(b) a certificate granted under section 29 of that Act (masters' and first mates' pilotage certificates) was in force in respect of the district at any time in any of those years in respect of which information was so given.

(3) If the Secretary of State considers that in the interests of efficiency and safety of navigation a competent harbour authority should exercise

pilotage functions both as respects its harbour and another area, he may by order provide—

    (a) that this Act shall apply to that authority as if its harbour included that other area; and

    (b) in a case where the other area is or falls within the harbour of another competent harbour authority, that that other authority shall not be a competent harbour authority for the purposes of this Act.

(4) A harbour authority which is not a competent harbour authority may apply to the Secretary of State to be treated for the purposes of this Act as such an authority and on such an application the Secretary of State may by order provide that the applicant shall be a competent harbour authority for the purposes of this Act.

(5) The Secretary of State may by order amend or revoke an order made under subsection (3) or (4) above if it appears to him to be appropriate to do so having regard to any change of circumstances which has occurred since the order was made.

(6) The Secretary of State shall maintain a list of the authorities which are for the time being competent harbour authorities for the purposes of this Act.

(7) Before making an order under this section the Secretary of State shall inform the persons he considers may be affected by the order of the terms of the proposed order and that they may within such reasonable period as he may specify object to the making of the order by giving him notice in writing.

(8) Where any person has duly objected under subsection (7) above to the making of a proposed order and has not withdrawn his objection, then if the Secretary of State makes an order in that form (or a substantially similar form) it shall be subject to special parliamentary procedure, and the Statutory Orders (Special Procedure) Act 1945 shall have effect accordingly, but as if—

    (a) sections 2 and 10(2) of that Act (which relate to preliminary proceedings) were omitted; and

    (b) that Act extended to Northern Ireland and, in the application of section 7(3) of that Act to Northern Ireland, for any reference to a local authority and the Secretary of State there were substituted respectively a reference to a district council and the Department of the Environment for Northern Ireland.

(9) For the purposes of subsection (1) above "harbour authority" does not include—

    (a) any authority excluded by virtue of section 58 of the Harbours Act 1964 from being taken as a harbour authority for the purposes of that Act;

    (b) a Queen's harbour master; or

    (c) any own account operator.

(10) For the purposes of subsection (1)(a) above powers exercisable by the harbour master for a harbour shall be taken to be exercisable by the harbour authority which appointed him.

(11) In this section "own account operator" means a statutory harbour undertaker within the meaning of section 42 of the Harbours Act 1964 or a harbour authority within the meaning of the Harbours Act (Northern Ireland) 1970 whose activities in the harbour in question relate wholly or mainly to ships resorting to the harbour wholly or mainly for the purpose of bringing or receiving goods which—

    (a) have been manufactured or produced by the statutory harbour undertaker or, as the case may be, the harbour authority or any connected person; or

(b) are to be used by him or any connected person for the manufacture or production of goods or electricity;

and for the purposes of this subsection a person is connected with a statutory harbour undertaker or, as the case may be, harbour authority, if he is a holding company or subsdiary of the undertaker, or authority, or a member of a consortium the members of which between them own, directly or indirectly, more than half the issued share capital of the undertaker or authority.

DEFINITIONS

"the appointed day": ss.1(2), 31(1).
"area": see s.1(1), (3).
"competent harbour authority": ss.1(1), 31(1).
"former pilotage district": ss.1(2), 31(1).
"functions": see General Note to s.31.
"harbour": ss.1(1), 31(1).
"harbour authority": s.31(1).
"master": s.31(1).
"own account operator": s.1(11).
"pilotage": s.31(1).
"pilotage authority": s.1(2); see also Pilotage Act 1983, s.68(1).
"pilotage certificate": see Pilotage Act 1983, s.20.
"pilotage district": see Pilotage Act 1983, s.68(1).
"Secretary of State": see General Note to s.31.
"ship": s.31(1).
"special parliamentary procedure": see Statutory Orders (Special Procedure) Act 1945 (c.18).
"statutory duties": s.31(1).
"statutory powers": s.31(1).

GENERAL NOTE

This section establishes which harbour authorities ("competent harbour authorities"—or "CHAs") are to exercise responsibility for pilotage under the new Act. So long as part of its harbour falls within an "active former pilotage district" (as defined by s.1(2)), the CHA has functions for pilotage throughout its area as a harbour authority. However, the mere fact that an authority responsible for more than one harbour becomes a CHA for one harbour does not mean that it becomes a CHA for another harbour unless "the necessary criteria are also fulfilled" with respect to the second harbour area.

By virtue of s.1(9), Queen's harbour masters cannot be competent harbour authorities. There is provision in ss.12 and 13 for the relationship between them and competent harbour authorities.

The description of "area" in s.1(1), (3) is relevant generally throughout the Act, though the term inevitably has a different meaning in relation to deep sea pilotage under s.23.

The concentration of pilotage responsibilities on individual harbour authorities could lead to undesirable inconvenience and expense in certain situations, particularly where a vessel proceeds through an estuary where there is more than one potential CHA. Therefore, where there are likely to be conflicting jurisdictions between different harbour authorities, the Secretary of State has power under s.1(3) to ensure that one or more authorities can be designated to exercise the appropriate functions. There is specific provision for this matter in s.12. See also s.13.

It is clear that the operation of s.1(3) is not restricted to cases where the Secretary of State extends a CHA's area of competence into the area of another harbour authority; it also provides for the inclusion of places outside any harbour area. In this respect, there is an apparent overlap (unacknowledged by the Act) with the procedure for a CHA to extend its pilotage jurisdiction to other places in which it thinks pilotage should be compulsory, under s.7(5), which requires the CHA to apply for a harbour revision order (or, in Northern Ireland, a harbour order) in order to do so. However, such overlap as may appear to exist is purely apparent, for the necessity for a harbour revision order under s.7(5) only occurs if the CHA wishes to extend pilotage jurisdiction beyond the area of its harbour. Once the Secretary of State has made an order under s.1(3), any additional area covered by that order comes within the area of the CHA's harbour, so it is no longer an area for which application for a harbour revision order is necessary.

Provision of pilotage services

General duties as to provision of pilotage services

2.—(1) Each competent harbour authority shall keep under consideration—

(a) whether any and, if so, what pilotage services need to be provided to secure the safety of ships navigating in or in the approaches to its harbour; and

(b) whether in the interests of safety pilotage should be compulsory for ships navigating in any part of that harbour or its approaches and, if so, for which ships and in which circumstances and what pilotage services need to be provided for those ships.

(2) Without prejudice to the generality of subsection (1) above, each competent harbour authority shall in performing its functions under that subsection have regard in particular to the hazards involved in the carriage of dangerous goods or harmful substances by ship.

(3) Each competent harbour authority shall provide such pilotage services as it considers need to be provided as mentioned in subsection (1)(a) and (b) above.

DEFINITIONS

"competent harbour authority": ss.1(1), 31(1).
"compulsory pilotage": see ss.7, 15–16.
"functions": see General Note to s.31.
"harbour": ss.1(1), 31(1).
"navigating": see s.31(2).
"pilotage": s.31(1).
"ship": s.31(1).

GENERAL NOTE

The CHA's duty with respect to the approaches to its harbour under s.2(1)(b), requires it to consider whether it should apply for a harbour revision order under s.7(5). The *duty* to consider areas outside its harbour under s.2(1)(b) only relates to the requirement of compulsory pilotage, but it is not prevented from considering the relevance of pilotage outside its area to its activities within its area.

Authorisation of pilots

3.—(1) Subject to subsection (3) and section 4 below, a competent harbour authority may authorise such persons to act as pilots in or in any part of the area in relation to which its duty under section 2(1) above is exercisable as it considers are suitably qualified to do so; and such an authorisation shall specify the area within which it has effect and may specify that it only has effect in relation to ships of a particular description.

(2) The authority may determine the qualifications in respect of age, physical fitness, time of service, local knowledge, skill, character and otherwise to be required from persons applying for authorisation and provide for the examination of such persons; and different qualifications may be required from persons who immediately before the appointed day were the holders of licences under section 12 of the Pilotage Act 1983, time-expired apprentice pilots or recognised assistant pilots.

(3) During the period of four years beginning with the appointed day a competent harbour authority shall not authorise any persons who were not immediately before the appointed day holders of full licences (that is to say, licences under that section other than licences for a limited period which are not renewable) unless the number of such persons applying to be authorised under this section who have the required qualifications falls short of the number the authority considers are required to be authorised.

(4) If at any time during that period there is such a shortfall, the competent harbour authority shall not authorise any person who was not immediately before that day a time-expired apprentice pilot or a recognised assistant pilot unless the number of such apprentice and assistant pilots applying to be authorised who have the required qualifications also falls short of that number.

(5) A competent harbour authority may suspend or revoke an authorisation granted by it under this section if it appears to it—

  (a) that the authorised person has been guilty of any incompetence or misconduct affecting his capability as a pilot;

  (b) that the authorised person has ceased to have the qualifications required from persons applying for authorisation by it under this section or has failed to provide evidence that he continues to have those qualifications;

  (c) that the number of persons for the time being authorised by it under this section exceeds the number required to be authorised; or

  (d) that it is appropriate to do so by virtue of the termination of any contract or other arrangement under which the services of pilots are provided within its harbour;

but the authorisation of a person who provides his services as a pilot under a contract for services may not be revoked by an authority by virtue of paragraph (c) above unless it gave him notice before the appointed day that the number of persons it proposed to authorise exceeded the number required to be authorised and it proposed to revoke his authorisation after allowing him a reasonable period from the appointed day to seek authorisation by another competent harbour authority.

(6) Before suspending or revoking an authorisation under subsection (5)(a) or (b) above, a competent harbour authority shall give written notice of its intention to do so to the authorised person, stating the reasons for which it proposes to act, and shall give him a reasonable opportunity of making representations.

(7) Where a competent harbour authority suspends or revokes an authorisation of any person by virtue of paragraph (c) or (d) of subsection (5) above, it shall give him notice in writing—

  (a) stating that the suspension or revocation was by virtue of that paragraph; and

  (b) specifying the duration of the authorisation in question and any previous authorisations granted to that person by the authority.

(8) If any person who is not an authorised pilot for an area describes himself whilst he is in that area as being such a pilot or so holds himself out as to indicate or be reasonably understood to indicate that he is such a pilot, he shall be guilty of an offence and liable on summary conviction to a fine not exceeding level 5 on the standard scale.

(9) A person who is an authorised pilot for a harbour for which the competent harbour authority is a local authority shall not by reason of his holding any office or employment as a pilot be disqualified for being a member of any committee of that local authority with any functions in respect of which knowledge or experience relevant to pilotage is material or for being a representative of the local authority on a joint committee of the authority and another authority with such functions.

(10) In this section—

  "local authority" means—

    (a) in England and Wales, a local authority within the meaning of the Local Government Act 1972;

    (b) in Scotland, a local authority within the meaning of the Local Government (Scotland) Act 1973; and

    (c) in Northern Ireland, a district council;

"time-expired apprentice pilot" means a person who has served the
full term of his apprenticeship as a pilot but is not the holder
of a licence under section 12 of the Pilotage Act 1983;
"recognised assistant pilot" means a person who acts as an assistant
to pilots in a pilotage district and is recognised as such an
assistant by the pilotage authority for the district but is not the
holder of such a licence.

DEFINITIONS
"the appointed day": ss.1(2), 31(1).
"assistant": see s.3(10).
"authorised pilot": ss.3, 31(1).
"competent harbour authority": ss.1(1), 31(1).
"functions": see General Note to s.31.
"harbour": ss.1(1), 31(1).
"licence": s.3(3); also see Pilotage Act 1983, s.12.
"local authority": s.3(10).
"pilot": s.31(1).
"pilotage": s.31(1).
"pilotage authority": s.1(2); see also Pilotage Act 1983, s.68(1).
"pilotage district": see Pilotage Act 1983, s.68(1).
"recognised assistant pilot": s.3(10).
"ship": s.31(1).
"the standard scale": Criminal Justice Act 1982, s.75.
"time-expired apprentice pilot": s.3(10).

GENERAL NOTE
The Act does not require uniform national qualifications for pilotage. These are matters
to be determined by individual CHAs in the light of local conditions.
Subss. (3)–(4) ensure that those concerned in providing pilotage services under the
Pilotage Act 1983 are to receive priority under the new system. So far as existing licensed
pilots are concerned, the phrase "which are not renewable" in subs. (3) makes it clear that
it is only provisional pilots, whose licences are issued for a limited period and are not
renewable, who are excluded from the priority provisions. The provisions in subs. (2)–(4)
relating to time-expired apprentice pilots and recognised assistant pilots (notably Manchester
Ship Canal helmsmen) give them a second level of priority for authorisation as pilots once
the supply of applications from former licensed pilots has dried up.
In relation to the provisions for suspension and revocation of the authorisation of pilots
in subss. (5)–(7), it should be borne in mind that those pilots who are employed pilots
remain entitled to the advantages of the unfair dismissal and redundancy provisions of the
Employment Protection (Consolidation) Act 1978.
The proviso to s.3(5) limits a CHA's power to suspend or revoke the authorisation of a
pilot where there are too many pilots in a port to cases where the pilots are employed by the
CHA. Therefore, self-employed pilots may be able to continue working even if trade in a
port falls away. It is contemplated that CHAs will nonetheless be able to keep costs under
control through their power to set the original number of authorisations, to set pilotage
charges, the terms of the contracts of agreements that will govern the provision of pilotage
services by agents or self-employed pilots, and the power to change the arrangements in the
port from an agency arrangement to direct employment.
With respect to the procedure in subs. (6) see *Moore* v. *Clyde Pilotage Authority,* 1943
S.C. 457; *Soames* v. *Corporation of Trinity House* (1950) 84 Ll.L.Rep. 432. See also *R.* v.
Trinity House (1855) 26 L.T.(O.S.) 103 (disapproved in *Moore's* case); *Conway* v. *Clyde
Pilotage Authority,* 1951 S.L.T.(Sh.Ct.) 74.
The effect of subs. (7) is, *inter alia,* to give a pilot a document which he can effectively use
as a reference, if it has been found necessary to suspend or revoke his authorisation on
grounds unconnected with his competence, conduct or qualifications.
Subs. (9) provides an exception to the general legislation, prohibiting employees of a local
authority from being members of committees of that local authority, in the case of pilotage
committees where the CHA is also the local authority. However, the exception is made
solely for the benefit of authorised pilots so does not, for example, permit harbourmasters
who were formerly pilots to sit on examination or disciplinary committees, however desirable
that might appear to be. *Cf. Conway* v. *Clyde Pilotage Authority,* 1951 S.L.T.(Sh.Ct.) 74,
76.

The fact that a person is authorised as a pilot under s.3 does not give him unfettered freedom to act as a pilot, for he is subject to the arrangements made by the CHA for the employment of pilots under s.4.

Employment etc. of authorised pilots

4.—(1) Subject to subsection (2) below, a competent harbour authority may make such arrangements as it considers appropriate for the provision of the services of authorised pilots in the area in relation to which its duty under section 2(1) above is exercisable (whether under a contract of employment or a contract for services).

(2) A competent harbour authority shall offer to employ under a contract of employment any person it authorises under section 3 above who is not already employed by it under such a contract ("the new pilot") unless—

(a) a majority of the relevant licence holders have agreed during the period beginning six months and ending three months before the appointed day that it need not do so; or

(b) a majority of the relevant authorised pilots have agreed on or after that day that it need not do so.

(3) For the purposes of subsection (2) above—

"relevant licence holders" means—

(a) in the case of a competent harbour authority whose harbour falls within more than one former pilotage district, the persons who at the time of the agreement were holders of full licences (within the meaning of section 3(3) above) for the pilotage district in which the area for which the new pilot is authorised falls;

(b) in the case of a competent harbour authority whose harbour falls within a former pilotage district in which another such authority's harbour also falls, the persons who at that time were holders of such licences for that district and, in the opinion of the Pilotage Commission, were then regularly providing their services as pilots within the part of the district in which the first-mentioned authority's harbour is situated;

(c) in any other case, all the persons who at that time were the holders of such licences for the former pilotage district in which the competent harbour authority's harbour falls; and

"relevant authorised pilots" means—

(i) in the case mentioned in paragraph (a) above, the persons who at the time of the agreement are authorised pilots for the area for which the new pilot has been authorised; and

(ii) in any other case the persons who at that time are authorised pilots for the harbour of the authority.

(4) A competent harbour authority may refuse to authorise any person who is not willing to provide his services as a pilot in accordance with the arrangements made for the provision of such services in its area.

(5) A competent harbour authority may pay into any pilots' benefit fund established under paragraph (i) of section 15(1) of the Pilotage Act 1983 such contributions as may be required by the rules governing that fund in respect of any authorised pilot providing his services under such arrangements as mentioned in subsection (1) above.

DEFINITIONS
"the appointed day": ss.1(2), 31(1).
"area": see s.1(1), (3).

"authorised pilot": ss.3, 31(1).
"competent harbour authority": ss.1(1), 31(1).
"former pilotage district": ss.1(2), 31(1).
"harbour": ss.1(1), 31(1).
"licence": s.3(3); see also Pilotage Act 1983, s.12.
"new pilot": s.4(2).
"pilot": s.31(1).
"pilots' benefit fund": s.4(5); see also Pilotage Act 1983, s.15(1)(h)–(i).
"Pilotage Commission": see Pilotage Act 1983, s.1(1).
"pilotage district": see Pilotage Act 1983, s.68(1).
"relevant authorised pilot": s.4(3).
"relevant licence holder": s.4(3).

GENERAL NOTE

In accordance with its duties as to the provision of pilotage services under s.2, a CHA is entitled to make arrangements as to such provision under s.4.

Where pilots are already directly employed by a harbour authority in its capacity as a pilotage authority, the authority is not obliged to make a fresh offer of employment or to upset existing arrangements. Otherwise, a CHA is obliged, under s.4(2), to offer a contract of employment to all pilots which it authorises. Since it is free, under subs. (1) to decide on what arrangements it makes—and, therefore, to decide only to offer a contract of employment—if the CHA does only offer a contract of employment, that is all that is available from it to authorised pilots. They are not bound to accept the offer but, if they do not, subs. (4) entitles the CHA to refuse to authorise them, although it does not entitle it to deprive them of any unexpired existing authorisation. If the CHA offers an arrangement whereby authorised pilots can operate as self-employed pilots, again, they are not bound to agree to that arrangement; however, they remain nonetheless entitled to be offered employment under subs. (2).

The CHA's obligation to employ under subs. (2) is not limited to employment solely as a pilot. Therefore, the employment may comprise other duties.

Where pilots have released a CHA from the obligation to offer employment, the CHA has the full range of options from which to choose, including self-employment, direct employment or agency arrangements which may involve either.

Temporary procedure for resolving disputes as to terms of employment

5.—(1) Where any dispute arises between a competent harbour authority and an authorised pilot or a person wishing to be authorised under section 3 above by the authority—

(a) as to what the terms of any provision in any contract of employment which is to be entered into between them should be; or

(b) whether the terms of any provision in any existing such contract between them should be modified,

and that dispute cannot be resolved by negotiation between them, the authority or the majority of the authorised pilots for its harbour may refer the dispute to an arbitration panel appointed in accordance with subsection (2) below and the panel shall determine what the terms of that provision should be and the kinds of contracts of employment between the authority and authorised pilots to which their determination is to apply ("relevant contracts").

(2) The arbitration panel referred to in subsection (1) above shall consist of three members, one, the Chairman, appointed by the Secretary of State, one, by a body appearing to the Secretary of State to be representative of harbour authorities throughout the United Kingdom and one by a body appearing to him to be representative of pilots throughout the United Kingdom.

(3) In making a determination under subsection (1) above the arbitration panel shall have regard to any general guidance issued by the Secretary of State as to the matters to be considered by them.

(4) Where the arbitration panel make a determination under subsection (1) above then, subject to any agreement to the contrary between the

parties and to the effect of any subsequent determination under this section—

(a) on and after the date on which the determination is made any relevant contracts entered into before that date shall have effect with the substitution for any inconsistent provision of a provision in the terms determined by the panel; and

(b) any relevant contracts entered into on or after that date shall contain a provision in those terms.

(5) The references to contracts in subsection (1) above do not include contracts of employment entered into before the appointed day for the provision of services as a pilot before that day.

(6) In the case of an authority whose harbour falls within more than one former pilotage district, for the reference in subsection (1) above to the majority of the authorised pilots for its harbour there shall be substituted a reference to the majority of the authorised pilots for the part of the harbour for which the person as to whose contract the dispute has arisen is or wishes to be authorised.

(7) Subject to the provisions of this section, the Secretary of State may by regulations make such provision as he thinks fit as respects the referral and determination of disputes under subsection (1) above and such regulations may, in particular, provide that the expenses of such referrals and determinations are to be borne by the Pilotage Commission or by such other person as the Secretary of State thinks fit.

(8) The preceding provisions of this section shall cease to have effect on such date (not being earlier than the expiry of the period of three years beginning with the appointed day) as the Secretary of State may by order prescribe, but no such order shall affect the terms of any contract continuing in force at that date.

DEFINITIONS

"the appointed day": ss.1(2), 31(1).
"authorised pilot": ss.3, 31(1).
"competent harbour authority": ss.1(1), 31(1).
"former pilotage district": ss.1(2), 31(1).
"harbour": ss.1(1), 31(1).
"harbour authority": s.31(1).
"pilot": s.31(1).
"Pilotage Commission": see Pilotage Act 1983, s.1(1).
"relevant contracts": s.5(1).
"Secretary of State": see General Note to s.31.

GENERAL NOTE

The object of s.5 is to provide transitional provisions for determining the terms of contracts of employment concluded as a result of the new Act. Existing contracts of employment are, by virtue of subs. (5), excluded from these provisions on the ground that those contracts already contain built-in arbitration procedures.

S.5 provides a temporary arbitration procedure for the resolution of disputes concerning the terms of contracts of employment, to which authorised pilots have a statutory right under s.4. There is no such arbitration procedure for the terms of contracts for services, though the right of self-employed pilots to contracts of employment under s.4, with the s.5 procedure for setting fair and reasonable terms, may be a relevant factor in negotiating the terms of contracts for services. Should such negotiations fail, self-employed pilots can fall back on their statutory rights as authorised pilots under ss.4–5.

The appointment of an arbitration panel under s.5(2) is a matter for the Secretary of State's discretion, exercisable within the limits of the subsection. The person appointed by a body appearing to the Secretary of State to be representative of harbour authorities need not be appointed by a body in any way representing the CHA concerned and could therefore be an appointee of an organisation representing competitors of that CHA, a real possibility given, for example, that Associated British Ports is currently not a member of the British Ports Association.

The chairman and/or members of such an arbitration panel may be different in different cases of dispute.

The Act provides no guarantees for the maintenance of previous levels of income, which must be negotiated so far as possible under subs. (1)(a) and this will no doubt be done with regard to productivity. The matters which might be referred to the panel include not only levels of earnings but other terms and conditions of employment, including pension arrangements, hours of working, redundancy payments, effects of the removal of authorisation on the contract of employment, and the length of notice to be given in contracts. So far as redundancy is concerned, it should be noted that self-employed pilots do not have the benefit of the redundancy provisions in the Employment Protection (Consolidation) Act 1978, which are dependent on the period for which an employee has been employed.

In the parliamentary debates, it was stated on behalf of the Government that, in the light of discussions with representatives of the ports and the pilots, the Secretary of State was considering guidelines under subs. (3) in relation to:

—the previous earnings of pilots in the port, taking account of both actual earnings and levels of earnings recommended under the former Letch agreements (suitably updated);

—the work rate, the volume of work (number of ships to be piloted) and the mix of work (*e.g.* range of sizes and types of vessels covered);

—earnings of pilots in comparable ports elsewhere in the country;

—the physical conditions under which pilotage is undertaken in the port;

—the physical and geographical characteristics of the ports, particularly including those relevant to navigational hazards;

—the earnings, conditions of employment and working patterns of senior staff of the harbour authority, including those of marine officers, in comparison with the working conditions and work patterns applied to pilots;

—any national guidelines agreed between representatives of the harbour authorities and of the pilots regarding the employment of pilots by the harbour authorities.

The national guidelines last referred to are proposed to include;

—an undertaking about the pilots' national pension fund (PNPF), subject to certain provisos about the future financial position of the fund, that benefits under the fund's rules will be maintained at levels no less favourable than those which apply at present;

—the early retirement benefits to be paid by the PNPF in association with the compensation scheme for pilots who lose their employment as a result of the reorganisation of pilotage under the Act will be maintained for the period of availability of that compensation scheme;

—in the event of redundancies becoming necessary after the end of the period for which the compensation scheme will be available, the terms offered to pilots will be no less favourable than those which would be payable under statutory requirements if previous service as a licensed self-employed pilot counted as employment.

Pilot boats

6.—(1) Ships regularly employed in pilotage services provided by or on behalf of any competent harbour authority (in this Act referred to as "pilot boats") shall—

(a) if they are operated by the authority, be approved by the authority; and

(b) otherwise be licensed by it;

and the authority shall not approve or license any ship under this subsection unless it is satisfied that it is suitable for use as a pilot boat.

(2) A competent harbour authority shall make such other provision as it considers necessary for the operation of pilot boats.

DEFINITIONS

"competent harbour authority": ss.1(1), 31(1).

"pilot boat": ss.6(1), 31(1).

"pilotage": s.31(1).

"ship": s.31(1).

GENERAL NOTE

Pilots regard the availability of suitable pilot boats—and not simply boats that are available for pilotage and other services—as a vital safety factor in the performance of their functions.

It was argued that there should be national supervision of the safety of pilot boats, an argument which the Government met, not by introducing a provision in this Act with that end, but by expressing the intention that the Secretary of State would bring forward additional measures to ensure the safety of pilot boats by exercising his existing power to make regulations under the Merchant Shipping Act 1979, s.21.

Compulsory pilotage

Pilotage directions

7.—(1) Subject to the provisions of this section, if a competent harbour authority considers that in the interests of safety it should do so, it shall direct that pilotage shall be compulsory for ships navigating in any area or part of an area in relation to which its duty under section 2(1) above is exercisable; and such a direction is referred to in this Act as a "pilotage direction".

(2) A pilotage direction—

    (a) may, subject to subsection (3) below, apply to all ships or all ships of a description specified in the direction (subject to any exceptions there specified);

    (b) shall specify the area and circumstances in which it applies;

    (c) may specifiy the circumstances in which an authorised pilot in charge of a ship to which it applies is to be accompanied by an assistant who is also an authorised pilot; and

    (d) may contain such supplementary provisions as the authority considers appropriate.

(3) A pilotage direction shall not apply to ships of less than 20 metres in length or to fishing boats of which the registered length is less than 47.5 metres.

(4) Before giving a pilotage direction a competent harbour authority shall consult—

    (a) the owners of ships which customarily navigate in the area to which the proposed direction would apply; and

    (b) any other persons who carry on harbour operations within the harbour of the authority;

or, in either case, such persons as it considers to be representative of them.

(5) If a competent harbour authority considers that pilotage should be compulsory for ships navigating in any area outside its harbour it shall apply for a harbour revision order to be made under section 14 of the Harbours Act 1964, or in Northern Ireland a harbour order under section 1 of the Harbours Act (Northern Ireland) 1970, to extend the limits within which the authority has jurisdiction for the purposes of pilotage to include that area and a pilotage direction given by it shall not apply to that area unless the limits have been so extended.

(6) A competent harbour authority shall arrange for any pilotage direction given by it to be published in such manner as to bring it to the notice of those persons likely to be interested.

DEFINITIONS
    "area": see s.1(1), (3).
    "assistant": see s.3(10).
    "authorised pilot": ss.3, 31(1).
    "competent harbour authority": ss.1(1), 31(1).
    "compulsory pilotage": see also ss.15–16.
    "harbour": ss.1(1), 31(1).
    "harbour operations": s.31(1).
    "harbour order": Harbours Act (Northern Ireland) 1970, s.1.
    "harbour revision order": Harbours Act 1964, s.14.
    "navigating". see s.31(2).

"pilot": s.31(1).
"pilotage": s.31(1).
"pilotage direction": ss.7(1), 31(1).
"ship": s.31(1).

GENERAL NOTE

The Act is not expressed to provide the exclusive means for making pilotage compulsory. This may, therefore, (albeit rarely, if at all) occur by other means—as it did under the Defence of the Realm (Consolidation) Act 1914, s.1(d) (see *The Nord* [1916] P. 53; *The Penrith Castle* [1918] P. 142).

In principle, however, the decision rests with competent harbour authorities. By s.2, they have a duty to consider whether pilotage should be made compulsory and, if so, in what circumstances. Subject to having the necessary jurisdiction over the relevant area (which may be extended under s.7(5)) and to having consulted interested parties under s.7(4), they have (under s.7(1)–(2)) a wide discretion as to the circumstances in which pilotage can be made compulsory.

The previous pilotage legislation contained a number of detailed provisions for vessels excepted from the requirement of compulsory pilotage. This is now also generally a matter for the authority's discretion (see s.7(2)(a)). However, it is specifically provided that ships of less than 20 metres in length and fishing boats of which the registered length is less than 47.5 metres cannot be included (s.7(3)). The effect of the subsection, is that most pleasure craft and all but the largest yachts will be exempted from compulsory pilotage, as will small fishing vessels.

The term "fishing boat" is not defined in this Act. In Pt. IV (Fishing Boats) of the Merchant Shipping Act 1894, unless the context otherwise requires, the expression "fishing boat" means a vessel of whatever size, and in whatever way propelled, which is for the time being employed in sea fishing or in the sea-fishing service. In the Merchant Shipping Act 1970, the term "fishing boat" has the same meaning as in Pt. IV of the 1894 Act, except that it includes a vessel which is being constructed for the purpose of being employed in sea fishing or in the sea-fishing service. The term "fishing vessel" appears in the Fishing Vessels (Safety Provisions) Act 1970 and is defined by s.9 thereof as meaning a vessel which is for the time being used for or in connection with sea fishing but not including a vessel used for fishing otherwise than for profit. The Merchant Shipping Act 1970, s.100(3), Sched. 5 deleted from the 1894 Act the exclusion from the definition therein of vessels used for catching fish otherwise than for profit.

The previous legislation specifically exempted "ships belonging to Her Majesty" from the requirement of compulsory pilotage (this may have included Royal Fleet Auxiliaries, see Chorley & Giles, *Shipping Law* (7th ed., 1980), p.256). There is no reference to Crown ships in the new Act but the general effect of the law is presumably unchanged in that, in the absence of contrary intention, statutes do not bind the Crown.

A CHA must, under subs. (4), consult interested persons before extending compulsory pilotage within the area for which it is competent—including such area as extended under s.1(3) (see General Note to s.1). Where it proposes to extend compulsory pilotage beyond its area, it has no direct powers but, under subs. (5), must seek a harbour revision order (or, in Northern Ireland, a harbour order), which is subject to objections to the Secretary of State. The effect of such an order is that it can exercise all of its functions as a CHA over the enlarged area, not only those in respect of compulsory pilotage, but the object of the subs. is not to give it other functions over that area. See also ss.12–13.

The fact that pilotage is not compulsory does not preclude a ship from taking a pilot or relieve it from liability where it is negligent not to take one (see *The Truculent* [1952] P. 1).

Pilotage exemption certificates

8.—(1) Subject to subsection (3) below, a competent harbour authority which has given a pilotage direction shall, on application by any person who is bona fide the master or first mate of any ship, grant a certificate (in this Act referred to as a "pilotage exemption certificate") to him if it is satisfied (by examination or by reference to such other requirements as it may reasonably impose)—

(a) that his skill, experience and local knowledge are sufficient for him to be capable of piloting the ship of which he is a master or first mate (or that and any other ships specified in the certificate) within its harbour or such part of its harbour as may be so specified; and

(b) in any case where it appears to the authority to be necessary in the interests of safety, that his knowledge of English is sufficient for that purpose.

(2) The requirements imposed under subsection (1) above—

(a) must not be unduly onerous having regard to the difficulties and danger of navigation in the harbour in question; and

(b) must not be more onerous than those required to be met by a person (other than a person who immediately before the appointed day was the holder of a licence under section 12 of the Pilotage Act 1983 or a time-expired apprentice pilot or recognised assistant pilot within the meaning of section 3 above) applying to the authority for authorisation under section 3 above.

(3) If the Secretary of State is satisfied, on application by a competent harbour authority, that it is appropriate to do so by reason of the unusual hazards involved in shipping movements within its harbour, he may direct that during such period (not exceeding three years) as he may specify, notwithstanding that the authority is satisfied as mentioned in subsection (1) above, it may refuse to grant pilotage exemption certificates under that subsection.

(4) Where a direction is given in respect of a competent harbour authority under subsection (3) above any pilotage exemption certificate granted by the authority shall cease to have effect and the authority shall notify the holders of such certificates of that fact.

(5) A pilotage exemption certificate shall not remain in force for more than one year from the date on which it is granted, but—

(a) if the holder continues to be the master or first mate of a ship, may be renewed annually by the competent harbour authority on application by the holder if the authority continues to be satisfied as mentioned in subsection (1) above; and

(b) on the application of the holder may be altered so as to refer to different ships from those to which it previously referred if the authority is so satisfied as respects those ships.

(6) A competent harbour authority may suspend or revoke a certificate granted by it under this section if it appears to it that the holder has been guilty of any incompetence or misconduct affecting his capability to pilot the ship of which he is a master or first mate or any other ships specified in the certificate.

(7) Before refusing an application by any person under this section for the grant, renewal or alteration of a certificate or suspending or revoking a certificate held by any person a competent harbour authority shall give him written notice of its intention to do so, stating the reasons for which it proposes to act, and shall give him a reasonable opportunity of making representations.

(8) A competent harbour authority may charge such fees in respect of any examination required to be taken for the purposes of this section or the grant, renewal or alteration of any pilotage exemption certificate as the authority considers reasonable for the purposes of meeting its administrative costs in connection therewith.

DEFINITIONS

"the appointed day": ss.1(1), 31(1).
"competent harbour authority": ss.1(1), 31(1).
"harbour": ss.1(1), 31(1).
"licence": s.3(3); see also Pilotage Act 1983, s.12.
"master": s.31(1).
"pilotage direction": ss.7(1), 31(1).
"pilotage exemption certificate": ss.8(1), 31(1).
"recognised assistant pilot": s.3(10).

"Secretary of State": see General Note to s.31.
"ship": s.31(1).
"time-experienced apprentice pilot": s.3(10).

GENERAL NOTE

Pilotage authorities have had a power to grant pilotage certificates to masters and first mates, in accordance with specified criteria under the Pilotage Act 1983, s.20, and the Act, in s.26, provided a procedure for appeal against the exercise of the authority's powers to the Secretary of State, which procedure was exclusive, except in relation to judicial review (*The Dana Anglia* [1982] 2 Lloyd's Rep. 14; see also *R.* v. *Trinity House London Pilotage Committee, ex p. Jensen* [1985] 2 C.M.L.R. 413).

The object of the new section is that, in a compulsory pilotage area, the CHA is obliged to issue a pilotage exemption certificate to a master or first mate who meets the relevant criteria. There is no power to restrict the issue, *e.g.,* as a means of discriminating to protect cabotage, because of the régime operating on a relevant ship (*e.g.* in relation to the physical conditions and the level of manning), the nationality of the applicant, the vessel's flag, the vessel's trading patterns and regularity with which it uses the port, or the fact that the more extensive grant of such certificates may contribute to the decline in the British merchant fleet and decrease the potential pool of British masters and first mates from which British pilots have traditionally been drawn. The Government's policy of reducing the costs of using British ports is underlined by the extension of the class of persons eligible for such certificates (previously it was mainly citizens of the EEC and the Commonwealth). The certificate need not be restricted to use on one ship.

Since a pilotage exemption certificate relates only to a master's or first mate's ability to navigate his vessel within the CHA's area, it is envisaged that the qualifications necessary for a certificate will not be as stringent or as extensive as for authorisation of a pilot, who will be required to handle a variety of sizes and types of vessel. Subs. (2) ensures that the requirements for a certificate must at the most be not more onerous than those for authorisation.

Under subs. (3), application can be made to the Secretary of State in cases of unusual hazards (which may relate to navigation, the nature of cargoes carried, etc.) to issue a direction granting CHA's a discretion for a limited period to refuse such certificates. However, the intention of the Act is that a CHA should only refuse to issue a pilotage exemption certificate on grounds relating to an individual's competence, experience and local knowledge, and not because the vessel is carrying a dangerous cargo, because the cargo does not in itself affect the master's competence to navigate the vessel. It is therefore envisaged that the Secretary of State's power under s.8(3), to exempt CHAs from the normal obligation to issue certificates, will only be exercised exceptionally.

Prevention of discrimination in favour of authority's ships

9. A competent harbour authority shall secure that any ship owned or operated by it and used by it in the exercise of its functions otherwise than under this Act is subject to the same obligations as respects pilotage whilst navigating within its harbour as any other ship.

DEFINITIONS
"competent harbour authority": ss.1(1), 31(1).
"functions": see General Note to s.31.
"harbour" ss.1(1), 31(1).
"navigating": see s.31(2).
"pilotage": s.31(1).
"ship": s.31(1).

Charging by authorities

Pilotage charges

10.—(1) A competent harbour authority may make reasonable charges in respect of the pilotage services provided by it.

(2) Without prejudice to the generality of subsection (1) above, the charges to be made under that subsection may include—

(a) charges for the services of a pilot authorised by the authority;
(b) charges in respect of any expenses reasonably incurred by such a pilot in connection with the provision of his services as a pilot;
(c) charges by way of penalties payable in cases where the estimated time of arrival or departure of a ship is not notified as required by the authority or the ship does not arrive or depart at the notified time;
(d) charges in respect of the cost of providing, maintaining and operating pilot boats for the area; and
(e) charges in respect of any other costs involved in providing and maintaining the pilotage organisation provided by the authority.

(3) A competent harbour authority which has given a pilotage direction may also make reasonable charges in respect of any ship navigating within the area to which the direction applies under the pilotage of a master or first mate who is the holder of a pilotage exemption certificate in respect of the area and ship in question.

(4) Different charges may be made under this section in different circumstances.

(5) A competent harbour authority shall arrange for the charges to be made by it under this section to be published in such manner as to bring them to the notice of those persons likely to be interested.

(6) Subsections (2) to (12) of section 31 of the Harbours Act 1964, or in Northern Ireland subsections (1) and (3) to (11) of section 7 of the Harbours Act (Northern Ireland) 1970, (right of objection to ship, passenger and goods dues) shall apply as respects charges imposed by an authority by virtue of this section as they apply as respects charges to which section 31 or, as the case may be, section 7 applies but—
(a) with the substitution for the references to the persons mentioned in section 31(2)(a) and (b) and (3)(b) or, as the case may be, section 7(1)(a) and (b) and (3)(b) of references to—
(i) the owners of ships which customarily navigate in the harbour in question;
(ii) any persons who carry on harbour operations within that harbour; and
(iii) any other harbour authority to whose harbour ships obtain access through that harbour,
or, in any of those cases, persons representative of them; and
(b) with the omission of section 31(2)(i) and (iii) or, as the case may be, 7(1)(i) and (iii).

(7) Charges imposed by a competent harbour authority under this section shall be recoverable as a civil debt or in any other manner in which ship, passenger and goods dues are recoverable by the authority.

(8) In subsection (7) above "ship, passenger and goods dues" has the same meaning as in the Harbours Act 1964 or, in Northern Ireland, the Harbours Act (Northern Ireland) 1970.

DEFINITIONS
  "area": see s.1(1), (3).
  "authorised pilot": ss.3, 31(1).
  "charges": *cf.* Harbours Act 1964, s.57(1); Harbours Act (Northern Ireland) 1970, s.38(1).
  "competent harbour authority": ss.1(1), 31(1).
  "goods": see Harbours Act 1964, s.57(1); Harbours Act (Northern Ireland) 1970, s.38(1).
  "harbour": ss.1(1), 31(1).
  "harbour authority": s.31(1).
  "harbour operations": s.31(1).
  "master": s.31(1).
  "navigate": see s.31(2).
  "navigating": see s.31(2).
  "pilot": s.31(1).

"pilot boat": ss.6(1), 31(1).
"pilotage": s.31(1).
"pilotage direction": ss.7(1), 31(1).
"pilotage exemption certificate": ss.8(1), 31(1).
"ship": s.31(1).
"ship, passenger and goods dues": Harbours Act 1964, s.57(j); Harbours Act (Northern Ireland) 1970, s.38(1).

GENERAL NOTE
Pilotage charges have traditionally been recoverable by proceedings *in rem* or *in personam* in the Admiralty Court, which has always had jurisdiction over pilotage services outside the body of a county (*The Nelson* (1805) 6 C.Rob. 227; *The Bee* (1822) 2 Dods. 498) and treated the pilot as a seaman and his remuneration as wages (Supreme Court Act 1981, s.20(2)(*l*); *The Ambatielos, The Cephalonia* [1923] P. 68; *cf. Ross* v. *Walker* (1765) 2 Wilson 264). Claims in the nature of pilotage also fall within the admiralty jurisdiction of county courts (County Courts Act 1984, s.27(1)(*h*)).

It is unlikely that a maritime lien exists for pilotage charges, since it is generally speaking the policy of admiralty law not to grant such secret liens in respect of ordinary commercial transactions such as the contract of pilotage (*The Ambatielos, The Cephalonia* [1923] P. 68, 72; *cf. La Constancia* (1846) 2 Wm.Rob. 460. See also *The St. Lawrence* (1880) 5 P.D. 250).

The Pilotage Act 1983, s.65, provided that, if a vessel, which had on board a licensed pilot, led another ship, which did not have a pilot on board, when that other ship could not be boarded due to particular circumstances, the same pilotage charges would be payable in respect of the ship so led as if the pilot had actually been on board and in charge of that ship. The section sought to ensure that, where a ship was led by a vessel which was the direct recipient of pilotage services, the second ship was not unjustly enriched and would have to make restitution for the benefit received. The provision is not reproduced in the 1987 Act but is presumably a matter with respect to which a CHA may decide to impose pilotage charges under s.10(1). If not, the second ship may be liable at common law.

Although there is a charge under s.8 for the administrative cost of issuing pilotage exemption certificates, an additional charge for the use of the port by ships piloted by certificated persons is also made under s.10(3) for the improvement in safety which a well-run pilotage service provides.

Agents and joint arrangements

Use of agents and joint arrangements

11.—(1) A competent harbour authority may arrange for its functions in relation to the provision of pilotage services (other than its functions under sections 2(1), 3(1), 4(2), 6(1)(b), 7(1), 8(1) above or section 28 below or its function of determining the qualifications to be required from persons applying for authorisation under section 3(2) above or any charge to be imposed under section 10(1) or (3) above) to be exercised on its behalf by such other persons as it thinks fit and may establish such companies as it thinks fit to exercise those functions on its behalf.

(2) A competent harbour authority may arrange for all or any of its functions relating to pilotage other than its duty under section 2(1) above to be exercised on its behalf by another competent harbour authority.

(3) Two or more competent harbour authorities may arrange to discharge any of their functions relating to pilotage jointly and such arrangements may provide for the discharge of such functions by a joint committee or any other body established by the authorities for that purpose.

(4) An authority which has entered into arrangements with another authority under subsection (2) or (3) above may withdraw from the arrangements on giving reasonable notice to the other authority.

DEFINITIONS
"competent harbour authority": ss.1(1), 31(1).
"functions": see General Note to s.31.
"pilotage": s.31(1).

GENERAL NOTE
For centuries, pilots have acted as self-employed persons and Trinity House, which currently has responsibility for nearly a half of the country's pilotage districts, has played a central role in pilotage affairs nationally. The essential decentralisation of pilotage matters to local CHAs has been effected with provision for self-employment to continue and, if CHAs decide to avail themselves of its services, with the possibility of use being made of Trinity House's long experience by arrangements with the recently formed Trinity House Agency Services Ltd. (THAS)—or, indeed, any other agency that may be formed. Such agencies will be able to offer their services to any CHA (thus, THAS is not confined to previous Trinity House districts) and can make different arrangements with pilots (whom they may contract with under contracts of service or for services). The effect of the legislation (including the abolition of the Pilotage Commission: s.26) ensures, however, that, apart from the minimal role of the Secretary of State, no body is guaranteed a central role in the administration of pilotage.

Information and directions as to joint arrangements

12.—(1) Where—

(a) the harbours of two or more competent harbour authorities fall wholly or partly within a single former pilotage district;

(b) access for ships to the harbour of a competent harbour authority is customarily available through the harbour of another competent harbour authority;

(c) there is any person other than the competent harbour authority who carries on harbour operations within the harbour of a competent harbour authority;

(d) there is any person who carries on harbour operations in a harbour (within the meaning of the Harbours Act 1964) which is not the harbour of a competent harbour authority and access to which is customarily available through the harbour of a competent harbour authority; or

(e) the harbour of a competent harbour authority and a dockyard port (within the meaning of the Dockyard Ports Regulation Act 1865) for which a Queen's harbour master has been appointed under that Act fall wholly or partly within a single former pilotage district,

the Secretary of State may require any of the authorities or, in the case of paragraph (c), (d) or (e) above, the authority concerned to provide him with such information as he may require concerning the arrangements made or proposed by the authorities or authority in question for the provision of pilotage services and that information shall be provided in such form as the Secretary of State may require.

(2) If the Secretary of State considers that any arrangements of which particulars are provided under subsection (1) above are not satisfactory he may—

(a) direct that they shall have effect subject to such modifications as he may specify in the direction; or

(b) direct the authorities or authority concerned to make different arrangements.

(3) If the statement provided under subsection (1) above is to the effect that no arrangements have been made or proposed by the authorities or authority in question for the provision of pilotage services in the area concerned and the Secretary of State considers that such arrangements should be made, he shall direct the authorities or authority in question to make appropriate arrangements.

(4) Section 11(4) above shall not apply to any arrangements made or modified by virtue of a direction under this section.

DEFINITIONS
"competent harbour authority": ss.1(1), 31(1).
"dockyard port": Dockyard Ports Act 1865, s.2.
"former pilotage districts": ss.1(2), 31(1).
"harbour": ss.1(1), 12(1)(d), 31(1).
"harbour operations": s.31(1).
"pilotage": s.31(1).
"pilotge district": see Pilotage Act 1983, s.68(1).
"Queen's harbour master": Dockyard Ports Act 1865, s.4.
"Secretary of State": see General Note to s.31.
"ship": s.31(1).

GENERAL NOTE
S.12 gives powers to the Secretary of State but, where he does not exercise them, does not ensure that such information will be given.
S.12(1)(d) was added to the Bill to enable the Secretary of State to ensure that proper arrangements are made for estuaries and for the resolution of disputes between the operator and the CHA.
See also s.1(3) and s.7(5) and the General Notes with respect to them. See also s.13.
The word "harbour", in relation to a competent harbour authority, is generally defined in s.1(1) (see s.31(1)). However, for the purposes of s.12(1)(d), the definition in the Harbours Act 1964, s.57(1) applies. The definition in the 1964 Act is similar to, but not identical with, that in the Harbours Act (Northern Ireland) 1970, s.38(1), to which reference is not made here, unlike elsewhere in the current Act, which applies to Northern Ireland: see s.33 and General Note thereto.

Resolution of disputes between authorities

13.—(1) Where any dispute arises between two or more competent harbour authorities concerning—
  (a) arrangements for the provision of pilotage services made by one authority which affect navigation in another authority's harbour;
  (b) arrangements made by two or more authorities for the discharge of their functions in relation to pilotage jointly; or
  (c) any statement required to be prepared or arrangements required to be made under section 12 above,
or between a competent harbour authority and such a person as mentioned in section 12(1)(c), (d) or (e) above concerning arrangements for the provision of pilotage services made by the authority which affect navigation in the harbour of the competent harbour authority or such a statement or arrangement, any party to the dispute may appeal to the Secretary of State.
  (2) On an appeal under subsection (1) above the Secretary of State shall settle the dispute in such manner as he considers appropriate and may in particular direct—
  (a) that such arrangements as are mentioned in that subsection shall not have effect or shall have effect subject to such modifications as he may specify; or
  (b) in the case of a dispute between two competent harbour authorities, that one authority only shall exercise functions under this Act in relation to any area in respect of which there is a dispute.
  (3) The arrangements mentioned in subsection (1) above include arrangements concerning which a previous dispute has been settled under subsection (2) above and arrangements made or modified by virtue of that subsection.

DEFINITIONS
"competent harbour authority": ss.1(1), 31(1).
"functions": see General Note to s.31.

"pilotage": s.31(1).
"Secretary of State": see General Note to s.31.

Accounts

Accounts

14.—(1) Regulations under section 42 of the Harbours Act 1964 may require any authority to which that section applies which is a competent harbour authority to make available for inspection by the public any statement of accounts required to be prepared by it under that section which relate to the activities of the authority (or any agent of the authority) in relation to pilotage.

(2) Regulations under section 30(1) of the Harbours Act (Northern Ireland) 1970 may require any harbour authority which is a competent harbour authority to make available for inspection by the public any statement of accounts to which that section applies which relates to any such activities of the authority (or any agent of the authority).

(3) Where any such activities of a competent harbour authority are carried out on its behalf by any agent, the agent shall furnish the authority with all such information concerning those activities as the authority may reasonably require to fulfil its obligations in relation to any such statement of accounts.

DEFINITIONS
"competent harbour authority": ss.1(1), 31(1).
"harbour authority": s.31(1).
"pilotage": s.31(1).

PART II

GENERAL PROVISIONS CONCERNING PILOTAGE

Compulsory pilotage

Compulsory pilotage

15.—(1) A ship which is being navigated in an area and in circumstances in which pilotage is compulsory for it by virtue of a pilotage direction shall be—

(a) under the pilotage of an authorised pilot accompanied by such an assistant, if any, as is required by virtue of the direction; or

(b) under the pilotage of a master or first mate possessing a pilotage exemption certificate in respect of that area and ship.

(2) If any ship is not under pilotage as required by subsection (1) above after an authorised pilot has offered to take charge of the ship, the master of the ship shall be guilty of an offence and liable on summary conviction to a fine not exceeding level 5 on the standard scale.

(3) If the master of a ship navigates the ship in an area and in circumstances in which pilotage is compulsory for it by virtue of a pilotage direction without notifying the competent harbour authority which gave the direction that he proposes to do so, he shall be guilty of an offence

and liable on summary conviction to a fine not exceeding level 2 on the standard scale.

DEFINITIONS
    "area": see ss.1(1), (3).
    "assistant": see s.3(10).
    "authorised pilot": ss.3, 31(1).
    "competent harbour authority": ss.1(1), 31(1).
    "compulsory pilotage": see also s.7.
    "master": s.31(1).
    "(being) navigated": see s.31(2).
    "pilotage": s.31(1).
    "pilotage direction": ss.7(1), 31(1).
    "pilotage exemption certificate": ss.8(1), 31(1).
    "ship": s.31(1).
    "the standard scale": Criminal Justice Act 1982, s.75.

GENERAL NOTE
    An authorised pilot has not "offered to take charge of the ship" under subs. (2) unless he has made a specific offer in relation to the particular movement of the vessel in question at the time his services are required. A general advertisement of the availability of pilotage services is insufficient (*Montague* v. *Babbs* [1972] 1 W.L.R. 176; see also *Babbs* v. *Press* [1971] 1 W.L.R. 1739) as is an offer to pilot the vessel at a later time (*The Ignition* [1983] 1 Lloyd's Rep. 382). A master is not obliged to seek out such an offer but he cannot avoid liability under the subsection if he fails to discharge his implied duty to keep a look-out for such an offer (*Rindby* v. *Brewis* (1926) 25 Ll.L.R. 26). If no offer is made, a ship may nonetheless lawfully navigate in a compulsory pilotage area without a pilot and without liability to pay pilotage charges (*Muller* v. *Trinity House* [1925] 1 K.B. 166).

Liability for ships under compulsory pilotage

16. The fact that a ship is being navigated in an area and in circumstances in which pilotage is compulsory for it shall not affect any liability of the owner or master of the ship for any loss or damage caused by the ship or by the manner in which it is navigated.

DEFINITIONS
    "compulsory pilotage": see ss.7, 15.
    "master": s.31(1).
    "(being) navigated": see s.31(2).
    "pilotage": s.31(1).
    "ship": s.31(1).

GENERAL NOTE
    At common law, it was considered unjust that shipowners should be held liable for the fault of a compulsory pilot, *i.e.* someone whom they were compelled to employ and who was entitled to override the authority of the master otherwise in charge of the ship (see *The Maria* (1839) 1 W. Rob. 95, 99; *The Ticonderoga* (1857) Swab. 215, 217; *The Halley* (1868) L.R. 2 P.C. 193, 202; *The Hector* (1883) 8 P.D. 218, 224; *The Beechgrove* [1916] 1 A.C. 364; *Workington Dock and Harbour Board* v. *Towerfield* (*Owners*) [1949] P. 10, *per* Bucknill L.J. [1951] A.C. 112).
    In 1910, the Convention for the Unification of certain rules of Law respecting Collisions was signed at Brussels (see Marsden, *Collisions at Sea,* 11th ed., paras. 1271 *et seq.*) Art. 5 provided: "The liability imposed by the preceding Article [for collisions] attaches in cases where the collision is caused by the fault of a pilot, even where the pilot is carried by compulsion of law." The current section is the result of Parliament's attempt to enact Art. 5 and to abolish the defence of compulsory pilotage. It attempts to do so generally, howsoever liability arises—whether under a public or local Act, under Defence of the Realm Regulations (*The Chyebassa* [1918] P. 201) or otherwise (see also *The Mostyn* [1926] P. 46, reversed [1928] A.C. 57). Nevertheless, it only does so domestically to the extent of the applicability of the Act, which only purports to extend to the United Kingdom, including Northern Ireland (s.33). Therefore, in accordance with the double actionability rule in *Phillips* v. *Eyre* (1870) L.R. 6 Q.B. 1 (to be interpreted in the light of *Boys* v. *Chaplin*

[1971] A.C. 356), a defendant in an English court may plead that the tort which he is alleged to have committed took place within a jurisdiction in which the defence of compulsory pilotage remains available, so defeating both the plaintiff's claim (see *The Halley, supra; The Arum* [1921] P. 12; *The Waziristan* [1953] 1 W.L.R. 1446) and the overall intent of Art. 5 of the Brussels Convention. Fortunately, the practical difficulties inherent in this situation are diminished by the extent to which the defence is not available in other jurisdictions, in accordance with the policy in Art. 5 of the Brussels Convention.

Rights of pilots

Right of authorised pilot to supersede unauthorised pilot

17.—(1) An authorised pilot may, within the harbour in relation to which or a part of which he is authorised, supersede as the pilot of a ship any unauthorised person who has been employed to pilot it.

(2) If the master of any ship navigates it in any part of a harbour under the pilotage of an unauthorised person without first notifying the competent harbour authority that he proposes to do so, he shall be guilty of an offence.

(3) If an unauthorised person pilots a ship within a harbour knowing that an authorised pilot has offered to pilot it, he shall be guilty of an offence.

(4) If the master of a ship navigating within a harbour knowingly employs or continues to employ an unauthorised person to pilot the ship after an authorised pilot has offered to pilot it, he shall be guilty of an offence.

(5) For the purposes of this section—

   (a) a person is an unauthorised person if he is neither an authorised pilot nor the holder of a pilotage exemption certificate in respect of the ship and the area in question; and

   (b) any person (other than the master or one of the crew of a ship) who is on the bridge of the ship or in any other position from which the ship is navigated (whether on board or elsewhere) shall be deemed to be piloting the ship unless he proves otherwise.

(6) Any person who is guilty of an offence under this section shall be liable on summary conviction to a fine not exceeding—

   (a) in the case of an offence under subsection (2) above, level 2 on the standard scale; and

   (b) in the case of an offence under subsection (3) or (4) above, level 4 on the standard scale.

(7) Subsections (1) to (4) above do not apply—

   (a) to a ship which a person is piloting or ordered to pilot in a dockyard port (within the meaning of the Dockyard Ports Regulation Act 1865) in the course of his duties as a servant of the Crown; or

   (b) if the competent harbour authority has directed that those subsections shall not apply to movements in its harbour or a specified part of its harbour for the purpose of changing a ship or a ship of a specified description from one mooring to another or of taking it into or out of any dock, to a ship or a ship of that description being moved in that harbour or that part for that purpose;

but nothing in paragraph (a) above shall be construed as derogating from any immunity which affects such a ship as there mentioned apart from that paragraph.

(8) A competent harbour authority shall not give a direction under subsection (7)(b) above unless the area in relation to which it will apply is either—

    (a) an area in relation to which a bye-law under section 38 of the Pilotage Act 1983 (exemptions from compulsory pilotage for ships moving within harbours, docks etc.) was in force immediately before the appointed day; or

    (b) a closed dock, lock or other closed work which is not in a former pilotage district.

DEFINITIONS

"the appointed day": ss.1(2), 31(1).
"area": see ss.1(1), (3).
"authorised pilot": ss.3, 31(1).
"competent harbour authority": ss.1(1), 31(1).
"compulsory pilotage": see ss.7, 15.
"dock": see Harbours Act 1964, s.57(1); Harbours Act (Northern Ireland) 1970, s.38(1).
"dockyard port": Dockyard Ports Act 1865, s.2.
"former pilotage district": ss.1(2), 31(1).
"harbour": ss.1(1), 31(1).
"master": s.31(1).
"(is) navigated": see s.31(2).
"navigating": see s.31(2).
"pilot": s.31(1).
"pilotage": s.31(1).
"pilotage district": see Pilotage Act 1983, s.68(1).
"pilotage exemption certificate": ss.8(1), 31(1).
"ship": s.31(1).
"standard scale": Criminal Justice Act 1982, s.75.
"unauthorised person": s.17(5).

GENERAL NOTE

An amendment specifically to *require* CHAs to have regard under subs. (7) to the size and nature of cargoes they carry or may carry, and so to give weight to safety considerations when issuing directions under subs. (7)(b), was withdrawn in the face of the Government's view that the term "ship of a specified description" *allows* them to consider the size of ship and the nature of its cargo.

Subs. (8) limits the power to make directions under subs. (7)(b) to areas where ship movements of the type described may presently be carried out by groups other than licensed pilots. The only area in subs. (7)(a)—*i.e.* one covered by a relevant bye-law made under the existing legislation—is the port of the present London pilotage district where work is carried out by watermen. Dock pilots working in a closed dock which currently falls outside a pilotage district, but which will fall within the area of a CHA, would lose their present immunity from supersession if, by virtue of subs. (8), subs. (7)(b) were not applied in such places.

Declaration as to draught etc. of ship

18.—(1) A pilot may require the master of any ship which he is piloting to declare its draught of water, length and beam, and to provide him with such other information relating to the ship or its cargo as the pilot specifies and is necessary to enable him to carry out his duties as the pilot of the ship.

(2) The master of a ship shall bring to the notice of any person who pilots the ship any defects in, and any matter peculiar to, the ship and its machinery and equipment of which the master knows and which might materially affect the navigation of the ship.

(3) Any master of a ship who—

    (a) refuses to comply with a request made to him in pursuance of subsection (1) above; or

    (b) makes a statement which is false in a material particular in answer to such a request, knowing it to be false or being reckless as to whether it is false, or fails without reasonable excuse to correct such a statement made by another person in

answer to such a request, although himself knowing it to be
false; or

(c) without reasonable excuse contravenes subsection (2) above,
shall be guilty of an offence.

(4) Any person who is guilty of an offence under this section shall be
liable on summary conviction to a fine not exceeding—

(a) in the case of an offence under subsection (3)(b) above, level 5 on
the standard scale, and

(b) in any other case, level 4 on the standard scale.

DEFINITIONS
 "master": s.31(1).
 "pilot": s.31(1).
 "ship": s.31(1).

Authorised pilot not to be taken out of his area

19.—(1) A master of a ship shall not without reasonable excuse take an
authorised pilot without his consent beyond the point up to which he has
been engaged to pilot the ship.

(2) A person who contravenes subsection (1) above shall be guilty of an
offence and liable on summary conviction to a fine not exceeding level 5
on the standard scale.

DEFINITIONS
 "authorised pilot": ss.3, 31(1).
 "master": s.31(1).
 "ship": s.31(1).
 "the standard scale": Criminal Justice Act 1982, s.35.

Facilities to be given for pilot boarding leaving ship

20.—(1) Where—

(a) the master of a ship, which is navigating in an area in circumstances in which pilotage is compulsory for it but is not under
the pilotage of an authorised pilot or a master or first mate
possessing a pilotage exemption certificate in respect of the
ship and the area, is offered the services of an authorised pilot;
or

(b) the master of a ship accepts the services of an authorised pilot
in any other circumstances,

he shall facilitate the pilot boarding and subsequently leaving the ship.

(2) If the master of any ship without reasonable excuse contravenes this
section he shall be guilty of an offence and liable on summary conviction
to a fine not exceeding level 4 on the standard scale.

DEFINITIONS
 "area": see ss.1(1), (3).
 "authorised pilot": ss.3, 31(1).
 "compulsory pilotage": see ss.7, 15.
 "master": s.31(1).
 "(is) navigating": see s.31(2).
 "pilotage": s.31(1).
 "pilotage exemption certificate": ss.8(1), 31(1).
 "ship": s.31(1).
 "the standard scale": Criminal Justice Act 1982, s.75.

GENERAL NOTE
 There is no obligation on the navigating ship to go and search for a pilot, but there is a
continuing obligation to take reasonable steps to keep a look-out for one (*Rindby* v.

Brewis (1926) 25 Ll.L.R. 27). A deliberate attempt to avoid taking on board a pilot will be an offence under this section.

As to the circumstances in which the master "is offered the services of an authorised pilot", *cf.* the General Note to s.15.

Misconduct by pilots

Misconduct by pilot endangering ship or persons on board ship

21.—(1) If the pilot of a ship—

    (a) does any act which causes or is likely to cause the loss or destruction of, or serious damage to, the ship or its machinery, navigational equipment or safety equipment, or the death of, or serious injury to, a person on board the ship; or

    (b) omits to do anything required to preserve the ship or its machinery, navigational equipment or safety equipment from loss, destruction or serious damage or to preserve any person on board the ship from death or serious injury,

and the act or omission is deliberate or amounts to a breach or neglect of duty or he is under the influence of drink or a drug at the time of the act or omission, he shall be guilty of an offence.

(2) A person who is guilty of an offence under this section shall be liable—

    (a) on summary conviction, to imprisonment for a term not exceeding 6 months or a fine not exceeding the statutory maximum or both; or

    (b) on conviction on indictment, to imprisonment for a term not exceeding 2 years or a fine or both.

DEFINITIONS

"pilot": s.31(1).

"ship": s.31(1).

"the statutory maximum": Criminal Justice Act 1982, s.74.

Limitation of liability

Limitation of liability in respect of pilots

22.—(1) The liability of an authorised pilot for any loss or damage caused by any act or omission of his whilst acting as such a pilot shall not exceed £1,000 and the amount of the pilotage charges in respect of the voyage during which the liability arose.

(2) For the purposes of subsection (1) above a person shall be deemed to be an authorised pilot notwithstanding that he is acting as a pilot of a ship navigating outside the area in relation to which he is authorised if—

    (a) he is piloting the ship to that area from a place where pilots authorised for that harbour regularly board ships navigating to it; or

    (b) he is piloting the ship from that harbour to a place where such pilots regularly leave ships navigating from it; and

    (c) in either case, the ship is one in respect of which he is authorised.

(3) Where, without any such personal act or omission by a competent harbour authority as is mentioned in Article 4 of the Convention in Part I of Schedule 4 to the Merchant Shipping Act 1979, any loss or damage to any ship, to any property on board any ship or to any property or rights of any kind is caused by an authorised pilot employed by it, the authority shall not be liable to damages beyond the amount of £1,000 multiplied by the number of authorised pilots employed by it at the date when the loss or damage occurs.

(4) Where, without any such personal act or omission as mentioned in subsection (3) above by a person providing pilotage services on behalf of a competent harbour authority ("the agent"), any such loss or damage as there mentioned is caused by an authorised pilot employed by him, the agent shall not be liable to damages beyond the amount of £1,000 multiplied by the number of authorised pilots employed by him providing pilotage services for that authority at the date when the loss or damage occurs.

(5) The limit of liability under this section shall apply to the whole of any losses and damages which may arise upon any one distinct occasion although such losses and damages may be sustained by more than one person.

(6) Where any proceedings are taken against any person ("the defendant") for any act or omission in respect of which liability is limited as provided by this section and other claims are or appear likely to be made in respect of the same act or omission, the court in which the proceedings are taken may—

(a) determine the amount of the liability;
(b) upon payment by the defendant of that amount into court, distribute that amount rateably amongst the claimants;
(c) stay, or in Scotland sist, any proceedings pending in any other court in relation to the same matter;
(d) proceed in such manner and subject to such requirements as the court thinks just—
    (i) as to making interested persons parties to the proceedings;
    (ii) as to the exclusion of any claimants whose claims are not made within a certain time;
    (iii) as to requiring security from the defendant; and
    (iv) as to payment of any costs.

(7) Nothing in subsection (3) or (4) above shall affect any liability which may be limited under section 17 or is excluded under section 18 of the Merchant Shipping Act 1979 (liabilities of shipowners).

(8) A competent harbour authority shall not be liable for any loss or damage caused by any act or omission of a pilot authorised by it under section 3 above by virtue only of that authorisation.

(9) In this section "the court" means—
(a) in England and Wales, the High Court;
(b) in Scotland, the Court of Session; and
(c) in Northern Ireland, the High Court.

DEFINITIONS
"the agent": s.22(4).
"area": see ss.1(1), (3).
"authorised pilot": ss.3, 31(1).
"competent harbour authority": ss.1(1), 31(1).
"the court": s.22(9).
"distinct occasion": see *Temperley's Merchant Shipping Acts*, 7th ed. (1976), para. 437, n.19.
"harbour": s.31(1).
"navigating": see s.31(2).
"pilot": s.31(1).
"pilotage": s.31(1).
"pilotage charges": see s.10.
"ship": s.31(1).
"shipowners": see Merchant Shipping Act 1979, s.18(4).

GENERAL NOTE
The limitation provisions in this section are framed generally in accordance with the limitation scheme to be found in the Merchant Shipping Act 1979, ss.17–18 and Sched. 4, Pt. I, enacting the Convention on Limitation of Liability for Maritime Claims 1976.

Subs. (8) provides that the mere fact that a CHA has authorised a pilot does not make it vicariously liable for the pilot's negligence. Moreover, a body which employs a pilot has been held not to be vicariously liable simply on the ground that it is his employer (see *Fowles* v. *Eastern and Australian SS. Co. Ltd.* [1916] 2 A.C. 556 (P.C.); *Oceanic Crest Shipping Co.* v. *Pilbara Harbour Services Pty. Ltd.* (1986) 60 A.L.J.R. 480 (H.C.A.); but *cf.* Rose, *The Modern Law of Pilotage* (1984), 35–37). But the section does not negative the vicarious liability of a CHA for the negligence in the course of his employment of a pilot whom it actually employs. Nor does it relieve it from its own negligence where it has failed to provide a proper pilotage service (see *Anchor Line (Henderson Brothers)* v. *Dundee Harbour Trustees, the Circassia* (1922) 38 T.L.R. 299 (H.L.)).

Deep sea pilotage

Deep sea pilotage certificates

23.—(1) The Secretary of State may authorise any body appearing to him to be competent to do so to grant certificates under this section ("deep sea pilotage certificates") in respect of such part of the sea falling outside the harbour of any competent harbour authority as he may specify.

(2) Any body for the time being authorised under this section may grant a deep sea pilotage certificate to any person on application by him if it is satisfied (by examination or by reference to such criteria as it may reasonably impose) that he is qualified to act as a pilot of a ship for the area in respect of which the body is authorised under subsection (1) above.

DEFINITIONS

"area": see General Note.
"competent harbour authority": ss.1(1), 31(1).
"deep sea pilotage certificate": see also s.28(3).
"harbour": s.31(1).
"pilot": s.31(1).
"Secretary of State": see General Note to s.31.
"ship": s.31(1).

GENERAL NOTE

The relevant "area" in s.23 is, by definition, different from the "area" of a competent harbour authority under s.1(1), (3).

PART III

WINDING-UP OF EXISTING PILOTAGE ORGANISATION

Abolition of pilotage authorities

24.—(1) On the appointed day every pilotage authority within the meaning of the Pilotage Act 1983 shall cease to exist as such an authority.

(2) Not later than such date as the Secretary of State may direct before the appointed day the Pilotage Commission shall submit to the Secretary of State proposals for a scheme or schemes to be made by him for the transfer of the relevant property, rights and liabilities of the pilotage authorities (including in particular liabilities in respect of pensions payable in respect of staff or former staff) and the arrangements to be made in accordance with section 25 below as respects their staff and any staff employed by persons licensed as pilots under section 12 of the Pilotage Act 1983 to whom the Commission considers the arrangements should also apply.

(3) Where only one competent harbour authority is to exercise functions under this Act in the harbours in the former pilotage district of a pilotage authority or, in the case of a pilotage authority which is the authority for

more than one district, in all the districts of the pilotage authority, the proposed scheme or schemes shall provide for any property, rights and liabilities of that pilotage authority which in the opinion of the Pilotage Commission have been used, have accrued or, as the case may be, have been incurred exclusively in connection with its pilotage functions to vest in that competent harbour authority.

(4) In the case of any pilotage authority to which subsection (3) above does not apply, the proposed scheme or schemes—

    (a) shall provide for the vesting in any competent harbour authority the Pilotage Commission considers appropriate or in the Commission itself of any property, rights and liabilities of the pilotage authority which, in the opinion of the Commission, have been used, have accrued or, as the case may be, have been incurred exclusively in connection with the authority's pilotage functions;

    (b) may make similar provision as to any such property, rights and liabilities which, in the opinion of the Commission have been used, have accrued or, as the case may be, have been incurred substantially but not exclusively in connection with those functions; and

    (c) may require any competent harbour authority the Commission considers appropriate to make provision to secure that the future payment of any pension which is payable in respect of staff or former staff of the pilotage authority and calculated by reference to remuneration paid and service given before the appointed day is properly funded or guaranteed.

(5) Proposals submitted under subsection (2) above may include such supplementary and incidental provision in connection with the matters there mentioned as the Pilotage Commission considers appropriate.

(6) Not later than three months before the appointed day the Secretary of State shall make a scheme or schemes giving effect to the proposals submitted to him under subsection (2) above with such modifications as he considers appropriate and on the appointed day the property, rights and liabilities of the pilotage authorities shall vest in accordance with the scheme or schemes.

(7) The modifications which may be made under subsection (6) above include the substitution for a provision for property of a person who is a pilotage authority to vest in a competent harbour authority or the Pilotage Commission of a provision for that person to retain that property and pay to the competent harbour authority or, as the case may be, the Commission such sum as may be agreed between them to be the value of the property at the appointed day.

(8) Nothing in this section shall require a scheme to make provision for the vesting in a competent harbour authority of any property, rights or liabilities already vested in it in its capacity as a pilotage authority.

(9) The Pilotage Commission may require any pilotage authority to furnish it within such time and in such form as the Commission may specify with such information as it considers necessary for the purpose of formulating the proposals to be submitted by it under this section; and any member of the Commission or person appointed by it for the purpose may inspect any books, documents or other records in the possession of the authority relating to any matter in respect of which information is required to be furnished under this subsection.

(10) Before submitting proposals for a scheme under subsection (2) above the Pilotage Commission shall consult the competent harbour authorities and pilotage authorities likely to be affected by the proposals and such persons or organisations as appear to it to be representative of the staff or former staff likely to be affected by them; and before making a scheme giving effect to those proposals the Secretary of State shall consider any representations concerning those proposals made to him by

any such authority or by any person or organisation which appears to him to be so representative.

(11) Where an order is made under section 1(3)(b) above in respect of an authority to which any property, rights or liabilities have been transferred under this section, the order shall, if the Secretary of State considers that it is appropriate for it to do so, make provision for the transfer of them to the authority which he considers should exercise pilotage functions within its harbour.

(12) References in this section and in section 25 below to a pilotage authority include references to any committee appointed by the authority under section 9(1)(e) of the Pilotage Act 1983.

DEFINITIONS
"the appointed day": ss.1(2), 31(1).
"competent harbour authority": ss.1(1), 31(1).
"former pilotage district": ss.1(2), 31(1).
"functions": see General Note to s.31.
"harbour": s.31(1).
"pilot": s.31(1).
"pilotage authority": s.24(12); see also s.1(2) and Pilotage Act 1983, s.68(1).
"Pilotage Commission": see Pilotage Act 1983, s.1(1).
"pilotage district": see Pilotage Act 1983, s.68(1).
"Secretary of State": see General Note to s.31.

Transfer of staff of pilotage authorities etc.

25.—(1) The arrangements to be made under a scheme under section 24 above as respects the staff of pilotage authorities shall apply—
(a) in the case of an authority which will continue to exist in another capacity on and after the appointed day, to such of the persons employed by it immediately before that day as the authority has determined are not required by it for its functions in that other capacity; and
(b) otherwise, to all the persons employed by the authority immediately before that day.

(2) Such a scheme shall provide—
(a) in the case mentioned in subsection (3) of section 24 above, that the staff to whom the scheme applies shall be employed on and after the appointed day by the competent harbour authority there mentioned; and
(b) in the case mentioned in subsection (4) of that section, that the staff to whom it applies shall be employed on and after that day by such competent harbour authority as the Pilotage Commission thinks fit or by the Commission.

(3) Such a scheme may make provision for the payment of compensation to staff of pilotage authorities for any loss of employment which is attributable to any provision made by or under this Act but no such scheme shall affect any person's right to compensation otherwise than under the scheme.

(4) Where such a scheme provides that an employee of a pilotage authority shall be employed by another person on and after the appointed day—
(a) the contract of employment between the employee and the pilotage authority shall not be terminated by the abolition of that authority but shall have effect from the appointed day as if originally made between him and that other person; and
(b) without prejudice to paragraph (a) above—
(i) all the pilotage authority's rights, powers, duties and liabilities under or in connection with such a contract shall

by virtue of this section be transferred on that day to that other person; and

(ii) anything done before that day by or in relation to the authority in respect of that contract or employee shall be deemed on and after that day to have been done by or in relation to that other person.

(5) Subsection (4) above is without prejudice to any right of an employee to terminate his contract of employment if a substantial change is made to his detriment in his working conditions but no such right shall arise by reason only of the change of employer effected by this section.

(6) Where a person formerly employed by a pilotage authority becomes employed by another person by virtue of this section—

(a) Schedule 13 to the Employment Protection (Consolidation) Act 1978 or, in Northern Ireland, Schedule 1 to the Contracts of Employment and Redundancy Payments Act (Northern Ireland) 1965 (computation of period of employment for the purposes of that Act) shall have effect in relation to him as if it included provision—

   (i) that the period of employment with the pilotage authority counted as a period of employment with that other person; and

   (ii) that the change of employer did not break the continuity of the period of employment; and

(b) the period of his employment with the pilotage authority shall count as a period of employment with his new employer for the purposes of any provision of his contract of employment with his new employer which depends on his length of service with him.

(7) Where the Pilotage Commission considers that arrangements under a scheme under section 24 above should also apply to an employee of a person licensed as a pilot under section 12 of the Pilotage Act 1983—

(a) subsections (2) and (3) above shall apply as if the employee were employed by the pilotage authority for the district for which his employer is licensed;

(b) the contract of employment between the employee and the licensed pilot shall have effect from the appointed day as if originally made between the employee and the person by whom the scheme provides that he shall be employed on and after that day; and

(c) without prejudice to paragraph (b) above, subsections (4)(b), (5) and (6) above shall apply as they apply to the transfer of an employee of a pilotage authority but with the substitution for the references in subsections (4)(b) and (6) to the pilotage authority of references to the licensed pilot.

(8) Nothing in paragraph 10 of Schedule 1 to the Pilotage Act 1983 (power of Commission to employ persons needed to assist it) shall prevent the Commission becoming the employer of any person under this section.

DEFINITIONS
"the appointed day": ss.1(2), 31(1).
"competent harbour authority": ss.1(1), 31(1).
"functions": see General Note to s.31.
"pilot": s.31(1).
"pilotage authority": s.24(12); see also Pilotage Act 1983, s.68(1).
"Pilotage Commission": see Pilotage Act 1983, s.1(1).
"pilotage district": see Pilotage Act 1983, s.68(1).

Abolition of Pilotage Commission

26.—(1) On such day as the Secretary of State may by order appoint the Pilotage Commission shall cease to exist and the Commission shall use its best endeavours to secure that its work is completed by that day.

(2) No later than six months before the day appointed under subsection (1) above the Pilotage Commission shall submit to the Secretary of State a scheme for the winding-up of the Commission and the disposal of the property, rights and liabilities of the Commission and the arrangements to be made as respects its staff, including in particular proposals concerning the payment of pensions in respect of staff or former staff and any compensation to be paid to staff for loss of employment; but the scheme shall not affect any person's right to compensation otherwise than under the scheme.

(3) The Secretary of State shall by order provide for the transfer of the property, rights and liabilities of the Pilotage Commission and the arrangements to be made as respects any staff of the Commission in accordance with the scheme (with or without modifications).

DEFINITIONS
"the appointed day": ss.1(2), 31(1).
"Pilotage Commission": see Pilotage Act 1983, s.1(1).
"Secretary of State": see General Note to s.31.

GENERAL NOTE
The Pilotage Commission, established under the Merchant Shipping Act 1979, is to be wound up but is to continue to exist during the transfer period and to have a statutory responsibility to advise and suggest schemes to the Secretary of State on transfer matters.

Functions and constitution of Pilotage Commission pending abolition

27.—(1) During the period beginning with the passing of this Act and ending immediately before the day appointed under section 26(1) above for the abolition of the Pilotage Commission.
    (a) the Commission shall give the Secretary of State such advice as he may request from it in connection with the reorganisation of pilotage services under this Act.
    (b) the Secretary of State may, if he considers it is appropriate to do so, exercise his power under paragraph 4 of Schedule 1 to the Pilotage Act 1983 (power to declare the office of any person who is a member of the Commission to be vacant) whether or not he is satisfied as mentioned in that paragraph;
and no person shall be entitled to any compensation for loss of an office declared vacant by virtue of paragraph (b) above.

(2) During the period mentioned in subsection (1) above, subsection (1) of section 2 of the Pilotage Act 1983 (Commission to consist of not less than 10 and not more than 15 persons appointed from among certain categories of persons) shall have effect with the substitution for "10" of "5"; and on and after the appointed day that section shall have effect with the following modifications—
    (a) in subsection (1) for the words from "from among the following" onwards there shall be substituted the words "and the Secretary of State shall appoint one member to be the Chairman of the Commission"; and
    (b) for subsection (2) there shall be substituted—
        "(2) It shall be the duty of the Secretary of State before appointing any person as a member or as Chairman of the Commission to consult on the appointment such persons as he considers are representative of the persons in the United Kingdom principally interested in the activities of the Commission.".

DEFINITIONS
"the appointed day": ss.1(2), 31(1).
"pilotage": s.31(1).

"the Pilotage Commission": see Pilotage Act 1983, s.1(1).
"Secretary of State": see General Note to s.31.

Pilots' compensation schemes

28.—(1) The Secretary of State shall make a scheme or schemes ("pilots' compensation schemes") under which payments are to be made for the purpose of compensating pilots for any loss of employment which may be suffered by them in consequence of the reorganisation of pilotage services under this Act.

(2) Subject to subsection (4) below, a pilots' compensation scheme shall require a competent harbour authority to make payments to or for the benefit of those persons—

(a) who immediately before the appointed day were licensed as pilots under section 12 of the Pilotage Act 1983 for the pilotage district in which its harbour is situated but were not then employed under a contract of employment by the pilotage authority for that district or any committee appointed by the authority under section 9(1)(e) of the Pilotage Act 1983;

(b) who either have no arrangements offered to them (whether by way of employment under a contract of employment or otherwise) for the provision of their services as authorised pilots after the appointed day or have such arrangements made with them which are terminated by the other party within such period as may be specified in the scheme;

(c) who are not at the relevant time holders of deep sea pilotage certificates; and

(d) who satisfy such further conditions as to eligibility as may be so specified;

and where there is more than one such authority in any former pilotage district, the payments to be made by each authority shall be determined by the Pilotage Commission.

(3) For the purposes of paragraph (c) of subsection (2) above—
  "the relevant time" means—

(a) in the case of a person who has no such arrangements as mentioned in paragraph (b) of that subsection offered to him, immediately before the appointed day; and

(b) in the case of a person who has such arrangements made with him which are terminated as there mentioned, immediately before the termination of those arrangements; and

  "deep sea pilotage certificate" means a certificate granted by virtue of section 9(1)(j) of the Pilotage Act 1983 or under section 23 above.

(4) In a case where such arrangements as mentioned in paragraph (b) of subsection (2) above are made for the provision of the services of any person in the harbour of a competent harbour authority other than the authority mentioned in that subsection, a pilots' compensation scheme shall require the payments in respect of that person to be made by that other authority.

(5) A pilots' compensation scheme may contain such provision as the Secretary of State may determine as to—

(a) the terms and conditions on which and the times at which payments are to be made; and

(b) the circumstances in which payments may be recovered from the persons to whom they are made.

(6) A pilots' compensation scheme may include provision enabling a competent harbour authority to require the whole or part of any existing fund constituted for the purpose of making payment by way of compen-

sation for loss of employment to pilots working in its harbour (whether vested in any person absolutely or as a trustee) to be applied towards any payments required to be made by the authority under the scheme.

(7) A pilots' compensation scheme may extend to one or more areas and different provision may be made in respect of different areas.

(8) The Secretary of State may arrange for the Pilotage Commission to administer any pilots' compensation scheme and any dispute arising as to the entitlement of any person to a payment under a pilots' compensation scheme shall be determined by the Commission.

(9) After the abolition of the Pilotage Commission its functions under this section may be exercised by such other person or persons as the Secretary of State may appoint after consultation with such persons as he considers are representative of the persons in the United Kingdom principally interested in pilotage.

(10) A pilots' compensation scheme may be varied or revoked by a subsequent such scheme.

DEFINITIONS
"the appointed day": ss.1(2), 31(1).
"area": see s.1(1), (3).
"authorised pilot": ss.3, 31(1).
"competent harbour authority": ss.1(1), 31(1).
"deep sea pilotage certificate": ss.23, 28(3).
"former pilotage district": ss.1(2), 31(1).
"harbour": s.31(1).
"pilot": s.31(1).
"pilotage": s.31(1).
"pilotage authority": s.24(12); see also s.1(2) and Pilotage Act 1983, s.68(1).
"Pilotage Commission": see Pilotage Act 1983, s.1(1).
"pilotage district": see Pilotage Act 1983, s.68(1).
"pilots' compensation fund": s.28(1).
"relevant time": s.28(3).
"Secretary of State": see General Note to s.31.

GENERAL NOTE
Subs. (2)(a) provides that pilots who are already employed—as, for example, by the Shetland and Orkney Islands councils—will not be eligible for the pilots' compensation scheme.

The current holder of a deep sea pilotage certificate is not automatically deprived of that certificate by subs. (2). However, if he wishes to qualify for participation in a pilots' compensation scheme, he must surrender the certificate and gets no additional compensation for loss of the certificate. He does not, therefore, have the opportunity of both benefitting from the pilots' compensation scheme and also having more time to seek increased work in the deep sea market to the detriment of full-time deep sea pilots. Nonetheless, the subs. will not inevitably diminish the availability of deep sea pilotage as such a person is not disentitled from applying for a fresh certificate. The CHA can then decide whether the issue of more certificates is then desirable and to ensure that no gaps are left in the coverage by British pilots which would otherwise be filled by Continental pilots in what is essentially an international market.

Funding of reorganisation

29.—(1) The Secretary of State may, on application by the Pilotage Commission (or, as respects any functions to be performed by virtue of section 28(9) above, any person appointed under that section), make a scheme for the recovery of—

(a) the expenses of the Commission (or any such person) in performing the functions of the Commission after the appointed day (including any arrangements to be made by the Commission under section 26(3) above); and

(b) any sums required by the Commission by virtue of this Act.

(2) A scheme made under subsection (1) above may provide for a charge to be imposed on any competent harbour authority and for the amount of such a charge to be determined by reference to such factors as the Secretary of State considers appropriate.

(3) A scheme made under subsection (1) above may be varied or revoked by a subsequent scheme made under that subsection.

(4) Before making a scheme under subsection (1) above or varying or revoking such a scheme the Secretary of State shall consult such persons as appear to him to be representative of those persons who are affected by it and he may, after considering any objections to the proposed scheme and consulting the Commission or any person appointed under section 28(9) above, modify the scheme; but the Secretary of State shall not make a scheme with a modification by virtue of which any amount payable under it is increased unless he has again consulted those persons.

(5) A competent harbour authority may recover any sums required by it by virtue of this Part of this Act by increasing any charges, dues or fees payable to it.

DEFINITIONS

"the appointed day": ss.1(2), 31(1).
"charges": see Harbours Act 1964, s.57(1); Harbours Act (Northern Ireland) 1970, s.38(1).
"competent harbour authority": ss.1(1), 31(1).
"functions": see General Note to s.31.
"Pilotage Commission": see Pilotage Act 1983, s.68(1).
"Secretary of State": see General Note to s.31.

PART IV

SUPPLEMENTARY

Orders and regulations

30.—(1) Any power to make an order or regulations under this Act shall be exercisable by statutory instrument.

(2) Any statutory instrument containing such an order or regulations (except an order made under section 1 to which subsection (8) of that section applies or an order made under section 33 below) shall be subject to annulment in pursuance of a resolution of either House of Parliament.

Interpretation

31.—(1) In this Act except where the context otherwise requires—
"the appointed day" means the date appointed for the coming into force of Part I of this Act;
"authorised pilot", in relation to any area, means a person authorised under section 3 above for that area and, in relation to any ship, a person so authorised in respect of ships of that description;
"competent harbour authority" has the meaning given in section 1 above;
"former pilotage district" has the meaning given in section 1(2) above;
"harbour", in relation to a competent harbour authority, has the meaning given in section 1 above;
"harbour authority" has the same meaning as in the Harbours Act 1964 ("the 1964 Act") or, in Northern Ireland, the Harbours Act (Northern Ireland) 1970 ("the 1970 Act");

"harbour operations" has the same meaning as in the 1964 Act or, in Northern Ireland, the 1970 Act;

"master" has the same meaning as in the Merchant Shipping Act 1894;

"pilot" has the same meaning as in the Merchant Shipping Act 1894 and "pilotage" shall be construed accordingly;

"pilot boat" has the meaning given in section 6 above;

"pilotage direction" has the meaning given in section 7(1) above;

"pilotage exemption certificate" means a certificate granted under section 8 above;

"ship" has the same meaning as in the 1964 Act or, in Northern Ireland, the 1970 Act and includes both British and foreign ships;

"statutory powers" and "statutory duties" have the same meanings as in the 1964 Act or, in Northern Ireland, mean powers or, as the case may be, duties which are statutory functions within the meaning of the 1970 Act.

(2) In this Act references to a ship navigating or being navigated include references to its moving or being moved within a harbour for the purpose of changing from one mooring to another or of being taken into or out of any dock.

DEFINITIONS

"dock": see Harbours Act 1964, s.57(1); Harbours Act (Northern Ireland) 1970, s.38(1).
"harbour": *cf.* s.12(1)(d).
"harbour authority": *cf.* s.1(9).

GENERAL NOTE

This section collects together those terms which are used generally throughout the Act.

Other definitions also appear throughout the Act and are occasionally qualified for specific purposes. These are noted in the Definition notes where appropriate.

For definition of certain terms relating to the pilotage system existing when this Act was passed, reference is made to the appropriate sections of the Pilotage Act 1983, which is repealed by this Act (s.32, Sched. 3).

The Pilotage Act 1983 was included in the Merchant Shipping Acts 1894–1984 (Pilotage Act 1983, s.70(1); Merchant Shipping Act 1984, s.14(1)). Now that this Act transfers responsibility for pilotage to harbour authorities, appropriate references are made to the principal harbour legislation but with no specific requirement that this Act be treated as uniform with it.

The word "functions" is used in this Act without definition. In the Harbours Act 1964, s.57(1) and the Pilotage Act 1983, s.68(1), "functions" is stated to include powers and duties.

In accordance with the normal practice, references to "the Secretary of State" throughout the Act are made without specifying the relevant Department. It is, at the time of writing, the Department of Transport.

It appears from what was said in the debates on the Bill that the word "ship" was assumed by the Government to be generally synonymous with "vessel" and not, therefore, to narrow the range of vessels to which the Act might apply.

Subs. (2)

Navigating or being navigated. Under the old scheme for compulsory pilotage, existing at the time the Merchant Shipping Act 1979 was passed and consolidated in the Pilotage Act 1983, the expression, "navigating" was used. The expression "being navigated" was brought in for the new scheme of compulsory pilotage introduced by the Merchant Shipping Act 1979 and consolidated in the Pilotage Act 1983. The mere change from active to passive voice in relation to navigation appears to have had only a terminological and not a legislative significance, so the two expressions are appropriately treated here as synonymous. See further Rose, *Modern Law of Pilotage* (1984), pp.23–25, 29–30.

Transitional and consequential provisions and repeals

32.—(1) The Secretary of State may by regulations make such transitional, consequential or incidental provision (including provision repealing

or amending any local enactment) as he considers necessary or expedient
for the purpose of giving effect to or in consequence of any provision of
this Act.

(2) In subsection (1) above "local enactment" includes an Act confirming a provisional Order, an instrument made under a local enactment and
an instrument in the nature of a local enactment made under any other
Act.

(3) Schedule 1 to this Act shall have effect for the purpose of making
transitional provision.

(4) The enactments mentioned in Schedule 2 to this Act shall have
effect with the amendments specified in that Schedule (which are consequential on the provisions of this Act).

(5) The enactments and instrument specified in Schedule 3 to this Act
are hereby repealed or, as the case may be, revoked to the extent specified
in the third column of that Schedule.

DEFINITION
"Secretary of State": see General Note to s.31.

Short title, commencement and extent

33.—(1) This Act may be cited as the Pilotage Act 1987.

(2) Subject to subsection (3) below, the provisions of this Act, except
section 27, shall come into force on such day as the Secretary of State
may by order appoint and different days may be appointed for different
provisions or for different purposes.

(3) The day appointed under subsection (2) above for the coming into
force of Part I of this Act shall be not less than nine months after the
passing of this Act.

(4) This Act extends to Northern Ireland.

DEFINITION
"Secretary of State": see General Note to s.31.

GENERAL NOTE
Specific references are made to the law operating in Northern Ireland in ss.1(8), (11),
3(10(c), 10(6), (8), 25(6) and 31(1).

SCHEDULES

Section 32(3)   SCHEDULE 1

TRANSITIONAL AND SAVING PROVISIONS

1. For the purposes of any provision of this Act which comes into force before Part I of
this Act and of the exercise of any powers conferred by this Act before that Part comes into
force by virtue of section 13 of the Interpretation Act 1978 (anticipatory exercise of powers),
a harbour authority shall be taken to be a competent harbour authority at any time if it
would be such an authority if that Part and any order made under section 1(3) or (4) of this
Act by virtue of the said section 13 had come into force immediately before that time and
the area which shall be taken to be its harbour shall be determined accordingly.

2.—(1) Where any dispute arises before the appointed day between a competent harbour
authority and any person who wishes to be authorised under section 3 of this Act by the
authority on or after that day as to what the terms of any provision in any contract of
employment which is to be entered into between them should be and that dispute cannot be
resolved by negotiation between them, the authority or any person or organisation which
represents the majority of the holders of licences under section 12 of the Pilotage Act 1983
for a pilotage district in which the authority's harbour falls may refer the dispute to an
arbitration panel appointed in accordance with section 5(2) of this Act, and the panel shall

determine what the terms of that provision should be and the kinds of contracts of employment between the authority and authorised pilots to which their determination is to apply ("material contracts").

(2) Subsections (3), (4), (5) (7) and (8) of section 5 of this Act shall apply for the purposes of this paragraph as if references in those subsections to subsection (1) of that section included references to sub-paragraph (1) above and references in subsection (4) to relevant contracts included references to material contracts.

(3) If regulations under subsection (7) of that section as it applies by virtue of sub-paragraph (2) above provide that the expenses of referrals and determinations under this paragraph are to be borne by the Pilotage Commission, section 3 of the Pilotage Act 1983 shall apply as if those expenses were expenses of the Commission in performing its functions.

(4) Where any such dispute as mentioned in subsection (1) of section 5 to this Act arises on or after the appointed day but before the competent harbour authority in question has authorised any persons under section 3 of this Act, for the reference in that subsection to the majority of the authorised pilots for its harbour there shall be substituted a reference to any person or organisation which represents the majority of the holders of licences under section 12 of the Pilotage Act 1983 for a former pilotage district in which the authority's harbour falls.

3. Where a competent harbour authority which proposes on or after the appointed day to direct that pilotage shall be compulsory for ships navigating in an area outside its harbour applies before that day for the making of the harbour revision order which will be required by virtue of section 7(5) of this Act and that area is an area in which pilotage is compulsory by virtue of an order under section 9(1)(i) of the Pilotage Act 1983—

   (a) before making the order the Secretary of State shall consult such persons as appear to him to be affected by it and, after considering any objections made by them, he may refuse to make the order, make the order in the form of the draft submitted to him or, if he considers that it should be modified, make the order in that form but with such modifications as he considers appropriate after consulting those persons again as to the modifications;

   (b) paragraphs 3, 4 and 5(c) of Schedule 3 to the Harbours Act 1964 (publication of notices concerning proposed harbour revision orders and provisions as to objections to them) shall not apply and the references in paragraph 4A(2) of that Schedule to an objection or a comment being duly made shall be taken to be references to the objection or comment being made in writing and stating the grounds on which it is made;

   (c) after the making of the order the direction shall apply to the area within the authority's limits of jurisdiction as extended by the order, notwithstanding that the order is not yet in force.

4.—(1) Any pilots' benefit fund established under paragraph (i) of section 15(1) of the Pilotage Act 1983 shall continue in existence notwithstanding the repeal of that section by this Act and the Secretary of State may by order make such provision as he considers appropriate as to—

   (a) the operation after the repeal of that section of the byelaws under which any such fund was established;

   (b) the appointment of the managers of any such fund and any powers to be exercisable as respects the management of the fund by the persons who are to appoint those managers; and

   (c) the powers of any such managers to amend or revoke the byelaws or any other provision governing the fund.

(2) Before making an order under sub-paragraph (1) above in respect of any fund the Secretary of State shall consult such persons or organisations as appear to him to be representative of competent harbour authorities and such persons or organisations as appear to him to be representative of the persons who may benefit from the fund.

5.—(1) Any pilotage certificate which immediately before the appointed day is in force under section 20 of the Pilotage Act 1983 shall continue in force during the period for which it was granted as if it had been granted under section 8 of this Act by the authority or authorities which are the competent harbour authorities as respects the area in relation to which the certificate was granted and section 8 of this Act shall apply accordingly.

(2) Where an application is made under section 8(5) of this Act by virtue of sub-paragraph (1) above to the competent harbour authority or one of the competent harbour authorities by which a certificate is deemed under that sub-paragraph to have been granted, the authority in question shall, if it renews the certificate under that section, issue the applicant with a copy of the certificate as it has effect by virtue of the application.

6.—(1) The Secretary of State shall, on application by any body which immediately before the appointed day was authorised under the Pilotage Act 1983 to grant deep sea pilotage certificates, authorise the body under section 23 of this Act to grant certificates under that section.

(2) Any deep sea pilotage certificate granted to any person by virtue of section 9(1)(*j*) of the Pilotage Act 1983 which is in force immediately before the appointed day in respect of any area shall continue in force during the period for which it was granted and may on application by him be renewed by any body authorised under section 23 of this Act in respect of the whole or part of that area on the same terms and conditions as if it had been granted by that body under section 23.

Section 32(4)   **SCHEDULE 2**

CONSEQUENTIAL AMENDMENTS

1.—(1) In the definition of "pilot boat" in subsection (4) of section 4 of the Pensions (Navy, Army, Air Force and Mercantile Marine) Act 1939 for the words "section 45 of the Pilotage Act 1983" there shall be substituted the words "section 6 of the Pilotage Act 1987".

(2) Sub-paragraph (1) above shall not affect the operation of any scheme made under that section before this paragraph comes into force.

2. The enactments and instruments with respect to which provision may be made by an Order in Council under section 1(1)(*h*) of the Hovercraft Act 1968 shall include this Act and any instrument made under it.

3. In the Offshore Petroleum Development (Scotland) Act 1975—
    (a) in section 6(2) the words "and, where appropriate, any pilotage authority" shall be omitted; and
    (b) for paragraph (*c*) of section 18 there shall be substituted—
        "(*c*) the Pilotage Act 1987."

4. At the end of section 35(3)(*b*)(ii) of the Finance Act 1980 there shall be inserted the words "or authorised by a competent harbour authority".

5. In section 27(2)(*a*) of the Oil and Gas (Enterprise) Act 1982 for the words "the Pilotage Act 1983" there shall be substituted the words "the Pilotage Act 1987".

Section 32(5)   **SCHEDULE 3**

REPEALS AND REVOCATIONS

Chapter or number	Short title	Extent of repeal or revocation
1975 c.8.	The Offshore Petroleum Development (Scotland) Act 1975.	In section 6(2), the words "and, where appropriate, any pilotage authority".
1975 c.24.	The House of Commons Disqualification Act 1975.	In Part II of Schedule 1, the entry relating to the Pilotage Commission.
1975 c.25.	The Northern Ireland Assembly Disqualification Act 1975.	In Part II of Schedule 1, the entry relating to the Pilotage Commission.
1979 c.39.	The Merchant Shipping Act 1979.	In section 50(2), the definition of "the Commission" and in the definition of "the Merchant Shipping Acts" the words "and the Pilotage Act 1983". Schedule 1.
1979 c.55.	The Justices of the Peace Act 1979.	Section 33(3)(*b*).

Chapter or number	Short title	Extent of repeal or revocation
1980 c.43.	The Magistrates' Courts Act 1980.	In Part III of Schedule 6, paragraph 4.
1981 c.69.	The Wildlife and Countryside Act 1981.	In section 36(7), in the definition of "relevant authority", the words "a pilotage authority".
1983 c.21.	The Pilotage Act 1983.	The whole Act.
S.I. 1985/170 (N.I. 1).	The Nature Conservation and Amenity Lands (Northern Ireland) Order 1985.	Article 20(6)(*f*).

BANKING ACT 1987*

(1987 c. 22)

ARRANGEMENT OF SECTIONS

PART I

REGULATION OF DEPOSIT-TAKING BUSINESS

The Bank of England and the Board of Banking Supervision

---

* Annotations by Geoffrey Harding, LL.M., Ph.D., Partner, Wilde Sapte.

An Act to make new provision for regulating the acceptance of deposits in the course of a business, for protecting depositors and for regulating the use of banking names and descriptions; to amend section 187 of the Consumer Credit Act 1974 in relation to arrangements for the electronic transfer of funds; to clarify the powers conferred by section 183 of the Financial Services Act 1986; and for purposes connected with those matters. [15th May 1987]

PARLIAMENTARY DEBATES

Hansard: H.C. Vol. 106, col. 540; Vol. 110, col. 1058; Vol. 115, col. 871; H.L. Vol. 485, cols. 10, 522, 546, 1213; Vol. 486, cols. 11, 695, 1236.

INTRODUCTION AND GENERAL NOTE

The Banking Act 1987 received the Royal Assent on May 15, 1987, immediately prior to the holding of the General Election, and following two other complementary financial measures, the Building Societies Act 1986 and the Financial Services Act 1986, also passed during the 1986/87 session. The scope of the Banking Act is narrower than its short title suggests in that it is primarily concerned with banking supervision in the interests of *depositors* and not with banking as a whole or with "banking law", or with specific questions concerning transactions between banks and their customers or with consumer protection. However, an independent Review Committee on Banking Services Law under the chairmanship of Professor R. B. Jack has been subsequently set up to examine the statute and common law relating to the provision of banking services within the U.K.

The Banking Act 1979 had provided the first statutory framework for the authorisation and supervision of deposit-taking businesses under the regulation of the Bank of England ("the Bank"). However, certain occurrences have highlighted the necessity to set up a more effective system of banking supervision within an adequate statutory framework. These occurrences include: accelerated developments in banking and in the general financial services sector; the significant increase over the past few years to nearly 298 recognised banks and 290 licensed deposit-takers with banks from 77 countries having offices in the U.K. (The Bank's Annual Report 1986/87 p.55); and in particular, the rescue of Johnson Matthey Bankers in October 1984 by the Bank. Following the publication in June 1985 of a report by a Review Committee, chaired by the Governor of the Bank (Cmnd. 9550 (1985)) which, amongst other recommendations, called for the abolition of the two-tier system of recognised banks and of licensed deposit-takers established by the Banking Act 1979, a Government White Paper *Banking Supervision* (Cmnd. 9695 (1985)) was published. The White Paper accepted much of the substance of the Review Committee's conclusion and endorsed the general recommendation that there should be no fundamental change in the nature of banking supervision. However, in the Foreword by the Chancellor of the Exchequer, it was emphasized at the outset that: "An effective system of banking supervision is as important as the banking system itself. For without it there will not be the confidence on which sound banking depends—from the confidence of the individual depositor that his money is safe, to confidence in Britain as one of the foremost financial centres in the world." The main proposals were:

—organisational changes including a new Bank of England Board of Banking Supervision to assist in the Bank's supervisory duties;

—that all authorised institutions be made subject to the same authorisation criteria and supervisory regime (it may be recalled that Johnson Matthey Bankers as a recognised bank was thereby made subject to a less stringent statutory control than a licensed deposit-taker would have been);

—that the use of the word "bank" as part of an institution's name should be limited to those with more than £5 million paid up equity;

—statutory provision for increased cooperation and dialogue between supervisors and auditors of authorised institutions;

—that greater information gathering powers should be granted to the Bank;

—notification of concentration of lending and other large exposures by authorised institutions be made to supervisors; and,

—by reason of the paramount importance attached to the protection of depositors, power be given for future amendments of the definitions of "deposit" and "deposit-taking business" by secondary legislation in order to keep up with changes in the financial world.

Further proposals included an amendment to the Consumer Credit Act 1974 to remove a possible constraint on the development of a national system for Electronic Funds Transfer at the Point of Sale (EFT-POS) in order to place an EFT-POS transaction in a similar position as a transaction on a current account effected by means of a cheque; and a proposal that the Bank should be given the power to prohibit any institution which carries on a business or which has a representative office in the U.K. from registering under or using a banking name which is misleading.

The Banking Bill was presented in the House of Commons in November 1986. It introduced a relatively small number of significant policy changes, but an issue such as the abolition of the two-tier system ending the distinction between recognised banks and licensed deposit-takers (and with it the separate systems of supervision and regulation) was so fundamental and so pervasive throughout the 1979 Act that a full new Bill was introduced instead of merely an amending enactment. One proposal, set out in the White Paper but not included in the Bill, was the amendment to the Consumer Credit Act to further the development of EFT-POS on the basis that it would be more appropriate for such a measure to be considered by the newly appointed Review Committee but in the end the amendment was brought into the Act.

In brief, the new Act seeks on the one hand to broaden and extend the functions of the Bank of England in the supervision of institutions in the banking sector, with the assistance of a new Board of Banking Supervision yet endeavours on the other hand to maintain the Bank's traditional flexibility in the exercise of its supervisory duties and powers.

OUTLINE OF THE ACT

A brief outline of what is to be found in the Act's several parts may prove helpful: a more detailed account appears in each of the annotations to the individual sections.

Part I

This lengthy Part sets out the duties and powers of the Bank of England which is given general supervisory and specific regulatory functions (s.1). A new Board of Banking Supervision consisting of three *ex-officio* members and six members independent of the Bank is established to provide a forum for advice on the exercise by the Bank of its regulatory functions (s.2 and Sched. 1). Only "authorised institutions," subject to exemptions, may accept a "deposit" (as defined) in the course of carrying on a "deposit-taking business" (as defined) (ss.3–6 and Sched. 2). The Treasury may, by order, amend these definitions (s.7). The procedure for applying for, the granting or refusing of an application for, and the minimum criteria for, authorisation are detailed (ss.8–10 and Sched. 3). An authorisation may be revoked or restricted by the Bank by notice (ss.11–14) or surrendered by the authorised institution (s.15). The Bank must publish a statement of principles in accordance with which it acts or proposes to act in carrying out its functions, powers and duties under the Act (s.16) and the Bank in its general report (s.1(3)), and on request, must make available a list of authorised institutions (s.17). It is an offence for a person to describe itself falsely as being authorised or falsely state or indicate that it may accept a deposit (s.18). The Bank is empowered in the interests of depositors or potential depositors to give directions to an institution which may in seeking written confirmation of the directions make written representation to the Bank (ss.19–20). Powers are provided to enable the Bank to serve a notice of objection on a prospective or existing controller of an authorised institution and sanctions against contraventions and restrictions on the sale of specified shares are created (ss.21–26). An appeals procedure is set up permitting institutions and specified persons to appeal to a specially constituted tribunal against a refusal or revocation of authorisation against a restriction or a direction, or against a decision of the Bank to serve a notice of objection. The constitution of, and the determination of such appeals by, the tribunal, its costs, procedure and evidence on appeals to the tribunal and further appeals on points of law are all provided for in ss.27–31. The Treasury is empowered to make regulations about deposit advertisements and to regulate the making of unsolicited calls seeking deposits. The power is given to the Bank to issue a direction restricting advertisements considered to be misleading. Contravention of such regulations and directions and the making of a fraudulent inducement to make a deposit are criminal offences (ss.32–35). There follow detailed provisions requiring each authorised institution to give the Bank notice of change of a director, controller or manager, and requiring the institution to make a report of any transactions entered into which expose large percentages of its available capital resources to risk of loss (ss.36–38). The Bank may obtain information and require production of documents from an institution or from a significant shareholder and it has right of entry to obtain such (ss.39 and 40). It may be noted that in s.39 and in others (such as in ss.41, 46 and 47) referred to in the relevant annotations, the provisions apply also to *former* authorised institutions. "Competent persons" may be appointed by the Bank to carry out investigations (s.41); persons suspected to be guilty of contravention of the Act may be required by the Bank to provide information, produce documents and attend and answer questions (s.42); the Bank may apply for a power of entry in certain circumstances (s.43) and the offence of obstruction of investigation is created (s.44). There are provisions concerning the keeping of audited accounts available for inspection (s.45); and the giving of notice to the Bank of the removal, non-reappointment, resignation, and retirement of auditors or qualification of accounts (s.46). A particularly significant provision is the relaxation of the auditor's and reporting accountant's duty of confidentiality or of loyalty or trust in the case of a matter which is relevant to any function of the Bank under this Act (s.47). Finally, there are provisions governing the repayment of unauthorised deposits and the treatment and application or distribution of moneys representing profits from unauthorised deposits (s.49).

Part II

These sections and the accompanying Sched. 4 contain the provisions continuing the Deposit Protection Board which administers the statutory scheme set up by the Banking Act 1979 for the protection of depositors. Unlike the newly-created protective scheme under the Building Societies Act 1986, the Deposit Protection Fund is a "standing fund" where contributions are levied at the outset on authorised institutions in the form of initial contributions (s.53). Further contributions may be levied where the amounts standing to the credit of the Fund drop below £3 million (in order to restore the Fund to at least £5 million and a maximum of £6 million) (s.54); or they may be levied in the form of special contributions where payments out are likely to exhaust the Fund (s.55). The minimum initial contribution required from each authorised institution is at least £10,000, with initial or further contributions not exceeding £300,000, and the total of contributions paid or to be paid (less certain repayments) must not exceed 0·3 per cent. of a contributory institution's "deposit base" (ss.56 and 57). A depositor with a "protected deposit" with an authorised institution which becomes insolvent (see s.59), or in relation to which an administration order is made under the Insolvency Act 1986, may receive a compensation payment of up to three-quarters of his protected deposit. "Protected deposit" is defined as the total liability of that institution to that depositor (principal amount of, and accrued interest on, sterling deposits) limited to a maximum of £20,000. The above figures and proportions may be amended by order (ss.58 and 60). There are detailed provisions for trustee and joint deposits (s.61), for the liability of the failed institution to the Board in respect of compensation payments (s.62) and for repayments of recovered money to contributory institutions (s.63). The Board has borrowing powers (s.64), and may request the Bank to obtain information from contributory institutions for the purpose of calculating contributions (s.65). The tax treatment of contributions to the Fund and repayments by the Board is stated (s.66).

Part III

This Part contains the detailed provisions controlling the use of banking names (size being the principal criterion) and of banking descriptions, each subject to exceptions (ss.67–69). The Bank is empowered to object to a name if considered misleading or otherwise undesirable (s.70) subject to appeal to the court (s.71). There are provisions linked to the Companies Act 1985 in respect of the registration of substitute corporate names by oversea companies where the Bank has notified its objection (s.72). Any contravention of a Pt. 3 provision is constituted an offence (s.73).

Part IV

This Part governs the regulation of names used, or to be used, by overseas institutions which establish representative offices in the U.K. in relation to their activities in the U.K. Prior notice must be given (s.75), and the Bank may object to any name proposed to be used or to any change in a name already being used (s.76), subject to a right of appeal to the court (s.77). Again, as in s.72, there are provisions concerning the registration of substitute corporate names by overseas institutions (s.78). There is a duty imposed on an overseas institution with a representative office in the U.K. by notice to provide information and documents (s.79). The Treasury is given power to make regulations imposing further requirements on such overseas institutions (s.80). S.81 creates an offence of contravening any of the provisions under this Part or of any requirement imposed under it.

Part V

Pt. V confirms the continuing obligation of secrecy on supervisors and on those who acquire supervisory information but new provisions are included enabling information to be disclosed through certain "gateways" or other supervisors. A general restriction is imposed (s.82) subject to specified exceptions (ss.83–85), on the disclosure of information relating to the business or other affairs of *any* person received under or for the purposes of this Act or of information obtained from a person who likewise received it or of information supplied by a relevant supervisory authority outside the U.K. (s.86). Provision is made for the disclosure of information to the Bank by certain other statutory supervisors (s.87).

Part VI
These provisions are largely miscellaneous and supplementary but they contain the important meanings of "controller" (and of its several sub-categories—s.105(3), (4) and (5)), "manager" (s.105(6)), "chief executive" (s.105(7)) and of "associate" (s.105(9)). The most significant provision (which did not appear in the earlier bills) is that of the amendment to s.187(3) of the Consumer Credit Act 1974 with regard to electronic transfer of funds which is examined in detail in the General Note to s.89.

EXTENT
The Act extends to Northern Ireland. It will be appreciated that as the following annotations to the individual sections are intended for those considering or advising on English law, there is no detailed reference to the Act's application under the law of Scotland or of Northern Ireland.

COMMENCEMENT
Apart from s.91 (powers for securing reciprocal facilities for banking and other financial business) which came into force on the passing of the Act, other sections come into force as the Treasury may appoint by order but different days may be appointed for different provisions or for different purposes of the same provision (s.110(2)). At the time of this publication the following provisions, came into force on July 15, 1987, namely those relating to restrictions on disclosure of information obtained by the Bank (Pt. V); the making of orders (s.102); interpretation (s.106); transitional provisions (s.107 in so far as it relates to Sched. 5, para. 14); certain consequential amendments and repeals (s.108(1) in in so far as that subsection relates to Sched. 6, para. 26(5) and s.108(2) in so far as it relates to certain entries in Sched. 7); the application of the Act to Northern Ireland (s.109); its short title and commencement (s.110); Sched. 5, para. 14; Sched. 6, para. 26(5) and certain entries in Sched. 7 (S.I. 1987 No. 1189). All other sections (apart from s.38—reports of large exposures to controllers) came into operation as from October 1 (S.I. 1987 No. 1664). It is proposed that s.38 will come into force on January 1, 1988.

ABBREVIATIONS
In the annotations, the following abbreviations are used:
Council Directive 77/780/EEC: First Council Directive 77/780/EEC of December 12, 1977, on the coordination of laws, regulations and administrative provisions relating to the taking up and pursuit of the business of credit institutions (O.J. 1977, L/322/30).
White Paper: Banking Supervision—Cmnd. 9695 (1985).
1979 Act: Banking Act 1979.
Standing Committee: The House of Commons Standing Committee E which considered the Banking Bill between December 11, 1986, and February 5, 1987.

PART I

REGULATION OF DEPOSIT-TAKING BUSINESS

The Bank of England and the Board of Banking Supervision

Functions and duties of the Bank of England

1.—(1) The Bank of England (in this Act referred to as "the Bank") shall have the powers conferred on it by this Act and the duty generally to supervise the institutions authorised by it in the exercise of those powers.

(2) It shall also be the duty of the Bank to keep under review the operation of this Act and developments in the field of banking which appear to it to be relevant to the exercise of its powers and the discharge of its duties.

(3) The Bank shall, as soon as practicable after the end of each of its financial years, make to the Chancellor of the Exchequer and publish in such manner as it thinks appropriate a report on its activities under this Act in that year; and the Chancellor of the Exchequer shall lay copies of every such report before Parliament.

(4) Neither the Bank nor any person who is a member of its Court of Directors or who is, or is acting as, an officer or servant of the Bank shall be liable in damages for anything done or omitted in the discharge or purported discharge of the functions of the Bank under this Act unless it is shown that the act or omission was in bad faith.

TRANSITIONAL PROVISION
Sched. 5, para. 1.

GENERAL NOTE
As in the case of the Banking Act 1979, the present Act seeks to afford the Bank of England a more formal statement of its functions, powers and authority—a far cry from its previously informal supervisory role when it operated as an adviser to the Treasury for the purposes of the Exchange Control Act 1947.

S.1 is new (apart from the requirement to make and publish an annual report—see s.4 of the 1979 Act) and serves to emphasise the Bank's primary duty to supervise the banking system over and above its specific regulatory functions and powers elsewhere provided in the Act.

Subs. (1)
This affirms the Bank's statutory powers and its fundamental duty to supervise the institutions authorised by it. Arrangements in other countries broadly vary as between those having a Central Bank as supervisor (U.K., Netherlands and Italy); a separate banking or regulatory Commission (Switzerland, Belgium, France and Canada); direct governmental regulation (Japan); and those where a Banking Supervisory Office reports to a government department (West Germany) (White Paper, Chap. 2 and Annex 2).

Subs. (2)
Although the Bank's direct statutory responsiblity to keep the operation of the Act under review should be self-evident, there also the duty to keep "developments in the field of banking" under review—a recognition of the rapid and increasingly sophisticated developments taking place in the financial and commercial world and an expectation that the Bank will take these developments into account in the discharge of its duties.

Subs. (3)
This re-enacts the requirements of the 1979 Act (s.4) and confirms the accountability of the Bank to Parliament. However, since the general supervisory duty of the Bank is more detailed and its powers more wide ranging under this Act, it may be expected that the scope and content of the annual report will be correspondingly augmented. This subsection should be read together with s.16(2) (material changes in the Bank's statement of principles), s.17(1) (list of authorised institutions to be contained in the annual report), and s.2(6) in that the Board of Banking Supervision's annual report will also be included in the Bank's report so providing Parliament with further information.

Subs. (4)
A similar provision for the granting of immunity from suit for damages to the Bank, its directors, staff and seconded personnel ("is acting as") is to be found in the Financial Services Act 1986 (s.187) in respect of S.R.O.s, etc. During the Committee Stage in the Lords (*Hansard,* H.L. Vol. 485, col. 1219) it was sought to extend the immunity to agents (*e.g.* accountants) but the amendment was withdrawn. The immunity is confined to liability in damages and would not serve to oust, say, any judicial review, or exclude acts or omissions shown to be in bad faith. Although this subsection recognises that the Bank as supervisor should not feel restrained from taking any necessary action in the interests of the banking system and of individual depositors, it is not above the law.

The Board of Banking Supervision

2.—(1) As soon as practicable after the coming into force of this section the Bank shall establish a committee to be known as the Board of Banking Supervision.

(2) The Board shall consist of—

(a) three ex officio members, namely, the Governor of the Bank for the time being, who shall be the chairman of the Board, the Deputy Governor of the Bank for the time being and the executive director of the Bank for the time being responsible for the supervision of institutions authorised under this Act; and

(b) six independent members, that is to say, members appointed jointly by the Chancellor of the Exchequer and the Governor, being persons having no executive responsibility in the Bank.

(3) It shall be the duty of the independent members to give such advice as they think fit to the ex officio members—

(a) on the exercise by the Bank of its functions under this Act, either generally or in any particular respect or in relation to a particular institution or institutions; and

(b) on any matter relating to or arising out of the exercise of those functions.

(4) The Bank shall make regular reports to the Board on matters which the Bank considers relevant to the discharge by the independent members of their duty under subsection (3) above and shall provide them with such other information as they may reasonably require.

(5) The ex officio members shall give written notice to the Chancellor of the Exchequer in any case in which it is decided that the advice of the independent members should not be followed and the independent members shall be entitled to place before the Chancellor the reasons for their advice.

(6) The Board shall prepare an annual report on its activities and that report shall be included in the report made by the Bank under section 1(3) above for the financial year in question.

(7) Section 1(4) above shall apply to an act or omission by a member of the Board in the discharge or purported discharge of his functions under this section as it applies to an act or omission of a person there mentioned in the discharge or purported discharge of the functions of the Bank.

(8) Schedule 1 to this Act shall have effect with respect to the Board.

DEFINITIONS
"authorised": s.106(1).
"the Bank": s.1.
"institution": s.106(1).
"notice": s.100.

GENERAL NOTE
The White Paper, whilst of the view that the Bank rather than any separate body should continue to exercise its supervisory role, proposed in Chapter 5 that a new Bank of England Board of Banking Supervision, bringing in independent commercial banking experience to assist the Governor in his supervisory responsibilities, should be established within the Bank as soon as possible before the new legislation took effect. S.2 requires the Bank, "as soon as practicable after the coming into force of this section," to establish a Board of Banking Supervision whose independent members shall give advice to its *ex-officio* members on the exercise by the Bank of its statutory functions. The Board is to consist of three *ex-officio* members (the Governor of the Bank (as Chairman), the Deputy Governor and the recently appointed Executive Director responsible for banking supervision) and six independent members. The Chancellor of the Exchequer must be informed in writing by the *ex-officio* members if the advice of the independent members is not followed and the independent

members *may* inform the Chancellor as to their reasons for the advice. The Board is required to give an annual report which is incorporated in the Bank's Annual Report (see s.1(3)). Members of the Board are afforded the same immunity from suit for damages as are the Bank, its members and officials under s.1(4). Sched. 1 to the Act provides a detailed housekeeping provision in respect of terms of, and removal from, office; the increase or reduction in number of members; proceedings and other facilities; and the remuneration of independent members.

Subs. (1)

In fact, at the time of writing, a "shadow" Board has been set up on a non-statutory basis. The six independent members are Mr. J. A. Caldecott, Mr. A. J. Hardcastle, Mr. N. J. Robson, Mr. D. Vander Weyer, Sir Donald Barron and Mr. H. Taylor. It seems that the "independent" members may nevertheless retain or take up banking posts.

In addition, as foreshadowed in the White Paper (Chap. 6), improvements and expansion are taking place in the Bank's internal organisation and personnel, including an augmenting of the Banking Supervision Division (with secondments from outside).

S.2 and Sched. 1 came into force on October 1, 1987, and the shadow Board as constituted continues, although this time on a statutory basis.

Subs. (2)

The Standing Committee on the Bill spent a considerable time during its First and Second Sitting agonising on the question of the number of independent members. The Bill originally provided for five, and an amendment was moved to enlarge the Board to comprise eight independent members and for the specific inclusion of a member each from the Building Societies Commission, the Securities and Investment Board together with the Director of the National Consumer Council (First and Second Sittings, December 11 and 16, 1986, cols. 414–450). The avowed aim was to shift power from the Board of Banking Supervision to the Goverment and as a measure to ensure that the Board did not resemble a "cosy club." Although the amendment was negatived, the number of independent members was increased from five to six before the Second Reading in the Lords. Para. 3(1) of Sched. 1 permits an increase or reduction in the independent members provided that any subsequent decrease does not reduce the majority held by independent members and, apparently, provided that it does not result in there being less than three *ex-officio* members and less than six independent members at any time.

Subs. (3)

Not only is it the duty of the independent members to give such advice "as they think fit" to the *ex-officio* members on matters of general supervisory policy but also on the Bank's exercise of its statutory functions in relation to particular institutions. The White Paper sets out in some detail the probable areas of advice (Chap. 5, para. 5.6).

Subs. (4)

In order that the independent members may discharge their duty under subs. (3) the Bank *must* regularly report to and provide the Board with such necessary information as they "may reasonably require". See also s.87(4).

Subs. (5)

Likewise, it is the *duty* of the *ex-officio* members to report to the Chancellor of the Exchequer in those instances where it is decided that the independent members' advice should not be followed. To this duty there was added at the Lords Committee stage (*Hansard*, H.L. Vol. 485, col. 1241) the explicit right granted to the independent members to approach the Chancellor of the Exchequer to explain the reasons for their advice. The entitlement of independent members to go above the head of the Governor of the Bank may prove an effective measure. In its first annual report (see under subs. (6)) it was stated that no disagreements had occurred during the period to February 28, 1987.

Subs. (6)

The Board *as an entity* is required to prepare an annual report for inclusion in the Bank's own report made under s.1(3). Its first report appeared as an annex to the Bank's annual report for the year ended February 28, 1987.

Subs. (7)

The same immunity as is given to the Bank, its directors and officials is extended to the Board's members.

Subs. (8)

Detailed provisions as to the appointment, removal from office, increase in members, procedure and remuneration of the Board's independent members are set out in Sched. 1 to the Act.

Restriction on acceptance of deposits

Restriction on acceptance of deposits

3.—(1) Subject to section 4 below, no person shall in the United Kingdom accept a deposit in the course of carrying on (whether there or elsewhere) a business which for the purposes of this Act is a deposit-taking business unless that person is an institution for the time being authorised by the Bank under the following provisions of this Part of this Act.

(2) Any person who contravenes this section shall be guilty of an offence and liable—

(a) on conviction on indictment, to imprisonment for a term not exceeding two years or to a fine or to both;

(b) on summary conviction, to imprisonment for a term not exceeding six months or to a fine not exceeding the statutory maximum or to both.

(3) The fact that a deposit has been taken in contravention of this section shall not affect any civil liability arising in respect of the deposit or the money deposited.

TRANSITIONAL PROVISIONS
Sched. 5, paras. 2(1), 3(1), 4 and 5.

DEFINITIONS
"authorised": s.106(1).
"the Bank": s.1(5).
"deposit": s.5.
"deposit-taking business": s.6.
"institution": s.106(1).
"the statutory maximum": Criminal Justice Act 1982, s.74; Magistrates' Courts Act 1980, s.32.

GENERAL NOTE
This section essentially ends the distinction between recognised banks and deposit-taking institutions introduced by the 1979 Act. Howver, although the two-tier system is abandoned, there still remains in this Act some element of distinction in that there is a qualification limit of at least £5 million of paid up equity capital required in order to use a name indicating that the person is a bank, etc. (s.67). S.3 represents the keystone of the Act setting up the new system of banking supervision in that it makes it an offence to accept a deposit in the course of carrying on a deposit-taking business unless the person is duly *authorised* by the Bank or is an *exempted* person (s.4 and Sched. 2).

Subs. (1)

Previously, under the two-tier system of supervision the applicants for recognised status essentially had to satisfy two criteria (initially by completing a questionnaire) over and above those for licensed deposit-takers (apart from the minimum net asset size requirement): a subjective criterion requiring that they enjoyed a high reputation and standing in the financial (and particularly banking) community, generally for a reasonable period of time; and that they provided a wide range of banking services *or* a highly specialised banking service (Sched. 2, para. 2 to the 1979 Act). The White Paper (Chap. 7) recognised that this classification did not necessarily reflect the merits of individual institutions and instead the new Act seeks to strengthen supervision generally and extends this to cover the *entire* recognised banking sector. Subs. (1) sets down the basic restriction on accepting a deposit (within the meaning of s.5) in the course of carrying on a deposit-taking business (within the meaning of s.6) similar to the provisions of s.1 of the Act of 1979. For a recent examination of the term "deposit" see *SCF Finance Co.* v. *Masri (No. 2)* [1986] 1 All E.R. 40. The acceptance of a deposit (in any currency) is caught if such acceptance occurs, whether directly or through an agent *in the U.K.* (which would include money sent from an overseas depositor to a deposit-taker in the U.K.); however, the deposit-taking business may be carried on *anywhere*.

Subs. (2)

A breach of the section is made a serious criminal office. The Bank annual report for 1986 (p.54) stated that some thirty investigations (mainly involving possible contraventions of s.1) were conducted which might have lead to prosecution. See also ss.48 and 49 concerning unauthorised acceptance of deposits in contravention of s.3.

Subs. (3)

A contravention of the section does not absolve the deposit-taker from civil liability in respect of the debt. This was referred to in *SCF Finance Co.* v. *Masri (supra)*. See also the inconsistent High Court decisions of *Stewart* v. *Oriental Fire and Marine Insurance Co.* [1985] Q.B. 988; *Bedford Insurance Co.* v. *Instituto de Resseguros do Brasil* [1985] Q.B. 966; and *Phoenix General Insurance Co. of Greece S.A.* v. *Halvanon Insurance Co.* [1986] 1 All E.R. 908 and the comment on these cases in *Phoenix General Insurance Co. of Greece S.A.* v. *Administratia Asigurarilor de Stat* [1987] 2 All E.R. 152.

Exempted persons and exempted transactions

4.—(1) Section 3 above shall not apply to the acceptance of a deposit by the Bank or by a person for the time being specified in Schedule 2 to this Act.

(2) The exemption of a person specified in that Schedule shall be subject to any restriction there specified in the case of that person.

(3) The Treasury may after consultation with the Bank by order amend that Schedule—

(a) by adding any person or relaxing any restriction; or

(b) by removing any person for the time being specified in it or imposing or extending any restriction.

(4) Section 3 above shall not apply to any transaction prescribed for the purposes of this subsection by regulations made by the Treasury.

(5) Regulations under subsection (4) above may prescribe transactions by reference to any factors appearing to the Treasury to appropriate and, in particular, by reference to all or any of the following—

(a) the amount of the deposit;

(b) the total liability of the person accepting the deposit to his depositors or to any other creditors;

(c) the circumstances in which or the purpose for which the deposit is made;

(d) the identity of the person by whom the deposit is made or accepted, including his membership of a class whose membership is determined otherwise than by the Treasury;

(e) the number of, or the amount involved in, transactions of any particular description carried out by the person accepting the deposit or the frequency with which he carries out transactions of any particular description.

(6) Regulations under subsection (4) above may make any exemption for which they provide subject to compliance with specified conditions or requirements.

(7) Any order under subsection (3)(a) above and any regulations under subsection (4) above shall be subject to annulment in pursuance of a resolution of either House of Parliament, and no order shall be made under subsection (3)(b) above unless a draft of it has been laid before and approved by a resolution of each House of Parliament.

DEFINITIONS

"the Bank": s.1.

"deposit": s.5.

S.4 and Sched. 2 together provide for exemptions of both persons and prescribed transactions from the prohibition on deposit-taking set down in s.3. S.4 is largely a continuation of s.2 of the 1979 Act and Sched. 2 updates Sched. 1 to the 1979 Act.

Subs. (1)
The Bank and persons listed in Sched. 2 are granted exemption. Essentially there are four main categories. First, those such as building societies, friendly societies, authorised insurance companies and credit unions each regulated under other enactments; secondly, those which are part of the public sector such as the National Savings Bank, local authorities, municipal banks and the Crown Agents; thirdly, those exempted by reason of their insignificant size and effect—penny-savings banks, loan societies and school banks; and finally those on a list of international, supranational and inter-governmental bodies.

Subs. (2)
Sched. 2 exemptions shall be subject to any restrictions specified in the Schedule itself. For example, para. 8 of Sched. 2 exempts authorised insurance companies only in relation to deposits accepted in the course of carrying on their authorised insurance business which is governed by the Insurance Companies Act 1982—they would not be exempted if they were to take deposits whilst carrying on, say, a banking business.

Subs. (3)
A power to amend by order the list of exemptions or restrictions is granted to the Treasury, after consultation with the Bank.

Subss. (4), (6)
The Treasury is empowered to exempt by regulation certain *transactions* by persons who are not authorised or exempted to accept certain deposits which may, for example, be governed by other legislation. For example, under regulations made under s.2(1) of the 1979 Act, these included acceptance of a deposit by a charity attracting neither interest nor a premium on repayment, and by a practising solicitor in the course of his profession. The exemptions *may* be made subject to compliance with specified conditions or requirements (subs. (6)).

Subs. (5)
The exemption of such transactions may be based on a wide variety of particular reasons and a list of factors are given similar to that given in s.2(5) of the 1979 Act. That relating to the identity of the person accepting the deposit represents the key factor, as the institution concerned is generally named or referred to in the exempt transaction. See, *e.g.,* Banking Act 1979 (Exempt Transactions) Regulations 1986 (S.I. 1986 No. 1712) which consolidated earlier regulations.

Subs. (7)
An order which serves to add a person or relax a restriction and regulations prescribing transactions are subject to the negative parliamentary procedure whereas an order which removes a person or imposes or extends any restriction necessitates the affirmative parliamentary procedure calling for greater debate and consideration.

Meaning of "deposit"

5.—(1) Subject to the provisions of this section, in this Act "deposit" means a sum of money paid on terms—

    (a) under which it will be repaid, with or without interest or a premium, and either on demand or at a time or in circumstances agreed by or on behalf of the person making the payment and the person receiving it; and

    (b) which are not referable to the provision of property or services or the giving of security;

and references in this Act to money deposited and to the making of a deposit shall be construed accordingly.

(2) For the purposes of subsection (1)(b) above, money is paid on terms which are referable to the provision of property or services or to the giving of security if, and only if—

(a) it is paid by way of advance or part payment under a contract for the sale, hire or other provision of property or services, and is repayable only in the event that the property or services is not or are not in fact sold, hired or otherwise provided;

(b) it is paid by way of security for the performance of a contract or by way of security in respect of loss which may result from the non-performance of a contract; or

(c) without prejudice to paragraph (b) above, it is paid by way of security for the delivery up or return of any property, whether in a particular state of repair or otherwise.

(3) Except so far as any provision of this Act otherwise provides, in this Act "deposit" does not include—

(a) a sum paid by the Bank or an authorised institution;

(b) a sum paid by a person for the time being specified in Schedule 2 to this Act;

(c) a sum paid by a person, other than a person within paragraph (a) or (b) above, in the course of carrying on a business consisting wholly or mainly of lending money;

(d) a sum which is paid by one company to another at a time when one is a subsidiary of the other or both are subsidiaries of another company or the same individual is a majority or principal share-holder controller of both of them; or

(e) a sum which is paid by a person who, at the time when it is paid, is a close relative of the person receiving it or who is, or is a close relative of, a director, controller or manager of that person.

(4) In the application of paragraph (e) of subsection (3) above to a sum paid by a partnership that paragraph shall have effect as if for the reference to the person paying the sum there were substituted a reference to each of the partners.

(5) In subsection (3)(e) above "close relative", in relation to any person, means—

(a) his spouse;

(b) his children and step-children, his parents and step-parents, his brothers and sisters and step-brothers and step-sisters; and

(c) the spouse of any person within paragraph (b) above.

DEFINITIONS
"authorised": s.106(1).
"the Bank": s.1.
"controller": s.105(3).
"director": s.105(2).
"institution": s.106(1).
"majority shareholder controller": s.105(4)(b).
"manager": s.105(6).
"principal shareholder controller": s.105(4)(c).
"subsidiary": s.106(2); Companies Act 1985, s.736.

GENERAL NOTE
As with the 1979 Act, this Act is directed primarily towards the maintenance of depositor protection and if an institution takes deposits it must (unless exempted) apply for authorisation. As most institutions would take deposits as defined, whether one falls within the meaning of a "deposit-taking business" under s.6 is the crucial test. The very wide definition of "deposit" largely follows that in s.1(4) of the 1979 Act. At Standing Committee stage in the House of Commons (Third Sitting, December 18, 1986, col. 81) it was stressed that one who takes a deposit is not necessarily in a deposit-taking business. The example was given of a subsidiary company taking deposits as part of a deposit-taking business and being

authorised whereas the parent may take the odd deposit and by definition would not be conducting a deposit-taking business.

Subs. (2)

Para. (a) *excludes* from the definition of a deposit for the purposes of subs. (1)(b), an advance or part payment for a *specific* item of a property or service and *not*, for example, moneys placed with investment managers for investment at their discretion or pending receipt of instructions from the client which in the Bank's view would be "deposits". An example of para. (b) would be the deposit payable at the time of exchange of contracts for house purchase and para. (c) would, for instance, exclude money paid at the inception of a furnished tenancy agreement to a landlord.

Subs. (3)

Certain of the stated *exclusions* are *included* ("Except so far as any provision of this Act otherwise provides") for the purposes of s.35(4) and s.60(9) and note also the effect of ss.52(5) and 57(5). In the case of para. (a) it is assumed that banks as sophisticated lenders do not require the protection of the Act!

Meaning of "deposit-taking business"

6.—(1) Subject to the provisions of this section, a business is a deposit-taking business for the purposes of this Act if—

    (a) in the course of the business money received by way of deposit is lent to others; or

    (b) any other activity of the business is financed, wholly or to any material extent, out of the capital of or the interest on money received by way of deposit.

(2) Notwithstanding that paragraph (a) or (b) of subsection (1) above applies to a business, it is not a deposit-taking business for the purposes of this Act if—

    (a) the person carrying it on does not hold himself out as accepting deposits on a day to day basis; and

    (b) any deposits which are accepted are accepted only on particular occasions, whether or not involving the issue of debentures or other securities.

(3) For the purposes of subsection (1) above all the activities which a person carries on by way of business shall be regarded as a single business carried on by him.

(4) In determining for the purposes of subsection (2)(b) above whether deposits are accepted only on particular occasions regard shall be had to the frequency of those occasions and to any characteristics distinguishing them from each other.

(5) For the purposes of subsection (2) above there shall be disregarded any deposit in respect of the acceptance of which the person in question is exempt from the prohibition in section 3 above and any money received by way of deposit which is not used in the manner described in subsection (1) above.

DEFINITIONS

"debenture": s.106(1); Companies Act 1985, s.744.

"deposit": s.5.

GENERAL NOTE

Again, as in the case of the definition of "deposit" (s.5) this s.6 wording closely follows the relevant provisions of s.1 of the 1979 Act.

Subs. (1)

Business. Not defined but wider than meaning of "credit institution" in Art. 1 of Council Directive 77/780/EEC ("whose business is to receive deposits or other repayable funds from the public and to grant credits for its own account").

To any material extent. Presumably not only relates to the proportion contributed by the capital sum or interest (as distinct from "wholly") but also to the actual total value of the sums involved in the financing of "any other activity."

Subs. (2)

The result of reading the two paragraphs conjunctively is that a business *is* a deposit-taking business if (1) it "holds itself out" as accepting deposits on a day to day basis notwithstanding that in practice it accepts only on "particular occasions"; or (2) does *not* so hold itself out but accepts deposits on other than "particular occasions."

Hold himself out. Probably sufficient for one to make it known, however informally, that one was ready and willing to accept deposits.

Subs. (3)

No matter what the vehicle may be through which a person chooses to carry on any of his business activities, that person is deemed for the purposes of s.6(1) and ultimately s.3(1) to be carrying on a single business.

Subs. (4)

This new provision reflects what has been the Bank of England's understanding of the term "particular occasions."

Subs. (5)

An "avoidance of doubt" provision!

Power to amend definitions

7.—(1) The Treasury may after consultation with the Bank by order amend the meaning of deposit or deposit-taking business for the purposes of all or any provisions of this Act.

(2) Without prejudice to the generality of the power conferred by subsection (1) above, an order under that subsection amending the meaning of deposit-taking business may provide for taking into account as activities of an institution the activities of any person who is connected with it in such manner as is specified in the order.

(3) Any order under this section shall be subject to annulment in pursuance of a resolution of either House of Parliament.

(4) An order under this section may contain such transitional provisions as the Treasury think necessary or expedient and may exclude or modify the effect of the order on any other enactment which is expressed to have effect in relation to a deposit or a deposit-taking business within the meaning of this Act.

DEFINITIONS
    "the Bank": s.1.
    "deposit": s.5.
    "deposit-taking business": s.6.
    "institution": s.106(1).

GENERAL NOTE

The White Paper (Chap. 4, para. 4.8) proposed that any new legislation should allow for future modification by secondary legislation of the definition of deposit and deposit-taking businesses to "cope with the needs of a rapidly changing banking system." Just as under the Financial Services Act 1986 (s.2) the definitions of "investments" and "investment business" may be adjusted to meet changing circumstances, so also will those of "deposit" and "deposit-taking business," thus recognising the ever-present need for flexibility of approach.

Subss. (1), (3)

Either definition may be altered by the Treasury, after consultation with the Bank, by order subject to the negative parliamentary procedure.

Subs. (2)

A power is also included to amend the definition of a "deposit-taking business" in such a manner that it takes into account activities of *connected persons* as specified in the order as well as of the activities of the institution itself.

Subs. (4)

It may be that any amending order will make changes which will necessitate the incorporation of transitional provisions to assist in any changeover and the possibility that such an order may affect other enactments is catered for.

Authorisations

Applications for authorisation

8.—(1) Any institution may make an application for authorisation to the Bank.

(2) Any such application—

   (a) shall be made in such manner as the Bank may direct; and

   (b) shall be accompanied by—

      (i) a statement setting out the nature and scale of the deposit-taking business which the applicant intends to carry on, any plans of the applicant for the future development of that business and particulars of the applicant's arrangements for the management of that business; and

      (ii) such other information or documents as the Bank may reasonably require for the purpose of determining the application.

(3) At any time after receiving an application and before determining it the Bank may by written notice require the applicant or any person who is or is to be a director, controller or manager of the applicant to provide additional information or documents.

(4) The directions and requirements given or imposed under subsections (2) and (3) above may differ as between different applications.

(5) Any information or statement to be provided to the Bank under this section shall be in such form as the Bank may specify; and the Bank may by written notice require the applicant or any such person as is mentioned in subsection (3) above to provide a report by an accountant or other qualified person approved by the Bank on such aspects of that information as may be specified by the Bank.

(6) An application may be withdrawn by written notice to the Bank at any time before it is granted or refused.

DEFINITIONS

   "authorisation": s.106(1).
   "the Bank": s.1.
   "controller": s.105(3).
   "deposit-taking business": s.6.
   "director": s.105(2).
   "documents": s.106(1).
   "institution": s.106(1).
   "manager": s.105(6).
   "notice": ss.99, 100.

GENERAL NOTE

This section provides the formal mechanism for application to the Bank for authorisation and is partly based on ss.3 and 5 of the 1979 Act and is partly new. Ss.8 to 14 of this Act provide for the whole procedure of applying for the granting (or refusing), revocation and restriction of authorisation. See also s.94(2) regarding false and misleading information.

Subs. (1)

This section should be read with s.106 (interpretation). In stating that any institution may apply for authorisation, sole traders are by definition excluded and partnerships and unincorporated bodies from non-EEC countries are no longer eligible. Under Council Directive 77/780/EEC partnerships in Member States may apply for authorisation (Arts. 1 and 3.).

Subss. (2), (4)

Although the Bank is free to direct the manner in which it is to be made, each application must be accompanied by a statement setting out the nature and scale of the intended deposit-taking business, plans for *future* development and particular arrangements for its management—all requirements of Council Directive 77/780/EEC, Art. 3.4, and "such other information or documents as the Bank may reasonably require". At Standing Committee stage (Third Sitting, December 18, 1986, col. 82) it was sought to give the Bank absolute discretion as to the information required but in the end this was not introduced for fear of deterring overseas banks who might not know what they would be asked. However, note that the Bank is not constrained as to its directions and requirements under subss. (2) and (3) with regard to different applications—presumably even if made by the same applicant at a subsequent date.

Subs. (3)

A new provision is the power given to the Bank to require the supply of documents or additional information from not only the applicant but also any present or intended director, controller or manager of the applicant.

Subs. (5)

Another new provision is the power given to the Bank requiring that specified aspects of information be reported on by an accountant or other suitably qualified person (see also ss.39(1)(b) and 47).

Grant and refusal of authorisation

9.—(1) The Bank may, on an application duly made in accordance with section 8 above and after being provided with all such information, documents and reports as it may require under that section, grant or refuse the application.

(2) The Bank shall not grant an application unless satisfied that the criteria specified in Schedule 3 to this Act are fulfilled with respect to the applicant.

(3) In the case of an application by an applicant whose principal place of business is in a country or territory outside the United Kingdom the Bank may regard itself as satisfied that the criteria specified in paragraphs 1, 4 and 5 of that Schedule are fulfilled if—

(a) the relevant supervisory authority in that country or territory informs the Bank that it is satisfied with respect to the prudent management and overall financial soundness of the applicant; and

(b) the Bank is satisfied as to the nature and scope of the supervision exercised by that authority.

(4) In determining whether to grant or refuse an application the Bank may take into account any matters relating—

(a) to any person who is or will be employed by or associated with the applicant for the purposes of the applicant's deposit-taking business; and

(b) if the applicant is a body corporate, to any other body corporate in the same group or to any director or controller of any such other body.

(5) No authorisation shall be granted to a partnership or unincorporated association if the whole of the assets available to it are owned by a single individual.

(6) An authorisation granted to a partnership shall be granted in the partnership name and, without prejudice to sections 11 and 12 below, shall not be affected by any change in the partners.

DEFINITIONS
    "authorisation": s.106(1).
    "the Bank": s.1.
    "controller": s.105(3).
    "deposit-taking business": s.6.

"director": s.105(2).
"documents": s.106(1).
"group": s.106(1).
"relevant supervisory authority": s.106(1).

GENERAL NOTE
S.9 and Sched. 3 are derived from s.3 and Sched. 2 to the 1979 Act.

Subss. (2), (3)
Apart from there being now only one list of criteria, (which must all be satisfied) these subsections follow subss. (3) and (5) of s.3 of the 1979 Act. The especial concern felt about the possible inadequacy of supervisory authorities in other parts of the world was aired during the Third Sitting of the Standing Committee (Third Sitting, December 18, 1986, cols. 83–88). Where applications are made in respect of a U.K. branch, by those whose principal place of business is outside the U.K. the Bank itself *must* take steps to satisfy itself that criteria 2, 3 and 6, specified in Sched. 3, are fulfilled. With regard to criteria 1, 4 and 5, the Bank *may* rely upon the information provided by the national supervisory authority in the country in which the applicant has his principal place of business, as to the applicant's "prudent management and overall financial soundness" provided that the Bank is itself satisfied with the "nature and scope" of the supervision exercised by that other authority. The Standing Committee reassured itself on the basis of the seven years' experience following the 1979 Act; it was noted that the Bank had power to probe if in doubt as to the particular institution and the system of supervision in the particular country (Third Sitting, December 18, 1986, col. 88).

Subs. (4)
This is new and in coming to a decision whether to grant or refuse an application, the Bank *may* take into account matters relating to any employee of the institution, to any person "associated" with (not defined) the institution and to other companies in its group or to any directors or controllers of any other such company.

Subs. (5)
In effect a requirement of the Council Directive 77/780/EEC, Art. 3.

Subs. (6)
Authorisation is granted in the partnership name and not in the name of the individual partners, and accordingly authorisation continues to apply irrespective of any subsequent change, subject to ss.21 to 25 (relating to the notification requirements of new or increased control).

Notice of grant or refusal

10.—(1) Where the Bank grants an application for authorisation it shall give written notice of that fact to the applicant.

(2) Where the Bank proposes to refuse an application for authorisation it shall give the applicant written notice of its intention to do so, stating the grounds on which it proposes to act and giving particulars of the applicant's rights under subsection (4) below.

(3) Where the ground or a ground for the proposed refusal is that the Bank is not satisfied that the criterion in paragraph 1 of Schedule 3 to this Act is fulfilled in the case of any such person as is there mentioned, the Bank shall give that person a copy of the notice mentioned in subsection (2) above, together with a statement of his rights under subsection (4) below.

(4) An applicant who is given a notice under subsection (2) above and a person who is given a copy of it under subsection (3) above may within such period (not being less than twenty-eight days) as is specified in the notice make written representations to the Bank; and where such representations are made the Bank shall take them into account before reaching a decision on the application.

(5) Where the Bank refuses an application it shall give written notice of that fact to the applicant and to any such person as is mentioned in

subsection (3) above, stating the reasons for the refusal and giving particulars of the rights conferred by section 27 below.

(6) Any notice under subsection (5) above shall be given before the end of the period of six months beginning with the day on which the application was received by the Bank or, where the Bank has under section 8 above required additional information or documents in connection with the application, before the end of whichever of the following first expires—

>(a) the period of six months beginning with the day on which the additional information or documents are provided;
>
>(b) the period of twelve months beginning with the day on which the application was received.

(7) The Bank may omit from the copy given to a person under subsection (3) above and from a notice given to him under subsection (5) above any matter which does not relate to him.

DEFINITIONS

>"authorisation": s.106(1).
>"the Bank": s.1.
>"documents": s.106(1).
>"notice": s.100.

GENERAL NOTE

This section provides in particular the more detailed mechanism to be followed by the Bank when refusing an application for authorisation. It follows, with an added requirement, the procedure laid down in s.5 of the 1979 Act.

Subs. (1)

Successful applicants are accordingly informed in writing and authorisation then takes immediate effect.

Subss. (2), (4), (5), (6)

Where the Bank is disposed to refuse, written notice of such intention, stating the grounds and the applicant's rights to make written representations within a period of at least 28 days, must be given to the applicant. Any such representations must be taken into account before the Bank makes its decision and the Bank is obliged to answer the applicant within six months of the date of receipt of the application (which may be extended to 12 months where additional information is sought under s.8(3)). A refusal must be given to the applicant in writing with reasons and giving particulars of the rights of appeal provided under s.27.

Subss. (3), (7)

This is a new provision which also appears elsewhere in the Act. (See s.13(4), (12).) Where the ground for refusal relates to the fitness and "properness" of a director, controller or manager (para. (1) of Sched. 3) then such person is to be given a copy of the notice given to the applicant under subs. (2) and a statement of his rights to make written representations (as also the applicant may). Any matter which does not relate to him may be omitted from the statement of his rights and from the notice of refusal. Probing amendments (which were later withdrawn) in Standing Committee (Fourth Sitting, January 13, 1987, cols. 111–115) disclosed that the greater majority of applicants were dealt with within eight months from application and in the case of the remainder the extra time remaining afforded the Bank the opportunity to arrive at a clear decision without undue pressure.

Revocation of authorisation

11.—(1) The Bank may revoke the authorisation of an institution if it appears to the Bank that—

>(a) any of the criteria specified in Schedule 3 to this Act is not or has not been fulfilled, or may not be or may not have been fulfilled, in respect of the institution;
>
>(b) the institution has failed to comply with any obligation imposed on it by or under this Act;
>
>(c) a person has become a controller of the institution in contravention

of section 21 below or has become or remains a controller after being given a notice of objection under section 22, 23 or 24 below;

(d) the Bank has been provided with false, misleading or inaccurate information by or on behalf of the institution or, in connection with an application for authorisation, by or on behalf of a person who is or is to be a director, controller or manager of the institution; or

(e) the interests of depositors or potential depositors of the institution are in any other way threatened, whether by the manner in which the institution is conducting or proposes to conduct its affairs or for any other reason.

(2) The Bank may revoke the authorisation of an institution if it appears to the Bank that the institution—

(a) has not accepted a deposit in the United Kingdom in the course of carrying on a deposit-taking business (whether there or elsewhere) within the period of twelve months beginning with the day on which it was authorised; or

(b) having accepted a deposit or deposits as aforesaid, has subsequently not done so for any period of more than six months.

(3) It in the case of an authorised institution whose principal place of business is in a country or territory outside the United Kingdom it appears to the Bank that the relevant supervisory authority in that country or territory has withdrawn from the institution an authorisation corresponding to that conferred by the Bank under this Part of this Act, the Bank may revoke the authorisation and shall do so if that country or territory is a member State.

(4) In the case of an authorised institution which is an authorised person under the Financial Services Act 1986 or holds a consumer credit licence under the Consumer Credit Act 1974 the Bank may revoke the authorisation if it appears to the Bank that the institution has ceased to be an authorised person under the said Act of 1986 (otherwise than at the request or with the consent of the institution) or that the licence under the said Act of 1974 has been revoked.

(5) The Treasury may after consultation with the Bank by order make provision corresponding to subsection (4) above in relation to any authorisation or licence granted under such other enactments as may appear to the Treasury to be appropriate; but any such order shall be subject to annulment in pursuance of a resolution of either House of Parliament.

(6) If in the case of an authorised institution wherever incorporated it appears to the Bank that—

(a) a winding-up order has been made against it in the United Kingdom; or

(b) a resolution for its voluntary winding up in the United Kingdom has been passed,

the Bank shall revoke the authorisation; and the Bank may revoke the authorisation of any authorised institution incorporated outside the United Kingdom if it appears to the Bank that an event has occurred in respect of it outside the United Kingdom which corresponds as nearly as may be to either of those mentioned in paragraphs (a) and (b) above.

(7) The Bank may revoke the authorisation of an authorised institution incorporated in the United Kingdom if it appears to the Bank that—

(a) a composition or arrangement with creditors has been made in respect of the institution;

(b) a receiver or manager of the institution's undertaking has been appointed; or

(c) possession has been taken, by or on behalf of the holders of any debenture secured by a charge, of any property of the institution comprised in or subject to the charge;

or, in the case of an authorised institution incorporated elsewhere, that an event has occurred in respect of it which corresponds as nearly as may be to any of those mentioned in paragraphs (a), (b) and (c) above.

(8) The Bank may revoke the authorisation of an authorised institution if it appears to the Bank that an administration order has been made in relation to the institution under section 8 of the Insolvency Act 1986.

(9) The Bank shall revoke the authorisation of an unincorporated institution if it appears to the Bank that a winding-up order has been made against it in the United Kingdom and may revoke the authorisation of such an institution if it appears to the Bank that—

(a) the institution has been dissolved; or

(b) a bankruptcy order, an award of sequestration, an order of adjudication of bankruptcy or a composition or arrangement with creditors has been made or a trust deed for creditors granted in respect of that institution or any of its members; or

(c) any event corresponding as nearly as may be to any of those mentioned in paragraph (b) above or in subsection (6)(a) or (b) or (7)(b) or (c) above has occurred in respect of that institution or any of its members; or

(d) the whole of the assets available to the institution have passed into the ownership of a single individual.

TRANSITIONAL PROVISION
Sched. 5, para. 2(2).

DEFINITIONS
"authorisation": s.106(1).
"the Bank": s.1.
"controller": s.105(3).
"debenture: s.106(1); Companies Act 1985, s.744.
"deposit": s.5.
"deposit-taking business": s.6.
"director": s.105(2).
"documents": s.106(1).
"institution": s.106(1).
"manager": s.105(6).
"relevant supervisory authority": s.106(1).

GENERAL NOTE
This section sets down the grounds upon which the Bank may, and in three instances must, revoke authorisation, and may well prove to be one of the most feared weapons in the Bank's armoury. S.12 provides, in less serious cases, for the authorisation to be restricted by the imposition of limits or conditions. S.11 continues and materially extends s.6 of the 1979 Act which itself reflected Art. 8 of the Council Directive 77/780/EEC. It may be noted that under s.19(1)(a) the Bank may give directions to an institution when notice of revocation of its authorisation is given. Revocation is clearly a serious step to take and the 1986 Bank of England annual report (on p.53) noted that the level of revocations was increasing, due, to some extent, to the growing number of investigations being carried out, but all of those in the period in question involved institutions with total liabilities of less than £10 million.

Subss. (1)–(4)
The Bank *may*, if there are reasonable grounds for so doing, revoke authorisation on a number of specific grounds, some of which were given in s.6 of the 1979 Act but two of which are new. S.11(1)(c) adds the ground of a person becoming a controller of an institution in contravention of the provisions in ss.21–24 (relating to notification of, and objection to, becoming a controller) and s.11(4) provides for power to revoke in the case of an institution which it appears has ceased to be an authorised person under the Financial Services Act 1986 or has had its consumer credit licence revoked under the Consumer Credit Act 1974. There is, as there was before, an extensive sweeping-up provision in para. (e) of s.11(1) where the interests of depositors or potential depositors are "in any other way threatened

. . . by the manner in which the institution is conducting *or proposes to conduct* its affairs *or for any other reason*" (emphasis added).

Under subs. (3) the Bank *must* revoke authorisation if the relevant supervisory authority in a Member State has withdrawn authorisation from an authorised institution whose principal place of business is in that particular Member State.

Subs. (5)

A useful provision enabling the extension of the provisions in subs. (4) correspondingly in relation to other appropriate enactments conferring authorisation or licensing functions on supervisory bodies.

Subss. (6), (9)

Revocation is *mandatory* where a winding-up order appears to the Bank to have been made in the U.K. against any incorporated or unincorporated institution or a resolution for its voluntary winding-up appears to have been passed in the case of any incorporated body. However, the Bank *may* revoke authorisation of an *unincorporated* institution if certain events (such as dissolution) appear to the Bank to have occurred (subs. (9)).

Subss. (7), (8)

Note that the Bank *may* revoke, amongst other grounds, if it appears to it that a receiver has been appointed (institution incorporated in U.K.) or that an administration order has been made under s.8 of the Insolvency Act 1986.

Restriction of authorisation

12.—(1) Where it appears to the Bank—
  (a) that there are grounds on which the Bank's power to revoke an institution's authorisation are exercisable; but
  (b) that the circumstances are not such as to justify revocation, the Bank may restrict the authorisation instead of revoking it.
(2) An authorisation may be restricted—
  (a) by imposing such limit on its duration as the Bank thinks fit;
  (b) by imposing such conditions as it thinks desirable for the protection of the institution's depositors or potential depositors; or
  (c) by the imposition both of such a limit and of such conditions.
(3) A limit on the duration of an authorisation shall not be such as to allow the authorisation to continue in force for more than three years from the date on which it is imposed; and such a limit may, in particular, be imposed in a case in which the Bank considers that an institution should be allowed time to repay its depositors in an orderly manner.
(4) The conditions imposed under this section may in particular—
  (a) require the institution to take certain steps or to refrain from adopting or pursuing a particular course of action or to restrict the scope of its business in a particular way;
  (b) impose limitations on the acceptance of deposits, the granting of credit or the making of investments;
  (c) prohibit the institution from soliciting deposits, either generally or from persons who are not already depositors;
  (d) prohibit it from entering into any other transaction or class of transactions;
  (e) require the removal of any director, controller or manager;
  (f) specify requirements to be fulfilled otherwise than by action taken by the institution.
(5) Any condition imposed under this section may be varied or withdrawn by the Bank; and any limit imposed under this section on the duration of an authorisation may be varied but not so as to allow the authorisation to continue in force for longer than the period mentioned in subsection (3) above from the date on which the limit was first imposed.

(6) An institution which fails to comply with any requirement or contravenes any prohibition imposed on it by a condition under this section shall be guilty of an offence and liable—

(a) on conviction on indictment, to a fine;

(b) on summary conviction, to a fine not exceeding the statutory maximum.

(7) The fact that a condition imposed under this section has not been complied with (whether or not constituting an offence under subsection (6) above) shall be a ground for the revocation of the authorisation in question but shall not invalidate any transaction.

(8) An institution whose authorisation is restricted by the imposition of a limit on its duration may apply under section 8 above for a new authorisation and, if that authorisation is granted, the restricted authorisation shall cease to have effect.

TRANSITIONAL PROVISION
Sched. 5, para. 3(1).

DEFINITIONS
"authorisation": s.106(1).
"the Bank": s.1.
"controller": s.105(3).
"deposit": s.5.
"director": s.105(2).
"institution": s.106(1).
"manager": s.105(6).
"the statutory maximum": Criminal Justice Act 1982, s.74; Magistrates' Courts Act 1980, s.32.

GENERAL NOTE
As revocation is such a serious action to take, the 1979 Act provided that the Bank may choose to allow an institution to continue its deposit-taking status by the Bank taking the step of revoking the existing recognition or licence and instead as a corrective measure granting a conditional licence for a period of up to one year (ss.7(1)(b) and 10). S.12 of the new Act allows the Bank to "restrict" the authorisation of an institution where one of the grounds for revocation has arisen but the Bank is of the view that circumstances are such that revocation is not justified (subs. (1)). S.16(1) preserves flexibility by requiring the Bank to publish a statement of principles as to how it will act, *inter alia,* in exercising its power to grant, revoke or restrict an authorisation.

Subss. (2)–(5)
A restriction may be of two kinds or a combination of both. It may allow the authorisation to continue in force for up to a maximum of three years and may in particular "be imposed in a case in which the Bank considers that an institution should be allowed time to repay its depositors in an orderly manner".

A question was raised in Standing Committee (Fourth Sitting, January 13, 1987, col. 116) as to the reason for the time limit but the forthcoming answer was not particularly helpful in stating that the time limit provided a reasonable but not unlimited period for an institution to repay depositors. The second type of restriction is the imposition of conditions (which may be varied or withdrawn) similar to those formerly imposed in s.10 of the 1979 Act but with the addition of further possible conditions which may prohibit any other transactions or specify requirements to be fulfilled by third parties.

Subss. (6), (7)
Any breach of a requirement or contravention of a prohibition imposed by a condition under this section constitutes a statutory offence and non-compliance with a condition shall be a ground for revocation of authorisation but does not in itself invalidate any transaction.

Subs. (8)
As a restricted authorisation with a limited duration (subs. (2)(a)) will lapse at the end of three years, an institution will be compelled to apply for a new authorisation under s.8.

Notice of revocation or restriction

13.—(1) Subject to section 14 below where the Bank proposes—

    (a) to revoke an authorisation; or

    (b) to restrict an authorisation; or

    (c) to vary the restrictions imposed on an authorisation otherwise than with the agreement of the institution concerned,

the Bank shall give to the institution concerned written notice of its intention to do so.

(2) If the proposed action is within paragraph (b) or (c) of subsection (1) above the notice under that subsection shall specify the proposed restrictions or, as the case may be, the proposed variation.

(3) A notice under subsection (1) above shall state the grounds on which the Bank proposes to act and give particulars of the institution's rights under subsection (5) below.

(4) Where—

    (a) the ground or a ground for a proposed revocation or for a proposal to impose or vary a restriction is that it appears to the Bank that the criterion in paragraph 1 of Schedule 3 to this Act is not or has not been fulfilled, or may not be or may not have been fulfilled, in the case of any person; or

    (b) a proposed restriction consists of or includes a condition requiring the removal of any person as director, controller or manager,

the Bank shall give that person a copy of the notice mentioned in subsection (1) above, together with a statement of his rights under subsection (5) below.

(5) An institution which is given a notice under subsection (1) above and a person who is given a copy of it under subsection (4) above may within the period of fourteen days beginning with the day on which the notice was given make representations to the Bank.

(6) After giving a notice under subsection (1) above and taking into account any representations made under subsection (5) above the Bank shall decide whether—

    (a) to proceed with the action proposed in the notice;

    (b) to take no further action;

    (c) if the proposed action was to revoke the institution's authorisation, to restrict its authorisation instead;

    (d) if the proposed action was to restrict the institution's authorisation, or to vary the restrictions on an authorisation, to restrict it or to vary the restrictions in a different manner.

(7) The Bank shall give the institution and any such person as is mentioned in subsection (4) above written notice of its decision and, except where the decision is to take no further action, the notice shall state the reasons for the decision and give particulars of the rights conferred by subsection (9) and section 27 below.

(8) A notice under subsection (7) above of a decision to revoke or restrict an authorisation or to vary the restrictions on an authorisation shall, subject to section 27(4) below, have the effect of revoking the authorisation or, as the case may be, restricting the authorisation or varying the restrictions in the manner specified in the notice.

(9) Where the decision notified under subsection (7) above is to restrict the authorisation or to vary the restrictions on an authorisation otherwise than as stated in the notice given under subsection (1) above the institution may within the period of seven days beginning with the day on which the notice was given under subsection (7) above make written representations to the Bank with respect to the restrictions and the Bank may, after taking those representations into account, alter the restrictions.

(10) A notice under subsection (7) above shall be given within the period of twenty-eight days beginning with the day on which the notice under subsection (1) above was given; and if no notice under subsection (7) is given within that period the Bank shall be treated as having at the end of that period given a notice under that subsection to the effect that no further action is to be taken.

(11) Where the Bank varies a restriction on an institution's authorisation with its agreement or withdraws a restriction consisting of a condition the variation or withdrawal shall be effected by written notice to the institution.

(12) The Bank may omit from the copy given to a person under subsection (4) above and from a notice given to him under subsection (7) above any matter which does not relate to him.

DEFINITIONS
  "authorisation": s.106(1).
  "the Bank": s.1.
  "controller": s.105(3).
  "director": s.105(2).
  "institution": s.106(1).
  "manager": s.105(6).
  "notice": s.100.

GENERAL NOTE
  The detailed process by which the revocation, or restriction or variation of the restriction, of an institution's authorisation is effected follows that set down in s.7 of, and Sched. 4 to, the 1979 Act. Note the right of the institution concerned and of any person referred to in subs. (4) to make representations to the Bank (which the Bank must take into account) and of their rights (after they each receive a notice of the Bank's decision to revoke or restrict an authorisation or to vary the restrictions) to appeal to the tribunal (under s.27).

Mandatory revocation and restriction in cases of urgency

14.—(1) No notice need be given under section 13 above in respect of—
  (a) the revocation of an institution's authorisation in any case in which revocation is mandatory under section 11 above; or
  (b) the imposition or variation of a restriction on an institution's authorisation in any case in which the Bank considers that the restriction should be imposed or varied as a matter of urgency.

(2) In any such case the Bank may by written notice to the institution revoke the authorisation or impose or vary the restriction.

(3) Any such notice shall state the reasons for which the Bank has acted and, in the case of a notice imposing or varying a restriction, particulars of the rights conferred by subsection (5) and by section 27 below.

(4) Subsection (4) of section 13 above shall apply to a notice under subsection (2) above imposing or varying a restriction as it applies to a notice under subsection (1) of that section in respect of a proposal to impose or vary a restriction; but the Bank may omit from a copy given to a person by virtue of this subsection any matter which does not relate to him.

(5) An institution to which a notice is given under this section of the imposition or variation of a restriction and a person who is given a copy of it by virtue of subsection (4) above may within the period of fourteen days beginning with the day on which the notice was given make representations to the Bank.

(6) After giving a notice under subsection (2) above imposing or varying a restriction and taking into account any representations made in accordance with subsection (5) above the Bank shall decide whether—
  (a) to confirm or rescind its original decision; or

(b) to impose a different restriction or to vary the restriction in a different manner.

(7) The Bank shall within the period of twenty-eight days beginning with the day on which the notice was given under subsection (2) above give the institution concerned written notice of its decision under subsection (6) above and, except where the decision is to rescind the original decision, the notice shall state the reasons for the decision.

(8) Where the notice under subsection (7) above is of a decision to take the action specified in subsection (6)(b) above the notice under subsection (7) shall have the effect of imposing the restriction or making the variation specified in the notice and with effect from the date on which it is given.

(9) Where a notice of the proposed revocation of an institution's authorisation under section 13 above is followed by a notice revoking its authorisation under this section the latter notice shall have the effect of terminating any right to make representations in respect of the proposed revocation and any pending appeal proceedings in respect of a decision implementing that proposal.

DEFINITIONS
   "authorisation": s.106(1).
   "the Bank": s.1.
   "institution": s.106(1).
   "notice": s.100.

GENERAL NOTE
   Whereas s.13 requires the Bank first to give notice of its intention to revoke, restrict or vary a restriction, in those circumstances where revocation is based on *mandatory* grounds (under s.11, *e.g.* winding-up order to be made against an authorised institution) or in circumstances where the Bank considers that the restriction should be imposed or varied "as a matter of urgency" (no examples given), the more protracted s.132 procedure need not be observed. Instead, notice of revocation, restriction or variation is served and the institution is immediately affected to the extent that the *notice of revocation* of authorisation terminates the right to make representations and any pending appeal proceedings (subs. (9)). In the case of an *imposition or variation of a restriction,* it may make representations which the Bank must take into account before confirming or rescinding its original decision or imposing a different restriction or varying the restriction in a different manner, and the institution must be informed of the rights of appeal under s.27 (subs. 3)).

Surrender of authorisation

15.—(1) An authorised institution may surrender its authorisation by written notice to the Bank.

(2) A surrender shall take effect on the giving of the notice or, if a later date is specified in it, on that date; and where a later date is specified in the notice the institution may by a further written notice to the Bank substitute an earlier date, not being earlier than that on which the first notice was given.

(3) The surrender of an authorisation shall be irrevocable unless it is expressed to take effect on a later date and before that date the Bank by notice in writing to the institution allows it to be withdrawn.

DEFINITIONS
   "authorised": s.106(1).
   "the Bank": s.1.
   "institution": s.106(1).
   "notice": s.99.

GENERAL NOTE
   Although the 1979 Act made no express provision for surrender of its authorisation by an institution, s.8(1)(c) of that Act referred to the giving of directions by the Bank "at any time after the institution has surrendered its recognition or licence". It may be noted that in the

case of ss.39(8), 41(6), 46(3) and 47(7) of this Act the provisions are expressed to apply in the case of *former* authorised institutions (for definition see s.106(1)) just as they apply to authorised institutions and ss.92(1) and 94(3) provide respectively for the winding-up of, and the particular statutory offence being committed by, a former authorised institution (see also ss.47(7) and 83(2)). Surrender subjects an institution to the s.3 restriction on acceptance of deposits, including in the Bank's view *renewal* of deposits and crediting interest on deposits.

Statement of principles

16.—(1) The Bank shall, as soon as practicable after the coming into force of this section, publish in such manner as it thinks appropriate a statement of the principles in accordance with which it is acting or proposing to act—

(a) in interpreting the criteria specified in Schedule 3 to this Act and the grounds for revocation specified in section 11 above; and

(b) in exercising its power to grant, revoke or restrict an authorisation.

(2) If in the course of a financial year of the Bank it makes a material change in the principles in accordance with which it is acting or proposing to act as mentioned in subsection (1) above it shall include a statement of the change in the report made by it for that year under section 1(3) above; and the Bank may, at any time, publish in such manner as it thinks appropriate a statement of the principles in accordance with which it is acting or proposing to act as mentioned in that subsection.

DEFINITIONS
"authorisation": s.106(1).
"the Bank": s.1.

GENERAL NOTE
The accountability of the Bank to Parliament has already been observed under s.1(3). Under s.4(3) of the 1979 Act the importance to be attached to making public the principles on which the Bank would act in its interpretation and application of the criteria for recognition or for a licence and of the grounds for revocation, was emphasised in its requiring the principles to be stated annually in the Bank's Annual Report. Under the present Act, again recognising that the Sched. 3 criteria for authorisation set only a *minimum* test, the Bank is required to publish as soon as practicable but "in such manner as it thinks appropriate" a statement of the principles in accordance with which it is acting or proposing to act in interpreting authorisation requirements and in exercising its powers of granting, revoking or restricting authorisation. Thereafter statements of principles are published at any time save that any "material change" in the principles must be included in the Bank's Annual Report. There appear to have been few major policy changes under the 1979 Act but the Bank's wide discretion in this connection is maintained.

Information as to authorised institutions

17.—(1) Every report made by the Bank under section 1(3) above shall contain a list of the institutions which are authorised under this Act at the end of the financial year to which the report relates.

(2) The Bank shall make available to any person on request and on payment of such fee, if any, as the Bank may reasonably require a list of the institutions which are authorised either at the date of the request or at such earlier date, being not more than one month earlier, as may be specified in the list.

(3) The Bank may give public notice of the fact that an institution has ceased to be authorised.

DEFINITIONS
"authorised": s.106(1).
"the Bank": s.1.
"institution": s.106(1).

GENERAL NOTE
This section (replacing s.4(2), (6) of the 1979 Act) requires the Bank to publish in its annual report, or on request on payment of a fee, a list of authorised institutions. In addition, the Bank is empowered to publish the names of those persons no longer authorised, but presumably not those where a restriction is in operation.

False statements as to authorised status

18.—(1) No person other than an authorised institution shall—
   (a) describe himself as an authorised institution; or
   (b) so hold himself out as to indicate or be reasonably understood to indicate that he is an authorised institution.

(2) No person shall falsely state, or do anything which falsely indicates, that he is entitled although not an authorised institution to accept a deposit in the course of carrying on a business which for the purposes of this Act is a deposit-taking business.

(3) Any person who contravenes this section shall be guilty of an offence and liable—
   (a) on conviction on indictment, to imprisonment for a term not exceeding two years or to a fine or to both;
   (b) on summary conviction, to imprisonment for a term not exceeding six months or to a fine not exceeding the statutory maximum or to both.

DEFINITIONS
"authorised": s.106(1).
"deposit": s.5.
"deposit-taking business": s.6.
"institution": s.106(1).
"statutory maximum": Criminal Justice Act 1982, s.74; Magistrates' Courts Act 1980, s.32.

GENERAL NOTE
The aim of this section, which did not appear in the 1979 Act, is to make it an offence (new) for any person (other than an authorised institution) to pass themselves off as authorised or entitled to accept a deposit in the course of a deposit-taking business. To this extent the Act is brought into a parallel position with s.200 of the Financial Services Act 1986, another instance of the avowed proposal to make the systems for the supervision of banks, of investment and securities business and of building societies as compatible as possible (*Hansard,* H.C. Vol. 106, col. 540).

Directions

Directions to institutions

19.—(1) The Bank may give an institution directions under this section—
   (a) when giving it notice that the Bank proposes to revoke its authorisation;
   (b) at any time after such a notice has been given to the institution (whether before or after its authorisation is revoked);
   (c) when giving the institution a notice of revocation under section 14(2) above by virtue of section 11(6)(b) above in the case of a members' voluntary winding up;
   (d) at any time after the institution has served a notice surrendering its authorisation, whether with immediate effect or with effect from a later date specified in the notice;
   (e) at or at any time after the expiry (otherwise than by virtue of section 12(8) above) of a restricted authorisation of the institution;
   (f) at any time after a disqualification notice has been served on

the institution under section 183 of the Financial Services Act 1986.

(2) Directions under this section shall be such as appear to the Bank to be desirable in the interests of the institution's depositors or potential depositors, whether for the purpose of safeguarding its assets or otherwise, and may in particular—

(a) require the institution to take certain steps or to refrain from adopting or pursuing a particular course of action or to restrict the scope of its business in a particular way;

(b) impose limitations on the acceptance of deposits, the granting of credit or the making of investments;

(c) prohibit the institution from soliciting deposits either generally or from persons who are not already depositors;

(d) prohibit it from entering into any other transaction or class of transactions;

(e) require the removal of any director, controller or manager.

(3) No direction shall be given by virtue of paragraph (a) or (b) of subsection (1) above, and any direction given by virtue of either of those paragraphs shall cease to have effect, if the Bank gives the institution notice that it is not proposing to take any further action pursuant to the notice mentioned in that paragraph or if the Bank's decision to revoke the institution's authorisation is reversed on appeal.

(4) No direction shall be given by virtue of paragraph (d) of subsection (1) above, and any direction given by virtue of that paragraph shall cease to have effect, if the Bank allows the institution to withdraw the surrender of its authorisation.

(5) No direction shall be given to an institution under this section after it has ceased to have any liability in respect of deposits for which it had a liability at a time when it was authorised; and any such direction which is in force with respect to an institution shall cease to have effect when the institution ceases to have any such liability.

(6) An institution which fails to comply with any requirement or contravenes any prohibition imposed on it by a direction under this section shall be guilty of an offence and liable—

(a) on conviction on indictment, to a fine;

(b) on summary conviction, to a fine not exceeding the statutory maximum.

(7) A contravention of a prohibition imposed under this section shall not invalidate any transaction.

TRANSITIONAL PROVISION
Sched. 5, para. 6.

DEFINITIONS
"authorisation": s.106(1).
"the Bank": s.1.
"controller": s.105(3).
"deposit": s.5.
"director": s.105(2).
"institution": s.106(1).
"manager": s.105(6).
"notice": ss.99, 100.
"statutory maximum": Criminal Justice Act 1982, s.74; Magistrates' Courts Act 1980, s.32.

GENERAL NOTE
This section and the next section replace, but largely unchanged, the provisions of ss.8 and 9 of the 1979 Act (and see Sched. 4, Pt. 1, to the 1979 Act). The Bank is empowered to give directions to an institution at the time of, or after, giving notice of revocation, after expiry of a restricted authorisation, after surrender or after service of a disqualification

notice under s.183 of the Financial Services Act 1986, and to protect the interests of depositors or *potential* depositors and to safeguard the institution's assets *or otherwise.*

Subs. (1)

Note, since the 1979 Act, the addition in para. (f) of the further ground of the serving of a disqualification notice under s.183 of the Financial Services Act 1986 (reciprocal facilities for financial business). At the Fourth Sitting of the Standing Committee (Fourth Sitting, January 13, 1987, col. 119) direction-making powers were extended to cover members' voluntary windings-up (new para. (c)) on the basis that depositors in such circumstances might not otherwise have sufficient protection under the Insolvency Act 1986.

Subs. (2)

The directions given must be such as appear in the eyes of the Bank to be desirable to protect the interests of depositors or potential depositors—not merely their deposits—whether to protect the institution's assets "or otherwise." The directions may well be far reaching in effect. (See also s.33 on advertisement directions.) The direction regarding the removal of any director, controller or manager (para. (e)) is new.

Subss. (3), (4), (5)

The power to give directions and the directions once made continue in force until such time as the Bank gives notice that it is not proceeding with the revocation (paras. (a) and (b) of subs. (1)), or if the decision to revoke is reversed on appeal, or if the Bank permits the institution to withdraw the surrender of its authorisation (para. (d)), or when the institution ceases to have any liability in respect of its deposits.

Subss. (6), (7)

Failure to comply with a requirement or contravention of a prohibition is a statutory offence but any such contravention would not invalidate any transaction.

Notification and confirmation of directions

20.—(1) A direction under section 19 above shall be given by notice in writing and may be varied by a further direction; and a direction may be revoked by the Bank by a notice in writing to the institution concerned.

(2) A direction under that section, except one varying a previous direction with the agreement of the institution concerned—

(a) shall state the reasons for which it is given and give particulars of the institution's rights under subsection (4) and section 27 below; and

(b) without prejudice to section 19(3), (4) and (5) above, shall cease to have effect at the end of the period of twenty-eight days beginning with the day in which it is given unless before the end of that period it is confirmed by a further written notice given by the Bank to the institution concerned.

(3) Where a direction requires the removal of a person as director, controller or manager of an institution the Bank shall give that person a copy of the direction (together with a statement of his rights under subsection (4) below) and, if the direction is confirmed, a copy of the notice mentioned in subsection (2)(b) above.

(4) An institution to which a direction is given which requires confirmation under subsection (2) above and a person who is given a copy of it under subsection (3) above may, within the period of fourteen days beginning with the day on which the direction is given, make written representations to the Bank; and the Bank shall take any such representations into account in deciding whether to confirm the direction.

(5) The Bank may omit from the copies given to a person under subsection (3) above any matter which does not relate to him.

DEFINITIONS
"the Bank": s.1.
"controller": s.105(3).

"director": s.105(2).
"institution": s.106(1).
"manager": s.105(6).
"notice": s.100.

GENERAL NOTE

This section sets out the notification procedures and the rights of the institution and of certain persons of which the direction requires the removal from office, including the rights of making representations (which the Bank must take into account in deciding whether to confirm any directions by further written notice to the institution) and of appealing to the tribunal pursuant to s.27. The Bank is obliged to give its reasons which, however, do not necessarily have to bear any direct relationship with the "remedy."

Objections to controllers

Notification of new or increased control

21.—(1) No person shall become a minority, majority or principal shareholder controller or an indirect controller of an authorised institution incorporated in the United Kingdom unless—

(a) he has served on the Bank a written notice stating that he intends to become such a controller of the institution; and

(b) either the Bank has, before the end of the period of three months beginning with the date of service of that notice, notified him in writing that there is no objection to his becoming such a controller of the institution or that period has elapsed without the Bank having served on him under section 22 or 23 below a written notice of objection to his becoming such a controller of the institution.

(2) Subsection (1) above applies also in relation to a person becoming a partner in an authorised institution which is a partnership formed under the law of any part of the United Kingdom.

(3) A notice under paragraph (a) of subsection (1) above shall contain such information as the Bank may direct and the Bank may, after receiving such a notice from any person, by notice in writing require him to provide such additional information or documents as the Bank may reasonably require for deciding whether to serve a notice of objection.

(4) Where additional information or documents are required from any person by a notice under subsection (3) above the time between the giving of the notice and the receipt of the information or documents shall be added to the period mentioned in subsection (1)(b) above.

(5) A notice served by a person under paragraph (a) of subsection (1) above shall not be regarded as a compliance with that paragraph except as respects his becoming a controller of the institution in question within the period of one year beginning—

(a) in a case where the Bank has notified him that there is no objection to his becoming such a controller, with the date of that notification;

(b) in a case where the period mentioned in paragraph (b) of that subsection has elapsed without any such notification and without his having been served with a written notice of objection, with the expiration of that period;

(c) in a case in which he has been served with a notice of objection which has been quashed on appeal, with the date on which it is quashed.

DEFINITIONS

"authorised": s.106(1).
"the Bank": s.1.
"controller": s.105(3).
"documents": s.106(1).
"indirect controller": s.105(5).
"institution": s.106(1).

"majority shareholder controller": s.105(4)(b).
"minority shareholder controller": s.105(4)(a).
"notice": ss.99, 100.
"principal shareholder controller": s.105(4)(c).

GENERAL NOTE

The White Paper (Chap. 14) noted that although the 1979 Act (s.14) required licensed deposit-takers to notify the Bank of changes in control (voting shareholdings of 15 per cent. and above) there was no provision for the Bank to object *before* the event. In practice, the Bank *expected* any institution, whether a recognised bank or licensed institution, to consult it in good time before any significant change in shareholders took place in order to discuss any future development of the business with any proposed new shareholder controllers. Should the Bank have had insufficient opportunity to satisfy itself that the minimum criteria would continue to be fulfilled, then it may have sought surrender of the institution's recognition or licence or considered revocation or the grant of a conditional licence. S.21 (to be read together with ss.22–26 which together provide for the checks on control changes in the banking sector, to which provisions significant additions were made during the Bill's passage through Parliament) requires notice to be given to the Bank by certain defined persons *before* any changes in individual shareholding take place in authorised institutions (including partnerships). The Bank then has a period of three months from being made aware as to the prospective controller to serve a notice of objection under s.22. See also s.94.

Subss. (1), (2)

Note the several classifications of "controller," "shareholder controller" and "indirect controller" and the sub-classifications, *i.e.* the requirements apply to persons with a 15 per cent. or more ownership of the voting power in an institution (which includes a U.K. partnership) and also to those who *propose* to increase such interest beyond 50 per cent. or 75 per cent. of such voting power; and to those who *contemplate* taking indirect control. Thus, *each* change in shareholdings leading to a change in the particular classification of shareholder controller necessitates service of a fresh notice on the Bank which is accordingly afforded a further opportunity of objecting. The three months' period specified in para. (b) of subs. (1) may seem a long period within which the Bank is left free to determine whether to serve a notice of objection, but presumably it is intended to enable the Bank to collect and evaluate information from many sources, both at home and from overseas. See also s.22(7) which may serve to extend the three month period if it would otherwise expire.

Subss. (3), (4)

The Bank may direct what information it requires from the prospective controller and if it calls for *additional* information or documents the three months' period is extended by the period of time elapsing between the giving of the further notice and the receipt of the information, etc. These provisions would presumably serve to encourage a prospective controller to give as much detailed information as he can at the outset so as not to prolong the period unduly.

Subs. (5)

Once the prospective controller has been expressly notified that the Bank has no objection to his proceeding, or the three months' period has elapsed with no notification and service of notice of objection, or the objection is quashed on appeal under s.27(3), he has thereupon one year within which to become a controller, otherwise he must serve notice afresh.

Objection to new or increased control

22.—(1) The Bank may serve a notice of objection under this section on a person who has given a notice under section 21 above unless it is satisfied—

    (a) that the person concerned is a fit and proper person to become a controller of the description in question of the institution;

    (b) that the interests of depositors and potential depositors of the institution would not be in any manner threatened by that person becoming a controller of that description of the institution; and

    (c) without prejudice to paragraphs (a) and (b) above, that, having regard to that person's likely influence on the institution as a controller of the description in question the criteria in Schedule 3 to this Act would continue to be fulfilled in the case of the institution or, if any of those criteria is not fulfilled, that that person is likely to undertake adequate remedial action.

(2) Before serving a notice of objection under this section the Bank shall serve the person concerned with a preliminary written notice stating that the Bank is considering the service on that person of a notice of objection; and that notice—

   (a) shall specify which of the matters mentioned in subsection (1) above the Bank is not satisfied about and, subject to subsection (5) below, the reasons for which it is not satisfied; and

   (b) shall give particulars of the rights conferred by subsection (3) below.

(3) A person served with a notice under subsection (2) above may, within the period of one month beginning with the day on which the notice is served, make written representations to the Bank; and where such representations are made the Bank shall take them into account in deciding whether to serve a notice of objection.

(4) A notice of objection under this section shall—

   (a) specify which of the matters mentioned in subsection (1) above the Bank is not satisfied about and, subject to subsection (5) below, the reasons for which it is not satisfied; and

   (b) give particulars of the rights conferred by section 27 below.

(5) Subsections (2)(a) and (4)(a) above shall not require the Bank to specify any reason which would in its opinion involve the disclosure of confidential information the disclosure of which would be prejudicial to a third party.

(6) Where a person required to give a notice under section 21 above in relation to his becoming a controller of any description becomes a controller of that description without having given the notice the Bank may serve him with a notice of objection under this section at any time within three months after becoming aware of his having done so and may, for the purpose of deciding whether to serve him with such a notice, require him by notice in writing to provide such information or documents as the Bank may reasonably require.

(7) The period mentioned in section 21(1)(b) above (with any extension under subsection (4) of that section) and the period mentioned in subsection (6) above shall not expire, if it would otherwise do so, until fourteen days after the end of the period within which representations can be made under subsection (3) above.

DEFINITIONS
   "the Bank": s.1.
   "controller": s.105(3).
   "documents": s.106(1).
   "institution": s.106(1).
   "notice": ss.99, 100.

GENERAL NOTE
   S.22 sets out the grounds and procedures for objection by the Bank. The Standing Committee in relation to a proposed amendment to involve the Treasury in any proposed change of control devoted a good deal of its discussion on the possible takeover of British banks by overseas financial institutions and on any protection against this afforded by references under the Fair Trading Act 1973 to the Monopolies and Mergers Commission and examined the reciprocal provisions of ss.183 and 185 of the Financial Services Act 1986 (Fifth and Sixth Sittings, January 15 and 20, 1987, cols. 125–158).

Subs. (1)
   Note the wide powers seemingly given to the Bank and in particular the placing of the onus of proof upon the person giving the notice under s.21 that he is a fit and proper person

(para. (a)). Again, not only are the interests of depositors and *potential* depositors of primary importance (para. (b)) but, amongst other things, it is confirmed that the tests in conducting a business must continue to be satisfied (see Sched. 3 and in particular paras. 4 and 5).

Subss. (2)–(5)

Similar procedures, as with a notice of revocation or restriction of an authorisation (s.13), are given, namely preliminary written notice from the Bank, right of the person concerned to make written representations (which the Bank must take into account in deciding whether to serve a notice of objection), and the definitive notice of objection must give reasons (except in this instance where disclosure of confidential information would prejudice a third person) and set out the rights of appeal conferred by s.27.

Subss. (6), (7)

If notice is either deliberately or unwittingly not given to the Bank then, it may serve a notice of objection *after* control has been acquired *at any time* (whether on the first or ninetieth day) of a three month period after becoming aware of the failure to serve a notice, without first giving preliminary notice of its intention. The provision of information and documents may be required. A person who contravenes s.21 may be guilty of an offence under s.25 and may also not be entitled to appeal to a tribunal (see s.27(3)). See the comparable provisions in the Insurance Companies Act 1982, ss.37 to 45 under which the Secretary of State has power, *inter alia*, to object to a new controlling shareholder of an insurance company. If the period would otherwise expire it may be further extended by virtue of subs. (7).

Objection by direction of the Treasury

23.—(1) The Treasury may direct the Bank to serve a notice of objection under this section on a person—
  (a) who has given notice under section 21 above of his intention to become a shareholder controller of any description of an institution; or
  (b) who has become such a controller without giving the required notice under that section,
if it appears to the Treasury that, in the event of his becoming or, as the case may be, as a result of his having become, such a controller, a notice could be served on the institution by the Treasury under section 183 of the Financial Services Act 1986 (disqualification or restriction of persons connected with overseas countries which do not afford reciprocal facilities for financial business).

(2) No direction shall be given in a case within subsection (1)(b) above more than three months after the Treasury becomes aware of the fact that the person concerned has become a controller of the relevant description.

(3) Any notice of objection served by virtue of a direction under this section shall state the grounds on which it is served.

DEFINITIONS
  "the Bank": s.1.
  "institution": s.106(1).
  "notice": ss.99, 100.
  "shareholder controller": s.105(4).

GENERAL NOTE
  The purpose of s.23 is to empower the Treasury, presumably in particularly sensitive or public interest matters, to direct the Bank to serve a notice of objection where a person either intends to become a shareholder controller (and has given the statutory notice) or has become a shareholder controller (*without* his giving it). The grounds are not set down here but are by reference to s.183 of the Financial Services Act 1986 (where by reason of the law of a foreign country or, by reason of any action taken by, or the practices of, the government, etc., in that country, U.K. persons are unable to carry on financial business on favourable reciprocal terms). See also s.91 of this Act.

Objection to existing shareholder controller

24.—(1) Where it appears to the Bank that a person who is a shareholder controller of any description of an authorised institution incorporated in the United Kingdom is not or is no longer a fit and proper person to be such a controller of the institution it may serve him with a written notice of objection to his being such a controller of the institution.

(2) Before serving a notice of objection under this section the Bank shall serve the person concerned with a preliminary written notice stating that the Bank is considering the service on that person of a notice of objection; and that notice shall—

(a) subject to subsection (5) below, specify the reasons for which it appears to the Bank that the person in question is not or is no longer a fit and proper person as mentioned in subsection (1) above; and

(b) give particulars of the rights conferred by subsection (3) below.

(3) A person served with a notice under subsection (2) above may, within the period of one month beginning with the day on which the notice is served, make written representations to the Bank; and where such representations are made the Bank shall take them into account in deciding whether to serve a notice of objection.

(4) A notice of objection under this section shall—

(a) subject to subsection (5) below, specify the reasons for which it appears to the Bank that the person in question is not or is no longer a fit and proper person as mentioned in subsection (1) above; and

(b) give particulars of the rights conferred by section 27 below.

(5) Subsections (2)(a) and (4)(a) above shall not require the Bank to specify any reason which would in its opinion involve the disclosure of confidential information the disclosure of which would be prejudicial to a third party.

DEFINITIONS
    "authorised": s.106(1).
    "the Bank": s.1.
    "institution": s.106(1).
    "notice": s.100.
    "shareholder controller": s.105(4).

GENERAL NOTE
    For completeness (and not within the proposals in the White Paper) the Bank was, during the passage of the Bill, granted the power to serve notice on an existing shareholder controller "of any description" that he is not or is no longer a fit and proper person to be such a controller. The procedure then follows that given in s.22.

Contraventions by controller

25.—(1) Subject to subsection (2) below, any person who contravenes section 21 above by—

(a) failing to give the notice required by paragraph (a) of subsection (1) of that section; or

(b) becoming a controller of any description to which that section applies before the end of the period mentioned in paragraph (b) of that subsection in a case where the Bank has not served him with a preliminary notice under section 22(2) above,

shall be guilty of an offence.

(2) A person shall not be guilty of an offence under subsection (1) above if he shows that he did not know of the acts or circumstances by virtue of which he became a controller of the relevant description; but where any person becomes a controller of any such description without

such knowledge and subsequently becomes aware of the fact that he has become such a controller he shall be guilty of an offence unless he gives the Bank written notice of the fact that he has become such a controller within fourteen days of becoming aware of that fact.

(3) Any person who—

(a) before the end of the period mentioned in paragraph (b) of subsection (1) of section 21 above becomes a controller of any description to which that subsection applies after being served with a preliminary notice under section 22(2) above;

(b) contravenes section 21 above by becoming a controller of any description after being served with a notice of objection to his becoming a controller of that description; or

(c) having become a controller of any description in contravention of that section (whether before or after being served with such a notice of objection) continues to be such a controller after such a notice has been served on him,

shall be guilty of an offence.

(4) A person guilty of an offence under subsection (1) or (2) above shall be liable on summary conviction to a fine not exceeding the fifth level on the standard scale.

(5) A person guilty of an offence under subsection (3) above shall be liable—

(a) on conviction on indictment, to imprisonment for a term not exceeding two years or to a fine or to both;

(b) on summary conviction, to a fine not exceeding the statutory maximum and, in respect of an offence under paragraph (c) of that subsection, to a fine not exceeding one tenth of the statutory maximum for each day on which the offence has continued.

DEFINITIONS
"the Bank": s.1.
"controller of any description": s.105(3), (4) & (5).
"notice": ss.99, 100.
"the standard scale": Criminal Justice Act 1982, s.37.
"the statutory maximum": Criminal Justice Act 1982, s.74; Magistrates' Courts Act 1980, s.32.

GENERAL NOTE
This section makes a contravention of s.21 a criminal offence with further back up power under s.26 to enable the Bank to place restrictions on and further to apply to the Court to require the sale of shares relevant to a contravention of s.21.

Subs. (1)
This is concerned with the failure of a person to give notice under s.21 or where the person gives the required notice and then becomes a controller without waiting out the full three months' period in circumstances where the Bank has not served the preliminary notice under s.22(2).

Subs. (2)
Examples of how this defence to an action under subs. (1) would operate were given by the Economic Secretary to the Treasury (Mr. Ian Stewart) during the Sixth Sitting of the Standing Committee (Sixth Sitting, January 28, 1987, col. 159): *e.g.* a beneficiary under a will or trust might unknowingly become a controller of a business; on becoming made aware of the fact, he must notify the Bank within 14 days thereafter.

Subs. (3)
It is also an offence for a person to become a controller after being served with a preliminary notice (s.22(2)) or to become or to continue to be a controller notwithstanding the serving of a definitive notice of objection on him.

Subss. (4), (5)

Circumstances giving rise to offences under s.25(3) carry heavier penalties than those for offences under subs. (1) or (2) including the maximum fine permitted. In addition, the perpetrator in all such cases has no right of appeal to the tribunal (s.27(3)).

Restrictions on and sale of shares

26.—(1) The powers conferred by this section shall be exercisable where a person—

(a) has contravened section 21 above by becoming a shareholder controller of any description after being served with a notice of objection to his becoming a controller of that description; or

(b) having become a shareholder controller of any description in contravention of that section continues to be one after such a notice has been served on him; or

(c) continues to be a shareholder controller of any description after being served under section 24 above with a notice of objection to his being a controller of that description.

(2) The Bank may by notice in writing served on the person concerned direct that any specified shares to which this section applies shall, until further notice, be subject to one or more of the following restrictions—

(a) any transfer of, or agreement to transfer, those shares or, in the case of unissued shares, any transfer of or agreement to transfer the right to be issued with them shall be void;

(b) no voting rights shall be exercisable in respect of the shares;

(c) no further shares shall be issued in right of them or in pursuance of any offer made to their holder;

(d) except in a liquidation, no payment shall be made of any sums due from the institution on the shares, whether in respect of capital or otherwise.

(3) The court may, on the application of the Bank, order the sale of any specified shares to which this section applies and, if they are for the time being subject to any restrictions under subsection (2) above, that they shall cease to be subject to those restrictions.

(4) No order shall be made under subsection (3) above in a case where the notice of objection was served under section 22 or 24 above—

(a) until the end of the period within which an appeal can be brought against the notice of objection; and

(b) if such an appeal is brought, until it has been determined or withdrawn.

(5) Where an order has been made under subsection (3) above the court may, on the application of the Bank, make such further order relating to the sale or transfer of the shares as it thinks fit.

(6) Where shares are sold in pursuance of an order under this section the proceeds of sale, less the costs of the sale, shall be paid into court for the benefit of the persons beneficially interested in them; and any such person may apply to the court for the whole or part of the proceeds to be paid to him.

(7) This section applies—

(a) to all the shares in the institution of which the person in question is a controller of the relevant description which are held by him or any associate of his and were not so held immediately before he became such a controller of the institution; and

(b) where the person in question became a controller of the relevant description of an institution as a result of the acquisition by him or any associate of his of shares in another company, to all the shares in that company which are held by him or any associate of his and were not so held before he became such a controller of that institution.

(8) A copy of the notice served on the person concerned under subsection (2) above shall be served on the institution or company to whose shares it relates and, if it relates to shares held by an associate of that person, on that associate.

(9) The jurisdiction conferred by this section shall be exercisable by the High Court and the Court of Session.

DEFINITIONS
"associate": s.105(9).
"the Bank": s.1.
"controller": s.105(3).
"institution": s.106(1).
"notice": s.100.
"shareholder controller": s.105(4).

GENERAL NOTE
This section will presumably provide a most effective sanction, to the extent that a person who becomes or continues as a shareholder controller in defiance of an objection notice may be divested of certain rights as a shareholder and that any improper control may be neutralised.

Subs. (2)
The restrictions which may be imposed individually or in combination include making void any transfer or agreement to transfer the shares or the right to be issued with them (para. (a)); the suspension of voting rights (para. (b)); the prohibition of any rights issue or offer (para. (c)); a total ban, except in a liquidation, on payments of any nature due on the shares (para. (d)).

Subss. (3), (4), (5)
The Bank may apply for a court order for the sale of the shares in question subject to any appeal procedures together with the lifting of any restriction which may have been imposed. These provisions permit the eventual release of such shares and presumably could require the offending controller to dispose of them.

Subss. (7), (8)
As controller includes an "associate" of his, the section would serve to prevent the fragmentation of a controlling interest among a number of other groups ("concert party").

Appeals

Rights of appeal

27.—(1) An institution which is aggrieved by a decision of the Bank—
    (a) to refuse an application by the institution for authorisation;
    (b) to revoke its authorisation otherwise than in a case in which revocation is mandatory under section 11 above;
    (c) to restrict its authorisation, to restrict it in a particular manner or to vary any restrictions of its authorisation; or
    (d) to give it a direction under section 19 above or to vary a direction given to it under that section,
may appeal against the decision to a tribunal constituted in accordance with section 28 below.

(2) Where—
    (a) the ground or a ground for a decision within paragraph (a), (b) or (c) of subsection (1) above is that mentioned in section 10(3) or 13(4)(a) above; or
    (b) the effect of a decision within paragraph (c) or (d) of that subsection is to require the removal of a person as director, controller or manager of an institution,
the person to whom the ground relates or whose removal is required may appeal to a tribunal constituted as aforesaid against the finding that there

is such a ground for the decision or, as the case may be, against the decision to require his removal.

(3) Any person on whom a notice of objection is served under section 22 or 24 above may appeal to a tribunal constituted as aforesaid against the decision of the Bank to serve the notice; but this subsection does does not apply to a person in any case in which he has failed to give a notice or become or continued to be a controller in circumstances in which his doing so constitutes an offence under section 25(1), (2) or (3) above.

(4) The revocation of an institution's authorisation pursuant to a decision against which there is a right of appeal under this section shall not have effect—

   (a) until the end of the period within which an appeal can be brought; and

   (b) if such an appeal is brought, until it is determined or withdrawn.

(5) The Tribunal may suspend the operation of a restriction or direction or a variation of a restriction or direction pending the determination of an appeal in respect of the decision imposing or varying the restriction or giving or varying the direction.

DEFINITIONS
  "authorisation": s.106(1).
  "the Bank": s.1.
  "controller": s.105(3).
  "director": s.105(2).
  "institution": s.106(1).
  "manager": s.105(6).
  "notice": s.100.

GENERAL NOTE
  This section and the remainder under the heading of Appeals (ss.27 to 31) correspond to ss.11 to 13 of the 1979 Act except that the unusual two-stage process in the 1979 Act of an appeal against a decision of the Bank being made nominally to the Chancellor of the Exchequer who referred the matter to a tribunal, is replaced by the more usual and no doubt speedier procedure of a direct appeal being taken by the tribunal itself (see for example Chapter IX (ss.96 to 101) of the Financial Services Act 1986).

Subs. (1)
  An appeal may be brought where the Bank decides to refuse an application for authorisation (see s.10(5)); to revoke its authorisation except where mandatory (see in this connection s.11(6) and (9)); to restrict or restrict in a particular manner or vary a restriction of its authorisation (s.12); or to issue or vary directions (ss.19 and 20).

Subs. (2)
  Where the ground for refusal, revocation or restriction of authorisation is that a person who is, or who is to be, a director, controller or manager is not a fit and proper person (Sched. 3, para. 1), or that the removal of such a person from office is required under a notice or direction, then that person has a right of appeal.

Subs. (3)
  Any person being served with a definitive notice may appeal. As mentioned under s.25 above, any person who fails to give notice in contravention of s.21 (*e.g.* s.22(6)) or who becomes or persists in continuing as a controller in defiance of a preliminary or definitive notice forfeits his right of appeal.

Subs. (4)
  Revocation of an authorisation is suspended until the time limit for an appeal to be brought has expired (prescribed by regulation—s.30(3)) or if the appeal is brought, it is later determined or withdrawn.

Subs. (5)

Note the power given to the tribunal (not in the 1979 Act) to determine whether the operation of a restriction or direction or variation of either shall be suspended during the hearing.

Constitution of tribunals

28.—(1) Where an appeal is brought under section 27 above a tribunal to determine the appeal shall be constituted in accordance with subsection (2) below.

(2) The tribunal shall consist of—

(a) a chairman appointed by the Lord Chancellor or, in a case where the institution concerned is a company registered in Scotland or has its principal or prospective principal place of business in the United Kingdom in Scotland, by the Lord Chancellor in consultation with the Lord Advocate; and

(b) two other members appointed by the Chancellor of the Exchequer.

(3) The chairman shall be a barrister, solicitor or advocate of at least seven years' standing; and the other two members shall be persons appearing to the Chancellor of the Exchequer to have respectively experience of accountancy and experience of banking.

(4) The Treasury may out of money provided by Parliament pay to the persons appointed as members of a tribunal under this section such fees and allowances in respect of expenses as the Treasury may determine and may also out of such money defray any other expenses of a tribunal.

DEFINITION
"institution": s.106(1).

GENERAL NOTE
Under The Banking Act 1979 (Appeals) Regulations 1980 (S.I. 1980 No. 353) the Chancellor of the Exchequer on receipt of a notice of appeal appointed three persons to hear the appeal on his behalf, the Chairman and one other to be a barrister or solicitor of at least seven years' standing, the other to be "experienced in matters of finance or accountancy" (reg. 7). Under the present Act, the tribunal is no longer merely advisory but stands in its own right and is able to make a binding determination rather than recommendations. It may be also noted that the *Lord Chancellor* appoints the legally qualified chairman, and the other two members (having experience of accountancy and banking respectively) are appointed by the Chancellor of the Exchequer, presumably anticipating the largely financial nature of the tribunal's work.

Determination of appeals

29.—(1) On an appeal under section 27(1) or (3) above the question for the determination of the tribunal shall be whether, for the reasons adduced by the appellant, the decision was unlawful or not justified by the evidence on which it was based.

(2) On any such appeal the tribunal may confirm or reverse the decision which is the subject of the appeal but shall not have power to vary it except that—

(a) where the decision was to revoke an authorisation the tribunal may direct the Bank to restrict it instead;

(b) where the decision was to impose or vary any restrictions the tribunal may direct the Bank to impose different restrictions or to vary them in a different way; or

(c) where the decision was to give or vary a direction the tribunal may direct the Bank to give a different direction or to vary it in a different way.

(3) Where the tribunal gives a direction to the Bank under subsection (2)(a), (b) or (c) above it shall be for the Bank to decide what restrictions should be imposed or how they should be varied or, as the case may be, what direction should be given or how a direction should be varied; and—

    (a) the Bank shall by notice in writing to the institution concerned impose the restrictions, give the direction or make the variation on which it has decided;

    (b) the institution may appeal to the tribunal against the Bank's decision,

and on any such appeal the tribunal may confirm the decision or give a further direction under paragraph (b) or (c) of subsection (2) above and, if it gives such a further direction, this subsection shall continue to apply until the Bank's decision is confirmed by the tribunal or accepted by the institution.

(4) Where the tribunal reverses a decision of the Bank to refuse an application for authorisation it shall direct the Bank to grant it.

(5) On an appeal under section 27(2)(a) above the question for the determination of the tribunal shall be whether, for the reasons adduced by the appellant, the finding of the Bank was not justified by the evidence on which it was based; and on an appeal under section 27(2)(b) above the question for the determination of the tribunal shall be whether, for the reasons adduced by the appellant, the decision requiring the appellant's removal was unlawful or not justified by the evidence on which it was based.

(6) A decision by the tribunal on an appeal under section 27(2)(a) above that a finding in respect of the appellant was not justified shall not affect any refusal, revocation or restriction wholly or partly based on that finding; but on an appeal under section 27(2)(b) above the tribunal may confirm or reverse the decision to require the removal of the appellant.

(7) Notice of a tribunal's determination, together with a statement of its reasons, shall be given to the appellant and to the Bank; and, unless the tribunal otherwise directs, the determination shall come into operation when the notice is given to the appellant and to the Bank.

(8) Notice of a tribunal's determination of an appeal under section 27(2) above shall also be given to the institution concerned and, where the determination is to reverse a decision to require the removal of the appellant as director, controller or manager of an institution, the determination shall not come into operation until notice of the determination has been give to that institution.

DEFINITIONS

    "authorisation": s.106(1).

    "the Bank": s.1.

    "controller": s.105(3).

    "director": s.105(2).

    "institution": s.106(1).

    "manager": s.105(6).

    "notice": s.100.

GENERAL NOTE

    This section sets down the tribunal's powers. Under the 1979 Act there was no further appeal from the decision of the Chancellor of the Exchequer other than on a point of law under s.13; see the parallel case of *R.* v. *Chief Registrar of Friendly Societies, ex p. New Cross Building Society* [1984] 2 All E.R. 27 under which the Court of Appeal held that the Chief Registrar had very wide discretionary powers to make orders and that the Courts may not substitute their judgment for his: the Building Societies Act 1986 has now established an appeals procedure (ss.46 to 49).

Subss. (1), (5)
   These subsections indicate the judicial review nature of the tribunal's role. The intended scope of the question directed for the determination of the tribunal "whether . . . the decision was unlawful or not justified by the evidence on which it was based" is not made apparent.

Subss. (2), (3), (4), (7), (8)
   The Tribunal may either confirm or reverse the decision of the Bank (in the latter case where the decision was to refuse authorisation, the tribunal *must* direct the Bank to grant it); or it has limited powers to direct a variation of that decision, *e.g.* a restriction of an authorisation instead of a revocation. Where the tribunal directs a variation, it is for the Bank (not the tribunal) to decide what the restriction or direction should be or how it should be varied. This is subject to a further appeal by the institution to the tribunal whereupon the tribunal may confirm such a decision or give a further direction. Provision is made for the time when the tribunal's determination of an appeal comes into operation.

Costs, procedure and evidence

   30.—(1) A tribunal may give such directions as it thinks fit for the payment of costs or expenses by any party to the appeal.
   (2) On an appeal under section 27(2) above the institution concerned shall be entitled to be heard.
   (3) Subject to subsection (4) below, the Treasury may, after consultation with the Council on Tribunals, make regulations with respect to appeals under this Part of this Act; and those regulations may in particular make provision—
   (a) as to the period within which and the manner in which such appeals are to be brought;
   (b) as to the manner in which such appeals are to be conducted, including provision for any hearing to be held in private, as to the persons entitled to appear on behalf of the parties and for enabling appeals to be heard notwithstanding the absence of a member of the tribunal other than the chairman;
   (c) as to the procedure to be adopted where appeals are brought both by an institution and a person who is or is to be a director, controller or manager of the institution, including provision for hearing the appeals together and for the mutual disclosure of information;
   (d) for requiring an appellant or the Bank to disclose or allow the inspection of documents in his or its custody or under his or its control;
   (e) for requiring any person, on tender of the necessary expenses of his attendance, to attend and give evidence or produce documents in his custody or under his control and for authorising the administration of oaths to witnesses;
   (f) for enabling an appellant to withdraw an appeal or the Bank to withdraw its opposition to an appeal and for the consequences of any such withdrawal;
   (g) for taxing or otherwise settling any costs or expenses which the tribunal directs to be paid and for the enforcement of any such direction;
   (h) for enabling any preliminary or incidental functions in relation to an appeal to be discharged by the chairman of a tribunal; and
   (j) as to any other matter connected with such appeals.
   (4) Regulations under this section with respect to appeals where the institution concerned—
   (a) is a company registered in Scotland; or
   (b) has its principal or prospective principal place of business in the United Kingdom in Scotland,
shall be made by the Lord Advocate after consultation with the Council on Tribunals which shall consult its Scottish Committee.

(5) A person who, having been required in accordance with regulations under this section to attend and give evidence, fails without reasonable excuse to attend or give evidence, shall be liable on summary conviction to a fine not exceeding the fifth level on the standard scale.

(6) A person who without reasonable excuse alters, suppresses, conceals, destroys or refuses to produce any document which he has been required to produce in accordance with regulations under this section, or which he is liable to be so required to produce, shall be guilty of an offence and liable—

(a) on conviction on indictment, to imprisonment for a term not exceeding two years or to a fine or to both;

(b) on summary conviction, to a fine not exceeding the statutory maximum.

(7) Any regulations made under this section shall be subject to annulment in pursuance of a resolution of either House of Parliament.

DEFINITIONS
"the Bank": s.1.
"controller": s.105(3).
"the Council on Tribunals": Tribunals and Inquiries Act 1971, s.1.
"director": s.105(2).
"documents": s.106(1).
"manager": s.105(6).
"the standard scale": Criminal Justice Act 1982, s.37.
"the statutory maximum": Criminal Justice Act 1982, s.74; Magistrates' Courts Act 1980, s.32.

GENERAL NOTE
This section should be read with ss.27–29 and s.31. The Tribunal is authorised to award costs and expenses and regulations may be made as to the time and manner in which appeals are to be brought, the conduct of the appeals, the evidence and appropriate procedure at and after the hearing, the disclosure or inspection of documents, the attendance of witnesses, the withdrawal of an appeal or of an opposition to appeal, the taxing of costs and the discharge of certain functions by the Chairman.

Subs. (2)
Where a person is appealing against a finding that he is not a fit and proper person (ss.10(3) or 13(4)(a)) or against a decision to require his removal, then the institution of which he is a director, controller or manager is also entitled to attend and be heard.

Subss. (3)–(7)
Before making the regulations with respect to appeals, the Treasury or the Lord Advocate (in the case of institutions registered in Scotland or having their principal or prospective principal place of business in Scotland) must consult with the Council on Tribunals. This Council is governed by the Tribunals and Inquiries Act 1971 and procedural rules for any of the listed tribunals may be approved or confirmed only after reference to and consultation with the Council (s.10). Sched. 6 (para. 4(2)) to this Act adds this appeal tribunal to the list in the Tribunal and Inquiries Act 1971. It may be noted that the procedural provisions given are *examples* only. Any regulations made are subject to the negative parliamentary procedure. To enable the tribunal to perform its functions effectively, it is made an offence for persons to fail to attend or give evidence, or without reasonable excuse to tamper with or refuse to produce documents required under the regulations. At the time of writing the Treasury, after consultation with the Council on Tribunals, have made The Banking Appeal Tribunal Regulations 1987 (S.I. 1987 No. 1299) coming into force on October 1, 1987.

Further appeals on points of law

31.—(1) An institution or other person who has appealed to a tribunal may appeal to the court on any question of law arising from the decision of the appeal by the tribunal and an appeal on any such question shall also lie at the instance of the Bank; and if the court is of opinion that the decision was erroneous in point of law, it shall remit the matter to the tribunal for re-hearing and determination by it.

(2) In subsection (1) above "the court" means the High Court, the Court of Session or the High Court in Northern Ireland according to whether—

(a) if the institution concerned is a company registered in the United Kingdom, it is registered in England and Wales, Scotland or Northern Ireland;

(b) in the case of any other institution, its principal or prospective principal place of business in the United Kingdom is situated in England and Wales, Scotland or Northern Ireland.

(3) No appeal to the Court of Appeal or to the Court of Appeal in Northern Ireland shall be brought from a decision under subsection (1) above except with the leave of that court or of the court or judge from whose decision the appeal is brought.

(4) An appeal shall lie, with the leave of the Court of Session or the House of Lords, from any decision of the Court of Session under this section, and such leave may be given on such terms as to costs, expenses or otherwise as the Court of Session or the House of Lords may determine.

DEFINITIONS
    "the Bank": s.1.
    "institution": s.106(1).

GENERAL NOTE
    This substantially re-enacts s.13 of the 1979 Act. An appeal lies from the tribunal to the High Court (or the Court of Session in Scotland or the High Court in Northern Ireland, as appropriate) but only on a point of law and if the decision was wrong in law it will be remitted for rehearing. An appeal lies to the Court of Appeal or to the Court of Appeal in Northern Ireland (and in Scottish cases to the House of Lords) with leave only.

Invitations to make deposits

Advertisement regulations

32.—(1) The Treasury may after consultation with the Bank and the Building Societies Commission make regulations for regulating the issue, form and content of deposit advertisements.

(2) Regulations under this section may make different provision for different cases and, without prejudice to the generality of subsection (1) above, may in particular—

(a) prohibit the issue of advertisements of any description (whether by reference to their contents, to the persons by whom they are issued or otherwise);

(b) make provision with respect to matters which must be, as well as matters which may not be, included in advertisements;

(c) provide for exemptions from any prohibition or requirement imposed by the regulations, including exemptions by reference to a person's membership of a class whose membership is determined otherwise than by the Treasury.

(3) Subject to subsection (4) below, any person who issues or causes to be issued in the United Kingdom an advertisement the issue of which is prohibited by regulations under this section or which does not comply with any requirements imposed by those regulations shall be guilty of an offence and liable—

(a) on conviction on indictment, to imprisonment for a term not exceeding two years or to a fine or to both;

(b) on summary conviction, to imprisonment for a term not exceeding six months or to a fine not exceeding the statutory maximum or to both.

(4) A person whose business it is to publish or arrange for the publication of advertisements shall not be guilty of an offence under this section if he proves that he received the advertisement for publication in the ordinary course of his business, that the matters contained in the advertisement were not (wholly or in part) devised or selected by him or by any person under his direction or control and that he did not know and had no reason for believing that publication of the advertisement would constitute an offence.

(5) In this section "a deposit advertisement" means any advertisement containing—

(a) an invitation to make a deposit; or

(b) information which is intended or might reasonably be presumed to be intended to lead directly or indirectly to the making of a deposit;

and for the purposes of this section an advertisement includes any means of bringing such an invitation or such information to the notice of the person or persons to whom it is addressed and references to the issue of an advertisement shall be construed accordingly.

(6) For the purposes of this section—

(a) an advertisement issued or caused to be issued by any person by way of display or exhibition in a public place shall be treated as issued or caused to be issued by him on every day on which he causes or permits it to be displayed or exhibited;

(b) an advertisement inviting deposits with a person specified in the advertisement shall be presumed, unless the contrary is proved, to have been issued to the order of that person.

(7) For the purposes of this section an advertisement issued outside the United Kingdom shall be treated as issued in the United Kingdom if it is directed to persons in the United Kingdom or is made available to them otherwise than in a newspaper, journal, magazine or other periodical publication published and circulating principally outside the United Kingdom or in a sound or television broadcast transmitted principally for reception outside the United Kingdom.

(8) Regulations under this section shall be subject to annulment in pursuance of a resolution of either House of Parliament.

DEFINITIONS
"the Bank": s.1.
"Building Societies Commission": Building Societies Act 1986, s.1.
"deposit": s.5.
"the statutory maximum": Criminal Justice Act 1982, s.74; Magistrates' Courts Act 1980, s.32.

GENERAL NOTE
This section corresponds closely with s.34 of the 1979 Act and enables the Treasury, after consulting the Bank and the Building Societies Commission, to make regulations controlling the issue, form and content of deposit advertisements (as defined in subs. (5)).

Subss. (1), (2)
The widest powers are given to the Treasury to make regulations for controlling deposit advertisements issued by such persons as building societies and overseas banks. The new Act is more comprehensive in two respects. The 1979 Act and the particular regulations made in the exercise of powers conferred under s.34 (Banking Act 1979 (Advertisements) Regulations 1985 (S.I. 1985 No. 220)) related only to advertisements soliciting deposits outside the U.K. and other Member States of the EEC. However, discussions had been taking place between the Bank and certain representative associations to establish guidelines governing advertisements and a code of conduct has been agreed (see the General Note to s.33). Note also the control by the Advertising Standards Authority.

Subs. (3)
This subsection and subs. (6) of s.33 set out the penalties for failing to comply with the regulations or with any directions.

Subs. (4)

Compare this defence available for publishers with that in respect of credit advertisements under s.47(2) of the Consumer Credit Act 1974. In addition in the case of "deposit advertisements" the publisher must also prove that the matters in the advertisement were not devised or selected by him or by any person under his direction or control.

Subs. (5)

In one respect "a deposit advertisement" is wider than that of "advertisement" in s.34(4) and (5) of the 1979 Act in so far as the new Act is not so concerned with the *form* of the advertising. It is the *contents* which are all important.

Subs. (6)

Similar wording as in s.34(5)(a) and (d) of the 1979 Act. Note in particular that, unless proved otherwise, the person who is specified in the advertisement shall be presumed to have issued it.

Subs. (7)

Presumably a "mail shot" sent to a person in the U.K. from abroad would be treated as an advertisement issued *in* the U.K.

Advertisement directions

33.—(1) If the Bank considers that any deposit advertisement issued or proposed to be issued by or on behalf of an authorised institution is misleading, the Bank may by notice in writing give the institution a direction under this section.

(2) A direction under this section may contain all or any of the following prohibitions or requirements—

(a) a prohibition on the issue of advertisements of a specified kind;

(b) a requirement that advertisements of a particular description shall be modified in a specified manner;

(c) a prohibition on the issue of any advertisements which are, wholly or substantially, repetitions of an advertisement which has been issued and which is identified in the direction;

(d) a requirement to take all practical steps to withdraw from display in any place any advertisements or any advertisements of a particular description specified in the direction.

(3) Not less than seven days before giving a direction under this section the Bank shall give the institution concerned notice in writing of its intention to give the direction stating the reasons for the proposed direction and giving particulars of the rights conferred by subsection (4) below.

(4) An institution to which a notice is given under subsection (3) above may within the period of seven days beginning with the day on which the notice was given make written representations to the Bank; and the Bank shall take any such representations into account in deciding whether to give the direction.

(5) A direction under this section may be varied by a further direction; and a direction may be revoked by the Bank by a notice in writing to the institution concerned.

(6) Any person who issues or causes to be issued an advertisement the issue of which is prohibited by a direction under this section or which does not comply with any requirements imposed by such a direction shall be guilty of an offence and liable—

(a) on conviction on indictment, to imprisonment for a term not exceeding two years or to a fine or to both;

(b) on summary conviction, to imprisonment for a term not exceeding six months or to a fine not exceeding the statutory maximum or to both.

(7) In this section "deposit advertisement" has the same meaning as in section 32 above and subsections (4) and (6) of that section shall apply also for the purposes of this section.

DEFINITIONS
"authorised": s.106(1).
"the Bank": s.1.
"deposit advertisement": s.32(5).
"institution": s.106(1).
"notice": s.100.
"the statutory maximum": Criminal Justice Act 1982, s.74; Magistrates' Courts Act 1980, s.32.

GENERAL NOTE
A code of conduct was agreed in March 1985 between the British Bankers' Association, the Building Societies Association, and the Finance Houses Association to deal with certain aspects of advertising of deposits. S.33 empowers the Bank to give written directions to authorised institutions in the case of advertisements considered to be misleading and as such provides a greater sanction to underpin such a code. Similar provisions appear in the Building Societies Act 1986 (s.50). It may be noted that the wording of s.33 is very similar, apart from some drafting alterations, to the wording of s.35 of the 1979 Act.

Unsolicited calls

34.—(1) The Treasury may after consultation with the Bank and the Building Societies Commission make regulations for regulating the making of unsolicited calls—
    (a) on persons in the United Kingdom; or
    (b) from the United Kingdom on persons elsewhere,
with a view to procuring the making of deposits.

(2) Regulations under this section may make different provision for different cases and, without prejudice to the generality of subsection (1) above, may in particular—
    (a) prohibit the soliciting of deposits from, and the making of agreements with a view to the acceptance of deposits from, persons on whom unsolicited calls are made and prohibit the procuring of such persons to make deposits or to enter into such agreements;
    (b) specify persons by whom or circumstances in which unsolicited calls may be made;
    (c) require specified information to be disclosed to persons on whom unsolicited calls are made.

(3) Any person who contravenes regulations made under this section shall be guilty of an offence and liable—
    (a) on conviction on indictment, to imprisonment for a term not exceeding two years or to a fine or to both;
    (b) on summary conviction, to imprisonment for a term not exceeding six months or to a fine not exceeding the statutory maximum or to both.

(4) In this section "unsolicited call" means a personal visit or oral communication made without express invitation.

(5) Regulations under this section shall be subject to annulment in pursuance of a resolution of either House of Parliament.

DEFINITIONS
"the Bank": s.1.
"Building Societies Commission": Building Societies Act 1986, s.1.
"deposit": s.5.
"the statutory maximum": Criminal Justice Act 1982, s.74; Magistrates' Courts Act 1980, s.32.

GENERAL NOTE
This section, which provides permissive powers to the Treasury (after consulting with the Bank and the Building Societies Commission), to make regulations to govern the practice

of the making of unsolicited calls ("cold calling"), is new and was not as such anticipated in the White Paper. It parallels provisions in the Financial Services Act 1976 (s.56) (providing another instance of the endeavours to bring consistency so far as is possible between the three sets of legislation regulating financial institutions). However, s.56 in essence provides that the practice of "cold calling" is prohibited unless effected in accordance with and except so far as permitted by regulations, whereas under the Banking Act the solicitation of deposits through "cold calling" is permitted unless and to the extent it is forbidden by regulations. The distinction was defended during the Sixth Sitting of the Standing Committee (Sixth Sitting, January 20, 1987, col. 173) on the basis that it is difficult to legislate in advance for "cold calling" for deposits (as contrasted with life assurance where the practice is traditional) until the nature and extent of any possible abuse is known.

Subss. (1), (2)
   As under s.32 the Bank *may* make regulations in the widest possible terms to apply to all "persons" including, say, building societies, and to regulate calls from the U.K. affecting persons outside the U.K.

Subs. (3)
   Again as with s.32(3) contravention of the regulations involves a criminal offence. Contrast s.56(2) of the Financial Services Act 1986 where no criminal offence is committed but there is a presumption that an investment agreement entered into during or as a consequence of "cold calling" is unenforceable.

Subs. (4)
   The same definition as in s.56(8) of the Financial Services Act 1980. Contrast also with s.48 of the Consumer Credit Act 1974 defining "canvassing off trade premises" which requires no less than six separate conditions to be satisfied for there to be "canvassing."

Fraudulent inducement to make a deposit

   35.—(1) Any person who—
      (a) makes a statement, promise or forecast which he knows to be misleading, false or deceptive, or dishonestly conceals any material facts; or
      (b) recklessly makes (dishonestly or otherwise) a statement, promise or forecast which is misleading, false or deceptive,
is guilty of an offence if he makes the statement, promise or forecast or conceals the facts for the purpose of inducing, or is reckless as to whether it may induce, another person (whether or not the person to whom the statement, promise or forecast is made or from whom the facts are concealed)—
            (i) to make, or refrain from making, a deposit with him or any other person; or
            (ii) to enter, or refrain from entering, into an agreement for the purpose of making such a deposit.
   (2) This section does not apply unless—
      (a) the statement, promise or forecast is made in or from, or the facts are concealed in or from, the United Kingdom or arrangements are made in or from the United Kingdom for the statement, promise or forecast to be made or the facts to be concealed;
      (b) the person on whom the inducement is intended to or may have effect is in the United Kingdom; or
      (c) the deposit is or would be made, or the agreement is or would be entered into, in the United Kingdom.
   (3) A person guilty of an offence under this section shall be liable—
      (a) on conviction on indictment, to imprisonment for a term not exceeding seven years or to a fine or to both;
      (b) on summary conviction, to imprisonment for a term not

exceeding six months or to a fine not exceeding the statutory maximum or to both.

(4) For the purposes of this section the definition of deposit in section 5 above shall be treated as including any sum that would be otherwise excluded by subsection (3) of that section.

DEFINITIONS

"deposit": s.5.

"the statutory maximum": Criminal Justice Act 1982, s.74; Magistrates' Courts Act 1980, s.32.

GENERAL NOTE

The wording of s.35 re-enacts and widens s.39 of the 1979 Act (which itself superseded s.1 of the Protection of Depositors Act 1963 and equivalent Northern Ireland legislation) and appears to be designed to follow the relevant provisions of s.47 of the Financial Services Act, making as consistent as possible the overall treatment of misleading, false or deceptive inducements or the dishonest concealment of material facts. Note the territorial limits.

Subs. (1)

Dishonestly. See *R.* v. *Feely* [1973] Q.B. 530 and *R.* v. *Ghosh* [1982] Q.B. 1053 (Theft Act 1968, s.1).

Recklessly, reckless. See *Commissioner of Police of the Metropolis* v. *Caldwell* [1982] A.C. 341; *R.* v. *Lawrence* [1982] A.C. 510. An attempt was made during the Sixth Sitting of the Standing Committee (Sixth Sitting, January 20, 1987, cols. 177–181) to replace "reckless" by "without due diligence" but it failed by reason of insufficient relevant case law on "due diligence."

Dishonestly or otherwise. Cf. *R.* v. *Mackinnon* [1959] 1 Q.B. 150. "Recklessly" entails a fraudulent state of mind. Note the extension of fraudulently inducing another to "refrain" from making deposits and that it need not be shown that the accused *intended* to induce— it is sufficient to show he was reckless as to whether the statement, etc., may induce another. Moreover the person who makes (or refrains from making) a deposit need not be the person to whom the statement, etc., is made or from whom material facts are concealed.

Subs. (2)

See *Secretary of State* v. *Markus* [1976] A.C. 35 on fraudulently inducing a person to take part in "any arrangements." "Arrangements" in (a) are not defined but note the very wide interpretation of the word "arrangements" given by Diplock L.J. in *Re British Basic Slag's Application* [1963] 1 W.L.R. 727 at pp.741–742 and 747.

Subs. (4)

This further widens "deposit" by importing into the definition items excluded by s.5(3) such as sums paid *by* an authorised institution, *e.g.* loans.

Information

Notification of change of director, controller or manager

36.—(1) Subject to subsection (3) below, an authorised institution shall give written notice to the Bank of the fact that any person has become or ceased to be a director, controller or manager of the institution.

(2) A notice required to be given under subsection (1) above shall be given before the end of the period of fourteen days beginning with the day on which the institution becomes aware of the relevant facts.

(3) The Bank may by a notice in writing wholly or partly dispense from the obligation imposed by subsection (1) above any authorised institution whose principal place of business is outside the United Kingdom.

(4) An institution which fails to give a notice required by this section shall be guilty of an offence and liable on summary conviction to a fine not exceeding the fifth level on the standard scale.

DEFINITIONS
"authorised": s.106(1).
"the Bank": s.1.
"controller": s.105(3).
"director": s.105(2).
"institution": s.106(1).
"manager": s.105(6).
"notice": s.99.
"the standard scale": Criminal Justice Act 1982, s.37.

GENERAL NOTE
S.14 of the 1979 Act required a licensed deposit-taker to give to the Bank 21 days' written notice of a change of its directors, controllers or managers. S.36 stipulates that all authorised institutions (with a possible dispensation for those whose principal place of business is *outside* the U.K.) must give notice within 14 days of becoming "aware of the relevant facts." If the Bank is satisfied that the relevant authority in the home country of an overseas bank is able to exercise sufficient supervisory control over its domestic financial institutions, it would probably feel disposed to dispense with the obligation imposed by subs. (1) (although the obligation to notify alterations in directors to the registrar of companies under s.692(1) of the Companies Act 1985 would still operate). Contrast the requirements of s.21 (*ante*) to give *prior* notification of the appointment of a shareholder controller.

Notification of acquisition of significant shareholding

37.—(1) A person who becomes a significant shareholder in relation to an authorised institution incorporated in the United Kingdom shall within seven days give written notice of that fact to the Bank.

(2) For the purposes of this section "a significant shareholder", in relation to an institution, means a person who, either alone or with any associate or associates, is entitled to exercise, or control the exercise of, 5 per cent. or more but less than 15 per cent. of the voting power at any general meeting of the institution or of another institution of which it is a subsidiary.

(3) Subject to subsection (4) below, any person who contravenes subsection (1) above shall be guilty of an offence.

(4) A person shall not be guilty of an offence under subsection (3) above if he shows that he did not know of the acts or circumstances by virtue of which he became a significant shareholder in relation to the institution; but where any person becomes such a shareholder without such knowledge and subsequently becomes aware of the fact that he has become such a shareholder he shall be guilty of an offence unless he gives the Bank written notice of the fact that he has become such a shareholder within fourteen days of becoming aware of that fact.

(5) A person guilty of an offence under this section shall be liable on summary conviction to a fine not exceeding the fifth level on the standard scale.

DEFINITIONS
"associate": s.105(9).
"authorised": s.106(1).
"the Bank": s.1.
"institution": s.106(1).
"notice": s.99.
"the standard scale": Criminal Justice Act 1982, s.37.
"subsidiary": s.106(2); Companies Act 1985, s.736.

GENERAL NOTE
This measure was introduced during the Bill's passage through the Standing Committee. This section, as also does s.41, provides an "early warning" of the possible increase of a controlling shareholding by an undesirable person. Where shareholders become entitled either alone or with others to control at least 5 per cent. but less than 15 per cent. of the voting power at any general meeting of a U.K. incorporated authorised institution (or

its holding company), the section requires this fact to be notified to the Bank within seven days of the acquisition. Such "significant shareholders" are then made subject to the Bank's powers to acquire information and to require assistance and the production of documents (see ss.39(10) and 41 (5)). S.37 should be read with Pt. VI of the Companies Act 1985 which requires nominee shareholdings of up to 5 per cent. to be disclosed to the company in question (note the exception in s.216(5)). Where the voting control is 15 per cent. or more, then the complementary provisions of s.21 of this Act will operate.

Reports of large exposures

38.—(1) An authorised institution, other than one whose principal place of business is outside the United Kingdom, shall make a report to the Bank if—

(a) it has entered into a transaction or transactions relating to any one person as a result of which it is exposed to the risk of incurring losses in excess of 10 per cent. of its available capital resources; or

(b) it proposes to enter into a transaction or transactions relating to any one person which, either alone or together with a previous transaction or previous transactions entered into by it in relation to that person, would result in its being exposed to the risk of incurring losses in excess of 25 per cent. of those resources.

(2) Subsection (1) above applies also where the transaction or transactions relate to different persons if they are connected in such a way that the financial soundness of any of them may affect the financial soundness of the other or others or the same factors may affect the financial soundness of both or all of them.

(3) If an authorised institution to which subsection (1) above applies has one or more subsidiaries which are not authorised institutions the Bank may by notice in writing to that institution direct that that subsection shall apply to it as if the transactions and available capital resources of the subsidiary or subsidiaries, or such of them as are specified in the notice, were included in those of the institution.

(4) The reports required to be made by an institution under subsection (1) above shall be made, in a case within paragraph (a) of that subsection, in respect of such period or periods and, in a case within paragraph (b) of that subsection, at such time before the transaction or transactions are entered into, as may be specified by notice in writing given to the institution by the Bank; and those reports shall be in such form and contain such particulars as the Bank may reasonably require.

(5) For the purposes of this section a transaction entered into by an institution relates to a person if it is—

(a) a transaction under which that person incurs an obligation to the institution or as a result of which he may incur such an obligation;

(b) a transaction under which the institution will incur, or as a result of which it may incur, an obligation in the event of that person defaulting on an obligation to a third party; or

(c) a transaction under which the institution acquires or incurs an obligation to acquire, or as a result of which it may incur an obligation to acquire, an asset the value of which depends wholly or mainly on that person performing his obligations or otherwise on his financial soundness;

and the risk of loss attributable to a transaction is, in a case within paragraph (a) or (b) above, the risk of the person concerned defaulting on the obligation there mentioned and, in a case within paragraph (c) above, the risk of the person concerned defaulting on the obligations there mentioned or of a deterioration in his financial soundness.

(6) Any question whether an institution is or would be exposed to risk as mentioned in subsection (1) above (or in that subsection as extended by subsection (2)) shall be determined in accordance with principles

published by the Bank or notified by it to the institution concerned; and those principles may in particular make provision for determining the amount at risk in particular circumstances or the extent to which any such amount is to be taken into account for the purposes of this section.

(7) For the purposes of this section the available capital resources of an institution (or, in a case within subsection (3) above, of an institution and its relevant subsidiary or subsidiaries) and the value of those resources at any time shall be determined by the Bank and notified by it to the institution by notice in writing; and any such determination, which may be varied from time to time, shall be made by the Bank after consultation with the institution concerned and in accordance with principles published by the Bank.

(8) The principles referred to in subsections (6) and (7) above may make different provision for different cases and those referred to in subsection (6) may, in particular, exclude from consideration, either wholly or in part, risks resulting from transactions of a particular description or entered into in particular circumstances or with persons of particular descriptions.

(9) An institution which fails to make a report as required by this section shall be guilty of an offence; but where an institution shows that at the time when the report was required to be made it did not know that the facts were such as to require the making of the report it shall not be guilty of an offence by reason of its failure to make a report at that time but shall be guilty of an offence unless it makes the report within seven days of becoming aware of those facts.

(10) An institution guilty of an offence under this section shall be liable on summary conviction to a fine not exceeding the fifth level on the standard scale.

(11) The Treasury may after consultation with the Bank by order—

  (a) amend subsection (1) above so as to substitute for either of the percentages for the time being specified in that subsection such other percentage as may be specified in the order;

  (b) make provision, whether by amending subsection (5) above or otherwise, with respect to the transactions and risks to be taken into account for the purposes of this section,

but any such order shall be subject to annulment in pursuance of a resolution of either House of Parliament.

(12) For the avoidance of doubt it is hereby declared that references in this section to "one person" include references to a partnership.

DEFINITIONS
  "authorised": s.106(1).
  "the Bank": s.1.
  "institution": s.106(1).
  "notice": s.100.
  "the standard scale": Criminal Justice Act 1982, s.37.
  "subsidiary": s.106(2); Companies Act 1985, s.736.

GENERAL NOTE
  The Bank issued a notice (BSD/1983/1) in April 1983 concerning, amongst other things, the size of individual exposures and the need to keep these within prudent limits. Consultative Papers were also issued on the issue of "Large Exposures Undertaken by Institutions Authorised under The Banking Act 1979", in July 1985, July 1986 and February 1987. The specific requirements imposed on a U.K. based authorised institution to report large credit exposures to the Bank arising from the Johnson Matthey Bankers collapse (conceivably also brought about by laxity in the reporting and supervising of large exposures) formed the basis of recommendations in Chapter 10 of the White Paper. S.38 (which is new) should also be read with ss.39 and 94. Any transaction or a related series of transactions which have already been entered into with one person or associated persons and carrying a potential loss in

excess of 10 per cent. of "available capital resources" (to be determined by the Bank after consultation with the institution concerned and in accordance with published principles), and those *proposed* to be entered into where the potential loss exceeds 25 per cent. of such resources, must be reported to the Bank. There are no requirements as to the form and content of the reports ("as the Bank may reasonably require"). The section imports a degree of flexibility into the procedures by leaving it to the Bank to determine exposure to risk "in accordance with principles published by the Bank" (subs. (6)) and the Bank determines the value of "available capital resources" (subs. (7)). A new statutory offence is created (subss. (9), (10)).

Subss. (1), (2), (11), (12)
Relating to any one person. This includes a partnership and also separate persons where these are connected in such a way that the financial soundness of any of them may affect the financial soundness of the others, or the same "factors" may affect the financial soundness of all of them. It may also include lending to governments. (Standing Committee, Seventh Sitting, January 22, 1987, col. 218). On the face of it, the scope of the requirements appear to be so wide as to embrace virtually every interdependent institution operating in the same system but for the Bank's power of definition in subs. (6). The percentages may be amended by order.

Subs. (3)
The requirement may extend to subsidiaries which are *not* themselves authorised with the result that their transactions and also their available capital resources would be included for the purpose of calculating the percentages in subs. (1).

Subs. (4)
The Bank may notify the frequency and prior notice required for subs. (1)(a) and (1)(b) cases respectively and the reports shall be in such form and contain such particulars as "reasonably" required by the Bank.

Subss. (5), (11)
This qualifies the apparently limitless scope of the "transaction or transactions relating to any one person" (subs. (1) to restrict it to the incurring or acquiring of obligations of one nature or another to the institution and limits the scope of the "risk of incurring losses" to the risk of the person defaulting or of "deterioration in its financial soundness". Such transactions and risks to be taken into account may be amended by order.

Subss. (6)–(8)
No definitions are given of "exposed to risk" or of "available capital resources" but the Bank may publish generally or notify the institution concerned as to the principles which will determine the question of exposure to risk, including the amount or extent to which such amount shall be taken into account and the Bank may, in accordance with published principles, determine and notify the institution of the value of its available capital resources. The Bank may exclude in part or full risks resulting from certain classes of transactions entered into in particular circumstances or with certain persons.

Power to obtain information and require production of documents

39.—(1) The Bank may by notice in writing served on an authorised institution—

    (a) require the institution to provide the Bank, at such time or times or at such intervals or in respect of such period or periods as may be specified in the notice, with such information as the Bank may reasonably require for the performance of its functions under this Act;

    (b) require the institution to provide the Bank with a report by an accountant or other person with relevant professional skill on, or on any aspect of, any matter about which the Bank has required or could require the institution to provide information under paragraph (a) above.

(2) The accountant or other person appointed by an institution to make any report required under subsection (1)(b) above shall be a person

nominated or approved by the Bank; and the Bank may require his report to be in such form as is specified in the notice.

(3) The Bank may—

    (a) by notice in writing served on an authorised institution require it to produce, within such time and at such place as may be specified in the notice, such document or documents of such description as may be so specified;

    (b) authorise an officer, servant or agent of the Bank, on producing evidence of his authority, to require any such institution to provide him forthwith with such information, or to produce to him forthwith such documents, as he may specify,

being such information or documents as the Bank may reasonably require for the performance of its functions under this Act.

(4) Where, by virtue of subsection (3) above, the Bank or any officer, servant or agent of the Bank has power to require the production of any documents from an authorised institution, the Bank or that officer, servant or agent shall have the like power to require the production of those documents from any person who appears to be in possession of them; but where any person from whom such production is required claims a lien on documents produced by him, the production shall be without prejudice to the lien.

(5) The power under this section to require an institution or other person to produce any documents includes power—

    (a) if the documents are produced, to take copies of them or extracts from them and to require that institution or person, or any other person who is a present or past director, controller or manager of, or is or was at any time employed by or acting as an employee of, the institution in question, to provide an explanation of any of them; and

    (b) if the documents are not produced, to require the person who was required to produce them to state, to the best of his knowledge and belief, where they are.

(6) If it appears to the Bank to be desirable in the interests of the depositors or potential depositors of an authorised institution to do so, it may also exercise the powers conferred by subsections (1) and (3) above in relation to any body corporate which is or has at any relevant time been—

    (a) a holding company, subsidiary or related company of that institution;

    (b) a subsidiary of a holding company of that institution;

    (c) a holding company of a subsidiary of that institution; or

    (d) a body corporate in the case of which a shareholder controller of that institution, either alone or with any associate or associates, is entitled to exercise, or control the exercise of, more than 50 per cent. of the voting power at a general meeting;

or in relation to any partnership of which that institution is or has at any relevant time been a member.

(7) If it appears to the Bank to be desirable to do so in the interests of the depositors or potential depositors of an authorised institution which is a partnership ("the authorised partnership") it may also exercise the powers conferred by subsections (1) and (3) above in relation to—

    (a) any other partnership having a member in common with the authorised partnership;

    (b) any body corporate which is or has at any relevant time been a member of the authorised partnership;

    (c) any body corporate in the case of which the partners in the authorised partnership hold more than 20 per cent. of the shares or any partner in the authorised partnership, either alone or with any associate or associates, is entitled to exercise, or control the exercise of, more than 50 per cent. of the voting power at a general meeting; or

(d) any subsidiary or holding company of any such body corporate as is mentioned in paragraph (b) or (c) above or any holding company of any such subsidiary.

(8) The foregoing provisions of this section shall apply to a former authorised institution as they apply to an authorised institution.

(9) The Bank may by notice in writing served on any person who is or is to be a director, controller or manager of an authorised institution require him to provide the Bank, within such time as may be specified in the notice, with such information or documents as the Bank may reasonably require for determining whether he is a fit and proper person to hold the particular position which he holds or is to hold.

(10) The Bank may exercise the powers conferred by subsections (1) and (3) above in relation to any person who is a significant shareholder of an authorised institution within the meaning of section 37 above if the Bank considers that the exercise of those powers is desirable in the interests of the depositors or potential depositors of that institution.

(11) Any person who without reasonable excuse fails to comply with a requirement imposed on him under this section shall be guilty of an offence and liable on summary conviction to imprisonment for a term not exceeding six months or to a fine not exceeding the fifth level on the standard scale or to both.

(12) A statement made by a person in compliance with a requirement imposed by virtue of this section may be used in evidence against him.

(13) Nothing in this section shall compel the production by a barrister, advocate or solicitor of a document containing a privileged communication made by him or to him in that capacity.

DEFINITIONS
  "associate": s.106(1).
  "authorised": s.106(1).
  "the Bank": s.1.
  "controller": s.105(3).
  "director": s.105(2).
  "documents": s.106(1).
  "former authorised institution": s.106(1).
  "holding company": s.106(2); Companies Act 1985, s.736.
  "institution": s.106(1).
  "manager": s.105(6).
  "notice": s.100.
  "related company": s.106(1).
  "shareholder controller": s.105(4).
  "the standard scale": Criminal Justice Act 1982, s.37.
  "subsidiary": s.106(2); Companies Act 1985, s.736.

GENERAL NOTE
  S.16 of the 1979 Act conferred power on the Bank to obtain information and require the production of documents but only from licensed deposit-takers and not from recognised banks. The White Paper (Chap. 9) proposed the reinforcement of the Bank's powers to enable it to require prudential data from all authorised institutions on a routine, and not merely on the then existing *ad hoc* basis, and s.39 materially extends these provisions. See ss.40 and 94 in this connection. Note the comparable powers of the Secretary of State to call for information under s.104 of the Financial Services Act 1986.

Subss. (1)–(3), (8)
  The Bank is empowered to require an authorised institution or former authorised institution (and companies within the same group) to provide information and documents "as the Bank may reasonably require for the performance of its functions under this Act."

It may be wondered whether any exercise of this wide general power would include a requirement that information, *inter alia*, relating to an institution's "plans for future development" be furnished as under s.16(1)(a) of the 1979 Act (which is also required in applications for authorisation under s.8 of this Act). The White Paper indicated (in para. 8.2) that any new legislation would empower the Bank to require the appointment of a second firm of accountants to carry out work not already satisfactorily carried out. Para. (b) of this subs. (1) provides for the requirement of this second opinion from an accountant "or other person with relevant professional skill", *i.e.* relevant to the performance of the particular supervisory activity under the new Act, on information which the Bank *may* but did not actually demand ("could require"). Such person must be nominated or approved by the Bank. Note in particular the provision in s.47(1) that any auditors' duties of confidentiality owed to an institution will not be breached by communications made in good faith to the Bank. Note the qualification "reasonably" on what the Bank may require in subss. (1) and (3).

Subs. (4)
Where the documents are held by a third person, the Bank or any officer, servant or agent has power to require their production subject to any lien on the documents (*e.g.* solicitors' lien for costs).

Subs. (5)
See the note to s.40(1).

Subss. (6), (7)
The powers conferred by subss. (1) and (3) may be exercised in respect of companies within the same group or any other partnership having a member in common with the "authorised partnership."

Subs. (10)
See the General Note to s.37.

Subs. (13)
The privilege limited to the legal profession with regard to documents and communications is confirmed and the Bank's powers do not extend to these (see ss.41(11) and 42(6).

Right of entry to obtain information and documents

40.—(1) Any officer, servant or agent of the Bank may, on producing if required evidence of his authority, enter any premises occupied by a person on whom a notice has been served under section 39 above for the purpose of obtaining there the information or documents required by that notice and of exercising the powers conferred by subsection (5) of that section.

(2) Any officer, servant or agent of the Bank may, on producing if required evidence of his authority, enter any premises occupied by any person on whom a notice could be served under section 39 above for the purpose of obtaining there such information or documents as are specified in the authority, being information or documents that could have been required by such a notice; but the Bank shall not authorise any person to act under this subsection unless it has reasonable cause to believe that if such a notice were served it would not be complied with or that any documents to which it would relate would be removed, tampered with or destroyed.

(3) Any person who intentionally obstructs a person exercising rights conferred by this section shall be guilty of an offence and liable on summary conviction to imprisonment for a term not exceeding six months or to a fine not exceeding the fifth level on the standard scale or to both.

DEFINITIONS
"the Bank": s.1.
"documents": s.106(1).
"notice": s.100.

"the standard scale": Criminal Justice Act 1982, s.37.

GENERAL NOTE

This section is new and provides further powers to support the Bank's powers to obtain information and require production of documents under s.39.

Subs. (1)

If, notwithstanding the sanctions in s.39(11), an authorised institution fails to provide the requisite information, report or documents, then the Bank may exercise a right of entry to obtain any of them and also to take copies or extracts, and require the provision of an explanation about them or their whereabouts if the documents are not produced.

Subs. (2)

The power may be exercised in circumstances where a notice "could" have been made under s.39 and where there is "reasonable" cause to believe that such a notice, if served, would not be complied with or the documents would be tampered with or suppressed.

Subs. (3)

Creates the statutory offence of obstruction.

Investigations

Investigations on behalf of the Bank

41.—(1) If it appears to the Bank desirable to do so in the interests of the depositors or potential depositors of an authorised institution the Bank may appoint one or more competent persons to investigate and report to the Bank on—

(a) the nature, conduct or state of the institution's business or any particular aspect of it; or

(b) the ownership or control of the institution;

and the Bank shall give written notice of any such appointment to the institution concerned.

(2) If a person appointed under subsection (1) above thinks it necessary for the purposes of his investigation, he may also investigate the business of any body corporate which is or has at any relevant time been—

(a) a holding company, subsidiary or related company of the institution under investigation;

(b) a subsidiary or related company of a holding company of that institution;

(c) a holding company of a subsidiary of that institution; or

(d) a body corporate in the case of which a shareholder controller of that institution, either alone or with any associate or associates, is entitled to exercise, or control the exercise of, more than 20 per cent. of the voting power at a general meeting;

or the business of any partnership of which that institution is or has at any relevant time been a member.

(3) If a person appointed under subsection (1) above thinks it necessary for the purposes of his investigation in the case of an authorised institution which is a partnership ("the authorised partnership") he may also investigate the business of—

(a) any other partnership having a member in common with the authorised partnership;

(b) any body corporate which is or has at any relevant time been a member of the authorised partnership;

(c) any body corporate in the case of which the partners in the authorised partnership hold more than 20 per cent. of the shares or any partner in the authorised partnership, either alone or with any associate or associates, is entitled to exercise, or control the exercise of, more than 20 per cent. of the voting power at a general meeting; or

(d) any subsidiary, related company or holding company of any such body corporate as is mentioned in paragraph (b) or (c) above or any holding company of any such subsidiary.

(4) Where a person appointed under subsection (1) above decides to investigate the business of any body by virtue of subsection (2) or (3) above he shall give it written notice to that effect.

(5) It shall be the duty of every person who is or was a director, controller, manager, employee, agent, banker, auditor or solicitor of a body which is under investigation (whether by virtue of subsection (1), (2) or (3) above), any person appointed to make a report in respect of that body under section 8(5) or 39(1)(b) above and anyone who is a significant shareholder in relation to that body within the meaning of section 37 above—

(a) to produce to the persons appointed under subsection (1) above, within such time and at such place as they may require, all documents relating to the body concerned which are in his custody or power;

(b) to attend before the persons so appointed at such time and place as they may require; and

(c) otherwise to give those persons all assistance in connection with the investigation which he is reasonably able to give;

and those persons may take copies of or extracts from any documents produced to them under paragraph (a) above.

(6) The foregoing provisions of this section shall apply to a former authorised institution as they apply to an authorised institution.

(7) For the purpose of exercising his powers under this section a person appointed under subsection (1) above may enter any premises occupied by a body which is being investigated by him under this section; but he shall not do so without prior notice in writing unless he has reasonable cause to believe that if such a notice were given any documents whose production could be required under this section would be removed, tampered with or destroyed.

(8) A person exercising powers by virtue of an appointment under this section shall, if so required, produce evidence of his authority.

(9) Any person who—

(a) without reasonable excuse fails to produce any documents which it is his duty to produce under subsection (5) above;

(b) without reasonable excuse fails to attend before the persons appointed under subsection (1) above when required to do so;

(c) without reasonable excuse fails to answer any question which is put to him by persons so appointed with respect to an institution which is under investigation or a body which is being investigated by virtue of subsection (2) or (3) above; or

(d) intentionally obstructs a person in the exercise of the rights conferred by subsection (7) above,

shall be guilty of an offence and liable on summary conviction to imprisonment for a term not exceeding six months or to a fine not exceeding the fifth level on the standard scale or to both.

(10) A statement made by a person in compliance with a requirement imposed by virtue of this section may be used in evidence against him.

(11) Nothing in this section shall compel the production by a barrister, advocate or solicitor of a document containing a privileged communication made by him or to him in that capacity.

DEFINITIONS
"associate": s.105(9).
"authorised": s.106(1).
"the Bank": s.1.
"controller": s.105(3).
"director": s.105(2).
"documents": s.106(1).
"former authorised institution": s.106(1).
"holding company": s.106(2); Companies Act 1985, s.736.
"institution": s.106(1).
"manager": s.105(6).
"notice": s.100.
"related company": s.106(1).
"shareholder controller": s.105(4).
"the standard scale": Criminal Justice Act 1982, s.37.
"subsidiary": s.106(2); Companies Act 1985, s.736.

GENERAL NOTE
The power of the Bank to appoint persons to carry out investigations of an authorised institution's business as laid down in s.17 of the 1979 Act, is further extended by enabling the Bank to investigate the ownership or control of an institution or of a *former* authorised institution and to enter its premises and also, under s.42, to investigate a suspected contravention of the Act. Note the comparable powers of the Secretary of State in the Financial Services Act 1986, ss.105 and 106.

Subs. (1)
The exercise of the power does not depend upon the existence of any particular circumstances—it need only appear "to the Bank desirable to do so in the interests of the depositors or potential depositors" of the authorised institution or of the former authorised institution. The investigators may, amongst other things, look into and report on ownership or control of the institution; note also ss.432 and 442 of the Companies Act 1985 regarding investigation of the membership of companies and their affairs.

Subss. (2)–(4)
The "competent" person also has a discretion to extend the investigation of incorporated bodies and authorised partnerships to other related bodies as listed by written notice to any such body.

Subss. (5), (11)
The duties of production of documents, attendances and giving of assistance extends, *inter alia*, to a banker, auditor or solicitor of the body under investigation but the solicitor's privilege with regard to documents and confidential communications is preserved.

Subs. (7)
Investigators have the power of entry but prior written notice must be given unless there is "reasonable" cause to believe that as a result relevant documents would be tampered with or suppressed.

Subs. (9)
Note the penalties, unless there is "reasonable" excuse, for not producing documents, attending or answering questions.

Investigation of suspected contraventions

42.—(1) Where the Bank has reasonable grounds for suspecting that a person is guilty of contravening section 3 or 35 above the Bank or any duly authorised officer, servant or agent of the Bank may by notice in writing require that or any other person—

(a) to provide, at such place as may be specified in the notice and either forthwith or at such time as may be so specified, such information as the Bank may reasonably require for the purpose of investigating the suspected contravention;

(b) to produce, at such place as may be specified in the notice and either forthwith or at such time as may be so specified, such documents, or documents of such description, as may be specified, being documents the production of which may be reasonably required by the Bank for that purpose;

(c) to attend at such place and time as may be specified in the notice and answer questions relevant for determining whether such a contravention has occurred.

(2) The Bank or a duly authorised officer, servant or agent of the Bank may take copies of or extracts from any documents produced under this section.

(3) Any officer, servant or agent of the Bank may, on producing if required evidence of his authority, enter any premises occupied by a person on whom a notice has been served under subsection (1) above for the purpose of obtaining there the information or documents required by the notice, putting the questions referred to in paragraph (c) of that subsection or exercising the powers conferred by subsection (2) above.

(4) Any person who without reasonable excuse fails to comply with a requirement imposed on him under this section or intentionally obstructs a person in the exercise of the rights conferred by subsection (3) above shall be guilty of an offence and liable on summary conviction to imprisonment for a term not exceeding six months or to a fine not exceeding the fifth level on the standard scale or to both.

(5) A statement made by a person in compliance with a requirement imposed by virtue of this section may be used in evidence against him.

(6) Nothing in this section shall compel the production by a barrister, advocate or solicitor of a document containing a privileged communication made by him or to him in that capacity.

TRANSITIONAL PROVISION
Sched. 5, para. 7(3).

DEFINITIONS
"the Bank": s.1.
"documents": s.106(1).
"notice": s.100.
"the standard scale": Criminal Justice Act 1982, s.37.

GENERAL NOTE
Para. 9.6 in Chapter 9 of the White Paper observed that although the 1979 Act provided for criminal offences which could (and in some cases could *only*) be committed by those not authorised under the Act, the Bank had no powers to obtain evidence to assist it in prosecuting. S.42 empowers the Bank to investigate the illegal taking of deposits (s.3) or a fraudulent inducement to make a deposit (s.35).

Subss. (1), (2)
Note the qualifying test of "reasonable grounds for suspecting" (see also s.43(1)). The suspected *person* may be required to provide information, produce documents and attend to answer questions, and copies of or extracts from documents produced may be taken.

Subs. (3)
Again the Bank's officer, servant or agent has power of entry after notice has been served, to exercise its powers under subss. (1) and (2).

Subs. (6)
The privilege of communications by or to a barrister, advocate or solicitor is confirmed.

Powers of entry in cases of suspected contraventions

43.—(1) A justice of the peace may issue a warrant under this section if satisfied on information on oath laid by an officer or servant of the

Bank or laid under the Bank's authority that there are reasonable grounds for suspecting that a person is guilty of such a contravention as is mentioned in section 42 above and—

(a) that that person has failed to comply with a notice served on him under that section; or

(b) that there are reasonable grounds for suspecting the completeness of any information provided or documents produced by him in response to such notice; or

(c) that there are reasonable grounds for suspecting that if a notice were served on him under that section it would not be complied with or that any documents to which it would relate would be removed, tampered with or destroyed.

(2) A warrant under this section shall authorise any constable, together with any other person named in the warrant and any other constables—

(a) to enter any premises occupied by the person mentioned in subsection (1) above which are specified in the warrant, using such force as is reasonably necessary for the purpose;

(b) to search the premises and take possession of any documents appearing to be such documents as are mentioned in subsection (1)(c) above or to take, in relation to any such documents, any other steps which may appear to be necessary for preserving them or preventing interference with them;

(c) to take copies of or extracts from any such documents;

(d) to require any person named in the warrant to answer questions relevant for determining whether that person is guilty of any such contravention as is mentioned in section 42 above.

(3) A warrant under this section shall continue in force until the end of the period of one month beginning with the day on which it is issued.

(4) Any documents of which possession is taken under this section may be retained—

(a) for a period of three months; or

(b) if within that period proceedings to which the documents are relevant are commenced against any person for any such contravention as is mentioned in section 42 above, until the conclusion of those proceedings.

(5) Any person who intentionally obstructs the exercise of any right conferred by a warrant issued under this section or fails without reasonable excuse to comply with any requirement imposed in accordance with subsection (2)(d) above shall be guilty of an offence and liable—

(a) on conviction on indictment, to imprisonment for a term not exceeding two years or to a fine or to both;

(b) on summary conviction, to imprisonment for a term not exceeding six months or to a fine not exceeding the statutory maximum or to both.

(6) A statement made by a person in compliance with a requirement imposed by virtue of this section may be used in evidence against him.

(7) In the application of subsection (1) above to Scotland, the reference to a justice of the peace includes a reference to a sheriff and for the reference to information on oath there shall be substituted a reference to evidence on oath; and in the application of that subsection to Northern Ireland for the reference to laying an information on oath there shall be substituted a reference to making a complaint on oath.

TRANSITIONAL PROVISION
  Sched. 5, para. 7(3).

DEFINITIONS
  "the Bank": s.1.
  "documents": s.106(1).

"notice": s.100.

"the statutory maximum": Criminal Justice Act 1982, s.74; Magistrates' Courts Act 1980, s.32.

GENERAL NOTE

An effective back-up provision to s.42 enabling the Bank to apply for a warrant from a J.P. (or sheriff in Scotland).

Subs. (1)

There must be "reasonable grounds for suspecting" that a person is guilty of a contravention under s.42 and that he has already failed to comply with the notice or where the information provided or documents produced are thought to be incomplete or that if a notice was served it would be ignored or documents would be suppressed, etc.

Subs. (2)

Note that in contrast to the rights of entry conferred on the Bank in ss.40(2), 41(7) and 42(3), any constable authorised "together with any other person named in the warrant and any other constables" may use reasonable force for the purpose of gaining entry and may take other steps appearing necessary to preserve or prevent interference with documents.

Subs. (5)

Note as contrasted with s.42(4) the heavier penalties imposed in the case of an intentional obstruction of the exercise of a right conferred by a warrant issued hereunder or on failure to comply without reasonable excuse with any requirement to answer questions under subs. (2)(d).

Obstruction of investigations

44.—(1) A person who knows or suspects that an investigation is being or is likely to be carried out—

(a) under section 41 above; or

(b) into a suspected contravention of section 3 or 35 above,

shall be guilty of an offence if he falsifies, conceals, destroys or otherwise disposes of, or causes or permits the falsification, concealment, destruction or disposal of, documents which he knows or suspects are or would be relevant to such an investigation unless he proves that he had no intention of concealing facts disclosed by the documents from persons carrying out such an investigation.

(2) A person guilty of an offence under this section shall be liable—

(a) on conviction on indictment, to imprisonment for a term not exceeding two years or to a fine or to both;

(b) on summary conviction, to imprisonment for a term not exceeding six months or to a fine not exceeding the statutory maximum or to both.

TRANSITIONAL PROVISION

Sched. 5, para. 7(3).

DEFINITIONS

"documents": s.106(1).

"the statutory maximum": Criminal Justice Act 1982, s.74; Magistrates' Courts Act 1980, s.32.

GENERAL NOTE

This new offence of obstructing investigations under s.41 or into suspected illegal deposit taking or fraudulent inducement to make deposits, was brought up, read and added to the Bill at the Eleventh Sitting of the Standing Committee (Eleventh Sitting, February 5, 1987, col. 293).

Accounts and auditors

Audited accounts to be open to inspection

45.—(1) An authorised institution shall at each of its offices in the United Kingdom at which it holds itself out as accepting deposits—

(a) keep a copy of its most recent audited accounts; and
(b) during normal business hours make that copy available for inspection by any person on request.

(2) An institution which fails to comply with paragraph (a) of subsection (1) above or with any request made in accordance with paragraph (b) of that subsection shall be guilty of an offence and liable on summary conviction to a fine not exceeding the fifth level on the standard scale.

(3) In the case of an institution incorporated in the United Kingdom the accounts referred to in subsection (1) above include the auditors' report on the accounts and, in the case of any other institution whose accounts are audited, the report of the auditors.

DEFINITIONS
"authorised": s.106(1).
"deposits": s.5.
"institution": s.106(1).
"the standard scale": Criminal Justice Act 1982, s.37.

GENERAL NOTE
Each authorised institution (the 1979 Act restricted the requirement to licensed deposit-takers) must keep a copy of its current audited accounts (and of the auditors' report) and make that copy available for inspection by any person so requesting it "at each of its *offices* in the United Kingdom at which it holds itself out as accepting deposits." (Emphasis added.)

Notification in respect of auditors

46.—(1) An authorised institution incorporated in the United Kingdom shall forthwith give written notice to the Bank if the institution—
   (a) proposes to give special notice to its shareholders of an ordinary resolution removing an auditor before the expiration of his term of office; or
   (b) gives notice to its shareholders of an ordinary resolution replacing an auditor at the expiration of his term of office with a different auditor,
or if a person ceases to be an auditor of the institution otherwise than in consequence of such a resolution.

(2) An auditor of an authorised institution appointed under section 384 of the Companies Act 1985 shall forthwith give written notice to the Bank if he—
   (a) resigns before the expiration of his term of office;
   (b) does not seek to be re-appointed; or
   (c) decides to include in his report on the institution's accounts any qualification as to a matter mentioned in section 236 or any statement pursuant to section 237 of that Act.

(3) The foregoing provisions of this section shall apply to a former authorised institution as they apply to an authorised institution.

(4) In the application of subsection (2) above to Northern Ireland for the references to sections 384, 236 and 237 of the Companies Act 1985 there shall be substituted references to Articles 392, 244 and 245 of the Companies (Northern Ireland) Order 1986.

(5) An institution or auditor who fails to comply with this section shall be guilty of an offence and liable on summary conviction to a fine not exceeding the fifth level on the standard scale.

DEFINITIONS
"authorised": s.106(1).
"the Bank": s.1.
"former authorised institution": s.106(1).
"institution": s.106(1).

"notice": s.100.
"the standard scale": Criminal Justice Act 1982, s.37.

GENERAL NOTE
This was another new provision proposed in the White Paper (Chap. 8, para. 8.2(iii)) following representations made by the professional bodies concerned. An authorised or former authorised, institution incorporated in the U.K. must immediately give the Bank written notice if it decides to remove before, or replace an auditor after, the expiry of his term of office or if a person otherwise ceases to be an auditor. The prior warning to the Bank would give it more time to object to any appointment. An auditor of any authorised institution must also give immediate written notice of his resignation or of not seeking reappointment or if he "decides" to qualify his opinion on the institution's accounts. "Decides" is imprecise as to time but see s.47 regarding the regular dialogue between the Bank and auditors.

Communication by auditor etc. with the Bank

47.—(1) No duty to which—
   (a) an auditor of an authorised institution; or
   (b) a person appointed to make a report under section 8(5) or 39(1)(b) above,
may be subject shall be regarded as contravened by reason of his communicating in good faith to the Bank, whether or not in response to a request made by it, any information or opinion on a matter to which this section applies and which is relevant to any function of the Bank under this Act.

(2) In relation to an auditor of an authorised institution this section applies to any matter of which he becomes aware in his capacity as auditor and which relates to the business or affairs of the institution or any associated body.

(3) In relation to a person appointed to make a report under section 8(5) or 39(1)(b) above this section applies to any matter of which he becomes aware in his capacity as the person making the report and which—
   (a) relates to the business of affairs of the institution in relation to which his report is made or any associated body of that institution; or
   (b) if by virtue of section 39(6) or (7) above the report relates to an associated body of an institution, to the business or affairs of that body.

(4) In this section "associated body", in relation to an institution, means any such body as is mentioned in section 39(6) or (7) above.

(5) If it appears to the Treasury that any accountants or class of accountants who are persons to whom subsection (1) above applies are not subject to satisfactory rules made or guidance issued by a professional body specifying circumstances in which matters are to be communicated to the Bank as mentioned in that subsection the Treasury may, after consultation with the Bank and such bodies as appear to the Treasury to represent the interests of accountants and authorised institutions, make regulations applying to those accountants and specifying such circumstances; and it shall be the duty of an accountant to whom the regulations apply to communicate a matter to the Bank in the circumstances specified by the regulations.

(6) Regulations under this section may make different provision for different cases and no such regulations shall be made unless a draft of them has been laid before and approved by a resolution of each House of Parliament.

(7) This section applies to the auditor of a former authorised institution as it applies to the auditor of an authorised institution.

DEFINITIONS
"authorised": s.106(1).
"the Bank": s.1.
"former authorised institution": s.106(1).
"institution": s.106(1).

GENERAL NOTE
The White Paper observed that the absence of a full-scale banking inspectorate increased the importance which should be attached to increased co-operation and discussion between supervisors and auditors of authorised institutions. The matter was examined in Chapter 8 of, and Annex 4 to, the White Paper, which gave guidance on the disclosure of information by auditors. The formulation adopted in s.47 closely follows s.109 of the Financial Services Act 1986 and s.82 of the Building Societies Act 1986 in order to provide a consistency to assist auditors and supervisors. There are differences, *e.g.* the Building Societies Act 1986 (s.82(5)) makes specific provision for auditors' annual reports to be passed *via* the society to the Building Socieites Commission—there is no provision as such in this Act. In general, s.47 makes it clear that auditors and reporting accountants are free to communicate to the Bank whether by written report, at a meeting or by any other means, on the institution's affairs on matters relevant to any of the functions of the Bank under this Act. The section applies to the auditor of a *former* authorised institution.
Note also s.83(2) of this Act.

Subs. (1)
In effect, a right is accorded to auditors of authorised institutions and to accountants and other qualified or professional persons reporting in connection with an application for authorisation under s.8 or providing information under s.39, to communicate with the Bank "any information or opinion" on a matter to which s.47 applies and which is relevant to the Bank's functions under the Act. Any restraint such as that imposed by a duty of confidence or trust otherwise owed to a client will be removed in order to facilitate the exercise of this right provided it is exercised in good faith and without malice. It should be noted that whereas there is no *statutory duty* to communicate imposed by this section upon auditors (subs. (1)(a), there may be a situation where they may become aware, during the ordinary course of their audit work or their examination, of, say, some adverse change in the circumstances of the institution whereupon they may be obliged to report to the Bank, and with expedition, to protect the interest of depositors.

Subss. (2)–(4)
The auditor (or the person appointed to make a report under s.8(5) or s.39(1)(b)) may disclose information about his client institution (or the institution he is reporting on) including information about its customers but not information obtained by him in other capacities, *e.g.* through his professional relationships with other clients. The information must relate to the business *or* affairs (note the printing error in subs. (3)(a)) of the authorised institution or, *e.g.*, its subsidiaries, fellow subsidiaries, holding company or related company.

Subs. (5)
It is expected that the professional bodies will introduce non-statutory rules or guidelines similar to those set out in Annex 4 of the White Paper specifying "circumstances" in which matters are to be communicated to the Bank. If any accountants are not covered by satisfactory rules or guidelines, the Treasury itself is granted a reserve power to bring forward rules, and accountants subject to the rules will be under a statutory duty to communicate to the Bank in the circumstances specified. The Treasury must first consult with the Bank and representative bodies such as the Institute of Chartered Accountants and the British Bankers' Association before making the regulations.
At the time of this publication the Auditing Practices Committee of the Consultative Committee of Accountancy Bodies has issued a *Banking Act 1987: Interim Guidance on Ad Hoc Reporting* (July 1987, TR663) and the Bank will be issuing a consultative paper "*The Bank of England's Relationship with Auditors and Reporting Accountants.*"

Subs. (6)
Any draft regulations are subject to the affirmative procedure thereby affording greater opportunity of debate and examination.

Unauthorised acceptance of deposits

Repayment of unauthorised deposits

48.—(1) If on the application of the Bank it appears to the court that a person has accepted deposits in contravention of section 3 above the court may—

(a) order him and any other person who appears to the court to have been knowingly concerned in the contravention to repay the deposits forthwith or at such time as the court may direct; or

(b) except in Scotland, appoint a receiver to recover those deposits;

but in deciding whether and, if so, on what terms to make an order under this section the court shall have regard to the effect that repayment in accordance with the order would have on the solvency of the person concerned or otherwise on his ability to carry on his business in a manner satisfactory to his creditors.

(2) The jurisdiction conferred by this section shall be exercisable by the High Court and the Court of Session.

DEFINITIONS
"the Bank": s.1.
"deposit": s.5.

GENERAL NOTE
This section (to be read with s.49) is new and provides another sanction enabling the Bank to apply to the High Court or Court of Session (as the case may be). The court may order any person who has accepted or has been knowingly concerned in accepting deposits in contravention of s.3 to repay or it may appoint a receiver to recover such deposits.

Subs. (1)
Knowingly. Cf. s.5 of the Financial Services Act 1986 where there are similar provisions, but there it is for the person to show that he "reasonably believed that his entering into" the agreement was not in contravention of the provisions relating to authorised or exempted persons. The court in s.48, has a discretion with regard to the timing of the repayments and must have regard to the effect that the terms of any order would have on that person's solvency or ability to carry on his business.

Profits from unauthorised deposits

49.—(1) If on the application of the Bank the court is satisfied that profits have accrued to a person as a result of deposits having been accepted in contravention of section 3 above the court may order him to pay into court or, except in Scotland, appoint a receiver to recover from him, such sum as appears to the court to be just having regard to the profits appearing to the court to have accrued to him.

(2) In deciding whether, and if so, on what terms to make an order under this section the court shall have regard to the effect that payment in accordance with the order would have on the solvency of the person concerned or otherwise on his ability to carry on his business in a manner satisfactory to his creditors.

(3) Any amount paid into court or recovered from a person in pursuance of an order under this section shall be paid out to such person or distributed among such persons as the court may direct, being a person or persons appearing to the court to have made the deposits as a result of which the profits mentioned in subsection (1) above have accrued or such other person or persons as the court thinks just.

(4) On an application under this section the court may require the person concerned to furnish it with such accounts or other information as it may require for determining whether any and if so, what profits have accrued to him as mentioned in subsection (1) above and for determining how any amounts are to be paid or distributed under subsection (3) above;

and the court may require any such accounts or other information to be verified in such manner as it may direct.

(5) The jurisdiction conferred by this section shall be exercisable by the High Court and the Court of Session.

DEFINITIONS
    "the Bank": s.1.
    "deposit": s.5.

GENERAL NOTE
A further weapon enabling the court, if it is satisfied that profits have accrued in respect of unauthorised deposits to the offender, to order that person to pay into court, or appoint a receiver to recover, such sums for the benefit of such persons as the court thinks just.

PART II

THE DEPOSIT PROTECTION SCHEME

The Board and the Fund

The Deposit Protection Board

50.—(1) The body corporate known as the Deposit Protection Board and the Fund known as the Deposit Protection Fund established by section 21 of the Banking Act 1979 shall continue to exist.

(2) The Deposit Protection Board (in this Part of this Act referred to as "the Board") shall—

    (a) hold, manage and apply the Fund in accordance with the provisions of this Part of this Act;

    (b) levy contributions for the Fund, in accordance with those provisions, from authorised institutions; and

    (c) have such other functions as are conferred on the Board by those provisions.

(3) Schedule 4 to this Act shall have effect with respect to the Board.

DEFINITIONS
    "authorised": s.106(1).
    "institution": s.106(1).

GENERAL NOTE
    Ss.50 to 66 comprising Pt. II continue the existence of the Deposit Protection Scheme and in particular the Deposit Protection Board ("the Board") set up under the 1979 Act (ss.21 to 33) and referred to in the "Summary of Minor Proposals" in Annex 1 of the White Paper. The concept of a scheme funded by the institutions in this particular financial sector and providing a partial reimbursement for those who suffer loss through the failure of any of the institutions had certain origins in the Policyholder Protection Act 1975. However, two main changes proposed in the White Paper have been made to this scheme; whereas under the 1979 Act there was power by order (under s.23(2)) to exclude overseas institutions from having to contribute to the Deposit Protection Fund ("the Fund") all authorised bodies will now be required to contribute. Furthermore, the minimum contribution is increased from £2,500 to £10,000 in line with the proposed increase in the minimum net assets criterion for authorisation (£250,000 to £1 million). Other changes are examined under the relevant sections. The Board includes as *ex-officio* members, the Governor (Chairman), Deputy Governor and Chief Cashier of the Bank. The Chairman appoints other members from the Bank together with three members who are directors, controllers or managers of contributory institutions. The Board, which determines its own procedure and financial year, is required to keep proper accounts and records and to prepare an annual report and accounts (Sched. 4).

22–68

The Deposit Protection Fund

51.—(1) The Fund shall consist of—

(a) any money which forms part of the Fund when this section comes into force;

(b) initial, further and special contributions levied by the Board under this Part of this Act;

(c) money borrowed by the Board under this Part of this Act; and

(d) any other money required by any provision of this Part of this Act to be credited to the Fund or received by the Board and directed by it to be so credited.

(2) The money constituting the Fund shall be placed by the Board in an account with the Bank.

(3) As far as possible, the Bank shall invest money placed with it under subsection (2) above in Treasury bills; and any income from money so invested shall be credited to the Fund.

(4) There shall be chargeable to the Fund—

(a) repayments of special contributions under section 55(2) below;

(b) payments under section 58 below;

(c) money required for the repayment of, and the payment of interest on, money borrowed by the Board; and

(d) the administrative and other necessary or incidental expenses incurred by the Board.

DEFINITIONS
  "the Bank": s.1.
  "the Board": s.50.

GENERAL NOTE
  The Fund continues and consists of the balance it holds on the coming into operation of the section; the three classes of contribution which it levies from all authorised institutions; borrowed moneys; other moneys to be credited to the Fund (*e.g.* under s.62 payments from liquidators of insolvent institutions); and income from Treasury bills in which the Board invests the Fund's money placed with it. The Fund is charged with repayment of special contributions, compensation payments to depositors, money to repay borrowings and interest thereon and the administrative, etc., expenses of the Board.

Contributions to the Fund

Contributory institutions and general provisions as to contributions

52.—(1) All authorised institutions shall be liable to contribute to the Fund and are in this Part of this Act referred to as "contributory institutions".

(2) Contributions to the Fund shall be levied on a contributory institution by the Board by the service on the institution of a notice specifying the amount due, which shall be paid by the institution not later than twenty-one days after the date on which the notice is served.

(3) Subject to section 56 below, on each occasion on which contributions are to be levied from contributory institutions (other than the occasion of the levy of an initial contribution from a particular institution under section 53 below)—

(a) a contribution shall be levied from each of the contributory institutions; and

(b) the amount of the contribution of each institution shall be ascertained by applying to the institution's deposit base the percentage determined by the Board for the purpose of the contribution levied on that occasion.

(4) Subject to section 57 below, the deposit base of an institution in relation to any contribution is the amount which the Board determines as

representing the average, over such period preceding the levying of the contribution as appears to the Board to be appropriate, of sterling deposits with the United Kingdom offices of that institution other than—
  (a) secured deposits;
  (b) deposits which had an original term to maturity of more than five years; and
  (c) deposits in respect of which the institution has in the United Kingdom issued a sterling certificate of deposit.

(5) In its application to this section, section 5(3) above shall have effect with the omission of paragraphs (b) and (c).

DEFINITIONS
  "authorised": s.106(1).
  "the Board": s.50.
  "deposit": s.5.
  "the Fund": s.51.
  "institution": s.106(1).
  "notice": s.100.

GENERAL NOTE
Ss.52 to 57 dealing with contributions to the Fund correspond to ss.23 to 27 of the 1979 Act. It was observed during the Eighth Sitting of the Standing Committee (Eighth Sitting, January 27, 1987, col. 229) that these provisions differ from those for the Building Societies Investor Protection Fund (Building Societies Act 1986, ss.24–25) which is not a "standing fund" by reason, in that sector, of the smaller number of building societies, the fact that if one building society gets into difficulties the others amalgamate with it so avoiding the need to call on the Fund and the fact that in the case of an authorised institution contingency arrangements under a standing fund should be able to respond more readily.

Subs. (1)
  There are now no exceptions; *all* authorised institutions are "contributory institutions."

Subss. (3), (4)
  Contributions are calculated by reference to a "deposit base" if there be one (see s.53(3)). The base (subject to the limits set in s.56) consists of the average, over a determined period, of sterling deposits which, on an interpretation of the stated exclusions, would include the current account credit balances of customers.

Subs. (5)
  In calculating the deposit base, s.5(3) applies but loans made by exempted persons such as building societies and loans made in the course of a business of lending, are *included*.

Initial contributions

53.—(1) Subject to subsection (4) below, where an institution becomes a contributory institution after the coming into force of this Part of this Act the Board shall levy from it, on or as soon as possible after the day on which it becomes a contributory institution, an initial contribution of an amount determined in accordance with subsection (2) or (3) below.

(2) Where the institution concerned has a deposit base, then, subject to section 56(1) below, the amount of an initial contribution levied under this section shall be such percentage of the deposit base as the Board considers appropriate to put the institution on a basis of equality with the other contributory institutions, having regard to—
  (a) the initial contributions previously levied under this section or under section 24(1) of the Banking Act 1979; and
  (b) so far as they are attributable to an increase in the size of the Fund resulting from an order under subsection (2) of section 54 below or subsection (2) of section 25 of that Act, further contributions levied under either of those sections.

(3) Where the institution concerned has no deposit base the amount of an initial contribution levied under this section shall be the minimum amount for the time being provided for in section 56(1) below.

(4) The Board may waive an initial contribution under this section if it appears to it that the institution concerned is to carry on substantially the same business as that previously carried on by one or more institutions which are or were contributory institutions.

TRANSITIONAL PROVISION
Sched. 5, para. 9.

DEFINITIONS
"the Board": s.50.
"contributory institutions": s.52(1).
"deposit base": s.52(4).
"the Fund": s.51.
"institution": s.106(1).

GENERAL NOTE
In essence, as in s.24 of the 1979 Act, each new contributory institution, which has a deposit base, must make an intitial contribution (unless the Board exercises its discretion and treats a new institution as being a continuation of a former (see subs. (4)). The initial contribution is calculated as such percentage of its deposit base as the Board thinks fit "to put the institution on a basis of equality" with the others and where it has no deposit base the initial contribution levied shall be the minimum amount stipulated (at present £10,000). The maximum amount of any initial contribution levied is maintained at £300,000 (s.56(2)).

Further contributions

54.—(1) If at the end of any financial year of the Board the amount standing to the credit of the Fund is less than £3 million the Board may, with the approval of the Treasury, levy further contributions from contributory institutions so as to restore the amount standing to the credit of the Fund to a minimum of £5 million and a maximum of £6 million.

(2) If at any time it appears to the Treasury to be desirable in the interests of depositors to increase the size of the Fund, the Treasury may, after consultation with the Board, by order amend subsection (1) above so as to substitute for the sums for the time being specified in that subsection such larger sums as may be specified in the order; but no such order shall be made unless a draft of it has been laid before and approved by a resolution of each House of Parliament.

(3) An order under subsection (2) above may authorise the Board forthwith to levy further contributions from contributory institutions so as to raise the amount standing to the credit of the Fund to a figure between the new minimum and maximum amounts provided for by the order.

DEFINITIONS
"the Board": s.50.
"contributory institutions": s.52(1).
"the Fund": s.51.
"institution": s.106(1).

GENERAL NOTE
This is virtually in the same form as s.25 of the 1979 Act with the same thresholds of £3 million, £5 million and £6 million respectively and the maximum amount which may be levied remains at £300,000 (s.56(2)). The Board in its report for the year ended February 28, 1985, indicated (p.2) that the Fund had fallen below the £3 million threshold and further contributions amounting to £5.1 million were levied.

Special contributions

55.—(1) If it appears to the Board that payments under section 58 below are likely to exhaust the Fund, the Board may, with the approval of the Treasury, levy special contributions from contributory institutions to meet the Fund's commitments under that section.

(2) Where at the end of any financial year of the Board there is money in the Fund which represents special contributions and will not in the opinion of the Board be required for making payments under section 58 below in consequence of institutions having become insolvent or subject to administration orders before repayments are made under this subsection the Board—

  (a) shall repay to the institutions from which it was levied so much (if any) of that money as can be repaid without reducing the amount standing to the credit of the Fund below the maximum amount for the time being specified in subsection (1) of section 54 above; and

  (b) may repay to those institutions so much (if any) of that money as can be repaid without reducing the amount standing to the credit of the Fund below the minimum amount for the time being specified in that subsection.

(3) Repayments to institutions under this section shall be made pro rata according to the amount of the special contribution made by each of them but the Board may withhold the whole or part of any repayment due to an institution that has become insolvent and, in the case of an institution that has ceased to be a contributory institution, may either withhold its repayment or make it to any other contributory institution which, in the opinion of the Board, is its successor.

DEFINITIONS
  "the Board": s.50.
  "contributory institutions": s.52(1).
  "the Fund": s.51.
  "institution": s.106(1).

GENERAL NOTE
  This section is similar to s.26 of the 1979 Act (in that it serves to ensure that there is sufficient to meet compensation payments under s.58) except for two important additions. First, s.26 *required* the Board at the end of any financial year to repay surplus special contributions whereas under s.55(2) the Board is granted the discretion to repay if in its opinion the monies will not be required for compensation payments under s.58. This discretion is qualified inasmuch as the Board *shall* thereafter repay provided that the Fund is not reduced below £6 million and *may* repay provided that the Fund remains at the figure of at least £5 million. Under the 1979 Act, the Board had to repay notwithstanding that the monies might be required. Secondly, under subs. (3) it has the discretion to withhold repayment to an institution which is insolvent or no longer a contributory institution. There are not, as such, any minimum or maximum levels for special contributions but the overall limit of 0·3 per cent. of an institution's deposit base will apply to aggregate net contributions (s.56(3)).

Maximum and minimum contributions

56.—(1) The amount of the initial contribution levied from a contributory institution shall be not less than £10,000.

(2) The amount of the initial contribution or any further contribution levied from a contributory institution shall not exceed £300,000.

(3) No contributory institution shall be required to pay a further or special contribution if, or to the extent that, the amount of that contribution, together with previous initial, further and special contributions made by the institution, after allowing for any repayments made to it under section 55(2) above or section 63 below, amounts to more than 0.3 per cent. of the institution's deposit base as ascertained for the purpose of the contribution in question.

(4) Nothing in subsection (3) above—

  (a) shall entitle an institution to repayment of any contribution previously made; or

(b) shall prevent the Board from proceeding to levy contributions from other contributory institutions in whose case the limit in that subsection has not been reached.

(5) The Treasury may from time to time after consultation with the Board by order—

(a) amend subsection (1) or (2) above so as to substitute for the sum for the time being specified in that subsection such other sum as may be specified in the order; or

(b) amend subsection (3) above so as to substitute for the percentage for the time being specified in that subsection such other percentage as may be specified in the order.

(6) No order shall be made under subsection (5) above unless a draft of it has been laid before and approved by a resolution of each House of Parliament.

TRANSITIONAL PROVISION
Sched. 5, para. 10.

DEFINITIONS
"the Board": s.50.
"contributory institutions": s.52(1).
"deposit base": s.52(4).
"institution": s.106(1).

GENERAL NOTE
This corresponds to s.27 of the 1979 Act with two modifications. First, the amount of the initial contribution levied from a new authorised institution is increased from £2,500 to £10,000 in line with the fourfold increase in the minimum net asset requirement for authorisation (subs. (1)). Secondly, subs. (5)(b) provides for the Treasury by order (affirmative parliamentary procedure) to change the maximum total of all contributions (at present 0.3 per cent. of an institution's deposit base).

Deposit base of transferee institutions

57.—(1) This section applies where the liabilities in respect of deposits of a person specified in Schedule 2 to this Act (an "exempted person") are transferred to an institution which is not such a person (a "transferee institution").

(2) If the transferee institution becomes a contributory institution on the occasion of the transfer or immediately thereafter it shall be treated for the purposes of section 53 above as having such deposit base as it would have if—

(a) sterling deposits with the United Kingdom offices of the exempted person at any time had at that time been sterling deposits with the United Kingdom offices of the transferee institution; and

(b) sterling certificates of deposit issued by the exempted person had been issued by the transferee institution.

(3) If the transferee institution is already a contributory institution at the time of the transfer, the Board shall levy from it, as soon as possible after the transfer, a further initial contribution of an amount equal to the initial contribution which it would have been liable to make if—

(a) it had become a contributory institution on the date of the transfer;

(b) its deposit base were calculated by reference (and by reference only) to the sterling deposits with the United Kingdom offices of the exempted person, taking sterling certificates of deposit issued by the exempted person as having been issued by the transferee institution; and

(c) the amount specified in section 56(2) above were reduced by the amount of any initial contribution which the transferee institution has already made.

(4) Whether or not the transferee institution is already a contributory institution at the time of the transfer it shall be treated for the purposes of the levying from it of any further or special contribution as having such deposit base as it would have if the sterling deposits with its United Kingdom offices and the sterling certificates of deposit issued by it included respectively sterling deposits with the United Kingdom offices of the exempted person and sterling certificates of deposit issued by that person.

(5) In its application to this section, section 5(3) above shall have effect with the omission of paragraphs (b) and (c).

DEFINITIONS
   "the Board": s.50.
   "contributory institutions": s.52(1).
   "deposit": s.5.

GENERAL NOTE
A new section to provide for a situation where the business of an exempted person (see Sched. 2) is transferred to a contributory institution such as in the circumstances where a building society has been acquired by a bank (Building Societies Act, s.97). Note again the widening of the definition of "deposit" for the purposes of this section (subs. (5)).

Payments out of the Fund

Compensation payments to depositors

58.—(1) Subject to the provisions of this section, if at any time an institution becomes insolvent and at that time—
   (a) it is an authorised institution; or
   (b) it is a former authorised institution (not being a recognised bank or licensed institution excluded by an order under section 23(2) of the Banking Act 1979),
the Board shall as soon as practicable pay out of the Fund to each depositor who has a protected deposit with that institution an amount equal to three-quarters of his protected deposit.

(2) Subject to the provisions of this section, if at any time an administration order is made under section 8 of the Insolvency Act 1986 in relation to an institution and at that time it is such an institution as is mentioned in subsection (1) above the Board shall pay out of the Fund to each depositor who has a protected deposit with that institution an amount equal to three-quarters of his protected deposit; and that payment shall be made as soon as practicable after the deposit is or becomes due and payable under the terms on which it was made or, if later, the approval of the administrator's proposals under section 24 of that Act.

(3) Where the Board is satisfied that a payment has been or will be made to a depositor in respect of his protected deposit under any scheme for protecting depositors or investors which is comparable to that for which provision is made by this Part of this Act or under a guarantee given by a government or other authority the Board may—
   (a) deduct an amount equal to the whole or part of that payment from the payment that would otherwise be made to him under subsection (1) or (2) above; or
   (b) in pursuance of an agreement made by the Board with the authority responsible for the scheme or by which the guarantee was given, make in full the payment required by that subsection and recoup from that authority such contribution to it as may be specified in or determined under the agreement.

(4) Where the Board makes such a deduction as is mentioned in paragraph (a) of subsection (3) above it may agree with the authority responsible for the scheme or by which the guarantee was given to

reimburse that authority to the extent of the deduction or any lesser amount.

(5) The Board may decline to make any payment under subsection (1) or (2) above to a person who, in the opinion of the Board, has any responsibility for, or may have profited directly or indirectly from, the circumstances giving rise to the institution's financial difficulties.

(6) There shall be deducted from any payment to be made by the Board in respect of a deposit under subsection (2) above any payment in respect of that deposit already made by the administrator; and where an institution becomes insolvent after an administration order has been in force in relation to it the payments to be made by the Board under subsections (1) and (2) above, taken together, in respect of a depositor's protected deposits with the institution shall not exceed an amount equal to three-quarters of those deposits.

(7) The Treasury may, after consultation with the Board, by order amend subsections (1), (2) and (6) above so as to substitute for the fraction for the time being specified in those subsections such other fraction as may be specified in the order; but no such order shall be made unless a draft of it has been laid before and approved by a resolution of each House of Parliament.

(8) Notwithstanding that the Board may not yet have made or become liable to make a payment under subsection (1) above in relation to an institution falling within that subsection—

    (a) the Board shall at all times be entitled to receive any notice or other document required to be sent to a creditor of the institution whose debt has been proved; and

    (b) a duly authorised representative of the Board shall be entitled—

        (i) to attend any meeting of creditors of the institution and to make representations as to any matter for decision at that meeting;

        (ii) to be a member of any committee established under section 301 of the Insolvency Act 1986;

        (iii) to be a commissioner under section 30 of the Bankruptcy (Scotland) Act 1985; and

        (iv) to be a member of a committee established for the purposes of Part IV or V of the Insolvency Act 1986 under section 101 of that Act or under section 141 or 142 of that Act or of a committee of inspection appointed for the purposes of Part XX or XXI of the Companies (Northern Ireland) Order 1986.

(9) Where a representative of the Board exercises his right to be a member of such a committee as is mentioned in paragraph (b)(ii) or (iv) of subsection (8) above or to be a commissioner by virtue of paragraph (b)(iii) of that subsection he may not be removed except with the consent of the Board and his appointment under that subsection shall be disregarded for the purposes of any provision made by or under any enactment which specifies a minimum or maximum number of members of such a committee or commission.

(10) Notwithstanding that the Board may not yet have made or become liable to make a payment under subsection (2) above in relation to an institution falling within that subsection—

    (a) the Board shall at all times be entitled to receive any notice or other document required to be sent to a creditor of the institution under Part II of the Insolvency Act 1986; and

    (b) a duly authorised representative of the Board shall be entitled—

        (i) to attend any meeting of creditors of the institution summoned under Part II of that Act and to make representations as to any matter for decision at that meeting; and

(ii) to be a member of any committee established under section 26 of that Act.

DEFINITIONS

"authorised": s.106(1).
"the Board": s.50.
"deposit": s.5.
"document": s.106(1).
"former authorised institution": s.106(1).
"the Fund": s.51.
"institution": s.106(1).
"notice": s.100.

GENERAL NOTE

This section and s.59 correspond with s.28 of the 1979 Act.

Subss. (1), (2), (5), (6), (7)

If an authorised institution or one which *was* an authorised institution (but not excluded as being incorporated or having its principal place of business outside the U.K.), becomes insolvent (as defined under s.59), or is an authorised institution or a *former* one in respect of which an administration order is made under s.8 of the Insolvency Act 1986 (and the administrator's proposals have been approved under s.24 of the Insolvency Act 1986), then each depositor who has a protected deposit (see s.60—limited to £20,000) shall be entitled to a payment out of the Fund "as soon as practicable" of up to three-quarters of such protected deposit. *Quare* "or if later"—possible non-entitlement of a depositor under either subs. (1) or subs. (2) if no s.24 meeting is held or it declines to approve the administrator's proposals. The Board has a discretion (subs. (5)) to exclude those who in the Board's opinion contributed to, or profited from the circumstances of the institution's financial difficulties. A deduction shall be made in respect of any payment already made by the administrator. The maximum of three-quarters may be amended by statutory instrument, the affirmative parliamentary procedure applying.

Subss. (3), (4)

An abatement may be made in the payment to a depositor otherwise to be made by the Board, or a recoupment made from another authority responsible for a comparable scheme for the protection of depositors or by which a guarantee was given. In the first case, the amount, deducted in the payment otherwise made to the depositor, may by agreement be reimbursed to the authority in whole or part.

Subss. (8)–(10)

The Board is entitled to be treated as a creditor as regards notices and other documents and may participate as a creditor in the insolvency or administration proceedings and as a member of any committee although no payment out of the Fund has been made. A possible extra member of the liquidation committee, being neither a creditor, contributor, nor a company member, is added (subs. (9)).

Meaning of insolvency

59.—(1) For the purposes of this Part of this Act a body corporate incorporated in the United Kingdom becomes insolvent—

    (a) on the making of a winding-up order against it;

    (b) on the passing of a resolution for a voluntary winding-up in a case in which no statutory declaration has been made under section 89 of the Insolvency Act 1986 or Article 534 of the Companies (Northern Ireland) Order 1986; or

    (c) on the holding of a creditor's meeting summoned under section 95 of that Act or Article 541 of that Order;

and a body corporate incorporated elsewhere becomes insolvent on the occurrence of an event which appears to the Board to correspond as nearly as may be to any of those mentioned in paragraphs (a), (b) and (c) above.

(2) For the purposes of this Part of this Act a partnership formed under the law of any part of the United Kingdom becomes insolvent—

(a) in England and Wales, on the making of a winding-up order against it under any provision of the Insolvency Act 1986 as applied by an order under section 420 of that Act;

(b) in Scotland, on the making of an award of sequestration on the estate of the partnership or on the making of a winding-up order against it by virtue of section 92 below;

(c) in Northern Ireland, on the making of an order of adjudication of bankruptcy against any of the partners;

and a partnership formed under the law of a member State other than the United Kingdom becomes insolvent on the occurrence of an event which appears to the Board to correspond as nearly as may be to any of those mentioned in paragraphs (a), (b) and (c) above.

(3) For the purposes of this Part of this Act an unincorporated association which is formed under the law of another member State and is not a partnership becomes insolvent on the occurrence of any event which appears to the Board to correspond as nearly as may be to any of those mentioned in subsection (1)(a), (b) or (c) or (2)(a), (b) or (c) above.

DEFINITION
  "the Board": s.50.

GENERAL NOTE
  The 1979 Act defined "insolvency" within s.28 (payments to depositors when an institution becomes insolvent) in subss. (3), (4) and (5). This section largely corresponds to those provisions save that the references are to the relevant provisions of the Insolvency Act 1986. It is left to the discretion of the Board in the case of a body incorporated outside the U.K. and in the case of a partnership and unincorporated association formed under the law of another Member State to determine whether or not it is insolvent.

Protected deposits

60.—(1) Subject to the provisions of this section, in relation to an institution in respect of which a payment falls to be made under section 58(1) above any reference in this Act to a depositor's protected deposit is a reference to the total liability of the institution to him immediately before the time when it becomes insolvent, limited to a maximum of £20,000, in respect of the principal amounts of and accrued interest on sterling deposits made with United Kingdom offices of the institution.

(2) Subject to the provisions of this section, in relation to an institution in respect of which a payment falls to be made under section 58(2) above any reference in this Act to a depositor's protected deposit is a reference to the liability of the institution to him in respect of—

(a) the principal amount of each sterling deposit which was made by him with a United Kingdom office of the institution before the making of the administration order and which under the terms on which it was made is or becomes due or payable while the order is in force; and

(b) accrued interest on any such deposit up to the time when it is or becomes due and payable as aforesaid;

but so that the total liability of the institution to him in respect of such deposits does not exceed £20,000.

(3) For the purposes of subsection (1) above no account shall be taken of any liability unless—

(a) proof of the debt which gives rise to it has been lodged with the liquidator of the insolvent institution; or

(b) in the case of an institution formed under the law of a country or territory outside the United Kingdom, an act has been done which appears to the Board to correspond as nearly as may be to the lodging of such a proof with the liquidator of the institution.

(4) For the purposes of subsection (2) above no account shall be taken of any liability unless a claim for repayment of the deposit which gives rise to it has been lodged with the administrator.

(5) The Treasury may, after consultation with the Board, by order amend subsections (1) and (2) above so as to substitute for the sum for the time being specified in those subsections such larger sum as may be specified in the order; but no such order shall be made unless a draft of it has been laid before and approved by a resolution of each House of Parliament.

(6) In determining the total liability of an institution to a depositor for the purposes of subsection (1) above, or the liability or total liability of an institution to a depositor for the purposes of subsection (2) above, no account shall be taken of any liability in respect of a deposit if—

(a) it is a secured deposit; or

(b) it is a deposit which had an original term to maturity of more than five years; or

(c) the institution is a former authorised institution and the deposit was made after it ceased to be an authorised institution or a recognised bank or licensed institution under the Banking Act 1979 unless, at the time the deposit was made, the depositor did not know and could not reasonably be expected to have known that it had ceased to be an authorised institution, recognised bank or licensed institution.

(7) Unless the Board otherwise directs in any particular case, in determining the total liability of an institution to a depositor for the purposes of subsection (1) or (2) above there shall be deducted the amount of any liability of the depositor to the institution—

(a) in respect of which a right of set-off existed immediately before the institution became insolvent or, as the case may be, subject to the administration order against any such sterling deposit as is referred to in subsection (1) or (2) above; or

(b) in respect of which such right would then have existed if the deposit in question had been repayable on demand and the liability in question had fallen due.

(8) Where an institution becomes insolvent after an administration order has been in force in relation to it the maximum applying under subsection (1) above to a depositor's protected deposit with the institution shall be reduced by the amount of his protected deposit or deposits with the institution taken into account for the purposes of subsection (2) above.

(9) For the purposes of this section and sections 61 and 62 below the definition of deposit in section 5 above—

(a) shall be treated as including—

(i) any sum that would otherwise be excluded by paragraph (a), (d) or (e) of subsection (3) of that section if the sum is paid as trustee for a person not falling within any of those paragraphs;

(ii) any sum that would otherwise be excluded by paragraph (b) or (c) of that subsection;

(b) subject to subsections (10) and (11) below, shall be treated as excluding any sum paid by a trustee for a person falling within paragraph (e) of subsection (3) of that section; and

(c) shall be treated as including any sum the right to repayment of which is evidenced by a transferable certificate of deposit or other transferable instrument and which would be a deposit within the meaning of section 5 as extended by paragraph (a) and restricted by paragraph (b) above if it had been paid by the person who is entitled to it at the time when the institution in question becomes insolvent.

(10) Where the trustee referred to in paragraph (b) of subsection (9) above is not a bare trustee and there are two or more beneficiaries that paragraph applies only if all the beneficiaries fall within section 5(3)(e) above.

(11) Subsection (10) above does not extend to Scotland and, in Scotland, where there are two or more beneficiaries of a trust the trustee of which is referred to in paragraph (b) of subsection (9) above that paragraph applies only if all the beneficiaries fall within section 5(3)(e) above.

Definitions
"authorised": s.106(1).
"bare trustee": s.106(1).
"the Board": s.50.
"deposit": s.5.
"former authorised institution": s.106(1).
"institution": s.106(1).
"liquidator": s.106(1).

General Note
The concept of depositor protection was discussed at length in relation to this section during the Eighth Sitting of the Standing Committee (Eighth Sitting, January 27, 1987, cols. 232–246) and reference was made to the balance to be made between the proper conditions of the market place (*i.e.* ensuring that there is no potential temptation for institutions knowing that their deposits are protected to conduct their business in a manner other than prudent) and a legislative desire to protect small investors. The Economic Secretary of the Treasury (Mr. Ian Stewart) reported some twelve cases only, involving 2,700 depositors to date, where claims have been made against the Fund—more than 90 per cent. having made deposits with less than £10,000. S.60 corresponds to s.29 of the 1979 Act with extensions which are noted later.

Subss. (1)–(4)
These together with s.58(1) comprise the heart of the Scheme. A depositor's "protected deposit" comprises the total liability of the institution to him up to the first £20,000 of each depositor's sterling deposits made into U.K. offices of the institution together with accrued interest, with a further "cap" of 75 per cent. of deposits covered (s.58(1)). In the case of a "protected investment" building society investors are limited to a maximum of £10,000 with a further "cap" of 90 per cent. of the "protected investment" (Building Societies Act 1986, s.27). As in the case of a insolvent institution where proof of debt must be lodged with the liquidator (or corresponding action taken in the case of an overseas institution) so also a claim for repayment of the deposit must first be lodged with the administrator. Failure to lodge proof or claim for repayment (as the case may be) would mean that the depositor would be ineligible to receive a compensation payment.

Subs. (5)
The "cap" of £20,000 may be *increased* under the affirmative parliamentary procedure.

Subs. (6)
There are three classes of security *excluded* from the calculation of the total liability.
Secured deposit. This is not defined but would appear to refer to monies deposited with an institution which has given some form of security in respect of them (see also s.52(4)(a)).
Ceased to be an authorised institution. E.g. see ss.11 and 15.
Or a recognised bank or licensed institution. See s.7 of the 1979 Act.

Subs. (7)
Note, in the absence of a contrary intention of the Board, the deductions to be made from the calculation of the total liability in respect of the institution's *right of set-off.* For the latest statement of law on this right, although it was in other circumstances, see *Re Charge Card Services* [1986] 3 W.L.R. 697.

Subs. (9)
The definition of "deposit" is widened where the sum is paid as trustee for a person who is not within the categories in paras. (a), (d) or (e) of subs. (3) but *excluding* where the sum is paid by a trustee for a close relative of the recipient, etc.

Trustee deposits, joint deposits etc.

61.—(1) In the cases to which this section applies sections 58 and 60 above shall have effect with the following modifications.

(2) Subject to the provisions of this section, where any persons are entitled to a deposit as trustees they shall be treated as a single and continuing body of persons distinct from the persons who may from time to time be the trustees, and if the same persons are entitled as trustees to different deposits under different trusts they shall be treated as a separate and distinct body with respect to each of those trusts.

(3) Where a deposit is held for any person or for two or more persons jointly by a bare trustee, that person or, as the case may be, those persons jointly shall be treated as entitled to the deposit without the intervention of any trust.

(4) Subsection (3) above does not extend to Scotland and, in Scotland, where a deposit is held by a person as nominee for another person or for two or more other persons jointly, that other person or, as the case may be, those other persons jointly shall be treated as entitled to the deposit.

(5) A deposit to which two or more persons are entitled as members of a partnership (whether or not in equal shares) shall be treated as a single deposit.

(6) Subject to subsection (5) above, where two or more persons are jointly entitled to a deposit and subsection (2) above does not apply each of them shall be treated as having a separate deposit of an amount produced by dividing the amount of the deposit to which they are jointly entitled by the number of persons who are so entitled.

(7) Where a person is entitled (whether as trustee or otherwise) to a deposit made out of a clients' or other similar account containing money to which one or more other persons are entitled, that other person or, as the case may be, each of those other persons shall be treated (to the exclusion of the first-mentioned person) as entitled to so much of the deposit as corresponds to the proportion of the money in the account to which he is entitled.

(8) Where an authorised institution is entitled as trustee to a sum which would be a deposit apart from section 5(3)(a) above and represents deposits made with the institution, each of the persons who made those deposits shall be treated as having made a deposit equal to so much of that sum as represents the deposit made by him.

(9) The Board may decline to make any payment under section 58 above in respect of a deposit until the person claiming to be entitled to it informs the Board of the capacity in which he is entitled to the deposit and provides sufficient information to enable the Board to determine what payment (if any) should be made under that section and to whom.

(10) In this section "jointly entitled" means—

    (a) in England and Wales and in Northern Ireland, beneficially entitled as joint tenants, tenants in common or coparceners;

    (b) in Scotland, beneficially entitled as joint owners or owners in common.

DEFINITIONS
"authorised": s.106(1).
"bare trustee": s.106(1).
"the Board": s.50.
"deposit": s.5.
"institution": s.106(1).

GENERAL NOTE
This section corresponds with s.30 of the 1979 Act. Ss.58 and 60 of this Act are modified where deposits are held by trustees or jointly by more than one person. In short, *for the purposes of this Act*, where a beneficiary (or beneficiaries) under a trust is entitled to call

upon the trustees to transfer the trust property to him absolutely, he is treated as the owner of the property (see also the Capital Gains Tax Act 1979, ss.46(2) and 52(1)). Under subs. (2) the trustees are treated as holding the deposit as a single and continuing body of persons so that in their hands there is a protected deposit up to a maximum of £20,000. However, where a beneficiary becomes absolutely entitled as against the trustee to a deposit, then the beneficiary and not the trustee will be entitled to compensation out of the Fund (subs. (3)). Again, where two or more persons are jointly entitled (not being trustees) to a deposit (subs. (6)), each is treated as having a separate protected deposit. Thus if two persons are jointly entitled to a deposit of £40,000, each would be treated as being entitled to a separate deposit of £20,000. Subs. (10) also refers to coparceners who since 1925 retained any rights they may have had in inherited *land*, as equitable interests in a legal estate vested in trustees for sale.

Liability of institution in respect of compensation payments

62.—(1) This section applies where—
  (a) an institution becomes insolvent or an administration order is in force in relation to it; and
  (b) the Board has made, or is under a liability to make, a payment under section 58 above by virtue of the institution becoming insolvent or of the making of that order;

and in the following provisions of this section a payment falling within paragraph (b) above, less any amount which the Board is entitled to recoup by virtue of any such agreement as is mentioned in subsection (3)(b) of that section, is referred to as "a compensation payment" and the person to whom such a payment has been or is to be made is referred to as "the depositor".

(2) Where this section applies in respect of an institution that is insolvent—
  (a) the institution shall become liable to the Board, as in respect of a contractual debt incurred immediately before the institution became insolvent, for an amount equal to the compensation payment;
  (b) the liability of the institution to the depositor in respect of any deposit or deposits of his ("the liability to the depositor") shall be reduced by an amount equal to the compensation payment made or to be made to him by the Board; and
  (c) the duty of the liquidator of the insolvent institution to make payments to the Board on account of the liability referred to in paragraph (a) above ("the liability to the Board") and to the depositor on account of the liability to him (after taking account of paragraph (b) above) shall be varied in accordance with subsection (3) below.

(3) The variation referred to in subsection (2)(c) above is as follows—
  (a) in the first instance the liquidator shall pay to the Board instead of to the depositor any amount which, apart from this section, would be payable on account of the liability to the depositor except in so far as that liability relates to any such deposit as is mentioned in section 60(6) above; and
  (b) if at any time the total amount paid to the Board by virtue of paragraph (a) above and in respect of the liability to the Board equals the amount of the compensation payment made to the depositor, the liquidator shall thereafter pay to the depositor instead of to the Board any amount which, apart from this paragraph, would be payable to the Board in respect of the liability to the Board.

(4) Where this section applies in respect of an institution in relation to which an administration order is in force—
  (a) the institution shall, at the time when the compensation payment

in respect of a deposit falls to be made by the Board, become liable to the Board for an amount equal to that payment; and

(b) the liability of the institution to the depositor in respect of that deposit shall be reduced by an amount equal to that payment.

(5) Where an institution becomes insolvent after an administration order has been in force in relation to it subsections (2) and (3) above shall not apply to any compensation payment to the extent to which the Board has received a payment in respect of it by virtue of subsection (4)(a) above.

(6) Where by virtue of section 61 above the compensation payment is or is to be made by the Board to a person other than the person to whom the institution is liable in respect of the deposit any reference in the foregoing provisions of this section to the liability to the depositor shall be construed as a reference to the liability of the institution to the person to whom that payment would fall to be made by the Board apart from that section.

(7) Where the Board makes a payment under section 58(4) above in respect of an amount deducted from a payment due to a depositor this section shall have effect as if the amount had been paid to the depositor.

(8) Rules may be made—

    (a) for England and Wales, under sections 411 and 412 of the Insolvency Act 1986;

    (b) for Scotland—

        (i) under the said section 411; and

        (ii) in relation to an institution whose estate may be sequestrated under the Bankruptcy (Scotland) Act 1985, by the Secretary of State under this subsection; and

    (c) for Northern Ireland, under Article 613 of the Companies (Northern Ireland) Order 1986 and section 65 of the Judicature (Northern Ireland) Act 1978,

for the purpose of integrating the procedure provided for in this section into the general procedure on a winding-up, bankruptcy or sequestration or under Part II of the Insolvency Act 1986.

DEFINITIONS

    "the Board": s.50.
    "deposit": s.5.
    "institution": s.106(1).
    "liquidator": s.106(1).

GENERAL NOTE

This section corresponds to s.31 of the 1979 Act and is designed to ensure that in a situation where the Board having made or being liable to make a payment under s.58 to a "depositor", the failed institution becomes liable to the Board for an amount equal to that payment less any recoupment under an agreement referred to in s.58(3)(b).

Subs. (1)

A "compensation payment" is a payment made by the Board under s.58 (by virtue of insolvency of, or of the making of an administration order in relation to, an institution) to the depositor. There may be deducted from such a payment any recoupment from an authority running a comparable scheme.

Subss. (2), (3)

A simple illustration may help. Suppose that an institution becomes insolvent and a depositor with that institution in the sum of £20,000 (not being a deposit as is mentioned in s.60(6)) receives or is due to receive a compensation payment of £15,000 by virtue of s.58(1). In brief, the section would operate as follows. The institution becomes liable to the Board for an amount equal to this compensation payment of £15,000 "as in respect of a contractual debt incurred immediately before" the insolvency (subs. (2)(a)). The institution's "liability to the depositor" is reduced by a corresponding amount (£20,000 less £15,000) and it will now have a liability to that depositor of £5,000 (subs. (2)(b)). The respective liabilities of the liquidator of the institution to the Board and to the depositor are *varied* in accordance with subs. (3). Assuming throughout that he has sufficient assets for distribution the liquidator must first pay to the Board, instead of to the depositor, £20,000 (on the assumption that falls no part of the deposit under s.60(6)) (subs. (3)(a)). However, as the total amount "paid" to the Board in this illustration is *greater* than the amount of the compensation payment of £15,000, the liquidator must then pay to the depositor, instead of to the Board, the balance of £5,000 (subs. (3)(b)).

Subss. (4), (5)

Where an administration order is in force and a compensation payment falls to be made the institution's liability (a) to the Board is for an amount equivalent to the compensation payment; and (b) to the depositor is reduced by that amount. Where payment has been received by the Board by virtue of subs. (4)(a) and that institution subsequently becomes insolvent, subss. (2) and (3) shall not apply in respect of any compensation payment to the extent of the amount of that payment.

Subs. (6)

Where under s.61 a compensation payment is, or is to be, made to a person other than one to whom the institution is liable (*e.g.* to a beneficiary instead of to trustees) references to "the liability to the depositor" should be read as being references to the liability of the institution to the person to whom that compensation payment would be required to be made by the Board as if s.61 were not in being.

Subs. (7)

Any payment made by the Board by way of reimbursement to other authorities operating comparable schemes or giving a guarantee under s.58(4) shall be treated under this section as having been paid to the depositor.

Subs. (8)

Ss.411 and 412 of the Insolvency Act 1986 respectively define the scope and extent of the power to make rules in respect of company and individual insolvency. Subs. (8) provides for such rules to integrate the procedure in s.62 into that for a winding up, bankruptcy, sequestration (Scotland) or in respect of the making of adminsitration orders.

Repayments in respect of contributions

Repayments in respect of contributions

63.—(1) Any money received by the Board under section 62 above ("recovered money") shall not form part of the Fund but, for the remainder of the financial year of the Board in which it is received, shall be placed by the Board in an account with the Bank which shall as far as possible invest the money in Treasury bills; and any income arising from the money so invested during the remainder of the year shall be credited to the Fund.

(2) The Board shall prepare a scheme for the making out of recovered money of repayments to institutions in respect of—

    (a) special contributions; and

    (b) so far as they are not attributable to an increase in the size of the Fund resulting from an order under subsection (2) of section 54 above, further contributions levied under that section,

which have been made in the financial year of the Board in which the money was received or in any previous such financial year.

(3) A scheme under subsection (2) above—

    (a) shall provide for the making of repayments first in respect of special contributions and then, if those contributions can be repaid in full (taking into account any previous repayments under this section and under section 55(2) above) in respect of further contributions;

    (b) may make provision for repayments in respect of contributions made by an institution which has ceased to be a contributory institution to be made to a contributory institution which, in the opinion of the Board, is its successor; and

(c) subject to paragraph (b) above, may exclude from the scheme further contributions levied from institutions which have ceased to be contributory institutions.

(4) Except where special or further contributions can be repaid in full, repayments to institutions under this section shall be made pro rata according to the amount of the special or further contribution made by each of them.

(5) If at the end of a financial year of the Board in which recovered money is received by it—

(a) that money; and

(b) the amount standing to the credit of the Fund, after any repayments made under section 55 above,

exceeds the maximum amount for the time being specified in section 54(1) above the Board shall as soon as practicable make out of the recovered money, up to an amount not greater than the excess, the repayments required by the scheme under subsection (2) above and may out of the recovered money make such further repayments required by the scheme as will not reduce the amounts mentioned in paragraphs (a) and (b) above below the minimum amount for the time being specified in section 54(1) above.

(6) If in any financial year of the Board—

(a) any of the recovered money is not applied in making payments in accordance with subsection (5) above; or

(b) the payments made in accordance with that subsection are sufficient to provide for the repayment in full of all the contributions to which the scheme relates,

any balance of that money shall be credited to the Fund.

TRANSITIONAL PROVISION
Sched. 5, para. 11.

DEFINITIONS
"the Bank": s.1.
"the Board": s.50.
"contributory institutions": s.52(1).
"the Fund": s.51.
"institution": s.106(1).

GENERAL NOTE
This section corresponds closely to s.32 of the 1979 Act. The purpose of this section is to ensure that any monies received from the liquidators of failed institutions under s.62 do not form part of the Fund but instead are repaid under a scheme prepared by the Board in respect of the refund of special and then further contributions made by contributory institutions.

Subs. (1)
"Recovered money" (received under s.62) is placed in an account with the Bank until the end of the Board's financial year and does not form part of the Fund. However, any *income* arising from the invested money during that period shall be credited to the Fund.

Subss. (2), (3), (4)
The Board must draw up a scheme for repaying out of recovered money: first, special contributions (s.55), and then (after taking into account previous repayments hereunder and under s.55(2) and disregarding an increase in the size of the Fund by Order under s.54(2)) any surplus in repayment of further contributions (s.54). Where payments in each case cannot be made in full they are made in proportion to the amounts of special or further contributions (as the case may be) made by institutions. The Board has a discretion to make repayments to successors of former contributory institutions and to exclude from the scheme *further contributions* made by institutions which are no longer contributory institutions.

Subs. (5)

If at the end of a financial year of the Board the total of (a) "recovered money" and of (b) the balance of the Fund remaining after repayments under s.55(2), exceeds the present maximum of £6 million, then the Board "shall as soon as practicable" out of the recovered money make the scheme repayments under subs. (2) up to an amount not greater than that excess; and make any further repayments under the scheme (presumably the discretionary payments under subs. (3)(b) and (c)) again out of the *recovered money* provided that the total of (a) and (b) above remaining does not fall below the present minimum amount of £5 million specified in s.54(1).

Subs. (6)

Any balance of recovered money not applied under the scheme is to be credited to the Fund. Moreover, if the moneys recovered from liquidators of failed institutions under s.62 are more than sufficient to repay *all* contributions in full under the scheme, again the balance is credited to the Fund.

Supplementary provisions

Borrowing powers

64.—(1) If in the course of operating the Fund it appears to the Board desirable to do so, the Board may borrow up to a total outstanding at any time of £10 million or such larger sum as, after consultation with the Board, the Treasury may from time to time by order prescribe.

(2) An order under subsection (1) above shall be subject to annulment in pursuance of a resolution of either House of Parliament.

(3) Any amount borrowed by virtue of this section shall be disregarded in ascertaining the amount standing to the credit of the Fund for the purposes of sections 54(1), 55(2) and 63(5) above.

TRANSITIONAL PROVISION
    Sched. 5, para. 12.

DEFINITIONS
    "the Board": s.50.
    "the Fund": s.51.

GENERAL NOTE
    As under s.26(3) to (5) of the 1979 Act, the Board may borrow (not merely for temporary purposes in this Act) up to a total outstanding amount at any time of £10 million subject to an increase in this maximum by order prescribed by the Treasury after consultation with the Board. Note the events where the borrowed sum is disregarded in calculating the amounts standing to the credit of the Fund to enable it to levy further contributions (s.54) in repayment of special contributions (s.55) or repayment of recovered money (s.63). These borrowing powers are wider than those conferred on the Building Societies Investor Protection Board (see s.26(14)–(16) of the Building Societies Act 1986).

Power to obtain information

65.—(1) If required to do so by a request in writing made by the Board, the Bank may by notice in writing served on a contributory institution require the institution, within such time and at such place as may be specified in the notice, to provide the Board with such information and to produce to it such documents, or documents of such a description, as the Board may reasonably require for the purpose of determining the contributions of the institution under this Part of this Act.

(2) Subsections (4), (5), (11) and (13) of section 39 above shall have effect in relation to any requirement imposed under subsection (1) above as they have effect in relation to a requirement imposed under that section.

(3) The Board may by notice in writing served on the liquidator of an insolvent institution or on the administrator of an institution under Part

II of the Insolvency Act 1986 require him, at such time or times and at such place as may be specified in the notice—

(a) to provide the Board with such information; and

(b) to produce to the Board such documents specified in the notice,

as the Board may reasonably require to enable it to carry out its functions under this Part of this Act.

(4) Where, as a result of an institution having become insolvent, any documents have come into the possession of the Official Receiver or, in Northern Ireland, the Official Assignee for company liquidations or in bankruptcy, he shall permit any person duly authorised by the Board to inspect the documents for the purpose of establishing—

(a) the identity of those of the institution's depositors to whom the Board are liable to make a payment under section 58 above; and

(b) the amount of the protected deposit held by each of the depositors.

DEFINITIONS

"the Bank": s.1.

"the Board": s.50.

"contributory institutions": s.52(1).

"documents": s.106(1).

"institution": s.106(1).

"liquidator": s.106(1).

"notice": s.100.

"protected deposit": s.60.

GENERAL NOTE

The Bank may on a written request from the Board require a contributory institution to supply information and documents to the Board as the Board may reasonably require to determine the contributions payable coupled with the supporting powers and sanctions as given in s.39. The Board has similar powers to be provided with information and documents by liquidators of failed institutions, or by administrators, and the Official Receiver must permit the inspection of documents in his possession for the purposes specified.

Tax treatment of contributions and repayments

66. In computing for the purposes of the Tax Acts the profits or gains arising from the trade carried on by a contributory institution—

(a) to the extent that it would not be deductible apart from this section, any sum expended by the institution in paying a contribution to the Fund may be deducted as an allowable expense;

(b) any payment which is made to the institution by the Board under section 55 (2) above or pursuant to a scheme under section 63 (2) above shall be treated as a trading receipt.

DEFINITIONS

"the Board": s.50.

"contributory institutions": s.52(1).

"the Fund": s.51.

"institution": s.106(1).

"the Tax Acts": Income and Corporation Taxes Act 1970, s.526(2); Interpretation Act 1978, Sched. 1.

GENERAL NOTE

As in s.33 of the 1979 Act, for the avoidance of doubt contributions made by a contributory institution to the Fund are fully deductible for tax as allowable expenses in computing its profits, and repayments made by the Board under s.55(2) or under a scheme in respect of recovered money under s.63(2) are deemed to be trading receipts of that institution.

PART III

BANKING NAMES AND DESCRIPTIONS

Restriction on use of banking names

67.—(1) Subject to section 68 below, no person carrying on any business in the United Kingdom shall use any name which indicates or may reasonably be understood to indicate (whether in English or any other language) that he is a bank or banker or is carrying on a banking business unless he is an authorised institution to which this section applies.

(2) This section applies to an authorised institution which—

    (a) is a company incorporated in the United Kingdom which has—

        (i) an issued share capital in respect of which the amount paid up is not less than £5 million (or an amount of equivalent value denominated wholly or partly otherwise than in sterling); or

        (ii) undistributable reserves falling within paragraph (a), (b) or (d) of section 264 (3) of the Companies Act 1985 or Article 272(3)(a), (b) or (d) of the Companies (Northern Ireland) Order 1986 of not less than that sum (or such an equivalent amount); or

        (iii) such undistributable reserves of an amount which together with the amount paid up in respect of its issued share capital equals not less than that sum (or such an equivalent amount); or

    (b) is a partnership formed under the law of any part of the United Kingdom in respect of which one or more designated fixed capital accounts are maintained to which there has been credited not less than £5 million (or such an equivalent amount).

(3) For the purposes of subsection (2)(a) above "share capital" does not include share capital which under the terms on which it is issued is to be, or may at the option of the shareholder be, redeemed by the company.

(4) For the purposes of subsection (2)(b) above "designated fixed capital account", in relation to a partnership, means an account—

    (a) which is prepared and designated as such under the terms of the partnership agreement;

    (b) which shows capital contributed by the partners; and

    (c) from which under the terms of that agreement an amount representing capital may only be withdrawn by a partner if—

        (i) he ceases to be a partner and an equal amount is transferred to a designated fixed capital account by his former partners or any person replacing him as their partner; or

        (ii) the partnership is otherwise dissolved or wound up.

(5) An authorised institution to which subsection (2) above applies whose issued share capital, undistributable reserves or designated fixed capital account is denominated wholly or partly otherwise than in sterling shall not be regarded as ceasing to be such an institution by reason only of a fluctuation in the rate of exchange of sterling unless and until it has ceased to satisfy any of the conditions in that subsection for a continuous period of three months.

(6) The Treasury may from time to time after consultation with the Bank by order amend subsection (2)(a) and (b) above so as to substitute for the sum for the time being specified in that subsection such other sum as may be specified in the order; but an order under this subsection shall be subject to annulment in pursuance of a resolution of either House of Parliament.

Transitional Provisions
Sched. 5, para. 13.

Definitions
"authorised": s.106(1).
"the Bank": s.1.
"institution": s.106(1).

General Note
Under s.36 of the 1979 Act, only recognised banks (and a few other institutions such as trustee savings banks or the National Girobank) could use a banking name. The White Paper in Chapter 7 (paras. 7.16 to 7.19) and in Annex 1 made proposals to control the use of misleading names. There was concern that permitting all to use "bank" in their name "would lend a more substantial aura to certain institutions than their size and standing merited" and accordingly these proposals have been largely followed in Part 3. Size is the principal criterion and s.67 provides that only authorised institutions with an issued share capital or undistributable reserves (companies) or with designated fixed capital accounts (partnerships) of at least £5 million may call themselves banks (*cf.* £1,000,000 of "net assets" required for authorisation—Sched. 3, para. 6).

Subs. (1)
Similar to s.36(1) of the 1979 Act. In defining a banking name the indication may also be in any language other than English (see also s.69(1) regarding the use of banking descriptions). The restriction applies to those carrying on *any* business in the U.K.

Subss. (2), (3), (4)
Authorised institutions may use a banking name if they are companies incorporated in the U.K. or partnerships formed under the law of any part of the U.K. and having either an issued share capital (not being capable of being redeemed) or certain undistributable reserves (or a combination of the two), or having "designated fixed capital accounts" (as the case may be) of not less than £5 million (or equivalent).

Subs. (5)
Where the particular authorised institution's capital account is denominated wholly or partly in a foreign currency and falls below the set level by reason only of exchange rate fluctuation, then that in itself would not cause the institution to be regarded as ceasing to be authorised unless it fails to satisfy the criteria in subs. (2) for a continuous three-month period.

Subs. (6)
The £5 million level may be *altered* by statutory instrument (after consultation with the Bank) by the negative parliamentary procedure.

Exemptions from s.67

68.—(1) Section 67 above does not prohibit the use of a name by a relevant savings bank, a municipal bank or a school bank if the name contains an indication that the bank or body is a savings bank, municipal bank or, as the case may be, a school bank.

(2) In subsection (1) above—

"relevant savings bank" means—
　　(i) the National Savings Bank; and
　　(ii) any penny savings bank;
"school bank" means a body of persons certified as a school bank by the National Savings Bank or an authorised institution.

(3) Section 67 above does not prohibit the use by an authorised institution which is a company incorporated under the law of a country or territory outside the United Kingdom or is formed under the law of a member State other than the United Kingdom of a name under which it carries on business in that country or territory or State (or an approximate translation in English of that name).

(4) Section 67 above does not prohibit the use by—

(a) an authorised institution which is a wholly-owned subsidiary of an authorised institution to which that section or subsection (3) above applies; or

(b) a company which has a wholly-owned subsidiary which is an authorised institution to which that section or subsection applies,

of a name which includes the name of the authorised institution to which that section or subsection applies for the purpose of indicating the connection between the two companies.

(5) Section 67 above does not prohibit the use by an overseas institution (within the meaning of Part IV of this Act) which has its principal place of business in a country or territory outside the United Kingdom and a representative office in the United Kingdom of the name under which it carries on business in that country or territory (or an approximate translation in English of that name) if—

(a) the name is used in immediate conjunction with the description "representative office"; and

(b) where the name appears in writing, that description is at least as prominent as the name;

and in this subsection "representative office" has the same meaning as in Part IV of this Act.

(6) Section 67 above does not apply to—

(a) the Bank;

(b) the central bank of a member State other than the United Kingdom;

(c) the European Investment Bank;

(d) the International Bank for Reconstruction and Development;

(e) the African Development Bank;

(f) the Asian Development Bank;

(g) the Caribbean Development Bank;

(h) the Inter-American Development Bank.

(7) The Treasury may, after consultation with the Bank, by order provide—

(a) that the prohibition in section 67 above shall not apply to any person or class of persons; or

(b) that that prohibition shall apply to a person mentioned in any of paragraphs (c) to (h) of subsection (6) above or a person previously exempted from it by virtue of an order under paragraph (a) above.

(8) An order under paragraph (a) of subsection (7) above shall be subject to annulment in pursuance of a resolution of either House of Parliament; and no order shall be made under paragraph (b) of that subsection unless a draft of it has been laid before and approved by a resolution of each House of Parliament.

(9) Nothing in section 67 above shall prevent an institution which ceases to be an authorised institution to which that section or subsection (4) above applies or ceases to be exempted from the prohibition in that section by virtue of subsection (1) above from continuing to use any name it was previously permitted to use by virtue of that provision during the period of six months beginning with the day when it ceases to be such an institution.

DEFINITIONS

"authorised": s.106(1).

"the Bank": s.1.

"institution": s.106(1).

"municipal bank": s.106(1).

"National Savings Bank Act 1971, s.16(4).

"penny savings bank": s.106(1).

"subsidiary": s.106(2); Companies Act 1985, s.736.

GENERAL NOTE

S.36(1) of the 1979 Act included a number of exemptions from the prohibition on using banking names and these have been carried into s.68. The Bank's 1986 annual report (p.54) gave some examples of abuses.

Subss. (1), (2)

A relevant savings bank, a municipal bank and a school bank (all as defined) may adopt these titles in the names they use.

Subss. (3), (4)

The exemption applies to U.K. branches (being authorised institutions) of any overseas incorporated company or of unincorporated bodies formed in other Member States using the name (or an approximate English translation) under which they carry on business in their own country. Moreover,

(a) a wholly-owned subsidiary (itself being an authorised institution) of an authorised institution which may use a banking name by virtue of s.67 or s.68(3); or

(b) a company having a wholly-owned subsidiary (itself being an authorised institution) to which s.67 or s.68(3) applies,

may use a name which includes the name of that (second) authorised institution in order to indicate the connection between the two.

Sub. (5)

Where an overseas institution has a representative office (see s.74(3)) in the U.K., it may use in the U.K. the name it uses abroad (or an approximate English translation), provided that such name is effected in immediate conjunction with the description "representative office" and, if in writing, the name must not have greater prominence than that description.

Subs. (6)

Exemption is given also to European Community central banks and other banks such as the "World Bank", all of which are listed in Sched. 2 as exempted persons under s.4(1).

Subss. (7), (8)

The Treasury may after consultation with the Bank make orders to delete from (by affirmative parliamentary procedure) or add to (by negative parliamentary procedure) the list of exempted persons.

Subs. (9)

A six-month period of grace is given to those institutions which cease to be authorised institutions to which s.67 or s.68(4) applies, or which cease to be exempt under s.68(1), during which period the previously permitted name may continue to be used.

Restriction on use of banking descriptions

69.—(1) No person carrying on any business in the United Kingdom shall so describe himself or hold himself out as to indicate or reasonably be understood to indicate (whether in English or in any other language) that he is a bank or banker or is carrying on a banking business unless he is an authorised institution or is exempted from the requirements of this subsection under the following provisions of this section.

(2) Subsection (1) above shall not be taken to authorise the use by an authorised institution to which the prohibition in section 67 above applies of any description of itself as a bank or banker or as carrying on a banking business which is in such immediate conjunction with the name of the institution that the description might reasonably be thought to be part of it.

(3) Subsection (1) above does not prohibit the use by a building society authorised under the Building Societies Act 1986 of any description of itself as providing banking services unless the description is in such immediate conjunction with its name that it might reasonably be thought to be part of it.

(4) Subsection (1) above does not prohibit a person from using the expression "bank" or "banker" (or a similar expression) where it is

necessary for him to do so in order to be able to assert that he is complying with, or entitled to take advantage of, any enactment, any instrument made under an enactment, any international agreement, any rule of law or any commercial usage or practice which applies to a person by virtue of his being a bank or banker.

(5) Subsection (1) above does not prohibit the use of a description by a relevant savings bank, a municipal bank or a school bank if the description is accompanied by a statement that the bank or body is a savings bank, a municipal bank or, as the case may be, a school bank; and for the purposes of this subsection "relevant savings bank" and "school bank" have the same meanings as in section 68 above.

(6) Subsection (1) above does not apply to—
  (a) the Bank;
  (b) the central bank of a member State other than the United Kingdom;
  (c) the European Investment Bank;
  (d) the International Bank for Reconstruction and Development;
  (e) the International Finance Corporation;
  (f) the African Development Bank;
  (g) the Asian Development Bank;
  (h) the Caribbean Development Bank;
  (i) the Inter-American Development Bank.

(7) The Treasury may, after consultation with the Bank, by order provide—
  (a) that the prohibition in subsection (1) above shall not apply to any person or class of persons; or
  (b) that that prohibition shall apply to a person mentioned in any of paragraphs (c) to (i) of subsection (6) above or a person previously exempted from it by an order under paragraph (a) above.

(8) An order under paragraph (a) of subsection (7) above shall be subject to annulment in pursuance of a resolution of either House of Parliament; and no order shall be made under paragraph (b) of that subsection unless a draft of it has been laid before and approved by a resolution of each House of Parliament.

DEFINITIONS
"authorised": s.106(1).
"the Bank": s.1.
"institution": s.106(1).
"municipal bank": s.103.
"relevant savings bank": s.68.
"school bank": s.68.

GENERAL NOTE
Unless a person is an authorised institution or is exempt under this section, it may not use banking *descriptions*. There is no capital requirement as in s.67(2) for the use of banking *names*. The object is to prevent any person from describing himself or from holding himself out in such a way as to indicate (in any language) that he is a bank or banker or carrying on a banking business (terms not defined).

Subss. (1), (2)
If authorised or exempt under this section, any person carrying on any business in the U.K. may use a banking description. However, an authorised institution which is prohibited from using a banking name by reason of having, for example, an issued share capital of less than £5 million, may not use a description in such immediate conjunction with the institution's name as might reasonably be thought to be part of the name.

Subs. (3)

A building society (now given wider financial powers under the Building Societies Act 1986) may hold itself out as providing *banking services* subject to the same immediate conjunction rule.

Subs. (4)

This subsection continues the provisions of s.36(2) and (3) of the 1979 Act and extends the relaxations to, say, building societies who may use banking descriptions to indicate that they are for instance, complying with and may benefit from any protection available under the Cheques Act 1957 or in other instances had a banker's lien.

Subss. (5)–(8)

Similar provisions in respect of exemptions and amendment by statutory instrument as with banking names under s.68(6)–(8).

Power to object to institution's names

70.—(1) Where an institution applies for authorisation under this Act it shall give notice to the Bank of any name it is using or proposes to use for the purposes of or in connection with any business carried on by it and the Bank may give the institution notice in writing—

(a) that it objects to the notified name; or

(b) in the case of an institution which is or will be obliged to disclose any name in connection with any business carried on by it by virtue of section 4 of the Business Names Act 1985 or Article 6 of the Business Names (Northern Ireland) Order 1986, that it objects to that name.

(2) Where an authorised institution proposes to change any name it uses for the purposes of or in connection with any business carried on by it or, in the case of such an institution as is mentioned in subsection (1)(b) above, any such name as is there mentioned, it shall give notice to the Bank of the proposed name and the Bank may within the period of two months beginning with the day on which it receives the notification give notice to the institution in writing that it objects to the proposed name.

(3) The Bank shall not give notice objecting to a name under subsection (1) or (2) above unless it considers that the name is misleading to the public or otherwise undesirable and, in the case of the use of a name by an authorised institution to which section 67 above applies—

(a) the whole of the name shall be taken into account in considering whether it is misleading or undesirable; but

(b) no objection may be made to so much of the name as it is entitled to use by virtue of that section.

(4) Where as a result of a material change in circumstances since the time when notice was given to the Bank under subsection (1) or (2) above or as a result of further information becoming available to the Bank since that time, it appears to the Bank that a name to which it might have objected under that subsection gives so misleading an indication of the nature of the institution's activities as to be likely to cause harm to the public, the Bank may give notice in writing to the institution objecting to the name.

(5) Any notice to be given by an institution under this section shall be given in such manner and form as the Bank may specify and shall be accompanied by such information or documents as the Bank may reasonably require.

TRANSITIONAL PROVISION
    Sched. 5, para. 2(3).

DEFINITIONS
    "authorisation": s.106(1).
    "the Bank": s.1.

"documents": s.106(1).
"institution": s.106(1).
"notice": s.100.

GENERAL NOTE

These are new provisions but are based on proposals in Annex 1 (para. 4) of the White Paper.

Subss. (1), (2), (5)

At the same time as an institution applies for authorisation it must also give notice to the Bank, in whatever manner and form the Bank may specify and accompanied by such information or documents as reasonably required by the Bank, of the name it uses or proposes to use and thereafter of any change in such name to enable the Bank to object, and also to object to the use of any business name in the circumstances specified in s.4 of the Business Names Act 1985.

Subs. (3)

The Bank may object only if the name is considered to be misleading to the public or otherwise undesirable. However, authorised institutions to which s.67 applies will have the whole of their name taken into account but may continue to use a *banking* name as part of the full name.

Subs. (4)

The Bank may at a later date (if there has been a material change of circumstances or further information becomes available) object to the use of a name which is so misleading as to harm the public.

Effect of notices under s.70 and appeals

71.—(1) Where the Bank has given notice to an authorised institution under section 70 above the institution shall not use the name to which the Bank has objected for the purposes of or in connection with any business carried on in the United Kingdom after the objection has taken effect; and for the purposes of this subsection the disclosure of a name in connection with such a business by virtue of section 4 of the Business Names Act 1985 or Article 6 of the Business Names (Northern Ireland) Order 1986 shall be treated (if it would not otherwise be) as use for the purposes of that business.

(2) For the purposes of this section an objection under section 70(1) or (2) above takes effect when the institution receives the notice of objection.

(3) An institution to which a notice of objection is given under section 70(1) or (2) above may within the period of three weeks beginning with the day on which it receives the notice apply to the court to set aside the objection and on such an application the court may set it aside or confirm it (but without prejudice to its operation before that time).

(4) For the purposes of this section an objection under section 70(4) above takes effect—

(a) in a case where no application is made under subsection (5) below, at the expiry of the period of two months beginning with the day on which the institution receives the notice of objection or such longer period as the notice may specify; or

(b) where an application is made under subsection (5) below and the court confirms the objection, after such period as the court may specify.

(5) An institution to which a notice of objection is given under section 70(4) above may within the period of three weeks beginning with the day on which it receives the notice apply to the court to set aside the objection.

(6) In this section "the court" means the High Court, the Court of Session or the High Court in Northern Ireland according to whether—

(a) if the institution concerned is a company registered in the United

Kingdom, it is registered in England and Wales, Scotland or Northern Ireland; and

(b) in the case of any other institution, its principal or prospective principal place of business in the United Kingdom is situated in England and Wales, Scotland or Northern Ireland.

DEFINITIONS
"authorised": s.106(1).
"the Bank": s.1.
"institution": s.106(1).
"notice": s.100.

GENERAL NOTE
These are consequential provisions to s.70. Once the institution has received notice of objection from the Bank under s.70(1) or (2) the institution is prohibited from using the name. The institution has a right of appeal to the *Court* (the High Court, the Court of Session or the High Court of Northern Ireland as the case may be) to have the objection set aside. Note that an objection by the Bank made subsequently pursuant to s.70(4) takes effect at a later period (subs. (4)).

Registration of substitute corporate name by oversea company

72.—(1) Where the Bank gives notice under section 70 above objecting to the corporate name of a company incorporated outside the United Kingdom, subsection (4) of section 694 of the Companies Act 1985 or, in Northern Ireland, paragraph (4) of Article 644 of the Companies (Northern Ireland) Order 1986 shall apply, subject to subsection (2) below, as it applies where a notice is served on a company under subsection (1) or (2) of that section or, as the case may be, paragraph (1) or (2) of that Article.

(2) No statement or further statement may be delivered under subsection (4) of section 694 or paragraph (4) of Article 644 by virtue of subsection (1) above unless the Bank has signified that it does not object to the name specified in the statement.

(3) Section 70(2) above shall not apply to a proposed change of a name which has been registered under section 694(4) of the Companies Act 1985 or Article 644(4) of the Companies (Northern Ireland) Order 1986 by virtue of subsection (1) above.

DEFINITIONS
"the Bank": s.1.
"notice": s.100.

GENERAL NOTE
Where the Bank gives a s.70 notice objecting to the corporate name of an overseas institution then s.694(4) of the Companies Act 1985 shall apply, subject to subs. (2), *i.e.* only if the Bank signifies that it does not object to the alternative name approved by the Secretary of State, may the overseas institution notify the registrar of companies of that name which is treated as being its corporate name and one which may be used lawfully for the purpose of its business. S.70(2) thereupon will not apply to such a registered name.

Offences under Part III

73. A person who contravenes any provision in this Part of this Act shall be guilty of an offence and liable on summary conviction to imprisonment for a term not exceeding six months or to a fine not exceeding the fifth level on the standard scale or to both and, where the contravention involves a public display or exhibition of any name or description, there shall be a fresh contravention on each day on which the person causes or permits the display or exhibition to continue.

DEFINITION
"the standard scale": Criminal Justice Act 1982, s.37.

GENERAL NOTE
The maximum penalties for contravening any provision of this Part (use of banking names, of banking descriptions and the detailed requirements of ss.70 to 72) were increased at the Ninth Sitting of the Standing Committee (Ninth Sitting, January 29, 1987, col. 263) to six months' imprisonment or a level 5 fine (currently £2,000) or both, recognising that the unlawful use of a banking name or description may be accompanied by an intent to deceive and profit from the deception. Note that an offending name or description on public display or exhibition constitutes the commission of a fresh offence on each of the days the display or exhibition continues.

PART IV

OVERSEAS INSTITUTIONS WITH REPRESENTATIVE OFFICES

Meaning of "overseas institution" and "representative office"

74.—(1) In this Part of this Act "overseas institution" means a person (other than an authorised institution or any person for the time being specified in Schedule 2 to this Act) who—

(a) is a body corporate incorporated in a country or territory outside the United Kingdom or a partnership or other unincorporated association formed under the law of such a country or territory; or

(b) has his principal place of business in such a country or territory, being, in either case, a person who satisfies one of the conditions mentioned in subsection (2) below.

(2) The conditions referred to in subsection (1) above are—

(a) that the person's principal place of business is outside the United Kingdom and the person is authorised by the relevant supervisory authority in a country or territory outside the United Kingdom;

(b) that the person describes himself or holds himself out as being authorised by such an authority in a country or territory outside the United Kingdom;

(c) that the person uses any name or in any other way so describes himself or holds himself out as to indicate or reasonably be understood to indicate (whether in English or any other language), that he is a bank or banker or is carrying on a banking business (whether in the United Kingdom or elsewhere).

(3) In this Part of this Act "representative office", in relation to any overseas institution, means premises from which the deposit-taking, lending or other financial or banking activities of the overseas institution are promoted or assisted in any way; and "establishment", in relation to such an office, includes the making of any arrangements by virtue of which such activities are promoted or assisted from it.

DEFINITIONS
"authorised": s.106(1).
"institution": s.106(1).
"the relevant supervisory authority": s.106(1).

GENERAL NOTE
Ss.74 to 81 comprising Pt. IV make specific provision for the representative offices of overseas institutions in the U.K. It was the practice of the Bank under the 1979 Act to expect,
over and above the legal requirements under s.40, to receive prior warning of the setting up of a representative office and to be assured that the local supervisory authorities had

knowledge of the proposals. The "London address" was not expected to involve or commit the overseas institution in, or to, business transactions as such. However, the 1979 Act was so drafted as to catch non-banking overseas businesses such as securities dealers yet not those institutions which are similar in their purpose to banks but which are not deposit-taking businesses within the meaning of the Act.

Part IV follows the proposals in Chapter 13 of the White Paper and is also more specific. The Bank sought to avoid a situation where the "London addresses" of dubious overseas institutions might seek to carry out illegal or undesirable activities *outside* the U.K. and its jurisdiction. Whilst not seeking the imposition of an authorisation system (but note the reserve powers of H.M. Treasury under s.80), the Bank proposed a strengthening of existing arrangements and powers to prevent the use of misleading names. S.74 defines "overseas institution," as being a person (i) who is incorporated, formed or having his principal place of business outside the U.K. and (ii) who is, or who holds himself out as being, authorised by the relevant supervisory authority outside the U.K., or who describes himself or holds himself out as carrying on a banking business. *Cf.* s.9(3) on application for authorisation.

Subs. (3)

The words " 'establishment,' in relation to such an office, includes the making of any arrangements by virtue of which such activities are promoted or assisted from it" were added as a Lords amendment (H.C. Vol. 115, col. 880) to require overseas banks still to notify, notwithstanding that an agent had *previously* established premises in the U.K. on behalf of an overseas bank.

Notice of establishment of representative office

75.—(1) An overseas institution shall not establish a representative office in the United Kingdom unless it has given not less than two months' notice to the Bank that it proposes to establish such an office and a notice under this subsection shall specify—

(a) any name the institution proposes to use in relation to activities conducted by it in the United Kingdom after the establishment of that office; and

(b) in the case of an institution which will be obliged to disclose any name in connection with those activities by virtue of section 4 of the Business Names Act 1985 or Article 6 of the Business Names (Northern Ireland) Order 1986, that name.

(2) Where an overseas institution has established a representative office in the United Kingdom before the date on which this Part of this Act comes into force and has not given notice of that fact to the Bank under section 40 of the Banking Act 1979 it shall give notice in writing to the Bank of the continued existence of that office within the period of two months beginning with that date; and the obligation of an overseas institution to give notice under this subsection in respect of the establishment of an office established within the period of one month ending with that date shall supersede any obligation to give notice in respect of that matter under that section.

(3) A notice under this section shall be given in such manner and form as the Bank may specify.

DEFINITIONS

"the Bank": s.1.
"institution": s.106(1).
"overseas institution": s.74(1).
"representative office": s.74(3).

GENERAL NOTE

Where s.40 of the 1979 Act required a new representative office to give the Bank one month's notice *after* establishment in the U.K. and those representative offices established before the section came into force were required to give notice six months from the appointed day, this section requires respectively two months' notice *before* establishment and two months from the appointed day for Part 4. The overseas institution must also inform the Bank of any name it proposes to use in connection with its activities and any name it may be obliged to disclose in connection with those activities under s.4 of the Business Names Act 1985.

Subs. (3)

Notwithstanding s.99, the Bank shall specify the manner and form of the notice.

Power to object to names of overseas institutions

76.—(1) An overseas institution which has established a representative office in the United Kingdom shall not change any name used by it in relation to activities conducted by it in the United Kingdom or, in the case of an institution which is obliged to disclose any name in connection with those activities as mentioned in section 75(1) above, that name unless it has given not less than two months' notice to the Bank of the proposed name.

(2) Where notice of a name is given to the Bank by an overseas institution under section 75(1) or subsection (1) above and it appears to the Bank that the name is misleading to the public or otherwise undesirable it may, within the period of two months beginning with the day on which that notice was given, give notice in writing to the institution that it objects to that name.

(3) Where it appears to the Bank that an overseas institution which has established a representative office in the United Kingdom before the date on which this Part of this Act comes into force is using a name in relation to activities conducted by it in the United Kingdom which is misleading to the public or otherwise undesirable, the Bank may give notice in writing to the institution that it objects to the name—

(a) in a case where the Bank was notified of the establishment of the representative office before that date, within the period of six months beginning with that date; and

(b) otherwise, within the period of six months beginning with the date on which the establishment of the representative office comes to the Bank's knowledge.

(4) Where, as a result of a material change in circumstances since the time when notice of a name was given to the Bank under section 75(1) or subsection (1) above or as a result of further information becoming available to the Bank since that time, it appears to the Bank that the name is so misleading as to be likely to cause harm to the public, the Bank may give notice in writing to the overseas institution in question that it objects to the name.

DEFINITIONS

"the Bank": s.1.
"institution": s.106(1).
"notice": ss.99 and 100.
"overseas institution": s.74(1).
"representative office": s.74(3).

GENERAL NOTE

The Bank is given similar powers as those in s.70 with regard to overseas institutions to object to a name of an overseas institution's representative office if such name appears to the Bank to be "misleading to the public or otherwise undesirable." During the Ninth Sitting of the Standing Committee (Ninth Sitting, January 29, 1987, col. 266) an example was advanced of what may be a misleading name namely, that of a small banking organisation in Ruritania calling itself the International Bank of the Western Hemisphere!

Effect of notices under s.76 and appeals

77.—(1) Where the Bank has given notice under section 76 above to an overseas institution the institution shall not use the name to which the

Bank has objected in relation to activities conducted by it in the United Kingdom after the objection has taken effect; and for the purposes of this subsection the disclosure of a name in connection with those activities as mentioned in section 75(1)(b) above shall be treated (if it would not otherwise be) as use of that name in relation to those activities.

(2) For the purposes of this section an objection under section 76(2) above takes effect when the institution receives the notice of objection.

(3) An institution to which a notice of objection is given under section 76(2) above may within the period of three weeks beginning with the day on which it receives the notice apply to the court to set aside the objection and on such an application the court may set it aside or confirm it (but without prejudice to its operation before that time).

(4) For the purposes of this section an objection under section 76(3) or (4) above takes effect—

    (a) in a case where no application is made under subsection (5) below, at the expiry of the period of two months beginning with the day on which the institution receives the notice of objection or such longer period as the notice may specify; or

    (b) where an application is made under subsection (5) below and the court confirms the objection, after such period as the court may specify.

(5) An institution to which a notice of objection is given under section 76(3) or (4) above may within the period of three weeks beginning with the day on which it receives the notice apply to the court to set aside the objection.

(6) In this section "the court" means the High Court, the Court of Session or the High Court in Northern Ireland according to whether the representative office of the institution in question is situated in England and Wales, Scotland or Northern Ireland.

DEFINITIONS
  "the Bank": s.1.
  "institution": s.106(1).
  "notice": s.100.
  "overseas institution": s.74(1).

GENERAL NOTE
  Again, these provisions follow those in s.71 relating to the Bank's objections to the use of a name by an authorised institution and to the right of such institution to apply to the Court to set the objection aside.

Registration of substitute corporate name by overseas institution

78.—(1) Where the Bank gives notice under section 76 above objecting to the corporate name of an overseas institution, subsection (4) of section 694 of the Companies Act 1985 or, in Northern Ireland, paragraph (4) of Article 644 of the Companies (Northern Ireland) Order 1986 shall apply, subject to subsection (2) below, as it applies where a notice is served on a company under subsection (1) or (2) of that section or, as the case may be, paragraph (1) or (2) of that Article.

(2) No statement or further statement may be delivered under subsection (4) of section 694 or paragraph (4) of Article 644 by virtue of subsection (1) above unless the Bank has signified that it does not object to the name specified in the statement.

(3) Section 76(1) above shall not apply to a change of a name which has been registered under section 694(4) of the Companies Act 1985 or Article 644(4) of the Companies (Northern Ireland) Order 1986 by virtue of subsection (1) above.

DEFINITIONS
"the Bank": s.1.
"notice": s.100.
"overseas institution": s.74(1).

GENERAL NOTE
Identical provisions (except these relate to s.76) as for s.72.

Duty to provide information and documents

79.—(1) The Bank may by notice in writing require any overseas institution which has established a representative office in the United Kingdom or has given notice to the Bank under section 75(1) above of its intention to establish such an office to provide the Bank with such information or documents as the Bank may reasonably require.

(2) Without prejudice to the generality of subsection (1) above, the Bank may by notice in writing require such an overseas institution to deliver to the Bank—

    (a) in the case of an overseas institution which is a company incorporated in the United Kingdom, copies of the documents which the company is required to send to the registrar of companies under section 10 of the Companies Act 1985 or Article 21 of the Companies (Northern Ireland) Order 1986;

    (b) in the case of an overseas institution to which section 691(1) of that Act or Article 641(1) of that Order applies, copies of the document which it is required to deliver for registration in accordance with that section or Article;

    (c) in the case of any other overseas institution (other than an individual), information corresponding to that which would be contained in the documents which it would be required to deliver as mentioned in paragraph (b) above if it were a company to which section 691(1) applied;

    (d) in the case of an overseas institution which is authorised to take deposits or conduct banking business in a country or territory outside the United Kingdom by the relevant supervisory authority in that country or territory, a certified copy of any certificate from that authority conferring such authorisation on it.

(3) An overseas institution to which a notice is given under subsection (1) or (2) above shall comply with the notice—

    (a) in the case of an institution which has established a representative office in the United Kingdom, before the end of such period as is specified in the notice; and

    (b) in the case of an institution which has given notice under section 75(1) above of its intention to establish such an office, before it establishes the office.

(4) If at any time an overseas institution which has been required to deliver information or documents to the Bank under subsection (2) above is required to deliver any document or give notice to the registrar of companies under section 18 or 288(2) of the said Act of 1985 or Article 29 or 296(2) of the said Order of 1986, it shall no later than the time by which it must have complied with that requirement deliver a copy of that document or give notice to the Bank.

(5) If at any time an overseas institution is required to furnish any document or give notice to the registrar of companies under section 692 or 696(4) of the said Act of 1985 or Article 642 or 646 of the said Order of 1986 (or would be so required if it were a company to which that section or Article applied), it shall no later than the time by which it must have complied with that requirement deliver a copy of that document to the Bank.

(6) If at any time a certificate of authorisation of which a copy was required to be delivered to the Bank under subsection (2)(d) above is amended or the authorisation is withdrawn, the overseas institution shall no later than one month after the amendment or withdrawal deliver a copy of the amended certificate or, as the case may be, a notice stating that the authorisation has been withdrawn to the Bank.

(7) The Treasury may after consultation with the Bank by order provide that sections 39 and 40 above shall apply in relation to overseas institutions as they apply in relation to authorised institutions; but no order shall be made under this section unless a draft of it has been laid before and approved by a resolution of each House of Parliament.

DEFINITIONS
"the Bank": s.1.
"documents": s.106(1).
"notice": ss.99 and 100.
"overseas institution": s.74(1).
"relevant supervisory authority": s.106(1).
"representative office": s.74(3).

GENERAL NOTE
The Bank may demand such information and documents as it may "reasonably require" from any overseas institution with a representative office in the U.K. or with the intention to establish such. In particular, it may demand by written notice:
—copies of the documents filed on a registration of an overseas institution incorporated in the U.K. (s.10 of the Companies Act 1985);
—copies of documents delivered by overseas companies establishing a place of business within the U.K. (s.691(1) of the Companies Act 1985);
—certified copies of certificates confirming, amending or withholding authorisation from overseas supervisory authorities;
—copies of documents amending charters, statutes, memorandum or articles of association (ss.18 and 692 of the Companies Act 1985), changes in directors or secretary or persons authorised to accept service (ss.288(2) and 692 of the Companies Act 1985); and
—a copy of the notice of the fact of cessation of the place of business in Great Britain (s.696(4) of the Companies Act 1985).
The Treasury, after consultation with the Bank, *may* extend the provisions of s.39 (power to obtain information and require production of documents) and of s.40 (right of entry, etc.) to overseas institutions, the affirmative parliamentary procedure to be adopted.

Regulations imposing requirements on overseas-based banks

80.—(1) The Treasury may, after consultation with the Bank, by regulations impose on overseas institutions which have established or propose to establish representative offices in the United Kingdom such requirements as the Treasury consider appropriate in connection with those offices and the activities conducted from them.

(2) Regulations under this section may in particular require the establishment or continued existence of a representative office to be authorised by the Bank and such regulations may make provision for—
(a) the granting and revocation of such authorisations;
(b) the imposition of conditions in connection with the grant or retention of such authorisations; and
(c) appeals against the refusal or withdrawal of such authorisations or the imposition of such conditions.

(3) No regulations shall be made under this section unless a draft of the regulations has been laid before and approved by a resolution of each House of Parliament.

DEFINITIONS
"authorised": s.106(1).
"the Bank": s.1.

"overseas institution": s.74(1).
"representative office": s.74(1).

GENERAL NOTE

The White Paper (Chap. 13, para. 13.6) noted that the Government had considered the possibility of requiring representative offices to obtain prior authorisation of supervisors but rejected this mainly through consideration of cost but remarked that if experience directed it, further restrictions could be introduced by Order.

As against the possibility of doubtful overseas institutions with banking names establishing offices in the U.K., s.80 (which is new) enables the Treasury, after consultation with the Bank, to make regulations imposing on such bodies an authorisation and supervision regime analogous to that applied on U.K. deposit-takers and overseas banks with branches here. These *reserve* powers may only be brought in by means of the affirmative parliamentary procedure affording an opportunity of full debate.

Offences under Part IV

81. A person who contravenes any provision in this Part of this Act or any requirement imposed under it shall be guilty of an offence and liable on summary conviction to imprisonment for a term not exceeding six months or to a fine not exceeding the fifth level on the standard scale or to both and, where the contravention involves a public display or exhibition of any name or description, there shall be a fresh contravention on each day on which the person causes or permits the display or exhibition to continue.

DEFINITION

"the standard scale": Criminal Justice Act 1982, s.37.

GENERAL NOTE

Similar provisions with regard to penalties for contravention of any part of this Act or of any requirements imposed are set down here, as in s.73, in respect of offences concerning banking names and descriptions.

PART V

RESTRICTION ON DISCLOSURE OF INFORMATION

Restricted information

82.—(1) Except as provided by the subsequent provisions of this Part of this Act—

(a) no person who under or for the purposes of this Act receives information relating to the business or other affairs of any person; and

(b) no person who obtains any such information directly or indirectly from a person who has received it as aforesaid,

shall disclose the information without the consent of the person to whom it relates and (if different) the person from whom it was received as aforesaid.

(2) This section does not apply to information which at the time of the disclosure is or has already been made available to the public from other sources or to information in the form of a summary or collection of information so framed as not to enable information relating to any particular person to be ascertained from it.

(3) Any person who discloses information in contravention of this section shall be guilty of an offence and liable—

(a) on conviction on indictment, to imprisonment for a term not exceeding two years or to a fine or to both;

(b) on summary conviction, to imprisonment for a term not exceeding three months or to a fine not exceeding the statutory maximum or to both.

TRANSITIONAL PROVISION
Sched. 5, para. 14.

DEFINITION
"the statutory maximum": Criminal Justice Act 1982; s.74; Magistrates' Courts Act 1980, s.32.

GENERAL NOTE
Part 5, comprising ss.82 to 87, deals with the issue of confidentiality of information obtained under, or for the purposes of, the Act and relating to the business or other affairs of any person. Ss.19 and 20 of the 1979 Act established this principle which it was agreed in Chapter 12 of the White Paper should be preserved, although amendments were proposed regarding the need for full dialogue between supervisors and auditors and for the relaxation of existing restrictions and the encouragement of the mutual exchange of information between supervisory authorities. Both the Building Societies Act 1986 (ss.53 and 54) and the Financial Services Act 1986 (Pt. VIII, ss.179 to 182) contain similar provision imposing restrictions on the disclosure of information and creating a series of exceptions.

S.82 imposes a duty of confidentiality (with exceptions later through controlled gateways) on *every* person who acquires information on any other person's business or other affairs.

Subs. (1)
The duty is general (subject to receipt of consent from persons to whom the information relates *and* from persons from whom the information is obtained and subject to other exceptions later specified in this section and elsewhere in Pt. V) and covers persons who acquire information by exchange with others.

Subs. (2)
Two other exceptions (apart from consent) to the general rule include information already in the public domain, and material in an abbreviated or aggregated form which prevents the business or other affairs of any particular person from being disclosed.

Subs. (3)
There are severe criminal sanctions against unlawful disclosure.

Disclosure for facilitating discharge of functions by the Bank

83.—(1) Section 82 above does not preclude the disclosure of information in any case in which disclosure is for the purpose of enabling or assisting the Bank to discharge its functions under this Act.

(2) Without prejudice to the generality of subsection (1) above, that section does not preclude the disclosure of information by the Bank to the auditor of an authorised institution or former authorised institution if it appears to the Bank that disclosing the information would enable or assist the Bank to discharge the functions mentioned in that subsection or would otherwise be in the interests of depositors.

(3) If, in order to enable or assist the Bank properly to discharge any of its functions under this Act, the Bank considers it necessary to seek advice from any qualified person on any matter of law, accountancy, valuation or other matter requiring the exercise of professional skill, section 82 above does not preclude the disclosure by the Bank to that person of such information as appears to the Bank to be necessary to ensure that he is properly informed with respect to the matters on which his advice is sought.

DEFINITIONS
"authorised": s.106(1).
"the Bank": s.1.
"former authorised institution": s.106(1).
"institution": s.106(1).

General Note

Corresponds to s.19(2) and (3) of the 1979 Act in so far as the Bank is permitted to disclose to enable or assist it to comply with its obligations under the Act (subs. (1)).

Subs. (2)

This relaxation of the general rule providing for disclosure of information by the Bank to auditors of an authorised institution (and also, in this subsection, of a *former* authorised institution) was recommended in the White Paper, if in the opinion of the Bank, it is in the interests of depositors to do so and to enable a full dialogue between supervisors and auditors to take place. However, the White Paper (Chap. 8, para. 8.3 and Annex 4) regarded such *bilateral* exchanges as being the exception and the *trilateral* exchange, with the authorised institution also present, as constituting the normal practice. See also s.47 for the correlative relaxation of the confidentiality rule in favour of auditors, etc.

Subs. (3)

To ensure that professional advisers are properly instructed, the Bank may disclose such information as is proper.

Disclosure for facilitating discharge of functions by other supervisory authorities

84.—(1) Section 82 above does not preclude the disclosure by the Bank of information to any person specified in the first column of the following Table if the Bank considers that the disclosure would enable or assist that person to discharge the functions specified in relation to him in the second column of that Table.

Table

Person	Functions
The Secretary of State.	Functions under the Insurance Companies Act 1982, Part XIV of the Companies Act 1985, Part XIII of the Insolvency Act 1986 or the Financial Services Act 1986.
An inspector appointed by the Secretary of State.	Functions under Part XIV of the Companies Act 1985.
A person authorised by the Secretary of State under section 44 of the Insurance Companies Act 1982.	Functions under that section.
The Chief Registrar of friendly societies, the Registrar of Friendly Societies for Northern Ireland and the Assistant Registrar of Friendly Societies for Scotland.	Functions under the enactments relating to friendly societies or under the Financial Services Act 1986.
The Industrial Assurance Commissioner and the Industrial Assurance Commissioner for Northern Ireland.	Functions under the enactments relating to industrial assurance.
The Building Societies Commission.	Functions under the Building Societies Act 1986 and protecting the interests of the shareholders and depositors of building societies.
The Director General of Fair Trading.	Functions under the Consumer Credit Act 1974.
A designated agency or transferee body or the competent authority (within the meaning of the Financial Services Act 1986).	Functions under the Financial Services Act 1986.

Person	*Functions*
A recognised self-regulating organisation, recognised professional body, recognised investment exchange, recognised clearing house or recognised self-regulating organisation for friendly societies (within the meaning of the Financial Services Act 1986).	Functions in its capacity as an organisation, body, exchange or clearing house recognised under the Financial Services Act 1986.
A person appointed under section 94, 106 or 177 of the Financial Services Act 1986.	Functions under the sections mentioned in column 1.
A recognised professional body (within the meaning of section 391 of the Insolvency Act 1986).	Functions in its capacity as such a body under the Insolvency Act 1986.
The Department of Economic Development in Northern Ireland.	Functions under Part XV of the Companies (Northern Ireland) Order 1986.
An inspector appointed by that Department.	Functions under Part XV of that Order.
The Official Receiver or, in Northern Ireland, the Official Assignee for company liquidations or for bankruptcy.	Investigating the cause of the failure of an authorised institution or former authorised institution in respect of which a winding-up order, bankruptcy order or order of adjudication of bankruptcy has been made.

(2) The Treasury may after consultation with the Bank by order amend the Table in subsection (1) above by—

(a) adding any person exercising regulatory functions and specifying functions in relation to that person;

(b) removing any person for the time being specified in the Table; or

(c) altering the functions for the time being specified in the Table in relation to any person;

and the Treasury may also after consultation with the Bank by order restrict the circumstances in which, or impose conditions subject to which, disclosure is permitted in the case of any person for the time being specified in the Table.

(3) An order under subsection (2) above shall be subject to annulment in pursuance of a resolution of either House of Parliament.

(4) Section 82 above does not preclude the disclosure by any person specified in the first column of the Table in subsection (1) above of information obtained by him by virtue of that subsection if he makes the disclosure with the consent of the Bank and for the purpose of enabling or assisting him to discharge any functions specified in relation to him in the second column of that Table; and before deciding whether to give its consent to such a disclosure by any person the Bank shall take account of such representations made by him as to the desirability of or the necessity for the disclosure.

(5) Section 82 above does not preclude the disclosure by the Bank of information to the Treasury if disclosure appears to the Bank to be desirable or expedient in the interests of depositors or in the public interest; and that section does not preclude the disclosure by the Bank

of information to the Secretary of State for purposes other than those specified in relation to him in subsection (1) above if the disclosure is made with the consent of the Treasury and—

(a) the information relates to an authorised institution or former authorised institution and does not enable the financial affairs of any other identifiable person to be ascertained and disclosure appears to the Bank to be necessary in the interests of depositors or in the public interest; or

(b) in any other case, disclosure appears to the Bank to be necessary in the interests of depositors.

(6) Section 82 above does not preclude the disclosure of information for the purpose of enabling or assisting an authority in a country or territory outside the United Kingdom to exercise—

(a) functions corresponding to those of—

(i) the Bank under this Act;

(ii) the Secretary of State under the Insurance Companies Act 1982, Part XIII of the Insolvency Act 1986 or the Financial Services Act 1986; or

(iii) the competent authority under Part IV of the Financial Services Act 1986;

(b) functions in connection with rules of law corresponding to any of the provisions of the Company Securities (Insider Dealing) Act 1985 or Part VII of the Financial Services Act 1986; or

(c) supervisory functions in respect of bodies carrying on business corresponding to that of building societies.

DEFINITIONS
"authorised": s.106(1).
"the Bank": s.1.
"former authorised institution": s.106(1).
"institution": s.106(1).

GENERAL NOTE
The White Paper (Chap. 12, para. 12.5) confirmed that existing restrictions should be relaxed to enable the Bank to disclose in the interests of depositors or in the wider public interest, information to other government departments (except the Revenue Departments). This new provision is included in this section.

Subss. (1)–(3)
The Bank may disclose to specific regulatory bodies information to enable or assist them to discharge their functions as specified. These include functions under the Insurance Companies Act 1982, the Companies Act 1985, the Insolvency Act 1986, the Financial Services Act 1986, the Building Societies Act 1986 and the Consumer Credit Act 1974. The Treasury, after consultation with the Bank, has permissive powers to amend the Table and restrict or qualify the relaxation from non-disclosure. The Banking Act 1987 (Disclosure of Information) (Specified Persons) Order 1987 (S.I. 1987 No. 1292) has added the Panel on Take-overs and mergers.

Subs. (4)
Information disclosed to any other supervisory body specified in subs. (1) may, to enable or assist that body to discharge its functions as specified, be passed on to unspecified third persons with the Bank's consent after any relevant representations may have been made and taken into account by the Bank.

Subs. (5)
The Bank may disclose to the Treasury (as in s.19(4) of the 1979 Act) and to other government departments (through the collective body "The Secretary of State") but *quaere* whether this would include the Inland Revenue in view of its regulation by the Treasury through the Commissioners of Inland Revenue (Inland Revenue Regulation Act 1890, s.1).

Subs. (6)

The Bank (and others) are not precluded by s.82 from also disclosing information to enable or assist overseas financial supervisory bodies to exercise those functions broadly corresponding to those of their U.K. counterparts.

Other permitted disclosures

85.—(1) Section 82 above does not preclude the disclosure of information—

(a) for the purpose of enabling or assisting the Board of Banking Supervision or the Deposit Protection Board or any other person to discharge its or his functions under this Act;

(b) for the purpose of enabling or assisting a person to do anything which he is required to do in pursuance of a requirement imposed under section 39(1)(b) above;

(c) with a view to the institution of, or otherwise for the purposes of, any criminal proceedings, whether under this Act or otherwise;

(d) in connection with any other proceedings arising out of this Act;

(e) with a view to the institution of, or otherwise for the purposes of, proceedings under section 7 or 8 of the Company Directors Disqualification Act 1986 in respect of a director or former director of an authorised institution or former authorised institution;

(f) in connection with any proceedings in respect of an authorised institution or former authorised institution under the Bankruptcy (Scotland) Act 1985 or Parts I to VII or IX to XI of the Insolvency Act 1986 which the Bank has instituted or in which it has a right to be heard;

(g) with a view to the institution of, or otherwise for the purposes of, any disciplinary proceedings relating to the exercise of his professional duties by an auditor of an authorised institution or former authorised institution or an accountant or other person nominated or approved for the purposes of section 39(1)(b) above or appointed under section 41 above;

(h) in pursuance of a Community obligation.

(2) Section 82 above does not preclude the disclosure by the Bank to the Director of Public Prosecutions, the Director of Public Prosecutions for Northern Ireland, the Lord Advocate, a procurator fiscal or a constable of information obtained by virtue of section 41, 42 or 43 above or of information in the possession of the Bank as to any suspected contravention in relation to which the powers conferred by those sections are exercisable.

(3) Section 82 above does not preclude the disclosure of information by the Deposit Protection Board to any person or body responsible for a scheme for protecting depositors or investors (whether in the United Kingdom or elsewhere) similar to that for which provision is made by Part II of this Act if it appears to the Board that disclosing the information would enable or assist the recipient of the information or the Board to discharge his or its functions.

DEFINITIONS

"authorised": s.106(1).

"the Bank": s.1.

"the Board of Banking Supervision": s.2.

"the Deposit Protection Board": s.50.

"director": s.105(2).

GENERAL NOTE

Disclosure may be made to the Board of Banking Supervision or the Deposit Protection Board (the latter as in s.19(4)(b) of the 1979 Act) and other persons and bodies for the purpose of this Act and for instituting criminal or other proceedings.

Subs. (1)
Subs. (1)(c) relates to specific charges and is not intended to be used for a "fishing expedition", *e.g.* into possible tax evasion. An example was given during the Tenth Sitting of the Standing Committee (Tenth Sitting, February 3, 1987, col. 273) of circumstances envisaged under subs. (1)(g). The Bank might require a second audit under s.39(1)(b) and an investigation under s.41 might show that auditors had been negligent or, in the case of a small institution, in league with the management. Subs. (1)(h) recognises that where EEC law exists, it cannot be overruled by this Act.

Subs. (2)
Information obtained as a result of investigation by or on behalf of the Bank under ss.41 to 43 into suspected contraventions may be passed on to the appropriate prosecuting authority.

Subs. (3)
The Deposit Protection Board may also disclose information to corresponding bodies in any country to enable or assist in the discharge of their functions.

Information supplied to Bank by relevant overseas authority

86. Section 82 above applies also to information which has been supplied to the Bank for the purposes of its functions under this Act by a relevant supervisory authority in a country or territory outside the United Kingdom but no such information shall be disclosed except as provided in that section or for the purpose of enabling or assisting the Bank to discharge those functions or with a view to the institution of, or otherwise for the purposes of, criminal proceedings, whether under this Act or otherwise.

DEFINITIONS
"the Bank": s.1.
"relevant supervisory authority": s.106(1).

GENERAL NOTE
This is similar to s.20(4) of the 1979 Act. Information received by the Bank from other overseas supervisory authorities may not be disclosed unless: (i) the appropriate consent is given; (ii) it has already been obtained from other sources; (ii) it is collected data so framed as not to disclose individual details (see s. 82 on these three exceptions); (iv) it enables or assists the Bank to discharge its functions; or (v) it is otherwise for the institution, or otherwise for the purposes of, any criminal proceedings.

Disclosure of information obtained under other Acts

87.—(1) After section 174(3) of the Consumer Credit Act 1974 there shall be inserted—
"(3A) Subsections (1) and (2) do not apply to any disclosure of information by the Director to the Bank of England for the purpose of enabling or assisting the Bank to discharge its functions under the Banking Act 1987 or the Director to discharge his functions under this Act."
(2) Information disclosed to the Bank under subsection (1) of section 449 of the Companies Act 1985 for the purpose of enabling or assisting it to discharge its functions under this Act or in its capacity as a competent authority under subsection (3) of that section may be disclosed—
(a) with the consent of the Secretary of State, in any case in which information to which section 82 applies could be disclosed by virtue of section 84(1) or (2) above; and
(b) in any case in which information to which section 82 above applies could be disclosed by virtue of any of the other provisions of this Part of this Act.
(3) Information disclosed to the Bank under paragraph (1) of Article 442 of the Companies (Northern Ireland) Order 1986 for the purpose of

enabling or assisting it to discharge its functions under this Act or in its capacity as a competent authority under paragraph (3) of that Article may be disclosed—

(a) with the consent of the Secretary of State, in any case in which information to which section 82 above applies could be disclosed by virtue of section 84(1) or (2) above; and

(b) in any case in which information to which section 82 above applies could be disclosed by virtue of any of the other provisions of this Part of this Act.

(4) Any information which has been lawfully disclosed to the Bank may be disclosed by it to the Board of Banking Supervision so far as necessary for enabling or assisting the Board to discharge its functions under this Act.

DEFINITIONS

"the Bank": s.1.
"the Board of Banking Supervision": s.2.

Subs. (1)

There is a general rule in s.174 of the Consumer Credit Act 1974 (subject to exceptions) that no information obtained under or by virtue of that Act about any individual or a business shall be disclosed without consent. Subs. (1) adds a further exception in favour of the Bank and of the Director-General of Fair Trading to enable or assist each to discharge its or his functions.

Subs. (2)

Where information relating to a body has been obtained by reason of the Secretary of State's power to require production of documents and to enter and search premises under ss.447 and 448 of the Companies Act 1985, that information may be disclosed to a competent authority (which includes the Bank) for the purpose of enabling or assisting the Bank to discharge its functions if it would otherwise come within the ambit of s.84 or of any other provisions of this Part. See Sched. 6, para. 18(7), for the consequential amendment to s.449(1)(f) and (1A) of the Companies Act 1985.

Subs. (4)

Almost as an afterthought, the Bank is permitted to disclose information to the Board of Banking Supervision See s.2(4).

PART VI

MISCELLANEOUS AND SUPPLEMENTARY

Exclusion of authorised institution's agreements from Consumer Credit Act 1974

88.—(1) The Consumer Credit Act 1974 shall be amended as follows.

(2) In section 16(1) (consumer credit agreements with certain bodies exempt from regulation) after paragraph (g) there shall be inserted ", or

(h) an authorised institution or wholly-owned subsidiary (within the meaning of the Companies Act 1985) of such an institution.".

(3) In section 16(3) (Secretary of State's duty to consult before making orders) after paragraph (e) there shall be inserted "or

(f) under subsection (1)(h) without consulting the Treasury and the Bank of England.".

(4) In section 189(1) (definitions) after the definition of "association" there shall be inserted—

"'authorised institution' means an institution authorised under the Banking Act 1987;".

GENERAL NOTE

The White Paper in Annex 1 (Summary of Minor Proposals) recommended that the Consumer Credit Act 1974 should be amended to bring into line the treatment of building societies and banks under that Act. The process was started in the case of building societies (see Building Societies Act 1986, s.120 and Sched. 18, paras. 10 and 19) to provide that first mortgage loans by banks and building societies will be exempted from the provisions of the Consumer Credit Act (save for advertisements and quotations requirements and of those sections dealing with extortionate credit bargains (ss.137 to 140) which apply to all "credit agreements"). The Consumer Credit (Exempt Agreements) (No. 2) (Amendment) Order 1987 (S.I. 1987 No. 1578) in art. 2(a) exempts agreements by an authorised institution or a wholly owned subsidiary of such. There appears to be a misprint in subs. (4): the definition is of "associate" (not "association") in s.189(1) of the Consumer Credit Act 1974.

Electronic transfer of funds

89. After section 187(3) of the Consumer Credit Act 1974 (arrangements to be disregarded in determining whether a consumer credit agreement is to be treated as entered into in accordance with prior or in contemplation of future arrangements between creditor and supplier) there shall be inserted—

"(3A) Arrangements shall also be disregarded for the purposes of subsections (1) and (2) if they are arrangements for the electronic transfer of funds from a current account at a bank within the meaning of the Bankers' Books Evidence Act 1879."

GENERAL NOTE

The White Paper (in Annex 1, para. 5) also recommended that the Consumer Credit Act 1974 be amended to ensure that a transaction effected by means of a plastic card operating on a bank current account (through the system known as electronic funds transfer at the point of sale "EFT/POS") be placed in a similar position (with the object and effect principally of excluding it from the provisions of Part V (except s.56) of the Consumer Credit Act relating to documentation and cancellation provisions) as a transaction effected by means of a cheque. The Banking Bill at first made no provision for this but when Lords' amendments were being considered in the Commons (*Hansard*, H.C. Vol. 115, col. 881) it was agreed that this new clause should go in in advance of the full review of banking services.

The means of effecting this in s.89 is, in essence, to exclude from the constituent "arrangements" included in the definition of debtor-creditor-supplier agreement in s.12(*b*) and 12(*c*) of the Consumer Credit Act 1974 those "arrangements" for the electronic transfer of funds from a current account. Such widening of the scope of s.187(3) creates an inroad into the concept of "connected lender". "Current account" is not defined but see *United Dominions Trust* v. *Kirkwood* [1966] 2 K.B. 431, 451, 457, 465 for some guidance. For the meaning of "a bank within the meaning of the Bankers' Books Evidence Act 1879" see Banking Act 1979, s.51 and Sched. 6, Pt. 1, para. (1), which have not been repealed by this Act (see Sched. 7). EFT/POS agreements in so far as they are debtor-creditor agreements enabling a debtor to overdraw on a current account would accordingly come within the determination limited to banks made by the Director General of Fair Trading under s.74(1)(*b*) of the Consumer Credit Act 1974 and issued on November 3, 1983, excluding them from the operation of Pt. V.

Disclosure of transactions by authorised institutions with chief executives and managers

90.—(1) For section 233(3) of the Companies Act 1985 there shall be substituted—

"(3) Subsections (1) and (2) do not apply in relation to any transaction, arrangement or agreement made by an authorised institution for any officer of the institution or for any officer of its holding company unless the officer is a chief executive or manager within the meaning of the Banking Act 1987; and references to officers in Part II of Schedule 6 shall be construed accordingly."

(2) For Article 241(3) of the Companies (Northern Ireland) Order 1986 there shall be substituted—

"(3) Paragraphs (1) and (2) do not apply in relation to any transaction, arrangement or agreement made by an authorised institution for any officer of the institution or for any officer of its holding company unless that officer is a chief executive or manager within the meaning of the Banking Act 1987; and references to officers in Part II of Schedule 6 shall be construed accordingly."

DEFINITIONS
"authorised": s.106(1).
"chief executive": s.105(7).
"institution": s.106(1).
"manager": s.105(6).

GENERAL NOTE
Ss.232 and 233 of the Companies Act 1985 require the accounts for a financial year of a company to comply with the relevant provisions of Sched. 6 to that Act regarding the disclosure of loans, quasi-loans and certain other transactions in favour of directors and other officers of the company. Certain exceptions and modifications applied in respect of recognised banks and in particular s.233(3) exempted transactions, etc., made by a recognised bank for any officers (including a director, manager or secretary) in respect of the requirements of Pt. 2 of Sched. 6. S.90 in its amendment exempts transactions, etc., made by authorised institutions but restricts the exemption in relation to the transactions made for officers other than those who are a chief executive or manager as defined in ss.105(7) and (6) respectively. See also Sched. 6, para. 18, to this Act which substitutes for the definitions of "recognised bank" that of "authorised institution" in the relevant provisions of the Companies Act 1985.

Powers for securing reciprocal facilities for banking and other financial business

91. For the avoidance of doubt it is hereby declared that a notice under section 183 of the Financial Services Act 1986 (disqualification or restriction of persons connected with overseas countries which do not afford reciprocal facilities for financial business) may be served on any person connected with the country in question who is carrying on or appears to the Secretary of State or the Treasury to intend to carry on in, or in relation to, the United Kingdom business of any of the descriptions specified in subsection (1) of that section whether or not it is of the same description as that affected by the less favourable terms which are the occasion for the service of the notice.

GENERAL NOTE
This section designed "for the avoidance of doubt" was introduced during the Lords' Debate at Report Stage (*Hansard*, H.L. Vol. 486, cols. 1256–1258) to clarify the meaning of s.183 of the Financial Services Act which deals with the issue of reciprocity. The reserve power, in securing reciprocal access for British financial businesses overseas, allows for the refusal, restriction or removal of authorisation in respect of the carrying on of banking, investment or insurance business in the U.K. if the country of origin of the institution involved does not allow reciprocal access in *any* of these sectors to British institutions. Thus, if there should be unfavourable treatment in an overseas country against U.K. *insurance* enterprises there might be corresponding action in the U.K. against a person connected with that overseas country carrying on a *banking* business in the U.K. ("whether or not it is of the same description as that affected . . ."). The new section seeks to make it clear that what is known as "cross-functionality" would apply. The section came into operation immediately on enactment (May 15, 1987). Once the whole of this Act is in operation s.185 of the Financial Services Act 1986 will have to be modified to refer to this Act in place of the 1979 Act. See para. 27(4) of Sched. 6.

Winding up on petition from the Bank

92.—(1) On a petition presented by the Bank by virtue of this section the court having jurisdiction under the Insolvency Act 1986 may wind up an authorised institution or former authorised institution if—

  (a) the institution is unable to pay its debts within the meaning of section 123 or, as the case may be, section 221 of that Act; or

  (b) the court is of the opinion that it is just and equitable that the institution should be wound up;

and for the purposes of such a petition an institution which defaults in an obligation to pay any sum due and payable in respect of a deposit shall be deemed to be unable to pay its debts as mentioned in paragraph (a) above.

(2) Where a petition is presented under subsection (1) above for the winding up of a partnership on the ground mentioned in paragraph (b) of that subsection or, in Scotland, on the ground mentioned in paragraph (a) or (b) of that subsection, the court shall have jurisdiction and the Insolvency Act 1986 shall have effect as if the partnership were an unregistered company within the meaning of section 220 of that Act.

(3) On a petition presented by the Bank by virtue of this section the High Court in Northern Ireland may wind up an authorised institution if—

  (a) the institution is unable to pay its debts within the meaning of Article 480 or, as the case may be, Article 616 of the Companies (Northern Ireland) Order 1986; or

  (b) the court is of the opinion that it is just and equitable that the institution should be wound up;

and for the purposes of such a petition an institution which defaults in an obligation to pay any sum due and payable in respect of a deposit shall be deemed to be unable to pay its debts as mentioned in paragraph (a) above.

(4) Where a petition is presented under subsection (3) above for the winding up of a partnership on the ground mentioned in paragraph (b) of that subsection, the court shall have jurisdiction and the said Order of 1986 shall have effect as if the partnership were an unregistered company within the meaning of Article 615 of that Order.

(5) For the purposes of this section the definition of deposit in section 5 above shall be treated as including any sum that would otherwise be excluded by subsection (3)(a), (b) or (c) of that section.

(6) This section applies to a company or partnership which has contravened section 3 above as it applies to an authorised institution.

DEFINITIONS
  "authorised": s.106(1).
  "the Bank": s.1.
  "deposit": s.5.
  "former authorised institution": s.106(1).
  "institution": s.106(1).

GENERAL NOTE
  Corresponds to s.18 of the 1979 Act as modified by s.219 of the Insolvency Act 1985 and then amended by the Insolvency Act 1986, Sched. 14. The Bank may petition for the winding-up of an authorised institution or *former* authorised institution not only where it is unable to pay its debts or had liabilities in excess of its assets but now also if the Court is of the opinion that it is "just and equitable." See *Re Goodwin Squires Securities, The Times*, March 22, 1983. Note the *inclusion* of certain payments, for the purposes of s.92, which would otherwise be excluded from the definition of "deposit" under s.5(3) (subs. (5)). The section will also apply to companies or partnerships guilty of illegal deposit-taking under s.3 (subs. (6)).

Injunctions

93.—(1) If on the application of the Bank, the Director of Public Prosecutions, the Lord Advocate or the Director of Public Prosecutions for Northern Ireland the court is satisfied—

(a)　that there is a reasonable likelihood that a person will contravene section 3, 18, 35, 67, 69, 71, or 77 above, a direction under section 19 above or regulations under section 32, 34, or 80 above; or

(b)　that any person has been guilty of any such contravention and that there is a reasonable likelihood that the contravention will continue or be repeated,

the court may grant an injunction restraining, or in Scotland an interdict prohibiting, the contravention.

(2) If on the application of the Bank, the Director of Public Prosecutions, the Lord Advocate or the Director of Public Prosecutions for Northern Ireland it appears to the court that a person may have been guilty of such a contravention as is mentioned in subsection (1) above the court may grant an injunction restraining, or in Scotland an interdict prohibiting, him from disposing of or otherwise dealing with any of his assets while the suspected contravention is investigated.

(3) The jurisdiction conferred by this section shall be exercisable by the High Court and the Court of Session.

DEFINITION
"the Bank": s.1.

GENERAL NOTE
This new section empowers the Bank and the prosecuting authorities as specified to apply to the High Court or the Court of Session (as the case may be) for injunctions restraining the likely, continued or repeated contraventions of the statutory provisions relating to illegal deposit-taking (s.3); false statements as to authorised status (s.18); false inducement to make a deposit (s.35); banking names or descriptions (ss.67 and 69); the use of names to which the Bank has objected (ss.71 and 77); the contravention of a direction under s.19; regulations concerning advertisements (s.32); unsolicited calls (s.34) or authorisation of overseas-based banks (s.80).

Subs. (2)
In addition, injunctions may be sought restraining a suspected person from disposing of or dealing with any of his assets during the investigation of the suspected contravention.

False and misleading information

94.—(1) Any person who knowingly or recklessly provides the Bank or any other person with information which is false or misleading in a material particular shall be guilty of an offence if the information is provided—

(a)　in purported compliance with a requirement imposed by or under this Act; or

(b)　otherwise than as mentioned in paragraph (a) above but in circumstances in which the person providing the information intends, or could reasonably be expected to know, that the information would be used by the Bank for the purpose of exercising its functions under this Act.

(2) Any person who knowingly or recklessly provides the Bank or any other person with information which is false or misleading in a material particular shall be guilty of an offence if the information is provided in connection with an application for authorisation under this Act.

(3) An authorised institution or former authorised institution shall be guilty of an offence if it fails to provide the Bank with any information in its possession knowing or having reasonable cause to believe—

(a) that the information is relevant to the exercise by the Bank of its functions under this Act in relation to the institution; and

(b) that the withholding of the information is likely to result in the Bank being misled as to any matter which is relevant to and of material significance for the exercise of those functions in relation to the institution.

(4) Any person who knowingly or recklessly provides any person appointed under section 41 above with information which is false or misleading in a material particular shall be guilty of an offence.

(5) Any person guilty of an offence under this section shall be liable—

(a) on conviction on indictment, to imprisonment for a term not exceeding two years or to a fine or to both;

(b) on summary conviction, to imprisonment for a term not exceeding six months or to a fine not exceeding the statutory maximum or to both.

DEFINITIONS

"authorised": s.106(1).
"the Bank": s.1.
"former authorised institution": s.106(1).
"institution": s.106(1).

GENERAL NOTE

This section brings in a new offence of *any* person misleading the Bank or in certain circumstances any other person and carries severe penalties. It was noted during the Tenth Sitting of the Standing Committee (Tenth Sitting, February 3, 1987, col. 275) that in view of the qualification "recklessly" it would be incumbent upon an officer of a subsidiary of a foreign bank to ensure that information provided from the parent for the supervisory authorities is checked independently. See also ss.96 and 98.

Subs. (1)

It is not only the Bank but any other person who may be supplied with information which is false or misleading, and the information may be provided not only under a statutory requirement but may be supplied voluntarily for the purposes of banking supervision.

Subs. (2)

The same provisions apply where the information relates to an application for authorisation.

Subs. (3)

If a less scrupulous authorised institution or *former* authorised institution fails to give the Bank information which is *in its possession* knowing or having *reasonable* cause to believe that such information is relevant to the Bank's statutory functions *and* the withholding of this information may mislead the Bank as to relevant materially significant matters with regard to the exercise of these functions, then an offence is committed.

Subs. (4)

Again, it is an offence to provide knowingly or recklessly false or misleading information to the competent persons investigating on behalf of the Bank under s.41.

Restriction of Rehabilitation of Offenders Act 1974

95.—(1) The Rehabilitation of Offenders Act 1974 shall have effect subject to the provisions of this section in cases where the spent conviction is for—

(a) an offence involving fraud or other dishonesty; or

(b) an offence under legislation (whether or not of the United Kingdom) relating to companies (including insider dealing), building societies, industrial and provident societies, credit unions, friendly societies, insurance, banking or other financial services, insolvency, consumer credit or consumer protection.

(2) Nothing in section 4(1) (restriction on evidence as to spent convictions in proceedings) shall prevent the determination in any proceeding arising out of any such decision of the Bank as is mentioned in section 27(1) or (3) above (including proceedings on appeal to any court) of any issue, or prevent the admission or requirement in any such proceedings of any evidence, relating to a person's previous convictions for any such offence as is mentioned in subsection (1) above or the circumstances ancillary thereto.

(3) A conviction for such an offence as is mentioned in subsection (1) above shall not be regarded as spent for the purposes of section 4(2) (questions relating to an individual's previous convictions) if—

(a) the question is put by or on behalf of the Bank and the individual is a person who is or is seeking to become a director, controller or manager of an authorised institution, a former authorised institution or an institution which has made an application for authorisation which has not been disposed of; or

(b) the question is put by or on behalf of any such institution and the individual is or is seeking to become a director, controller or manager of that institution,

and the person questioned is informed that by virtue of this section convictions for any such offence are to be disclosed.

(4) Section 4(3)(b) (spent conviction not to be ground for excluding person from office, occupation etc.) shall not—

(a) prevent the Bank from refusing to grant or revoking an authorisation on the ground that an individual is not a fit and proper person to be a director, controller or manager of the institution in question or from imposing a restriction or giving a direction requiring the removal of an individual as director, controller or manager of an institution; or

(b) prevent an authorised institution, a former authorised institution or an institution which has made an application for authorisation which has not yet been disposed of from dismissing or excluding an individual from being a director, controller or manager of the institution,

by reason, or partly by reason, of a spent conviction of that individual for such an offence as is mentioned in subsection (1) above or any circumstances ancillary to such a conviction or of a failure (whether or not by that individual) to disclose such a conviction or any such circumstances.

(5) For the purposes of subsections (3) and (4) above an application by an institution is not disposed of until the decision of the Bank on the application is communicated to the institution.

(6) This section shall apply to Northern Ireland with the substitution for the references to the said Act of 1974 and section 4(1), (2) and (3)(b) of that Act of references to the Rehabilitation of Offenders (Northern Ireland) Order 1978 and Article 5(1), (2) and (3)(b) of that Order.

DEFINITIONS
  "authorisation": s.106(1).
  "authorised": s.106(1).
  "the Bank": s.1.
  "controller": s.105(3).
  "director": s.105(2).
  "former authorised institution": s.106(1).
  "institution": s.106(1).
  "manager": s.105(6).

GENERAL NOTE
  This section makes provision for the disclosure of convictions which would otherwise be treated as spent by virtue of the Rehabilitation of Offenders Act 1974 and for convictions

for those offences specified in subs. (1) to be taken into account in the discharge of the Bank's statutory functions. See, *e.g.*, Sched. 3, para. 1.

Offences

96.—(1) Where an offence under this Act committed by a body corporate is proved to have been committed with the consent or connivance of, or to be attributable to any neglect on the part of any director, manager, secretary or other similar office of the body corporate, or any person who was purporting to act in any such capacity, he, as well as the body corporate, shall be guilty of that offence and be liable to be proceeded against and punished accordingly.

(2) Where the affairs of a body corporate are managed by its members, subsection (1) above shall apply in relation to the acts and defaults of a member in connection with his functions of management as if he were a director of the body corporate.

(3) In the case of a person who by virtue of subsection (1) or (2) above or section 98(6) or (7) below is guilty of an offence under section 12(6) or 19(6) above the penalty that can be imposed on conviction on indictment shall be imprisonment for a term not exceeding two years or a fine or both.

(4) In any proceedings for an offence under this Act it shall be a defence for the person charged to prove that he took all reasonable precautions and exercised all due diligence to avoid the commission of such an offence by himself or any person under his control.

(5) No proceedings for an offence under this Act shall be instituted—

   (a) in England and Wales, except by or with the consent of the Director of Public Prosecutions or the Bank; or

   (b) in Northern Ireland, except by or with the consent of the Director of Public Prosecutions for Northern Ireland or the Bank.

(6) In relation to proceedings against a building society incorporated (or deemed to be incorporated) under the Building Societies Act 1986 subsection (5) above shall have effect with the substitution for references to the Bank of references to the Building Societies Commission.

(7) In relation to proceedings against a friendly society within the meaning of section 7(1)(a) of the Friendly Societies Act 1974 the reference in paragraph (a) of subsection (5) above to the Bank shall include a reference to the Chief Registrar of friendly societies; and in relation to proceedings against a friendly society within the meaning of section 1(1)(a) of the Friendly Societies Act (Northern Ireland) 1970 the reference in paragraph (b) of that subsection to the Bank shall include a reference to the Registrar of Friendly Societies for Northern Ireland.

<small>DEFINITIONS</small>
   "director": s.105(2).
   "manager": s.105(6).

<small>GENERAL NOTE</small>
   Corresponds with s.41 of the 1979 Act with extensions to cover the situations of building societies and friendly societies affected by the provisions of this Act. Similar provisions are made in s.733 of the Companies Act 1985, s.202 of the Financial Provisions Act 1986 and s.112 of the Building Socieites Act 1986.

Summary proceedings

97.—(1) Summary proceedings for any offence under this Act may, without prejudice to any jurisdiction exercisable apart from this subsection, be taken against an institution, including an unincorporated institution, at any place at which it has a place of business, and against an individual at any place at which he is for the time being.

(2) Notwithstanding anything in section 127(1) of the Magistrates' Courts Act 1980, any information relating to an offence under this Act which is triable by a magistrates' court in England and Wales may be so tried if it is laid at any time within three years after the commission of the offence and within six months after the relevant date.

(3) Notwithstanding anything in section 331 of the Criminal Procedure (Scotland) Act 1975, summary proceedings for such an offence may be commenced in Scotland at any time within three years after the commission of the offence and within six months after the relevant date; and subsection (3) of that section shall apply for the purposes of this subsection as it applies for the purposes of that section.

(4) Notwithstanding anything in Article 19(1) of the Magistrates' Courts (Northern Ireland) Order 1981, a complaint relating to such an offence which is triable by a court of summary jurisdiction in Northern Ireland may be so tried if it is made at any time within three years after the commission of the offence and within six months after the relevant date.

(5) In this section—
> "the relevant date" means the date on which evidence sufficient in the opinion of the prosecuting authority to justify proceedings comes to its knowledge; and
> "the prosecuting authority" means the authority by or with whose consent the proceedings are instituted in accordance with section 96 above or, in Scotland, the Lord Advocate.

(6) For the purposes of subsection (5) above, a certificate of any prosecuting authority as to the date on which such evidence as is there mentioned came to its knowledge shall be conclusive evidence of that fact.

DEFINITION
"institution": s.106(1).

GENERAL NOTE
This section provides for the jurisdiction of the Courts in the U.K. and for time limits for summary proceedings. See also s.731 of the Companies Act 1985, s.203 of the Financial Services Act 1986, and s.111 of the Building Societies Act 1986.

Offences committed by unincorporated associations

98.—(1) Proceedings for an offence alleged to have been committed under this Act by an unincorporated association shall be brought in the name of that association (and not in that of any of its members) and, for the purposes of any such proceedings, any rules of court relating to the service of documents shall have effect as if the association were a corporation.

(2) A fine imposed on an unincorporated association on its conviction of an offence under this Act shall be paid out of the funds of the association.

(3) Section 33 of the Criminal Justice Act 1925 and Schedule 3 to the Magistrates' Courts Act 1980 (procedure on charge of offence against a corporation) shall have effect in a case in which an unincorporated association is charged in England or Wales with an offence under this Act in like manner as they have effect in the case of a corporation so charged.

(4) In relation to any proceedings on indictment in Scotland for an offence alleged to have been committed under this Act by an unincorporated association, section 74 of the Criminal Procedure (Scotland) Act 1975 (proceedings on indictment against bodies corporate) shall have effect as if the association were a body corporate.

(5) Section 18 of the Criminal Justice Act (Northern Ireland) 1945 and Schedule 4 to the Magistrates' Courts (Northern Ireland) Order 1981 (procedure on charge of offence against a corporation) shall have effect in a case in which an unincorporated association is charged in Northern Ireland with an offence under this Act in like manner as they have effect in the case of a corporation so charged.

(6) Where a partnership is guilty of an offence under this Act, every partner, other than a partner who is proved to have been ignorant of, or to have attempted to prevent the commission of the offence, shall also be guilty of that offence and be liable to be proceeded against and punished accordingly.

(7) Where any other unincorporated association is guilty of an offence under this Act, every officer of the association who is bound to fulfil any duty whereof the offence is a breach, or if there is no such officer then every member of the committee or other similar governing body, other than a member who is proved to have been ignorant of, or to have attempted to prevent the commission of the offence, shall also be guilty of that offence and be liable to be proceeded against and punished accordingly.

GENERAL NOTE
  This represents an updating of s.42 of the 1979 Act. Ss.202 and 203 of the Financial Services Act 1986 have comparable provisions.

Service of notices on the Bank

99.—(1) No notice required by this Act to be given to or served on the Bank shall be regarded as given or served until it is received.

(2) Subject to subsection (1) above, any such notice may be given or served by telex or other similar means which produce a document containing the text of the communication.

Service of other notices

100.—(1) This section has effect in relation to any notice, direction or other document required or authorised by or under this Act to be given to or served on any person other than the Bank.

(2) Any such document may be given to or served on the person in question—
  (a) by delivering it to him; or
  (b) be leaving it at his proper address; or
  (c) by sending it by post to him at that address; or
  (d) by sending it to him at that address by telex or other similar means which produce a document containing the text of the communication.

(3) Any such document may—
  (a) in the case of a body corporate, be given to or served on the secretary or clerk of that body; and
  (b) in the case of any other description of institution, be given to or served on a controller of the institution.

(4) For the purposes of this section and section 7 of the Interpretation Act 1978 (service of documents by post) in its application to this section, the proper address of any person to or on whom a document is to be given or served shall be his last known address, except that—
  (a) in the case of a body corporate or its secretary or clerk, it shall be the address of the registered or principal office of that body in the United Kingdom; and
  (b) in the case of any other description of institution or a person having

control or management of its business, it shall be that of the principal office of the institution in the United Kingdom.

(5) If the person to or on whom any document mentioned in subsection (1) above is to be given or served has notified the Bank of an address within the United Kingdom, other than his proper address within the meaning of subsection (4) above, as the one at which he or someone on his behalf will accept documents of the same description as that document, that address shall also be treated for the purposes of this section and section 7 of the Interpretation Act 1978 as his proper address.

DEFINITIONS
"the Bank": s.1.
"controller": s.105(3).
"documents": s.106(1).
"institution": s.106(1).

GENERAL NOTE
These sections correspond with and update s.45 of the 1979 Act. None of the terms "given," "delivery" or "served" is defined. Notification may be effected by telex "or other similar means which produce a document containing the text of the communication" which no doubt would include transmission by means of a facsimile process. Note the exceptions to these general provisions where the Bank may prescribe the form and content of notices in, *e.g.* ss.70(5) and 75(3).

Evidence

101.—(1) In any proceedings, a certificate purporting to be signed on behalf of the Bank and certifying—
  (a) that a particular person is or is not an authorised institution or was or was not such an institution at a particular time;
  (b) the date on which a particular institution became or ceased to be authorised;
  (c) whether or not a particular institution's authorisation is or was restricted;
  (d) the date on which a restricted authorisation expires; or
  (e) the date on which a particular institution became or ceased to be a recognised bank or licensed institution under the Banking Act 1979,
shall be admissible in evidence and, in Scotland, shall be sufficient evidence of the facts stated in the certificate.

(2) A certificate purporting to be signed as mentioned in subsection (1) above shall be deemed to have been duly signed unless the contrary is shown.

DEFINITIONS
"authorised": s.106(1).
"the Bank": s.1.
"institution": s.106(1).

GENERAL NOTE
This section corresponds with s.44 of the 1979 Act and extends it to include the certification of a restriction of a particular institution's authorisation (para. (c)) and when such restriction expires (para. (d)). Note that the particular certificate need no longer be signed by the Chief Cashier or Deputy Chief Cashier but that it is sufficient, in the absence of contrary evidence, that the certificate purports to be signed on behalf of the Bank. Similar provisions relating to the means of proving documents appear in s.113 of the Building Societies Act 1986.

Orders and regulations

102. Any power of the Treasury to make orders or regulations under this Act shall be exercisable by statutory instrument.

Municipal banks

103.—(1) References in this Act to a municipal bank are to a company within the meaning of the Companies Act 1985 which—

(a) carries on a deposit-taking business,

(b) is connected with a local authority as mentioned in subsection (2) below, and

(c) has its deposits guaranteed by that local authority in accordance with subsection (5) below.

(2) The connection referred to in paragraph (b) of subsection (1) above between a company and a local authority is that—

(a) the company's articles of association provide that the shares in the company are to be held only by members of the local authority; and

(b) substantially all the funds lent by the company are lent to the local authority.

(3) Where on 9th November 1978 a company or its predecessor—

(a) was carrying on a deposit-taking business, and

(b) was connected with a local authority as mentioned in subsection (2) above,

that local authority or its successor may for the purposes of this Act resolve to guarantee deposits with the company.

(4) A resolution passed by a local authority under subsection (3) above may not be rescinded.

(5) Where a local authority has passed a resolution under subsection (3) above or under section 48(3) of the Banking Act 1979, that local authority and any local authority which is its successor shall be liable, if the company concerned defaults in payment, to make good to a depositor the principal and interest owing in respect of any deposit with the company, whether made before or after the passing of the resolution.

(6) For the purposes of this section—

(a) one company is the predecessor of another if that other succeeds to its obligations in respect of its deposit-taking business; and

(b) one local authority is the successor of another if, as a result of, or in connection with, an order under Part IV of the Local Government Act 1972 or Part II of the Local Government (Scotland) Act 1973 (change of local government area), it becomes connected as mentioned in subsection (2) above with a company formerly so connected with that other local authority.

DEFINITIONS
"deposit": s.5.
"deposit-taking business": s.6.
"local authority": s.106(1).

GENERAL NOTE
This defines "a municipal bank" which, for example, is included in the list of exempted persons in Sched. 2. It corresponds exactly with s.48 of the 1979 Act.

Scottish 1819 savings banks

104.—(1) This section applies to any savings bank established before 28th July 1863 under an Act passed in the 59th year of King George III entitled an Act for the Protection of Banks for Savings in Scotland.

(2) For the purposes of Part II of this Act a savings bank to which this section applies becomes insolvent on the making of a winding-up order

against it under Part V of the Insolvency Act 1986 or on the making of an award of sequestration on the estate of the bank.

(3) A savings bank to which this section applies shall be regarded as a relevant savings bank for the purposes of sections 68 and 69 above.

GENERAL NOTE

Inadvertently, no provision was made in the 1979 Act for what are known as Scottish 1819 Savings Banks which are any savings banks established before July 28, 1863, under the Protection of Banks for Savings in Scotland Act 1819 and which have not since become trustee savings banks. S.6 of the Trustee Savings Banks 1985 cured the defect in providing that any savings bank will be treated for the purposes of the Banking Act 1979 as an "institution" within the meaning of that Act for the purposes of being granted recognition or a licence.

S.104 now provides that for the purposes of any claim being made against the Deposit Protection Fund such a savings bank becomes insolvent on the making of a winding-up order against it under Pt. V of the Insolvency Act 1986 or on the making up of an order of sequestration. Subs. (3) confirms that for the purpose of banking names and banking descriptions a Scottish 1819 savings bank is treated as a relevant savings bank. At the time of writing it is understood that there is only one such bank still extant.

Meaning of "director", "controller", "manager", and "associate"

105.—(1) In the provisions of this Act other than section 96 "director", "controller", "manager" and "associate" shall be construed in accordance with the provisions of this section.

(2) "Director", in relation to an institution, includes—

(a) any person who occupies the position of a director, by whatever name called; and

(b) in the case of an institution established in a country or territory outside the United Kingdom, any person, including a member of a managing board, who occupies a position appearing to the Bank to be analogous to that of a director of a company registered under the Companies Act 1985;

and in the case of a partnership "director", where it is used in subsections (6) and (7) below, includes a partner.

(3) "Controller", in relation to an institution, means—

(a) a managing director of the institution or of another institution of which it is a subsidiary or, in the case of an institution which is a partnership, a partner;

(b) a chief executive of the institution or of another institution of which it is a subsidiary;

(c) a person who, either alone or with any associate or associates, is entitled to exercise, or control the exercise of, 15 per cent. or more of the voting power at any general meeting of the institution or of another institution of which it is a subsidiary; and

(d) a person in accordance with whose directions or instructions the directors of the institution or of another institution of which it is a subsidiary or persons who are controllers of the institution by virtue of paragraph (c) above (or any of them) are accustomed to act.

(4) A person who is a controller of an institution by virtue of paragraph (c) of subsection (3) above is in this Act referred to as a "shareholder controller" of the institution; and in this Act—

(a) a "minority shareholder controller" means a shareholder controller in whose case the percentage referred to in that paragraph does not exceed 50;

(b) a "majority shareholder controller" means a shareholder controller in whose case that percentage exceeds 50 but not 75; and

(c) a "principal shareholder controller" means a shareholder controller in whose case that percentage exceeds 75.

(5) A person who is a controller of an institution by virtue of subsection (3)(d) above is in this Act referred to as "an indirect controller" of the institution.

(6) "Manager", in relation to an institution, means a person (other than a chief executive) who, under the immediate authority of a director or chief executive of the institution—

(a) exercises managerial functions; or

(b) is responsible for maintaining accounts or other records of the institution.

(7) In this section "chief executive", in relation to an institution, means a person who, either alone or jointly with one or more other persons, is responsible under the immediate authority of the directors for the conduct of the business of the institution.

(8) Without prejudice to subsection (7) above, in relation to an institution whose principal place of business is in a country or territory outside the United Kingdom, "chief executive" also includes a person who, either alone or jointly with one or more other persons, is responsible for the conduct of its business in the United Kingdom.

(9) In this Act "associate", in relation to a person entitled to exercise or control the exercise of voting power in relation to, or holding shares in, a body corporate, means—

(a) the wife or husband or son or daughter of that person;

(b) any company of which that person is a director;

(c) any person who is an employee or partner of that person;

(d) if that person is a company—

    (i) any director of that company;

    (ii) any subsidiary of that company; and

    (iii) any director or employee of any such subsidiary; and

(e) if that person has with any other person an agreement or arrangement with respect to the acquisition, holding or disposal of shares or other interests in that body corporate or under which they undertake to act together in exercising their voting power in relation to it, that other person.

(10) For the purposes of subsection (9) above "son" includes stepson and "daughter" includes step-daughter.

DEFINITIONS

"institution": s.106(1).

"subsidiary": s.106(2); s.736 of the Companies Act 1985.

GENERAL NOTE

These definitions in the marginal heading follow those in s.49 of the 1979 Act but in addition the particular definition of controller appearing within para. (c) of subs. (3) is further defined as a "shareholder controller" under which further sub-categories appear with reference to the percentage exercise of voting power. Further, a controller within the meaning of para. (d) of subs. (3) is referred to as an "indirect controller." These sub-categories are in particular relevant to the prior notification procedure required under s.21. The definition in subs. (3)(c) covering persons "either alone or with any associate or associate" is presumably intended to include any parties "acting in concert."

A manager is a person who "exercises managerial functions; or is responsible for maintaining accounts or other records . . ." but this is limited in that he must be "under the immediate authority of a director or chief executive of the institution." The definition of "associate" is taken from s.49(7) of the 1979 Act but also includes a person who has "an agreement or arrangement" with the person entitled to exercise or control the exercise of voting power with respect to the acquisition, holding or disposal of shares.

Interpretation

106.—(1) In this Act—

"associate" has the meaning given in section 105(9) above;

"authorisation" means authorisation granted by the Bank under this Act and "authorised" shall be construed accordingly;

"the Bank" means the Bank of England;

"bare trustee", in relation to a deposit, means a person holding the deposit on trust for another person who has the exclusive right to direct how it shall be dealt with subject only to satisfying any outstanding charge, lien or other right of the trustee to resort to it for the payment of duty, taxes, costs or other outgoings;

"controller" has the meaning given in section 105(3) above;

"director" has the meaning given in section 105(2) above;

"debenture" has the same meaning as in the Companies Act 1985;

"deposit" and "deposit-taking business" have the meaning given in sections 5 and 6 above but subject to any order under section 7 above;

"documents" includes information recorded in any form and, in relation to information recorded otherwise than in legible form, references to its production include references to producing a copy of the information in legible form;

"former authorised institution" means an institution which was formerly an authorised institution or a recognised bank or licensed institution under the Banking Act 1979 and continues to have a liability in respect of any deposit for which it had a liability at a time when it was an authorised institution, recognised bank or licensed institution;

"group", in relation to a body corporate, means that body corporate, any other body corporate which is its holding company or subsidiary and any other body corporate which is a subsidiary of that holding company;

"indirect controller" has the meaning given in section 105(5) above;

"institution", except in the expression "overseas institution" means—

(a) a body corporate wherever incorporated;

(b) a partnership formed under the law of any part of the United Kingdom;

(c) a partnership or other unincorporated association of two or more persons formed under the law of a member State other than the United Kingdom; or

(d) a savings bank to which section 104 above applies;

"liquidator", in relation to a partnership having its principal place of business in Scotland, includes a trustee appointed on the sequestrated estate of the partnership under the Bankruptcy (Scotland) Act 1985;

"local authority" means—

(a) in England and Wales, a local authority within the meaning of the Local Government Act 1972, the Common Council of the City of London or the Council of the Isles of Scilly;

(b) in Scotland, a local authority within the meaning of the Local Government (Scotland) Act 1973; and

(c) in Northern Ireland, a district council within the meaning of the Local Government Act (Northern Ireland) 1972;

"manager" has the meaning given in section 105(6) above;

"municipal bank" has the meaning given in section 103 above;

"penny savings bank" has the same meaning as in the National
        Savings Bank Act 1971;
"related company" has the meaning given in paragraph 92 of
        Schedule 4 to the Companies Act 1985, taking references to a
        company as including any body corporate;
"relevant supervisory authority", in relation to a country or territory
        outside the United Kingdom, means the authority discharging
        in that country or territory functions corresponding to those of
        the Bank under this Act;
"shareholder controller", "minority shareholder controller", "major-
        ity shareholder controller" and "principal shareholder control-
        ler" have the meaning given in section 105(4) above.

(2) Section 736 of the Companies Act 1985 (meaning of subsidiary and
holding company) shall apply for the purposes of this Act.

(3) Any reference in this Act to any provision of Northern Ireland
legislation within the meaning of section 24 of the Interpretation Act 1978
includes a reference to any subsequent provision of that legislation which,
with or without modification, re-enacts the provision referred to in this
Act.

GENERAL NOTE
    It may be noted that in the definition of "institution" a s.104 savings bank is included.

Transitional provisions

107. Schedule 5 to this Act shall have effect with respect to the
transitional matters there mentioned.

GENERAL NOTE
    This section brings in the transitional provisions to serve as a passage as between the old
legislation and the new Act. The principal matters as set out in Sched. 5 are:
    —deemed grant of authorisation to existing recognised banks and licensed institutions
        with back-dating so that no fresh application need be made (para. 2);
    —conditional licences under the 1979 Act are to be treated as restricted authorisations
        (para. 3);
    —certain applications under the 1979 Act subject to appeal may continue (para. 4);
    —revocations (para. 5), directions (para. 6), the imposition of requirements and the
        carrying out of investigations under the 1979 Act (para. 7) shall continue in operation;
    —the Deposit Protection Board shall carry on with its ordinary or alternate members
        retaining office (paras. 8 to 10);
    —certain banking names in use by "deemed" authorised institutions may continue to
        be used (para. 13).

Minor and consequential amendments, repeals and revocations

108.—(1) The enactments mentioned in Schedule 6 to this Act, shall
have effect with the amendments there specified, being minor amendments
and amendments consequential on the provisions of this Act, but subject
to any savings there mentioned.

(2) The enactments mentioned in Part I of Schedule 7 to this Act and
the instruments mentioned in Part II of that Schedule are hereby repealed
or revoked to the extent specified in the third column of those Parts.

GENERAL NOTE
    Sched. 6 sets out the necessary minor and consequential amendments—for the most part
substituting the reference to authorised institutions for the previous "recognised bank" or
"licensed institution" under the 1979 Act. Sched. 7 provides for necessary repeals, the main
being the 1979 Act. The sections remaining in operation are s.38 (amendments to the
Consumer Credit Act 1974, the principal one being that the Director-General of Fair
Trading shall make a determination excluding debtor-creditor agreements operating on a
current account from most of the provisions of Pt. V—see the General Note to s.89); s.47

(retention of defence of contributory negligence to banks where proof of absence of negligence would be a defence under the Cheques Act 1957); s.51 (consequential amendments and repeals); s.52 and Sched. 6.

Northern Ireland

109.—(1) This Act extends to Northern Ireland.

(2) Subject to any Order made after the passing of this Act by virtue of subsection (1)(a) of section 3 of the Northern Ireland Constitution Act 1973, the regulation of banking shall not be a transferred matter for the purposes of that Act but shall for the purposes of subsection (2) of that section be treated as specified in Schedule 3 to that Act.

Short title and commencement

110.—(1) This Act may be cited as the Banking Act 1987.

(2) Section 91 above shall come into force on the passing of this Act and the other provisions of this Act shall come into force on such day as the Treasury may by order appoint; and different days may be appointed for different provisions or different purposes.

GENERAL NOTE

Subs. (2)

S.91 providing powers for securing reciprocal facilities for banking and other financial business came into force immediately on May 15, 1987. The Banking Act 1987 (Commencement No. 1) Order 1987 (S.I. 1987 No. 1189) brought into force on July 15, 1987, the provisions of Pt. V of the Act relating to restrictions on the disclosure of information obtained by the Bank pursuant to this Act, the making of orders under the Act, the interpretation section (s.106), certain consequential amendments and repeals, the short title and commencement. The Banking Act 1987 (Commencement No. 2) Order 1987 (S.I. 1987 No. 1664) has brought the remaining sections into force save for s.38 (reports of large exposures) and the entry in Part 1 of Sch. 7 relating to s.193 of the Financial Services Act 1986.

SCHEDULES

Section 2   SCHEDULE 1

THE BOARD OF BANKING SUPERVISION

Terms of office

1.—(1) The independent members of the Board shall hold office for five years except that some of those first appointed may be appointed to hold office for shorter and different periods so as to secure that all the members do not retire simultaneously.

(2) An independent member may resign his office by written notice to the Bank and the Chancellor of the Exchequer.

(3) A person shall vacate his office as an independent member if he takes up a post with executive responsibility in the Bank.

(4) Subject to sub-paragraph (3) above, a person who has ceased to be an independent member of the Board shall be eligible for re-appointment.

Removal from office

2. An independent member may be removed by the Bank with the consent of the Chancellor of the Exchequer if it is satisfied—

(a) that he has been absent from meetings of the Board for more than three months without the permission of the Board;

(b) that he has become bankrupt, that his estate has been sequestrated or that he has made an arrangement with or granted a trust deed for his creditors;

(c) that he is incapacitated by physical or mental illness; or

(d) that he is otherwise unable or unfit to discharge his functions as a member of the Board.

Increase of number of members

3.—(1) The Treasury may, after consultation with the Bank, by order increase or, subject to section 2(2) of this Act, reduce the number of ex officio or independent members of the Board, provided always that there shall be a majority of independent members on the Board.

(2) Any order under this paragraph shall be subject to annulment in pursuance of a resolution of either House of Parliament.

Proceedings

4.—(1) The quorum for a meeting of the Board shall be one ex officio member and three independent members.

(2) Subject to sub-paragraph (1) above, the Board shall determine its own procedure.

Facilities, remuneration and allowances

5. The Bank shall make such provision as it thinks necessary for providing the Board with facilities for the exercise of its functions and for providing remuneration, allowances or other benefits for or in respect of the independent members.

DEFINITIONS
"the Bank": s.1.
"the Board": s.2.

GENERAL NOTE
Sched. 1 provides for the constitution of the new Board and sets out the terms on which its members will hold office.

Para. 1(3)
Although independent members may not hold any position of "executive responsibility" in the Bank, they may still as independent members hold positions with authorised institutions subject to the Bank's statutory supervision.

Para. 3(1)
The number of *ex-officio* or independent members may be increased by order provided that there always remains a majority of independent members. The number may be reduced but "subject to section 2(2)" which may be interpreted to mean that there must be always at least three *ex-officio* members and at least six independent members on the Board.

Section 4(1)   SCHEDULE 2

EXEMPTED PERSONS

1. The central bank of a member State other than the United Kingdom.

2. The National Savings Bank.

3. A penny savings bank.

4. A municipal bank.

5. A building society incorporated (or deemed to be incorporated) under the Building Societies Act 1986.

6.—(1) A friendly society within the meaning of section 7(1)(a) of the Friendly Societies Act 1974 or section 1(1)(a) of the Friendly Societies Act (Northern Ireland) 1970.

(2) This paragraph applies only to the acceptance of deposits in the course of carrying out transactions permitted by the rules of the society.

7. A society registered under either of the Acts mentioned in paragraph 6 above other than such a society as is there mentioned.

8.—(1) Any institution which is for the time being authorised under section 3 or 4 of the Insurance Companies Act 1982 to carry on insurance business of a class specified in Schedule 1 or 2 to that Act.

(2) This paragraph applies only to the acceptance of deposits in the course of carrying on the authorised insurance business.

9. A loan society whose rules are certified, deposited and enrolled in accordance with the Loan Societies Act 1840.

10. A credit union within the meaning of the Credit Unions Act 1979 or the Credit Unions (Northern Ireland) Order 1985.

11. A body of persons certified as a school bank by the National Savings Bank or an authorised institution.

12. A local authority.

13. Any other body which by virtue of any enactment has power to issue a precept to a local authority in England or Wales or a requisition to a local authority in Scotland.

14. The Crown Agents for Oversea Governments and Administrations.

15. The European Atomic Energy Community.

16. The European Coal and Steel Community.

17. The European Economic Community.

18. The European Investment Bank.

19. The International Bank for Reconstruction and Development.

20. The International Finance Corporation.

21. The International Monetary Fund.

22. The African Development Bank.

23. The Asian Development Bank.

24. The Caribbean Development Bank.

25. The Inter-American Development Bank.

DEFINITIONS

"local authority": s.106(1).

"municipal bank": s.106(1).

"National Savings Bank Act 1971": s.16(4).

"penny savings bank": s.106(1).

GENERAL NOTE

This list of persons exempted from the restriction on accepting deposits in the course of carrying on a deposit-taking business updates Sched. 1 to the 1979 Act. See the annotation to s.4.

Sections 9, 11, 13(4),
16(1), and 22   SCHEDULE 3

MINIMUM CRITERIA FOR AUTHORISATION

Directors etc. to be fit and proper persons

1.—(1) Every person who is, or is to be, a director, controller or manager of the institution is a fit and proper person to hold the particular position which he holds or is to hold.

(2) In determining whether a person is a fit and proper person to hold any particular position, regard shall be had to his probity, to his competence and soundness of judgement for fulfilling the responsibilities of that position, to the diligence with which he is fulfilling or likely to fulfil those responsibilities and to whether the interests of depositors or potential depositors of the institution are, or are likely to be, in any way threatened by his holding that position.

(3) Without prejudice to the generality of the foregoing provisions, regard may be had to the previous conduct and activities in business or financial matters of the person in question and, in particular, to any evidence that he has—

(a) committed an offence involving fraud or other dishonesty or violence;

(b) contravened any provision made by or under any enactment appearing to the Bank to be designed for protecting members of the public against financial loss due to dishonesty, incompetence or malpractice by persons concerned in the provision of banking, insurance, investment or other financial services or the management of companies or against financial loss due to the conduct of discharged or undischarged bankrupts;

(c) engaged in any business practices appearing to the Bank to be deceitful or oppressive or otherwise improper (whether unlawful or not) or which otherwise reflect discredit on his method of conducting business;

(d) engaged in or been associated with any other business practices or otherwise conducted himself in such a way as to cast doubt on his competence and soundness of judgement.

Business to be directed by at least two individuals

2. At least two individuals effectively direct the business of the institution.

Composition of board of directors

3. In the case of an institution incorporated in the United Kingdom the directors include such number (if any) of directors without executive responsibility for the management of its business as the Bank considers appropriate having regard to the circumstances of the institution and the nature and scale of its operations.

Business to be conducted in prudent manner

4.—(1) The institution conducts, or, in the case of an institution which is not yet carrying on a deposit-taking business, will conduct its business in a prudent manner.

(2) An institution shall not be regarded as conducting its business in a prudent manner unless it maintains or, as the case may be, will maintain net assets which, together with other financial resources available to the institution of such nature and amount as are considered appropriate by the Bank, are—

(a) of an amount which is commensurate with the nature and scale of the institution's operations; and

(b) of an amount and nature sufficient to safeguard the interests of its depositors and potential depositors, having regard to the particular factors mentioned in sub-paragraph (3) below and any other factors appearing to the Bank to be relevant.

(3) The particular factors referred to above are—

(a) the nature and scale of the institution's operations; and

(b) the risks inherent in those operations and, if the institution is a body corporate, in the operations of any other body corporate in the same group so far as capable of affecting the institution.

(4) An institution shall not be regarded as conducting its business in a prudent manner unless it maintains or, as the case may be, will maintain adequate liquidity, having regard to the relationship between its liquid assets and its actual and contingent liabilities, to the times at which those liabilities will or may fall due and its assets mature, to the factors mentioned in sub-paragraph (3) above and to any other factors appearing to the Bank to be relevant.

(5) For the purposes of sub-paragraph (4) above the Bank may, to such extent as it thinks appropriate, take into account as liquid assets, assets of the institution and facilities available to it which are capable of providing liquidity within a reasonable period.

(6) An institution shall not be regarded as conducting its business in a prudent manner unless it makes or, as the case may be, will make adequate provision for depreciation or diminution in the value of its assets (including provision for bad or doubtful debts), for liabilities which will or may fall to be discharged by it and for losses which it will or may incur.

(7) An institution shall not be regarded as conducting its business in a prudent manner unless it maintains or, as the case may be, will maintain adequate accounting and other records of its business and adequate systems of control of its business and records.

(8) Those records and systems shall not be regarded as adequate unless they are such as to enable the business of the institution to be prudently managed and the institution to comply with the duties imposed on it by or under this Act and in determining whether those systems are adequate the Bank shall have regard to the functions and responsibilities in respect of them of any such directors of the institution as are mentioned in paragraph 3 above.

(9) Sub-paragraphs (2) to (7) above are without prejudice to the generality of sub-paragraph (1) above.

(10) For the purposes of this paragraph "net assets", in relation to a body corporate, means paid-up capital and reserves.

Integrity and skill

5. The business of the institution is or, in the case of an institution which is not yet carrying on a deposit-taking business, will be carried on with integrity and the professional skills appropriate to the nature and scale of its activities.

Minimum net assets

6.—(1) The institution will at the time when authorisation is granted to it have net assets amounting to not less than £1 million (or an amount of equivalent value denominated wholly or partly otherwise than in sterling).

(2) In this paragraph "net assets", in relation to a body corporate, means paid-up capital and reserves.

(3) The Treasury may, after consultation with the Bank, by order vary the sum specified in sub-paragraph (1) above.

(4) Any order under sub-paragraph (3) above shall be subject to annulment in pursuance of a resolution of either House of Parliament.

TRANSITIONAL PROVISION
    Sched. 5, para. 3(2).

DEFINITIONS
    "the Bank": s.1.
    "controller": s.105(3).
    "deposit-taking business": s.6.
    "director": s.105(2).
    "institution": s.106(1).
    "manager": s.105(6).

GENERAL NOTE
These criteria are based closely on those in Sched. 2 to the 1979 Act which the White Paper (Chap. 7, para. 7.7) considered to "have proved to be the better prudential criteria for both recognised banks and licensed deposit-takers." There is of course now one list, drafted in more detail than previously, with one entirely new provision (para. 3).

Para. 1
Each person who is or is to be a director, controller or manager must be a fit and proper person to hold that particular position. Regard must be had to certain factors in determining whether a person is "fit and proper" and his honesty, competence, diligence and judgment and previous conduct and activities in business or financial matters are all taken into account. In particular any evidence as to his criminal record is relevant (see s.95(3)). Convictions for fraud or other dishonesty or violence, or contravention of any provision designed to protect the public against dishonesty, etc., by persons in the banking sector, or engagement in business practices appearing to the Bank to be "deceitful or oppressive or otherwise improper," or engagement in any business practices so as to cast doubt on his competence and soundness of judgment are all relevant. It is clear that the integrity as well as the competence of the person in question is all important. The Bank in its annual report for 1984 stated (p.42) that the Bank takes, a "cumulative approach," *i.e.* several instances of imprudent conduct taken individually may not amount to failure but, when taken collectively, may confirm that a criterion has not been fulfilled. The person concerned is in practice required to complete a questionnaire relating to his background, business record and experience, and inquiries are made of outside sources by the Bank. Existing occupants of offices also undertake to keep the Bank informed of any material changes in circumstances. Two examples of reasons for concluding that the "fit and proper" criterion was not fulfilled were given in the Bank's annual report for 1986 (p.53), *e.g.* the provision of false or misleading information to the Bank in statistical returns.

Para. 2
The business of the institution must be directed by at least two individuals. This requirement was set down in the Council Directive 77/780/EEC (Art. 3.2). This is often referred to as the "four eyes" criterion, *i.e.* at least two persons with executive authority (general or active partners or senior executives) must take an active role in the affairs of the institution. In its interpretation and application of this criterion, the Bank has indicated that both persons must have sufficient experience and knowledge of the business and the necessary authority to detect and resist any imprudence, dishonesty or other irregularities by the other person. See the Bank's annual report for 1984 (pp.42–43); three cases where the Bank concluded that this criterion was not fulfilled were given in the annual report for 1986 (p.53).

Para. 3
A U.K. authorised institution will be required to include on its Board of Directors one or more non-executive directors, the number to be determined by the Bank of England, having regard to the circumstances of the institution and the nature and scope of its operations. The appointment of an "audit committee" is encouraged. This is a *new* provision.

Para. 4

This key criterion ("the prudent manner" criterion) provides that the business of the institution must be conducted in a prudent manner. In place of setting down the prudential requirements in detail, there are a number of conditions to be taken into account in determining whether a particular institution is conducting its business in a prudent manner. These include (1) maintenance of adequate capital resources, depending on the nature and scope of the institution's operations; the resources must be of an amount and nature sufficient to safeguard depositors' and potential depositors' interests (see, for example, the Bank's paper "The Measurement of Capital (September, 1980)); (2) the maintenance of adequate liquidity (the Bank published a paper "The Measurement of Liquidity" (July 1982) to provide the basis for assessing the adequacy of liquidity of deposit-taking institutions for purposes of the Bank's continuing supervision; note also BSD/1986/4); (3) adequate provision for the depreciation or diminution in the value of its assets (including provision for bad or doubtful debts); and (4) a *new* statutory requirement that each authorised institution must, in order to be regarded as carrying on its business prudently, maintain adequate accounting and other records and adequate business control systems and records. For systems and records to be "adequate" they must be such as to enable the business of the institution to be prudently managed and to enable the institution to comply with its duties under the Acts; the Bank is also to have regard to the functions and responsibilities (in respect of systems) of the non-executive directors mentioned in para. 3. This particular requirement relates to the provisions governing auditors contained in ss.45 to 47. Examples of reasons for deciding that the "prudent conduct" criterion had not been fulfilled were given in the Bank's annual report for 1986 (p.53), *e.g.* exposures imprudently large in relation to capital.

Para. 5

The business of the institution must be conducted with integrity and the professional skills "appropriate to the nature and scale of its activities." No examples are given as to the meaning of these terms.

Para. 6

The institution must have, at the time of authorisation, net assets (paid up capital and reserves) amounting to not less than £1,000,000 or its equivalent in other currencies. This sum may be varied by order. Under the 1979 Act the minimum net asset figure was £5,000,000 for recognised banks and £250,000 for licensed institutions.

Section 50   SCHEDULE 4

THE DEPOSIT PROTECTION BOARD

Constitution

1.—(1) The Board shall consist of three ex officio members, namely—
   (a) the Governor of the Bank for the time being, who shall be the chairman of the Board;
   (b) the Deputy Governor of the Bank for the time being; and
   (c) the Chief Cashier of the Bank for the time being;
and such ordinary members as shall from time to time be appointed under sub-paragraph (2) below.

(2) The Governor of the Bank shall appoint as ordinary members of the Board—
   (a) three persons who are directors, controllers or managers of contributory institutions; and
   (b) persons who are officers or employees of the Bank.

(3) Each ex officio member of the Board may appoint an alternate member, being an officer or employee of the Bank, to perform his duties as a member in his absence.

(4) Each ordinary member of the Board may appoint an appropriately qualified person as an alternate member to perform his duties as a member in his absence; and for this purpose a person is appropriately qualified for appointment as an alternate—
   (a) by a member appointed under paragraph (a) of sub-paragraph (2) above, if he is a director, controller or manager of a contributory institution; and
   (b) by a member appointed under paragraph (b) of that sub-paragraph, if he is either an officer or an employee of the Bank.

(5) Ordinary and alternate members of the Board shall hold and vacate office in accordance with the terms of their appointment.

Expenses

2. The Board may pay to its members such allowances in respect of expenses as the Board may determine.

Proceedings

3.—(1) The Board shall determine its own procedure, including the quorum necessary for its meetings.

(2) The validity of any proceedings of the Board shall not be affected by any vacancy among the ex officio members of the Board or by any defect in the appointment of any ordinary or alternate member.

4.—(1) The fixing of the common seal of the Board shall be authenticated by the signature of the chairman of the Board or some other person authorised by the Board to act for that purpose.

(2) A document purporting to be duly executed under the seal of the Board shall be received in evidence and deemed to be so executed unless the contrary is proved.

Accounts, audit and annual report

5.—(1) The Board may determine its own financial year.

(2) It shall be the duty of the Board—

     (a) to keep proper accounts and proper records in relation to the accounts; and

     (b) to prepare in respect of each of its financial years a statement of accounts showing the state of affairs and income and expenditure of the Board.

(3) A statement of accounts prepared in accordance with sub-paragraph (2)(b) above shall be audited by auditors appointed by the Board and the auditors shall report to the Board stating whether in their opinion the provisions of sub-paragraph (2) above have been complied with.

(4) A person shall not be qualified to be appointed as auditor by the Board under sub-paragraph (3) above unless—

     (a) he is a member of, or a Scottish firm in which all the partners are members of, one or more bodies of accountants established in the United Kingdom and for the time being recognised for the purposes of section 389(1)(a) of the Companies Act 1985; or

     (b) he is for the time being authorised to be appointed as auditor of a company under section 389(1)(b) of that Act as having similar qualifications obtained outside the United Kingdom.

(5) It shall be the duty of the Board, as soon as practicable after the end of each of its financial years, to prepare a report on the performance of its functions during that year.

(6) It shall be the duty of the Board to publish, in such manner as it thinks appropriate, every statement of account prepared in accordance with sub-paragraph (2)(b) above and every report prepared in accordance with sub-paragraph (5) above.

TRANSITIONAL PROVISION
     Sched. 5, para. 8.

DEFINITIONS
     "the Bank": s.1.
     "contributory institutions": s.52(1).
     "controller": s.105(3).
     "director": s.105(2).
     "documents": s.106(1).
     "manager": s.105(6).

GENERAL NOTE
     This Schedule is in the same form as constituted by Sched. 5 to the 1979 Act with the additional provision that the Board may pay its members allowances to cover expenses "as the Board may determine" (para. 2). See also the General Note to s.50.

SCHEDULE 5

Transitional Provisions

First report by Bank of England

1. If this Act comes into force in the course of a financial year of the Bank of England its first report under section 1 of this Act shall include a report on its activities during that year under the Banking Act 1979 (in this Schedule referred to as "the former Act").

Existing recognised banks are licensed institutions

2.—(1) Any institution (within the meaning of this Act) which at the coming into force of section 3 of this Act or by virtue of paragraph 4 or 5 below is
  (a) a recognised bank; or
  (b) a licensed institution,
under the former Act shall be deemed to have been granted an authorisation under this Act.

(2) In relation to any such institution the reference in paragraph (a) of section 11(2) of this Act to the day on which it was authorised shall be construed as a reference to the day on which it was recognised or licensed under the former Act; and in relation to an institution recognised under the former Act by virtue of Part II of Schedule 3 to that Act that paragraph shall have effect with the omission of the words "in the United Kingdom".

(3) In relation to any such institution the reference in section 70(4) of this Act to the time when notice was given to the Bank under subsection (1) shall be construed as a reference to the day on which it first applied for recognition or a licence under the former Act.

Conditional licences

3.—(1) Any conditional licence in force under the former Act when section 3 of this Act comes into force or granted by virtue of paragraph 4 or 5 below shall be treated as an authorisation granted under this Act subject to restrictions (as to duration and conditions) corresponding to those applying to the conditional licence; but no institution shall be guilty of an offence under section 12 of this Act by reason only of a contravention of or failure to comply with a condition which is treated as a restriction of such an authorisation except so far as the condition is attributable to a variation under this Act.

(2) In relation to an application for authorisation made by an institution holding a conditional licence which by virtue of this paragraph is treated as a restricted authorisation, paragraph 6(1) of Schedule 3 to this Act shall have effect with the substitution for the reference to £1 million of a reference to £250,000.

Applications subject to appeal

4.—(1) Where an application for recognition or a licence under the former Act has been refused by the Bank and at the coming into force of section 3 of this Act—
  (a) an appeal is pending against that refusal; or
  (b) the time for appealing against that refusal has not expired,
the repeal of the former Act shall not preclude the determination, or the bringing and determination, of the appeal and the grant or refusal of recognition or a licence as a result of that determination.

(2) Sub-paragraph (1) above does not apply to an appeal by a licensed institution against a refusal to grant it recognition.

Revocation

5.—(1) Where the Bank has given an institution a notice under section 7(3) or (4) of the former Act and the proceedings pursuant to that notice under the provisions of Schedule 4 to that Act have not been concluded at the coming into force of section 3 of this Act the repeal of that Act shall not affect the operation of those provisions in relation to that notice.

(2) Paragraph 2 above does not apply to an institution which is a recognised bank or licensed institution at the coming into force of section 3 of this Act if its recognition or licence is subsequently revoked by virtue of this paragraph.

Directions

6.—(1) The repeal of the former Act shall not affect the continued operation of any direction under section 8 of that Act which has been confirmed in accordance with section

9 before the repeal and any such direction may be varied or revoked as if given under section 19 of this Act.

(2) A direction may be given under section 19 of this Act to an institution which was a recognised bank or licensed institution under the former Act if—

(a) its recognition or licence under that Act was revoked or surrendered; or

(b) a disqualification notice has been served on it under section 183 of the Financial Services Act 1986;

but subsection (5) of section 19 shall apply to it as it applies to an authorised institution, taking references to the time when it was authorised as references to the time when it was recognised or licensed under the former Act.

Information and investigations

7.—(1) The repeal of the former Act shall not affect the operation of any requirement imposed under section 16 of that Act before the repeal or any powers exercisable under that section in relation to any such requirement.

(2) The repeal of the former Act shall not affect the operation of section 17 of that Act in any case in which a person or persons to carry out an investigation under that section have been appointed before the repeal.

(3) Sections 42, 43 and 44 of this Act shall have effect in relation to a contravention of section 1 or 39 of the former Act as they have effect in relation to a contravention of section 3 or 35 of this Act.

Members of Deposit Protection Board

8. Any person who is an ordinary member or alternate member of the Deposit Protection Board at the coming into force of Part II of this Act shall be treated as having been appointed under Schedule 4 to this Act.

Initial contributions by excluded institutions

9.—(1) On or as soon as possible after the coming into force of Part II of this Act the Deposit Protection Board shall levy an initial contribution from each authorised institution which by virtue of an order under section 23(2) of the former Act did not have such a contribution levied from it under section 24 of that Act.

(2) The amount of the initial contribution to be levied from an institution under this paragraph shall be the amount of the initial contribution that would have been levied from it under that section if it had not been exempted from levy by virtue of the order.

Maximum contributions

10. For the purposes of section 56(3) of this Act there shall be taken into account any contribution or repayment made under any provision of the former Act which corresponds to any provision of this Act.

Insolvencies before commencement of Part II

11. This Act does not affect the operation of sections 28 to 31 of the former Act in relation to any insolvency occurring before the coming into force of Part II of this Act; but section 63 of this Act shall apply (instead of section 32 of that Act) to any money received by the Board under section 31.

Borrowing

12. Any sum borrowed by virtue of section 26(3) of the said Act of 1979 shall, so far as outstanding at the coming into force of Part II of this Act, be treated as having been borrowed under section 64 of this Act.

Use of banking names

13.—(1) Subject to sub-paragraph (2) below, section 67 of this Act does not prohibit the use by an institution which is incorporated in or is a partnership formed under the law of any part of the United Kingdom and is deemed to be an authorised institution by virtue of paragraph 2 above of a name which was its registered business or company name immediately before the coming into force of Part III of this Act or of section 36 of the former Act.

(2) Sub-paragraph (1) above shall cease to apply—

(a) in the case of an incorporated institution, if the total value in sterling of its issued share capital and undistributable reserves falls below their total value at the coming into force of Part III of this Act; or

(b) in the case of a partnership in respect of which one or more designated fixed capital accounts are maintained, if the total value in sterling of those accounts falls below their value at that time.

(3) Section 67 of this Act does not prohibit the use by—

(a) an authorised institution which is a wholly-owned subsidiary of an institution to which sub-paragraph (1) above applies; or

(b) a company which has a wholly-owned subsidiary which is an institution to which that sub-paragraph applies,

of a name which includes the name of the institution to which that sub-paragraph applies for the purpose of indicating the connection between the two companies.

(4) In sub-paragraph (2) above "share capital" and "designated fixed capital account" have the same meaning as in subsection (2) of section 67 of this Act and "undistributable reserves" means such reserves as mentioned in paragraph (a)(ii) of that subsection.

Restriction on disclosure of information

14. In section 82(1) of this Act the reference to information received under or for the purposes of this Act includes a reference to information received under or for the purposes of the former Act.

GENERAL NOTE

See the General Note to s.107. Throughout the foregoing annotations, references to the relevant paragraph of this Schedule are included before the General Note in respect of each section of the Act to which transitional provisions apply.

Section 108(1)   SCHEDULE 6

MINOR AND CONSEQUENTIAL AMENDMENTS

The Bankers' Books Evidence Act 1879

1.—(1) For subsection (1)(a) of section 9 of the Bankers' Books Evidence Act 1879 there shall be substituted—

"(a) an institution authorised under the Banking Act 1987 or a municipal bank within the meaning of that Act;".

(2) This paragraph does not affect the operation of the said Act of 1879 in relation to any entry in any banker's book made or transaction carried out before this paragraph comes into force.

The Agricultural Credits Act 1928

2.—(1) In the definition of "Bank" in section 5(7) of the Agricultural Credits Act 1928 for the words "a recognised bank or licensed institution within the meaning of the Banking Act 1979" there shall be substituted the words "an institution authorised under the Banking Act 1987".

(2) This paragraph does not affect the validity of, or the rights and obligations of the parties to, an agricultural charge within the meaning of the said Act of 1928 made before this paragraph comes into force.

The Agricultural Credits (Scotland) Act 1929

3.—(1) In the definition of "Bank" in section 9(2) of the Agricultural Credits (Scotland) Act 1929 for the words "a recognised bank or licensed institution within the meaning of the Banking Act 1979" there shall be substituted the words "an institution authorised under the Banking Act 1987".

(2) This paragraph does not affect the validity of, or the rights and obligations of the parties to, an agricultural charge within the meaning of the said Act of 1929 made before this paragraph comes into force.

The Tribunals and Inquiries Act 1971

4.—(1) In section 8(2) of the Tribunals and Inquiries Act 1971 after the word "paragraph" there shall be inserted "2A".

(2) In Part I of Schedule 1 to that Act after paragraph 2 there shall be inserted—

"Banking   2A. An appeal tribunal constituted under section 28 of the Banking Act 1987 (c.22)."

The Solicitors Act 1974

5. In paragraph (a) of the definition of "bank" in section 87(1) of the Solicitors Act 1974 for the words "a recognised bank within the meaning of the Banking Act 1979" there shall be substituted the words "an institution authorised under the Banking Act 1987" and paragraph (b) of that definition shall be omitted.

The Home Purchase Assistance and Housing Corporation Guarantee Act 1978

6. In paragraph 7 of Part I of the Schedule to the Home Purchase Assistance and Housing Corporation Guarantee Act 1978 for the words "Recognised banks, within the meaning of the Banking Act 1979" there shall be substituted the words "Institutions authorised under the Banking Act 1987".

The Credit Unions Act 1979

7.—(1) In section 8 of the Credit Unions Act 1979 for subsections (2) and (3) there shall be substituted—

"(2) In this section and section 9 below "deposit" has the meaning given in section 5 of the Banking Act 1987."

(2) In the definition of "authorised bank" in section 31(1) of that Act for paragraph (a) there shall be substituted—

"(a) an institution authorised under the Banking Act 1987 or a municipal bank within the meaning of that Act;"

and the words from "and so long" to "that Schedule" shall be omitted.

The Crown Agents Act 1979

8. In section 8(5)(ii) of the Crown Agents Act 1979 for the words "a recognised bank within the meaning of the Banking Act 1979" there shall be substituted the words "an institution authorised under the Banking Act 1987".

The Solicitors (Scotland) Act 1980

9. In section 35(2) of the Solicitors (Scotland) Act 1980 for paragraph (e) there shall be substituted—

"(e) an institution authorised under the Banking Act 1987;"

and paragraph (f) shall be omitted.

The British Telecommunications Act 1981

10. In the definition of "bank" in section 67(4) of the British Telecommunications Act 1981 for paragraph (b) there shall be substituted—

"(b) an institution authorised under the Banking Act 1987;".

The Supreme Court Act 1981

11. In section 40(6) of the Supreme Court Act 1981 for the words "the Banking Act 1979" there shall be substituted the words "the Banking Act 1987".

The Housing (Northern Ireland) Order 1981

12. In Schedule 10 to the Housing (Northern Ireland) Order 1981 for paragraph 4(b) there shall be substituted—

"(b) institutions authorised under the Banking Act 1987."

The Finance Act 1982

13. In paragraph 14(1)(o) of Schedule 7 to the Finance Act 1982 for the words "a recognised bank or licensed institution within the meaning of the Banking Act 1979" there shall be substituted the words "an institution authorised under the Banking Act 1987".

The Duchy of Cornwall Management Act 1982

14. In section 6 of the Duchy of Cornwall Management Act 1982—
(a) in subsection (3)(b) and (c) for the words "a recognised bank" there shall be substituted the words "an authorised institution"; and
(b) for subsection (4) there shall be substituted—
   "(4) In this section "authorised institution" means an institution authorised under the Banking Act 1987.".

The County Courts Act 1984

15. In the definition of "deposit-taking institution" in section 147(1) of the County Courts Act 1984 for the words "the Banking Act 1979" there shall be substituted the words "the Banking Act 1987".

The Finance Act 1984

16. For paragraph 2(1)(b) of Schedule 8 to the Finance Act 1984 there shall be substituted—
   "(b) any institution authorised under the Banking Act 1987 or any municipal bank within the meaning of that Act;".

The Inheritance Tax Act 1984

17. In section 157(5) of the Inheritance Tax Act 1984 for the words "a recognised bank or licensed institution" there shall be substituted the words "or an authorised institution" and for paragraph (b) there shall be substituted—
   "(b) "authorised institution" means an institution authorised under the Banking Act 1987."

The Companies Act 1985

18.—(1) In section 209(5)(a)(i) of the Companies Act 1985 for the words "a recognised bank or licensed institution within the meaning of the Banking Act 1979" there shall be substituted the words "an authorised institution".
(2) In section 232(5) of that Act for the words "recognised banks" there shall be substituted the words "authorised institutions".
(3) In section 234(1) of that Act for the words "a recognised bank", wherever they occur, there shall be substituted the words "an authorised institution".
(4) In section 247(3)(c) of that Act for the words "a recognised bank or licensed institution within the meaning of the Banking Act 1979" there shall be substituted the words "an authorised institution".
(5) In section 257(1) of that Act for paragraph (a) there shall be substituted—
   "(a) "banking company" means a company which is an authorised institution;".
(6) In sections 338(4), 339(4), 343(1)(a) and 344(2) of that Act for the words "a recognised bank", wherever they occur, there shall be substituted the words "an authorised institution".
(7) In section 449(1)(f) and (1A) of that Act for the words "the Banking Act 1979" there shall be substituted the words "the Banking Act 1987".
(8) In section 744 of that Act the definition of "recognised bank" shall be omitted and after the definition of "articles" there shall be inserted—
   ""authorised institution" means a company which is an institution authorised under the Banking Act 1987;".
(9) In Schedule 6 to that Act, in paragraph 4 for the words "a recognised bank" and "that recognised bank" there shall be substituted respectively the words "an authorised institution" and "that authorised institution" and in the heading to Part III for the words "RECOGNISED BANKS" there shall be substituted the words "AUTHORISED INSTITUTIONS".

The Trustee Savings Banks Act 1985

19. In paragraph 11 of Schedule 1 to the Trustee Savings Banks Act 1985—
(a) sub-paragraph (3) shall be omitted; and

(b) in sub-paragraph (4) for the words "a licensed institution for the purposes of the Banking Act 1979" there shall be substituted the words "an institution authorised under the Banking Act 1987".

The Bankruptcy (Scotland) Act 1985

20. In section 73(1) of the Bankruptcy (Scotland) Act 1985 for the definition of "appropriate bank or institution" there shall be substituted the following—
""appropriate bank or institution" means the Bank of England, an institution authorised under the Banking Act 1987 or a person for the time being specified in Schedule 2 to that Act;".

The Housing Act 1985

21. In the definition of "bank" in section 622 of the Housing Act 1985 for paragraph (a) there shall be substituted—
"(a) an institution authorised under the Banking Act 1987, or".

The Housing Associations Act 1985

22. In the definition of "bank" in section 106(1) of the Housing Associations Act 1985 for paragraph (a) there shall be substituted—
"(a) an institution authorised under the Banking Act 1987, or".

The Credit Unions (Northern Ireland) Order 1985

23.—(1) In the definition of "authorised bank" in Article 2(2) of the Credit Unions (Northern Ireland) Order 1985 for sub-paragraph (a) there shall be substituted—
"(a) an institution authorised under the Banking Act 1987 or a municipal bank within the meaning of that Act;".
(2) In Article 25 of that Order for paragraphs (2) and (3) there shall be substituted—
"(2) In this Article and Article 26 "deposit" has the meaning given in section 5 of the Banking Act 1987":

The Finance Act 1986

24. In Schedule 7 to the Finance Act 1986—
(a) in paragraphs 8(1) and 11(1)(c) for the words "a recognised bank or licensed institution (within the meaning of the Banking Act 1979)" there shall be substituted the words "an institution authorised under the Banking Act 1987";
(b) in paragraph 8(2) for the words "recognised bank or licensed institution" there shall be substituted the words "authorised institution."

The Insolvency Act 1986

25.—(1) For paragraph (b) of section 8(4) of the Insolvency Act 1986 there shall be substituted—
"(b) an authorised institution or former authorised institution within the meaning of the Banking Act 1987".
(2) In section 422 of that Act for paragraphs (a) and (b) there shall be substituted the words "authorised institutions and former authorised institutions within the meaning of the Banking Act 1987".

The Building Societies Act 1986

26.—(1) In section 18(17) of the Building Societies Act 1986 for the words "the Banking Act 1979" there shall be substituted the words "the Banking Act 1987".
(2) In section 25(5) of that Act before the definition of "the expenses attributable to the insolvency" there shall be inserted the words—
""authorised institution" means an institution authorised under the Banking Act 1987";
and the definitions of "recognised bank" and "licensed institution" shall be omitted.
(3) In section 25(7) and 27(3) of that Act for the words "recognised bank, licensed institution" there shall be substituted the words "authorised institution".
(4) In section 53(5) of that Act for the words "Banking Act 1979" and the words "section 19 of that Act other than subsection (4)(a)" there shall be substituted respectively the words "Banking Act 1987" and "Part V of that Act other than section 84(5)".

(5) Section 54(4) and (5) of that Act shall be omitted.

(6) In section 98(3)(c) of that Act for the words "a recognised bank or licensed institution for the purposes of the Banking Act 1979" there shall be substituted the words "an authorised institution for the purposes of the Banking Act 1987".

(7) In sections 102(2)(a) and 107(12) of that Act for the words "Banking Act 1979" there shall be substituted the words "Banking Act 1987".

(8) In Schedule 8 to that Act—

(a) in paragraph 7 of Part III for the words "recognised banks or licensed institutions" there shall be substituted the words "authorised institutions"; and

(b) in paragraph 7 of Part IV before the definition of "conveyancing services" there shall be inserted the words—

""authorised institution" means an institution which is authorised under the Banking Act 1987".

and the definitions of "recognised bank" and "licensed institution" shall be omitted.

The Financial Services Act 1986

27.—(1) In section 75(6)(e) of the Financial Services Act 1986 for the words "Banking Act 1979" and "section 2" there shall be substituted respectively the words "Banking Act 1987" and "section 4(4)".

(2) In section 105(7) of that Act for the words "a recognised bank or licensed institution within the meaning of the Banking Act 1979" and "bank, institution" there shall be substituted respectively the words "an institution authorised under the Banking Act 1987" and "institution".

(3) In section 180(1)(f) and (6) of that Act for the words "the Banking Act 1979" there shall be substituted the words "the Banking Act 1987".

(4) In section 185 of that Act—

(a) in subsection (1) for the words "a recognised bank or licensed institution within the meaning of the Banking Act 1979" there shall be substituted the words "an authorised institution within the meaning of the Banking Act 1987"; and

(b) in subsection (2) for the words "recognition or licence", "Banking Act 1979" and "a recognised bank or licensed institution" there shall be substituted respectively the words "authorisation", "Banking Act 1987" and "an authorised institution".

(5) In section 186 of that Act—

(a) in subsection (4) for the words "recognition or licence" there shall be substituted the word "authorisation"; and

(b) in subsection (5) the words from "or, as" to "1979" shall be omitted.

(6) In paragraph 2(2)(a) of Schedule 5 to that Act for the words "a recognised bank or licensed institution within the meaning of the Banking Act 1979" there shall be substituted the words "an authorised institution within the meaning of the Banking Act 1987".

The Companies (Northern Ireland) Order 1986

28.—(1) In Article 2(3) of the Companies (Northern Ireland) Order 1986—

(a) after the definition of "articles" there shall be inserted—

""authorised institution" means a company which is an institution authorised under the Banking Act 1987;"

(b) the definition of "recognised bank" shall be omitted.

(2) In Article 217(5)(a)(i) of that Order for the words "a recognised bank or licensed institution within the meaning of the Banking Act 1979" there shall be substituted the words "an authorised institution".

(3) In Article 240(5) of that Order for the words "recognised banks" there shall be substituted the words "authorised institutions".

(4) In Article 242(1) of that Order for the words "a recognised bank", wherever they occur, there shall be substituted the words "an authorised institution".

(5) In Article 255(3)(c) of that Order for the words "a recognised bank or licensed institution within the meaning of the Banking Act 1979" there shall be substituted the words "an authorised institution".

(6) In Article 265(1) of that Order for paragraph (a) there shall be substituted—

"(a) "banking company" means a company which is an authorised institution".

(7) In Articles 346(4), 347(4), 351(1)(a) and 352(2) of that Order for the words "a recognised bank", wherever they occur, there shall be substituted the words "an authorised institution".

(8) In Article 442(1)(f) and (1A) of that Order for the words "the Banking Act 1979" there shall be substituted the words "the Banking Act 1987".

(9) In Schedule 6 to that Order, in paragraph 4 for the words "a recognised bank" and "that recognised bank" there shall be substituted respectively the words "an authorised institution" and "that authorised institution", in paragraphs 14(a) and 17(a) for "(7)" there shall be substituted "(6)" and in the heading to Part III for the words "RECOGNISED BANKS" there shall be substituted the words "AUTHORISED INSTITUTIONS".

GENERAL NOTE
See *e.g.*, the General Notes to ss.87, 88(2), 90, 91 and 108.

Section 108(2)   SCHEDULE 7

REPEALS AND REVOCATIONS

PART I

ENACTMENTS

Chapter	Short title	Extent of repeal
1974 c. 47.	The Solicitors Act 1974.	In section 87(1), in the definition of "bank", paragraph (b) and the word "and" immediately preceding it.
1974 c. 53.	The Rehabilitation of Offenders Act 1974.	Section 7(2)(g).
1979 c. 34.	The Credit Unions Act 1979.	In section 31(1), in the definition of "authorised bank" the words from "and so long" to "that Schedule". Schedule 3.
1979 c. 37.	The Banking Act 1979.	The whole Act except sections 38, 47, 51 and 52 and Schedule 6.
1980 c. 43.	The Magistrates' Courts Act 1980.	In Schedule 7, paragraph 184.
1980 c.46.	The Solicitors (Scotland) Act 1980.	In section 35(2), paragraph (f) and the word "and" immediately preceding it.
1981 c. 31.	The Insurance Companies Act 1981.	In Schedule 4, paragraph 27.
1982 c. 50.	The Insurance Companies Act 1982.	In Schedule 5, paragraph 21.
1984 c. 46.	The Cable and Broadcasting Act 1984.	In Schedule 5, paragraph 36.
1985 c.6.	The Companies Act 1985.	Section 331(5). In section 744, the definition of "recognised bank". In Schedule 6, in paragraphs 14(a) and 17(a) the figure "(5)" and the words "recognised bank".
1985 c. 9.	The Companies Consolidation (Consequential Provisions) Act 1985.	Section 20. In Schedule 2, the entries relating to the Banking Act 1979.
1985 c. 58	The Trustee Savings Banks Act 1985.	Section 6. In Schedule 1, paragraphs 8, 9 and 11(3). Schedule 3.
1986 c.53.	The Building Societies Act 1986.	In section 25(5), the definitions of "recognised bank" and "licensed institution". Section 54(4) and (5). In Schedule 8, in paragraph 7 of Part IV the definitions of "recognised bank" and "licensed institution". In Schedule 18, paragraph 13.

Chapter	Short title	Extent of repeal
1986 c. 60.	The Financial Services Act 1986.	Section 185(7) In section 186(5), the words from "or, as" to "1979". Section 193. In Schedule 13, paragraphs 3 and 4.

PART II

INSTRUMENTS

Number	Title	Extent of revocation
S.I. 1978/1908 (N.I. 27).	The Rehabilitation of Offenders (Northern Ireland) Order.	Article 8(2)(*f*).
S.I. 1986/1032 (N.I. 6).	The Companies (Northern Ireland) Order 1986.	In Article 2(3), the definition of "recognised bank". In Schedule 6, in paragraphs 14(*a*) and 17(*a*) the figure "(5)" and the words "recognised bank".
S.I. 1986/1035 (N.I. 9).	The Companies Consolidation (Consequential Provisions) (Northern Ireland) Order 1986.	In Schedule 1, the entries relating to the Banking Act 1979.

GENERAL NOTE

See the General Notes to ss.89 and 108(2).

REGISTER OF SASINES (SCOTLAND) ACT 1987

(1987 c. 23)

An Act to make provision as to the methods of keeping the Register of Sasines.   [15th May 1987]

PARLIAMENTARY DEBATES
Hansard: H.C. Vol. 107, col. 357; Vol. 108, col. 1196; Vol. 113, col. 673; H.L. Vol. 486, cols. 448, 1433; Vol. 487, cols. 246, 423.
The Bill was considered in the Second Scottish Standing Committee on February 4, 1987.

Regulations prescribing methods of operation in the Register of Sasines

1.—(1) Subject to the following provisions of this section, the Secretary of State may by regulations prescribe methods of operation in the Register of Sasines and these methods shall apply in place of methods of operation provided for in any enactment prior to the coming into force of this Act, notwithstanding the provisions of such enactments.

(2) In subsection (1) above, "methods of operation" means—

    (a) the manner of recording a deed and of keeping the Register, including the medium in which a deed may be recorded and the Register kept;

    (b) the making available of the Register to the public for inspection,

and different provision may be made for different cases or classes of case.

(3) Nothing in this Act, or in regulations under this Act, or done under or by virtue of such regulations shall affect—

    (a) any rule of law relating to the information—

        (i) to be recorded in the Register; or

        (ii) to be made available to the public; or

    (b) the evidential value of the Register or of an extract from the Register.

(4) Methods of keeping the Register prescribed in accordance with subsection (1) above may apply to records of deeds, notwithstanding that they were recorded before the coming into force of the regulations.

(5) Any reference, however expressed, in any enactment to—

    (a) a particular book, volume or folio; or

    (b) a method of recording a deed or keeping the Register

which has been superseded by virtue of regulations made under this Act shall be construed as a reference to such document or method as has so superseded it.

(6) In this Act—

    "enactment" includes any Act of Parliament, whether public, general, local or private, any Act of Sederunt and any instrument made under any enactment;

any reference to the Register of Sasines shall be construed in accordance with section 2 of The Land Registers (Scotland) Act 1868.

Making of regulations

2.—(1) Before making regulations under this Act, the Secretary of State shall consult such persons or bodies as appear to him to be appropriate.

(2) Regulations under this Act shall be made by statutory instrument which shall be subject to annulment in pursuance of a resolution of either House of Parliament.

Citation commencement and extent

3.—(1) This Act, which may be cited as the Register of Sasines (Scotland) Act 1987, shall come into force on the expiry of the period of two months beginning with the day on which it is passed.

(2) This Act extends to Scotland only.

IMMIGRATION (CARRIERS' LIABILITY) ACT 1987

(1987 c. 24)

An Act to require carriers to make payments to the Secretary of State in respect of passengers brought by them to the United Kingdom without proper documents.   [15th May 1987]

PARLIAMENTARY DEBATES
Hansard: H.C. Vol. 111, col. 872; Vol. 112, col. 705; Vol. 113, col. 591; H.L. Vol. 486, cols. 360, 857; Vol. 487, cols. 247, 545.

Liability of carriers for passengers without proper documents

1.—(1) Where a person requiring leave to enter the United Kingdom arrives in the United Kingdom by ship or aircraft and, on being required to do so by an immigration officer, fails to produce—

(a) either a valid passport with photograph or some other document satisfactorily establishing his identity and nationality or citizenship; and

(b) if he is a person who under the immigration rules requires a visa for entry into the United Kingdom, a visa valid for that purpose.

the owners or agents of the ship or aircraft shall, in respect of that person, be liable to pay the Secretary of State on demand the sum of £1,000 or such other sum as may be prescribed.

(2) No liability shall be incurred under subsection (1) above in respect of any person who is shown by the owners or agents to have produced to them or an employee of theirs the document or documents specified in that subsection when embarking on the ship or aircraft for the voyage or flight to the United Kingdom.

(3) In subsection (1) above "prescribed" means prescribed by an order made by the Secretary of State by statutory instrument subject to annulment in pursuance of a resolution of either House of Parliament.

(4) For the purposes of this section a document shall be regarded as being what it purports to be unless its falsity is reasonably apparent.

(5) Any sums received by the Secretary of State under this section shall be paid into the Consolidated Fund.

Short title, interpretation, extent and commencement

2.—(1) This Act may be cited as the Immigration (Carriers' Liability) Act 1987.

(2) In this Act any expression which is also used in the Immigration Act 1971 has the same meaning as in that Act.

(3) This Act extends to Northern Ireland; and section 36 of the said Act of 1971 (power to extend any of its provisions to the Channel Islands and the Isle of Man) shall apply also to the provisions of this Act.

(4) This Act has effect in relation to persons arriving in the United Kingdom at any time after 4th March 1987 except persons arriving by a voyage or flight for which they embarked on the ship or aircraft in question on or before that date.

CROWN PROCEEDINGS (ARMED FORCES) ACT 1987*

(1987 c. 25)

An Act to repeal section 10 of the Crown Proceedings Act 1947 and to provide for the revival of that section in certain circumstances.

[15th May 1987]

PARLIAMENTARY DEBATES

Hansard: H.C. Vol. 107, col. 354; Vol. 110, col. 567; Vol. 114, col. 925; H.L. Vol. 486, col. 1421; Vol. 487, cols. 209, 609.

The Bill was considered in Standing Committee C on March 18, 1987.

GENERAL NOTE

Reform of the law relating to the privileges of the Crown in litigation and its immunity from liability in tort had been proposed in 1927 by a Committee presided over by the Attorney General, Sir Gordon Hewart (later Lord Hewart L.C.J.) (Cmd. 2842). Legislation was not introduced until 20 years later when the position of the Crown in actions in tort again became a matter of controversy after the courts refused to continue to sanction the procedure by which actions which in essence were against government departments were brought against individuals "nominated" as defendants (*Adams* v. *Naylor* [1946] A.C. 543; *Royster* v. *Cavey* [1947] 1 K.B. 204). S.2 of the Crown Proceedings Act 1947 introduced a wide degree of liability in tort on the part of the Crown. Apart, however, from limitations to liability arising from the terms of that section, s.9 continued the immunity of the Post Office (except in the case of registered post) and even extended that immunity to the individual wrongdoer. The Post Office and its employees retained their immunities when it ceased to be a government department and became an independent, public corporation (Post Office Act 1969, s.29). (A similar immunity in the case of British Telecom and its employees which was conferred by the British Telecommunications Act 1981, s.23, was removed by the Telecommunications Act 1984, s.109 and Sched. 7.) S.10 of the Crown Proceedings Act 1947 dealt with cases of death or physical injury suffered by members of the armed forces arising from the acts of other members of the armed forces (subs. (1)) or from the condition or nature of any land or vehicle being used for the purposes of the armed forces or of any equipment or supplies similarly being used (subs. (2)). In the case of both subsections the Crown was immune from liability if the Secretary of State certified that the death or injury was, for pension purposes, attributable to service in the armed forces. In the case of subs. (1) immunity was also conferred on the member of the armed forces causing the death or injury if at the time of the act complained of he was on duty. (For a detailed account of the section see O. Hood Phillips, *Constitutional and Administrative Law* (7th ed., 1987), pp.711–713).

Perhaps, inevitably, the passing of the Crown Proceedings Act 1947 highlighted the anomalous cases where the Crown retained immunities and privileges from the general law. In the nineteen sixties, for instance, the courts began to assert a jurisdiction over claims by ministers to Crown Privileges which, not surprisingly, they had been prepared to yield at the height of the War (*Duncan* v. *Cammell Laird* [1942] A.C. 624; *Conway* v. *Rimmer* [1968] A.C. 910; see further O. Hood Phillips, *op. cit.* 718–723). The absurdity of public health and hygiene legislation not applying to the kitchens of National Health Service hospitals was abolished by the National Health Service (Amendment) Act 1986—although the general rule that statutes do not bind the Crown unless by express words or necessary implication which was preserved by s.40(2)(*f*) of the Crown Proceedings Act 1947 was unaffected. Dissatisfaction with s.10 of the 1947 Act had manifested itself at least as long ago as 1975 when a private member's Bill to repeal the section had been unsuccessfully introduced into the House of Commons. The Courts, in two recent decisions, displayed some ingenuity in restricting the scope of the section (*Bell* v. *Secretary of State for Defence* [1986] Q.B. 322 (C.A.); *Pearce* v. *Secretary of State for Defence* [1987] 2 W.L.R. 782). (For an unsuccessful attempt to evade s.10 see *Brown* v. *Lord Advocate*, 1984 S.L.T. 146.) In 1987 Mr. Winston Churchill, with the support of the government and members of all parties, successfully introduced a Bill which received Royal Assent as the Crown Proceedings (Armed Forces) Act 1987.

At the time of the introduction of the 1947 Bill there was no doubt that clause 10 had

---

* Annotations by Paul Jackson, LL.D., Professor of Law, University of Reading.

been included at the insistence of the Service Departments. Viscount Jowitt, L.C. frankly told the House of Lords, "That the short and the long of it is that I am under an obligation either to get this clause as it is or to withdraw my Bill." (*Hansard*, H.L. Vol. 146, col. 382.) Circumstances had, however, in the view of members of both Houses changed markedly since 1947. Then the War had ended but the United Kingdom was still largely on a war footing with a huge amateur army, as opposed to the small, professional army of the nineteen eighties. Public opinion, in the view of Mr. Churchill had changed, "Throughout society there is now much less willingness to accept that the special circumstances of life in the armed forces justify depriving the service man or service woman of the rights enjoyed by his or her fellow citizens, particularly in peacetime, and particularly in circumstances that are similar to those experienced by other disciplined forces that are engaged on hazardous duties, such as the police and the fire brigades. This change of opinion is undeniably in the right direction and we in Parliament must respond to it." (*Hansard*, H.C. Vol. 110, col. 568.) A further important distinction between 1947 and 1987 was that payments by way of pensions and disability allowances to members of the armed forces no longer compared with damages recoverable in actions in the courts, contrary to the position as envisaged when clause 10 was originally debated. (It could also be objected that as s.10 had been interpreted the provision relating to the certification by the Secretary of State that an injury was attributable to military service could well be entirely worthless; immunity from liability was conferred by the issuing of a certificate even if subsequently no benefit was paid (*Adams* v. *War Office* [1955] 1 W.L.R. 1116; affirmed, *Bell* v. *Secretary of State for Defence* [1986] Q.B. 322 (C.A.)). The only issue which divided members in welcoming the Bill was whether its provisions ought to be made retrospective. All agreed that not to do so would cause injustice to those injured before the Act came into effect. Some, on the other hand, were also concerned about the injustice to defendants who might be sued for incidents which had occurred long ago. A majority was determined, in the face of Government opposition, not to lose the Bill for the sake of the attempt to make it retrospective. (See further, *infra*.) Crown immunity generally was seen as an "obscure" or "outdated, medieval" concept, to be subject to a process of gentle erosion or, in the view of one member, to "a wholesale re-examination. . . . Instead of it being done on a piecemeal basis—a bit here, a bit there, and a bit somewhere else—I should prefer the Government to say that they are prepared to give up Crown immunity completely. If, however, the Government believe that Crown immunity is needed in certain key, specific areas, let them make a case for retaining it. That would be very much better understood by the general public." (*Hansard*, H.C. Vol. 110, col. 582.)

Repeal of s.10 of the Crown Proceedings Act 1947

1. Subject to section 2 below, section 10 of the Crown Proceedings Act 1947 (exclusions from liability in tort in cases involving the armed forces) shall cease to have effect except in relation to anything suffered by a person in consequence of an act or omission committed before the date on which this Act is passed.

DEFINITIONS

"Anything suffered by a person in consequence of an act or omission": s.5(2).

The effect of the definition section is to ensure that s.1 extends to both subsections of s.10 of the 1947 Act, *i.e.* injuries caused by acts or omissions and injuries caused by the nature or condition of land or vehicles.

GENERAL NOTE

S.1 repeals s.10 of the Crown Proceedings Act 1947 subject to the power of the Secretary of State to revive it within the limits set by s.2.

The repeal applies only to anything suffered by a person in consequence of an act or omission committed after the date on which the Act was passed [May 15, 1987]. The Government has, however, agreed to meet claims on an *ex gratia* basis relating to the period between the passing of the Act and December 8, 1986 (*infra*). The language of the section (which follows closely that of s.10 in the 1947 Act) leaves open the possibility, accepted by the Court of Appeal in *Bell* v. *Secretary of State for Defence* [1986] Q.B. 322, of a continuing act or omission which, although beginning before the Act is continuing and causes the thing suffered—for example, cancer arising from negligent failure to provide appropriate protective equipment after the Act. (See too *Pearce* v. *Secretary of State for Defence* [1987] 2 W.L.R. 782).

The refusal of the Government to agree to s.1 having retrospective effect was rather disingenuously justified on the ground that retrospective legislation is, as a general principle, to be deprecated. That is not a principle to which governments of any party can be said to adhere with any regularity. (See, for example, O. Hood Phillips, *op. cit.* 53). A more attractive argument was the injustice of exposing members of the armed forces to possible liability in negligence many years after the occurrence of the act complained of. Even that argument would have lost most of its weight in the light of a government assurance that it would pay any damages awarded in such cases, as it has committed itself to do in cases falling within s.1 where the negligence relates to actions committed in the course of service duties (Mr. Freeman, *Hansard*, H.C. Vol. 114, col. 935). The difficulty of proving negligence after many years might also in practice be thought to provide a limit to possible litigation, particularly in the light of the payment (however inadequate in some cases) of pensions and disability allowances, in effect on a "no-fault" basis. A compromise which was suggested without success was the establishment of a fund to meet claims for a limited period made in relation to acts committed before the 1987 Act. The proponents of such a scheme relied on analogous provisions under the Coal Industry Act 1975 and the Pneumoconiosis Etc. (Workers' Compensation) Act 1979. The analogy was rejected by the Government on the ground that the legislation related to cases where questions of liability were not necessarily relevant. Clearly the issue will be raised again if, in due course, it is established that the incidence of radiologically induced diseases is significantly higher than average among the twenty thousand servicemen who took part in the British nuclear test programme—where indeed it will be argued that questions of liability in terms of negligence are not relevant. The only element of retroactivity accepted by the Government was the payment on an *ex gratia* basis of compensation for claims relating to the period between the enactments of the Act and December 8, 1986, when the Secretary of State for Defence had announced that the Government accepted that the section ought to be repealed.

S.1 merely removes the prohibition on members of the armed forces suing other members or the Crown in the circumstances where the prohibition formerly applied. It does not alter the law of evidence or the substantive law of tortious liability. In the course of the debates on the Bill it was recognised that litigation between members of the armed forces in the circumstances covered by s.1 might raise questions of withholding evidence on the grounds of national security. The government view was that no difficulty would be caused because the Crown would "where appropriate" admit liability and discussion could continue on the quantum of damages (*Hansard*, H.C. Vol. 114, col. 937). Whether conduct in a particular case was negligent as a matter of law will remain to be determined by the court in each case. Conduct which might be negligent in some circumstances in civilian life because of its hazardous character with no counter-balancing justification may not be so in the context of military life. The Attorney-General, Sir Hartley Shawcross, during the Second Reading of the 1974 Bill said,

> "It is necessary in the course of Service training, in order to secure the efficiency of the forces, to exercise them in the use of live ammunition, in flying in close formation and, in the Navy, in battle conditions, with, perhaps, destroyers dashing about with lights out, and so on. These operations are highly dangerous and, if done by private citizens, would, no doubt, be extremely blameworthy".

Nothing in s.1 provides a remedy for injuries sustained in such circumstances unless the dangerous activity can be shown to be negligent.

Damages recovered under s.1 will be in addition to payments under the existing no-fault scheme for compensation.

Revival of s.10

2.—(1) Subject to the following provisions of this section, the Secretary of State may, at any time after the coming into force of section 1 above, by order—

(a) revive the effect of section 10 of the Crown Proceedings Act 1947 either for all purposes or for such purposes as may be described in the order; or

(b) where that section has effect for the time being in pursuance of an order made by virtue of paragraph (a) above, provide for that section to cease to have effect either for all of the purposes for which it so has effect or for such of them as may be so described.

(2) The Secretary of State shall not make an order reviving the effect of the said section 10 for any purposes unless it appears to him necessary or expedient to do so—

    (a) by reason of any imminent national danger or of any great emergency that has arisen; or

    (b) for the purposes of any warlike operations in any part of the world outside the United Kingdom or of any other operations which are or are to be carried out in connection with the warlike activity of any persons in any such part of the world.

(3) Subject to subsection (4) below, an order under this section describing purposes for which the effect of the said section 10 is to be revived, or for which that section is to cease to have effect, may describe those purposes by reference to any matter whatever and may make different provision for different cases, circumstances or persons.

(4) Nothing in any order under this section shall revive the effect of the said section 10, or provide for that section to cease to have effect, in relation to anything suffered by a person in consequence of an act or omission committed before the date on which the order comes into force.

(5) The power to make an order under this section shall be exercisable by statutory instrument subject to annulment in pursuance of a resolution of either House of Parliament.

GENERAL NOTE

S.2 reflects the views of the government and most members of both Houses that s.10 of the Crown Proceedings Act 1947 remains appropriate in times of war or other emergencies. S.10 may be revived from time to time as required by statutory instrument, to be made by the Secretary of State, subject to annulment by a resolution of either House.

Subs. (2)

    An order reviving s.10 cannot be made unless it appears to the Secretary of State to be "necessary or expedient to do so" for either of the reasons in paras. (a) and (b).

The use of such subjective language ("if it appears") does not of itself exclude judicial review (*Secretary of State for Education* v. *Tameside M.B.C.* [1977] A.C. 1014). Such words "*may* confer an absolute discretion on the Executive. Sometimes they do, but sometimes they do not" (*Att.-Gen. of St. Christopher, Nevis and Anguilla* v. *Reynolds* [1980] A.C. 637, at 657, *per* Lord Salmon). Judicial attitudes have changed from the days of *Liversidge* v. *Anderson* [1942] A.C. 206, which was described by Lord Reid in *Ridge* v. *Baldwin* [1964] A.C. 40, as a "very peculiar decision." Lord Diplock in *I.R.C.* v. *Rossminster* [1981] A.C. 952, 1011 thought that "the time has come to acknowledge openly that the majority of this House in *Liversidge* v. *Anderson* were expediently and, at that time, perhaps, excusably, wrong and the dissenting speech of Lord Atkin was right." Thus an order made by the Secretary of State could be open to challenge on the ground, for example, that no reasonable Secretary of State *could* believe it was necessary or expedient to make an order. Secondly, an order might be challenged on the ground that the facts which led to its making did not constitute an "imminent national danger" or "great emergency" or "warlike operations". The jurisdiction of the Courts to investigate such matters might be said to be established by *Council of Civil Service Unions* v. *Minister for the Civil Service* [1985] A.C. 374 where the House of Lords maintained that an exercise of ministerial power on the ground of national security was open to challenge in the absence of evidence that a question of national security was involved. While their Lordships recognised the existence of non-justiciable matters, such as the making of treaties and the defence of the realm they were referring to prerogative powers and such judicial non-intervention would not apply to disputes over the limits of statutory powers.

Nonetheless, despite the existence of jurisdiction to review orders made under subs. (2) it may be doubted whether the courts would be keen to interfere in such a sensitive area. Moreover the terms "imminent national danger" and "great emergency" are sufficiently vague to allow, on any view, a wide discretion to the Secretary of State. In the case of "warlike operations" the same consideration might be thought to apply. The phrase is clearly intended to extend beyond war *stricto sensu*. Where the existence of a state of war is in question the courts defer to the view of the Foreign Office (*R.* v. *Bottrill, ex p. Kuechenmeister* K.B. 41). Beyond that, the question may still be one for the court but, as has been suggested, it cannot be a question with which the courts would be happy to be involved.

The fact that an order made under the subsection has been laid before both Houses does not preclude judicial review (*Hoffmann La Roche* v. *Secretary of State for Trade and Industry* [1975] A.C. 295). But such laying may give rise to judicial reluctance to become involved in what may be regarded as a matter of "political judgment" (*R.* v. *Secretary of State for the Environment, ex p. Nottinghamshire County Council* [1986] A.C. 240).

Since subs. (2)(b) relates to warlike operations "in any part of the world *outside the United Kingdom*" the question cannot arise of attempting to revive s.10 by reference, for example, to the state of affairs in Northern Ireland. On the other hand disturbances in one part of the United Kingdom might well give rise to "imminent national danger" or "great emergency" under subs. (2)(a).

Consequential adaptations of existing enactments etc.

3.—(1) Except in so far as an order under section 2 above otherwise provides, any reference to section 10 of the Crown Proceedings Act 1947 in any Act passed, or subordinate legislation made, before the passing of this Act shall be construed as a reference to that section as it from time to time has effect by virtue of this Act.

(2) Subsection (1) above shall apply, as it applies to express references to the said section 10—

(a) to the references to that section which are comprised in the references in the said Act of 1947 to or to the provisions of that Act itself; and

(b) to any other references to the said section 10 which are comprised in references to that Act, in references to enactments generally or in references to any description of enactments.

(3) In this section "subordinate legislation" has the same meaning as in the Interpretation Act 1978.

Expenses

4. There shall be paid out of money provided by Parliament any expenses incurred by a Minister of the Crown or Government department in consequence of the provisions of this Act.

GENERAL NOTE

This section makes provision for the cost of implementing the terms of the Act. To estimate the costs with any precision before the Act has been in operation for some time is impossible. The memorandum accompanying the Bill originally envisaged costs rising to £20,000,000 in 1997–98 and remaining steady thereafter. To the amazement and horror of members of both Houses nearly half that figure was to go on legal costs. The Treasury Solicitor's Department, for example, envisaged appointing 52 additional staff at an annual average cost of £32,000 each. Subsequently the estimated total figure was reduced to £13,040,000, of which, however, almost one half is still attributable to legal costs. Damages were estimated at £7,000,000. Claimants' legal costs were estimated at £4,600,000. Twenty-four additional legal staff for the Ministry of Defence were estimated to be required, at a cost of £700,000. Other additional staff would cost £190,000 and legal aid for unsuccessful claimants, £450,000.

Short title, interpretation and extent

5.—(1) This Act may be cited as the Crown Proceedings (Armed Forces) Act 1987.

(2) For the purposes of the application of any provision of this Act in relation to subsection (2) of section 10 of the Crown Proceedings Act 1947 references in this Act to anything suffered by any person in consequence of an act or omission committed before a particular date shall include references to anything which—

(a) would not, apart from this subsection, be regarded as suffered in consequence of an act or omission; but

(b) is suffered in consequence of the nature or condition at a time before that date of any land, premises, ship, aircraft, hovercraft, or vehicle or of any equipment or supplies.

(3) This Act shall extend to Northern Ireland.

GENERAL NOTE

Subs. (2)

See General Note to s.1, *supra.*

Subs. (3)

The Crown Proceedings Act 1947 did not extend to Northern Ireland. Provision instead was made by s.53 for the extension of its provisions to Northern Ireland by Order in Council, subject to such exceptions and modifications as appeared to His Majesty to be expedient.

A distinction was recognised with regard to questions of liability between liability of the Crown in right of His Majesty's Government in the United Kingdom and in right of His Majesty's Government in Northern Ireland. In 1947, however, Northern Ireland possessed its own Governor and Legislature. In 1987 responsibility for governing the Province rested with Parliament at Westminster and a Secretary of State. In such circumstances it is not surprising that Parliament legislated for the whole of the United Kingdom. (Whether, in any circumstances, a distinction could be drawn between the Crown in right of the United Kingdom and in right of Northern Ireland in a case where Her Majesty's forces were involved may be open to doubt). Subs. (3) thus ensures one rule throughout the United Kingdom in cases involving the liability of members of the armed forces.